Caravan and Camp
in Britain 2001

Compiled and edited by George Gurney

Mirador Books
Hereford

Copyright © 2001 Mirador Books
ISBN 1 870009 30 4

Mirador Books, Hillsboro, How Caple, Hereford HR1 4TE

**Typeset by
Butford Technical Publishing
Birlingham, Pershore WR10 3AB
Printed and bound by The Cromwell Press
Aintree Ave, White Horse Business Park,
Trowbridge BA14 0XB**

Contents

Free to buyers of this book Beginner's guide to DIY holidays out of doors – see page 9

Introduction

This guide lists campsites in Britain open to all. It groups all campsites of an acceptable standard accommodating six or more tents or caravans into sixteen regions based on the new county boundaries. This division seems logical enough since most campers and caravanners first choose the region they want to visit and second the campsite at which they propose to stay. With the aim of making both choices easier, each region has an introduction indicating in broad terms the areas best for camping and caravanning within it.

The guide attempts to cater as much for the adventure camper as for the family caravanner. The regional introductions indicate scenic drives as well as long-distance footpaths and the information on each campsite includes its telephone number for those who need or prefer to book their pitch in advance, though not all sites accept bookings.

The symbols used to describe the facilities at campsites are those which, for most of us, are immediately recognisable, thereby avoiding the need for the reader to refer constantly to a key when comparing the amenities of one site with another.

Where the information has been supplied to us we give details of campsite charges. However low these may be they may still give cause for complaint in that the camper or caravanner can get so little in return. Most of us would happily pay more for the kind of facilities so common on the Continent and so rare in Britain, and no system of classification that is not backed by authority is going to change this state of affairs. The AA's pennant scheme makes a valuable contribution to the raising of site standards in Britain. We have played our part by eliminating from the guide any sites not equipped with flush lavatories and showers—although a few sites without showers are included because there is no alternative anywhere near.

Publication of campsite charges is in no way binding on the site operator concerned and there is nothing to prevent him increasing his prices halfway through the season should he decide to do so. Readers often complain of other malpractices, such as quoting what appears to be an inclusive price then adding on various items as extras. Any camper or caravanner who considers the charges on a particular campsite exorbitant can not only avoid it next time but warn his fellow campers to do the same. Alternatively he can telephone or write beforehand to find out how much he is expected to pay—usually not more than £5 a night for a four-person family, though this figure can go up to £7 or more on one of the really top-class sites.

The aim of this guide is to make camping and caravanning in Britain easier and so more enjoyable. We should therefore be grateful to any readers willing to help us make it so by sending us details of any corrections or additions to the information on campsites or of any not already listed that they would like to see included in the guide. Provided of course that these are open to all.

Specimen entry

Place name in alphabetical order within the region

Population, early closing and market days

Sights of tourist interest in place named or within a few miles, followed by tourist office (if any)

Grid reference on map at start of regional section

Recommended restaurant in or near place named

Distance and direction of site from centre of place under which it is listed, the place name in brackets following the road number indicating which route to take. See note below.

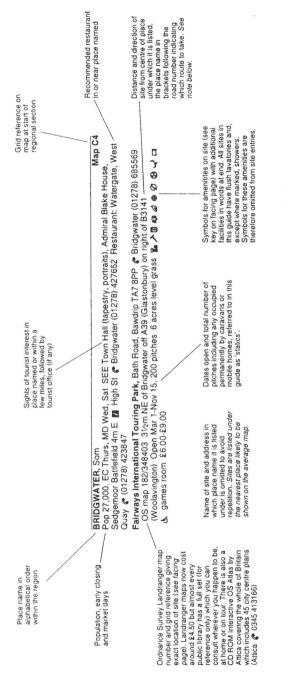

BRIDGWATER, Som
Pop 27,000. EC Thurs, MD Wed, Sat SEE Town Hall (tapestry, portraits), Admiral Blake House, Sedgemoor Battlefield 4m E ⓘ High St ☎ Bridgwater (01278) 427652 Restaurant: Watergate, West Quay ☎ (01278) 423847

Map C4

Fairways International Touring Park, Bath Road, Bawdrip TA7 8PP ☎ Bridgwater (01278) 685569 OS map 182/348403 3½m NE of Bridgwater off A39 (Glastonbury) on right of B3141 (Woolavington) Open Mar 1-Nov 15, 200 pitches 6 acres level grass ♿ games room £6.00-£9.00

Ordnance Survey Landranger map number and grid reference giving exact location of site (see facing page). Landranger maps now cost around £4.50 but almost every public library has a full set (for reference only) which you can consult wherever you happen to be, at home or on tour. There is also a CD ROM interactive OS Atlas by Attica covering the whole of Britain which includes 45 city centre plans (Attica ☎ 0345 413166)

Name of site and address in which place name it is listed under is omitted to avoid repetition. Sites are listed under the nearest place likely to be shown on the average map.

Dates open and total number of pitches including any occupied permanently by caravans or mobile homes, referred to in this guide as 'statics'.

Symbols for amenities on site (see key on facing page) with additional facilities in words at end. All sites in this guide have flush lavatories and, except where marked, showers. Symbols for these amenities are therefore omitted from site entries.

To give detailed directions for finding a site would either mean a more expensive guide or fewer sites. In any case most sites are now signposted from the nearest numbered road. Taking the place under which a site is listed as the starting point, as this guide does, enables you to pinpoint it on a suitable map. That way you can approach it from wherever you happen to be. There is no need to go to the place concerned.

How to use this book

This guide groups campsites into regions then lists them alphabetically under key towns likely to be shown on the average map. The name of the campsite, its address and telephone number is followed by the Ordnance Survey grid reference. As metric scale 1:50 000 maps covering the whole of Britain have now been introduced, these are the ones that have been used.

Pinpointing a site on an OS map is easy enough. The first number or numbers before the oblique stroke refer to the relevant map in this series, the six numbers that follow being the grid reference. In this, the first three figures give the east–west location of the place referred to, the second the north–south, the first two figures in each case relating to the number of the kilometre square shown at the edge of the map, the third figure to tenths of the square. For example, the grid reference for the church of Llanbedrog in North Wales is 123/329315, that is, map number 123, east–west square 32 and north–south square 31, the

third figure representing tenths of the square. (The maps at the beginning of each regional section show each of the key towns in the region and the major roads leading to them.)

The OS grid reference in each entry is followed by the distance and direction of the campsite from the *centre* of the key town under which it appears. Then comes the inclusive opening dates and the permitted number of tents or caravans or both the campsite can accept, including any there semi-permanently.

Prices supplied by the site operator are for two people with car and tent or caravan per night. Awnings are invariably charged extra as are mains electric hook-ups.

While every care was taken to ensure that the information in this guide was accurate at the time of going to press neither the author nor the publisher can accept any liability for errors or omissions.

Key to symbols

₤	shop	⊠	swimming pool
✗	restaurant	⊕	games area
♀	bar	↵	children's playground
⏁	takeaway food	⊡	TV
✗	off licence	⬤	winter storage for caravans
⊟	launderette	Ⓟ	parking obligatory (P)
▣	mains electric hook-ups	⊗	no dogs
∂	gas supplies	⊂⊃	caravan hire
⊛	chemical disposal point	⌂	bungalow hire
∅	payphone	♿	facilities for disabled

Additional facilities given in words at end.

Except where marked, all sites in this guide have flush lavatories and showers. Symbols for these amenities have therefore been omitted from site entries.

Key to the regions

1 Northumbria
Northumberland
Tyne and Wear
Durham

2 Cumbria

3 Northeast
Cleveland
Humberside
North Yorkshire
South Yorkshire
West Yorkshire

4 Northwest
Lancashire
Greater Manchester
Merseyside
Cheshire

5 East Midlands
Derbyshire
Nottinghamshire
Lincolnshire
Leicestershire
Northamptonshire

6 Central England
Shropshire
Staffordshire
West Midlands
Hereford and Worcester
Warwickshire
Gloucestershire

7 East Anglia
Cambridgeshire
Norfolk
Suffolk
Essex

8 London and Home Counties
Berkshire
Oxfordshire
Buckinghamshire
Bedfordshire
Hertfordshire
Greater London

9 Southern England
Hampshire
Surrey
Kent
East Sussex
West Sussex
Isle of Wight

10 Southwest
Avon
Wiltshire
Dorset
Somerset

11 West Country
Cornwall
Devon

12 North Wales
Gwynedd
Clwyd

13 Central and South Wales
Dyfed
Powys
Gwent
South Glamorgan
Mid Glamorgan
West Glamorgan

14 South Scotland
Dumfries and Galloway
Borders

15 Central Scotland
Strathclyde
Central
Tayside
Fife
Lothian

16 North Scotland
Western Isles
Highland
Grampian

As a buyer of *Caravan and Camp in Britain 2001* you are entitled to a free copy of the booklet Beginner's Guide to DIY Holidays Out of Doors. If you would like us to send you the booklet please complete the order form below, detach this page and post it to us (stamp required). Please enclose 2 x 27 p stamps to cover postage and packing and allow 14 days for delivery.

FREE
p & p only

ORDER FORM (please use BLOCK CAPITALS)

Please send me a copy of the Beginner's Guide to DIY Holidays Out of Doors

Name . . . .

Address . . . .

Postcode . . . . Signed . . . .

RETURN to Mirador Books, Hillsboro, How Caple, Hereford HR1 4TE

If you would like your name to be added to our mailing list for news of forthcoming books and any reductions for orders placed prior to publication please tick box ☐

1 Northumbria

Bounded on the north and south by the Scottish and Yorkshire borders and on the east and west by the North Sea and the Pennines, Northumbria is made up of Northumberland, Durham and the new county of Tyne and Wear—a triangular and mainly built-up area embracing Newcastle, Whitley Bay and Sunderland.

North of Newcastle is a wildly beautiful coastline of rolling dunes and springy turf punctuated by fishing harbours and modest resorts, and guarded by impressive castles like massive Warkworth near the mouth of the Coquet, fortress home of the fighting Percys. Beyond, on the Great North Road and the threshold of Scotland is Berwick, its old quarter on the north bank of the Tweed contained within the massive ramparts. Offshore is Holy Island, dominated by its castle and melancholy priory ruins, and the Farne Islands, with their colonies of grey seals. Holy Island is linked to the mainland by a mile-long causeway uncovered at low tide, and there are boats to the Farnes from Seahouses.

Inland, from the natural barrier of the Pennine Fells in the south to the rolling Cheviots in the north, is wild and remote country laced by the dales or valleys of Wear, Coquet, Tees and Tyne and bisected by Hadrian's Wall, northernmost frontier of the Roman Empire, begun by order of Emperor Hadrian in AD122, which formed a continuous frontier across England from Wallsend to Bowness on Solway until abandoned in 383. A convenient centre for exploring the wall and the national park to the north of it is Hexham, near the important Roman sites of Housesteads and Corbridge. Linking Heddon on the Wall and Greenhead is the old military road B6318, which runs on or beside the wall at many points.

Main features of the national park are the Border Forest around Kielder, the beautiful river valleys and the Pennine Way, a route for walkers which passes through Once Brewed, Bellingham and Byrness to cross the Scottish border. Another ancient road which can be followed by walkers is the Devil's Causeway north of Hexham. Otterburn, famed for its tweed and as the site of the battle in 1388 between the Percys of England and the Douglases of Scotland, is well placed as a touring centre.

One of the newest sights in the region is Kielder Reservoir, the largest man-made lake in Europe, with plenty of scope for recreation.

Other sights include the fortresses of Alnwick, Bamburgh, Staindrop, Dunstanburgh and Raby, the churches of Escomb, Bywell and Hexham, the great cathedral of Durham and the ancient priory of Finchale. Three important museums are the Beamish near Stanley in Durham, the Grace Darling at Bamburgh and the Trailside Centre at Kielder.

Campsites, not numerous in Northumbria, exist in the national park, along the Northumbrian coast and at each of the main tourist centres.

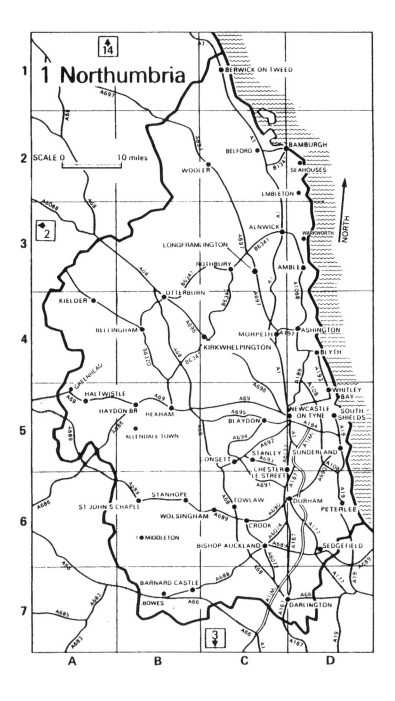

ALNWICK, Northumberland **Map C3**
Pop 7,000 EC Wed MD Sat SEE castle, church of SS Mary and Michael, Bondgate Tower, Alnwick
Fair (last Sun Jun) ⬛The Shambles, Northumberland Hall ✆Alnwick (01665) 510665 Restaurant:
White Swan, Bondgate Within ✆(01665) 602109

Cherry Tree Farm, Edlingham NE66 2BL ✆Whittingham (01665) 574635 OS map 81/115090 5m
W of Alnwick on B6341 (Rothbury) Open Apr-Sept, 1 acre, gentle slope 20 pitches No showers
£4.50

ALWINTON–see Rothbury

ASHINGTON, Northumberland **Map D4**
Pop 27,789. EC Wed, MD Fri, Sat SEE Wansbeck riverside park, Bothal castle and church
Restaurant: Queen's Head 6m W at Morpeth ✆(01670) 512083

Wansbeck Riverside Park, NE63 8TX ✆Ashington (01670) 812323 OS map 81/257863 ½m SW
of Ashington off A1068 (Bedlington) Open all year 75 pitches (enclosed) 5½ acres, part level,
hard standings 🔋🔲🔳🔷🔶🔛⬅️♿ boating, fishing £4.50-£8.00

BAMBURGH, Northumberland **Map C2**
Pop 450. EC Wed SEE Bamburgh Castle, Grace Darling museum Restaurant: Lord Crewe Arms
✆(01668) 214243

Bradford Kaims Caravan Park, NE69 7BW ✆(01668) 214432 OS map 75/165315 2m S of
Bamburgh on B1341 (Lucker) Open Easter-Oct 40 acres 350 pitches (270 static)
🔋➶🔲🔷🔶🔳🔛 £3.00

Glororum Caravan Park, Glororum NE69 7AW ✆Bamburgh (01668) 214457 OS map 75/166334
1½m SW of Bamburgh on B1341 (Adderstone) Open Apr-Oct 20 acres 250 pitches (150 static)
Level grass, sheltered 🔋➶🔲🔛🔳🔷🔶⬅️ £9.00-£12.00

BARNARD CASTLE, Co. Durham **Map B7**
Pop 5,700. EC Thur, MD Wed SEE ruined castle, Bowes museum, market cross ⬛43 Galgate
✆Teesdale (01833) 690909 Restaurant: King's Head, Market Pl ✆(01833) 38356

Bendholm Farm Caravan Park, Egglestone DL12 0AX ✆Teesdale (01833) 650457 OS map
92/990246 6m NW of Barnard Castle off B6278 (Stanhope) Open Mar-Oct 5 acres 99 pitches (65
static) Level grass and hard standing, sheltered 🔲🔛🔳🔷🔶🔛 £6.00

Thorpe Hall, Wycliffe DL12 9TW ✆Teesdale (01833) 627230 *Friendly site in grounds of country
house* OS map 92/104142 4m SE of Barnard Castle off A66 on Wycliffe road near Greta Bridge
Open Apr-Oct 2 acres 27 pitches (16 static) Level grass, sheltered 🔲🔛🔳🔷🔶 milk £8.00-£9.00

West Roods Working Farm, Boldron DL12 9SW ✆Teesdale (01833) 690116 OS map 92/032139
2m SW of Barnard Castle off A66 (Scotch Corner-Bowes) Open May-Oct, 6 pitches Level and
sloping grass, hard standings 🔛🔷⬅️ b and b £7.00-£9.00

Winston Caravan Park, Winston on Tees DL2 3RH ✆Darlington (01325) 730228 OS map 92/140168
5½m E of Barnard Castle on A67 (Darlington) Open Mar-Oct 3 acres 31 pitches (11 static) 3
acres level grass and hard standing, sheltered 🔋✖🔲🔛🔳🔷🔛 river bathing £8.00-£10.00

BEADNELL–see Seahouses

BELFORD, Northumberland **Map C2**
Pop 460. EC Thurs SEE St Mary's church Restaurant: Blue Bell, Market Place ✆(01668) 213543

Blue Bell Farm, West Street NE70 7QS ✆Belford (01668) 213362 OS map 75/107339 ¼m W of
Belford on B6349 (Wooler) Open Mar-Oct 75 pitches (45 static) 5 acres mainly level
✖♀⬅️🔲🔛🔳🔷🔛🏠♿ £7.50-10.00

Budle Bay Camp, Waren Mill NE70 7EE ✆Bamburgh (01668) 214598 OS map 75/146341 2m E
of Belford on B1342 (Bamburgh) Open Mar-Oct 250 pitches 6 acres mainly level grass, hard
standings, sheltered 🔋✖♀🔲🔛🔳🔷⬅️🔛 £7.50-£8.50

Waren Caravan Park, Waren Mill NE70 7EE ✆Bamburgh (01668) 214366 Fax (01668) 214224 OS
map 75/155343 2m E of Belford on B1342 (Bamburgh) Open Apr-Oct 480 pitches (300
static)–booking advisable 100 acres level grass and hard standings, sheltered
🔋✖♀⬅️➶🔲🔛🔳🔷🔲🔛⬅️🔛🔳♿ £7.50-£10.50

For other sites near Belford see also Bamburgh

BELLINGHAM, Northumberland **Map B4**
Pop 800 EC Tues, Sat See Kielder forest (largest in Europe), Kielder reservoir (largest in Britain)
15m NW ⬛Main St ✆(01434) 2220616 Restaurant: Cheviot ✆(01660) 220216

Brown Rigg Camping Caravan Park, NE48 2JY ✆(01434) 220175 OS map 80/835826 ½m S of
Bellingham on B6320 (Hexham) Open Easter-Oct 80 pitches 5 acres level grass and hard
standings, sheltered 🔋🔲🔛🔳🔷🔶⬅️🔲 fishing permits, indoor play area £8.00-£9.50

For other sites near Bellingham see Kielder

BERWICK ON TWEED, Northumberland   **Map C1**
Pop 11,600. EC Thur, MD Wed, Fri, Sat Small and ancient seaport of great charm at mouth of river Tweed SEE ramparts, castle remains, Jacobean bridge, Trinity church ⛟ Castlegate Car Park ☎ Berwick on Tweed (01289) 330733 Restaurant: Queen's Head, Sandgate ☎ (01289) 307852

Haggerston Castle Caravan Park, Beal TD15 2PA ☎ (01289) 381333 OS map 75/042435 6m SE of Berwick on Tweed on A1 (Alnwick) Open all year 1,255 pitches (1100 static) Level grass, sheltered ▮▮▮▮▮▮▮▮▮▮▮▮▮▮▮▮ boating, tennis, putting green, 9 hole par 3 golf course, bike hire, live entertainment £9.00-£22.00 (Mastercard/Visa)

Marshall Meadows Farm, A1 Road TD15 1UT ☎ (01289) 330735 OS map 75/982567 2½m N of Berwick on Tweed off A1 (Dunbar) Open Apr-Oct 105 pitches (65 static) Level grass, sheltered ▮▮▮▮▮ £4.00-£7.00

Ord House Country Park, East Ord TD15 2NS *Well equipped site in pleasant surroundings* ☎ (01289) 305288 OS map 75/981516 1½m SW of Berwick on Tweed off bypass and East Ord road Open Mar-Jan–must book peak periods 280 pitches (200 static) Level grass and hard standing, sheltered ▮▮▮▮▮▮▮▮▮▮▮▮ family room, crazy golf £8.30-£12.75 (Mastercard/ Visa/Delta/Switch)

BISHOP AUCKLAND, Co. Durham   **Map C6**
Pop 15,840. EC Wed, MD Sat SEE 12c church, Roman hypocaust at Vinovium (Binchester) ⛟ Town Hall, Market Pl ☎ (01388) 604922 Restaurant: Queen's Head, Market Pl ☎ (01388) 603477

Witton Castle, Witton le Wear DL14 0DE ☎ Witton le Wear (01388) 488230 OS map 92/154304 4m NW of Bishop Auckland on A68 (West Auckland-Tow Law) Open Mar-Oct 499 pitches (315 static) Level/sloping grass, sheltered ▮▮▮▮▮▮▮▮▮▮▮▮▮▮▮▮ paddling pool, putting, pets corner, flyfishing £7.50-£14.40

BLAYDON, Tyne and Wear   **Map C5**
Pop 4000. EC Wed SEE Derwent Walk country park, Gibside chapel at Rowlands Gill 2m S Restaurant: Black Bull, Bridge St ☎ (0191) 414 2846

Derwent Park Camping, Rowland's Gill NE39 1LG ☎ Rowland's Gill (01207) 543383 OS map 88/168586 3½m S of Blaydon on A694 (Consett) near junction with B6314 beside river Derwent Open Apr-Sept 4 acres 72 pitches (25 static) Level grass and hard standings, sheltered ▮▮▮▮▮▮▮▮▮ £9.30 (Mastercard/Visa/Eurocard)

BOWES, Co Durham   **Map B7**
SEE Norman keep, St Giles church, Mickle Fell (2,591ft) NW Restaurant: Fox and Hounds 4m N at Cotherstone ☎ (01833) 650241

East Mellwaters DL12 9RH ☎ Teesdale (01833) 628269 OS map 92/968127 1m W of Bowes off A66 (Appleby) Open Mar-Oct, 2 acres, gentle slope, 12 pitches Grass, sheltered ▮▮ (snack) fishing, bathing £4.00-£6.00 (Mastercard/Visa)

CASTLESIDE–see Consett

CONSETT, Co. Durham   **Map C5**
Pop 30,000. EC Wed, MD Fri, Sat SEE moors, Roman baths at Ebchester 2m N Restaurant: Bellamys near bus station ☎ (01207) 503654

Allensford Park Camping Site, Allensford, Castleside DH8 9BA *Secluded riverside location in Derwent valley* ☎ Consett (01207) 505572 OS map 88/082504 2½m SW of Consett off A68 (Tow Law-Hexham) Open Mar-Oct 80 pitches (50 static) Level grass, sheltered ▮▮▮▮▮▮▮▮ £8.50-£9.50

Byreside Farm, Hamsterley NE17 7RT ☎ Ebchester (01207) 560280 OS map 88/124562 3m NE of Consett off B6310 (Rowlands Gill) at Medomsley Open all year 40 pitches–booking advisable 3 acres part level, grass and hard standing ▮▮▮▮▮ £4.80

Manor Park Caravan Site, Broadmeadows, Castleside DH8 9HD ☎ Consett (01207) 501000/503706 OS map 88/104461 3½m S of Consett off A68 (Tow Law) via Castleside Open Apr-Oct 40 pitches (10 static) Part level grass, sheltered ▮▮▮▮▮▮▮▮▮ £5.50-£7.00

COTHERSTONE–see Barnard Castle

CRASTER–see Embleton

Finchale Abbey Farm

4m N of Durham off A167 (Chester le Street) and Newton Hall/Brasside road, near Finchale Priory.
Well-equipped site in pleasant setting beside river Wear, with level grass and hard standing.

Contact Mr or Mrs Welsh on 0191 386 6528   www.FinchaleAbbey.co.uk

---

DARLINGTON, Co. Durham   **Map D7**
Pop 97,210. EC Wed, MD Mon, Thurs, Sat SEE North Road rail museum, St Cuthbert's church
🅸 West Row ☎ Darlington (01325) 382698 Restaurant: Cricketers, Parkgate ☎ (01325) 384444

Newbus Grange, Neasham DL2 1PE ☎ Darlington (01325) 720973 OS map 93/320097 5m SE of
Darlington off A167 (Northallerton) Open Mar-Dec 150 pitches (130 static) Level grass 🗑🏠🔌
£12.50 inc awning and electrics

DURHAM, Co. Durham   **Map D6**
Pop 24,750. EC. Wed, MD Sat SEE Cathedral, Norman castle, Gulbenkian Museum of Oriental Art
🅸 Market Pl ☎ Durham (0191) 384 3720 Restaurant: Three Tuns, New Elvet ☎ (01385) 64326

Finchale Abbey Farm, Finchale Priory DH1 5SH ☎ Durham 0191-386 6528 OS map 88/295468
4m N of Durham off A167 (Chester le Street) and Newton Hall/Brasside road, beside river Wear
Open all year 180 pitches (100 static)–adv booking 6 acres level grass and hard standing,
sheltered 🅇 café, takeaway food 🗑🔌🅐🔌🅓🅧🔌🔌🅓🛁 fishing £7.50

Grange Park (Caravan Club), Meadow Lane, Carville DH1 1TL ☎ Durham 0191-384 4778 OS map
88/303446 2m NE of Durham off A1(M) on A690 (Sunderland) Open all year 10½ acres 120
pitches Level grass and hard standing, sheltered 🗑🔌🅐🔌🅓🔌🛁 £5.50-£6.50

EMBLETON, Northumberland   **Map D3**
Pop 300. EC Wed SEE castle, old church, vicarage with pele tower Restaurant: Craster 2m S at
Craster ☎ (01665) 576230/576233

Dunstan Hill (Camping Club), Craster NE66 3TQ ☎ (01665) 576310 OS map 75/236214 ½m SE
of Embleton on left of Craster road Open Mar 24-Nov 3 150 pitches Level grass and hard
standings 🗑🔌🅐🔌🅓🛁 games room, late arrivals enclosure £11.60-£14.60

Proctors Stead, Craster NE66 3TF ☎ Craster (01665) 576613 OS map 75/248202 1½m S of
Embleton on Craster road Open Mar-Oct 60 pitches 3 acres level grass and hard standings,
sheltered 🅇🗑🔌🅐🔌🅓🔌🅧 £6.50

GREENHEAD, Northumberland   **Map A4**
SEE Roman Wall, Featherstone Castle Restaurant: Holmhead, Hadrian's Wall ☎ (01697) 247402

Roam-n-Rest Caravan Park, Raylton House CA6 7HA ☎ (01697) 747213 OS map 86/656654 ¼m
W of Greenhead on right of A69 (Brampton) Open Mar-Oct 20 pitches (5 static) 1 acre level
grass, sheltered 🔌🅐🔌🔌 £6.50-£7.00

HALTWHISTLE, Northumberland   **Map A5**
Pop 2,500. EC Wed, MD Thurs SEE Hadrian's Wall, Featherstone Castle, 13c parish church of Holy
Cross, South Tyne valley S, Blenkinsopp Hall gardens 1m W 🅲 Church Hall, Main St ☎ Haltwhistle
(01434) 322002 Restaurant: Milecastle Inn, Military Rd ☎ (01434) 321372

Seldom Seen Caravan Park, NE49 0NE ☎ Haltwhistle (01434) 320571 OS map 86/87/718638 1m
E of Haltwhistle off A69 (Hexham) Open Mar-Jan 70 pitches (50 static) Level grass, sheltered
🛁🔌🅐 club room, fishing £8.00

Yont the Cleugh, Coanwood NE49 0QN ☎ Haltwhistle (01434) 320274 OS map 87/685585 4½m
S of Haltwhistle off Alston road Open Mar-Jan 107 pitches (77 static) 9 acres level grass and
hard standings, sheltered 🛁🗑🔌🅐🔌🅓🔌🔌 quoit pitch, bar meals £7.50-£9.00

HAYDON BRIDGE, Northumberland   **Map B5**
Pop 1,800. EC Wed SEE 18c bridge, old church, Langley Castle SW Restaurant: Anchor
☎ (01434) 684427

Poplars Riverside Park, Eastland Ends NE47 6BY ☎ Haydon Bridge (01434) 684427 OS map
87/836642 ¼m W of Haydon Bridge on A69 (Carlisle-Newcastle) Open Mar-Oct 43 pitches (30
static) 2½ acres level grass, sheltered 🗑🔌🅐🔌🅓🔌🅧 fishing £9.00

MANOR PARK
Castleside, Consett
Tel (01207) 501000/503706   Fax (01207) 509271

Open April-October. Part level grass, sheltered

HEXHAM, Northumberland   **Map B5**
Pop 10,000. EC Thurs, MD Tues, Fri SEE Housesteads Roman Camp, abbey church ⚿Manor
Office, Hallgate ☏Hexham (01434) 605225 Restaurant: Beaumont ☏(01434) 602331

Barrasford Park NE48 4BE ☏Hexham (01434) 681210 OS map 87/935738 5½m N of Hexham off
A68 (Corbridge-Carter Bar) Open Apr-Oct 150 pitches (120 static) no adv bkg 60 acres woodland
Hard standings, grass sloping, sheltered ⚑♀◨♥◍◉∅● £8.50

Causey Hill Caravan Park, Bensons Fell Farm, Causey Hill NE46 2JN ☏Hexham (01434) 602834
OS map 87/925627 1¼m SW of Hexham off B6305 (Alston) Open Apr-Oct–must book public
holidays 145 pitches Level/sloping grass and hard standing ⚑◨♥◍◉ £6.50-£9.50

Fallowfield Dene, Acomb NE46 4RP ☏Hexham (01434) 603553 OS map 87/938678 2m NW of
Hexham off A69 (Carlisle) on A6079 (Wall) in Acomb village Open Apr-Oct 160 pitches (80 static)
10 acres mainly level, grass and hardstanding ⚑◨♥♥◍●⚅ £6.50-£7.50

Heathergate Country Park, Lowgate NE46 2NN ☏(0402) 359131 OS map 87/902641 2m W of
Hexham off B6305 (Alston) Open Mar-Oct, 65 pitches (55 static) Level grass ◨♥◍◉∅⚘●▭
£12.00-£14.00

Hexham Racecourse, High Yarridge NE47 2JP OS map 87/918623 1½m S of Hexham off B6035
(Alston) Open Apr 25-Sept 28, 60 pitches Grass, level, open ◨♥◍◉∅◉⚘▢ £6.20

KIELDER, Northumberland   **Map A4**
Pop 330 Restaurant: Riverside Hall 15m SE at Bellingham ☏(01660) 220254

Kielder Forest Camp Site, NE48 1EP ☏Kielder (01434) 250291 OS map 80/627938 ¼m N of
Kielder centre near Forestry Commission visitor centre Open Apr-Sept 70 pitches 10 acres level
grass and hard standings, sheltered ⚑⚲◨♥◍◉∅⚘⚅ access to forest walks and cycle
routes £7.00-£8.50

KIRKWHELPINGTON, Northumberland   **Map C4**
SEE Bartholomew's church, river bridge Restaurant: The Hadrian 6m SW at Wall ☏(01434) 681232

Raechester Farm, NE19 2RH ☏Otterburn (01830) 540345 OS map 81/979871 2m NW of
Kirkwhelpington on right of A696 (Carter Bar) Open Easter-Sept 15 pitches ½ acre mainly level
grass and hard standing ✗ (snack) ♀ £3.50-£5.50

LONGFRAMLINGTON, Northumberland   **Map C3**
Pop 280 SEE Coquet valley and Swarland forest walk NE Restaurant: Granby on A697 ☏(01665)
570228

Percy Wood Caravan Park, Chesterhill, Swarland NE65 9JW *Peaceful site in mixed woodland 2m
from A1* ☏(01670) 787649 OS map 81/159040 2m NE of Longframlington at Swarland adj golf
course–signposted Open Mar-Jan 120 pitches (60 static) Level grass and hard standings,
sheltered ⚑◨♥◍◉∅◉⚘▭ full service pitches £8.00-£10.00 inc elect

MIDDLETON IN TEESDALE, Co Durham   **Map B6**
Pop 1,200 EC Wed MD alt Tues SEE church, old clock tower, High Force waterfall 5m NW
⚿Middleton Crafts, courtyard of Teesdale Hotel ☏(01833) 640400 Restaurant: Teesdale, Market Pl
☏(01833) 640264

Cote House Caravan Park, Cote House Farm DL12 0PN ☏(01833) 640515 OS map 91/951233
1m S of Middleton in Teesdale off B6277 (Barnard Castle) by Grassholme reservoir Open Mar-Oct
102 pitches (82 static) Level grass, sheltered by woodland ◍⚘ fishing £5.00

Daleview Caravan Park DL12 0NG ☏Teesdale (01833) 640233 OS map 92/948248 ½ W of
Middleton in Teesdale on Brough Road Open Mar-Oct, 4½ acres, 80 pitches (64 static) Level
grass and hard standing, sheltered ⚑✗ (snack) ♀◨◍▭ £3.00-£6.50

MORPETH, Northumberland   **Map C4**
Pop 16,000. EC Thurs, MD Wed SEE courthouse, parish church, clock tower ⚿Council Offices,
High Street ☏(01670) 511323 Restaurant: Queens Head, Bridge Street ☏(01670) 512083

Forget-me-Not Caravan Park, Longhorsley NE65 8QY ☏Longhorsley (0167088) 364 OS map
81/126946 7m NW of Morpeth off A697 (Wooler) Open Mar-Oct 60 pitches Hard standings and
grass ⚑✗♀◨♥◍◉∅◉⚘▢●▭ £7.00-£9.00

NEWCASTLE ON TYNE, Tyne and Wear   **Map D5**
Pop 267,600. EC Wed, MD Tues, Thurs, Sat, Sun SEE Civic Centre, cathedrals, museums
🅩 Central Library, Princess Square ☎ Newcastle on Tyne (0191) 2610610 Restaurant: Swallow,
Newgate Arcade ☎ 0191-232-5025

OTTERBURN, Northumberland   **Map B4**
Pop 300 SEE Otterburn Tower, Battle of Otterburn Memorial, Pennine Way Restaurant: Percy
Arms, Main St ☎ (01830) 520261

Border Forest Caravan Park, Cottonshope, Burnfoot NE19 1TF ☎ Otterburn (01830) 520259 OS
    map 80/780014 8m NW of Otterburn on A68 (Carter Bar) Open Mar-Oct, 3 acres, 45 pitches 3
    acres level grass 🔲🔌⊕∅🔤 £7.50

ROTHBURY, Northumberland   **Map C3**
Pop 2,000. EC Wed SEE Cragside Gardens, Callaby Castle, Brinkburn Priory 🅩 Nat Park Info
Centre, Church St ☎ (01669) 620887 Restaurant: Granby 3m E at Longframlington ☎ (01665)
570228

Clennell Hall, Alwinton NE65 7BG ☎ (01669) 650341 Fax (01669) 650341 OS map 80/928072
    10m NW of Rothbury off B6341 (Alwinton) Open all year 70 pitches 13 acres level grass
    ✗ 🍴 ⊷🔲🔌∅↩♿ sep pitches, games room, lic club £7.00-£10.00

Coquetdale Caravan Park, Whitton NE65 7RU ☎ Rothbury (01669) 620549 OS map 81/056008
    ½m SW of Rothbury on Newtown road Open Easter-Oct 250 pitches (200 static) Level grass,
    sheltered 🔲🔌∅⊕∅⊕↩ fishing, swimming near £8.00-£13.00 (2000)

ROWLAND'S GILL–see Blaydon

ST JOHN'S CHAPEL, Co. Durham   **Map B6**
Restaurant: Golden Lion, Market Pl ☎ (01388) 537231

Briton Hall, Westgate in Weardale DL13 1LN OS map 81/905380 1m E of St John's Chapel on
    A689 (Stanhope) Open Mar-Oct 50 pitches 🔲∅ fishing, bathing £1.50-£4.00

Weardale Caravan Site, Westgate in Weardale DL13 2JT ☎ Weardale (01388) 537733 OS map
    92/903383 2m E of St John's Chapel on A689 (Stanhope) Open Apr-Oct 45 pitches 🔲∅🔌 (25)
    £3.00-£5.00

SEAHOUSES, Northumberland   **Map D2**
Pop 1,800. EC Wed SEE fishing port, marine life centre, fishing museum 🅩 Seafield Rd
☎ Seahouses (01665) 720884 Restaurant: Olde Shop, Main St ☎ (01665) 720200

Beadnell Links, The Harbour, Beadnell NE67 5BN ☎ Seahouses (01665) 720526 OS map
    75/233287 2m S of Seahouses off B1340 Open Apr-Oct 167 pitches (150 static)–no
    tents 10 acres level grass 🔲🔌∅⊕∅ £9.00-£15.50 (Mastercard/Visa/Switch)

Beadnell Park (Camping Club), Anstead NE67 5BX ☎ Seahouses (01665) 720586 OS map
    75/231297 2m S of Seahouses on right of B1340 (Beadnell) Open Mar-Sept 150 marked pitches
    Level grass, sheltered Last arrival 2100 🔲 £10.40-£13.60

Seafield Park, Seafield Road NE68 7SP ☎ Seahouses (01665) 720628 OS map 75/207322 In
    centre of Seahouses on Bamburgh road Open Mar-Dec 230 pitches (207 static) Level grass and
    hard standings, sheltered ✗🔲🔌∅⊕∅⊕↩🔲🔤♿ £9.00-£18.00 (all cards)

Swinhoe Links, Beadnell NE67 5BW ☎ Seahouses (01665) 720589 OS map 75/230285 1½m S of
    Seahouses on B1340 (Beadnell) Open Apr-Oct 163 pitches (140 static) 24 acres level grass
    🔌🔲∅⊕∅⊕↩🔤 £5.50-£6.50

STANHOPE, Co. Durham   **Map B6**
Pop 2000 Attractive old market and quarrying town, main centre for walks on moors flanking
Weardale SEE 18c castle, lime trees, St Thomas church 🅩 Durham Dales Centre, Castle Gdns
☎ (01388) 527650 Restaurant: Teesdale 12m S at Middleton in Teesdale ☎ (01833) 640264

Stanhope Caravan Park, Melton House DL13 2PF ☎ (01388) 528398 OS map 92/992392 ¼m S
    of Stanhope off A689 (Wolsingham) Open Mar-Oct 70 pitches 🔲🔌∅ £3.00-£5.00

STANLEY, Co. Durham   **Map C5**
Pop 14,380. EC Wed, MD Thurs SEE Beamish Open Air Museum (industrial archaeology) 1m N
Restaurant: Blue Boar Tavern, Front St (off A693) ✆(01207) 231167

Bobby Shafto Caravan Park, Beamish DH9 0RY *Tranquil site in wooded setting* ✆Tyneside
(0191) 370 1776 OS map 88/232545 2m E of Stanley off A693 (Chester le Street) and Beamish
museum road Open Mar-Oct, 8 acres, level, sheltered grass 75 pitches (40 static)
🐾♿🚿♨️🅿️⊕∅⊕☐ £9.50-£10.50 (Mastercard/Visa)

Harperley Country Park, Tanfield Lea DH9 8TB ✆Stanley (01207) 234011 OS map 88/171535
1m NW of Stanley off A693 (Leadgate) Open Apr-Oct 25 pitches (hard standings) ✖🅿️∅ hotel
facilities £4.00-£6.00

WOLSINGHAM, Co. Durham   **Map C6**
Pop 2,840. EC Wed SEE Killhope Wheel lead mine 2m W Restaurant: Queen's Head 10m SE at
Bishop Auckland ✆(01388) 603477

Bradley Mill Caravan Park, DL13 3JH ✆(01388) 527285 OS map 92/107360 2m E of
Wolsingham on A689 (Crook) Open Apr-Oct–booking preferable 120 pitches (100 static) Level
grass and hard standing, sheltered 🅿️♿⊕∅🔌🚽 £5.00-£10.00

The Eilands, Frosterley, Landieu Weardale DL13 2SJ ✆(01388) 527230 OS map 92/040368 1½m
W of Wolsingham off A689 (Stanhope) at Frosterley, by river Wear Open Mar-Oct 100 pitches–no
tents 15 acres level/sloping grass, sheltered 🐾🅿️♿∅🔌🚽 £6.50-£7.50

WOOLER, Northumberland   **Map C2**
Pop 1,830. EC Thurs, MD Mon, Wed, Sat SEE Ancient British Camps 🅿️Bus Station Car Park
✆Wooler (01668) 281602 Restaurant: Ryecroft, Ryecroft Way ✆(01668) 281233

Riverside Caravan Park NE71 6QG ✆Wooler (01668) 281447 OS map 75/997278 ¼m SE of
Wooler off A697 (Newcastle) Open Easter-Oct 400 pitches (333 static) Level grass, sheltered
🐾✖♿🔌🅿️♿⊕∅☐⊕🔌♿ riding stables, trout fishing, family club with entertainment £9.50-
£18.00 inc club membership

  Clennel Hall, Alwinton
NW of Rothbury at edge of national park
Tranquil rural site with modern facilities – Open all year
Tel (01669) 650341

2 Cumbria

CUMBRIA

Cumbria replaces the old counties of Cumberland, Westmorland and that part of 'Lancashire across the sands' which juts out into Morecambe Bay. Bounded on the north and south by the estuaries of the Kent and Esk and on the east and west by the Pennines and the Irish Sea, the region is centred on the Cumbrian Mountains which reach their highest point in the 3200ft Scafell Pikes north of Eskdale. The lakes fan out from Scafell like the spokes of a wheel, forming the essential element in a beautiful landscape noted less for its benevolent climate than for its spectacular variations of colour and contour, and the crowds that swamp the more accessible resorts in season. Yet May and June are usually the sunniest and driest months.

Best known of the lakes are Derwentwater (the acknowledged 'queen'), Windermere, Ullswater, Buttermere, Coniston, Thirlmere, Rydal and Bassenthwaite; but the undisputed hub of the lakes is Keswick, its limestone buildings typical of Cumbrian architecture.

Main gateways to the region are Kendal and Penrith. A miniature railway runs from Eskdale to Ravenglass, near the coast, and ferries operate on the larger lakes, some linking up with bus services, but public transport generally is poor. For walkers at least

distances are short, since most of Cumbria is contained within a fifteen mile radius of Scafell. Main roads are feasible for most vehicles, but many secondary roads are narrow and gradients on both major and minor roads can be as steep as one in three. Some passes like Honister, Hardknott, Wrynose and Newlands are particularly dangerous and many others are unfit for anything on wheels.

Coastal resorts include Grange over Sands and, farther north, smaller and quieter Silloth, Seascale and St Bees. The most remote parts of Cumbria are the contrasting peninsulas of Furness and Cartmel, newly won from Lancashire. Where a railway now crosses Morecambe Bay to link them with the mainland travellers once had to make the dangerous journey on foot at low tide. Both areas are rewarding for the amateur archaeologist—among recent finds are flint tools, stone circles and Iron Age camps.

Cumbria is best appreciated in its quiet valleys, like lovely Eskdale, where Beckfoot is a popular centre for climbing Scafell. Other centres for walkers and climbers are Ambleside for the Langdale Pikes and Keswick for the 3000ft Skiddaw Peak. There are many regarding discoveries to be made in the Eden Valley (for which Appleby is the obvious centre) as there are in the remote country adjoining the Scottish border.

This is not a region rich in historic buildings. The Roman fort on Hardknott and the bath-house at Ravenglass are noteworthy, as are the castles of Carlisle, Cockermouth, Wetherall and Muncaster and the country houses of Levens Hall and Abbots Hall. There are Wordsworth museums at Grasmere and Cockermouth.

Most campsites in the lakes are simply equipped and in quiet situations. The widest choice is around Carlisle, at Penrith and Silloth, but all the major centres—and other places on the coast—have several sites.

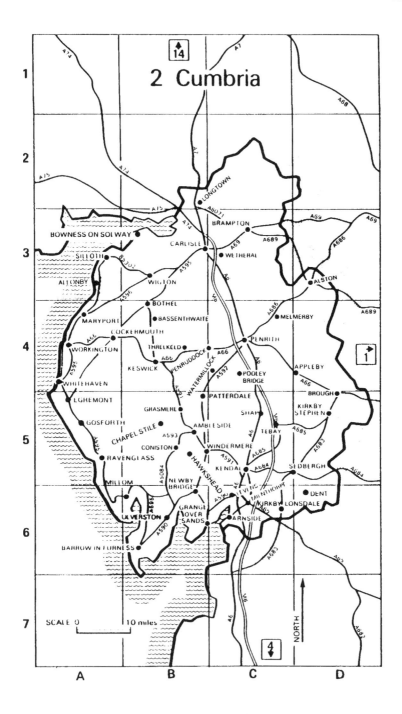

ALLONBY, Cumbria   **Map A3**
Pop 650 SEE extensive sands of Allonby Bay Restaurant: Waverley 5m S at Maryport ☎(01900)
812115

Blue Dial Caravan Park, CA15 6PB ☎Allonby (01900) 881277 OS map 85/075407 1m S of
Allonby on B5300 (Maryport) Open Apr-Oct 150 pitches ▣⊟⊘⊕∅⌄⎯⊡ £5.00-£6.00

Manor House Caravan Park, Edderside Road, CA15 6RA ☎Allonby (01900) 881236 OS map
85/092450 1m NE of Allonby off B5300 (Silloth) on Edderside road Open Mar-Oct 180 pitches
(160 static) Level grass ⚑✕⚲⇢↗▣⊟⊘⊕∅⊕⌄⎯⊡ fitness room & sauna £4.00-£7.00
(Mastercard/Amex)

Mealo House Farm, CA15 6PB ☎(01900) 881210 OS map 85/079416 ½m S of Allonby near junct
of B5300 (Maryport) and Hayton road Open Apr-Oct 140 pitches (120 static) Level grass
▣⊟⊘⊕∅⊕⌄ £6.00-£8.00 (Mastercard/Visa)

Spring Lea Caravan Park, CA15 6QF ☎Allonby (01900) 881331 OS map 85/086433 On B5300
(Maryport-Silloth) in Allonby near beach Open Apr-Oct 131 pitches (96 static) 5 acres level grass
and hard standings ✕⚲⇢▣⊟⊕∅▱ (indoor) ⌄⊡ sauna, games room £8.00-£10.00
(Mastercard/Visa/Switch)

ALSTON, Cumbria   **Map D3**
Pop 1,930 EC Tues MD Sat SEE market cross, church, Pennine Way, Gilderdale Forest SW
🚉Railway Station ☎(01434) 381696 Restaurant: Victoria, Front Street ☎(01498) 381269

Horse and Wagon Caravan Park, Nentsbury CA9 3LH ☎Nentsbury (01434) 382805 OS map
87/764452 3m E of Alston on A689 (Durham) Open Mar-Oct 3 acres, mainly level grass,
sheltered, 36 pitches (26 static) ▣⊟⊘⊕∅⌄⎯⊕ £7.50-£9.50

AMBLESIDE, Cumbria   **Map B5**
Pop 2,560. EC Thurs, MD Wed SEE lake Windermere, House on the Bridge, Stock Ghyll Force,
White Craggs rock garden 1m W 🚉Old Courthouse, Church Street ☎(01539) 432582 Restaurant:
Queens, Market Pl ☎(01539) 432206

Skelwith Fold Caravan Park, Skelwith Fold LA22 0HX *In grounds of former manor near lakeside*
☎(01539) 432277 OS map 90/355029 1½m SW of Ambleside off B5286 (Hawkshead) Open
Mar-Nov 15, 450 pitches (300 static) Level, sheltered hard standing ⚑↗▣⊟⊘⊕∅⊕⌄⎯⊕ (15)
♿ £8.50-£9.50

For other sites near Ambleside see Coniston, Hawkshead and Windermere

APPLEBY, Cumbria   **Map D4**
Pop 2,330. EC Thurs, MD Sat SEE St Lawrence church, High Cross, 16c Moot Hall, castle, Eden
Valley 🚉Moot Hall, Boroughgate ☎Appleby (017683) 51177 Restaurant: Tufton Arms,
Boroughgate ☎(017683) 51593

Low Moor, Kirkby Thore CA10 1XG ☎Kirkby Thore (017683) 61231 OS map 91/626260 4½m NW
of Appleby on A66 (Penrith) Open Apr-Oct 37 pitches (25 static) 2 acres, level/gentle slope, grass
⊟⊘⊕∅⊡ £5.00

Silver Band Caravan Park, Silver Band, Knock CA16 6DL ☎Kirkby Thore (017683) 61218 OS
map 91/675276 5m N of Appleby off A66 (Penrith) at Kirkby Thore on Knock road at Silverband
Open Mar-Oct (weekends Nov-Feb)—must book 12 pitches ½ acre, sloping grass
⚑↗⊟⊘⊕⎯⊡ £6.00-£7.50

Three Greyhounds, Great Asby CA16 6EX ☎Appleby (017683) 51428 OS map 91/682132 2m S
of Appleby off B6260 (Tebay) on Great Asby road Open Mar-Oct 18 pitches 3 acres mainly level
grass ⚲⇢⊟⊕⊕⎯ £6.00

Wild Rose Caravan and Camping Park, Ormside CA16 6EJ *Top level facilities meticulously
maintained* ☎Appleby (017683) 51077 OS map 91/697165 2m SSE of Appleby off B6260
(Orton) Open all year 40 acres 440 pitches (200 static) Caravans, hard standing and grass
Tents, level and slightly sloping grass Shelter available all areas ⚑✕⇢↗▣⊟⊘⊕∅▱
(heated) ⊕⌄☐♿fishing, farm produce, cycle hire, indoor toddlers' playroom, mini-golf, safety-
surfaced outdoor playpark, teenage games room £7.40-£12.15 (inc hot water and heated pool)
(Mastercard/Visa)

ASPATRIA–see Cockermouth

AYSIDE–see Newby Bridge

**Some site operators make it a rule that cars must be left in a separate parking area away from
caravans and tents, which can be inconvenient when shopping by car. But it does minimise
traffic noise and the risk to children.**

BARROW IN FURNESS, Cumbria   Map B6
Pop 60,000. EC Thurs, MD Wed, Fri, Sat SEE ruins of Furness Abbey, Walney Island nature reserves, Biggar village ℹ Civic Hall, Duke Street ☎ Barrow in Furness (01229) 870156 Restaurant: Victoria Park, Victoria Rd ☎ (01229) 821159

Longlands Caravan Park, Kirkby in Furness LA17 7XZ ☎ Kirkby in Furness (01229) 889342 OS map 96/239836 8m N of Barrow in Furness off A595 (Whitehaven) Open Mar-Oct 130 pitches ▵▿

South End Caravan Site, Walney Island LA14 3YQ *Site near sea and nature reserves* ☎ Barrow in Furness (01229) 472823/471556 OS map 96/208633 3½m S of Barrow in Furness on unclass road, via Biggar Open Mar-Oct 150 pitches (100 static) Sloping grass ▵▿ (indoor heated) ▵▿ lic club, bowling green £8.00-£12.00 (Mastercard/Visa)

BASSENTHWAITE, Cumbria   Map B4
Pop 400 SEE old church at lakeside Restaurant: Pheasant Inn ☎ (01768) 776234

Trafford Caravan Park, Low Wood CA12 4QH ☎ (01768) 776298 OS map 90/228316 1m W of Bassenthwaite on A591 (Bothel-Keswick) Open Mar-Oct 80 pitches (50 static) Level grass and hard standing ▵▿ farm produce £6.00-£10.00 inc elect

North Lakes Caravan Park, Bewaldeth CA13 9SY ☎ (01768) 776510 OS map 89/207354 2m NW of Bassenthwaite on A591 (Bothel-Keswick) at Bewaldeth Open Mar-Nov, 30 acres, level grass and hard standings, 145 pitches (50 static) ▵▿ £8.00

Robin Hood Caravan Park CA12 4RJ ☎ Bassenthwaite Lake (01768) 776334 OS map 89/207354 ½m N of Bassenthwaite off Caldbeck road Open Mar-Nov, 2 acres, part level 35 pitches (20 static) grass and hard standing level/sloping, sheltered ▵▿ fishing, pony trekking £5.00-£15.00

BOTHEL, Cumbria   Map B4
Restaurant: Pink House 3m NE at Mealsgate ☎ (01697) 371229

Larches Caravan Park, Mealsgate CA5 1LQ ☎ (016973) 71379 OS map 85/206416 2m NE of Bothel on right of A595 (Carlisle) Open Mar-Oct, 273 pitches (100 static) Grass and hard standing, sheltered ▵▿ £6.80-£8.80

Skiddaw View Caravan Park, Sunderland CA5 2JG ☎ (01697) 320919 OS map 89/90/180370 1m S of Bothel off A591 (Keswick) on Sunderland road Open Apr 11-Oct 31 96 pitches (76 static) ▵▿ sauna £5.00-£10.00 (all cards)

BOWNESS ON SOLWAY, Cumbria   Map B3
Pop 300 SEE remains of Hadrian's Wall, mudflats and marshes Restaurant: Crown and Mitre 10m SE at Carlisle ☎ (01228) 25491

Cottage Caravan Park, Port Carlisle CA5 5DJ ☎ (01697) 351317 OS map 85/242612 2m E of Bowness on Solway off coast road Open Mar-Oct 237 pitches (200 static) Grass, level, sheltered, some hard standing ▵▿ bar meals, beer garden £7.00-£8.50

BOWNESS ON WINDERMERE–see Windermere

BRAITHWAITE–see Keswick

BRAMPTON, Cumbria   Map C3
Pop 3,400. EC Thurs, MD Wed SEE church with Burnes Jones windows, Moot Hall, Prince Charlie's house ℹ Moot Hall ☎ Brampton (016977) 3433 Restaurant: Farlam Hall ☎ (01697) 773600

Irthing Vale Holiday Park, Old Church Lane CA8 2AA ☎ Brampton (016977) 3600 OS map 86/523614 ½m N of Brampton off A6071 (Longtown) Open Mar-Oct 50 pitches (23 static) 4½ acres level grass ▵▿ £8.00

BEGINNER'S GUIDE TO DIY OUTDOOR HOLIDAYS

free to buyers of this year's guide –

see order form on p9

CARK IN CARTMEL–see Grange over Sands

CARLISLE, Cumbria   Map B3
Pop 70,000. EC Thurs, MD all except Thurs and Sun SEE cathedral, castle, Tullie House museum, market cross, tithe barn ▊Old Town Hall, Greenmarket ✆Carlisle (01228) 512444 Restaurant: Crown and Mitre, English St ✆(01228) 25491

Cairndale Caravan Park, Cumwhitton, CA4 9BZ ✆(01768) 896280 OS map 86/519522 6m SE of Carlisle off A69 (Brampton) via Great Corby Open Mar-Oct 20 pitches (15 static) Hard standings, level, sheltered ▯ £5.00-£5.50

Dalston Hall Caravan Park, Dalston CA5 7JX ✆Carlisle (01228) 710165 OS map 85/375517 3m W of Carlisle on B5299 (Dalston) Open Mar-Oct 60 pitches Level grass and hard standing ▯ fishing, 9-hole golf £6.00-£7.50 (Visa)

Dandy Dinmont Caravan Site, Blackford CA6 4EA ✆(01228) 674611 OS map 85/397622 4m N of Carlisle off A7 (Longtown) Open Mar-Oct 4.5 acres 47 pitches Level grass and hard standings ▯ £6.50-£8.00

Orton Grange Caravan Park, Wigton Road CA5 6LA ✆(01228) 710252 OS map 85/357517 4m SW of Carlisle on A595 (Wigton) Open all year 7 acres 72 pitches (22 static) Level, grass and hard standings, sheltered ▯ (heated) ▯ games room, accessory shop £7.20-£9.00

For other sites near Carlisle see Bowness on Solway, Brampton, Longtown and Wigton

---

COCKERMOUTH, Cumbria   Map A4
Pop 6,290. EC Thurs, MD Mon SEE Wordsworth House, ruined castle, Moorland Close, birthplace of Fletcher Christian of Mutiny on the Bounty fame ▊Town Hall, Market Street ✆Cockermouth (01900) 822634 Restaurant: Wordsworth, Main St ✆(01900) 822757

Graysonside Farm Caravan Park, Lorton Road CA13 9TQ ✆Cockermouth (01900) 826972 OS map 89/134292 1m E of Cockermouth on B5292 (Buttermere) Open Mar-Sept, 12 pitches ▯(£1.50/wk under cover) £4.00

Inglenook Caravan Park, Fitzbridge, Lamplugh CA14 4SH ✆Lamplugh (01946) 861240 OS map 89/084205 6½m SSW of Cockermouth off A5086 (Egremont) Open all year, 58 pitches (28 static) Level/sloping grass and hard standings ▯ £7.00-£9.00

Violet Bank Caravan Park, Simonscales Lane, off Lorton Road CA13 9TG ✆Cockermouth (01900) 822169 OS map 89/125295 ½m S of Cockermouth on B5292 (Lorton/Buttermere) Open Mar-Nov 120 pitches (90 static) ▯ Level/sloping grass and hard standing £5.90-£6.90

Wheatsheaf Inn, Low Lorton CA13 9UW ✆(01900) 85268 OS map 89/153263 4m SE of Cockermouth on B5289 (Buttermere) Open Mar-Oct 15 pitches Level grass, sheltered ▯ £8.50-£12.50

Whinfell Hall Caravan Park, Lorton CA13 0RQ ✆(01900) 822260 OS map 89/150254 3½m SSE of Cockermouth off B5289 (Borrowdale) Open Mar-Oct 4 acres, level, 52 pitches (16 static) Level grass and hard standing ▯ £6.00-£8.00

Wyndham Caravan Park, Keswick Road CA13 9SF ✆(01900) 822571/825238 OS map 89/133312 1m E of Cockermouth on old Keswick road Open Mar-Oct 132 pitches (102 static) Level grass and hard standing, sheltered ▯ dancing, snooker, family social club, amusement arcade £7.60-£12.00

CONISTON, Cumbria   **Map B5**
Pop 1,060 EC Wed SEE Ruskin Museum, parish church, Donald Campbell Memorial, Tennyson's home, Coniston Water, Coniston Old Man 2,633ft, Tarn Hows (NT) ∎ Yewdale Rd ☏ Coniston (01539) 441533 Restaurant: Black Bull, Yewdale Rd ☏ (01539) 441335

Coniston Hall, Haws Bank LA21 8AS ☏ Coniston (01539) 441223 OS map 96/304964 ¾m S of Coniston off A593 (Millom) via Haws Bank by Coniston Water Open Mar-Oct, 20 acres, level/gentle slope, grass and hard standings 200 pitches–no trailer caravans ⬛✕🅿🅰⊕ boating, fishing £8.50

Hoathwaite Farm, Torver LA21 8AX *Basic site in superb secluded setting with lake access* ☏ Coniston (01539) 441349 OS map 96/296949 2m S of Coniston off A593 (Broughton in Furness) before Torver Open all year 34 pitches 30 acres level/sloping grass ⊕ lake access *No showers* £3.50-£5.00

Pier Cottage Caravan Park LA21 8AJ ☏ Coniston (01539) 441497 OS map 96/310973 ¼m E of Coniston off B5285 (Hawkshead) by lake Open Mar-Oct, 1 acre, level, sheltered 10 pitches–no tents–must book ⊕ £9.00-£10.00

DENT, Cumbria   **Map D6**
Pop 300 SEE Dentdale, Dales Way, St Andrew church Restaurant: Sun Inn, Main St ☏ (01539) 625208

Conder Farm, LA10 5QT ☏ (01539) 625277 OS map 98/706868 In Dent off Cowgill road Open all year 48 pitches Sloping grass £6.00-£6.50

High Laning Caravan Camping Park, LA10 5QJ ☏ Dent (01539) 625239 OS map 98/738469 In two sections on W edge of Dent Open Mar-Sept/all year 40 pitches 3½ acres level grass ⬛✕🛈⇦↗🅿🅱🅰⊕∅⤳🍴🏪🏠♿

EGREMONT, Cumbria   **Map A5**
Pop 8,030. EC Wed, MD Fri SEE castle ruins ∎ 12 Main Street ☏ Egremont (01946) 820693 Restaurant: Roseneath 6m NW at Low Moresby ☏ (01946) 861572

Home Farm Caravan Park, Rothersyke CA22 2UD ☏ (01946) 820797 and 824023 OS map 89/993094 2m SW of Egremont on B5345 (Calder Bridge-St Bees) Open Mar-Nov 18 pitches Hard standings and grass, level, sheltered 🛈🅱🅰⊕⊕ £8.00-£12.00

Tarside Caravan Site, Braystone, Beckermet CA21 2YL ☏ (01946) 841308 OS map 89/005063 2m S of Egremont–signposted from B5345 Open all year 200 pitches (150 static) Level grass and hard standing ✕🅿⇦↗🛈🅱🅰⊕∅🏪🏠 fishing £4.00-£5.00

ESKDALE–see Gosforth

GILCRUX–see Cockermouth

GOSFORTH, Cumbria   **Map A5**
SEE Gosforth Cross in churchyard Restaurant: Westlakes at junct of A595 and B5344 ☏ (01946) 725221

Church Stile Farm, Wasdale, Seascale CA20 1ET ☏ (01946) 725388 OS map 89/124040 4m E of Gosforth on unclass (Nether Wasdale) road Open Mar-Nov 80 pitches (30 static)–no touring caravans 🛈🅰⊕ £5.00-£6.00

Fisherground Farm Campsite, Eskdale CA19 1TF ☏ Eskdale (01946) 723319 OS map 89/153002 7m SE of Gosforth on unclass (Eskdale Green/Boot) road Open Mar-Nov 150 pitches–no caravans Level grass, sheltered 🛈🅱🅰⊕∅⤳🏠 adventure playground, miniature railway, camp fires permitted £9.00

Seven Acres Caravan Park, Holmrook CA19 1YD ☏ (01946) 725480 OS map 89/073019 1m S of Gosforth centre off A595 (Broughton-Whitehaven) Open Mar 1-Nov 15 103 pitches (65 static) 7 acres level grass and hard standings, part sheltered 🛈🅱🅰⊕∅⤳🏪 £8.00

GRANGE OVER SANDS, Cumbria   **Map B6**
Pop 3,470. EC Thurs SEE Cartmel Priory gatehouse 2m W, Holker Hall 3m SW ∎ Victoria Hall, Main Street ☏ (01539) 534026 Restaurant: Grange, Lindale Rd ☏ (014484) 3666

Meathop Fell (Caravan Club), Meathop LA11 6RB ☏ (01539) 532912 OS map 96/438805 5m N of Grange over Sands on A590 (Levens Bridge) Open all year, level, hard standings, 150 pitches 🅱🅰⊕∅⤳♿ dog walk £6.00-£8.00

Old Park Wood Caravan Site, Holker, Cark in Cartmel LA11 7PP ☏ (01539) 558266 OS map 96/335782 3m W of Grange over Sands off B5277 (Cark) Open Mar-Oct–must book public holidays 367 pitches (325 static) Level grass and hard standings ⬛↗🛈🅱🅰⊕∅🖿⊕⤳ £13.50

GREYSTOKE–see Penruddock

HAWKSHEAD, Cumbria   **Map B5**
Pop 690. EC Thurs SEE Esthwaite Water, forest, Theatre in the Forest 3m S of Grizedale Main
car park ☎(01539) 436525 Restaurant: Queen's Head ☎(01539) 436271

Croft Caravan and Camp Site, North Lonsdale Road, LA22 0NX ☎Hawkshead (01539) 436374
   OS map 96/353982 ¼m SE of Hawkshead centre on B5286 (Near Sawrey) Open Mar-Oct 100
   pitches (20 static) Level grass sheltered TV room £10.50 (Mastercard/Visa)

Grizedale Hall (Camping Club), LA22 0GL ☎(01229) 860257 OS map 97/337943 3m S of
   Hawkshead on left of Satterthwaite road Open Apr-Sept, 60 pitches–tents and trailer tents and
   m/vans only, adv booking min 2 nights 3 acres level, sheltered, forest setting parent
   and child room, recreation room £9.60-£12.10

Hawkshead Hall Farm, LA22 0NN ☎Hawkshead (01539) 436221 OS map 96/351988 ½m N of
   Hawkshead centre on right of B5286 (Ambleside) near junction with B5285 (Coniston) Open Mar-
   Oct, 60 pitches 3½ acres gentle slope, grass and hard standings No showers £5.00

Waterson Ground Farm, Outgate LA22 0NJ ☎Hawkshead (01539) 436225 OS map 96/351994
   1m N of Hawkshead on left of B5286 (Ambleside) near junction with Borwick Lodge road Open
   Mar 1-Oct 15, 50 pitches 6 acres level grass £4.50-£5.00

INGS–see Windermere

KENDAL, Cumbria   **Map C5**
Pop 21,590. MD Sat SEE parish church, museum, Sizergh castle (NT) 3m SW Town Hall,
Highgate ☎Kendal (01593) 725758 Restaurant: Woolpack, Stricklandgate ☎(01539) 723852

Ashes Lane Camping Caravan Park, Ashes Lane, Staveley LA8 9JS ☎(01539) 821119 OS map
   97/479964 3m NW off Kendal off A591 (Windermere) Open Mar-Jan 22 acres, part level, 350
   pitches (50 static) £6.00-£15.00

Low Park Wood (Caravan Club), Sedgwick LA8 0JZ ☎(01539) 560186 OS map 97/509878 3m
   SSW of Kendal off M6 at Junction 36 Open Easter-Oct 180 pitches no tents–must book Hard
   standing £7.50-£15.00 (Mastercard/Visa)

Pound Farm, Crook LA8 8JZ ☎Crook (01539) 821220 OS map 97/471953 3m NW of Kendal off
   A591 (Windermere) on left of B5284 (Bowness) Open Mar 1-Nov 14 34 pitches–bkg advised 2
   acres level grass and hard standings, sheltered £5.50-£8.50

Ratherheath Lane Camping Caravan Park, Chain House, Bonning Gate LA8 8JU ☎Crook (01539)
   821154 OS map 97/479957 3m NW of Kendal off A5284 (Crook) in Ratherheath Lane Open Mar
   1-Nov 15 20 pitches Level grass £7.50-£9.50

KESWICK, Cumbria   **Map B4**
Pop 4,850 EC Wed, MD Sat SEE Derwentwater, Southey's grave, Castlerigg stone circle Moot
Hall, Market Square ☎Keswick (01768) 772645 Restaurant: Queen's, Main St ☎(01768) 773333

Burns Farm, St Johns in the Vale CA12 4RR ☎Threlkeld (01768) 779225 OS map 90/308242
   2½m E of Keswick off A66 (Penrith) on Castlerigg Stone Circle road Open Mar-Oct 37 pitches 2
   acres level grass £5.00-£7.50

Burnside Caravan Site, Underskiddaw CA12 4PF ☎Keswick (01768) 72950 OS map 89/265245
   1m NW of Keswick on A591 (Bothel)–A66 roundabout Open Mar 15-Oct 31, 49 pitches (25 static)
   2½ acres level grass and hard standing £9.00-£11.50

Castlerigg Hall, Castlerigg CA12 4TE ☎Keswick (01768) 772437 OS map 89/285225 1m SE of
   Keswick off A591 (Grasmere) Open Apr-Oct 150 pitches Level grass and hard standing
   breakfast £9.50-£11.20 (Mastercard/Visa)

Dalebottom Holiday Park, Dalebottom, Naddle CA12 4TF ☎Keswick (01768) 772176 OS map
   90/294220 2m SE of Keswick on left of A591 (Ambleside) Open Mar-Oct 60 pitches 7 acres
   level/sloping grass, sheltered £6.00-£9.00

Derwentwater Caravan Park, Crowe Park Rd, CA12 5EN *Quiet lakeside park in woodland 3 min
   from town centre* ☎Keswick (01768) 772579 OS map 90/256235 ½m W of Keswick centre via
   Tithebarn Street, by lake Open Mar 1-Nov 14 210 pitches (160 static)–no tents, no awnings 17½
   acres hard standings, sheltered private beach–pitches with all mains services
   £8.40-£9.20

Scotgate Caravan Site, Braithwaite CA12 5TF ☎Braithwaite (01768) 778343 OS map 90/235236
   2½m W of Keswick at junction of A66 (Cockermouth) and B5292 (High Lorton) Open Mar-Oct 9
   acres, 150 pitches (35 static) no adv bkg Level grass and hard standing
   £7.00-£15.00 (Mastercard/Visa)

For other sites near Keswick see Bassenthwaite

Church Stile Farm in Wasdale near Gosforth

Your base for visiting Wastwater, England's deepest lake and Scafell Pike, England's highest peak (3205m). A sheltered site on a working farm, toilet block cleaned twice daily, country walks, fell climbing, beach 6m, Muncaster Castle, Ravenglass and Eskdale miniature railway 9m. Restaurant/bar nearby. *No touring caravans.*

KIRKBY LONSDALE, Cumbria   **Map C6**
Pop 1,500. EC Wed, MD Thurs SEE Devil's Bridge, St Mary's church ℹ Main Street ☎ (01524) 271437 Restaurant: Pheasant Inn 1m NE at Casterton ☎ (01524) 271230

Wood Close Caravan Park, Casterton LA6 2SE ☎ (01524) 271597 OS map 97/619783 ½m SE of Kirkby Lonsdale centre off A65 (Skipton) opposite junction with A683 (Lancaster) Open Mar-Oct 84 pitches (54 static) Grass, some hard standings, part level, sheltered ▓🖸🕿🖉⊕∅⊕↩🖭& fishing, golf £3.50-£13.00

KIRKBY STEPHEN, Cumbria   **Map D5**
Pop 1,520. EC Thurs, MD Mon SEE Cloister, church, Wharton Hall ℹ Market Sq ☎ Kirkby Stephen (01768) 371199 Restaurant: King's Arms, Market Sq ☎ (01768) 371378

Bowber Head, Ravenstonedale CA17 4NL ☎ (01539) 623254 OS map 91/740032 4½m SW of Kirkby Stephen off A683 (Sedbergh) Open all year 26 pitches Level/sloping grass 🖸🕿🖉⊕∅⊕ TV hook-ups £6.00-£12.00

Pennine View Caravan Park, Station Road CA17 4SZ ☎ Kirkby Stephen (01768) 371717 OS map 91/772075 ¼m S of Kirkby Stephen centre off A685 (Tebay) Open Mar-Nov 58 pitches Level grass and hard standing, sheltered 🖸🖉⊕∅🕿↩🖭& £10.00-£11.10

LAMPLUGH–see Cockermouth

LEVENS, Cumbria   **Map C6**
Pop 895. EC Thurs SEE Levens Hall 1m SE, Sizergh Castle 1m NE Restaurant: Heaves ☎ (01539) 560396

Sampool Caravan Park, LA8 8EQ ☎ (01539) 552265 OS map 97/479843 1m SW of Levens off A590 (Levens Bridge-Lindale) near river Kent Open Mar-Oct 200 pitches (185 static)–no tents 18 acres level grass and hard standings ▓🖸🕿🖉⊕∅↩ fishing £6.00-£8.00

LONGTOWN, Cumbria   **Map B2**
Pop 2,200 EC Wed SEE church, St Michael's Well ℹ Arthuret Rd ☎ (01228) 791876 Restaurant: Graham Arms, English St ☎ (01228) 791213

Camelot Caravan Park, Sandysike CA6 5SZ ☎ Longtown (01228) 791248 OS map 85/390667 1½m S of Longtown on A7 (Carlisle) Open Mar-Oct, 20 pitches 1½ acres level grass and hard standings, sheltered ▓🕿🖉⊕🖭 dog walk £6.00-£7.00

Oakbank Country Park CA6 5NA ☎ Longtown (01228) 791108 OS map 85/368702 1m N of Longtown off A7 (Langholm) on Chapelknowe road Open all year 24 pitches 60 acres level/sloping grass and hard standing ▓✗🕿⊕⊕↩& fishing (trout, carp, salmon) £5.00-£10.50

MELMERBY, Cumbria   **Map C4**
Restaurant: Shepherds Inn off A686 ☎ (01768) 881217

Cross Fell Caravan and Camping Park, Ousby CA10 1QA ☎ (01768) 881374 OS map 91/620350 1m S of Melmerby on Skirwith road in Ousby Open Mar-Jan 38 pitches Level grass ✗♀⌐↗🖸🕿🖉⊕∅ £6.00-£7.00

Melmerby Caravan Park CA10 1HE ☎ Langwathby (01768) 881311 OS map 91/615373 In Melmerby on A686 (Alston) Open Mar-Oct 45 pitches (40 static) Level grass and hard standing, sheltered ▓✗🖸🕿🖉⊕∅🖭 £8.00

Cause for Complaint

If you have cause for complaint while staying on a site take the matter up with the manager or owner. If you are still not satisfied set the facts down in writing and send photocopies to anyone you think might be able to help, starting with the editor of this guide and the local (licensing) authority for the area where the site is located.

MILLOM, Cumbria   **Map B6**
Pop 7,340. EC Wed SEE folk museum, Holy Trinity church Restaurant: Punchbowl Inn 2m N at The
Green ☎ (01229) 772605

Butterflowers, Port Haverigg LA18 4HB ☎Millom (01229) 772880 OS map 96/158784 1½m SW
of Millom off A5093 (Silecroft) Open all year 189 pitches (79 static) 9 acres level grass
🔌🏪⌀♦⌀⛺ (heated) ⚡🏕📮 £10.00 (Mastercard/Visa/Switch)

Silecroft Caravan Site, Silecroft LA18 4NX ☎Millom (01229) 772659 OS map 96/124812 4m N of
Millom off A5093 (Broughton in Furness) Open Mar-Oct 184 pitches (124 static) Level grass and
hard standing 🏕🔌🏪♦⌀⊕🅿⚡📮 £6.00-£7.00

MILNTHORPE, Cumbria   **Map C6**
Pop 1,050 SEE Milnthorpe Sands, Kent Valley Restaurant: Blue Bell 1m N at Heversham
☎ (01539) 562018

Fell End Caravan Park, Slackhead Road, Hale LA7 7BS ☎Milnthorpe (01539) 562122 OS map
97/503778 3m S of Milnthorpe off A6 (Carnforth) Open all year 28 acres 305 pitches (215 static)
Caravans, hard standing (shingle), sheltered Tents, level and sloping, grass, sheltered
🏕✖🍴🔄🏹🔌🏪 (10amp) ⌀♦⌀⊕⚡🚪🏪♿ Satellite TV aerial hook-ups £13.00-£16.00 (all
cards)

Hall More Caravan Park, Hale LA7 7BP ☎Milnthorpe (01539) 563383 OS map 97/502771 ½m N
of Milnthorpe off A6 (Kendal) Open Mar-Oct 100 pitches (56 static) 7 acres level grass and hard
standing, sheltered 🔌🏪⌀⌀ fishing, pony trekking £12.00-£14.00 (Mastercard/Visa)

Millness Hill Park, Crooklands LA7 7NU ☎ (01539) 567306 OS map 97/537826 2m E of
Milnthorpe near junction 36 of M6 Open Mar-Oct 75 pitches (30 static) Caravans, grass,
sheltered. Tents, part sheltered 🔌🏪⌀♦⌀⛺ (children's) ⊕⚡🚪📮🏪 £6.50-£8.00

Water's Edge Caravan Park, Crooklands LA7 7NN ☎Crooklands (01539) 567708 OS map
97/535835 3m NE of Milnthorpe off B6385 (Endmoor) on A65 at Crooklands (M6 junction 36)
Open Mar-Nov, 48 pitches 3 acres level grass and hard standings 🏕🍴🏹🔌🏪⌀♦⌀⊕🅿🚪🏪♿
solarium £7.00-£14.00 (Mastercard/Visa)

NEWBY BRIDGE, Cumbria   **Map B6**
SEE lake Windermere, Haverthwaite railway Restaurant: Swan ☎ (01539) 531681

Bigland Hall Caravan Park, Haverthwaite LA12 8PJ ☎Newby Bridge (01539) 531702 OS map
96/339838 2½m SW of Newby Bridge on B5278 (Cark) Open Mar-Oct–must book peak periods
144 pitches (48 static) Hard standings 🏕🔌🏪⌀♦⌀ £7.00-£10.00

Black Beck Caravan Park, Bouth, LA12 8JN ☎ (01229) 861274 OS map 96/335853 3m SW of
Newby Bridge off A590 (Ulverston) Open Mar-Oct 305 pitches (235 static) 38 acres level grass
sheltered 🏕🏹🔌🏪⌀♦⌀⚡🏪♿ £6.50-£14.00

Hill of Oaks and Blakeholm Caravan Estate, Tower Wood LA23 3PJ ☎ (01539) 531578 OS map
96/385894 2½m N of Newby Bridge on A592 (Windermere) Open Mar-Oct 258 pitches (215
static) Hard standings, sheltered ⌀ bathing, fishing, boating (private lake frontage) £12.50-
£16.00

Oak Head Caravan Park, Ayside LA11 6JA ☎ (01539) 531475 OS map 96/389839 1m SE of
Newby Bridge off A590 (Grange over Sands) at Ayside Open Mar-Oct 130 pitches (70 static) 5
acres level/sloping grass, and hard standings, sheltered 🔌🏪⌀♦⌀♿ £7.50-£10.00

Park Cliffe Camping and Caravan Estate, Birks Road LA23 3PG ☎ (01539) 531344 OS map
96/391911 3m NE of Newby Bridge off A592 (Windermere) Open Mar-Oct 250 pitches (50 static)
25 acres hard standings and level/sloping grass, sheltered 🏕✖🍴🔄🏹🔌🏪⌀♦⌀⚡🏪 £10.00-
£12.80 (Mastercard/Visa)

For other sites near Newby Bridge see also Ulverston and Windermere

PATTERDALE, Cumbria   **Map B5**
Pop 440 SEE Aira Force, Helvellyn 3,200ft, Ullswater ℹ2m NW at Glenridding ☎ (01768) 482414
Restaurant: Patterdale ☎ (01768) 482231

Gillside Farm, Glenridding CA11 0QQ ☎Glenriding (01768) 482346 OS map 90/385175 1m N of
Patterdale on A592 (Penrith) Open Mar-Oct 90 pitches (25 static) Grass, level, some hard
standings 🔌🏪⌀⌀📮 dairy produce £8.00-£10.00

Sykeside Campsite, Brotherswater CA11 0NZ ☎Glenridding (01768) 482239 OS map 90/408132
3m S of Patterdale on A592 (Windermere) Open all year 80 pitches 🏕✖🍴🏹🔌🏪⌀ £2.50-
£7.50

**There's usually no objection to your walking onto a site to see if you might like it but always
ask permission first. Remember that the person in charge is responsible for safeguarding the
property of those staying there.**

PENRITH, Cumbria   **Map C4**
Pop 12,090. EC Wed, MD Tues SEE castle ruins, monuments in St Andrew's church, old inns,
Brougham castle 2m SE ■Penrith museum, Middlegate ✆Penrith (01768) 867466 Restaurant:
George, Devonshire St ✆(01768) 862696

Lowther Caravan Park, Elysian Fields, Eamont Bridge CA10 2JB ✆Penrith (01768) 863631 OS
map 90/524282 1m S of Penrith on A6 (Shap) Open Mar-Oct–no adv booking 575 pitches (375
static) Level grass and hard standing, sheltered 🔣 fishing £8.50-
£9.50

Thacka Lea Caravan Park, Thacka Lea CA11 9HX ✆Penrith (01768) 863319 OS map 90/509308
½m N of Penrith off A6 (Carlisle) Open Mar-Oct 25 pitches Grass and hard standing,
level/sloping, sheltered 🔣 £6.50

For other sites near Penrith see Melmerby, Penruddock, Pooley Bridge and Watermillock

PENRUDDOCK, Cumbria   **Map C4**
Pop 400 Restaurant: Swiss Chalet 3m SE at Pooley Bridge ✆(01768) 483215

Beckses Caravan Park CA11 0RX ✆Greystoke (01768) 483224 OS map 90/418278 1m W of
Penruddocck on B5288 (Greystoke-Keswick) adj Beckses Garage Open Mar 20-Oct 31, 3 acres,
45 pitches (18 static) 3 acres level/sloping grass, hard standings, sheltered 🔣
£7.00

Gill Head Farm, Troutbeck CA11 0ST ✆(017687) 79652 OS map 90/380269 3m SW of
Penruddock off A66 (Keswick) on right of A5091 (Ullswater) Open Easter-Oct, 55 pitches 15
acres level grass and hard standings, sheltered 🔣 fishing £7.00-£10.00

Hopkinsons' Whitbarrow Hall Caravan Park, Berrier CA11 0XB ✆(01768) 483456 OS map
90/405289 3m NW of Penruddock off A66 (Keswick) at Sportsman Inn on Hutton Roof
road–signposted Open Mar-Oct 248 pitches (167 static) Level grass and hard standing, sheltered
🔣 games room £8.50

Thanet Well Caravan Park, Greystoke CA11 0XX *Family site in rolling countryside* ✆(01768)
484262 OS map 90/397351 5m N of Penruddock via Greystoke and Lamonby road (signposted)
Open Mar-Oct, 85 pitches (65 static) Grass and hard standings, part level, sheltered
🔣 £8.00-£9.50

Troutbeck Head Caravan Park, Troutbeck CA11 0SS *Quiet secluded family-run park* ✆(01768)
483521 OS map 90/385256 3m SW of Penruddock off A66 (Keswick) on A5091 (Ullswater)–M6
junction 40 Open Mar-Jan 15, 120 pitches (75 static)–no tents Level/sloping grass and hard
standing, sheltered 🔣 £7.00-£8.00

For other sites near Penruddock see also Threlkeld

POOLEY BRIDGE, Cumbria   **Map C4**
Pop 265 SEE Ullswater, Iron Age fort W ■The Square ✆(01768) 486530 Restaurant: Howtown
4m SW at Howtown ✆(01768) 486514

Hill Croft Caravan Park CA10 2LT ✆Pooley Bridge (01768) 486363 OS map 90/476243 ½m E of
Pooley Bridge on Roehead road Open Mar-Oct, 325 pitches (200 static) 10 acres, part sloping
grass and hard standing 🔣 £8.50-£12.00

Park Foot Caravan Camping Park, Howtown Road CA10 2NA ✆Pooley Bridge (017684) 86309
OS map 90/469235 1m S of Pooley Bridge on lakeside road Open Easter-Oct 430 pitches (130
static) Caravans, grass and hard standing Tents, grass, part level, sheltered
🔣 bar meals, lake access for water sports, tennis, pony
trekking, fell walking, children's club, bike hire £9.00-£20.00 (most cards)

Waterfoot Caravan Park CA11 0JF ✆Pooley Bridge (01768) 486302 OS map 90/462243 ½m W
of Pooley Bridge on A592 (Penrith-Ullswater) Open Mar-Oct 180 pitches (123 static)–no tents–adv
booking by phone only Level/sloping grass and hard standing, sheltered 🔣
£12.00-£14.00 inc electricity

PORT CARLISLE–see Bowness on Solway

❊ ❊ ❊   **Beckses Caravan Park**   ❊ ❊ ❊
                         Penruddock, Penrith CA11 0RX
                              Tel (01768) 483224

Small pleasant site with up-to-date facilities on fringe of
Lake District national park within easy reach of M6, Ullswater and Keswick.

Park Foot, Pooley Bridge

Open Easter-
October.

On lakeside road with lake access for water sports.
Bike hire, tennis, pony trekking, fell walking.

Tel. (01768) 486309

Grass
and hard
standings.

RAVENGLASS, Cumbria   **Map A5**
Pop 266. EC Sat SEE narrow gauge railway, Muncaster castle and gardens, museum
🛈 Ravenglass and Eskdale Railway Station ☎ Ravenglass (01229) 717278 Restaurant: Pennington
Arms, Main St ☎ (01229) 717222
Walls Caravan-Camping Park, CA18 1SR ☎ Ravenglass (01229) 717250 OS map 96/088965 ½m
   E of Ravenglass off A595 Gosforth-Bootle road Open Feb 28-Nov 15, 5 acres, 60 pitches Grass
   and hard standings, sheltered 🏕️🗑️📞🍴✳️⊘📞 £3.50-£10.00

SEDBERGH, Cumbria   **Map C5**
Pop 2,110. EC Thurs, MD Wed SEE parish church, Quaker meeting house 🛈 72 Main Street
☎ Sedbergh (01539) 620125 Restaurant: Oakdene Country, Garsdale Rd ☎ (01539) 620280
Lincoln's Inn, Firbank LA10 5EE ☎ Sedbergh (01539) 620567 OS map 97/631923 2m W of
   Sedbergh on A684 (Kendal) Open Mar-Oct 13 pitches–no trailer caravans ½ acre level grass
   ✳️ 🚻 £3.00
Pinfold Caravan Park, LA10 5JL ☎ Sedbergh (01539) 620576 OS map 98/667919 ½m E of
   Sedbergh on Hawes road Open Mar-Oct 84 pitches (56 static)–adv bkg for caravans only Level
   grass and hard standing, sheltered 🗑️📞🍴✳️⊘ £10.00-£12.00 (all cards)

SILLOTH, Cumbria   **Map A3**
Pop 2,580. EC Tues SEE Hadrian's Wall 🛈 The Green ☎ Silloth (01697) 331944 Restaurant: Golf,
Criffel St ☎ (01697) 331438
Hylton Park Holiday Centre, Eden Street CA5 4AY ☎ Silloth (01697) 331707 OS map 85/113534
   ½m S of Silloth on B5300 (Maryport) Open Mar-Oct 257 pitches (213 static) Level grass and hard
   standings, sheltered 🍴✳️ £10.50-£13.70
Moordale Caravan Park, CA7 4JZ ☎ Silloth (01697) 331375 OS map 85/105518 2m S of Silloth
   on B5300 (Maryport) adj golf course and beach Open Mar-Oct 118 pitches (65 static) 7 acres
   level grass and hard standings 🗑️📞🍴✳️🔌💡📞🚻 £7.00-£9.00
Rowanbank Caravan Park, Beckfoot CA5 4LA *Quiet family run coastal site* ☎ Silloth (01697)
   331653 OS map 85/096497 2m SW of Silloth on B5300 (Maryport) in Beckfoot–signposted Open
   Mar 1-Nov 15 50 pitches 3½ acres level grass and hard standing, part sheltered
   🗑️📞🍴✳️⊘🔌🚻 £8.50
Seacote Caravan Park, Skinburness Road CA5 4QJ ☎ Silloth (01697) 331121 OS map 85/105550
   1m N of Silloth on Skirnburness road Open Mar 1-Nov 15 100 pitches (80 static)–no tents Level
   grass and hard standings sheltered 🗑️📞🍴✳️⊘💡📞🚻 £10.00 inc electricity
The Solway Holiday Village, CA5 4QQ ☎ Silloth (01697) 331236 OS map 85/118548 ½m N of
   Silloth off Skinburness road Open Mar-Oct 300 pitches (200 static) 120 acres level grass
   🏕️🍽️🍺🔌🗑️📞🍴✳️⊘🚻🔌🚽 (large screen) 📞🏪 golf, pool and snooker, health studio, bowling
   alley, sports hall, tennis, kids' club, farm animals £7.00-£12.00 (Mastercard/Visa/Switch)
Stanwix Park Holiday Centre, CA5 4HH ☎ Silloth (01697) 332666 Fax (01697) 332666 OS map
   85/108527 1m S of Silloth on B5300 (Maryport) Open Easter-Oct 348 pitches (221 static) Level
   grass, sheltered 🏕️🍽️🍺🔌🏹🗑️📞🍴✳️⊘🚻 (heated) ✳️🔌🚽💡📞🚻🏪 indoor leisure centre,
   tenpin bowling, dancing, pony trekking £13.40-£16.70 (2000) (Mastercard/Visa)
Tanglewood Caravan Park, Causeway Head CA5 4PE ☎ Silloth (01697) 331253 OS map
   85/131534 1m E of Silloth on B5302 (Wigton) Open Easter-Oct–must book peak periods 90
   pitches (59 static) Level grass and hard standing, sheltered 🍺🏹🗑️📞🍴✳️⊘🐕🚽🚻 club house
   £8.00-£10.00

**The restaurants recommended in this guide are of three kinds – inns and pubs, restaurants
proper and those forming part of hotels and motels. They all serve lunch and dinner – at a
reasonable price – say under £10 a head. We shall be glad to have your comments on any
you use this season and if you think they are not up to standard to have your suggestions for
alternatives.**

STAVELEY–see Kendal

TEBAY, Cumbria   **Map C5**
Pop 580 Restaurant: Tebay Mountain Lodge, Orton ✆(015396) 24351
Tebay Caravan Park, Orton CA10 3SB ✆Orton (01539) 624511 OS map 91/608061 Signposted from Westmorland sevice areas on M6 between junctions 38 and 39 Open Mar 15-Oct 70 pitches–no tents Hard standings, sheltered £8.50

ULVERSTON, Cumbria   **Map B6**
Pop 11,970. EC Wed, MD Thurs SEE parish church, crystal works, Laurel and Hardy museum, Swarthmoor Hall ℹ️Coronation Hall, County Sq ✆(01229) 587120 Restaurant: Bay Horse, Canal Foot ✆(01229) 53972
Bardsea Leisure Park, Priory Road LA12 9QE *Former quarry attractively landscaped* ✆Ulverston (01229) 584712 OS map 97/296765 1m S of Ulverston on A5087 (Bardsea) Open all year 171 pitches (88 static) 10 acres level grass and hard standings, sheltered £7.95-£15.00 (all cards)

WATERMILLOCK, Cumbria   **Map C4**
Pop 460 SEE Ullswater, Aira Force 2m SW Restaurant: Pooley Bridge Inn 3m NE at Pooley Bridge ✆(01768) 483215
Cove Caravan Camping Park CA11 0LS ✆Pooley Bridge (01768) 486549 OS map 90/431236 1½m N of Watermillock off A592 (Penrith) at Brackenrigg Inn on Penruddock road Open Mar-Oct, 2½ acres, 89 pitches (38 static) 5 acres level/sloping grass and hard standings, sheltered £6.80-£8.50
Knotts Hill Caravan Chalet Park CA11 0JR ✆Pooley Bridge (01768) 486328 OS map 90/435218 1m W of Watermillock off A592 (Windermere) at Gowbarrow Lodge Open Mar-Oct 100 pitches–no tents Level/gently sloping woodland, hard standings £10.00
Quiet Site CA11 0LS *Good facilities, charming location* ✆Ullswater (01768) 486337 OS map 90/431237 2m N of Watermillock off Penruddock road Open Mar-Nov, 83 pitches (23 static) Grass and hard standing, level/sloping, part sheltered children's room £8.00-£12.00
Ullswater Caravan Camping and Marine Park CA11 0LR ✆(01768) 486666 Fax (01768) 486095 OS map 90/436230 ½m SW of Watermillock off A592 (Windermere) near junct 40 of M6 Open Mar 1-Nov 14, 7 acres, 210 pitches (sep area for tents) (55 static) Grass and hard standing, level/sloping, part sheltered (35) boat launching and mooring 1 mile £10.00 (Mastercard/Visa/Switch)

WHITEHAVEN, Cumbria   **Map A4**
Pop 26,710. EC Wed, MD Thurs, Sat SEE museum in market hall, pottery craft centre, St Bees Head ℹ️Market Place ✆Whitehaven (01946) 695678 Restaurant: Roseneath, Low Moresby ✆(01946) 61572
St Bees Chalet and Trailer Park, CA27 0ES ✆St Bees (01946) 822777 OS map 89/962119 3m S of Whitehaven off B5345 (St Bees) Open all year 380 pitches (200 static) 22 acres level/sloping grass and hard standings £6.00-£8.00
Seacote Caravan Park, CA27 0ES ✆St Bees (01946) 822777 OS map 89/123456 4m S of Whitehaven off B5345 (St Bees) on seafront by beach Open all year 65 pitches Level grass £9.00-£10.50

WIGTON, Cumbria   **Map B3**
Pop 4,720. EC Wed, MD Tues SEE St Mary's church Restaurant: Wheyrigg Hall 3m W on B5302 (Silloth) ✆(01697) 361242
Clea Hall Holiday Park, Westward CA7 8NQ ✆(01697) 342880 OS map 85/274499 4½m S of Wigton off B5305 (Penrith) Open Mar-Oct 106 pitches (90 static) Level/sloping grass baths, library, lounge £10.00-£12.00

Help us make CARAVAN AND CAMP IN BRITAIN better known to site operators – and thereby more informative – by showing them your copy when booking in.

WINDERMERE, Cumbria   **Map B5**
Pop 7,320. EC Thurs SEE lake, steamboat museum, viewpoint of Orrest Head, aquarium, Belle Isle
🔲 Victoria Street ☏ Windermere (015394) 46499 Restaurant: Applegarth, College Rd ☏ (01539)
443206

Fallbarrow Park, Bowness on Windermere LA23 3DL ☏ (01539) 444422 OS map 96/402972 1m
    SW of Windermere centre on A592 (Ullswater-Newby Bridge) by lake Open Mar 15-Oct 31–must
    book peak periods 340 pitches (248 static)–no tents Level grass and hard standing, sheltered
    🛒✖♀↩♪🗄🪑⊘∅☯↩⛁ serviced pitches, slipway, boating, swimming £14.50-£20.50
    (inc electricity)

Ings Caravan Park, Ings LA8 9QF ☏ (01539) 821426 OS map 97/444990 2m E of Windermere off
    A591 (Kendal) near Ings Garage Open Mar-Oct 71 pitches (58 static) Level grass and hard
    standing 🗄🪑⊘∅⛁ £8.00-£10.00

Lambhowe Caravan Park, Lyth Valley, Crosthwaite LA8 8JE *Well-run site within reach of lake*
    ☏ (01539) 568483 OS map 97/423915 5m SE of Windermere on A5074 (Howe) Open Mar-Nov
    15–must book peak periods 125 pitches (111 static) Grass and hard standings, level, sheltered
    ♀🗄🪑⊘∅⊘ £10.00-£12.00

Limefitt Park, LA23 1PA ☏ (01539) 432300 OS map 90/416030 4m N of Windermere on A592
    (Ullswater) Open Easter-Oct 210 pitches (45 static) Grass and hard standing, level/sloping
    🛒✖♀↩♪🗄🪑⊘∅☯↩⊘⛁ fishing £9.50-£13.00 inc elect

White Cross Bay Caravan Park, Ambleside Road LA23 1LF ☏ Windermere (01539) 443937 OS
    map 90/393006 1½m NW of Windermere on A591 (Ambleside) Open Mar-Nov–must book public
    holidays 312 pitches (187 static)–no tents Level grass and hard standings, sheltered
    🛒✖♀↩🗄♪🪑⊘∅☯↩▪⛁🏠 lake access/slipway, marina, tennis £12.00-£16.00
    (Mastercard/Visa)

For other sites near Windermere see Ambleside and Kendal

3 Northeast

Once the largest county in England, Yorkshire is now divided administratively into the north, south and west—and even parts of these have been lost to Cleveland and Humberside, which not only includes much of what used to be known as the East Riding but crosses the river to take in industrial Lincolnshire and the coast as far as Cleethorpes and beyond. And Cleveland in the north not only contains the industrial Tees but much of the Durham coast as well.

A striking feature of the region is still its diversity of landscape. In the east, between inland Northallerton and the boisterous coastal resorts of Whitby and Scarborough, are the spacious North York Moors, where flat topped heather-clad hills are separated by wooded dales. Since most roads go round rather than through them the moors are strictly for walkers—who can cross the area in an east–west direction on the Lyke Wake Walk between Ravenscar and Osmotherley. A pleasant centre on the southern edge of the moors, now a national park, is Pickering. Almost as rewarding are the Cleveland and Hambleton Hills, the northern and western extensions of the moors. Sights which ought not to be missed are the majestic twelfth-century ruins of Rievaulx Abbey west of Helmsley and Wade's Causeway, a well-preserved section of Roman road near Hunt House south of Grosmont.

Looping down from seaside Filey to the Humber near industrial Hull are the Wolds, a chalk mass of dry uplands and steep-sided valleys, once used only for sheep grazing but now intensively farmed. In the western half of the region—mainly within the triangle linking Sedbergh, Aysgarth and Skipton—are the sparsely populated and scenic Yorkshire Dales, another national park bisected by the sixty miles long River Ure flowing through Wensleydale. Other dales or valleys, topped by wild fells and stretches of open moor, are Littondale, Wharfedale, Nidderdale, Airedale and—reached via the spectacular Buttertubs Pass—Swaledale. A well-known sight in Airedale is Malham Cove, a great natural amphitheatre 300ft high. Near Hawes in Wensleydale is Hardraw Force, England's highest waterfall. Often windy and wet, the dales abound in potholes and caverns, the most striking probably being the Victoria Caves beneath Ingleborough Common near Ingleton. The park is crossed by the Dales Way, which follows riverside paths from Ilkley to Windermere.

The east-flowing streams of the dales drop down to the Vale of York, through which the Great North Road rides a ridge not far from the ancient capital and its superb minster.

The low shore of Holderness on the Humber estuary east of the Wolds slopes gradually to Spurn Head, a long spit of sand, but at Boulby near Saltburn in the north are England's highest cliffs. Along the wholly unspoiled coast between these two places are resorts large and small, most at the edge of firm sands. Near Bridlington is Flamborough Head, with its sea-girt caves and tiny bays enclosing pebble beaches.

Getting around in Humberside is now made much easier by the new Humber bridge, a major feat of engineering which spans the river between Barton on the south and Hessle on the north bank.

Campsites are numerous in the northeast. Those inland are often simple; those on the coast, where the choice is greatest, often well equipped.

ACASTER MALBIS–see York

ALDBROUGH, Humberside   **Map G2**
Restaurant: Medio 10m W at Hull ☎(01482) 507070
Royal Hotel, Cliff Top, Seaside Road HU11 4SB ☎Aldbrough (01964) 527786 OS map 107/257395
1m NE of Aldbrough on road to beach, near sea Open Apr-Sept 8 pitches 2 acres mainly level
✗ (snack) ⚑⚉ £2.00-£3.00

AYSGARTH, N Yorks   **Map B4**
Pop 170. EC Wed Most popular village in Wensleydale SEE mile long stretch of waterfalls, parish
church, carriage museum, Nat Park centre Restaurant: George and Dragon ☎(01969) 663358
Street Head Caravan Site, Newbiggin, Bishopdale DL8 4TE ☎Wensleydale (01969)
663472/663571 OS map 98/998861 1½m S of Aysgarth on right of B6160 (Kettlewell) Open
Mar-Oct 100 pitches (50 static) Grass and hard standing, level, sheltered ⚑✗⚉⊡⚑⚉⊕⊘⚑
£8.00-£13.00
Westholme Caravan Park, DL8 3SP ☎Wensleydale (01969) 663268 OS map 98/106883 1m E of
Aysgarth on A684 (Leyburn) Open Mar-Oct–must book public holidays and Jul-Aug 113 pitches
(44 static) Level grass and hard standing, sheltered ⚑✗⚉⊡⚑⚉⊕⊘⊕✈⊡ trout fishing
£7.00-£9.70

ATWICK–see Hornsea

BARMSTON–see Skipsea

BARNSLEY, S Yorks   **Map E6**
Pop 223,900. MD Mon, Wed, Fri, Sat SEE Cannon Hall Park, Town Hall, Cooper art gallery ℹ Civic
Hall, Eldon Street ☎Barnsley (01266) 206757 Restaurant: Armstrongs, Shambles St ☎(01226)
240113
Earths Wood Caravan Park, Bank End Lane, Barnsley Road, Clayton West, HD8 9LJ
☎Huddersfield (01484) 863211 and 864266 OS map 110/265102 6m NW of Barnsley off A636
(Denby Dale) on High Hoyland road (junction 38 of M1) Open Mar-Oct 45 pitches 3 acres level
grass, sheltered ⊡⚑⊕⊘⚹ £6.00
Green Springs Touring Park, Rockley Lane, Worsbrough S75 3DS ☎Barnsley (01226) 288298
OS map 111/330019 2m S of Barnsley off A61 on Pilley road near junct 36 of M1 Open Apr-Oct
65 pitches Grass, part level, hard standings, sheltered ⚑ (10 amp) ⚉⊕⚑◔ £6.50

BARTON UPON HUMBER, S. Humberside   **Map G4**
Pop 8,620. EC Thurs SEE suspension bridge, churches, museum, country park ℹ Humber Bridge
Viewing Area, (North Bank) ☎Hessle (01482) 640852 Restaurant: George, George St ☎(01652)
632433
Barton Broads, Chemical Lane DN18 5JW ☎Barton upon Humber (01652) 634742 OS map
112/035225 ½m E of Barton upon Humber on A1077 (Barrow) Open all year 35 pitches
⚑⚲⚉⊕⚑⊡ fishing £3.50-£4.50
Silver Birches Tourist Park, Waterside Road, DN18 5BA ☎Barton upon Humber (01652) 632509
OS map 112/028247 ½m N of Barton upon Humber on Waterside Road Open Easter-Oct
25 pitches Level grass, sheltered ⊡⚑⚉⊕⊘⊕✈⚿ £6.50

BEDALE, N Yorks   **Map C4**
SEE church of St Gregory, market place, Bedale Hall, Snape Castle 3m S ℹ Bedale Hall, North End
☎(01677) 424604 Restaurant: Leeming Motel 1m NE near A1 at Leeming Bar ☎(01677) 423611
Boot and Shoe Inn, Thirn HG4 4AU ☎Bedale (01677) 460219 OS map 99/217860 3m SW of
Bedale off Thornton Watlass road Open Apr-Oct 10 pitches 1 acre gentle slope ✗ (snack) ⚉ *No
showers* £3.00-£3.50
Pembroke Caravan Park, Leases Road, Leeming Bar DL7 9BW ☎Bedale (01677) 422608/422652
OS map 99/285905 2m NE of Bedale off A684 (Northallerton) near A1 Open Apr-Sept 25 pitches
Level grass, sheltered, some hard standings ⚑⊷⚑⚉⊕⊘✈⚑⊡ £5.50-£7.00

BEVERLEY, N Humberside   **Map F3**
Pop 17,180. MD Wed, Sat SEE Minster, North Bar Museum, market cross ℹ Guildhall, Register Sq
☎Hull (01482) 867430 Restaurant: Beverley Arms, North Bar Within ☎(01482) 869241
Lakeminster Park, Hull Road, Woodmansey HU17 0PN ☎Hull (01482) 882655 OS map
107/049384 1m SE of Beverley on A1174 (Hull) Open all year 80 pitches (30 static) Level grass,
sheltered ⚑⚉⊷⊡⚑⚉⊕⊘⊡⚑⚹⌂ fishing £8.00-£10.00

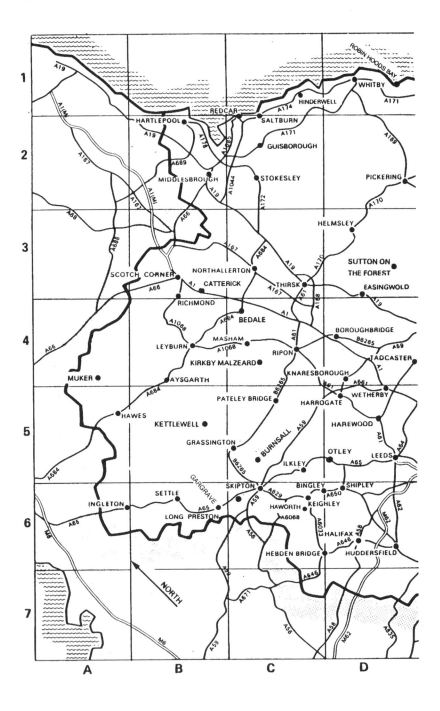

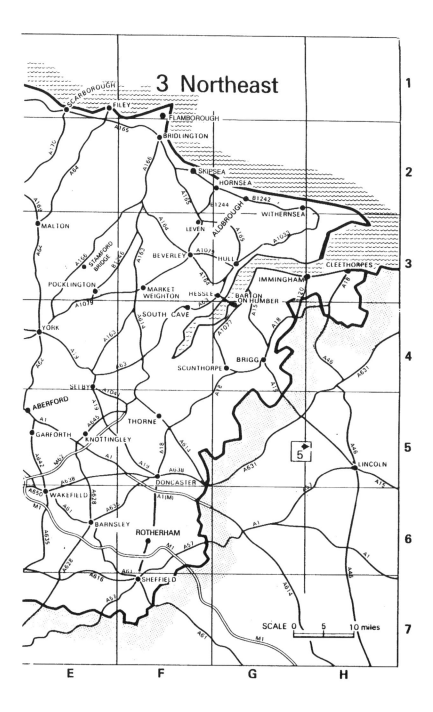

3 Northeast

SCALE 0   5   10 miles

3. NORTHEAST

BINGLEY, W Yorks Map D6
Pop 13,300. EC Tues, MD Wed, Fri, Sat SEE All Saints Church, stocks, cross and market house, Leeds-Liverpool canal locks Restaurant: Bankfield, Bradford Rd ☎(01274) 567123

Harden and Bingley Caravan Park, Harden BD16 1DF ☎(01535) 273810 OS map 104/089379 2m SW of Bingley off B6429 (Harden) near Malt Shovel Inn Open Apr-Oct 3 acres 96 pitches (81 static) Level/sloping grass and hard standing, sheltered ▣▣▣▣▣▣▣ woodland walks £8.00-£11.00

BISHOPTHORPE-see York

BOROUGHBRIDGE, N Yorks Map D4
Pop 2,500. EC Thurs, MD Mon SEE Roman Museum at Aldborough ▣Fishergate ☎Boroughbridge (01423) 323373 Restaurant: Crown, Horsefair ☎(01423) 322328

Bluebell Caravan Park, Kirby Hill YO5 9DN ☎Boroughbridge (01423) 322380 OS map 99/392680 1m N of Boroughbridge on B6265 (Ripon) Open May-Sept 10 pitches Grass, sloping £6.00

Old Hall Caravan Park, Langthorpe YO5 9BZ ☎Boroughbridge (01423) 322130/323190 OS map 99/391673 ½m W of Boroughbridge off B6265 (Ripon) Open Apr-Oct 120 pitches (98 static) Level grass ▣▣▣▣▣▣▣▣ £7.50-£8.80

BRIDLINGTON, N Humberside Map F2
Pop 30,000. EC Thurs, MD Wed, Sat SEE Bayle Gate, museum, zoo, Sewerby Hall and Park, Flamborough Head 2m NE ▣Prince Street ☎(01262) 673474 Restaurant: Monarch, South Marine Drive ☎(01262) 674447

Poplars Touring Park, 45 Jewison Lane, Sewerby YO15 1DX ☎Bridlington (01262) 677251 OS map 101/196699 2m NE of Bridlington off Flamborough road adj motel Open Mar-Nov 30 pitches Grass and hard standing, sheltered ▣▣▣ hotel and pub near £7.00-£12.00 (2000)

Shirley Caravan Park, Jewison Lane YO16 5YG ☎Bridlington (01262) 676442 OS map 101/192701 2m N of Bridlington off A165 (Scarborough) on B1255 (Flamborough) Open Mar-Oct 420 pitches (375 static)–no tents 25 acres level grass and hard standing ▣▣▣▣▣▣▣▣▣ ▣ (indoor heated) ▣▣▣▣ £6.50-£12.00

Thorpe Hall Caravan Camping Park, Rudston YO25 4JE ☎Kilham (01262) 420393/420574 OS map 101/109677 4½m W of Bridlington on B1253 (Rudston) Open Mar-Oct 90 pitches Grass, level, sheltered ▣▣▣▣▣▣▣▣▣▣ baths, fishing £5.00-£10.00

CASTLE HOWARD-see Malton

CAWOOD-see Selby

CLAPHAM-see Ingleton

CLEETHORPES, S Humberside Map H3
Pop 35,770. EC Thurs (winter), MD Wed SEE leisure park, beacon ▣43 Alexandra Road ☎Cleethorpes (01472) 200220 Restaurant: Kingsway, Kingsway ☎(01472) 601122

Municipal Camping Park, Humberston DN36 4HG ☎Cleethorpes (01472) 813395 OS map 113/372063 2m S of Cleethorpes off A1031 (Mablethorpe) Open Apr-Sept 50 pitches ▣▣▣▣ £3.80-£5.00

CONSTABLE BURTON-see Leyburn

EASINGWOLD, N Yorks Map D3
Pop 3,640. EC Wed, MD Fri SEE market cross, Bull Ring, Byland Abbey ▣Chapel Lane ☎(01347) 821530 Restaurant: George, Market Pl ☎(01347) 821698

Easingwold Caravan Camping Park, Thirsk Road Y06 3NF ☎Easingwold (01347) 821479 OS map 100/510708 1m N of Easingwold on A19 (Thirsk) Open Mar-Oct 50 pitches (30 static) 5 acres grass, gentle slope/level, sheltered ▣▣▣ £6.00-£15.00

Holly Brook Caravan Park, Pennycarr Lane, off Stillington Road YO61 3EU ☎Easingwold (01347) 821906 OS map 100/534684 1m SE of Easingwold off Stillington road Open Mar-Dec 30 pitches–adults only Level grass and hard standing, sheltered ▣▣▣▣▣▣▣▣ fridge/freezer, microwave, small library £7.50

The Alders Caravan Park, Home Farm, Alne YO61 1TB ☎(01347) 838722 OS map 100/497654 2m SW of Easingwold in Alne Open Mar-Oct 40 pitches 6 acres level grass and hard standings ▣▣▣▣▣ £6.50-£9.50

FANGFOSS-see Stamford Bridge

FILEY, N Yorks   **Map E1**
Pop 5,480. EC Wed SEE Promenade Gardens, beach ▨John Street ☏Scarborough (01723)
512204 Restaurant: Crown 7½m NW at Scarborough ☏(01723) 373491

Blue Dolphin Holiday Park, Gristhorpe Bay YO14 9PU ☏(01723) 515155 OS map 101/090833
2m N of Filey on A165 (Scarborough)–signposted Open Mar-Oct 701 pitches (272 static) 12
acres level grass ⬛✖♀↩↗▣➡⌀⊕∅⊡ (heated) ✿↵☎ disco, cabaret, putting green
£8.00-£16.00

Filey Brigg Touring Caravan Site and Country Park, North Cliff YO14 0XX ☏(01723) 366212 OS
map 101/120814 ½m N of Filey centre on Church Cliff Drive Open Easter-Oct 140 pitches
⬛▣➡⌀✿ path to beach £5.00-£10.00 (Mastercard/Visa)

Lebberston Touring Caravan Park, Lebberston YO11 3PE ☏(01723) 585723 OS map
101/081822 3m NW of Filey off A165 (Scarborough) on B1261 (Lebberston) Open Mar-Oct 50
pitches–no tents 7½ acres level/sloping grass and hard standing, sheltered ⬛ (mobile)
↗▣➡⌀⊕∅✿ dog walk, separate pitches £6.00-£10.00 (2000)

Muston Grange Caravan Park, YO14 0HU ☏(01723) 512167 OS map 101/1137797 1½m SW of
Filey on A1039 (Bridlington) Open Easter-Oct 15 220 pitches–no tents 10 acres level/sloping
grass ⬛▣➡⌀⊕↵& £5.75-£8.25

Reighton Sands Holiday Village, Reighton Gap YO14 9SJ ☏(01723) 890476 OS map
101/145759 4m SE of Filey off A165 (Bridlington) Open Mar-Sept 657 pitches (135 static) Grass,
part level, hard standings ⬛✖♀↩↗▣➡⌀⊕∅⊡↵ £5.95-£12.00

Spring Willows Caravan Park, Main Road, Staxton YO12 4SB ☏(01723) 891505 OS map
101/023799 3m W of Filey on A1039 (Staxton) via Muston Open Mar-Oct 184 pitches Grass and
hard standing, sheltered ⬛✖♀↩▣➡⌀⊕∅⊡ (indoor) ✿↵□➡& sauna, solarium, games
room, lounge, children's club

For other sites near Filey see Scarborough

FLAMBOROUGH, Humberside   **Map F1**
Pop 1800 SEE St Oswald's church, lighthouse, museum, Flamborough Head 5m NE, Danes Dyke
3m NE Restaurant: Royal Dog and Duck, Tower St ☏(01262) 850206

Old Mill Caravan Park, Bempton YO16 5XD ☏Flamborough (01262) 673565 OS map 101/183705
2m W of Flamborough off B1255 (Bridlington) at Marton Open Apr-Oct 55 pitches Level grass,
sheltered ▣➡⊕∅□➡❖ £6.50-£9.50

FYLINGDALES–see Whitby

FYLINGTHORPE–see Robin Hood's Bay

GALPHAY–see Kirkby Malzeard

GARGRAVE, N Yorks   **Map B6**
Pop 8000 SEE Eshton Hall N Restaurant: Anchor on A65 ☏(01756) 748666

Eshton Road Caravan Park, Eshton Road BD23 3PN ☏(01756) 749229 OS map 103/936546
¼m NE of Gargrave centre on Hetton road by Liverpool–Leeds canal Open all year 30 pitches (24
static) 1 acre level grass and hard standing, sheltered ▣➡⌀⊕ £12.00

GRASSINGTON, N Yorks   **Map C5**
Pop 1,300. EC Thurs SEE old moorland lead mines, museum, Linton church ▨National Park
Centre, Hebden Rd ☏(01756) 752774 Restaurant: Wilson Arms 1m SW at Threshfield
☏(01756) 752666

Howgill Lodge, Barden BD23 6DJ ☏Burnsall (01756) 720655 OS map 104/065592 6m SE of
Grassington off B6160 (Ilkley) Open Mar-Oct 40 pitches Level grass and hard standing
⬛✖▣➡⌀⊕∅➿ B&B £9.00-£15.00 (all cards)

Threaplands House Farm, Cracoe BD23 6LD ☏Cracoe (01756) 730248 OS map 98/986606 2m
S of Grassington off B6265 (Skipton) Open Mar-Oct 30 pitches 8 acres level grass
⬛➡⌀⊕□➿ £7.00

Wood Nook Caravan Site, Skirethorns, Threshfield BD23 5NU ☏Grassington (01756) 752412 OS
map 98/974641 1¾m W of Grassington off Threshfield road Open Apr-Oct 40 pitches (10 static)
Level/sloping grass and hard standings, sheltered ⬛▣➡⌀⊕∅↵➿ £7.00-£8.50

**Charges quoted are the minimum and maximum for two people with car and caravan or tent.
They are given only as a guide and should be checked with the owner of any site at which
you plan to stay.
Remember to ask whether hot water or use of the pool (if any) is extra and make sure that
VAT is included.**

GREAT BROUGHTON–see Stokesley

GUISBOROUGH, Cleveland   **Map C2**
Pop 19,100. EC Wed, MD Thurs, Sat SEE Upleathen Church, smallest in England Restaurant:
Moor Cock, West End Rd ☎(01287) 632342

Margrove Park Touring Caravan Park, Boosbeck TS12 3BZ ☎Guisborough (01287) 653616 OS
   map 94/652156 3m E of Guisborough off A171 (Whitby) Open Apr-Oct 100 pitches Level grass
   ⊕◉● £6.00

Tocketts Mill Caravan Park, off Skelton Road TS14 6QA ☎Guisborough (01287) 610182 OS map
   94/626182 2m NE of Guisborough off A173 (Skelton) Open Mar-Oct 100 pitches (75 static)
   Level grass, sheltered ♀◻●∅∅⊕↩ £9.00-£11.00

HAREWOOD, N Yorks   **Map D5**
SEE Harewood House 1m SW Restaurant: Ladbroke 6m E at Wetherby ☎(01937) 563881

  Maustin Caravan Park, Kearby cum Netherby LS22 4DP ☎(0113) 288 6234 OS map 104/344474
   3m NE of Harewood on A61 Harrogate road Open Mar-Oct 100 pitches (75 static)–no facs for
   children Level grass, sheltered ✗♀↩⟋◻●∅⊕∅□⌂⅄ bowling £10.00
   (Mastercard/Visa/Switch)

┌──┐

                                      HARROGATE
Shaws Trailer Park
Knaresborough Road HG2 7NE   Tel (01423) 884432

1m E of Harrogate on A59 (York) opposite hospital.
Well-equipped site with level/sloping grass and hard standings.
Open all year.

└──┘

HARROGATE, N Yorks   **Map D5**
Pop 65,000. EC Wed, MD daily SEE Valley Gardens, The Stray, Pump Room Museum, moors and
dales, Ripley Castle 4m NW ◪Royal Bath Assembly Rooms, Crescent Road ☎Harrogate (01423)
525666 Restaurant: Bay Horse Inn, Burnt Yates ☎(01423) 770230

Bilton Park, Village Farm, Bilton Lane HG1 4DH ☎Harrogate (01423) 863121/565070 OS map
   104/318573 2m NE of Harrogate off A59 ring road at Dragon Hotel Open Apr-Oct 95 pitches (70
   static) Level grass ▲●∅⊕↩● (30)□ farm produce, fishing £8.00-£11.00

Chequers Inn Motor Lodge, Bishop Thornton HG3 3JN ☎Harrogate (01423) 770173 OS map
   99/268638 6m NNW of Harrogate off A59 (Knaresborough) and B6165 (Ripley) Open Apr-Oct 70
   pitches (50 static) Level grass, sheltered ✗♀◻●∅⊕ horse riding £5.00

High Moor Farm, Skipton Road HG3 2LT ☎Harrogate (01423) 563637/564955 OS map
   104/244559 4m W of Harrogate on A59 (Skipton) Open Apr-Oct 340 pitches (180 static) Level
   grass and hard standing ▲✗♀↩⟋◻●∅⊕∅□↩◉●□ lic club, golf £8.75-£9.00

Ripley Caravan Park, Ripley HG3 3AU ☎Harrogate (01423) 770050 OS map 104/291599 3½m N
   of Harrogate off A61 (Ripon) on B6165 (Knaresborough) Open Easter-Oct 100 pitches Level
   grass and hard standings ▲◻●∅⊕∅□ (indoor-heated) ◉↩□⅄ nursery playroom, sauna
   £6.95-£8.50 (2000)

Rudding Holiday Park, Follifoot HG3 1JH *Set in gardens of Rudding Park* ☎Harrogate (01423)
   870439 OS map 104/345302 2m SE of Harrogate off A661 (Wetherby) Open Mar 22-Nov 3, 141
   pitches (80 static) Level/sloping grass and hard standing, sheltered ▲✗♀↩⟋◻●∅⊕∅□
   (outdoor-heated) ◉↩●⌂⅄ 18 hole golf course, serviced pitches £7.00-£22.00
   (Mastercard/Visa/Switch)

Shaws Trailer Park, Knaresborough Road HG2 7NE ☎Harrogate (01423) 884432 OS map
   104/325557 1m E of Harrogate on A59 (Knaresborough) Open all year 211 pitches (146 static)
   Level/sloping grass and hard standings ◻●∅⊕∅● £5.00-£8.50

HATFIELD–see Thorne

HAWES, N Yorks   **Map A5**
Pop 1,300. EC Wed, MD Tues SEE Waterfalls ⚹Dales Countryside Museum, Station Yard
✆Hawes (01969) 667450 Restaurant: Rose House Main St ✆(01969) 667324

Bainbridge Ings Caravan Camping Site, DL8 3NU ✆Hawes (01969) 667354 OS map 98/875894
½m E of Hawes off A684 (Leyburn) Open Apr-Oct 85 pitches (15 static) Level grass 🚐🖊❂🔲
£7.00-£7.50

Shaw Ghyll Farm, Simonstone DL8 3LY ✆Hawes (01969) 667359 OS map 98/865933 2m N of
Hawes on Muker road Open Mar-Oct 30 pitches 3 acres level grass, sheltered 🚐🖊❂∅ £6.00

HAWORTH, W Yorks   **Map C6**
Pop 350 SEE Old Vicarage (home of Bronte sisters), Keighley steam railway ⚹2 West Lane
✆(01535) 642313 Restaurant: Old White Lion ✆(01535) 642313

Upwood Holiday Park, Blackmoor Rd, Oxenhope BD22 9SS ✆(01535) 644242 OS map
104/044355 1m SE of Haworth at Oxenhope Open Apr-Oct 139 pitches (30 static) Grass, level,
open ✕🍴⇥🚐🖊❂∅🔲🌀↩🚻🔲👐 £5.00-£9.00 (Mastercard/Visa/Switch)

HEBDEN BRIDGE, W Yorks   **Map D6**
SEE Weavers' cottages, Hardcastle Crags 3m NW ⚹Bridge Gate ✆(01422) 843831 Restaurant:
Walkley's, Clog Mill (lunch only) ✆(01422) 842061

High Greenwood House, Heptonstall HX7 7AZ ✆Hebden Bridge (01422) 842287 OS map
103/969308 3½m NW of Hebden Bridge off A646 (Todmorden) on Widdop road Open May-Oct
50 pitches 5 acres, level grass and hard standings 🚐🖊🔲 £6.50-£9.50

HELMSLEY, N Yorks   **Map D3**
Pop 1,460. EC Wed, MD Fri SEE Castle ruins, Rievaulx Terrace frescoes 2m NW, Rievaulx Abbey
3m NW, N Yorks moors ⚹Town Hall ✆(01439) 770173 Restaurant: Feathers, Market Pl ✆(01439)
770275

Foxholme Touring Caravan and Camping Park, Harome YO62 5JG *Peaceful site in wooded
countryside* ✆Helmsley (01439) 770416 OS map 100/661831 4m SE of Helmsley off A170
(Pickering) Open Apr-Oct 60 pitches Level grass, some hard standings, sheltered 🛒⇥🚐🖊❂∅
£7.00-£8.00

Golden Square Caravan Park, Golden Square, Oswaldkirk YO6 5YQ ✆Ampleforth (01439) 788269
OS map 100/605798 2m S of Helmsley off B1257 (Malton) on Ampleforth road Open Mar-Oct
129 pitches Level grass and hard standing, sheltered 🛒⇥↗🚐🖊❂∅🌀↩🚻 (25-45)
🔲🖐♿ fishing, swimming, pony trekking near £6.00-£8.00

Wombleton Caravan Park, Moorfield Lane, Wombleton YO62 5RY ✆Kirkbymoorside (01751)
431684 OS map 100/665827 3m SE of Helmsley off A170 (Pickering) on Wombleton road Open
Mar-Oct 88 pitches–couples only Level grass and hard standing, sheltered 🛒⇥🚐🖊❂∅↩🚻
£6.00-£10.00

Wren's of Ryedale Camping Park, Nawton YO62 7SD ✆Helmsley (01439) 771260 OS map
100/656841 3m E of Helmsley off A170 (Pickering) Open Mar-Oct 45 pitches Level grass,
sheltered 🛒⇥🚐🖊❂∅↩🚻🔲 bike hire £6.00-£7.50

HIGH HAWSKER–see Whitby

HINDERWELL, N Yorks   **Map C1**
Pop 1,500 Restaurant: Ellerby Country Inn 1½m S at Ellerby ✆(01947) 840342

Fern Farm, High Street TS13 5JH ✆Whitby (01947) 840350 OS map 94/792168 On A174 in
Hinderwell opposite Badger and Hounds Inn Open Mar-Oct 20 pitches Level/sloping grass,
sheltered 🚐❂ £4.00

Runswick Bay Caravan Park, Runswick Bay TS13 5HR ✆Whitby (01947) 840997 OS map
94/804163 1m S of Hinderwell on Runswick Bay road Open Mar-Oct 40 pitches 5 acres level
grass sheltered ⇥❂ £3.00-£5.00

Serenity Touring Caravan Camping Park, High St TS13 5JH *Family run park near sea and shops*
✆Hinderwell (01947) 841122 OS map 94/793166 In village on A174 (Whitby-Saltburn) Open
Mar-Oct 40 pitches 3 acres level/sloping grass, sheltered 🚐🖊❂ £7.00-£7.50

HOLMFIRTH–see Huddersfield

**If you caravan or camp with your dog be prepared when on a campsite to keep it on a lead at
all times. Many sites now charge for dogs and some ban them altogether.**

HORNSEA, N Humberside   **Map G2**
Pop 7,270. EC Wed, MD Sun SEE Hornsea Mere (freshwater lake now bird sanctuary), Holderness museum of village life, Hornsea pottery ∎75 Newbegin ✆(01964) 536404 Restaurant: Dacre Arms 5m W at Brandesburton ✆(01964) 542392

Four Acres Caravan Park, Hornsea Road, Atwick YO25 8DG ✆Hornsea (01964) 536940 OS map 107/193506 2m N of Hornsea on B1242 (Skipsea) Open Mar-Oct 54 pitches 4 acres level grass, sheltered ♥⌀⊕☻↵ £7.00-£10.00

Longbeach Leisure Park, South Cliff HU18 1TL *Landscaped park overlooking Bridlington bay with direct beach access* ✆(01964) 532506 OS map 107/213465 ¼m S of Hornsea centre at South Cliff, by sea Open Mar-Oct 450 pitches (350 static) 90 acres level grass, sheltered ⛽🗑♥⌀⊕∅☻↵♥⛵ 9 hole pitch and putt £10.00-£12.00 inc

Springfield Farm, Atwick Road HU18 1EJ ✆Hornsea (01964) 532112 OS map 107/195484 ¾m N of Hornsea on B1242 (Bridlington) Open Mar 28-Oct 31, 30 pitches Level grass and hard standing, part sheltered ♥⌀❀ £6.00

HUDDERSFIELD, W Yorks   **Map D6**
Pop 123,160. EC Wed, MD Mon, Thurs SEE town hall, Roman relics, Castle Hill Tower, Kirklees Hall, Holmfirth postcard museum ∎3 Albion Street ✆Huddersfield (01484) 430808 Restaurant: Solo Mio (Italian), Imperial Arcade, Market St ✆(01484) 542828

Holme Valley Camping Caravan Park, Thongsbridge, Holmfirth HD7 2TD ✆Huddersfield (01484) 665819 Fax (01484) 663870 OS map 110/153104 6m S of Huddersfield on A6024 (Holmfirth) Open all year 62 pitches 4½ acres level grass and hard standing, sheltered ⛽🏹🗑♥⌀⊕∅↵🚐⛓ fishing, solarium £6.00-£8.00 (Mastercard/Visa)

HULL, N Humberside   **Map G3**
Pop 271,000. EC Thurs, MD Tues, Fri, Sat SEE Wilberforce House Museum, St Mary's Curch, Humber Bridge at Hessle 2m W ∎Central Library, Albion Street ✆Hull (01482) 223344 Restaurant: Waterfront, Dagger Lane, Old Town ✆(01482) 227222

Burton Constable Country Park, Old Lodges, Sproatley HU11 4LN ✆(01964) 562508 OS map 107/186357 7m NE of Hull off A165 (Bridlington) Open Mar 1-Nov 1, 175 pitches (50 static) 20 acres level/sloping grass, sheltered ⛲🗑♥⌀⊕∅↵ boating, wind surfing, fishing £6.75-£7.50

For other sites near Hull see also Barton upon Humber, Beverley, Hornsea, South Cave and Withernsea

INGLETON, N Yorks   **Map A6**
Pop 1,930. EC Thurs, MD Fri Tourist village where in 1884 the Ingleton improvement society christened the wooded gorges of the Doe and Twiss the ingleton Glens and built the bridges and paths that now make up the Falls Walk SEE Norman church, Ingleborough Mountain (2,373ft) with subterranean lake, White Scar Cave, Thornton Force ∎Community Centre Car Park ✆(01524) 241049 Restaurant: Royal 7m NW at Kirkby Lonsdale ✆(01524) 271217

Flying Horseshoe Hotel, Clapham LA2 8ES ✆(015242) 51229 OS map 98/733679 4m SE of Ingleton off A65 (Settle) on Keasden road near rail station Open Mar-Oct 46 pitches Level grass and hard standing ✗⛲⟵♥⌀⊕∅☻ fishing near £7.00-£10.00 (Mastercard/Visa)

Goat Gap Inn, Clapham LA2 8JB ✆Ingleton (01524) 241230 OS map 98/714703 2m E of Ingleton on A65 (Kirkby Lonsdale-Settle) Open Mar-Oct 15 pitches Level/sloping grass and hard standing, sheltered ✗⛲⟵🏹♥⌀☻🚐 £6.00-£8.00 (Mastercard/Visa)

Goodenbergh Caravan Park, Bentham LA2 7EW ✆(01524) 262022 OS map 97/638705 3m SW of Ingleton via Burton in Lonsdale off Low Bentham road Open Apr-Oct 140 pitches (130 static) Level grass and hard standing, sheltered ⛽♥⌀⊕∅🚐▭ pony trekking £6.50

Riverside Caravan Park, Wenning Avenue, Bentham LA2 7HS ✆Bentham (01524) 261272 OS map 98/666688 3m SW of Ingleton off High Bentham road Open Mar-Oct 200 pitches (170 static) 20 acres level grass, sheltered 🗑♥⌀⊕∅☻↵▢🚐 fishing £8.40 (2000)

Trees Caravan Park, Westhouse LA6 3DN ✆Ingleton (01524) 241511 OS map 98/672737 1m W of Ingleton on left of A65 (Kendal) Open Apr-Oct 29 pitches – booking advisable 2½ acres level grass, sheltered ♥⌀⊕∅🚐 £7.50

CHECK BEFORE ENTERING

Beware less-than-honest site operators who give us one price for the following year and then increase it once the season gets underway. So note the charges for any site featured in this guide and before pulling in verify how much you will have to pay, and for what. If on leaving the charges turn out to be higher, ask why the difference.

KEIGHLEY, W Yorks   **Map C6**
Pop 47,610. EC Tues, MD Wed, Fri, Sat SEE Cliffe Castle Museum, Keighley-Worth Valley Railway
Restaurant: Bridge Inn 3m NW at Silsden ☎(01535) 653144

Dales Bank Holiday Park, Low lane, Horn Lane (off Bradley Road), Silsden BD20 9JH ☎Keighley
(01535) 653321 OS map 104/036483 5m N of Keighley off A629 (Skipton) Open Apr-Oct 52
pitches Level grass, sheltered ⚑✗⚐⚑⚑⊘⊕⊘⊗ £5.50-£6.50

Springs Farm Caravan Park, Lothersdale BD20 8HH ☎Cross Hills (01535) 632533 OS map
103/944450 10m NW of Keighley off A629 (Skipton) on Lothersdale Road Open Apr-Oct, 3½
acres 37 pitches (18 static) Must book tents and m/caravans–preferred for caravans Grass,
gentle slope, hard standing ⚑⊘⊕⚑⊗ fly fishing £6.50-£8.50

See also Haworth

KETTLEWELL, N Yorks   **Map B5**
Pop 320 EC Thurs SEE Wharfedale, Great Whernside (2,310ft), Kilnsey Crag, moors Restaurant:
Racehorses ☎(01756) 760233

Fold Farm BD23 5RJ ☎(01756) 760886 OS map 98/975725 ¼m NE of Kettlewell centre Open all
year 20 pitches–no caravans – booking advisable ½ acre grass, sloping £7.50

KINGSTON UPON HULL–see Hull

KIRKBY MALZEARD, N Yorks   **Map C4**
Restaurant: King's Head 4m N at Masham ☎(01765) 689295

Gold Coin Farm, Galphay HG4 3NJ ☎(01765) 658508 OS map 99/253724 1m SE of Kirkby
Malzeard on Ripon road Open Apr-Oct, 6 pitches Level grass ⊕ *No showers* £3.00

Winksley Banks Holiday Park, Winksley Banks, Galphay HG4 3NS ☎Kirkby Malzeard (01765)
658439 OS map 99/247718 1½m SE of Kirkby Malzeard on Winksley road Open Mar-Oct 96
pitches (90 static) 5 acres level grass, sheltered ⚑⚑⊘⊕⊘⊗⚐⚑⚑⚑⚑ trout and coarse
fishing £9.00-£13.00 (Mastercard/Visa)

Woodhouse Farm Caravan and Camping Park, Winksley HG4 3PG ☎(01765) 658309 OS map
99/240715 2m S of Kirkby Malzeard off Grantley road Open Apr-Oct 200 pitches (25 static)
Grass and hard standing, level, sheltered ⚑⚑⚑⊘⊕⊘⊗⚐⚑⚑ paddling pool, fishing lake
£7.00-£8.00 (Mastercard/Visa/Switch)

KNARESBOROUGH, N Yorks   **Map D4**
Pop 13,000. EC Thurs, MD Wed SEE castle ruins, St Roberts' chapel, old manor house and chemist
shop, Mother Shipton's Cave, Nidderdale NW ⚑Market Place ☎Harrogate (01423) 866886
Restaurant: Bond End Wine Bar, Bond End ☎(01423) 863899

Allerton Park, Allerton Mauleverer HG5 0SE ☎(01423) 330569 OS map 105/416576 4m E of
Knaresborough on A59 (Harrogate-York) near junct with A1 Open Feb-Jan 130 pitches Grass,
sloping, sheltered ⚑⚑⚑⊘⊕⊘⊗⚐⚑⚑ £8.50-£11.00

Kingfisher Caravan Park, Low Moor Lane, Farnham HG5 9DQ ☎(01423) 869411 OS map
104/350606 2m NW of Knaresborough off B6055 (Boroughbridge) Open Mar-Oct 135 pitches (40
static) Level grass and hard standing, sheltered ⚑⚑⚑⊘⊕⚐⚑⚑ £6.00-£12.50

Vintage France

192pp ISBN 1-870009-04-5

Tours of the major vineyard areas make a celebratory start with Champagne in the north and end
with Cognac and the Loire in the west. In between come Alsace, the Jura, Burgundy, Beaujolais, the
Rhone Valley, Provence, Armagnac and the world-famous Bordelais around Bordeaux. Each
vineyard area is described in terms of its history and landscape with individual wines related to the
places where they are made and can be tasted. Most of these areas still provide quiet roads, fine
scenery and local restaurant meals at local prices. **For details of publication and possible
reductions on cover price write to Frederick Tingey at Hillsboro, How Caple HR1 4TE.**

KNOTTINGLEY, W Yorks   **Map E5**
SEE Old Pump, 14c arcade and racecourse at Pontefract 2m NW Restaurant: Wentbridge House,
4m S at Wentbridge ☎(01977) 620444

West Park, Great North Road, Darrington WF8 3HY ☎(01977) 620382 OS map 111/486167 2½m
S of Knottingley on A1 (Doncaster) Open all year 30 pitches 🖪 £5.00

LEEDS, W Yorks   **Map D5**
Pop 750,000. MD daily SEE Cathedral (RC), town hall, museum, City square, Kirkstall Abbey and
Abbey House Museum, Middleton Railway, Roundhay Park, Tropical World, Royal Armouries 🛈 19
Wellington St ☎Leeds (0113) 2478301/2 Restaurant: Metropole, King St ☎(0113) 245 0841

Roundhay Park, Elmete Lane LS8 2LG ☎Leeds (0113) 265 2354 OS 104/338374 4m NE of
    Leeds city centre off A58 (Wetherby) Open Mar 30-Oct 26 60 pitches Grass and hard standing,
    level, sheltered 🖪🖳🖉🌑🖉⌇🖢 dog walk £9.00-£9.50

LEEMING BAR–see Bedale

LEVEN, Humberside   **Map F3**
Pop 300 Restaurant: Esplanade 6m E at Hornsea ☎(01964) 532616

Dacre Lakeside Park, Brandesburton YO25 8SA ☎(01964) 543704 OS map 107/118468 3m N of
    Leven off A165 (Bridlington) Open Mar-Oct 120 marked pitches 6 acres level grass by lake
    🖢🖵🖪🖉🌑🖉🖢 late arrivals enclosure, wind surfing £7.50-£8.00

LEYBURN, N Yorks   **Map B4**
🛈Thornborough Hall ☎Wensleydale (01969) 23069 Restaurant: Golden Lion, Market Pl ☎(01969)
622161

Akebar Park, Wensleydale DL8 5LY ☎(01677) 650201 OS map 99/193907 5m E of Leyburn on
    A684 (Northallerton) Open Mar-Oct–family camping only 300 pitches (150 static) Level grass,
    sheltered 🖢✕🖵⟿🖈🖪🖉🖳 (indoor heated) 🌑🖭 sauna, tennis, fishing, barbecue, golf, bowling
    green £5.00-£6.50

Constable Burton Hall Caravan Park, DL8 5LJ *Walled site in grounds near country house*
    ☎(01677) 450428 OS map 99/161911 3½m E of Leyburn on A684 (Bedale) Open Easter-Oct
    120 pitches Level/sloping grass, sheltered 🖪🖳🖉🌑🖉 £7.50-£10.00 (2000)

Lower Wensleydale Caravan Park, Harmby DL8 5NU ☎Wensleydale (01969) 623366 OS map
    99/128901 1m E of Leyburn off A684 (Bedale) on Bellerby road Open Apr-Nov 100 pitches–no
    tents (exc trailer tents) 10 acres level/sloping grass and hard standing, sheltered 🖪🖳🌑 £8.40-
    £9.20

LINTON ON OUSE–see York

LOTHERDALE–see Skipton

MALTON, N Yorks   **Map E3**
Pop 4,320. EC Thurs, MD Tues, Fri, Sat SEE St Michael's church, Roman Museum, Old Malton
Priory, Flamingoland zoo 🛈58 Market Place ☎(01653) 600048 Restaurant: Green Man, Market St
☎(01653) 602662

Castle Howard Caravan and Camping Park, Coneysthorpe YO60 7DD ☎(01653) 648316
    OS map 100/705710 5m W of Malton off A64 (York) Open Mar-Oct 192 pitches (120 static) Level
    grass, sheltered 🖢🖪🖳🖉🌑🖉 fishing £8.50 (inc hot water)

Robin Hood Caravan and Camping Park, Green Dyke Lane, Slingsby YO62 7AP ☎Hovingham
    (01653) 628391 OS map 100/700749 6m NW of Malton off B1257 (Slingsby) Open Apr-Oct
    43 pitches Level grass and hard standings, sheltered 🖢🖈🖪🖳🖉🌑🖉🌑⌇🖱🖭🖢 battery
    charging £9.00-£15.00

MASHAM, N Yorks   **Map C4**
Pop 1,000. EC Thurs, MD Wed SEE Norman church, Saxon cross, brewery Restaurant: King's
Head, Market Pl ☎(01765) 689295

Black Swan Caravan and Camping, Black Swan Hotel, Fearby HG4 4NF ☎Ripon (01765) 689477
    OS map 99/194809 1m W of Masham off A6108 (Ripon-Leyburn) on Fearby road at rear of Black
    Swan hotel Open Mar-Oct 100 pitches Grass, level, part sheltered 🖢✕🖵🖪🖳🖉🖉⌇🖱🖭🏠
    £8.00-£9.00 (all cards)

FACTS CAN CHANGE

**We do our best to check the accuracy of the entries in this guide but changes can and do
occur after publication. So if you plan to stay at a site some distance from home it makes
sense to ring the manager or owner before setting off.**

MIDDLESBROUGH, Cleveland   **Map B2**
Pop149,100. MD daily Once village on S bank of river Tees now heart of conurbation of Teesside born in 1830s with extension of Stockton-Darlington railway SEE parks, bridges, museum, cathedral (RC), Newham Grange Farm Museum, Capt Cook's Birthplace Museum, Stockton Transport Museum 4m NW ☎ 125 Albert Road ☎ Middlesbrough (01642) 245750 Restaurant: Blue Bell 4m SE at Marton ☎ (01642) 593939

Middlesbrough Caravan Park, Prissick Sports Centre, Marton Road TS4 3SA ☎ Middlesbrough (01642) 311911 OS map 93/512166 ½m S of Middlesbrough on A172 (York) Open Easter-Oct 22 pitches Level grass ❋ £5.00

MUKER, N Yorks   **Map A4**
Pop 650 SEE Swaledale, waterfalls Restaurant: Tan Hill Inn (one highest pubs in England) 4m NW at Keld ☎ (01833) 628246

Usha Gap DL11 6DW ☎ (01748) 886214 OS map 98/900980 ½m W of Muker on right of B6270 (Hawes) by river Open all year 24 pitches 1 acre level grass £7.50-£8.00

NORTHALLERTON, N Yorks   **Map C3**
Pop 10,300. EC Thurs, MD Wed, Sat SEE church, Porch House, old inns ☎ Applegarth Car Park ☎ Northallerton (01609) 776864 Restaurant: Golden Lion, Market Pl ☎ (01609) 772404

Cote Ghyll Caravan Park, North End, Osmotherley DL6 3AH ☎ Osmotherley (01609) 883425 OS map 99/456972 5¾m NE of Northallerton off junction of A684 (Guisborough) and A19 (Thirsk-Middlesbrough) Open Apr-Oct 77 pitches (18 static) Grass level/sloping, sheltered ▣❋❋❋ £7.50

Hutton Bonville Caravan Park, Church Lane, Hutton Bonville DL7 0NR ☎ Great Smeaton (01609) 881416 OS map 93/356005 4m N of Northallerton off A167 (Darlington) Open Apr-Oct 75 pitches (70 static) Grass, sloping ▣❋❋❋❋ £7.50

OTLEY, W Yorks   **Map D5**
Pop 14,130 SEE Chevin Hill (900ft), medieval bridge, old inns, Bramhope chapel SE ☎ 8 Boroughgate ☎ Otley (0113) 247 7707 Restaurant: Chevin Lodge, York Gate ☎ (01493) 467818

Yorkshire Clarion Clubhouse, Chevin End, West Chevin Road, Menston LS29 6BL OS map 104/187442 1m SW of Otley on Menston road Open Apr-Oct 20 pitches—no adv booking 1 acre level grass, sheltered ❋ £2.50-£3.50

PATELEY BRIDGE, N Yorks   **Map C5**
Pop 1,900. EC Thurs SEE Bronze Age relics, Stump Cross Caverns 4m W, How Stean Gorge in Upper Nidderdale ☎ 14 High St ☎ (01423) 711147 Restaurant: Sportman's Arms 3m N at Wath in Nidderdale ☎ (01423) 711306

Heathfield Caravan Park, Wath Rd HG3 5PY ☎ (01423) 711652 OS map 99/150670 1½m NW of Pateley Bridge off Ramsgill road in Nidderdale Open Mar-Oct 180 pitches (170 static)—no tents ❋▣❋❋❋❋ £7.50

Manor House Farm, Summerbridge HG3 4JS ☎ (01423) 780322 OS map 99/203605 3½m SE of Pateley Bridge off B6165 (Knaresborough) Open Mar 21-Oct 31, 60 pitches (50 static) Hard standings, sheltered ▣❋❋❋❋ baths £8.00-£12.00

Riverside Caravan Park HG3 5HL ☎ (01423) 711383 OS map 99/154658 ½m N of Pateley Bridge on Low Wath road Open Apr-Oct—booking (3 nights or more) 158 pitches (110 static) Level grass and hard standings, sheltered ▣❋❋❋❋ £7.50

Studfold Farm, Lofthouse in Nidderdale HG3 5SG ☎ (01423) 755210 OS map 99/099733 7m NW of Pateley Bridge on Stean road at head of Nidderdale Open Apr-Oct—must book 80 pitches (60 static) Level grass, sheltered ❋❋❋❋ farm produce £7.00-£9.25

Westfield Farm, Heathfield HG3 5BX ☎ (01423) 711880/711410 OS map 99/133666 1½m NW of Pateley Bridge off Ramsgill road via Heathfield Open Apr-Oct 30 pitches—family camping only 1½ acres level/sloping grass, sheltered ❋❋❋

See also Harrogate

Cause for Complaint

If you have cause for complaint while staying on a site take the matter up with the manager or owner. If you are still not satisfied set the facts down in writing and send photocopies to anyone you think might be able to help, starting with the editor of this guide and the local (licensing) authority for the area where the site is located.

PICKERING, N Yorks   Map D2
Pop 6,200. EC Wed, MD Mon SEE church (15c murals), castle ruins, steam railway, Beck Isle Museum of Rural Life ▣ Eastgate Car Park ☎ Pickering (01751) 473791 Restaurant: White Swan, Market Pl ☎ (01751) 472288

Black Bull Inn, Malton Road YO18 8EA ☎ Pickering (01751) 472528 OS map 100/802815 1m S of Pickering on A169 (Malton) at rear of inn Open Mar-Oct 36 pitches 4 acres level grass
✗ ♁ ▤ ▣ ◈ ❂ ⌁ 🏠 £8.00

Overbrook Caravan Park, Maltongate, Thornton Dale YO18 7SE ☎ Pickering (01751) 474417 OS map 100/834822 2½m E of Pickering off A170 (Scarborough) Open Mar-Oct, 2½ acres, 50 pitches–no children Level grass, sheltered, hard standings ▤ ▣ ◈ ❂ ▣ 🏠 £6.00-£8.50

Rosedale Caravan and Camping Parks, Rosedale Abbey YO18 8SA ☎ (01751) 472272 OS map 100/723960 9m NW of Pickering off A170 (Helmsley) via Wrelton Open Mar-Oct–no adv booking for tents on public holidays 225 pitches Grass and hard standings ▣ ✗ ▤ ▣ ◈ ⌁ ▣ fishing £3.10-£3.90

Spiers House Caravan and Camp Site, Forestry Commission, Cropton YO18 8ES ☎ (01751) 417591 OS map 100/758918 5m NW of Pickering off Rosedale Abbey road, via Cropton Open Mar 27-Oct 3–adv booking min 7 nights 150 pitches Grass sloping ▣ ▤ ▣ ◈ ❂ ❸ ⌁ ♿ forest trail £6.00-£7.00

Sun Inn, Normanby YO6 6RH ☎ Kirkbymoorside (01751) 431051 OS map 100/736816 6m SW of Pickering off A170 (Helmsley) via Marton by River Severn Open Apr-Oct–adv booking preferred 18 pitches ✗ fishing £4.50-£5.00

Upper Carr Caravan Park, Malton Road YO18 7JP ☎ Pickering (01751) 473115 OS map 100/802815 1½m S of Pickering off A169 (Malton) Open Mar-Oct 80 pitches Grass and hard standing, level, sheltered ▣ ✗ ▤ ▣ ◈ ❂ ⌁ ▣ 🏠 ♿ pets corner, nature trail £7.00-£9.50 (Mastercard/Visa)

Vale of Pickering Caravan Park, Carr House Farm, Allerston YO18 7PQ *Outstanding site in lovely country* ☎ (01723) 859280 OS map 101/879808 4½m E of Pickering off A170 (Scarborough) on B1415 (Malton) Open Mar-Oct 120 pitches 8 acres level grass and hard standing, sheltered ▣ ✗ ▤ ▣ ◈ ❂ ⌁ ▢ ▣ ♿ £6.00-£9.00

Wayside Caravan Park, Wrelton YO18 8PG ☎ (01751) 472608 Fax (01751) 472608 OS map 100/764858 2½m W of Pickering off A170 (Helmsley) Open Easter-Oct 160 pitches (80 static) 10 acres level grass ▣ ▤ ▣ ◈ ❂ ❂ ♿ £8.50-£13.00 (Mastercard/Visa/Delta/Switch)

RICHMOND, N Yorks   Map B3
Pop 7,240. EC Wed, MD Sat SEE Holy Trinity church, Green Howards' regimental museum, castle ruins, Greyfriars Tower, Georgian Theatre ▣ Friary Garden, Victoria Road ☎ Richmond (01748) 850252/825994 Restaurant: Frenchgate, Frenchgate ☎ (01748) 852067

Brompton on Swale Caravan Park DL10 7EZ *Well maintained riverside park* ☎ Richmond (01748) 824629 OS map 93/201004 1½m E of Richmond on B6271 (Catterick Bridge) by river Swale Open Apr-Oct–must book peak periods 150 pitches (23 static) Level grass ▣ ✗ ▤ ▣ ◈ ❂ ❸ ⌁ ▢ ▣ (40 not on site) ▱ 🏠 ♿ on site fishing, scenic walks £6.90-£10.40

Fox Hall Caravan Park, Ravensworth DL11 7JZ *Separate gravelled pitches in woodland setting* ☎ (01325) 718344 OS map 93/545678 5m NW of Richmond on Ravensworth road Open Apr-Oct 65 pitches (55 static) 3½ acres level grass and hard standings, sheltered ▤ ▣ ◈ ⌁ £7.50

Swaleview Caravan Park, Reeth Road DL10 4SF ☎ Richmond (01748) 823106 OS map 92/134013 2½m W of Richmond on A6108 (Leyburn) by River Swale Open Mar-Oct 150 pitches (100 static) Grass, level, sheltered ▣ ▤ ▣ ◈ ❂ ❸ ⌁ ▱ £8.00

RIPLEY–see Harrogate

RIPON, N Yorks   **Map C4**
Pop 12,500. EC Wed, MD Thurs SEE Cathedral, St Wilfrid's church, almshouses, racecourse, Fountains Abbey 3m SW, Newby Hall 3m SE ◪ Minster Rd ☏ Ripon (01765) 604625 Restaurant: Unicorn, Market Pl ☏ (01765) 602202

River Laver Holiday Park, Studley Rd HG4 2QR ☏ (01765) 690508 OS map 99/297708 1m W of Ripon on B6265 (Fountains Abbey) Open Mar-Dec 100 pitches (50 static)–no tents 5 acres level hard standing, sheltered 🏕️ £8.50-£11.00 (Mastercard/Visa)

Sleningford Watermill Caravan Park, North Stainley HG4 3HQ ☏ Ripon (01765) 635201 OS map 99/280783 5m NNW of Ripon on A6108 (Leyburn) Open Apr-Oct 90 pitches (25 static) Grass and hard standing, level, sheltered 🏕️ fly fishing, canoeing £7.50-£11.50 (midweek off peak £5.00)

Ure Bank Touring Caravan-Camping Park, Ure Bank Top HG4 1JD ☏ Ripon (01765) 602964 OS map 99/317726 1m NE of Ripon off A61 (Thirsk) Open Mar-Oct 401 pitches (200 static)–no single sex groups Hard standing, level/sloping grass, sheltered 🏕️ £9.00-£11.00

Yorkshire Hussar Inn Holiday Caravan Park, Markington HG3 3NR ☏ Ripon (01765) 677327 OS map 99/287649 5m S of Ripon off A61 (Harrogate) Open Mar-Oct 95 pitches (75 static) Level grass and hard standing, sheltered 🏕️ horse riding £7.50-£10.00

For other sites near Ripon see also Kirkby Malzeard

ROBIN HOOD'S BAY, N Yorks   **Map D1**
Pop 750 Attractive old fishing and smuggling village, with main street feeding intricate maze of alleys and steps. SEE Fylingdales Moor W Restaurant: Victoria, Station Rd ☏ (01947) 880205

Middlewood Farm Holiday Park, Fylingthorpe Y022 4UF *Small family park with luxury facs and magnificent views* ☏ Whitby (01947) 880414 OS map 94/945045 ¼m SW of Robin Hood's Bay in Fylingthorpe Open Easter-Oct 150 pitches (30 static) 6 acres level grass, sheltered 🏕️ £6.50-£10.50 (Mastercard/Visa/Switch/Solo)

ROSEDALE ABBEY–see Pickering

ROTHERHAM, S Yorks   **Map F6**
Pop 82,000 EC Thurs MD Mon, Fri, Sat SEE ancient bridge with chapel, All Saints church, museum and art gallery ◪ Central Library, Walker Pl ☏ Rotherham (01709) 823611 Restaurant: Moat House, Moorgate Road ☏ (01709) 364902

Thrybergh Country Park, Doncaster Road, Thrybergh S65 4NU ☏ Rotherham (01709) 850353 OS map 111/474963 3m NE of Rotherham on A630 (Doncaster) Open all year 26 pitches booking advisable 3 acres, level grass and hard standing, sheltered 🏕️ trout fishing £5.40

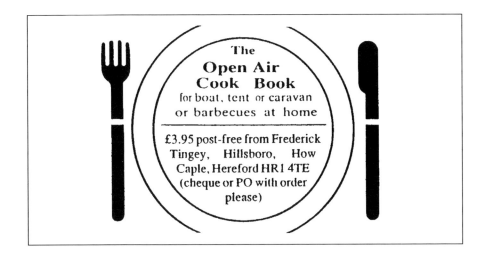

SCARBOROUGH, N Yorks   **Map E1**
Pop 41,770. EC Wed, MD Thurs SEE St Mary's church, spa, ballroom theatre and concert hall, zoo and marineland, miniature railway ■ St Nicholas Cliff ☎ Scarborough (01723) 373333 Restaurant: Palm Court, St Nicholas Cliff ☎ (01723) 368161

Arosa Caravan and Camping Park, Ratten Row, Seamer YO12 4QB ☎ Scarborough (01723) 862166 OS map 101/012830 4m S of Scarborough off A64 (Malton) Open Mar 1-Jan 4 105 pitches ▨▨▨▨▨▨▨ farm produce, B&B, lic club, bar meals £8.50-£10.50

Brown's Caravan Park, Cayton Bay YO11 3NN ☎ (01723) 582303 OS map 101/065840 3m SE of Scarborough off A165 (Filey) Open Apr-Sept 145 pitches (110 static) Level grass ✗ (bar snacks) ▨▨▨▨▨▨▨▨▨ £8.00

Cayton Village Caravan Park, Mill Lane, Cayton Bay YO11 3NN ☎ (01723) 583171 (Winter 01904 624630) OS map 101/058834 3m S of Scarborough off A165 (Filey) in Cayton village Open Easter-Oct 200 pitches Level grass and hard standing, sheltered ▨▨▨▨▨▨▨▨▨▨▨ dog walk £6.00-£10.00 (Mastercard/Visa/Switch)

Flower of May Holiday Park, Lebberston Cliff YO11 3NU ☎ Scarborough (01723) 584311 OS map 101/084833 4½m S of Scarborough off A165 (Filey) Open Easter-Oct–booking advisable 484 pitches (184 static) Level grass and hard standing ▨▨▨▨▨▨▨▨▨ (indoor heated) ▨▨▨▨ (peak season) ▨▨ bowling, squash, golf £7.00-£11.50

Jacob's Mount Caravan Camping Park, Stepney Road YO12 5NL ☎ Scarborough (01723) 361178 OS map 101/013870 2m SW of Scarborough on A170 (Pickering) Open Apr-Oct 200 pitches (44 static) Level grass and hard standings, sheltered ▨▨▨▨▨▨▨▨▨▨▨▨ serviced pitches £6.50-£10.00

Jasmine Caravan Park, Snainton YO13 9BE ☎ Scarborough (01723) 859240 OS map 101/930813 9m SW of Scarborough off A170 (Pickering) Open Mar-Jan 100 pitches Grass, level, sheltered ▨▨▨▨▨▨▨▨▨▨ £6.00-£10.00 (Mastercard/Visa/Switch)

Merry Lees Caravan Park, Staxton YO12 4NN *Woodland park overlooking lake popular with 60 species of birds* ☎ (01944) 710080 OS map 101/020800 6m S of Scarborough on right off A64 (Malton) Open Mar-Oct 80 pitches 8 acres level grass, sheltered ▨▨▨▨▨ £6.00-£11.00 (Mastercard/Visa)

St Helens Caravan and Camping Park, Wykeham YO13 9QD ☎ Scarborough (01723) 862771 OS map 101/957836 5m SW of Scarborough on A170 (Pickering) Open all year 250 pitches Level/sloping grass and hard standing, sheltered ▨▨▨▨▨▨▨▨▨ baby care units, games room £6.50-£8.50

Scalby Close Camping Park, Burniston Road YO13 0DA ☎ Scarborough (01723) 365908 OS map 101/026913 2m N of Scarborough on A165 (Burniston) Open Mar-Oct 50 pitches 3 acres level grass and hard standing, sheltered ▨▨▨▨▨▨▨ £6.00 (Mastercard/Visa)

Scalby Manor Touring Caravan Camping Park, Burniston Rd YO13 0DA ☎ (01723) 366212 (day) OS map 101/025911 2m N of Scarborough centre on A165 (Whitby) coast road Open Easter-Oct, 375 pitches 20 acres level grass ▨▨▨▨▨▨▨▨▨▨ £5.00-£10.00 (Mastercard/Visa)

SCOTCH CORNER, N Yorks   **Map B3**
Pop 400. EC Wed SEE Easby Abbey ruins, Richmond Castle 4m SW, Stanwick Fort ■ Pavilion Service Area, A1 ☎ (01325) 377677 Restaurant: Scotch Corner, Gt North Rd ☎ (01748) 822943

Scotch Corner Caravan Park, DL10 6NS *Well equipped, well maintained* ☎ (01748) 824424 (winter) 822530 (summer) OS map 93/214047 ¼m SW of Scotch Corner on A6108 (Richmond) Open Easter-mid Oct 96 pitches Level grass ▨▨✗▨▨▨▨ £8.50-£10.00

SELBY, N Yorks   **Map E4**
Pop 10.960. EC Thurs, MD Mon SEE Abbey Church, market cross, toll bridge ■ Bus Station, Park Street ☎ Selby (01757) 703263 Restaurant: Londesborough Arms, Market Pl ☎ (01757) 707355

Bay Horse Inn, York Road, Barlby YO8 5JH ☎ Selby (01757) 703878 OS map 105/630340 2m N of Selby on A19 (York) in Barlby Open all year 10 pitches Level grass, sheltered ▨▨▨▨ £3.00-£5.00

Cawood Holiday Park Caravan and Camping Centre, Ryther Road, Cawood YO8 3TT ☎ (01757) 268450 Fax (01757) 268537 OS map 105/571380 4m NNW of Selby on B1223 (Tadcaster) near junction with B1222 (York) Open Mar-Jan 60 pitches Level/sloping grass and hard standing, sheltered ▨▨✗▨▨▨▨▨▨▨▨ (indoor) ▨▨▨▨▨ fishing, entertainment, pool room £8.50-£12.00 (all cards)

Some site operators make it a rule that cars must be left in a separate parking area away from caravans and tents, which can be inconvenient when shopping by car. But it does minimise traffic noise and the risk to children.

SETTLE, N Yorks   Map B6
Pop 2,310. EC Wed, MD Tues SEE museum, Flowing Well at Giggleswick, Stainforth Foss at
Stainforth 3m N ◪ Town Hall, Cheapside ✆ (01729) 825192 Restaurant: Royal Oak, Market Pl
✆ (01729) 822561

Knight Stainforth Hall, BD24 ODP ✆ Settle (01729) 822200 OS map 98/815672 2½m N of Settle
off A65 (Kirkby Lonsdale) at Stackhouse Lane beside River Ribble Open Mar-Oct 160 pitches (60
static) Level/sloping grass, hard standings ⬛◻◻◻◉⬤◉◭⬛ £7.50

Langcliffe Caravan Park, Langcliffe Place, Langcliffe BD24 9LX ✆ (01729) 822387 OS map
98/818652 ½m N of Settle off A65 (Ingleton) and B6479 (Horton in Ribblesdale) Open Mar-Oct
60 pitches (53 static) 5 acres mainly level grass and hard standing ◻◻◉◻◉◭▣ fishing
£8.00-£12.00

SHEFFIELD, S Yorks   Map F7
Pop 544,200. EC Thurs, MD daily except Thurs SEE cathedral, city museum, Cutlers' Hall, New
Crucible Theatre, Abbeydale Industral Hamlet (18c), Kelham Industrial Museum ◪ Peace Gardens
✆ Sheffield (0114) 2734671 Restaurant: Norfolk Arms, Manchester Rd ✆ (0114) 2308253

Fox Hagg Farm, Lodge Lane, Rivelin S6 5SN ✆ Sheffield (0114) 2305589 OS map 110/292868
3m W of Sheffield off A57 (Glossop) near John Thomas Inn Open Apr-Oct 100 pitches (20 static)
Level grass and hard standing ◻◻◉◭▣ £6.75

SHIPLEY, W Yorks   Map D6
Restaurant: Aagrah (Indian), Westgate ✆ (01274) 594660

Crook Farm, Shipley Glen, Baildon BD17 5ED ✆ (01274) 584339 OS map 104/135393 2½m NW
of Shipley off Glen road Open Mar-Jan 160 pitches (100 static) Grass and hard standing
⬛♀◻◻◻◉◉⬛ bar meals, mobile shop calls, childrens room £8.00

SILSDEN–see Keighley

SKIPSEA, Humberside   Map F2
Pop 540 Small seaside resort overlooking extensive sandy beach SEE castle ruins, 12c church, All
Saints church 2m N at Barmston Restaurant: Star Inn 4m W at North Frodingham ✆ (01262) 488365

Beach Bank Caravan Park, South Field Lane, Ulrome YO25 8TU ✆ (01262) 468491 OS map
107/175565 1½m NE of Skipsea on coast road Open Mar-Oct 60 pitches 2½ acres level/sloping
grass, on cliff top ⬛✕◻◻◻◉◉ £6.00

Far Grange Park, YO25 8SY ✆ (01262)468293/468248 OS map 107/187531 1½m S of Skipsea
off B1242 (Hornsea) by sea Open Mar-Oct 814 pitches (630 static) 63 acres level grass
⬛✕♀◭◭◻◻◻◉◻◻◉◭⬛◭⬛ tennis amusements, beach near £11.00-£14.00

Low Skirlington Caravan Park, YO25 8SY ✆ (01262) 468213 and 468358 OS map 107/185525
1½m S of Skipsea off B1242 (Hornsea) by sea Open Mar-Oct 725 pitches (450 static)
⬛✕◻◻◻◻◻⬛ £9.00

Mill Farm Country Park, Mill Lane YO25 8SS ✆ (01262) 468211 OS map 107/166555 ¼m N of
Skipsea centre off B1242 (Bridlington) via Cross St Open Mar 2-Oct 6 54 pitches 6 acres level
grass and hard standing, sheltered ◻◉◉◻ farm walk £6.95-£8.50

Skipsea Sands Caravan Park, Mill Lane, YO25 8TZ ✆ (01262) 468210 OS map 107/175563 1m
E of Skipsea by sea Open Mar-Nov 36 acres, 740 pitches (650 static) Level grass
⬛✕♀◭◻◻◻◉◻◻ (indoor) ◉◭⬛ £10.50-£12.50

Planning a tour in Europe?

Then choose one of the itineraries mapped and described in *Tour Europe* and have the homework
done for you. Each chapter presents a complete holiday – a step by step account of how to enjoy
touring for a fortnight through one of ten chosen regions in seven countries, each rewarding in
itself, from the scenic splendour of the Austrian lake district adjoining Mozart's Salzburg to the
wooded wonderland of the Ardennes/Eifel, from the castle-studded Loire valley to the sun-baked
Italian Marches, and much more. Linking all the local information are touring directions and a
sketch map, with each route forming a circuit so that it can be left and picked up again at any point.

**Reserve your copy at a special pre-publication price by writing to Frederick Tingey (TE),
Hillsboro, How Caple HR1 4TE.**

Moor Lodge Caravan Park
Blackmoor Lane, Bardsey LS17 9DZ

Tranquil, immaculate country park for adults only off A58,
a mere 30 minutes York, Leeds, the Dales or Harrogate.

Superb shower block. £6.00 per night with this advert. Open all year.

Tel: 01937 572424

SKIPTON, N Yorks   **Map C6**
Pop 13,000. EC Tues, MD Mon SEE castle, church, Craven museum, old corn mill ⓘ 9 Sheep St
☎ (01756) 792809 Restaurant: Black Horse, Market Place ☎ (01756) 792145

Overdale Trailer Park, Harrogate Road BD23 6AA ☎ Skipton (01756) 3480 OS map 104/001525
½m E of Skipton on A59 (Harrogate) Open all year–must book 194 pitches (174 static) 🏠⌀⊕⌂
£4.00-£6.50

Springs Caravan Park, Lothersdale BD20 8HH ☎ Cross Hills (01535) 632533 OS map 103/944450
5m S of Skipton off A629 (Keighley) and A6068 (Colne) at Cross Hills Open Apr-Oct–adv booking
preferred 37 pitches–must book m/vans and tents Grass and hard standing 🏠⌀⊕🏠⊗🏠
fishing £6.50-£8.50

Tarn Caravan Park, Stirton BD23 3LQ ☎ Skipton (01756) 795309 OS map 103/977534 1¼m NW
of Skipton off B6265 (Grassington) Open Apr-Oct 260 pitches (226 static)–no tents Level/sloping
grass and hard standings ✗♟🏠⌀⊕⌀⊕ one dog (no alsatians, rottweilers, dobermans, etc.)
£8.00-£12.00 (Mastercard/Visa/Switch)

SLINGSBY–see Malton

STAMFORD BRIDGE, Humberside   **Map E4**
Pop 2,500 SEE stone bridge and weir Restaurant: Feathers 7m SE at Pocklington ☎ (01759)
303155

Fangfoss Old Station Caravan Park, Fangfoss YO41 5QB ☎ Wilberfoss (01759) 380491 OS map
105/748528 3m SE of Stamford Bridge off A1079 (York-Hull) on Fangfoss road at
Wilberfoss–signposted Open Mar-Oct 75 pitches Level grass and hard standing, sheltered
♟⇗🏠🏠⌀⊕⌀⊕⌂🏠⌂ £6.00-£9.00 (Mastercard/Visa)

Weir Caravan Park, Stamford Bridge YO41 1AN ☎ Stamford Bridge (01759) 371377 OS map
105/710557 ¼m NW of Stamford Bridge centre off A166 (York) Open Mar-Oct 150 pitches (108
static) Level grass and hard standing, sheltered 🏠🏠⌀⌀⊕⌂⌂ fishing, boating £8.00-£10.50

STILLINGFLEET–see York

STOKESLEY, N Yorks   **Map C2**
SEE church of SS Peter and Paul, town hall, packhorse bridge, Cleveland Hills Restaurant: Ayton
Hall 2m NE at Great Ayton ☎ (01642) 723595

Carlton Caravan Park, The Elms, Carlton in Cleveland TS9 7DJ ☎ Stokesley (01642) 712550 OS
map 93/509042 4m SW of Stokesley off A172 (Thirsk) Open Mar-Oct 25 pitches Level grass,
sheltered ♟✗⌀⊕⌂⌂ pets corner, post office £5.00-£8.00

Toft Hill Farm, Kirkby in Cleveland TS9 7HJ ☎ (01642) 712469 OS map 93/540043 3m S of
Stokesley via Kirkby Open Apr-Oct 60 pitches 4 acres level/sloping grass, sheltered ⊕ £4.50

White House Farm, Little Broughton TS9 5JE ☎ Stokesley (01642) 778238 OS map 93/555071
3m SE of Stokesley off B1257 (Helmsley) on Ingleby Greenhow road Open Mar-Oct 60 pitches
(35 static) 10 acres level grass 🏠🏠⊕⌀⌂🖐 fishing £6.00-£7.00

STRENSALL–see York

SUTTON ON THE FOREST, N Yorks   **Map D3**
Pop 950 SEE Georgian houses, Sutton Hall and gardens, vicarage where Sterne wrote Tristram
Shandy Restaurant: George 7m NW at Easingwold ☎ (01347) 821698

Goosewood Caravan Park YO61 1ET ☎ (01347) 810829 OS map 100/599627 1½m SE of Sutton
on the Forest off York road Open Mar-Jan 75 pitches – booking advisable–no tents 20 acres
level, woodland setting, grass and hard standings, sheltered ♟⇗🏠🏠⌀⊕⌀⊕⌂🏠🏠 on site
fishing £8.50-£10.50

THIRSK, N Yorks   Map C3
Pop 6,830. EC Wed, MD Mon SEE church, Thirsk Hall, Golden Fleece Inn, Byland Abbey ruins
🅩14 Kirkgate ✆(01845) 522755 Restaurant: Golden Fleece, Market Pl ✆(01845) 523108

Beechwood Caravan Park, Beechwood House, South Kilvington YO7 2LZ ✆Thirsk (01845) 522348
   OS map 99/426838 1m N of Thirsk on A61/A19 (Middlesbrough) Open Mar-Oct 30 pitches 1½
   acres level grass and hard standings 🔌⊕ flat rental £7.00 (2000)

Carlton Minniott Park, Carlton Minniott YO7 4NJ ✆Thirsk (01845) 523106 OS map 99/40816 2m
   W of Thirsk off A61 (Ripon) on right of Sandhutton road Open Apr-Oct 40 pitches 5 acres level
   grass, sheltered Fishing and boating lake 🔌 £7.00-£9.50 inc elect

Nursery Garden Caravan Park, Rainton YO7 3PG ✆and fax (01845) 577277 OS map 99/388756
   5m SW of Thirsk off A168 (Boroughbridge) via Asenby near junct 49 of A1M Open Mar-Oct 74
   pitches (52 static) Level grass, sheltered 🗑🔌⌀⊕⌀🌳✨⊡🔄 games room, tourist info £10.00-
   £11.00

Quernhow Cafe Camping Park, Great North Road, Sinderby YO7 4LG ✆Thirsk (01845) 567221
   OS map 99/337813 8m W of Thirsk on northbound carriageway of A1, 3m N of junction with A61
   Open all year 40 pitches Grass, level, sheltered ✖⌁🔥🔌⌀⌀⊕🍴 tennis £7.00-£8.60

Sowerby Caravan Park, Sowerby YO7 3AG ✆Thirsk (01845) 522753 OS map 99/437804 ½m SE
   of Thirsk on Dalton road beyond bridge under A168, by river Open Apr-Oct 110 pitches (85 static)
   6 acres level grass and hard standings 🛒🗑🔌⌀⊕⌀⊕✨🔥 £6.50-£7.00

White Rose Leisure Park, Hutton Sessay YO7 3BA ✆Thirsk (01845) 501215 OS map 100/476763
   5m SE of Thirsk off A19 (York) near inn Open Mar-Oct 220 pitches (120 static) Level grass,
   sheltered 🛒✖⌁⌁🗑⌀⊕⌀⊡⊕✨🔥🔥 £12.50

York House Caravan Park, Balk, Sutton under Whitestonecliffe YO7 2AQ ✆Thirsk (01845) 597495
   OS map 100/476808 3m E of Thirsk off A170 (Pickering) on Bagby-Sutton road Open Apr-Oct
   195 pitches Level grass 🛒🗑🔌⌀⊕✨🔥 farm produce £8.50

THORNE, S Yorks   Map F5
Pop 11,740. EC Thurs, MD Tues, Fri, Sat SEE parish church Restaurant, Belmont, Horsefair Green
✆(01405) 812320

Hatfield Waterpark, DN7 6EQ *Watersports centre in delightful setting* ✆(01302) 841572 OS map
   111/668097 3m SW of Thorne off A18 (Doncaster) Open Apr-Oct 75 pitches Level grass,
   sheltered ⊕⌀✨🔥 fishing £4.50-£6.60

THRESHFIELD–see Grassington

ULROME–see Skipsea

WAKEFIELD, W Yorks   Map E6
Pop 76,290. EC Wed, MD daily except Wed, Sun SEE cathedral, old bridge with chantry chapel,
museum, Heath Hall 1½m E 🅩Town Hall, Wood Street ✆Wakefield (01924) 295000/1 Restaurant:
Swallow, Queen St ✆(01924) 837211

Nostell Priory Holiday Park, Top Park Wood, Nostell WF4 1QD *Friendly site in mature woodland*
   ✆Wakefield (01924) 863938 OS map 111/420175 6m SE of Wakefield off A638 (Doncaster)
   Open Apr-Sept 140 pitches (80 static) Grass and hard standings, level, sheltered
   🗑🔌⌀⊕⌀✨🔥 (30) ⊡ £8.00-£8.50

WENSLEYDALE–see Leyburn

WETHERBY, W Yorks   Map D5
Pop 10,200. EC Wed, MD Mon SEE bridge, old inns, National Hunt racecourse, Branham Park 4m
S 🅩Council Offices, 24 Westgate ✆Wetherby (01937) 5862706 Restaurant: George and Dragon,
High St ✆(01937) 582888

Moor Lodge Caravan Park, Blackmoor Lane, Bardsey LS17 9DZ ✆Collingham Bridge (01937)
   572424 OS map 104/355425 5½m SSW of Wetherby off A58 (Leeds) Open all year 72 pitches
   (60 static)–adults only Level grass 🗑🔌⌀⊕⌀✨ £6.00

The restaurants recommended in this guide are of three kinds – inns and pubs, restaurants
proper and those forming part of hotels and motels. They all serve lunch and dinner – at a
reasonable price – say under £10 a head. We shall be glad to have your comments on any
you use this season and if you think they are not up to standard to have your suggestions for
alternatives.

WHITBY, N Yorks   **Map D1**
Pop 13,400. EC Wed, MD Sat SEE abbey ruins, Pannett Park aviary and museum, Capt Cook's house, town hall, promenade ▨Langborne Rd ☏Whitby (01947) 602674 Restaurant: Magpie, Pier Rd ☏(01947) 602058

Burnt House Caravan Park, Ugthorpe YO21 2BG ☏Whitby (01947) 840448 OS map 94/783112 6m W of Whitby on right of A171 (Guiesborough) Open Mar-Oct 140 pitches (40 static) 7 acres level grass and hard standing ▨▨▨▨▨▨▨▨ £8.50

Grouse Hill Caravan Park, Flask Bungalow Farm, Fylingdales YO22 4QH ☏Whitby (01947) 880543 OS map 94/929003 8m SE of Whitby off A171 (Scarborough) Open Easter-Oct—must book peak periods 300 pitches 14 acres level/sloping grass, sheltered ▨▨▨▨▨▨▨▨▨▨▨ £6.00-£7.00

Ladycross Plantation Caravan Park, Egton YO21 1UA *Peaceful woodland site convenient for coast and North York Moors* ☏(01947) 895502 OS map 94/821080 5m W of Whitby off A171 (Guisborough) Open Mar-Oct 100 pitches 28 acres level grass, sheltered ▨▨▨▨▨▨▨▨ £7.50 (Mastercard/Visa)

Northcliffe Holiday Park, High Hawsker YO22 4LL *Clifftop location with fine views* ☏Whitby (01947) 880477 OS map 94/940080 4m S of Whitby off A171 (Scarborough) on B1447 (Robin Hood's Bay) Open Easter-Oct 201 pitches (171 static) level grass and hard standing ▨▨▨▨▨▨▨▨▨▨▨▨▨ tea room, football pitch £7.00-£11.00 (Mastercard/Visa)

Rigg Farm Caravan Park, Stainsacre YO22 4LP ☏Whitby (01947) 880430 OS map 94/915062 3m SE of Whitby off B1416 (Ruswarp-Scarborough) Open Mar-Oct 29 pitches 3 acres grass and hard standing, level, sheltered ▨▨▨▨▨▨▨▨ games room, laundry £7.50-£8.50

Sandfield House Farm, Sandsend Road YO21 3SR ☏Whitby (01947) 602660 OS map 94/879116 1m NW of Whitby on left of A174 (Sandsend) opp golf course Open Mar 15-Oct 30, 50 pitches 10 acres level grass and hard standing ▨▨▨▨▨▨▨ tennis £7.00-£9.25

Ugthorpe Caravan Park, Ugthorpe YO21 2BE ☏(01947) 840518 OS map 94/785115 6m NW of Whitby off A171 (Guisborough) Open Apr-Oct 90 pitches (70 static) ▨▨▨▨▨▨▨▨▨▨ £8.00

Whitby Holiday Park, Saltwick Bay YO22 4JX ☏Whitby (01947) 602664 OS map 94/916108 1m E of Whitby at Saltwick Bay Open Easter-Oct 175 pitches ▨▨▨▨▨▨▨▨▨▨ beach access £7.00-£11.00

York House Caravan Park, High Hawsker YO22 4LW ☏Whitby (01947) 880354 OS map 94/927074 3m SE of Whitby on Sneaton Thorpe road Open Mar-Oct 100 pitches (41 static) Level/sloping grass, sheltered ▨▨▨▨▨▨▨▨▨ £6.50-£8.00

WITHERNSEA, Humberside   **Map G2**
Pop 7000 SEE medieval church, Spurn Point 10m SE Restaurant: Shakespeare Inn 9m W at Hedon ☏(01482) 898371

Easington Beach Caravan Park, Easington HU12 0TY ☏Withernsea (01964) 650293 OS map 113/410188 8m SE of Withernsea off B1445 (Easington) Open Mar-Dec 350 pitches (300 static) ▨▨▨▨▨▨▨▨▨ (indoor) ▨▨ club, pets corner, badminton, putting green £4.00-£6.00

Sandy Beach Caravan Park, Kilnsea HU12 0UB ☏(01964) 650256 and 650372 OS map 113/415158 9m SE of Withernsea off B1445 (Easington) near Spurn Point Open Mar-Oct 420 pitches (350 static) Level grass and hard standing ▨▨▨▨▨▨▨▨▨▨▨▨▨ £7.50

YORK, N Yorks   **Map E4**

Pop 97,240. EC Wed, MD daily SEE Minster, Nat Railway museum, castle museum, city walls, The Shambles De Grey Rooms, Exhibition Square York (01904) 621756 and 6 Rougler St (01904) 620557 Restaurant: Betty's, St Helen's Sq (01904) 659142

Chestnut Farm Caravan Park, Acaster Malbis YO23 2UQ York (01904) 704676 OS map 105/588461 3m SW of York off A64 (Leeds) via Copmanthorpe Open Apr-Oct 81 pitches (56 static) Level grass, sheltered £8.00-£11.00

Home Farm Camping Caravan Park, Moreby, Stillingfleet YO19 6HN *Small working farm overlooking river Ouse* (01904) 728263 OS map 105/596438 4m S of York off A19 (Selby) on B1222 (Cawood) Open Feb-Dec 25 pitches Level grass, sheltered

Hundred Acre Farm Caravan Park, Pottery Lane, Strensall YO3 5TW York (01904) 490020 OS map 100/618622 7m N of York off A64 (Malton) via Strensall Open Mar-Oct 21 pitches 1 acre level grass sheltered (heated), nature reserve £5.50

Linton Leisureways, Linton Lock, Linton on Ouse YO30 2AZ *Secluded site in lovely countryside* (01347) 848486 OS map 100/502604 6m NW of York off A19 (Northallerton) at Shipton, by river Ouse Open Mar-Oct 90 pitches Level grass, sheltered £6.00

Moor End Farm, Acaster Malbis YO23 2UQ York (01904) 706727 OS map 105/589457 4m S of York off A64 (Leeds) via Bishopthorpe or Copmanthorpe Open Apr-Oct 15 pitches Level grass, sheltered £8.00-£9.00

Moorside Caravan Park, Moorside Farm, Flaxton Road, Strensall YO3 5XF York (01904) 491865 OS map 100/647614 6m NE of York off A1237 (northern bypass) on Strensall road Open Easter-Oct 55 pitches–no children under 16, area for adults only 5 acres level grass and hard standing fishing £7.00-£9.00 (2000)

Mount Pleasant Holiday Park, Acaster Malbis YO23 2UA York (01904) 707078 OS map 105/583443 5m S of York off A64 (Leeds) via Bishopthorpe Open Mar-Nov–no adv booking 284 pitches (224 static) Level grass and hard standing first aid £8.50-£11.00 (Mastercard/Visa/Switch)

Naburn Lock Caravan Camping Park, Naburn YO19 4RU York (01904) 728697 OS map 105/599453 4m S of York off A19 (Selby) on B1222 (Stillingfleet) Open Apr-Oct 100 pitches Level grass, sheltered with bays holding 3 to 6 pitches 7 acres level grass fishing, horse riding, bike hire, hot air balloon trips, river bus to York £9.50

Poplar Farm, Acaster Malbis YO2 1UH York (01904) 706548 OS map 105/591455 3m S of York off A64 (Leeds) via Bishopthorpe Open Apr-Sept 130 pitches (80 static) Level grass and hard standing fishing, boating, regular river bus to York £8.00

Post Office Caravan Park, Acaster Malbis YO2 1UL York (01904) 702448 OS map 105/582433 4m S of York off A64 (Leeds) via Bishopthorpe by River Ouse Open Apr-Oct 76 pitches (65 static) Level grass, sheltered £5.50-£6.00

Rawcliffe Caravans, Manor Lane, Shipton Road YO3 6TZ York (01904) 624422 OS map 105/582551 2m NW of York off A19 (Thirsk) Open all year 120 pitches Level grass and hard standing petanque pitches, invalid room £8.00-£11.80 (Mastercard/Visa)

Riverside Caravan Camping Park, Ferry Lane, Bishopthorpe YO2 1SB *Secluded riverside location on level grass* York (01904) 704442 OS map 105/600475 2m S of York at Bishopthorpe on W bank of river Ouse Open Apr-Oct 25 pitches 1 acre grass, level, sheltered boat hire, riverbus to city £5.00-£10.50 (Mastercard/Visa)

Swallow Hall, Crockey Hill YO1 4SG York (01904) 448219 OS map 105/657462 5m S of York off A19 (Selby) on Wheldrake road Open Mar-Oct 40 pitches 5 acres level grass, sheltered 18-hole golf, driving range, tennis £7.50-£12.00

For other sites near York see also Easingwold, Malton, Selby, Stamford Bridge and Sutton on the Forest

4 Northwest

Lancashire may no longer be the most densely populated county in Europe, now that it has lost ground to newly created Merseyside (Liverpool and Birkenhead) and Greater Manchester. Yet in the south, at least, industrial towns are still more numerous than villages. Cheshire consists mainly of a rolling plain centred on the medieval walled city of Chester, as famous for its Rows, or arcaded streets, as for its Roman relics.

The largest single open space in the region is the Forest of Bowland northeast of Preston, southern gateway to which is Clitheroe in the Ribble Valley. Fell and moor rather than forest, Bowland is fine walking country with few human settlements. North of Chester is the Wirral Peninsula, ridge and vale country in the centre but wholly industrial on either side. Between Northwich and Chester is the small Delamere Forest, dotted with lakes. Elsewhere, apart from the Cheshire farmlands, there is little but built up areas and industrialized moorland.

The coast of Lancashire is probably most scenic around Morecambe Bay, noted for its sunsets. Pleasant coastal resorts are Southport and Lytham St Annes, out of earshot of the funfairs and bingo halls of Blackpool, the pleasure ground for people living in the nearby industrial towns, with their staggered holidays or 'wakes'. West of Bowland is Lancaster, topped by its magnificent castle (part prison), housing a superb collection of armorial bearings. The Lune flows south into Lancaster along the Trough of Bowland. West of the river is the only undeveloped corner of the Lancashire coast, a wooded district between Carnforth and Silverdale on the Cumbrian border, isolated behind its saltings at the edge of Morecambe Bay.

Other sights in the region are the castles of Chester, Hawarden and Beeston, and the country houses of Moreton Old Hall, Bramhall, Tatton Park and Tabley Hall.

Most campsites in the region, often well equipped, are—like the towns—grouped together rather than dispersed. So the choice is usually wide at the larger centres and resorts but non-existent elsewhere.

ACCRINGTON, Lancs   **Map C3**
Pop 35,890. EC Wed, MD Tues, Fri, Sat ▮Town Hall, Blackburn Rd ☏(01254) 386807 Restaurant:
Abbey, Bank St ☏(01254) 235727

Harwood Bar Caravan Park, Mill Lane, Great Harwood BB6 7UQ ☏Great Harwood (01254)
884853 OS map 103/752338 2½m N of Accrington off A680 (Whalley) at Sunnyside Open Feb-
Dec–must book peak periods 143 pitches (117 static) Hard standing, sloping, sheltered
🛏🔌🚿🚾🅿 £5.00-£9.00

ACTON BRIDGE–see Northwich

BLACKPOOL, Lancs   **Map A3**
Pop 147,000. EC Wed SEE seafront, Tower (518ft), winter gardens, zoo park, model village (Stanley
park), electric trams, illuminations (Sept-Oct) ▮1 Clifton Street ☏(01253) 421623/425212 and
Pleasure Beach, Ocean Boulevard ☏(01253) 403223 Restaurant: Cottage, Newhouse Rd
☏(01253) 464081

Gillett Farm, Peel Road, Peel FY4 5JU ☏(01253) 761676 OS map 102/356323 2m E of Blackpool
off A583 (Kirkham) on Peel road near junct 4 of M55 Open Mar-Oct 175 pitches (100 static) 12
acres sloping grass and hard standings 🛏🚿🔌🚾 £6.00-£12.00 (Mastercard/Visa)

Mariclough Hampsfield Camp Site, Preston New Road, Peel FY4 5JR *Small friendly site in open
countryside* ☏Blackpool (01253) 761034 OS map 102/357327 4m E of Blackpool on A583
(Preston) Open Mar-Nov–caravans must book peak periods 70 pitches Level grass and hard
standing, sheltered 🛏🚿🔌🚾 £6.00-£7.00

Marton Mere Park, Mythop Road FY4 4XN ☏Blackpool (01253) 767544 OS map 102/337354
2½m E of Blackpool off junction 4 of M55 (Preston) Open Mar-Oct 93 acres, 1351 pitches (920
static) no tents 93 acres hard standings, sheltered 🛏✗🍴 (indoor heated) tennis,
bowling green £8.00-£14.00 (Mastercard/Visa/Switch)

Newton Hall Holiday Centre, Staining Road, Staining FY3 0AX ☏(01253) 882512 OS map
102/338366 2½m NE of Blackpool off B5266 (Singleton) at Newton Arms hotel Open Mar-Oct
525 pitches–no tents Level grass and hard standings 🛏🍴 (indoor)
fishing, amusement arcade £9.00-£14.00

Pipers Height Caravan Camping Park, Peel Road, Peel FY4 5JT ☏Blackpool (01253) 763767
OS map 102/355325 2½m SE of Blackpool off A583 (Kirkham) on Peel road Open Mar-Nov 154
pitches–families only Grass and hard standing, level, sheltered 🛏✗🍴
family room, entertainment mid and peak season £6.00-£11.00

Redleigh Orchard Touring Caravan Park, Cropper Road FY4 5LB ☏Blackpool (01253) 691459
OS map 102/347324 3m SE of Blackpool off A583 (Preston) Open Mar-Oct–must book peak
periods 15 pitches–no tents Level grass and hard standing, sheltered 🔌🚿 £8.00 inc elect

Richmond Hill Caravan Site, 352 St Anne's Road FY4 2QN ☏Blackpool (01253) 344266 OS map
102/320332 ½m S of Blackpool off A584 (Lytham) Open Mar-Oct 15 pitches Grass and hard
standing, sheltered 🚿🔌 £10.25

BOLTON LE SANDS, Lancs   **Map B2**
Pop 500 SEE Sands of Morecambe Bay Restaurant: Royal Station 2m N at Carnforth ☏(01524)
733636

Bolton Holmes Farm, off Mill Lane, LA5 8ES ☏Carnforth (01524) 732854 OS map 97/480693 1m
NW of Bolton le Sands off A6 (Carnforth) Open Mar-Oct 75 pitches Level/sloping grass 🚿🔌🚾
£5.50 (2000)

Detron Gate Farm LA5 9TN ☏Carnforth (01524) 732842 OS map 97/485685 ½m W of Bolton le
Sands off A6 (Lancaster) Open Mar-Oct 150 pitches (42 static) Level/sloping grass
🛏🚿🔌🚾 £4.50-£6.25

Morecambe Lodge Caravan Park LA5 8JP ☏Carnforth (01524) 823260 OS map 97/471674 1m
SW of Bolton le Sands off A5105 (Morecambe) Open Mar-Oct 211 pitches (181 static)–no tents
13 acres level grass and hard standing, sheltered 🚿🔌🚾 serviced pitches, access to beach
£6.00-£11.00

Sandside Farm Caravan Site, Sandside Farm, St Michael's Lane LA5 8JS ☏Hest Bank (01524)
822311 OS map 97/475680 ½m SW of Bolton le Sands off A6 (Lancaster) Open Mar-Oct 165
pitches (35 static) Level/sloping grass, sheltered, some hard standings 🛏🚿🔌🚾
£9.00-£10.50 (Mastercard/Visa)

**Help us make CARAVAN AND CAMP IN BRITAIN better known to site operators – and thereby
more informative – by showing them your copy when booking in.**

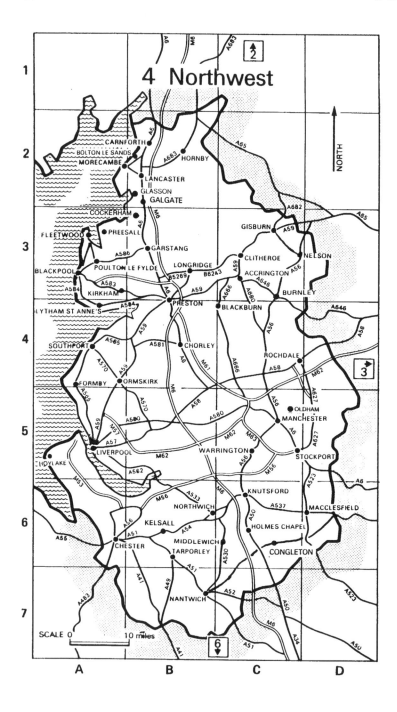

CARNFORTH, Lancs   Map B2
SEE Steamtown Railway Museum, Halton church 5m S, Borwick Hall 2m NE, Leighton Hall 3m N
Restaurant: Holmere Hall, Yealand Conyers ☎(01524) 735353

Capernwray House Caravan Site, Capernwray LA6 1AE ☎Carnforth (01524) 732363 OS map
  97/530718 2½m NE of Carnforth off B6254 (Over Kellet) Open Mar-Oct–66 pitches 17 acres,
  level/sloping, grass and hard standings, sheltered 🛁🗑🚿🅿⊕∅↩🔌🚃 B&B £10.00-£12.00

Hawthorns Caravan Park, Nether Kellet LA6 1EA ☎Carnforth (01524) 732079 OS map 97/514686
  2m SE of Carnforth off B6254 (Kirkby Lonsdale) via Over Kellet Open Mar-Oct 70 pitches (50
  static) Level grass and hard standing 🗑🚿🅿⊕∅⊕↩🔌 9 hole putting green, library £8.00-
  £11.50

Holgates Caravan Park, Cove Road, Silverdale LA5 0SH ☎Silverdale (01524) 701508 OS map
  97/455759 5m NW of Carnforth on Arnside road Open Dec-Nov–must book peak periods 420
  pitches (350 static) Hard standings and grass, part level, part sheltered 🛁✗🍽♨🗑🚿🅿⊕∅🚃
  (heated) ⊕↩🚃 £13.50-£15.00

Netherbeck Caravan Park, North Road LA5 9NG ☎Carnforth (01524) 735133 OS map 97/508711
  1m NE of Carnforth on Borwick road near junct 35 of M6 Open Mar-Oct–must book public
  holidays 52 pitches (32 static) Grass part-sloping, sheltered 🚿🅿∅↩🚃 £4.00

Old Hall Caravan Park, Capernwray LA6 1AD ☎Carnforth (01524) 733276 OS map 97/533707
  2½m NE of Carnforth off B6254 (Kirkby Lonsdale) on Capernwray road Open Mar-Oct–advisable
  to book 198 pitches (160 static) Level hard standings, sheltered 🗑🚿🅿⊕∅⊕↩🔌♿
  £12.00-£14.00

CHESTER, Ches   Map A6
Pop 116,000. EC Wed, MD daily except Wed SEE The Rows, cathedral, city walls, gates and
towers, High Cross, Roman amphitheatre, Dee Bridge, old inns, Grosvenor museum, zoo and
gardens, river and canal (boat trips) ℹ Town Hall, Northgate Street ☎Chester (01244) 317962
Restaurant: Blossoms, St John St ☎(01244) 323186

Chester Southerly Caravan Park, Balderton Lane, Marlston-cum-Lache CH4 9LF
  ☎(01244) 671308 and (0976) 743388 OS map 117/385624 3m S of Chester off A55/A483
  (Wrexham) Open Mar-Nov–adv booking advisable 90 pitches Level grass and hard standings
  🛁🗑🚿🅿⊕∅↩♿ £8.00-£10.00 (inc showers)

Fairoaks Camping Caravan Park, Rake Lane, Little Stanney CH2 4HS ☎0151-355 1600 OS map
  117/410738 4m N of Chester on A5117 (Mold) Open Mar-Oct 130 pitches 8 acres level grass
  and hard standing, sheltered 🛁🗑🚿🅿⊕∅↩♿ £7.00-£7.50

Netherwood House, Whitchurch Road CH3 6AF ☎Chester (01244) 335583 Fax (01244) 336066
  OS map 117/447648 2m SE of Chester on A41 (Whitchurch) Open Mar-Oct 15 pitches, must
  book 1½ acres level grass, sheltered 🚿⊕∅ £6.20-£8.80 (2000)

See also Kelsall

CLITHEROE, Lancs   Map C3
Pop 13,670. EC Wed, MD Mon, Tues, Fri, Sat SEE Pendle Hill (1,830ft), castle keep, Sawley Abbey,
Castle House Museum ℹMarket Pl ☎(01200) 25566 Restaurant: Swan and Royal, Castle St
☎(01200) 23130

Shireburn Caravan Park, Waddington Road, near Edisford Bridge BB7 3LB ☎Clitheroe (01200)
  423422 OS map 103/727418 1½m W of Clitheroe off B6243 (Longridge) Open Mar-Oct 200
  pitches (180 static) Level grass and hard standings, sheltered 🛁🗑🚿🅿∅🚃 fishing, lic club
  £10.00-£11.00

Three Rivers Park, Eaves Hall Lane, West Bradford BB7 3JG ☎Clitheroe (01200) 423523
  Fax (01200) 442383 OS map 103/736451 2m N of Clitheroe off B6478 (Slaidburn) at Waddington
  Open all year 250 pitches (150 static) Grass, level, hard standings, sheltered
  🛁✗🍽↩🗑🚿🅿⊕∅🚃 (indoor) ⊕↩🔌🚃 lic club, entertainment w/ends £12.50-£15.50
  (Mastercard/Visa)

COCKERHAM, Lancs   Map B3
Pop 350 Restaurant: Victoria 2m N at Glasson Dock ☎(01524) 751423

Cockerham Sands Country Park, LA2 0BB ☎(01524) 751387 OS map 102/430544 3m NW of
  Cockerham off A588 (Lancaster) at Upper Thurnham on Cockersand Abbey road, near sea Open
  Mar-Oct 270 pitches (261 static) Grass and hard standings 🛁🍽↩🗑🚿🅿⊕∅🚃 (Jun-Sept)
  ↩🚃 £11.00-£16.00

Moss Wood Caravan Park, Crimbles Lane LA2 0ES ☎(01524) 791041 OS map 102/455513 1m
  SW of Cockerham on A588 (Poulton le Fylde) Open Mar-Oct 200 pitches (175 static) 2½ acres
  hard standings, sheltered 🛁🗑🚿🅿⊕ £7.00-£9.00

GALGATE, Lancs   Map B2
Restaurant Hampson House ☎(01524) 751158

Laundfields, Stoney Lane LA2 0JZ ☎Galgate (01524) 751763 OS Map 102/485553 ½m E of
Galgate centre on right of Dolpinholme road, near junction 33 of M6 Open Mar-Oct 20 pitches
½ acre level grass ▦✿ £5.00

GARSTANG, Lancs   Map B3
EC Wed, MD Thurs SEE castle ruins, parish church, Wyre bridge ▣Discovery Centre, Council
offices, High St ☎(01995) 602125 Restaurant: Owd Tithebarn, Church St ☎(01995) 602923

Bridge House Marina, Nateby Crossing Lane, Nateby PR3 0JJ ☎Garstang (01995) 603207 OS
map 102/483457 ½m W of Garstang off Nateby road by Lancaster canal Open Mar-Jan 70
pitches (20 static)–no tents Level grass and hard standing ▦▤▦◪◪◪↲ £7.50

Claylands Farm, Cabus PR3 1AJ *Well maintained park close to river and woodland walks* ☎Forton
(01524) 791242 OS map 102/496485 2m N of Garstang off A6 (Lancaster)–signposted Open
Mar-Jan 4 98 pitches (68 static) 4 acres gentle slope, grass and hard standing
▦✕▦▤▦◪◈◪◉↲& £11.00 inc elect (Mastercard/Visa)

Six Arches Caravan Park, Scorton PR3 1AL ☎Forton (01524) 791683 OS map 102/502485 3m N
of Garstang on A6 (Lancaster) Open Mar-Oct–must book 310 pitches (275 static)–no tents Grass
and hard standing, level, sheltered ▦↲↗▤▦◪◪◪▭☗◉↲▭☖ paddling pool, fishing, lic club
£11.00-£13.00

Smithy Caravan Park, Cabus Nook Lane, Winmarleigh PR3 1AA ☎Garstang (01995) 606200 OS
map 102/482482 1½m N of Garstang off A6 (Lancaster) on Winmarleigh road via Cabus Open
Mar-Jan 90 pitches (70 static) Grass and hard standing, part level ▦▤▦◪◈◪▭ private
fishing lake £8.00-£15.00

RIMINGTON CARAVAN PARK
Hardacre Lane, Rimington BB7 4EE

1m south of Gisburn off Nelson road
Level grass and hard standing, sheltered

Open March-October. Licensed club.

GISBURN, Lancs   Map C3
Pop 350. MD Thurs Restaurant: Stirk House ☎(01200) 445581

Rimington Caravan Park, Hardacre Lane, Rimington BB7 4EE ☎Gisburn (01200) 445355 OS
map 103/862471 1m S of Gisburn off A682 (Nelson) Open Mar-Oct 150 pitches (130 static)
Level grass and hard standing, sheltered ▦▤▦◪◈◪◉▦ (30) lic club £7.00-£8.00

GLASSON DOCK, Lancs   Map A2
Pop 1500 Restaurant: Victoria, Victoria Terr ☎(01524) 751423

Marina Caravan Park, Glasson Dock LA2 0BP ☎Lancaster (01524) 751787 OS map 102/443560
In Glasson on B5290 Open Mar-Dec 143 pitches (123 static) Grass and hard standings
▦▤▦◪◈◪▭◉▭▦& £9.50-£10.50

HOLMES CHAPEL, Ches   Map C6
Pop 4750 Restaurant: Swan, Station Rd ☎(01477) 532259

Mount Pleasant Caravan Site, Goostrey CW4 8JS ☎Holmes Chapel (01477) 532263 OS map
118/768700 2m NNE of Holmes Chapel off A50 (Knutsford) Open all year 110 pitches (90 static)
Grass, level, open, sheltered, some hard standings ▤▦◪◈ £4.50-£5.00

HOYLAKE, Merseyside   Map A5
Pop 33,220 EC Wed SEE promenade, Dee estuary Restaurant: Linos, Market St ☎0151 632 1408

Wirral Country Park, Station Road, Thurstaston, Wirral L61 0HN ☎0151-648 5228 OS map
108/234838 3m SE of Hoylake off A540 (Heswall) via Thurstaston Open Apr 12-Nov 2, 8 acres
90 pitches ▤▦◪◪↲ £6.20-£13.80 (Mastercard/Visa)

GARSTANG
Six Arches Caravan Park
Scorton PR3 1AL

Grass and hard standing, level, sheltered. 35 pitches for motorhomes and trailer caravans.

Well equipped park by river Wyre, within easy reach of Blackpool, Morecambe and the Lake District. Family entertainment, heated outdoor pool and fishing. Brochure on request.

Tel (01524) 791683

KELSALL, Ches   **Map B6**
SEE Delamere forest NE Restaurant: Willington Hall 2m S at Willington ☎(01829) 752321
Northwood Hall Country Touring Park, CW6 0RP ☎(01829) 752569 OS map 117/517680 1m W of Kelsall on A54 (Chester) Open all year 30 pitches 5 acres level/gentle slope, some hard standings 🔲🅿◢✪🕙⤴💀🏠🏠 £7.00-£8.50

KIRKHAM, Lancs   **Map A3**
Pop 6,990. EC Wed, MD Thurs SEE church, fish-stone circle Restaurant: Queens Arms, Poulton St (A585) ☎(01772) 686705
Whitmore Caravan Park, Bradshaw Lane, Greenhalgh PR4 3HQ ☎(01253) 836224 OS map 102/401356 2m NNW of Kirkham off A585 (Fleetwood) Open Mar-Oct 25 pitches Level grass and hard standing, sheltered 🅿◢✪💀 coarse fishing £11.00

KNUTSFORD, Ches   **Map C6**
Pop 13,800. EC Wed MD Fri, Sat SEE 17c Unitarian chapel (Mrs Gaskell's grave), Gaskell memorial tower, Sessions House, 18c Georgian church 🅸 Council Offices, Toft Rd ☎(01565) 632018 Restaurant: White Lion, King St ☎(01565) 632018
Woodlands Park, Wash Lane, Allostock WA16 9LG OS map 118/736707 4m S of Knutsford off A50 (Holmes Chapel) on right of B5082 (Northwich) near lake Open Mar 1-Jan 6 50 pitches–no motor cycles Level grass 🏋🔲🅿◢✪∅ £9.00-£10.00

LANCASTER, Lancs   **Map B2**
Pop 45,120. EC Wed, MD daily SEE castle, cathedral, St Mary's church, Town Hall gardens, Town Hall Museum, Maritime Museum 🅸29 Castle Hill ☎(01524) 732878 Restaurant: Orient Express, Parliament St ☎(01524) 733332
Crook-O-Lune Caravan Park, Caton LA2 9HP ☎Caton (01524) 770216 Fax (01524) 771694 OS map 97/539642 4m NE of Lancaster on A683 (Kirkby Lonsdale) near river Lune Open Feb-Nov 184 pitches (158 static) Level grass and hard standing ✕🍴🔲◢✪ £9.50-£10.00

LYTHAM ST ANNE'S, Lancs   **Map A4**
Pop 42,150. EC Wed SEE St Anne's Pier, Lifeboat memorial, parish church, Lowther gardens, Motive Power Museum, Fairhaven Lake 🅸290 Clifton Drive South ☎Lytham (01253) 725610 Restaurant: Queens, Central Beach ☎(01253) 737316
Bank Lane Caravan Park, Warton PR4 1TB ☎(01772) 633513 OS map 102/403276 5m E of Lytham off A584 (Preston) at Warton Bank Open Mar-Oct 230 pitches (180 static) 14 acres level grass and hard standing, sheltered 🏋🔲🅿◢✪∅⤴💀 £8.50-£12.00
Eastham Hall Caravan Park, Saltcotes Road FY8 4LS ☎Lytham (01253) 737907 OS map 102/380289 2½m E of Lytham St Anne's off A584 (Preston) Open Mar-Oct 400 pitches (170 static)–no tents Grass and hard standing, level, sheltered 🏋🔲🅿◢✪∅✪⤴💀 (50) £10.00-£11.50 (most cards)
Seaview Caravan Park, Bank Lane Warton PR4 1TD ☎Freckleton (01772) 679336 OS map 102/405273 3m E of Lytham St Anne's off A584 (Preston) Open Mar-Nov 192 pitches (76 static) 6 acres grass 🏋🔲🅿◢ £10.00

MACCLESFIELD, Ches   **Map D6**
Pop 33,600. EC Wed, MD daily SEE Silk museum, market stone, St Michael's church, Capesthorne Hall 4½m W 🅸Town Hall, Market Place ☎Macclesfield (01625) 504114 Restaurant: Oliver's Bistro, Chestergate ☎(01625) 832003
Capesthorne Hall Caravan Park, SK11 9JY ☎Chelford (01625) 861779/861221 OS map 118/840728 4½m W of Macclesfield off A537 (Knutsford) on right of A34 (Congleton) in grounds of stately home Open Easter-Oct 33 pitches–no tents or trailer tents Level grass, part sheltered 🔲🅿✪∅♿ gardens, angling in season £11.50-£13.50

MORECAMBE, Lancs   **Map A2**
Pop 40,660. EC Wed, MD Tues, Sat SEE Marineland, autumn illuminations, sands (guided walks
across) ℹ Central Promenade ☎ Morecambe (01524) 582808/9 Restaurant: Elms, Elms Rd
☎ (01524) 411501

Glen Caravan Park, Westgate LA3 3EL ☎ Morecambe (01524) 423896 OS map 97/435629 1m E
of Morecambe off B5321 (Skerton) on Westgate road Open Mar-Oct 70 pitches (51 static) 3
acres level grass and hard standing, sheltered (20) £6.50-£8.00

Greendales Farm Caravan Park, Carr Lane, Middleton LA3 3LH ☎ (01524) 852616 OS map
102/418584 5m S of Morecambe off A589 (Heysham) and Overton road Open all year 20 pitches
1 acre hard standing and level grass £6.75-£8.85

Hawthorne Camping Site, Carr Lane, Middleton Sands LA3 3LL ☎ (01524) 852074 OS map
102/415573 3½m SW of Morecambe off A589 (Heysham) via Middleton and coast road Open
Apr-Sept 73 pitches Level grass and hard standings £10.00

Melbreak Camp, Carr Lane, Middleton LA3 3LH ☎ (01524) 852430 OS map 102/418584 3m S of
Morecambe off A589 (Middleton) on Carr Lane near holiday camp Open Mar-Oct 50 pitches (20
static) 2 acres level grass and hard standing £6.25-£6.75

Regent Leisure Park, Westgate LA3 3DF ☎ Morecambe (01524) 413940 OS map 97/428630 ½m
SE of Morecambe off B5273 (Lancaster) Open Mar-Jan, 324 pitches (300 static) Hard standing,
level, sheltered lic club, evening entertainment, snooker,
pool, children's indoor adventureland £10.00-£15.00

Riverside Caravan Park, Oxcliffe Hall Farm, Heaton with Oxcliffe LA3 3ER *Small friendly farm site
on river estuary* ☎ (01524) 844193 OS map 97/448617 2m E of Morecambe off B5273 (Scale
Hall) on Heaton road Open Mar-Oct 100 pitches (20 static) Level grass £5.50-
£6.75

Venture Caravan Park, Langridge Way, Westgate LA4 4TQ ☎ Morecambe (01524) 412986 OS
map 97/435632 ¼m S of Morecambe off A589 (Heysham) Open Mar-Oct 316 pitches (260 static)
17 acres level grass amusements £9.00-£13.00

NANTWICH, Ches   **Map B7**
Pop 11,120. EC Wed Old market town still with medieval street pattern SEE St Mary's church,
Welsh Row, museum ℹ Church House, Church Walk ☎ Nantwich (01270) 610983/610880
Restaurant: Crown, High St ☎ (01270) 625283

Brookfield Caravan Park, Shrewbridge Road CW5 7AD ☎ Nantwich (01270) 569176 OS map
118/652516 ½m S of Nantwich centre off A530 (Whitchurch) adj park and river Open Easter-
Sept, 25 pitches–no adv booking 1 acre, level grass Fishing £3.80-£6.50

NORTHWICH, Ches   **Map B6**
Pop 17,090. EC Wed, MD Tue, Fri, Sat SEE Budworth Mere, Anderton Lift linking river Weaver and
Trent and Mersey Canal, Marbury Country Park Restaurant: Quincey's, London Rd ☎ (01606)
845524

Daleford Manor Caravan Park, Dalefords Lane, Sandiway CW8 2BT ☎ Sandiway (01606) 883391
OS map 118/605698 4m SW of Northwich off A556 (Manchester-Chester) and Foxwist Green
road Open Mar-Oct 42 pitches (30 static)–no tents Level grass and hard standing, sheltered
£5.00-£7.00

Lamb Cottage, Dalefords Lane, Whitegate CW8 2BN ☎ Sandiway (01606) 882302 Fax (01606)
882302 OS map 118/614693 4m SW of Northwich off A556 (Manchester-Chester) Open Mar-Oct
100 pitches Grass, level, sheltered £5.50-£6.50

Woodbine Cottage, Warrington Road, Acton Bridge CW8 3QB ☎ Weaverham (01606) 852319 and
77900 OS map 117/590755 4m NW of Northwich on A49 (Warrington) via Weaverham Open Mar
1-Oct 21–must book public holidays 50 pitches Grass and hard standing (40)
£7.00-£10.00

OLDHAM, Gtr Manchester   **Map D5**
Pop 104,000 EC Thurs MD Mon, Fri, Sat SEE art gallery, crypt of parish church, Town hall, Bluecoat
school ℹ Central library, Union St ☎ 0161 627 1024 Restaurant: King George, Hollins Rd ☎ 0161
624 5170

Moorlands Caravan Park, Ripponden Rd, Denshaw OL3 5UN *Good touring centre with splendid
moorland views* ☎ (01457) 874348 OS map 109/977120 5m NE of Oldham on A672
(Huddersfield) near junct 22 of M62 Open all year 42 pitches 2½ acres level, hard standings and
level grass £4.50-£5.50

The distance and direction of a campsite is given from the centre of the key town under
which it appears, the place name in parentheses following the road number indicating which
route to take.

ORMSKIRK, Lancs   **Map A4**
SEE church of SS Peter and Paul Restaurant: Bull and Dog 4m NE at Lathom ✆(01704) 894418

Abbey Farm, Dark Lane L40 5TX ✆Ormskirk (01695) 572686 OS map 108/433099 1½m NE of Ormskirk via Derby Street amd Greetby Hill, near Burscough Abbey Open all year–must book peak periods 104 pitches (44 static) Level grass and hard standings, sheltered ▦♪▯▦◈⊕∅ ❸↩☙ library, games room, fishing £8.25-£12.50 (Mastercard/Visa)

Shaw Hall Caravan Park, off Smithy Lane, Scarisbrick L40 8HJ ✆Halsall (01704) 840298 OS map 108/397115 3m NW of Ormskirk off A570 (Southport) Open Mar-Jan 345 pitches (300 static) Level grass and hard standing ▦⚲▯▦◌◈∅↩☐ lic club, bowling green £12.00-£15.00 (Mastercard/Visa)

POULTON LE FYLDE, Lancs   **Map A3**
SEE St Chad's church Restaurant: Anna's Bistro, Breck Rd ✆(01253) 882336

Kneps Farm Holiday Park, River Road, Thornton Cleveleys FY5 5LR ✆Cleveleys (01253) 823632 OS map 102/354430 2m N of Poulton le Fylde off B5412 (Thornton) Open Mar-Nov 15–must book peak periods 150 pitches (80 static) 10 acres level grass and hard standing ▦♪▯▦◌◈∅❸↩☙☖ sep pitches £10.00-£12.50 (Mastercard/Visa)

Meadowcroft and Queensgate Caravan Park, Garstang Road, Great Eccleston PR3 0ZQ ✆Great Eccleston (01995) 670266 OS map 102/415403 3m E of Poulton le Fylde on A586 (Garstang-Blackpool) Open Mar-Oct 91 pitches (83 static) Level grass and hard standing ▯▦◌◈∅ £8.00

PREESALL, Lancs   **Map A3**
Restaurant: Saracens Head, Park Lane (B5377) ✆(01253) 810346

Glenfield Caravan Park, Smallwood Hey Rd, Pilling PR3 6HE ✆(01253) 790782 OS map 102/399483 2m E of Preesall off A588 (Cockerham) in Pilling village Open Mar-Oct 140 pitches (130 static) 8½ acres level grass ▯▦◌◈∅ £7.00-£8.50

Maaruig Touring Caravan Park, 71 Pilling Lane FY6 0HB ✆(01253) 810404 OS map 102/364490 1m N of Preesall off B5377 (Knott End) Open Mar 1-Jan 4 28 pitches Grass and hard standing, level, sheltered ▯▦◈ £9.00

Sunset Park, Sower Carr Lane, Hambleton FY6 9EQ ✆(01253) 700222 OS map 102/373425 3m S of Preesall off A588 (Poulton) Open Mar-Oct 105 pitches (70 static) Level grass and hard standing ▦⚲▯▦◌◈∅☐ (indoor children's) ❸↩☐ spa bath, sauna, fishing £10.00-£14.00 (Mastercard/Visa)

Willowgrove Caravan Park, Sandy Lane FY6 0EJ ✆(01253) 811306 OS map 102/366480 1m N of Preesall off B5377 (Knott End) Open Mar-Oct 200 pitches (137 static) Level grass ▦▯▦◌◈∅↩☙ coarse fishing, bird watching £8.00-£11.50

PRESTON, Lancs   **Map B4**
Pop 126,000. MD Daily except Thurs SEE Roman Museum (Ribchester), Crown Court Hall, parish church, shopping precinct, Harris museum, Fulwood barracks (military museum) ▮Guildhall, Lancaster Road ✆Preston (01772) 253731 Restaurant: Tiggi's (Italian), Guildhall St ✆(01772) 658527

Royal Umpire Touring Park, Croston PR5 7JB ✆Preston (01772) 600257 OS map 108/504190 5m S of Preston on A581 (Chorley-Southport) at Croston Open all year 201 pitches 60 acres grass and hard standing, part sheltered ▦✕↩♪▯▦◌◈∅❸↩☙ £7.00-£14.80 inc elect

ROCHDALE, Gtr Manchester   **Map C4**
Pop 94,110. EC Tues, MD daily except Tues SEE St Chad's church, town hall, museum, John Bright's grave, Co-op museum ▮Clock Tower, Town Hall ✆(01706) 356592 Restaurant: Egerton Arms off B6222 at North Heywood ✆(01706) 346183

Hollingworth Lake Caravan Park, Rakewood, Littleborough OL15 0AT ✆Littleborough (01706) 378661 OS map 109/943146 4m NE of Rochdale off A68 (Milnrow) and B6225 (Littleborough) at The Fish Inn on Rakewood road Open all year 75 pitches (40 static) 5 acres, grass and hard standing, sheltered ▦▯▦◌◈∅☙☖ £8.00-£12.00

SANDIWAY–see Northwich

Cause for Complaint

If you have cause for complaint while staying on a site take the matter up with the manager or owner. If you are still not satisfied set the facts down in writing and send photocopies to anyone you think might be able to help, starting with the editor of this guide and the local (licensing) authority for the area where the site is located.

SILVERDALE–see Carnforth

SOUTHPORT, Merseyside   **Map A4**
Pop 89,750. EC Tues SEE St Cuthbert's church, Floral Hall and gardens, zoo, Birkdale Sands,
Ribble estuary 🄸112 Lord St ✆Southport (01704) 533333 Restaurant: Legh Arms, 5m NE at Mere
Brow ✆(01772) 812225

Brooklyn Caravan Park and Country Club, Gravel Lane, Banks PR9 8BU ✆Southport (01704)
    228534 OS map 108/392198 4m NE of Southport on A565 (Preston) Open Mar 1-Jan 7 250
    pitches (150 static) Level grass, sheltered 🝆✕🛈🛢🛍🗘⊕⌀⤙🟥🖾 £8.50-£9.00

Leisure Lakes Caravan Park, Mere Brow PR4 6JX *Well equipped site in spacious parkland with
    facs for watersports* ✆Hesketh Bank (01772) 813446 OS map 108/415187 5m NE of Southport
    off A565 (Preston) at Mere Brow Open all year 86 pitches 8 acres level grass and hard standings
    ✕🝆⤙🛈🗘🛍⊕⌀🟢⤙🛁 golf driving range £7.00-£11.00 (Mastercard/Visa/Switch)

STOCKPORT, Gtr Manchester   **Map C5**
Pop 289,000 EC Thurs, MD Tues, Fri, Sat SEE Art Gallery Museum, Bramall Hall 2½m S
🄸Graylaw House, Chestergate ✆0161 474 3320/1 Restaurant: Alma Lodge, Buxton Rd ✆0161-
483 4431

Elmbeds Caravan and Camping Park, Elmbeds Road, Higher Poynton SK12 1TG ✆Poynton
    (01625) 872370 OS map 109/945829 5m SE of Stockport off A523 (Macclesfield) Open Apr-Oct
    70 pitches (50 static) Level/sloping grass and hard standing, sheltered 🗘🛍⊕⌀ £5.00-£10.00

THORNTON CLEVELEYS–see Poulton le Fylde

WARRINGTON, Ches   **Map C5**
Pop 176,000. EC Thurs, MD daily except Thurs SEE parish church, museum and library, town hall,
Barley Mow inn 🄸21 Rylands St ✆Warrington (01925) 442180/444400 Restaurant: Patten Arms,
Parker St ✆(01925) 436602

Holly Bank Caravan Park, Warburton Bridge Road, Rixton WA3 6HU ✆0161 775 2842 OS map
    109/692904 5½m E of Warrington off A57 (Irlam) near Junction 21 of M6 Open all year 75
    pitches Level grass and hard standing, sheltered 🝆🛈🗘🛍⊕⌀🟢⤙🟥 £12.00-£15.00

WARTON–see Lytham

WEETON–see Poulton le Fylde

WINSFORD–see Middlewich

5   East Midlands

The essentially rural East Midlands consists of the five shires of Derby, Leicester, Lincoln, Northampton and Nottingham. Derbyshire is the most scenic of this group, containing as it does much of the Peak District, dramatic in the upper half, softer and more gentle in the lower, with its high fells and beautiful dales, homely villages, handsome spa towns and subterranean rivers and caves. The three main rivers—Dane, Dove and Manifold—rise at Axe Edge to flow through the well known valleys to which they give their names. Chapel en le Frith is a handy base for the northern half, and Buxton—where the Pennines roll down into the dales—for the southern. Some of the most impressive scenery can be reached only on foot, for example on the trail between Tissington and Buxton, or the ridge walk from Mam Tor near Castleton to Lose Hill. Peak Pathfinder bus services operate in season from Buxton and Ashbourne to Dovedale. Two historic Derbyshire buildings not to be missed are Peveril Castle near Castleton and, farther south, Chatsworth House.

Adjoining Derbyshire on the east is Nottinghamshire. Its distinctive and appealing scenery includes the central plateau cut by treelined valleys, the wolds in the southeast, the Trent Valley in the east, with steep buffs lining the river at Gunthorpe and Hazelford, and the glades and clearings of gently rolling Sherwood Forest around Edwinstowe. Routes for walkers include the Fosse Way, the Trent Ridgeway between Radcliffe and East Bridgeford and the Soar Ridgeway above Thrumpton. Important sights are the castles of Nottingham and Newark, the houses of Newstead Abbey and Wollaton Hall and the parks of Thoresby and Welbeck.

Nottinghamshire's neighbour on the east is Lincolnshire, in which the landscape shifts from the Belvoir Hills, forming the western border, to the limestone ridge from Barrowby Hill to Lincoln and the low ground around the Wash, which is patterned with canals and flood banks and appropriately called Holland. In the south is flat and fertile farmland, some of it around Spalding dazzling with tulips in spring. Along the coast are firm sands sheltered by dunes; south of Skegness is an extensive nature reserve. The two most historic buildings in the county are probably the cathedral and Norman castle of Lincoln.

Leicestershire, a small county famed for its hunting, is most pastoral in the east and south, where the tow-paths of its disused canals provide excellent routes for walkers. Between Leicester, Ashby and Loughborough is Charnwood Forest, where crags and moorland alternate with woods. There are grand churches at Kelton, Empingham, Market Harborough and Staunton Harold.

Southernmost county in the region is Northamptonshire, green and peaceful away from the industrial towns of Kettering, Rothwell, Wellingborough and Corby. As well as Yardley Chase and the Forest of Rockingham round the Welland Valley there are numerous Saxon churches and country houses worth seeing.

Campsites are well distributed throughout the region in the Peak and dales, the Trent Valley and Sherwood Forest, on the Lincolnshire coast and the main transit routes.

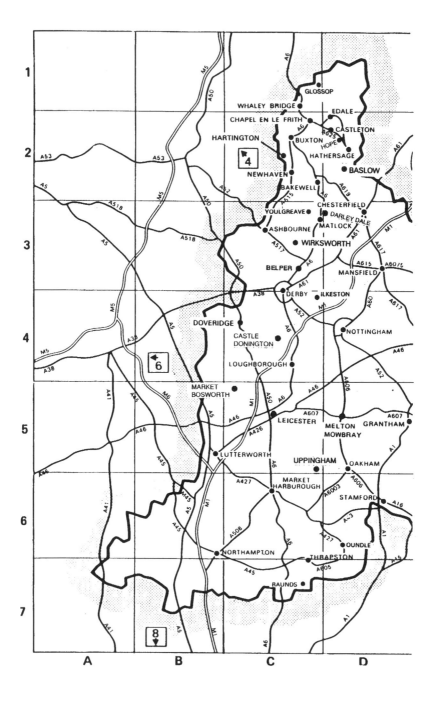

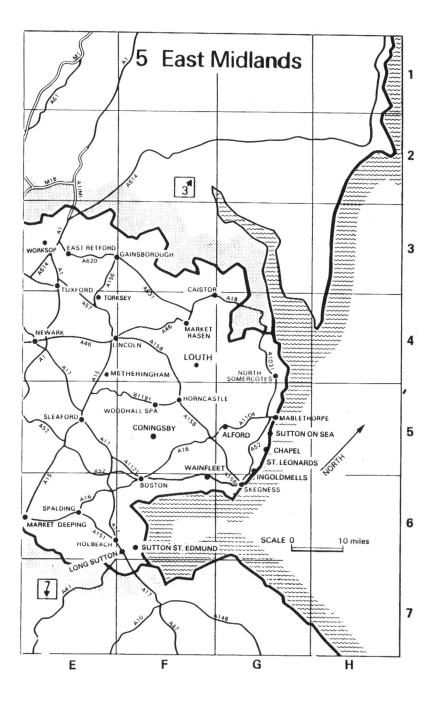

ALFORD, Lincs   **Map G5**
Pop 2,500 SEE museum, church Restaurant: Half Moon, West St ☎(01507) 463477
Woodthorpe Hall Leisure Park LN13 0DD ☎(01507) 450294 OS map 122/436803 3½m N of
Alford on left of A1104-B1373 (Withern) Open Mar 15-Jan 1, 200 pitches (150 static)–booking
advisable Level grass and hard standings, sheltered ⚑⬛⊘ golf, fishing £10.00-£12.00
(Mastercard/Visa)

ALPORT–see Youlgreave

ANCASTER–see Sleaford and Grantham

ASHBOURNE, Derbys   **Map C3**
Pop 5,970. EC Wed, MD Thurs, Sat SEE 13c church, Manifold Valley 3m NW, Dovedale 2m NW
🖥13 Market Place ☎(01335) 343666 Restaurant: Smiths Tavern, St Johns St ☎(01335) 342264
Bank Top Farm, Fenny Bentley DE6 1LF *Working dairy farm with viewing gallery*
☎(01335) 350250 OS map 119/183498 2m N of Ashbourne off A515 (Buxton) on B5056
(Bakewell) Open Easter-Sept 50 pitches Level/sloping grass, sheltered ⚑⬛⊕
£5.90-£9.50
Blackwall Plantation (Caravan Club), Blackwall, Kirk Ireton DE4 4JC ☎(01335) 370903 (0800-
2000 hrs) OS map 119/253498 6m E of Ashbourne off A517 (Belper) and Kirk Ireton road Open
Apr-Oct 134 pitches–adv booking advisable 25 acres level grass and hard standings in woodland
⬛⊘⊕ £8.00-£12.00
Callow Top Holiday Park, Buxton Road DE6 2AQ ☎(01335) 344020 OS map 119/172477 ½m N
of Ashbourne on A515 (Buxton) Open Easter-Nov 150 pitches (40 static) Level grass
⚑✕⚋⬛⊘⊕⊘⊟ (heated) ⊕⚐⊡⛺⬥⚙ pub and pub food, games room, cycle hire,
fishing £9.50 (most cards)
Gateway Caravan Park, Osmaston DE6 1NA ☎Ashbourne (01335) 344643 OS map 119/193451
1½m SE of Ashbourne off A52 (Derby) on Osmaston road Open all year 200 pitches Level grass
and hard standings, sheltered ⚑⚋⬛⊘⊕⊘⊡⬥ pool room, club room £6.25-£8.25
Highfield Farm, Fenny Bentley DE6 1LE ☎(01335) 350228 OS map 119/174510 2½m N of
Ashbourne on A515 (Buxton) Open Mar-Oct 105 pitches (55 static) Level grass and hard
standing, sheltered ⚑⬛⬛⊘⊕⊘⊟ (indoor) ⊕⚐⬛℗⚊ farm produce £10.50
(Mastercard/Visa)
Rivendale Caravan and Leisure Park, Buxton Road, Alsop in le Dale ☎(01332) 843000 OS map
119/164562 6m N of Ashbourne off A515 (Buxton) 105 pitches Level grass and
hard standings, sheltered ⚑✕⚋⚹⬛⬛⊘⊕⊘⊕⚐⊡⬥ games room, lounge £6.80-£9.50
(Mastercard/Visa/ Switch/Solo)
Sandybrook Country Park, DE6 2AQ ☎Ashbourne (01335) 300000 OS map 119/178483 1m N of
Ashbourne on A515 (Buxton) Open Apr-Oct 50 pitches Sloping grass, sheltered ⬛⊘⊕⊘
£7.50 (most cards if prepaid)

BAKEWELL, Derbys   **Map C2**
Pop 3,940. EC Thurs, MD Mon SEE Vernon monuments in church, Saxon cross, almshouses, old
bridge, Old House museum, Haddon Hall 2m SE, Chatsworth House 3m NE 🖥Old Market Hall,
Bridge Street ☎Bakewell (01629) 813227 Restaurant: Aitch's Wine Bar ☎(01629) 813895
Greenhills Caravan Park, Crow Hill Lane DE4 1PX ☎(01629) 813052 OS map 119/195698 1m
NW of Bakewell off A6 (Buxton) Open Mar-Oct 140 pitches (65 static) Level grass, sheltered
⚑⚋⬛⬛⊘⊘⚊ lic club £10.50 (all cards)
Haddon Grove Farm, Over Haddon DE4 1JF ☎Bakewell (01629) 812343 OS map 119/177663
4m SW of Bakewell off B5055 (Monyash) Open Mar-Oct 10 pitches Grass, partly level, sheltered
⬛⊡ £2.00-£4.00
Mill Farm, Haddon Grove, Over Haddon DE45 1JF ☎(01629) 812013 OS map 119/180662 3m W
of Bakewell off B5055 (Monyash) at Haddon Grove Open all year 10 pitches 2 acres level/sloping
grass and hard standings ⊕⚊ £4.00

BASLOW, Derbys   **Map D2**
Pop 1,200 SEE St Anne's church, 17c bridge, Derwent valley, Chatsworth House 2m S Restaurant: Cavendish ☎ (01246) 882311

Chatsworth Park (Caravan Club), DE4 1PN ☎ (01246) 582226 (0800-2000 hrs) OS map 119/260720 ½m E of Baslow off A619 (Sheffield) Open Mar 15-Oct 123 pitches–no tents Level, walled, grass and hard standing 🗑🚿🅿⊗♨✓♿ all-weather pitches £8.80-£16.00 (most cards)

Stocking Farm, Calver S30 1XA ☎ Hope Valley (01433) 630516 OS map 119/247747 2m NW of Baslow off A623 (Chapel en le Frith) on Calver Mill road Open Apr-Oct, 20 pitches–bkg adv 1 acre gentle slope grass, hard standing £6.00-£6.50

See also Stoney Middleton

BELPER, Derbys   **Map C3**
Pop 16,450 SEE Alport Height NW, Wirksworth parish church NW Restaurant: Remy, Bridge Street ☎ (01773) 852246

The Firs Farm, Crich Lane, Nether Heage, Ambergate DE56 2JH ☎ Ambergate (01773) 852913 OS map 119/355507 ½m N of Belper off A6–signposted Open all year 60 pitches Level grass, some hard standings ⊸🚿🅿⊗♨⊘▱🛒 sauna £8.00

BOSTON, Lincs   **Map F6**
Pop 26,640. EC Thurs, MD Wed, Sat SEE St Botolph's church, Guildhall museum, Dominican Friary ▨ Blackfriars Arts Centre, Spain Lane ☎ Boston (01205) 356656 Restaurant: New England, Wide Bargate ☎ (01205) 865225

Oak Tree Caravan Park, Firth Bank, Anton's Gowt PE22 7BG ☎ Boston (01205) 860369 OS map 131/280435 2m W of Boston off A1121 (Swineshead Bridge) Open Mar 16-Oct 30, 40 pitches (32 static) Level grass, sheltered ✗🍴⊸🚿🅿⊗❸🛒 children's room, games room £10.00 (most cards)

Orchard Park, Frampton Lane, Hubberts Bridge PE20 3QU ☎ (01205) 290328 OS map 131/273433 3½m W of Boston off A1121 (Sleaford) on B1192 (Kirton End) Open all year 188 pitches (128 static) Level grass, sheltered ☎🍴🗑🚿🅿⊗♨⊘✓🛒♿ £8.00-£10.00

Plough Inn, Swineshead Bridge PE20 3PT ☎ Boston (01205) 820300 OS map 131/219428 7m W of Boston on left of A17 (Sleaford-Spalding) near junction with A1121 Open Apr-Sept 30 pitches Level grass, sheltered ⊗✓ fishing £7.00

White Cat Caravan and Camping Park, Shaw Lane, Old Leake PE22 9LQ ☎ Boston (01205) 870121 OS map 122/415512 8m NE of Boston on A52 (Skegness) Open Mar-Nov 40 pitches Level grass, sheltered ☎🚿🅿⊗⊘✓🛒▱ £5.75-£6.75

BUXTON, Derbys   **Map C2**
Pop 20,790. EC Wed, MD Tues, Sat SEE The Crescent (of 18c houses), Pavilion gardens, Corbar Woods, Grimlow Woods, Peak Rail Steam Centre, Cat and Fiddle Inn 4m NW ▨ The Crescent ☎ Buxton (01298) 25106 Restaurant: Hartington, Broad Walk ☎ (01298) 22638

Cold Springs Farm, SK17 6SS ☎ Buxton (01298) 22762 OS map 119/044747 1m NW of Buxton on left of A5002/5004 (Whaley Bridge) Open Mar-Nov 40 pitches 4 acres grass, gentle slope 🗑⊗⊘❖ flat rental £3.50

Cottage Farm Caravan Park, Blackwell SK17 9TQ ☎ (01298) 85330 OS map 119/126717 6m E of Buxton off A6 (Bakewell) on Blackwell road Open Mar-Oct 30 pitches 3 acres level grass and hard standings ☎🚿🅿⊗⊘▱ £6.00

Grin Low (Caravan Club), Grin Low Rd, Landanlow SK17 6UJ *Imaginative development of old quarry* ☎ (01298) 77735 (0800-2000 hrs) OS map 119/046722 2m SW of Buxton off A53 (Leek) on Harpur Hill road Open Mar-Nov 132 pitches–booking advisable in season Level grass, mainly hard standing, sheltered 🗑🚿🅿⊗✓ £12.00-£16.00 (2000) (Mastercard/Visa/Switch)

Limetree Park, Dukes Drive SK17 9RP ☎ Buxton (01298) 22988 OS map 119/068726 1m S of Buxton off A6 (Bakewell) and A515 (Ashbourne) Open Mar-Oct 135 pitches (36 static) 9 acres, Level/gentle slope grass and hard standings ☎🗑🚿🅿⊗♨⊘✓▱🛒 (35) ▱🏪♿ £8.25-£10.50 (most cards)

Pomeroy Caravan Camping Park, Street House Farm, Flagg SK17 9QG ☎ (01298) 83259 OS map 119/116675 5m SE of Buxton on A515 (Ashbourne) Open Easter-Oct–must book public holidays 40 pitches Level grass 🗑🚿🅿⊗▱ £6.00-£6.50

Thornheyes Farm, Longridge Lane, Peak Dale SK17 8AD ☎ (01298) 26421 OS map 119/078756 1½m N of Buxton off A6 (Chapel en le Frith) Open Easter-Nov 15 pitches 2 acres level/sloping grass 🚿🅿⊗▱ £5.00-£7.25

CAISTOR, Lincs   **Map F4**
Restaurant: White Hart 10m S at Ludford ☎(01472) 781664

Nettleton Lodge LN7 6JQ ☎Caistor (01472) 851501 OS map 112/091009 2m W of Caistor on
B1205 (Waddingham) Open Apr-Oct 150 pitches �▮▮▮ country club, fishing £4.00-£6.00

CASTLE DONINGTON, Leics   **Map C4**
Pop 5350 SEE Donington Hall, church, Old Key House, Kings Mills village, motor racing circuit
Restaurant: Priest House 1m W at Kings Mills by river Trent ☎(01332) 810649

Park Farmhouse Caravan Park, Melbourne Rd, Isley Walton DE74 2RN ☎(01332) 862409 OS
map 129/418253 1½m SW of Castle Donington off Ashby de la Zouch road at Isley Walton near
junct 24 of M1 Open Mar-Nov 65 pitches 5 acres mainly level grass, sheltered
✗▮▮▮▮▮▮▮▮ £9.00-£13.00

CASTLETON, Derbys   **Map D2**
Pop 510. EC Wed SEE Peveril Castle ruins, Peak, Blue John and Treak Cliff caverns, Winnats
Gorge and Speedwell cavern 3m W Restaurant: Castle ☎(01433) 620578

Losehill Hall (Caravan Club) S30 2WB ☎(01433) 620636 OS map 110/154834 ½m NE of
Castleton on left of A625 (Hathersage) Open Mar-Jan–must book public holidays and week ends
95 pitches ▮▮▮▮▮▮▮▮ £7.50-£8.00

Rowter Farm, S33 8WA ☎(01433) 620271 OS map 110/132820 2½m W of Castleton off Buxton
road via Winnats Pass Open Easter-Oct 30 pitches 4 acres level grass £5.00

CHAPEL EN LE FRITH, Derbys   **Map C2**
SEE church, stocks, Market cross, old inns Restaurant: King's Arms, Market Pl ☎(01298) 812105

Hayfield Campsite, Kinder Road, Hayfield SK12 5LE ☎(01663) 745394 OS map 110/052875 4m
N of Chapel en le Frith off A624 (Glossop) at Hayfield Open Apr-Oct 90 pitches–no caravans
Grass, level ▮▮▮ drying room £7.50-£8.60

CHAPEL ST LEONARDS, Lincs   **Map G5**
SEE Hogsthorpe church 1m W Restaurant: Ship, Sea Lane ☎(01754) 872975

Eastfields Touring Park, Chapel Point PE24 5UX ☎Skegness (01754) 874499 OS map
122/563733 ½m N of Chapel St Leonards centre at Chapel Point near beach Open Easter-Oct 80
pitches – no tents 3 acres level grass ▮▮▮▮▮▮▮ fishing lake £9.00-£12.00

Hill View Lakes Touring Caravan Park, Skegness Road, Hogsthorpe PE24 5NR ☎Skegness
(01754) 872979 OS map 122/541714 1m SW of Chapel St Leonards on left of A52 (Mablethorpe)
Open Mar 15-Oct 31 90 pitches Level grass ▮▮▮▮▮▮▮▮ coarse fishing adj £10.00 inc elect
and awning

Robin Hood Leisure Park, South Rd PE24 5TR ☎(01754) 874444 OS map 122/560715 On S
edge of Chapel St Leonards in South Road Open Mar-Oct 770 pitches (650 static)–no tents–no
adv booking 40 acres level grass ▮✗▮▮▮▮▮▮▮▮▮▮▮▮▮▮▮▮▮▮▮ betting shop,
theatre club £5.50-£11.00

CHATSWORTH–see Baslow

CHESTERFIELD, Derbys   **Map D3**
Pop 97,000. EC Wed (not town centre), MD Mon, Fri, Sat SEE parish church, Bolsover Castle 6m E,
Hardwick Hall 8m SE ℹPeacock Tourist Information and Heritage Centre, Low Pavement
☎Chesterfield (01246) 207777 Restaurant: Portland, West Bars ☎(01246) 234502

Batemans Mill Holiday Park, Old Tupton S42 6AE ☎(01246) 862296 OS map 119/370641 4½m
S of Chesterfield off A61 (Alfreton) and Ashover road at Old Tupton Open all year 51 pitches
✗▮▮▮▮▮▮ £6.00-£7.00 (most cards)

CONINGSBY, Lincs   **Map F5**
Pop 1,400 SEE church (with largest clock in Eng), village of Tumby 1m N, Tattershall castle
Restaurant: Leagate Inn, Leagate Rd ☎(01526) 342370

Orchard Caravans, Chapel Hill LN4 4PZ ☎Coningsby (01526) 342414 OS map 122/207540 2m S
of Coningsby off A153 (Sleaford) at Chapel Hill Open all year–must book peak periods 48 pitches
Level grass, sheltered ▮▮▮▮▮▮▮▮▮▮▮▮ boat moorings, fishing £6.00-£9.00

Tattershall Park Country Club, Tattershall LN4 4LR ☎Coningsby (01526) 343193 OS map
122/207573 1m SW of Coningsby on left of A153 (Sleaford) Open Easter-Oct 150 pitches (90
static) Level grass and hard standing, sheltered ▮✗▮▮▮▮▮▮▮▮▮▮▮▮▮▮▮▮ boating,
fishing, pony trekking, squash, windsurfing, riding school, nature walks, gym, sauna, solarium
£6.00-£8.00

Willow Holt Caravan Camping Park, Lodge Road, Tattershall LN4 4JS ☎Coningsby (01526)
343111 OS map 122/200596 1½ NW of Coningsby on left of B1192 (Woodhall Spa) Open Mar
15-Oct 90 pitches Level grass and hard standing ▮▮▮▮▮▮▮ fishing £7.00-£8.00

DARLEY DALE, Derbys   **Map D3**
Pop 1500 Famous Peak District beauty spot in Derwent valley Restaurant: Grouse Inn, Dale Road
North ✆ (01629) 734357

Darwin Forest Country Park, Darley Moor DE4 5LN ✆ (01629) 732428 OS map 119/302649 2m
NE of Darley Dale on left of B5057 (Chesterfield) Open all year 48 pitches Level grass and hard
standings sheltered by woodland tennis, mini golf
£10.00-£12.00 (Mastercard/Visa/Switch)

Grouse and Claret, Station Yard, Station Rd, Rowsley DE4 2EB ✆ (01629) 733233 OS map
119/258660 2m N of Darley Dale on A6 (Bakewell) at junction with B6012 (Baslow) at rear of
eating house adj river Open all year 29 pitches Level standing, sheltered £8.50-
£11.50 (most cards)

DERBY, Derbys   **Map C3**
Pop 217,000. MD Tues, Thurs, Fri, Sat SEE Cathedral, RC church of St Mary by Pugin, St Mary's
bridge and chapel, Crown Derby Works and Museum, Kedleston Hall 3½ NW, Elvaston Castle
Country Park 4m SE Assembly Rooms, Market Place ✆ Derby (01332) 255802 Restaurant:
Gondola (Italian), Osmaston Rd ✆ (01332) 332895

Elvaston Castle Country Park (Caravan Club), Borrowash road, Elvaston DE7 3EP ✆ Derby
(01332) 573735 (0830-1800 hrs) OS map 129/412332 4m SE of Derby off A6 (Loughborough) on
B5010 (Borrowash) Open Apr-Oct 55 pitches–must book peak season and weekends 3 acres
level grass, sheltered woodland walks, nature trails £5.00-£12.50 (Mastercard/Visa)

Shardlow Marina, London Road, Shardlow DE7 2GL ✆ Derby (01332) 792832 OS map
129/444303 7m SE of Derby on left of A6 (Loughborough) at Shardlow Open Mar-Oct 70 pitches
Level grass and hard standings, sheltered fishing £8.00-£10.75

DOVERIDGE, Derbys   **Map C4**
Pop 350 Restaurant: Cavendish Arms ✆ (01889) 563820

Cavendish Caravan Camping, Derby Rd DE6 5JR ✆ Uttoxeter (01889) 562092 OS map
128/122342 ½m NE of Doveridge centre on old A50 (Derby-Stoke on Trent) Open Apr-Oct, 15
pitches 2 acres part level grass *No showers* £3.00

EAST RETFORD–see Retford

EDALE, Derbys   **Map D2**
Moorland village at start of long distance (250m) Pennine way. SEE Mam Tor, Edale valley
Restaurant: Castle 3m SE at Castleton ✆ (01433) 620578

Coopers Caravan and Campsite, Newfold Farm, S30 2ZD ✆ (01433) 670372 OS map 110/121859
In Edale adj post office Open all year 25 pitches Sloping grass £6.50

Fieldhead Campsite S30 2ZF ✆ Hope Valley (01433) 670386 OS map 110/124856 In Edale betw
station and church Open all year 45 pitches–tents only–weekends only Nov-Mar Level grass,
sheltered £8.00-£8.50

Upper Booth Farm S33 7ZS ✆ Hope Valley (01433) 670250 OS map 110/103853 2m W of Edale
on Jacobs Ladder road, by stream and Pennine Way Open all year 40 pitches–no trailer or motor
caravans 3 acres level grass

FENNY BENTLEY–see Ashbourne

GLOSSOP, Derbys   **Map D1**
Pop 24,140. EC Tues, MD Thurs, Fri, Sat SEE Dinting Railway Centre, Saxon cross, Snake Pass,
Peak National Park The Gatehouse, Victoria St ✆ Glossop (01457) 855920 Restaurant: Firenze
(Italian), High St ✆ (01457) 861054

Crowden Campsite, Crowden SK14 7HZ ✆ Glossop (01457) 866057 OS map 110/073994 4m NW
of Glossop off B6105 on A628 (Manchester) via Tintwhistle Open Mar-Oct 45 pitches–no trailer or
motor caravans Grass, level £9.60-£12.10

GRANTHAM, Lincs   **Map D5**
Pop 30,500. EC Wed, MD Thurs, Sat SEE market cross, St Wulfram's church, old inns, Belton
House 2½m NE Guild Hall Centre, St Peters Hill ✆ Grantham (01476) 566444 Restaurant: Angel
and Royal, High St ✆ (01476) 565816

Old Hall Farm, Sudbrook, Ancaster NG32 3RY ✆ (01400) 230262 OS map 130/984455 6m NE of
Grantham on B6403 (Colsterworth-Newark) Open all year 10 pitches 2½ acres level grass £5.00

**The distance and direction of a campsite is given from the centre of the key town under
which it appears, the place name in parentheses following the road number indicating which
route to take.**

HARTINGTON, Derbys   **Map C2**
Pop 340 SEE Beresford Dale, Dovedale S Restaurant: Charles Cotton, Market pl ☎(01298) 84229

Barracks Farm, Beresford Dale SK17 0HQ ☎Hartington (01298) 84261 OS map 119/118575 2m S of Hartington off B5054 (Warslow) Open Apr-Oct 100 pitches (35 static) 10 acres level grass £5.00-£6.00

Chapel Farm, Heathcote SK17 0AY ☎Hartington (01298) 84312 OS map 119/147602 1m SE of Hartington in Heathcote village Open Mar-Oct 20 pitches–booking advisable 3 acres gentle slope *No showers*, farm produce £2.00

HATHERSAGE, Derbys   **Map D2**
Pop 1,420. SEE Castle earthworks, Iron Age Fort, church with Robin Hood associations Restaurant: Hathersage Inn, Main St ☎(01433) 650259

North Lees Campsite, Birley Lane S12 3BP ☎Hope Valley (01433) 650838 OS map 110/235832 1½m N of Hathersage off A625 via Jaggers Lane Open Apr-Sept 45 pitches – booking advisable 1½ acres gentle slope £5.00

Swallow Holme Caravan Park, Station Road, Bamford S33 0BN ☎Hope Valley (01433) 650981 OS map 110/207825 2m NW of Hathersage off A625 (Chapel en le Frith) on A6013 (Bamford) Open Easter-Oct 60 pitches (40 static) Level grass and hard standings, sheltered ▫▫▫ £9.00

HOLBEACH, Lincs   **Map E6**
Pop 4,760. EC Wed, MD Thurs SEE church, bulbfields (Apr-May) Restaurant: Rose and Crown, West End ☎(01406) 423941

Delph Bank Touring Park, Old Main Rd, Fleet Hargate PE12 8LL ☎Holbeach (01406) 422910 OS map 131/393248 2m E of Holbeach on B1515 (Fleet Hargate) Open Mar-Oct 45 pitches–grass, sheltered–adults only ▫▫▫▫▫ dog walk £6.50

Whaplode Manor Caravan Park, Saracens Head PE12 8AZ ☎Holbeach (01406) 422837 OS map 131/341278 2m N of Holbeach on A17 (Sleaford) Open Easter-Nov 20 pitches 1 acre, level grass, sheltered ✗▫▫▫▫▫▫▫ £5.50 (Mastercard/Visa)

HOPE, Derbys   **Map D2**
Pop 230 Moorland village in Hope valley at heart of Northern Peak district. SEE caves, Roman fort S, Ladybower reservoir N Restaurant: Poachers Arms, Castleton Rd ☎(01433) 620380

Laneside Caravan Park, S30 2RR ☎Hope Valley (01433) 620215 OS map 110/180830 ¼m E of Hope on A625 (Hathersage) Open Apr-Oct–must book peak periods 120 pitches Level grass and hard standing, sheltered ▫▫▫▫▫▫▫ £9.00-£10.00 (Delta/Switch)

HORNCASTLE, Lincs   **Map F5**
Pop 4,200. EC Wed, MD Thurs, Sat SEE St Mary's church, Bain valley ▨Trinity Centre, Spilsby Rd ☎(01507) 526636 Restaurant: Fighting Cocks, West St ☎(01507) 527307

Ashby Park, West Ashby LN9 5PP ☎(01507) 527966 OS map 122/251726 2m N of Horncastle between A153 (Louth) and A158 (Lincoln) Open all year 90 pitches 4 acres level grass, sheltered, in 50 acre Ashby Park ✗▫▫▫▫▫▫▫ (indoor) ⅃ fishing £7.50-£11.00 (all cards)

HUBBERTS BRIDGE–see Boston

INGOLDMELLS, Lincs   **Map G5**
Pop 6120 Modest resort N of Skegness overlooking extensive beaches of fine sand backed by dunes SEE Gunby Hall (NT) 6m W, Burgh le Marsh church and windmill 4m SW Restaurant: County 3m S at Skegness ☎(01754) 612461

Country Meadows Holiday Park, Anchor Lane PE25 1LZ ☎(01754) 874455 and 873351 OS map 122/565697 1m N of Ingoldmells off A52 (Mablethorpe) and road to beach on right Open Easter-Oct 200 pitches (100 static) 6 acres level grass ▫▫▫▫▫▫▫ £6.00

Greenacres, Bolton's Lane PE25 1JJ ☎(01754) 872263 OS map 122/564684 ¼m S of Ingoldmells centre off A52 (Skegness) near sea Open Easter-Oct 150 pitches 7 acres level ▫▫▫ £3.00

Hardy's Tourer Park, Sea Lane PE25 1PG ☎Skegness (01754) 874071 OS map 122/566688 ¼m E of Ingoldmells centre on road to Ingoldmells Point Open Mar 15-Oct 15, 175 pitches 10 acres level grass and hard standing ▫▫▫▫▫▫▫ £6.00

Ingoldale Park, Roman Bank, PE25 1LL ☎(01754) 872335 OS map 122/570683 ½m S of Ingoldmells on old Roman Bank road near junct with A52 Open Mar 15-Oct 27 110 pitches–no tents Level grass, sheltered ✗▫▫▫▫▫▫▫▫▫▫▫▫▫ £6.00

Valetta Farm, Mill Lane, Addlethorpe PE24 4TB ☎(01754) 763758 OS map 122/553674 1m SW of Ingoldmells off A52 (Skegness) and Burgh le Marsh road, in Mill Lane Open Mar 15-Oct 15, 35 pitches 2 acres mainly level grass ▫▫▫▫ £6.00-£9.00

LINCOLN, Lincs   **Map E4**
Pop 78,000. EC Wed, MD daily SEE cathedral, castle, courthouse, Stonebow with Guildhall above, county museum ▣9 Castle Hill ☎(01522) 529828 Restaurant: White Hart, Bailgate ☎(01522) 526222

Hartsholme Country Park, Skellingthorpe Road LN6 0EY ☎Lincoln (01522) 873578 OS map 121/943691 3m SW of Lincoln off A46 bypass on Skellingthorpe road Open Mar-Oct 50 pitches Grass, level, sheltered ▱▤⊕◔↵⬡ lake fishing (permit) £4.50-£10.70

LONG SUTTON, Lincs   **Map F6**
Pop 3,000 SEE church, Sutton Bridge river port E Restaurant: Rose and Crown 7m S at Wisbech ☎(01945) 583187

Foreman's Bridge Caravan Park, Sutton Road, Sutton St James PE12 0HU ☎Sutton St James (01945) 440346 OS map 131/412196 2m SW of Long Sutton off B1390 (Sutton St James) by river Open Mar-Nov 40 pitches 2 acres part level grass ▱▤▰⬡⊕⊘◙▭⬡ cycle hire £8.00

Laurel Park, Huntsgate, Gedney Broadgate PE12 0DJ ☎(01406) 364369 OS map 131/405222 2m W of Long Sutton off A17 (Holbeach) at Gedney roundabout on Gedney Broadgate road Open Apr-Dec 14 pitches 2 acres, grass, mainly level ▤▰⬡⊕◔↵▰ £4.50

LOUTH, Lincs   **Map F4**
Pop 13,295 EC Thurs, MD Wed SEE church, town hall, market hall Restaurant: Priory, Eastgate ☎(01507) 602930

Manby Caravan Park, Manby LN11 8SX ☎(01507) 328232 OS map 122/395876 3m E of Louth on B1200 (Saltfleet) at Manby Open Mar 15-Oct 31, 125 pitches Level grass and hard standing, sheltered ▱✕⬡▰▤▰⬡⊕⊘▭◔⬡⬡ £7.50 (Mastercard/Access)

MABLETHORPE, Lincs   **Map G5**
Pop 7,450. EC Wed (winter), MD Thurs SEE church, sands, Queens Park ▣Entertainment Centre, Central Promenade ☎(01507) 472496 Restaurant: Bacchus 3m S at Sutton on Sea ☎(01521) 441204

Denehurst Hotel Caravan Camping, Alford Road LN12 1PX ☎Mablethorpe (01507) 472951 OS map 122/496846 ¾m W of Mablethorpe on right of A1104 (Alford) past junct with A1031 Open Mar-Oct 20 pitches Level grass, sheltered ✕⬡▰⊘ tea gardens £5.00-£7.00 (Mastercard/Visa)

Holivans, Quebec Road LN12 1QH ☎Mablethorpe (01507) 473327 OS map 122/498865 1m N of Mablethorpe on coast road Open Easter-Sept 192 pitches (165 static) Level grass ⬡➚▤▰⊘⊘⊕▭ lic club £6.50-£7.50

Kirkstead Holiday Park, North Road, Trusthorpe LN12 2QD ☎Mablethorpe (01507) 441483 OS map 122/515838 1m S of Mablethorpe on A52 (Skegness) Open Mar-Nov 100 pitches (65 static) 6 acres level grass ▱⬡▰▤▰⊘⊕◔↵▭⬡▭⬡ children's room, clubhouse, bar meals £8.50-£13.50 (all cards)

Mermaid Caravan and Tent Park, Seaholme Road LN12 2NX ☎Mablethorpe (01507) 473273 OS map 122/500846 ½m SW of Mablethorpe off Seacroft Road Open Mar 15-Oct 20 600 pitches (300 static) Level grass ▱⬡➚▤▰⊘⊕⊘↵⬡ lic club/bar £3.50-£8.00

Seacroft Holiday Estate, Mainbridge, Trusthorpe LN12 2PN ☎(01507) 472421 OS map 122/513830 1½m SE of Mablethorpe on A52 (Skegness) Open Mar-Nov 245 pitches (230 static)–no tents 20 acres level grass ▱▤▰⊘⊘↵▭⬡⬡ clubhouse £7.00-£12.00

Trusthorpe Springs Leisure Park, Trusthorpe Hall, Mile Lane, Trusthorpe LN12 2QQ ☎(01507) 441384 OS map 122/500838 1m S of Mablethorpe off A1104 at Cross Inn in Mile Lane Level grass and hard standings, sheltered Open Mar-Oct 152 pitches (130 static)–no tents ▱✕⬡▤⊘⊕⊘▭↵▭⬡ £7.00

St Vincents Caravan Camping Park, Seaholme Rd LN12 2NX ☎(01507) 472287 OS map 122/505842 In South Mablethorpe off Seaholme Road Open Mar-Oct 48 pitches–no adv bkg 1½ acres level grass, part sheltered ✕⬡▰⊘⊕⊘ £4.00-£7.00

CHECK BEFORE ENTERING

Beware less-than-honest site operators who give us one price for the following year and then increase it once the season gets underway. So note the charges for any site featured in this guide and before pulling in verify how much you will have to pay, and for what. If on leaving the charges turn out to be higher, ask why the difference.
The outdoor holidaymaker gets a better deal in France. There site charges are governed by law and must be displayed at the site entrance.

MANSFIELD, Notts   **Map D3**
Pop 100,000. EC Wed, MD Mon, Thurs, Fri, Sat SEE parish church, Moot hall, Clumber Park,
Newstead Abbey (Byron assoc) 4m S, Sherwood Forest Restaurant: Bella Napoli (Italian), Leeming
St ☎(01623) 652376

Shardaroba, Silverhill Lane, Teversal NG17 3JJ ☎(01623) 551838 OS map 120/472615 3m W of
Mansfield off A38 (Alfreton) and B6014 (Tibshelf) Open Mar-Oct 100 pitches 6 acres level grass
and hard standings 🔲🔌🥤◔⛄ late arrivals area

Sherwood Forest Caravan Park, Edwinstowe NG21 9HW ☎(0800) 146505 OS map 120/593651
5m NE of Mansfield off A6075 (Edwinstowe) on B6030 Open Feb-Nov 150 pitches 20 acres level
grass 🔝🔲🔌◔⛄◔🍴⛄⤴◻🍴⛄ £7.00-£9.95

MARKET BOSWORTH, Leics   **Map C5**
Pop 1800 SEE Bosworth battlefield 1m S (now country park) Restaurant: Olde Red Lion, Park St
☎(01455) 291713

Bosworth Water Trust, Far Coton Lane CV13 6PD *Park with 20 acres of lakes for sailing and
fishing* ☎(01455) 291876 OS map 140/385030 1m SW of Market Bosworth off B585 (Sheepy
Magna) by Ashby canal Open all year 20 pitches 5 acres level grass and hard standings 🔌⤴
fishing £7.50

MARKET DEEPING, Lincs   **Map E6**
Pop 9,260 Restaurant: Deeping Stage, Market Pl ☎(01778) 343234

Deepings Caravan Camping Park, Outgang Road, Towngate East PE6 8LQ ☎Market Deeping
(01778) 344335 OS map 142/166116 2m NE of Market Deeping off A16 (Spalding) Open Feb-
Dec 45 pitches level grass and hard standings 🔌◔⛄◔🍴⛄ £6.00-£7.50

Tallington Lakes Leisure Park, Tallington PE9 4RJ ☎Market Deeping (01778) 347000 OS map
142/095095 3m W of Market Deeping off A16 (Stamford) on Barholm road Open all year 341
pitches (241 static) level grass and hard standings ✕🍴⤴🔲🔌◔⤴◻ wind surfing, water skiing,
canoeing, jet skiing, dinghy sailing, dry slope skiing, quad bike track, tennis court £7.50-£10.00
(Mastercard/Visa/Switch)

MARKET HARBOROUGH–see Lutterworth

MARKET RASEN, Lincs   **Map F4**
Pop 2,780. EC Thurs, MD Tues, Wed SEE St Thomas's church, racecourse Restaurant: White Hart
5m E at Ludford ☎(01507) 313489

The Racecourse, Legsby Road LN8 3EA ☎Market Rasen (01673) 842307 OS map 121/115880
1m SE of Market Rasen off A631 (Louth) Open Mar 31-Oct 1 55 pitches Level grass
🔲🔌🔌◔⛄◔🍴⛄⤴◻ golf £5.40-£9.20

Walesby Woodland Caravan Park, Walesby Rd LN8 3UN ☎Market Rasen (01673) 843285 OS
map 113/117906 1½m N of Market Rasen off B1203 (Tealby) Open Mar-Oct 64 pitches Level
grass, sheltered 🔝🔲🔌◔⛄◔🍴⛄⤴◻🍴⛄⛄ £8.00-£8.50 (Mastercard/Visa)

Camping Caravanning Through France

160pp ISBN 1-870009-23-1 £6.50 net in UK only

A unique guide which describes and maps main-road routes crossing the country from
north to south which start at ports served by tunnel or ferry from Britain. These are
backed by link routes leading from and joining up with them so that, for example, those
arriving at one port can pick up a route starting from another. Every campsite on or near
the routes is pinpointed and historic sights, shopping for food and good-value restaurants
noted at places along the way.

Each route leads to or passes near a popular holiday location and in a separate section
are featured regions by the sea or inland where outdoor holidaymakers are
welcomed and catered for. A brief description of each region is followed by a selection
of campsites chosen for their location or amenities.

**Publication is planned for Easter 2001 and to reserve your copy write to Frederick
Tingey (CCF), Hillsboro, How Caple HR1 4TE. Copies ordered prior to publication
cost only £5.00 post-free. Send no money now.**

MATLOCK, Derbys   Map C3
Pop 19,560. EC Thurs, MD Tues, Fri SEE High Tor (673ft), Hall Leys Park, Riber castle, Fauna Reserve, Heights of Abraham by cable car, Tramway Museum 4m SE at Crich, Haddon Hall 5m NW ⓘThe Pavillion, Matlock Bath ☎Matlock (01629) 855082 Restaurant: New Bath 1m S on A6 at Matlock Bath ☎(01629) 583275

Birchwood Farm, Wirksworth Road, Whatstandwell DE4 5HS ☎Wirksworth (01629) 822280 OS map 119/315551 6m S of Matlock off A6 (Belper) on B5035 (Wirksworth) adj Midshires Way Open Mar-Oct 44 pitches (20 static) 4 acres level/sloping grass 🏕 table tennis, farm produce £6.00-£8.00

Haytop Country Park, Whatstandwell DE4 5HP ☎Ambergate (01773) 852063 OS map 119/331538 6m SE of Matlock off A6 (Derby) at Whatstandwell bridge Open all year 60 pitches (30 static) 65 acres level/sloping grass and hard standings 🏕 farm produce, fishing, canoeing (own boats) £8.00-£16.00

Merebrook Caravan Park, Whatstandwell DE4 5HH ☎Ambergate (01773) 857010/852154 OS map 119/332555 5m S of Matlock on A6 (Derby) beside River Derwent Open all year 196 pitches (116 static) Grass, part level, sheltered 🏕 fishing £7.00-£9.00

Middle Hills Farm, Grangemill DE4 4HY ☎(01629) 650368 OS map 119/230595 4m W of Matlock on A5012 (Buxton) beyond Holly Bush Inn Open Easter-Oct 60 pitches 4 acres level grass, sheltered 🏕 £5.00-£7.00

Packhorse Farm, Matlock Moor DE4 5LF ☎Matlock (01629) 582781 OS map 119/322517 2m NE of Matlock off A615 (Alfreton) Open all year–must book public holidays 30 pitches 🏕 sep pitches, farm produce £7.00-£8.00

Pine Groves Caravan Park, High Lane, Tansley DE4 5BG ☎Dethick (01629) 534815 and 534670 OS map 119/343586 2½m E of Matlock off A615 (Alfreton) Open Apr-Oct 100 pitches 8 acres level grass, sheltered 🏕 £8.00

Sycamore Caravan Camping Park, Lant Lane, Tansley DE4 5LF ☎Matlock (01629) 55760 OS map 119/327617 2½m NE of Matlock off A632 (Chesterfield) Open Mar 15-Oct 31, 70 pitches (35 static) Level grass 🏕 £8.00-£10.00

Wayside Farm, Matlock Moor DE4 5LF ☎Matlock (01629) 582967 OS map 119/322620 2m NE of Matlock off A632 (Chesterfield) at site sign Open all year 30 pitches Level/sloping grass, hard standing, sheltered 🏕 children's pet corner £8.00

For other sites near Matlock see Wirksworth and Youlgreave

METHERINGHAM, Lincs   Map E4
Restaurant: Harvey's 9m NW at Lincoln ☎(01522) 21886

White Horse Inn Holiday Park, Dunston Fen LN4 3AP ☎Metheringham (01526) 398341 OS map 121/130660 6m ENE of Metheringham off B1188 (Lincoln) on unclass via Dunston by river Open Feb-Dec 42 pitches (32 static) Level grass, sheltered 🏕 fishing, moorings, games room £5.00-£10.00

NEWARK, Notts   Map E4
Pop 24,600. EC Thurs, MD Wed, Fri, Sat SEE Church of St Mary Magdalene, Beaumond Cross, Town Hall, facades of Market Square, old inns, folk museum ⓘGilstrap Centre, Castlegate ☎Newark (01636) 78962 Restaurant: Crown and Mitre, Castlegate ☎(01636) 703131

Al Carapark, Vicarage Lane, North Muskham NG23 6HS ☎Newark (01636) 76558 OS map 120/121/792589 3¼m N of Newark off A1 (East Retford) Open Mar-Oct 30 pitches 🏕 £5.00

Carlton Manor Touring Park, Carlton on Trent NG23 6NW ☎(01530) 835662 and 0771 2083909 (mobile) OS map 120/791641 7m N of Newark on A1 (Doncaster) Open Easter-Oct 22 pitches 🏕 fishing Level grass, sheltered £6.00-£7.75

Milestone Caravan Park, Cromwell NG23 6JE ☎Newark (01636) 821244 OS map 120/798622 5½m N of Newark off A1 (Doncaster) in village Open all year 60 pitches 8 acres level grass and hard standing 🏕 £8.00-£9.00

FOLLOW THE COUNTRY CODE

Guard against all risk of fire. Fasten all gates. Keep dogs under proper control. Keep to the paths across farmland. Avoid damaging fences, hedges and walls. Leave no litter. Safeguard water supplies. Protect wildlife, plants and trees. Go carefully on country roads and be prepared for slow-moving vehicles like tractors. Respect the life of the countryside.

NEWHAVEN, Derbys   **Map C2**
Restaurant: Dales 2m W at Hartington ☎(01298) 84235

Newhaven Caravan Camping Park, SK17 0DT ☎(01298) 84300 OS map 119/166603 ¼m N of
Newhaven at junction of A515 (Buxton) and A5012 (Grangemill) Open Mar-Oct 198 pitches (73
static) Level grass and hard standing, sheltered 🔒🏹🗄🍴🌀☀🌿😊🍴 sep pitches £7.50-£8.50

Waterloo Inn, Biggin SK17 0DH ☎(01298) 84284 OS map 119/153595 ½m SW of Newhaven off
A515 (Ashbourne) near Biggin church Open all year 20 pitches–booking advisable 2 acres grass,
part level–*No showers* 🔌🍴 Bar meals £4.00-£7.00

NORTHAMPTON, Northants   **Map B6**
Pop 162,200. EC Thurs, MD Wed, Fri, Sat SEE Abingdon Park Museum, church of Holy Sepulchre,
Lamport Hall and garden, Queen Eleanor cross 2m S, Althorp House 5m NW 🅸Visitor Centre, St
Giles Sq ☎(01604) 722677 Restaurant: Napoleon, Welford Rd ☎(01604) 713899

Billing Aquadrome, Little Billing NN3 4DA ☎Northampton (01604) 408181 OS map 152/808615
3m E of Northampton off A45 (Wellingborough) Open Mar 21-Oct 30, 1990 pitches (995 static)
Level grass, sheltered 🔒✗🍴🔌🗄🍴🌀🌿⬛🍴😊♿ club rooms, fishing, lakes £9.50

Overstone Solarium, Sywell NN6 0BD ☎Northampton (01604) 645255 OS map 152/822672 6m
NE of Northampton off A43 (Kettering) near Sywell Airport and A4500 at Ecton Open Apr-Oct
1,000 pitches (800 static)–no tents 🔒🗄🍴🌿☀🌀⬛😊🍴🚐 lic club £8.00-£12.00

NORTH SOMERCOTES, Lincs   **Map G4**
Restaurant: Priory 8m W at Louth ☎(01507) 602930

Lakeside Park LN11 7RB ☎North Somercotes (01507) 358428/358315 OS map 113/432960) ½m
SE of North Somercotes on A1031 (Mablethorpe) Open Apr-Oct 450 pitches (300 static) Level
grass and hard standing 🔒✗🍴🔌🗄🍴🌀☀🌿⬛😊🍴♿ lic club, sauna £8.00-£17.00 (most
cards)

NOTTINGHAM, Notts   **Map D4**
Pop 271,000. EC Mon (large stores), MD daily SEE parish church, cathedral, castle, arboretum, Trip
to Jerusalem Inn, Salutation Inn (13c), annual Goose Fair 🅸Smithy Row ☎(0115) 947 0661
Restaurant: Café Royal, Upper Parliament St ☎(0115) 941 3444

Holme Pierrepont Caravan Camping Park, National Water Sports Centre, Adbolton Lane, Holme
Pierrepont NG12 2LU ☎Nottingham (0115) 982 4721 OS map 129/620390 5m SE of Nottingham
off A52 (Grantham) Open Apr-Oct 360 pitches Grass, level 🔒🗄🍴🌀🌿🍴♿ fishing, boating
£5.00-£7.50

New Moor Farm Trailer Park, Calverton NG14 6FZ ☎Nottingham (0115) 965 2426 OS map
129/615490 7m N of Nottingham off A614 (Ollerton) Open all year 140 pitches (80 static) Level
grass and hard standing 🔒🗄🍴 fishing £5.75

Thornton's Holt, Stragglethorpe, Radcliffe on Trent NG12 2JZ ☎Nottingham (0115) 933 2125–Fax
(0115) 933 3318 OS map 129/636337 3½m E of Nottingham off A52 (Grantham) on
Cotgrave/Cropwell Bishop road Open all year (limited facs Nov 2-Mar 31) 90 pitches Level grass
and hard standings, sheltered 🔒🗄🍴🌀☀🌿⬛ (indoor heated) 😊🍴♿ first aid, barbecue,
games room £7.00-£8.00

OAKHAM, Leics   **Map D5**
Pop 8,850. EC Thurs, MD Wed, Sat SEE Castle ruins, horseshoe collection, Rutland County
Museum, Butter cross, stocks, parish church 🅸Oakham Library, Catmos Street ☎(01572) 724329
Restaurant: Wheatsheaf, Northgate ☎(01572) 723458

Ranksborough Hall Leisure Centre, Milton Road, Langham LE15 7ER ☎Oakham (01572) 722984
OS map 130/833115 2m N of Oakham on A606 (Melton Mowbray) Open all year 273 pitches (84
static) Level grass and hard standing 🔒🗄🌿⬛ (indoor), crazy golf, squash, solarium
£8.00-£11.00

See also Uppingham

OUNDLE, Northants   **Map D6**
Pop 3,450 EC Wed MD Thurs SEE public school, St Peter's church, old Talbot inn, almshouses,
Barnwell Country Park and Marina 1m S 🅸West St ☎(01832) 274333 Restaurant: Talbot, New St
☎(01832) 273621

The George, Glapthorn Road PE8 4PR ☎Oundle (01832) 272324 OS map 141/035890 ½m N of
Oundle on Glapthorn road Open all year, 1 acre, 23 pitches *No showers* £2.00

**Help us make CARAVAN AND CAMP IN BRITAIN better known to site operators – and thereby
more informative – by showing them your copy when booking in.**

RETFORD, Notts   **Map E3**
Pop 18,400 EC Wd MD Thurs SEE St Swithin's church, ◪Amcott House, Grove St ☏Retford (01777) 860780 Restaurant: White Hart, The Square ☏(01777) 703761

Crookford Caravan Camping Park, Crookford Hill, Elkesley DN22 8BT ☏(01777) 703670 OS map 120/6757512 3m S of Retford off A638 (Tuxford) Open Apr 15-Oct 31, 3 acres, 50 pitches ◢ £5.00

Ferry Boat Inn, Church Laneham DN22 0NQ ☏(01777) 703350 OS map 121/815767 6m E of Retford off A57 (Saxilby) Open Apr-Sept 40 pitches ✗♀ £5.00

Manor House Caravan Park, Laneham DN22 2NJ ☏(01777) 228428 OS map 121/819771 6m E of Retford off A57 (Saxilby) Open Mar-Oct 190 pitches (170 static) 15 acres level grass ▣◢⊛∅◞ £6.50

SKEGNESS, Lincs   **Map G6**
Pop 14,550. EC Thurs (Oct-May), MD daily (summer) SEE St Clement's church, Natureland (aquarium and marine zoo) ◪Embassy Centre, Grand Parade ☏Skegness (01754) 764821 Restaurant: Vine Hotel, Vine Rd ☏(01754) 763018

Elms Touring Park, Addlethorpe PE24 4TR ☏Skegness (01754) 872266 OS map 122/546690 3½m NW of Skegness off A158 (Horncastle) at Gunby Open Mar 15-Oct 15–must book peak periods 200 pitches Level grass, sheltered ▣▣∅◉▣ fishing £8.00

North Shore Holiday Centre, Elmhirst Avenue, off Roman Bank PE25 1SN ☏Skegness (01754) 763815 OS map 122/566646 ½m N of Skegness off A52 (Sutton on Sea) Open Apr-early Oct 625 pitches (375 static) Level grass and hard standing ▣↪≯▣◢∅◉◞▢▣⊛⊡▣d. lic club, mini-golf, tennis, bowls £7.50

Richmond Drive Carapark, Richmond Drive PE25 3TQ ☏Skegness (01754) 762097 OS map 122/559624 ¼m SW of Skegness off A52 near station Open Mar-Nov–must book public holidays 724 pitches (550 static)–level grass ▣✗♀◞▣▣◢⊛∅▣ (indoor heated) ◞▢▣▣d. post office, amusements, lic hotel £8.00-£13.50

Southview Leisure Park, Burgh Road PE25 2LA ☏Skegness (01754) 874893 OS map 122/543647 1m W of Skegness off A158 (Burgh le Marsh) Open mid Mar-mid Oct 300 pitches (225 static) ▣▢▣▣ fishing lake, lic club, cabaret, bowling green, amusement arcade £5.00-£7.50

SLEAFORD, Lincs   **Map E5**
Pop 8,890. EC Thurs, MD Mon, Fri, Sat SEE St Denis church, Carre Hospital (almhouses), Handley monument ◪The Mill, Money's Yard, 76 Carre St ☏(01529) 414294 Restaurant: Rose and Crown, Watergate ☏(01529) 303350

Low Farm Touring Park, Spring Lane, Folkingham NG34 0SJ ☏Folkingham (01529) 497322 OS map 130/070333 9m S of Sleaford off A15 (Bourne) Open Easter-Oct, 36 pitches 2½ acres level/sloping grass, sheltered ▣▣⊛▣ £7.00-£8.00

Woodland Waters, Willoughby Road, Ancaster NG32 3RT *Picturesque park set in 72 acres of woods and lakes* ☏(01400) 230888 OS map 130/977436 5m W of Sleaford on A153 (Grantham) Open all year 64 pitches Level grass, sheltered ✗♀▣⊛◞▣▣ fishing £5.00-£7.00

SOUTHWELL–see Newark

SPALDING, Lincs   **Map E6**
Pop 19,000. EC Thurs, MD Tues SEE church, Ayscoughfee Hall with bird museum and gardens, White Horse Inn, bulbfields (Apr-May) ◪Ayscoughfee Hall, Churchgate ☏Spalding (01775) 725468 Restaurant: Lincolnshire Poacher, Double St ☏(01775) 766490

Lake Ross Caravan Park, Dozens Bank, West Pinchbeck PE11 3NA ☏Spalding (01775) 761690 OS map 131/211223 2¼m W of Spalding on A151 (Bourne) near Pode Hole Bridge Open Apr-Oct 28 pitches Level grass, sheltered ▣♀▣▣◢⊛∅◉▢▣ fishing £7.50

STAMFORD, Lincs   **Map D6**
Pop 16,650. EC Thurs, MD Fri, Sat Handsome country town noted for its stone built houses and medieval churches. SEE St Martin's area S of river (18c High St), Browne's Hospital, museum, Burghley House 2m SE ◪Arts Centre, St Mary's St ☏(01780) 55611 Restaurant: Bull and Swan, High St (St Martins, B1081) ☏(01780) 63558

Casterton Taverner Motor Inn, Castleton Hill PE9 4DE ☏(01780) 481481 OS map 141/006085 2m NW of Stamford on B1081 (Great Casterton) Open all year 30 pitches 1¾ acres level grass and hard standing, sheltered ▣▣▣⊛∅ pub, petrol, pizza bar £4.95-£7.75

STONEY MIDDLETON, Derbys   **Map D2**
Pop 1080 Restaurant: Bridge ¼m SE at Calver Bridge ☎(01433) 630415

Peakland Caravan Park, High St S32 4TL ☎(01433) 631414 OS map 119/223754 ¼m SW of
Stoney Middleton centre in High Street Open Apr-Oct 32 pitches–no trailer caravans Level grass
▯♉⌂ £8.00

SUTTON ON SEA, Lincs   **Map G5**
Pop 3,150 EC Thurs SEE sands, Huttoft windmill and granary Restaurant: Bacchus, High Street
☎(01507) 441204

Cherry Tree Park, Huttoft Road LN12 2RU ☎Sutton on Sea (01507) 441626 OS map 122/525802
1½m S of Sutton on Sea on left of A52 (Skegness) near beach Open Mar-Oct 60 pitches 2½
acres, level grass ▯♉∅⊛∅↲& £6.00-£8.00

Hawthorn Farm (Caravan Club), Crabtree Lane LN12 2RS ☎(01507) 441503 (0800-2000 hrs) OS
map 122/519801 1½m S of Sutton on Sea off A52 (Skegness) Open Apr-Oct 120 pitches–must
book 8½ acres level, open ♉∅⊛& £8.00-£10.00 (Mastercard/Visa)

Jolly Common, Sea Lane, Huttoft LN13 9RW ☎(01507) 490236 OS map 122/524776 3m S of
Sutton on Sea off A52 (Skegness) Open Mar 15-Oct 31, 55 pitches 9 acres, level Fishing lake
£5.50-£8.00

SUTTON ST EDMUND, Lincs   **Map F6**
SEE Crowland Abbey 8m W Restaurant: Queens 5m SE at Wisbech ☎(01945) 583933

Orchard View Caravan Camping Park, Broadgate PE12 OLT ☎Wisbech (01945) 700482 OS map
142/365108 1m S of Sutton St Edmund on left of Parson Drove road Open Apr-Oct 37 pitches 6
acres level grass and hard standings ⚒♈⚲♉∅⊛∅↲⚑⌂& £5.00-£8.00

SUTTON ST JAMES–see Long Sutton

TATTERSHALL–see Coningsby

THRAPSTON, Northants   **Map C7**
SEE Nene Valley lakes to N Restaurant: Woolpack on A604 near main bridge ☎(01832) 732578

Mill Marina, Midland Road NN14 4JR ☎Thrapston (01832) 732850 OS map 141/994781 ½m S of
Thrapston on Denford road Open Apr-Dec–must book summer weekends 42 pitches Level
grass, part sheltered ⚲▯♉∅⊛∅⚑⌂ fishing, slipway £8.00-£11.00

TORKSEY, Lincs   **Map E4**
Restaurant: White Swan at Torksey Lock ☎(01427) 71653

Little London Caravan Park LN1 2EL ☎Torksey (01427) 71322 OS map 121/840778 1m S of
Torksey on A156 (Lincoln) near junction with A1133 Open Mar-Oct 7½ acres 400 pitches
✗⚲▯♉∅⊛∅⌂⊡ lic club £6.00

TUXFORD, Notts   **Map E3**
Pop 2,600. EC Wed SEE parish church, grammar school, ancient lock-up Restaurant: Newcastle
Arms, Market pl ☎(01777) 870208

Greenacres Touring Park, Lincoln Road NG22 0JW ☎Tuxford (01777) 870264 Fax (01777)
872512 OS map 120/755720 1m ENE of Tuxford on A6075 (Lincoln) Open Apr-Oct 79 pitches
(20 static) grass and hard standing ⚒▯♉∅⊛∅⊛↲⚑⌂& £7.50

Longbow Caravan Park, Milton NG22 0PP ☎(01777) 838067 OS map 120/717736 2m N of
Tuxford off A1 (Doncaster) on Milton/Walesby road Open all year 1 acre 20 pitches Grass and
hard standing, level ▯♉∅⊛↲⌂⊡⌂ £6.50

Orchard Park Caravan Camping Park, Marnham Road NG22 0PY *Quiet sheltered park in old
orchard* ☎Tuxford (01777) 870228 OS map 120/753708 1m E of Tuxford off A6075 (Lincoln)
Open Mar 15-Oct 31, 65 pitches 5 acres level grass, sheltered ▯♉∅⊛∅⚑& £7.00-£8.50

UPPINGHAM, Leics   **Map C5**
Pop 2760 EC Thurs MD Fri SEE Uppingham School, church, Lyddington village (Bede House) 2m
S, Rutland Water 3m W Restaurant: Vaults, High St ☎(01572) 823259

Old Rectory, Belton in Rutland LE15 9LE ☎(01572) 717279 OS map 141/819009 3m W of
Uppingham off A47 (Peterborough-Leicester) on Belton road Open Jan-Dec 15 pitches
Level/sloping grass ▯♉⊛∅⌂ £5.00-£10.00

**Some site operators make it a rule that cars must be left in a separate parking area away from
caravans and tents, which can be inconvenient when shopping by car. But it does minimise
traffic noise and the risk to children.**

WAINFLEET ALL SAINTS, Lincs   Map F6
SEE 15c turreted Magdalen school, Croft church (interior) 2m NE, nature reserve 5m E Restaurant: Red Lion, High St ☎ (01754) 880301

Riverside Caravan Park, Wainfleet Bank PE24 4ND ☎ Skegness (01754) 880205 OS map 122/480593 2m W of Wainfleet All Saints on B1195 (Spilsby) at Wainfleet Bank Open Mar 15-Oct 10, 30 pitches Grass, sheltered ▢▢▢▢▢ (30) ▢ £5.50

Swan Lake Leisure Park, Culvert Road, Thorpe Culvert PE24 4NJ ☎ Skegness (01754) 881456 OS map 122/464606 2m NW of Wainfleet All Saints off B1195 (Spilsby) on Thorpe Culvert road Open Mar-Nov 60 pitches 7 acres level grass ▢▢▢▢▢ (25) ▢▢ fishing £5.00-£8.50

WHALEY BRIDGE, Derbys   Map C1
SEE Goyt valley Restaurant: White Horse, Lower Macclesfield Rd, Horwich End ☎ (01663) 732617

Ringstones Caravan Park, Yeardsley Lane, Furness Vale SK23 7EB ☎ Whaley Bridge (01663) 732152 OS map 110/005824 1½m N of Whaley Bridge off A6 (Stockport) Open Mar-Oct 20 pitches Level grass, sheltered ▢▢ £7.00

WHATSTANDWELL–see Matlock

WOODHALL SPA, Lincs   Map F5
Pop 2,440. EC Wed SEE springs and mineral baths, Wellington monument, Tower on the Moor ▢ Cottage Museum, Iddesleigh Rd ☎ (01526) 353775 Restaurant: Petwood, Stixwould Rd ☎ (01526) 352411

Bainland Country Park, Horncastle Road LN10 6UX ☎ Woodhall Spa (01526) 352903 OS map 122/215640 1m NE of Woodhall Spa on B1191 (Horncastle) Open all year, 150 pitches Level grass and hard standing ▢▢▢▢▢▢▢▢▢▢ (heated) ▢▢▢ (satellite) ▢▢▢▢ tennis, golf, sauna, jacuzzi, croquet, boules, sunbed, trampoline, bowling green £9.00-£30.00 (Mastercard/Visa/Switch)

Jubilee Park, Stixwould Road LN10 6QH ☎ Woodhall Spa (01526) 352448 OS map 122/192635 ½m N of Woodhall Spa on Stixwould road Open Apr-Nov 1, 90 pitches (27 static)–must book high season Level grass and hard standing ▢ (café) ▢▢▢ (heated) ▢▢▢ bowling, putting greens, tennis, cycle hire £3.50-£7.50

Roughton Moor Caravan Park LN10 6UU ☎ Woodhall Spa (01526) 352312 OS map 122/205663 2m NE of Woodhall Spa on B1191 (Horncastle) Open all year 120 pitches (70 static) ▢▢ £3.50-£4.50

WORKSOP, Notts   Map E3
Pop 36,380 EC Thurs, MD Wed, Fri, Sat SEE Priory Church, 13c Lady Chapel, 14c gatehouse, old market cross ▢ Library, Memorial Ave ☎ (01909) 501148 Restaurant: Cottage, 30 Park St ☎ (01909) 474379

Clumber Park (Caravan Club), Lime Tree Ave, Clumber Park S80 3AE ☎ (01909) 484758 (0800-2000 hrs) OS map 120/624763 4½m SE of Worksop off A57 (Newark)–signposted Open Mar-Oct 162 pitches–must book w/ends and BH ▢▢▢▢ £7.50-£15.00

Riverside Caravan Park, Worksop Cricket Club, Central Ave S80 1ER ☎ Worksop (01909) 474118 OS map 120/583791 ½m SW of Worksop centre off junction of A60 and A57–signposted Open all year 60 pitches 5 acres, level grass, hardstanding ▢▢▢▢ clubhouse, coarse fishing £7.50-£8.00

YOULGREAVE, Derbys   Map C3
Pop 1,210 SEE church, Arbor Low 3m W, Bradford Dale Restaurant: George Inn, Church St ☎ (01629) 636292

Harthill Hall Farm, Alport DE4 1LH ☎ (01629) 636203 OS map 119/227646 1m NE of Youlgreave off Rowsley road at junct with B5056 (no access for caravans via Alport) Open Mar-Nov 32 pitches ▢ £4.00

Hopping Farm DE4 1NA ☎ Youlgreave (01629) 636302 OS map 119/209631 1m S of Youlgreave off Dale End road Open Apr-Sept, 1½ acres 15 pitches Must book ▢ £8.00

CARAVAN STORAGE

Many sites in this guide offer caravan storage in winter but some will also store your caravan in summer, which for those of us able to tour several times a year saves towing over long distances. Sites most conveniently placed for this are those on or near popular routes to the West Country and Scotland.

6   Central England

Central England is made up of Shropshire and Staffordshire in the north, Warwickshire and the recently combined Hereford and Worcester in the centre and Gloucestershire in the south. To these are added the new county of West Midlands, embracing Coventry, Birmingham and Wolverhampton, which is wholly industrial. Yet the region retains enough unspoiled landscape to make it one of the most attractive in Britain.

Divided by the Severn and bordered on the west by Wales, Shropshire is wild in the northwest, soft in the south. West and south of Shrewsbury are the scenic uplands: the geological freak of the Wrekin, the oldest mountain in Britain which takes only an hour to climb; the 1600ft high long Mynd above Church Stretton; the narrow spine of wooded Wenlock Edge extending from Craven Arms to Ironbridge and famed for its views, and to the southwest the Clee Hills, topped by ancient British camps. Around these heights are the fascinating old towns of Shrewsbury, with its half timbered houses and inns; medieval Much Wenlock and ancient Ludlow, moated by the Teme and dominated by its great castle. Long Mynd is traversed by the venerable Portway track and near Newcastle one of the best preserved sections of Offa's Dyke cuts across the treeless Clun Forest.

In adjoining Staffordshire is Cannock Chase near Rugeley, a vast area of woods and moorland, and east of Stoke on Trent is Hawksmoor nature reserve.

Fine walking country exists in the rich countryside of Hereford and Worcester, from Bewdley in the west high above the Severn to the pleasant reaches of other rivers: the willow hung Avon winding down to Pershore and Bredon Hill, and the Teme flowing through hopfields and orchards to its junction with the Severn. West of the plain of Malvern are the Malvern Hills, with a nine-mile walk on the saddleback ridge to the Herefordshire Beacon, 1114ft high. From the cathedral city of Hereford the River Wye flows south into Gloucestershire, most striking feature of which is the Cotswold Hills, rising up from the Severn and rolling east into Oxfordshire. Ross on Wye is an acknowledged centre for the Wye Valley, with its famous beauty spots of Symonds Yat and the reaches below Goodrich castle. On the left bank of the river is the Forest of Dean, with its magnificent woods of oak and birch. The Teme Valley northwest of Worcester forms part of a forty-five mile waymarked drive through attractive scenery. A popular centre in the Cotswolds is Cirencester, where the old roads Icknield Way and Ermine Street join the equally ancient Fosse Way. The Cotswold Way also crosses the district, on an escarpment from Chipping Campden to Bath via Duntisbourne and Slimbridge.

Southwest of Stratford on Avon in Warwickshire charming villages line the Stour; and Stratford itself is the heart of Shakespeare country; his birthplace is in Henley Street, his grave in the churchyard by the river and Anne Hathaway's cottage at Shottery. Not far away are the beautiful reaches of the Avon south of Kenilworth, its castle is almost as imposing as Warwick's, further south.

Most campsites in the region are recommended more for their setting than for their amenities.

ALCESTER, Warwicks   **Map E5**

Pop 5290 EC Thurs SEE town hall and houses in Butter, Church and Henley streets, 1 Malt Mill Lane (Shakespeare assns), Ragley Hall and Park (adventure trails) 2m SW Restaurant: Arrow Mill on Evesham road at Arrow ☎(01789) 762419

Island Meadow Caravan Park, The Mill House, Aston Cantlow B95 6JP ☎ and Fax (01789) 488273 OS map 151/135597 3m NE of Alcester off B4089 (Wootton Wawen)–access via Little Alne advisable Open Mar-Oct–must book peak periods 80 pitches (56 static) Grass, level, sheltered ▨▸▨▨▨◈▨❾▭⅃ fishing £8.00-£10.50

ALSTONEFIELD, Staffs   **Map E1**

Pop 780 SEE Manifold Valley SW, Dove Dale S Restaurant: Dales 3m N at Hartington ☎(01298) 84235

The George DE6 2FX ☎(01335) 310205 OS map 119/132556 ¼m E of Alstonefield centre on Tissington road at rear of hotel Open all year 15 pitches–no adv booking–no trailer caravans 1 acre level grass and hard standing, walled ✖♀ £5.75

See also Longnor and Warslow

ASTON MUNSLOW, Shrops   **Map B4**

Pop 300 SEE Millichope Park NE, nature trail (Wolverton Wood) Restaurant: Sun Inn at Corfton ☎(01584) 861239

Glebe Farm, Diddlebury SY7 9DH *Secluded wooded paddock on farm* ☎(01584) 841221 OS map 137/508855 ½m SW of Aston Munslow off B4368 (Craven Arms) on Peaton road Open all year 6 pitches Level grass, sheltered £4.00-£6.00

BERKELEY, Glos   **Map C8**

Pop 1,390 EC Wed SEE parish church, castle, Slimbridge Wildfowl Trust 6m NE Restaurant: Old School House, Canonbury St ☎(01453) 811711

Hogsdown Farm, Lower Wick GL11 6DS ☎(01453) 810224 OS map 162/710973 1½m SE of Berkeley off B4066 (Dursley) on Lower Wick road Open all year 40 pitches Level grass and hard standing, sheltered ▨▨▨▨◈⦰❾✔▨▭ £7.50

BERROW–see Tewkesbury

BEWDLEY, H and Worcs   **Map D5**

Pop 9,920. EC Wed, MD Tues, Sat SEE Wyre Forst, Tudor houses and inns, Telford bridge, Severn valley Rly to Bridgnorth 🆔St George's Hall, Load Street ☎Bewdley (01299) 404740 Restaurant: Black Boy, Kidderminster Rd ☎(01299) 403523

Woodlands Holiday Home Park, Dowles Road DY12 3AE ☎(01299) 403208/403294 OS map 138/773767 1½m NW of Bewdley on left of B4194 (Bridgnorth) by Wyre Forest Open Mar-Jan 150 pitches (140 static)–no tents ▨▨▨◈⦰✔ £7.00 inc elect

BIDFORD ON AVON, Warwicks   **Map E6**

Pop 3,190 SEE 13c church, 15c bridge Restaurant: Arrow Mill 3m N on A422 at Arrow ☎(01789) 762419

Cottage of Content Inn, Barton B50 4NP ☎(01789) 772279 OS map 150/107511 1m SE of Bidford on Avon off B4085 (Evesham) in Barton village Open Mar-Oct 25 pitches ✖♀ *No showers* £5.00

BIRMINGHAM, West Midlands   **Map E4**

Pop 1,017,300 EC Wed (suburbs) MD daily SEE Museum of Science and Industry, Botanic Gardens, Midlands Arts Centre, National Exhibition Centre 🆔National Exhibition Centre ☎0121-780 4321 and 2 City Arcade ☎0121-643 2514 Restaurant: Bell 7m SE via A453 at Tanworth in Arden ☎(01564) 742212

Chapel Lane Park (Caravan Club), Chapel Lane, Wythall B47 6JX ☎(01564) 826483 (0800-2000 hrs) OS map 139/073750 7m S of Birmingham centre off A435 (Evesham) near junction 3 of M42 Open all year 90 pitches, hard standings ▨▨▨⦰❒▨ £8.50-£9.00

BISHOP'S CASTLE, Shrops   **Map A4**

SEE church Restaurant: Castle, Market Sq ☎(01588) 638403

The Old School Caravan Park, Shelve, Minsterley SY5 0JQ ☎(01588) 650410 OS map 137/336990 6m N of Bishops Castle on A488 (Shrewsbury) Open Mar-Oct 13 pitches ▨◈⦰ TV hook-up £5.50

Powis Arms, Lydbury North SY7 8AU ☎(01588) 680254 OS map 137/349858 3m SE of Bishop's Castle on right of B4385 (Leintwardine) in grounds of 18c coaching inn Open Apr-Oct 15 pitches 1 acre level grass ✖♀▨⦰ £5.00

See also Wentnor

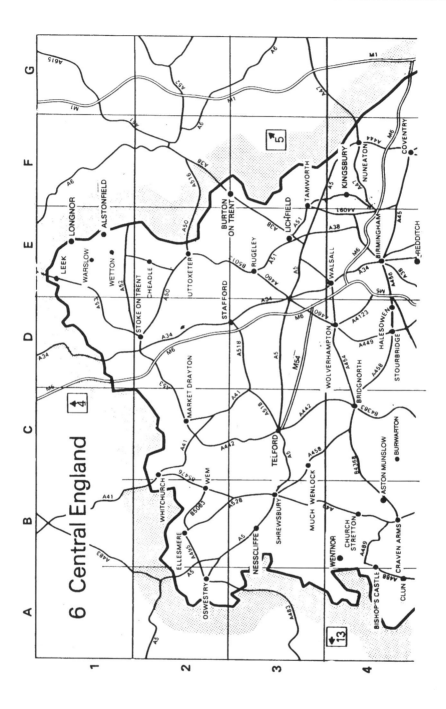

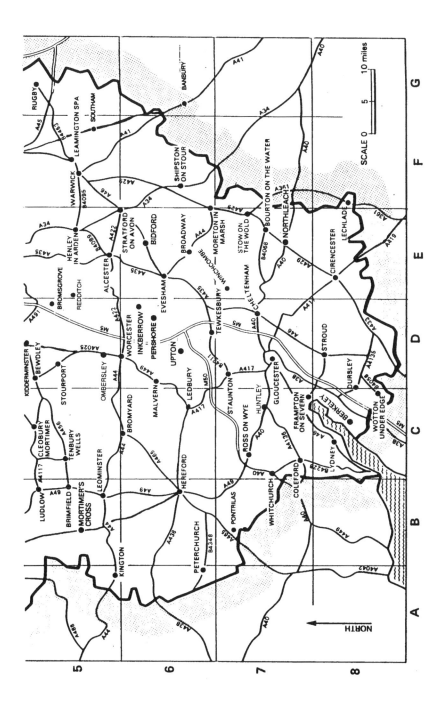

CHELTENHAM
Freedom Camping and RV Park
Bamfurlong Lane, Staverton GL51 6SL   **Tel (01452) 712705**

Open February to November inc.
£6.00-£8.50 for two people per night (Mastercard, Visa, Switch accepted)

BOURTON ON THE WATER, Glos   **Map E7**
Pop 2,710. EC Sat SEE aquarium, Birdland, model village Restaurant: Old New Inn, High St
☎(01451) 820467

Folly Farm, Notgrove GL54 3BY *Basic site in area of outstanding natural beauty* ☎Cotswold
   (01451) 820285 OS Map 163/124206 2½m W of Bourton on the Water on A436 (Andoversford)
   Open all year 20 pitches Level grass, sheltered ▣✦ £8.00-£10.00

BRIDGNORTH, Shrops   **Map C4**
Pop 11,120. EC Thurs, MD Mon, Sat SEE Bishop Percy's House, cliff railway, castle ruins, town hall,
Northgate museum, Severn Valley Rly to Bewdley ⓲Library, Listley Street ☎Bridgnorth (01746)
763358 Restaurant: Bear Inn, Northgate (High Town) ☎(01746) 763250

Stanmore Hall Touring Park, Stourbridge Road WV15 6DT ☎Bridgnorth (01746) 761761 OS map
   138/922742 2m E of Bridgnorth on A458 (Stourbridge) Open all year 131 pitches (all weather,
   serviced) Grass and hard standing, sheltered ▤▣▣𝄄✦✹✦ £10.60-£12.20 (all cards)
See also Burwarton

BRILLEY–see Kington

BROADWAY, H and Worcs   **Map E6**
Pop 2,380. EC Thurs SEE Lygon Arms, Elizabethan houses, Fish Inn, church, Broadway Tower
country park ⓲Cotswold Court ☎Broadway (01386) 852937 Restaurant: Crown and Trumpet,
Church St (Snowshill road) ☎(01386) 853202

Leedons Park, Childswickham Road WR12 7HB ☎Broadway (01386) 852423 OS map
   150/080385 1m NW of Broadway off A44 (Evesham) Open all year 480 pitches Grass, level, part
   sheltered ▤⚲▣▣𝄄▤ (heated) ✹✦▢▣ kitchen facs £5.00-£10.00 (Mastercard/Visa/Switch)

BROMYARD, H and Worcs   **Map C6**
Pop 3200 SEE Norman church, Lower Brockhampton House 2m E, Bromyard Downs NE
⓲Heritage Centre, Rowberry St ☎(01885) 482038 Restaurant: Herefordshire House ☎(01886)
884252

Boyce Caravan Park, Stanford Bishop, Bringsty WR6 5UB ☎(01885) 483439 (evenings) OS map
   149/697526 3m E of Bromyard off A44 (Worcester) and B4220 (Malvern) Open Mar-Oct 114
   pitches (90 static) Level grass, part sheltered ▣▣𝄄✹𝄄 coarse fishing £7.50

BROOME–see Craven Arms

BURWARTON, Shrops   **Map C4**
Pop 350 SEE Brown Clee Hill and woods W Restaurant: Pheasant Inn 2m NE on B4364 at
Neenton ☎(01746) 787247

Three Horseshoes Inn, Wheathill WV16 6QT ☎(01584) 823206 OS map 138/600819 In village on
   B4364 Open Apr-Oct 45 pitches level grass ⴲ↩𝄄✹𝄄▣ £3.00

CHEADLE, Staffs   **Map E2**
Pop 10,870. EC Wed, MD Fri, Sat Attractive market town amid rolling hills and moorland SEE
church (RC), Hawksmoor nature reserve 2m E Restaurant: Royal Oak, High St ☎(01538) 753116

Hales Hall Caravan Camping Park, Oakamoor Road ST10 4QR ☎Cheadle (01538) 753305 OS
   map 119/021441 1m NE of Cheadle on B5417 (Oakamoor) Open Easter-Oct–must book public
   holidays 80 pitches (30 static) Level/sloping grass and hard standing, sheltered
   ▤✕ⴲ⚲▣▣𝄄✹𝄄▤ (heated) ✹✦▢▣ £7.50-£8.50

Quarry Walk Park, Coppice Lane, Freehay ST10 1RQ ☎(01538) 723412 OS map 128/045404 2m
   S of Cheadle off A522 (Uttoxeter) in Freehay on Great Gate road Open all year 40 pitches 46
   acres level grass and hard standings, sheltered ▣▣𝄄✹𝄄✹✦ £7.50-£8.50

Star Caravan Camping Park, Cotton, Oakamoor ST10 3DW ☎Oakamoor (01538) 702256/702219
   OS 119/067456 3m NE of Cheadle on B5417 (Cotton) near Star Inn Open Feb-Dec 170 pitches
   (50 static) Level/sloping grass and hard standing, sheltered ▤▣▣𝄄✹𝄄✹✦▣ £8.00

Camping Caravanning Through France

160pp ISBN 1-870009-23-1 £6.50 net in UK only

A unique guide which describes and maps main-road routes crossing the country from north to south which start at ports served by tunnel or ferry from Britain. These are backed by link routes leading from and joining up with them so that, for example, those arriving at one port can pick up a route starting from another. Every campsite on or near the routes is pinpointed and historic sights, shopping for food and good-value restaurants noted at places along the way.

Each route leads to or passes near a popular holiday location and in a separate section are featured regions by the sea or inland where outdoor holidaymakers are welcomed and catered for. A brief description of each region is followed by a selection of campsites chosen for their location or amenities.

Publication is planned for Easter 2001 and to reserve your copy write to Frederick Tingey (CCF), Hillsboro, How Caple HR1 4TE. Copies ordered prior to publication cost only £5.00 post-free. Send no money now.

CHELTENHAM, Glos   **Map D7**
Pop 85,000. EC Wed, MD Thurs SEE Pittville Park, museum, colleges, Rotunda, Regency houses, mineral springs 🛈 The Promenade ☎ Cheltenham (01242) 522878 Restaurant: Bayhill Inn, St Georges Place (behind bus station) ☎ (01242) 524388

Freedom Camping and RV Park, Bamfurlong Lane, Staverton GL51 6SL ☎ Churchdown (01452) 712705 OS map 163/899217 3m W of Cheltenham off A40 (Gloucester), B4063 (Staverton) and Badgeworth road Open all year 50 pitches 2 acres level grass and hard standings, sheltered 🖻🖳🅰⊕∅🖳 pets corner £6.50-£8.40 (Mastercard/Visa/Switch/Delta)

Cheltenham Racecourse (Caravan Club), Prestbury Park GL50 4SH ☎ Cheltenham (01242) 523102 OS map 163/960250 1½m NE of Cheltenham on A436 (Evesham) Open Mar-Oct 84 pitches Grass and hard standing 🖻🖳🅰⊕∅ £6.20-£11.65

Stansby Caravan Park, Reddings Road, The Reddings GL51 6RS ☎ Gloucester (01452) 712168 (24 hrs) OS map 163/907208 2m W of Cheltenham off A40 (Gloucester) (near junct 11 of M5) Open Feb-Dec 30 pitches Level grass and hard standing, sheltered 🖳🅰⊕ £6.00-£6.50

CHURCH STRETTON, Shrops   **Map B4**
Pop 3,890. EC Wed, MD Thurs SEE parish church, Long Mynd (NT), Cardingmill Valley, Acton Scott Farm Museum 2m S off A49 🛈 Church Street ☎ Church Stretton (01694) 723133 Restaurant: Green Dragon SW at Little Stretton ☎ (01694) 722925

Small Batch Caravan and Camping Site, Ashes Valley, Little Stretton SY6 6PW *Basic site in fine walking country* ☎ Church Stretton (01694) 723358 OS map 137/441920 1½m SW of Church Stretton off A49 (Craven Arms) Open Easter-Sept 37 pitches Grass, level ⊕ £8.00

Wayside Inn, Marshbrook SY6 6QE ☎ Marshbrook (01694) 781208 OS map 137/441898 2½m S of Church Stretton at junc of A49 (Ludlow) and B4370 (Bishops Castle) Open all year 40 pitches 2 acres, level grass, sheltered ✖ bar meals, *No showers* £4.00

FOLLOW THE COUNTRY CODE

Guard against all risk of fire. Fasten all gates. Keep dogs under proper control. Keep to the paths across farmland. Avoid damaging fences, hedges and walls. Leave no litter. Safeguard water supplies. Protect wildlife, plants and trees. Go carefully on country roads and be prepared for slow-moving vehicles like tractors. Respect the life of the countryside.

CIRENCESTER, Glos   **Map E8**
Pop 15,530. EC Thurs, MD Mon, Tues, Fri SEE parish church, Corinium museum, Roman wall, Chedworth Roman Villa 7m N ℤCorn Hall, Market Place ☏Cirencester (01285) 654180 Restaurant: King's Head, Market Pl ☏(01285) 653322

Cotswold Hoburne, Broadway Lane, South Cerney GL7 5UQ ☏Cirencester (01285) 860216 OS map 163/055958 4m SE of Cirencester off A419 (Swindon) Open Easter-Oct–must book peak periods 540 pitches (154 static) Hard standings ▣✕♀⊸▣▣⊘⊘▢ (2) ⊕↲▢◈▱⊜⛉ club house, tennis courts £8.00-£19.00 (inc showers and elect)

Mayfield Touring Park, Perrot's Brook GL7 7BH ☏Cirencester (01285) 831301 OS map 163/020055 2m N of Cirencester on A435 (Cheltenham) Open all year, 72 pitches Grass, sloping, and hard standing ▣▣▣⊘⊕⊘⊕▣⊘ £5.40-£9.40 (Mastercard/Visa/Switch)

CLUN, Shrops   **Map A4**
Pop 820 Restaurant the Old Post Office, the Square ☏(01743) 236019

Bush Farm, Clunton SY7 0HU ☏(01588) 660330 OS map 137/337811 2m E of Clun off B4368 (Craven Arms) at Clunton, by river Clun Open Apr-Oct 40 pitches 2 acres level grass and hard standings, sheltered ▣⊕▣⛉◲ archery, fishing £6.00-£8.00

COLEFORD, Glos   **Map C7**
Pop 4,360. EC Thurs SEE ruined 14c church, Forest of Dean ℤ27 Market Place ☏(01594) 836307 Restaurant: Dog and Muffler 1m N at Joyford (off B4432) ☏(01594) 832444

Braceland Site, (Forest Enterprise) GL16 8BA ☏Dean (01594) 833376 OS map 162/569129 1½m N of Coleford off B4432 (Ross) at Berry Hill Open Mar-Oct 600 pitches 20 acres level grass, sheltered ▣⊕▣ £5.00-£9.00

Forest of Dean Camping Ground, Christchurch GL16 7NN ☏Dean (01594) 833057 OS map 162/569129 2m N of Coleford off B4432 (Ross) at Berry Hill Open all year, 280 pitches Level/sloping grass and hard standing ▣▣▣⊘⊕⊘↲▣⊘⛉ £5.00-£9.00

Woodland View Camping Park, Sling GL16 8JA ☏Dean (01594) 835127 OS map 162/582085 1½m S of Coleford on B4228 (Chepstow) near Lambsquay Hotel Open Mar 1-Oct 31 3½ acres, part level grass and hard standing, 20 pitches ▣▣⊘⊕ £6.00-£9.50

COVENTRY, W Midlands   **Map F4**
Pop 320,000. MD daily exc Thurs SEE cathedral remains and new cathedral, St Mary's Hall, Holy Trinity church, Lady Godiva statue, art gallery, new city centre ℤBroadgate ☏(01203) 630084 Restaurant: Campanile, Wigston Road, Walsgrave ☏(01203) 622311

Hollyfast Caravan Park, Wall Hill Road, Allesley CV5 9EL ☏(02476) 336411 OS map 140/300833 2m NW of Coventry off A4114 (Birmingham) Open all year 75 pitches 10 acres level grass and hard standings, sheltered ▣⊕⊕↲▢⛉ £7.00-£9.00

CRAVEN ARMS, Shrops   **Map B4**
Pop 1,370. EC Wed, MD Fri, Sat SEE Stokesay Castle, Iron Age hill fort Restaurant: Craven Arms, Shrewsbury Rd ☏(01588) 673331

Engine and Tender Inn, Broome SY7 0NT ☏(01588) 660275 OS map 137/401812 2½m SW of Craven Arms off B4367 (Clungunford) Open all year 25 pitches Level/sloping grass, sheltered ⊸▣▱ (1) £5.00-£6.00

Kevindale, Broome SY7 0NT ☏(01588) 660326 OS map 137/403809 2m SW of Craven Arms on B4367 (Bucknell) in Broome village Open Apr-Sep 12 pitches 4 acres level grass £5.00-£6.00

CROSSWAY GREEN–see Stourport on Severn

DURSLEY, Glos   **Map D8**
Pop 27,200. EC Thurs Restaurant: Black Horse 1m SW at North Nibley ☏(01453) 846841

Tudor Caravan and Camping Site, Shepherds Patch, Slimbridge GL2 7BP ☏Dursley (01453) 890483 OS map 162/685981 4½m W of Dursley off A4135 (Slimbridge) Open all year–must book peak periods 75 pitches Level grass and hard standing, sheltered ✕▣⊘⊕ £7.75-£8.00

EDGERLEY–see Nesscliffe

Cause for Complaint

If you have cause for complaint while staying on a site take the matter up with the manager or owner. If you are still not satisfied set the facts down in writing and send photocopies to anyone you think might be able to help, starting with the editor of this guide and the local (licensing) authority for the area where the site is located.

ELLESMERE, Shrops   **Map B2**
Pop 2,470. EC Thurs, MD Tues SEE Kynaston Monument, half timbered houses, The Mere (lake)
🅸Meres Visitor Centre, The Mere ☎(01691) 622981 Restaurant: Grange 1m N on A528 ☎(01691)
623495
Fernwood Caravan Park, Lyneal SY12 0QF ☎(01948) 710221 OS map 126/453338 4m SE of
   Ellesmere off B5063 (Wem) Open Mar-Nov 66 acres 225 pitches (165 static) no tents Level grass
   🐾🗄🔌🅰⊕∅🛒�'🚐🛗 coarse fishing £10.00-£14.00 inc elect

EVESHAM, H and Worcs   **Map E6**
Pop 15,270. EC Wed SEE abbey ruins, churches, local history museum, Abbey park and gardens,
riverside 🅸Almonry Museum, Abbey Gate ☎Evesham (01386) 446944 Restaurant: Waterside on
A44 ☎(01386) 442420
Ranch Caravan Park, Honeybourne WR11 5QG ☎Evesham (01386) 830744 OS map 150/115445
   5m E of Evesham off B4035 (Bretforton) Open Mar-Nov 300 pitches (180 static) no tents Level
   grass, sheltered–some hard standing 🐾🗄🔌🅰⊕∅🖳 (heated) 🚲🚐🚐 lic club £9.00-£16.50
   (Mastercard/Visa)
Weir Meadow Holiday and Touring Park, Lower Leys WR11 5AB ☎Evesham (01386) 442417 OS
   map 150/044439 In Evesham off A44 (Chipping Norton) by River Avon Open Apr-Oct 185 pitches
   (100 static)–no tents Level grass and hard standing 🗄🔌🅰∅🚲🚐🛗 boating, fishing £6.85-
   £8.85

GLOUCESTER, Glos   **Map D7**
Pop 92,000. MD daily SEE cathedral, folk museum, New Inn, canal, Prinknash Abbey 5m SE,
regimental museum 🅸St Michael's Tower, The Cross ☎Gloucester (01452) 421188 Restaurant:
Fountain, Westgate St ☎(01452) 522562
Gable Farm, Moreton Valence GL2 7ND ☎Gloucester (01452) 720331 OS map 162/787100 6m S
   of Gloucester on A38 (Bristol) near Junction 13 of M5 Open Mar-Nov 40 pitches Level grass and
   hard standing, sheltered 🔌🅰⊕🚐 £4.50-£5.30
Red Lion, Wainlodes Hill, Norton GL2 9LW ☎Gloucester (01452) 730251 OS map 162/848258 5m
   N of Gloucester off A38 (Tewkesbury) by River Severn Open all year 60 pitches Grass and hard
   standing, level 🐾🍽🔌🅰∅🚐🏠 bar snacks, fishing £8.00
Staunton Court, Ledbury Rd, Staunton GL19 3QS ☎(01452) 840230 OS map 150/782292 7m
   NW of Gloucester on A417 (Ledbury) Open all year 40 pitches 4½ acres level/sloping grass,
   sheltered 🔌⊕🚐 fishing £5.50-£7.00 inc elect
See also Huntley and Tewkesbury

HANLEY SWAN–see Malvern

HAY ON WYE–see Central and South Wales

HEREFORD, H and Worcs   **Map B6**
Pop 48,700. EC Thurs, MD daily except Tues, Sun SEE cathedral, The Old House, 15c Wye Bridge
🅸1 King St ☎(01432) 268430 Restaurant: Bunch of Carrots Inn 2m SE at Hampton Bishop
☎(01432) 870237
Lucks-All, Mordiford HR1 4LP ☎Holme Lacy (01432) 870213 OS map 149/567362 5m SE of
   Hereford off B4077 (Ledbury) on B4224 (Mordiford) by River Wye Open Easter-Oct 80 pitches 10
   acres level grass 🐾🗄🔌🅰⊕∅🕀🚲🚐🚐🛗 £6.50-£9.50 (all cards exc Switch and Amex)

HONEYBOURNE–see Evesham

HUGHLEY–see Much Wenlock

HUNTLEY, Glos   **Map C7**
Pop 250 SEE Newent Wood 1m NW, falconry centre 3m N at Newent Restaurant: Red Lion
☎(01452) 870251
Forest Gate, GL19 3EU *Convenient base for Forest of Dean and Severn Vale* ☎(01452) 831192
   OS map 162/718194 In Huntley near junct of A40 and A4136 (Mitcheldean) Open Mar-Oct 30
   pitches 3 acres level grass, sheltered 🐾🔌🅰⊕∅ B&B £9.00 (Mastercard/Visa)

INKBERROW, H and Worcs   **Map D6**
Pop 2,540 Restaurant: Old Bull Inn on A422 ☎(01386) 792428

Wheelbarrow Castle, Radford WR7 4LR ☎Inkberrow (01386) 792207 OS map 150/012549 1½m
  S of Inkberrow off A422 (Worcester) on Abbots Morton road in Radford Open all year 15 pitches
  3 acres level, sheltered ♀↩ lic club, games room *No showers* £4.00

KIDDERMINSTER, H and Worcs   **Map D5**
Pop 50,6000. EC Wed. MD Tues, Thurs, Fri, Sat SEE St Mary's church, Severn Valley Rlwy, Wyre
Forest, Staffs and Worcs canal 🖼Severn Valley Railway Stn, Comberton Hill ☎(01562) 829400
Restaurant: King and Castle, Severn Valley Railway Stn, Comberton Hill ☎(01562) 747505

Brown Westhead Park (Camping Club), Wolverley DY10 3PX ☎Kidderminster (01562) 850909
  OS map 138/833792 2m N of Kidderminster off A449 (Wolverhampton) on B4189 (Wolverley)
  Open Mar 20-Oct 30 120 pitches Level/sloping grass, sheltered 🖎🗈🖾🗭❀🗭↩& £10.60-
  £13.90

KINGTON, Herefordshire   **Map A5**
Pop 2,040. EC Wed, MD Tues SEE Hergest Ridge 1m W 🖼Council Offices, Mill Street ☎Kington
(01544) 230202 Restaurant: Royal Oak, Church St ☎(01544) 230484

Penlan Caravan Park, Brilley HR3 6JW ☎(01497) 831485 OS map 148/272515 4½m S of
  Kington off Brilley road Open Easter-Oct 12 pitches 2 acres level/sloping grass, sheltered
  🗈🖾❀🗭 £8.00-£12.00

KNIGHTON ON TEME–see Tenbury Wells

LECHLADE, Glos   **Map F8**
SEE Georgian houses, church, river Isis Restaurant: Trout Inn, St John's Bridge ☎(01367) 252313

Bridge House GL7 3AG ☎Lechlade (01367) 252348 OS map 163/219991 ¼m S of Lechlade on
  A361 (Swindon) near river bridge Open Mar-Oct 51 pitches 4½ acres level grass, open
  🗈🖾❀🗭& £7.00-£9.00

St John's Priory Caravans, Faringdon Road GL7 3EZ ☎Faringdon (01367) 252360 OS map
  163/224989 ½m E of Lechlade on A417 (Faringdon) Open Mar-Oct 100 pitches (74 static) Level
  grass, sheltered 🖾🗭❀ £5.00-£10.00

LEDBURY, H and Worcs   **Map C6**
Pop 4,985 EC Wed, MD Tues, Wed SEE Church Lane, Birtsmorton Court SE 7m 🖼 Church Lane
☎(01531) 636147 Restaurant: Feathers ☎(01531) 635266

Russells End Caravan Park, Bromsberrow HR8 1PB ☎Ledbury (01531) 650687 OS map
  150/755330 4½m SE of Ledbury on A417 (Gloucester) near junct 2 of M50 Open Mar-Oct, 60
  pitches 🗈🖾🗭❀🗭🗭 £3.00-£6.50

See also Gloucester

LEEK, Staffs   **Map E1**
Pop 19,500. EC Thurs, MD Wed SEE parish church, Nicholson Institute, Prince Charlie's house, 17c
almshouses, Rudyard lake 3m NW, N Staffs Railway Museum 2m S 🖼Market Place ☎(01538)
381000 Restaurant: Flintlock ☎(01538) 361032

Glencote Caravan Park, Churnet Valley, Station Road, Cheddleton ST13 7EE ☎(01538) 360745
  Fax (01538) 361788 OS map 118/982524 3m S of Leek off A520 (Stone) near canal-side pub
  Open Apr-Oct, 6 acres 60 pitches Grass and hard standing, level, sheltered 🗈🖾❀🗭🗭↩🗭
  fishing, barbecue area £9.00 (Mastercard/Visa/Switch)

LICHFIELD, Staffs   **Map E3**
Pop 26,310 EC Wed MD Mon, Fri, Sat SEE cathedral, Birthplace of Dr Samuel Johnson, Museum,
St John's Hospital (almshouses) with church adj 🖼Donegal House, Bore St ☎Lichfield (01543)
252109 Restaurant: George, Bird St ☎(01543) 414822

Willowbrook Farm, Alrewas DE13 7BA ☎(01283) 790217 OS map 128/183157 5m NE of
  Lichfield on E side of (dual carriageway) A38 (Burton on Trent) Open all year 3 acres, level grass,
  20 pitches 🖾❀🗭 Fishing *No showers* £2.50-£4.00

LONGNOR, Staffs   **Map E1**
Pop 300 SEE church, Dovedale E, Manifold Valley S Restaurant: Old Cheshire Cheese, High St
☎(01298) 83218

Longnor Wood Just for Adults Caravan Park, Newtown, Fawfieldhead SK17 0NG *Secluded
  haven for mature tourist* ☎Longnor (01298) 83648 OS map 119/072641 1m SW of Longnor off
  Leek road Open Apr or Easter-Oct 11 acres, grass, part sloping, hard standing 46 pitches (14
  static) 🖎✔🗈🖾🗭❀🗭🗭🗭🗭 putting, croquet, boules £6.00-£12.00

LUDLOW, Shrops   **Map B5**
Pop 8,130. EC Thurs, MD Mon, Fri, Sat SEE castle, old inns, museum, craft centre ⁊Castle Street
⁊Ludlow (01584) 875053 Restaurant: Church Inn, Buttercross ⁊(01584) 872174

Orleton Rise Caravan Park, Green Lane, Orleton SY8 4JE ⁊(01584) 831617 OS map
137/138/477680 5m S of Ludlow off B4361 (Leominster), ½m from Maidenhead Inn Open Mar
14-Oct 31, 104 pitches (87 static)–no tents Level grass and hard standing, sheltered ⌗⌀⊛⌀
£9.50

LYNEAL–see Ellesmere

MALVERN, H and Worcs   **Map D6**
Pop 30,160. EC Wed, MD Fri SEE College, Priory church, St Anne's well, grave of Elgar at Little
Malvern, Malvern Hills ⁊Winter Gardens, Grange Road ⁊(01684) 892289 Restaurant: Cottage in
the Wood 2m S at Malvern Wells ⁊(01684) 573487

Oakmere Caravan Park, Hanley Swan WR8 0DZ ⁊Hanley Swan (01684) 310375 OS map
150/803428 3m SE of Malvern on B4209 (Upton on Severn) Open Easter-Oct 90 pitches (70
static) Hard standings and level grass, sheltered ⌗⌀⊛⌀⊛⌁⌂ £6.50-£8.50

Riverside Caravan Park, Little Clevelode WR13 6PE ⁊Hanley Swan (01684) 310475 OS map
150/832462 3½m E of Malvern on B4424 (Worcester) by River Severn Open Apr-Oct 220 pitches
(140 static) Level grass, sheltered ⌖⌕⌁⌂⌗⌀⊛⌀⊛⌁⌂⌑⌻ fishing, boating, tennis
£6.00 (1999)

See also Tewkesbury and Upton on Severn

MORETON IN MARSH, Glos   **Map E6**
Pop 2,570 EC Wed SEE White Hart Royal Hotel (Charles II associations), Redesdale Hall, old
houses ⁊Council Offices, High St ⁊Moreton in Marsh (01608) 650881 Restaurant: Redesdale
Arms, High St ⁊(01608) 650308

Moreton in Marsh Park (Caravan Club), Bourton Road GL56 0BT ⁊Moreton in Marsh (01608)
650519 (0800-2000 hrs) OS map 151/201323 ½m W of Moreton in Marsh centre on right of A44
(Evesham) Open all year 180 pitches Level grass and hard standing ⌂⌗⌀⊛⌀⊛⌁⌖
£10.20-£14.00

MORTIMERS CROSS, H and Worcs   **Map B5**
Famous as site of decisive battle in Wars of Roses SEE battle museum Restaurant: Angel Inn 2m
SE at Kingsland ⁊(01568) 708355

Pearl Lake Leisure Park, Shobdon HR6 9NQ *Picturesque lakeside park with lovely on-site walks*
⁊(01568) 708326 OS map 149/394623 1m W of Mortimer's Cross on right of B4362 (Presteigne)
Open Mar 1-Jan 7 165 pitches (150 static) Level grass and hard standings ⌂⌗⌀⌀⌁ serviced
pitches, 9 hole golf course, bowling green, 15-acre lake and 20-acre woodland £7.50-£11.00

Shobdon Airfield Touring Park, Shobdon HR6 9NR ⁊(01568) 708369 OS map 149/400610 3m
W of Mortimer's Cross off B4362 (Presteigne) and Pembridge road Open Mar-Oct 3 acres 25
pitches level grass and hard standing ✗⌕⊛ gliding, flying lessons inc microlight £2.00-£5.00
(most cards)

MUCH WENLOCK, Shrops   **Map C3**
Pop 2530 Small town which grew up round priory founded 680 and twice demolished SEE ruined
priory, Guildhall, old houses, Benthall Hall 4m NE, Shipton Hall 6m SW, Corvedale 2m S, Wenlock
Edge SW ⁊Museum, High St ⁊(01952) 727679 Restaurant: George and Dragon, High St
⁊(01952) 727312

Mill Farm, Hughley SY5 6NT ⁊(01746) 785208 OS map 138/563982 4m SW of Much Wenlock off
A458 (Shrewsbury) via Harley Open Mar-Oct–must book peak periods 125 pitches (88 static)
Level grass and hard standing, sheltered ⌂⌗⌀⊛⌀⊛⌑⌻ pony trekking, fishing £7.50

NESSCLIFFE, Shrops   **Map B3**
Pop 300 SEE Earthwork on hill, half-timbered church at Melverley 4m SW on Severn Restaurant:
Old Three Pigeons opp Kynaston Cave ⁊(01743) 741279

Cranberry Moss Camping and Caravan Site, Kinnerley SY10 8DY ⁊Nesscliffe (01743) 741444
OS map 126/365212 2m NW of Nesscliffe off A5 (Oswestry) on left of B4396 (Knockin) Open
Apr-Sept 60 pitches 4 acres level/sloping grass ⌖⌗⌀⊛⌀⌁ £5.75-£7.25

Royal Hill Camping, Edgerley SY10 8ES ⁊Nesscliffe (01743) 741242 OS map 126/352175 2m
SW of Nesscliffe on Melverley road Open Apr-Oct 25 pitches Level grass ⌀⊛⌀⌁⌻ freezer
pack service £4.50

NOTGROVE–see Bourton on the Water

NUNEATON, Warwicks   **Map F4**
Pop 72,000. MD Sat SEE churches, museum, Arbury Hall 3m SW ■ Library, Church Street
✆ Nuneaton (01203) 384027 Restaurant: Railway Tavern, Bond St ✆ (01203) 382015

Wolvey Villa Farm Caravan Camping Park, Wolvey LE10 3HF ✆ (01455) 220493/220630 OS
  map 140/428869 6m SE of Nuneaton off B4114 (Rugby)–Wolvey signed from Junct 2 of M6 and
  Junct 1 of M69 Open all year–must book peak periods 110 pitches Level grass and hard standing
  (winter), sheltered putting green, fishing £6.00-£6.30

OAKAMOOR–see Cheadle

OMBERSLEY, H and Worcs   **Map D5**
Pop 375 SEE timbered cottages and inns, Holt Fleet lock on river Severn W Restaurant: Crown and
Sandys Arms ✆ (01905) 620252

Holt Fleet Farm, Ombersley WR6 6NW ✆ Worcester (01905) 620512 OS map 150/825634 1m W
  of Ombersley off A4133 near Holt Fleet lock by river Severn Open Apr-Oct 338 pitches (188
  static) Level grass lic club £3.75-£6.50

Little Meadow, Lenchford, Shrawley WR6 6TB ✆ (01905) 620246 OS map 150/813643 2m W of
  Ombersley off A443 (Great Witley) on right of B4196 (Stourport) Open Mar 7-Jan 6 72 pitches 5
  acres level grass, sheltered £7.00-£9.00

OSWESTRY, Shrops   **Map A2**
Pop 13,210. EC Thurs, MD Wed SEE parish church, King Oswald's Well, Llwyd Mansion, Offa's
Dyke ■ Mile End Services (A5) ✆ (01691) 662488 and Heritage Centre, The Old School, Church St
✆ (01691) 662753 Restaurant: Wynnstay, Church St ✆ (01691) 655261

Royal Oak, Treflach SY10 9HE ✆ Oswestry (01691) 652455 OS map 126/258254 3m SW of
  Oswestry off A483 (Welshpool) via Trefonen by Offa's Dyke Open Apr-Oct 1 acre, level, 12
  pitches–no adv booking £5.00

PERSHORE, H and Worcs   **Map D6**
Pop 6850 EC Thurs SEE abbey, 14c bridge over river Avon ■ 19 High St ✆ (01386) 554262
Restaurant Angel, High St ✆ (01386) 552046

Eckington Riverside Caravan Park, Eckington WR10 3DD ✆ Pershore (01386) 750985 OS map
  150/922423 2m S of Pershore off A4104 (Upton) on B4080 (Tewkesbury) Open Mar 1-Nov, 85
  pitches (50 static) 5 acres level grass, sheltered fishing £5.00

PETERCHURCH, H and Worcs   **Map A6**
SEE Golden Valley Restaurant: Rhydspence Inn 5m N at Whitney on Wye ✆ (01497) 831262

Bridge Inn, Michaelchurch Escley HR2 0JW ✆ (01981) 510646 OS map 161/317341 5m SW of
  Peterchurch off B4348 (Kingstone) Open Mar-Oct 12 pitches Grass and hard standings
  children's area £7.00 (Mastercard/Visa)

Poston Mill Park, Vowchurch HR2 0SF ✆ Peterchurch (01981) 550225 Fax (01981) 550885 OS
  map 161/356371 1½m SE of Peterchurch on B4348 (Kingstone) Open all year 92 pitches (82
  static) Level grass and hard standings, sheltered serviced
  pitches, TV hookups £7.50-£12.00 (Mastercard/Visa)

REDDITCH, H and Worcs   **Map E5**
Pop 73,000 EC Wed MD daily exc Sun SEE National Needle Museum in Forge Mill, Bordesley
abbey ruins ■ Civic Sq, Alcester St ✆ (01527) 60806 Restaurant: Old Washford Mill 2m S on
B4497 at Washford by river Arrow ✆ (01527) 23068

Outhill Caravan Park, Outhill, Studley B80 7DY ✆ (01527) 852160 OS map 150/107663 3m E of
  Redditch off A4189 (Henley in Arden) on left of Studley road Open Apr-Oct 30 pitches–no tents
  10 acres level grass £3.00

ROSS ON WYE, H and Worcs   **Map C7**
Pop 8,000 EC Wed MD Thurs, Sat SEE House of `Man of Ross', market hall, St Mary's church,
Prospect Walk, Plague Cross, river Wye, Goodrich Castle 3m SW ■ The Swan, Edde Cross St
✆ Ross on Wye (01989) 762768 Restaurant: Orles Barn 1m W at Wilton ✆ (01989) 762155

Broadmeadow Caravan Park, Broadmeadow HR9 7BH ✆ (01989) 768076 Fax (01989) 566030
  OS map 162/607246 On E edge of Ross on Wye, access via Station Approach off Gloucester
  road Open Apr-Oct 150 pitches Level grass and hard standing £12.00-
  £13.00 (all cards)

RUGBY, Warwicks   **Map G5**
Pop 59,040. EC Wed, MD Mon, Fri, Sat Birthplace of football SEE Rugby School, Stanford castle
and park NE 5m ℹ️Public Library St Matthew's St ☎(01788) 535348 Restaurant Three
Horseshoes, Sheep St ☎(01788) 574585

Lodge Farm Caravan Site, Bilton Lane, Long Lawford CV23 9DU ☎Rugby (01788) 560193 OS
   map 140/477749 1½m W of Rugby off A428 (Coventry) at Long Lawford on Bilton Lane Open
   Apr-Oct 35 pitches 5 acres level grass sheltered 🚽🏪⊕♨⛽🛍️ £5.00-£7.00

RUGELEY, Staffs   **Map E3**
Pop 24,400. EC Wed, MD Tues, Thurs, Fri, Sat SEE ruined parish church, market hall, Cannock
Chase 1mW Restaurant: Old Farmhouse 3m SE on A513 at Armitage ☎(01543) 490353

Silvertrees Caravan Park, Stafford Brook Road, Penkridge Bank WS15 2TX ☎Rugeley (01889)
   582185 OS map 128/014172 2m W of Rugeley off A51 (Penkridge) Open Apr-Oct 100 pitches
   (50 static)–no tents 30 acres, level grass and hard standing, sheltered 📻🚽🏪⊕⊘🛍️♨⚡🛍️
   tennis £8.00-£10.00

SHIPSTON ON STOUR, Warwicks   **Map F6**
Pop 3050 EC Thurs Small town on Stour in typical Cotswold countryside Restaurant: White Bear,
High St ☎(01608) 661558

Mill Farm, Long Compton CV36 5NZ ☎(01608) 684663 OS map 151/280332 4m S of Shipston on
   Stour off A34 (Oxford) on Barton on the Heath road Open Easter-Oct 10 pitches 3½ acres level
   grass 🚽⊕ *no showers* £5.00

SHOBDON–see Mortimers Cross

SHREWSBURY, Shrops   **Map B3**
Pop 87,300 EC Thurs, MD Tues, Wed, Fri, Sat SEE abbey church, 15c Grope Lane, St Mary's
church, Roman city of Wroxeter 6m SE, Condover Hall 5m S ℹ️The Square ☎Shrewsbury (01743)
350761 Restaurant: Coach and Horses, Swan Hill ☎(01743) 365661

Bridge Inn, Dorrington SY5 7ED ☎Dorrington (01743) 718209 OS map 126/475037 6m S of
   Shrewsbury on left of A49 (Ludlow) Open all year, 2 acres, 24 pitches Level/sloping grass
   ✖🍴🏪⊕⊘♨🚽♿ £5.00-£7.00

Cartref, Fords Heath SY5 9GD ☎Yockleton (01743) 821688 OS map 126/415116 4m W of
   Shrewsbury on A458 (Welshpool)–signposted from bypass Open May-Oct 35 pitches Level
   grass, sheltered 📻🚽⊕⊘♨♨♿ £6.00-£10.00

Oxon Touring Park, Welshpool Road SY3 5FB ☎(01743) 340868 OS map 126/455138 2m W of
   Shrewsbury off A458 (Welshpool) near junct with A5–follow signs for Oxon Park and Ride Open
   all year 130 pitches with mains services Level grass and hard standing, sheltered
   ⚡📻🚽🏪⊕⊘♨♿ £10.60-£12.60 (all major cards)

Severn House, Montford Bridge SY4 1ED ☎(01743) 850229 OS map 126/435155 4m NW of
   Shrewsbury off A458 (Welshpool) on B4380 (Oswestry) by river Severn Open Apr-Oct 25 pitches
   1¼ acres grass and hard standings, sheltered £5.00-£6.00

SLIMBRIDGE–see Dursley

SOUTHAM, Warwicks   **Map F5**
Pop 1,700 SEE old bridge, 'Mint' House, Grand Union and Oxford Canals Restaurant: Old Mint,
Coventry St (A423) ☎(01926) 812339

Holt Farm CV47 1NJ ☎Southam (01926) 812225 OS map 151/455593 3m SE of Southam off
   Priors Marston road–signposted from A423 bypass Open Mar-Oct 45 pitches 1½ acres level
   grass part sheltered 🏪⊕ £7.00

STAUNTON–see Gloucester

STOKE ON TRENT, Staffs   **Map D2**
Pop 250,000. EC Thurs, MD Wed, Fri, Sat SEE St Peter's church, town hall, Arnold Bennett
museum at Corbridge, Wedgewood, mining and potteries museums, canal by boat ℹ️Potteries
Shopping Centre, Quadrant Rd, Hanley ☎(01782) 284600 Restaurant: Victoria Inn 2m W at
Newcastle under Lyme ☎(01782) 615569

Trentham Gardens, Stone Rd, Trentham ST4 8AX ☎(01782) 657341 OS map 118/863407 4m S
   of Stoke on Trent on right of A34 (Stafford) near junct 15 of M6–signposted Open all year 250
   pitches–bkg advisable 30 acres level wooded meadowland, secluded ⚡✖🍴📻🚽🏪⊕⊘♨♿
   fishing £5.50-£8.50

**There's usually no objection to your walking onto a site to see if you might like it but always
ask permission first. Remember that the person in charge is responsible for safeguarding the
property of those staying there.**

Stratford on Avon Racecourse

1m SW off B439 (Evesham) on Luddington road
Open March-October   250 pitches on level grass

£7.00 a night for two   Tel (01789) 267949
Spring and autumn discounts

STOURPORT, H and Worcs   **Map D5**
Pop 19,050. EC Wed, MD Fri SEE canal basin and locks, caves, nature reserve, Harrington Hall 5m
E Restaurant: Holly Bush Inn, Milton St ☎(01299) 822569

Lickhill Manor Caravan Park DY13 8RL ☎Stourport (01299) 871041 or 822024 OS map
138/797718 ½m W of Stourport off B4195 (Bewdley) on Lickhill road Open all year 240 pitches
(120 static) Level grass and hard standings ▯▯◻⊕◻◻◻◻◻◻◻ fishing £6.00-£10.00
(Mastercard/Visa)

Lincomb Lock Caravan Park, Worcester Road, Titton DY13 9QR ☎Stourport (01299) 823836 OS
map 138/825690 ½m SE of Stourport off A4025 (Worcester) at signs Open Mar-Nov 250 pitches
(118 static)–no tents Level grass, sheltered ▯◻⊕◻◻◻◻ fishing £8.50

Shorthill Caravan Camping Centre, Kidderminster Road, Crossway Green DY13 9SH
☎Hartlebury (01299) 250571 OS map 138/841689 3m SE of Stourport on A449 (Kidderminster-
Worcester) at rear of Little Chef Open all year 25 pitches level grass and hard standing
✕▯◻⊕◻◻◻ £8.00

STOW ON THE WOLD, Glos   **Map E7**
Pop 1,650. EC Wed SEE town hall, St Edward's hall and church, market cross, Cotswold Farm Park
(Guiting Power) ℹHollis House, The Square ☎(01451) 831082 Restaurant: Queens Head, The
Square ☎(01451) 830563

New Inn, Nether Westcote OX7 6SD ☎(01993) 830827 OS map 163/227205 4m SE of Stow on
the Wold off A424 (Burford) on Nether Westcote road Open Apr-Oct 25 pitches
✕♀◻◻▯◻⊕◻ farm produce £7.00-£9.00

STRATFORD ON AVON, Warwicks   **Map E5**
Pop 21,220. EC Thurs, MD Tues, Fri SEE Shakespeare's birthplace (Henley St), Holy Trinity church,
old inns, almshouses, Mary Arden's house at Wilmcote 3m NW, Anne Hathaway's cottage at
Shottery ℹBridgefoot ☎(01789) 293127 Restaurant: White Swan, Rother St ☎(01789) 297022

Avon Park, Warwick Road CV37 0NS ☎Stratford on Avon (01789) 293438 OS map 151/210560
½m NE of Stratford on Avon on A46 (Warwick) Open Mar-Oct 260 pitches (180 static) Level
grass ▮▯◻◻⊕◻ fishing, river launch to Stratford £8.00-£10.00

Dodwell Park, Evesham Road CV37 9ST ☎(01789) 204957 OS map 151/168537 2m SW of
Stratford on Avon on B439 (Bidford) Open all year 50 pitches Grass and hard standings, part
level, part sheltered ▮◻▯▯◻⊕◻◻ £9.00-£10.00 (Mastercard/Visa/Switch)

The Racecourse, Luddington Road CV37 9SE ☎(01789) 267949 OS map 151/187536 1m SW of
Stratford on Avon off B439 (Evesham) Open Mar-Oct 250 pitches Level grass ▯▯⊕◻◻◻
£7.00 (Mastercard/Visa/Switch)

See also Alcester

SYMONDS YAT–see Coleford

TELFORD, Shrops   **Map C3**
Pop 103,000 SEE Ironbridge Gorge (various ex of industrial archaeology) 3m S, Wrekin hill 3m SW
ℹTelford Centre ☎(01952) 291370 Restaurant: Falcon 2m W at Wellington ☎(01952) 255011

Church Farm, Rowton TF6 6QY ☎(01952) 770381 OS map 127/615199 6m NW of Telford on
A442 (Whitchurch) Open all year 12 pitches Level grass, part sheltered ▯⊕◻ children's play
barn, campers' kitchen *No showers* £3.50-£7.00

Severn Gorge Caravan Park, Bridgnorth Road, Tweedale TF7 4JB ☎Telford (01952) 684789 OS
map 127/704052 3m S of Telford off A442 (Bridgnorth) at Tweedale Open all year 10 acres, level
grass and hard standings, secluded woodland, 100 pitches ▮▯▯◻⊕◻◻◻◻◻◻ fishing
£8.50-£10.00 (2000) (most cards)

TENBURY WELLS, H and Worcs   **Map C5**
Pop 2460 EC Thurs MD Tues, Fri SEE Burford House Gardens W, Teme Valley Restaurant:
Peacock Inn 2m E on A456 at Newnham Bridge ☎(01584) 810506

Knighton on Teme Caravan Park, WR15 8NA ☎(01584) 781246 OS map 138/633698 3m E of
  Tenbury Wells off A456 (Bewdley) at Newnham Bridge on Knighton on Teme road Open Mar-Dec
  95 pitches (90 static) Level grass, sheltered ▣🅰⊕∅↩ £6.00-£7.00

Westbrook Park, Little Hereford SY8 9AU ☎(01584) 711280 OS map 138/547680 3m W of
  Tenbury Wells off A456 (Ludlow) on Leysters road by river Teme Open Mar-Oct 50 pitches Level
  grass, sheltered ▣🅰🅰⊕ £6.00

TEWKESBURY, Glos   **Map D6**
Pop 9,550. EC Thurs, MD Wed, Sat SEE Norman abbey, museum, medieval merchants' houses
▮Tewkesbury Museum, 64 Barton Street ☎Tewkesbury (01684) 295027 Restaurant: Black Bear,
High St ☎(01684) 292202

Croft Farm Leisure and Water Park, Bredons Hardwick GL20 7EE ☎Tewkesbury (01684) 772321
  OS map 150/911354 2m NE of Tewkesbury on Bredons Hardwick road (B4080) opp Cross Keys
  Inn Open Mar-Dec 6 acres, part sloping grass and hard standing 76 pitches ✗🝳▣🅰🅰⊕🅖
  ↩🝳 fishing, boating, boardsailing, health and fitness centre £8.00-£10.00 (most cards)

Dawleys Caravan Park, Owls Lane, Shuthonger GL20 6EQ ☎(01684) 292622 OS map
  150/886353 2m N of Tewkesbury off A38 (Worc) Open Mar 16-Oct 31 110 pitches (90 static)
  Level/sloping grass, sheltered ▣🅰⊕∅🅖↩ £6.00-£9.00

Mill Avon Holiday Park, Gloucester Road GL20 5SW ☎Tewkesbury (01684) 296876 OS map
  150/888323 ¼m S of Tewkesbury on A38 (Gloucester), at rear of car park Open Mar-Oct—must
  book public holidays 55 pitches (24 static) Part hard standing, level grass, open ▣🅰🅰⊕∅🝳
  £10.00-£14.00

Sunset View Touring Park, Church End Lane, Twyning GL20 6EH ☎Tewkesbury (01684) 292145
  OS map 150/889357 1½m N of Tewkesbury off A38 (Worcester) near Junction 1 of M50 Open all
  year 45 pitches level grass 🅰🅰⊕∅🝳🝳 horse riding £8.00

Three Counties Caravan Park, Sledge Green, Berrow WR13 6JW ☎Birtsmorton (01684) 833439
  OS map 150/809347 6m W of Tewkesbury on A438 (Ledbury) near bridge under M50 Open Mar
  18-Oct 21 50 pitches Grass, level/sloping, sheltered 🅰⊕∅🝳 £7.75

See also Winchcombe and Upton on Severn

UPTON ON SEVERN, H and Worcs   **Map D6**
Pop 2,260 EC Thurs SEE church, bridge, old houses ▮Pepperpot, Church St ☎(01684) 594200
Restaurant: White Lion, High St ☎(01684) 592551

Anchor Inn, Welland WR13 6LN ☎(01684) 592317 OS map 150/813403 3m W of Upton on
  Severn on A4104 (Little Malvern) in village Open all year. 1 acre level grass 42 pitches
  ✗🝳🅰⊕∅ £6.00-£10.00 (most cards)

UTTOXETER, Staffs   **Map E2**
Pop 11,270. EC Thurs, MD Wed, Sat SEE parish church, racecourse Restaurant: Vaults, Market
Place ☎(01889) 562997

The Racecourse (Caravan Club), Wood Lane ST14 8BD ☎Uttoxeter (01889) 564172 OS map
  128/100330 ½m SE of Uttoxeter off B5017 (Draycott) on Marchington road Open Mar 17-Nov 15,
  83 pitches 3 acres level grass ▣🅰🅰⊕∅🅖↩🝳 £8.70-£12.65 (inc free racing) (1999)
  (Mastercard/Visa)

WARWICK, Warwicks   **Map F5**
Pop 21,930. EC Thurs, MD Sat County town founded in Saxon times on spur above river Avon
SEE 14c castle, Lord Leycester's Hospital, St Mary's church ▮Court House, 2 Jury Street
☎Warwick (01926) 492212 Restaurant: Woolpack, Market Pl ☎(01926) 496191

The Racecourse (Caravan Club), Hampton Street CV34 6HA ☎Warwick (01926) 495448 OS map
  151/277647 ½m W of Warwick off A429 (Stratford) on B4095 (Henley) Open Apr-Nov
  55 pitches—no tents Level grass and hard standing ▣ 🝳 £13.40-£15.25 (all cards)

The Racecourse, Hampton Street CV34 6HN ☎Warwick (01926) 495448 OS map 151/277645
  ¼m SW of Warwick centre on right of B4095 (Henley) in centre of racecourse Open Mar-Nov 60
  pitches 2 acres level grass and hard standings 🅰🅰⊕∅↩🝳 £6.70-£7.50

WELLAND—see Upton on Severn

WEM, Shrops   **Map B2**
SEE parish church, Lowe Hall Restaurant: Grange 6m W at Ellesmere ☎(01691) 623495
Lower Lacon Caravan Park, Lower Lacon SY4 5RP ☎Wem (01939) 232376 OS map 126/532302
  1m NE of Wem on B5065 (Prees) Open all year, 270 pitches (50 static) Level grass and hard
  standing, sheltered (35) café £10.50-£11.00 (all cards)

WENTNOR, Shrops   **Map B4**
Pop 320 SEE Long Mynd 1m E, Linley Woods W Restaurant: Crown Inn ☎(01588) 640613
Cwnd House Farm, SY9 5EQ ☎(01588) 650237 OS map 137/383950 1½m NE of Wentnor off
  Bridges road Open May-Oct 10 pitches level grass £6.00
Green Caravan and Camping Park SY9 5EF ☎Linley (01588) 650605 OS map 137/382933 ½m
  NW of Wentnor at The Green on Bridges road Open Easter-Oct 140 pitches Level grass and
  hard standing, sheltered £6.50 (Mastercard/Visa)

WHITCHURCH, Shrops   **Map C7**
Pop 7,240. EC Wed, MD Fri SEE parish church (with tomb of John Talbot in porch), almshouses
  ℹ Civic Centre, High Street ☎Whitchurch (01948) 664577 Restaurant: Willey Moor Lock Tavern,
  Tarporley Rd (A49) ☎(01948) 663274
Brook House Farm, Grindley Brook, SY13 4QJ ☎Whitchurch (01948) 664557 OS map
  117/526425 1m N of Whitchurch on A41 (Chester) Open Mar-Nov 25 pitches Level grass,
  sheltered £4.00-£6.00
Green Lane Farm Caravan Park, Prees SY13 2AH ☎Whitchurch (01948) 840460 OS map
  126/568347 4½m SE of Whitchurch off A41-A442 (Telford) on Prees road Open Mar-Oct 20
  pitches 3 acres level grass sheltered £6.00-£9.00

WINCHCOMBE, Glos   **Map E7**
Pop 4,790. EC Thurs SEE St Peter's church, Belas Knap long barrow, Sudeley Castle S ℹ Town
Hall ☎Cheltenham (01242) 602925 Restaurant: White Hart, High St ☎(01242) 602359
Brooklands Farm Touring Caravan Park, Alderton GL20 8NX ☎Alderton (01242) 620259 OS
  map 150/015322 2m N of Winchcombe on B4077 (Tewkesbury-Stow on the Wold) Open Mar-Jan
  80 pitches 10 acres level grass and hard standing, sheltered, by lake games
  room, dog walk, coarse fishing, skittle alley £6.50-£9.75

WOLVEY–see Nuneaton

WOODMANCOTE–see Cheltenham

WORCESTER, H and Worcs   **Map D6**
Pop 75,000. EC Thurs, MD Wed, Fri, Sat Industrial town cut in two by river Severn, here a navigable
waterway SEE Cathedral, Commandery, Guildhall, 15c Greyfriars, Royal Porcelain Works, Elgar
museum 2m NW at Broadheath ℹ Guildhall, High St ☎Worcester (01905) 723471 Restaurant:
Star, Foregate St ☎(01905) 24308
Coppice Leisure Park, Ockeridge Wood, Wichenford WR6 6YP ☎(018866) 888305 OS map
  150/791625 8m NW of Worcester off A443 (Tenbury) Open Mar 1-Jan 6 150 pitches (138
  static)–no tents lic club £6.50
Court Meadow Caravan Park, Kempsey WR5 3JL ☎Worcester (01905) 820295 OS map
  150/848495 2m S of Worcester off A38 (Tewkesbury) at Kempsey Open all year 150 pitches (85
  static)–no tents Grass and hard standings slipway, moorings £5.00-£7.50
Mill House, Hawford WR3 7SE ☎Worcester (01905) 451283 OS map 150/847601 3½m N of
  Worcester on A449 (Kidderminster) near river bridge Open Easter-Oct 150 pitches 10 acres level
  grass fishing £6.00
See also Ombersley

7 East Anglia

East Anglia is composed of Norfolk, Suffolk, Essex and Cambridgeshire, the last increased in size since it absorbed the former Huntingdonshire.

Beyond the metropolitan area southernmost Essex has a varied landscape of field and river and a deeply indented coast line. The mudflats of the deep river estuaries, the habitat of many species of wildfowl, give way to sandy beaches at Southend, Clacton and Frinton. Highlights of inland Essex are the glades and uplands of Epping Forest, the villages of the Rodings, the town of Saffron Walden, the most attractive in the county, and ancient Colchester, oldest recorded town in Britain. There are also the stately homes of Audley End and Steeple Bumpstead, the pretty villages of Finchingfield, Cavendish and Newport and the churches of Greensted and Thaxted. A long distance footpath, the Essex Way, runs for fifty-five miles from Epping to Dedham.

The secretive charm of rural Suffolk, with its moated farmhouses, can be discovered in the Constable country around East Bergholt near the Essex border and the ancient wool district around Lavenham. Uncommercialized resorts along the constantly-eroded coastline include charming Aldeburgh and Southwold and Dunwich, slowly being devoured by the sea.

North Norfolk is best known for its Broads between Norwich and Yarmouth, a sprawling network of rivers and shallow reed fringed lakes formed from age-old peat diggings. Popular centres for cruising on the Broads are Hickling, Potter Heigham and Wroxham. Important nature reserves line the coast between the attractive resorts of Cromer and Hunstanton on the Wash, notably on the saltings east of Wells. Also on the Wash is the graceful port of King's Lynn. Thetford Forest, spilling over into Suffolk, encloses the wild heaths of Breckland, but the neolithic flint mines of Grimes Graves are definitely in Norfolk. Antique Norwich has a wealth of historic buildings and a long tradition of immigration from the Low Countries. Two walkers' routes in Norfolk are the ancient roads of Peddars Way and Icknield Way. Important buildings include the abbey church of Wymondham, the ruined fortress of Castle Rising where Edward III imprisoned his mother Isabella, and the stately homes of Felbrigg Blickling, Oxburgh and Holkham.

Cambridgeshire encloses part of the Great Fen, marshland which until reclaimed from the sea stretched from Lincoln to Cambridge. The heart of Fenland is the Isle of Ely, its great cathedral like a tall ship in the flat landscape. Here sections of the original marshland have been preserved in their primeval state at Wood Walton Fen and Wicken Fen. Northwest of Cambridge the 60ft high Devil's Dyke bisects the equally old Icknield Way. Major sights in Cambridge itself are the medieval King's and Trinity Colleges and the Backs by the river Cam. The superb Norman cathedral of Peterborough is worth a detour, as are the country houses of Wimpole and Hinchingbrooke and the pretty villages of Alconbury, Grantchester and Haslingfield.

The greatest concentrations of campsites are at the popular coast resorts, with less of a choice in the Broads, the Essex estuaries and inland Suffolk. Amenities are not usually extensive, even on the coast.

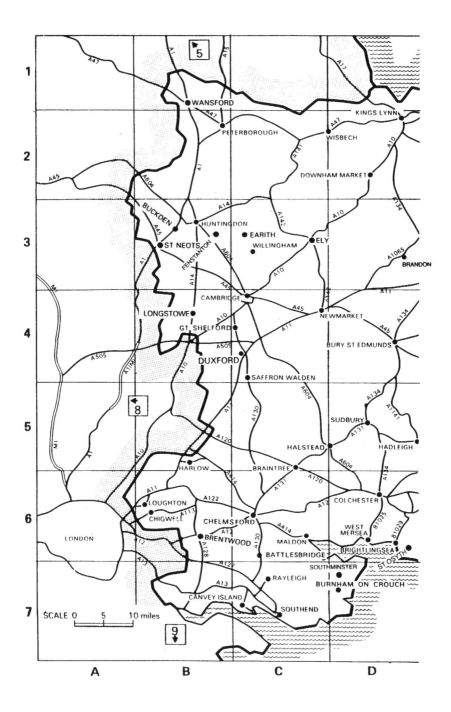

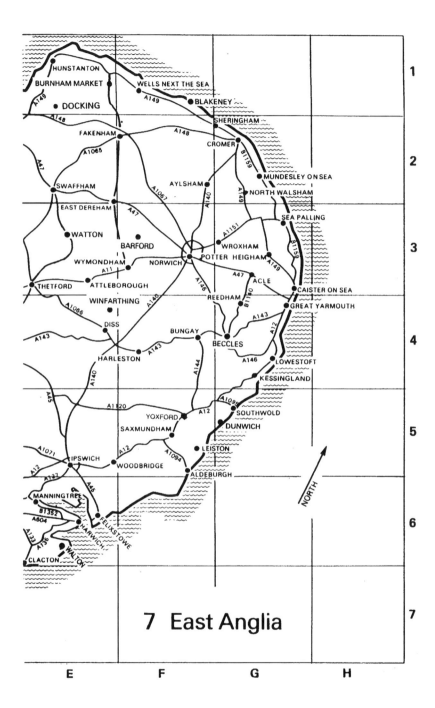

7 East Anglia

ACLE, Norfolk   **Map G3**
Pleasant market town near river Bure Restaurant: Bridge by river Bure ☎(01493) 750288

Broad Farm Camping, Main Road, Burgh St Margaret NR29 3AF ☎(01493) 369273 OS map
134/446142 3m NE of Acle off A1064 (Caister on Sea) Open Easter-Sept 500 pitches Level
grass ⚓✗♀⊶🗑🔌⌀🖵 (heated) ✪❀ £5.00-£12.00

Bureside Holiday Park, Boundary Farm, Oby NR29 3BW ☎(01493) 369233 OS map 134/405151
3m N of Acle off B1152 (Martham) Open Whitsun-Sept 175 pitches Level grass ⚓🗑⌀🖵
(heated) ↙ boating (slipway) fishing lake £7.00

Clippesby Holidays, Clippesby NR29 3BL ☎(01493) 367800 OS map 134/423144 3m NE of Acle
off A1064 (Caister) and B1152 (Martham) Open May-Sept, 100 pitches 34 acres, level grass,
sheltered ⚓✗♀🗑🔌⌀⊕∅🖵 (heated) ✪↙🚽♿ putting, tennis, bowls £8.50-£15.75 (most
cards)

ALDEBURGH, Suffolk   **Map F5**
Pop 2,910. EC Wed Quiet unspoiled resort with long pebble beach SEE church with memorial to
George Crabbe, 16c Moot Hall ℹ The Cinema, High St ☎(01728) 453637 Restaurant: White Lion,
Market Pl ☎(01728) 452720

Church Farm Caravan Site, Thorpeness Road IP15 5BH ☎Aldeburgh (01728) 453433 OS map
156/463569 ¼m N of Aldeburgh off A1094 (Snape) Open Apr-Oct 112 pitches Grass, level, open
⌀🚍 farm produce £2.00-£3.00

ATTLEBOROUGH, Norfolk   **Map E3**
Pop 6,000. EC Wed, MD Thurs SEE parish church, Attleborough Hall Restaurant: Griffin, Church St
☎(01953) 452149

Applewood, Banham Zoo, The Grove, Banham NR16 2HE ☎Quidenham (01953) 888370 OS map
144/058876 5m S of Attleborough on B1113 (Stowmarket) Open all year 100 pitches 8 acres
level grass ⚓✗♀⊶⤳🗑🔌⌀⊕∅↙🍴♿ farm shop £8.50-£10.00 (most cards)

Oak Tree Caravan Park, Norwich Road NR17 2JX ☎Attleborough (01953) 455565 OS map
144/057690 ½m NE of Attleborough on old A11 (Norwich) Open all year, 30 pitches 3 acres, level
grass 🔌⌀⊕ £6.50-£7.50

AYLSHAM, Norfolk   **Map F2**
Pop 4,800, EC Wed, MD Mon, Fri SEE Blickling Hall 1½m NW Restaurant: Rising Sun 3m SE at
Coltishall ☎(01603) 737440

Haveringland Hall Park,Cawston NR10 4PN ☎(01603) 871302 OS map 133/156214 4m SW of
Aylsham off B1145 (Cawston) Open Apr-Oct 100 pitches (60 static) 25 acres grass, level,
sheltered 🗑🔌⌀⊕∅🍴🚍♿ fishing by permit in 12 acre lake, woodland walks £7.80-£9.50

Landguard House, Erpingham NR11 7QB ☎(01263) 761219 OS map 133/204324 4m N of
Aylsham on Erpingham rd Open Apr-Oct 25 pitches 1½ acres, mainly level grass ✗ (snack)
♀🔌 £3.50

Top Farm, Marsham NR10 5QF ☎Aylsham (01263) 732282 OS map 133/182244 2m SW of
Aylsham off A140 (Norwich-Cromer) and Cawston road Open all year, 25 pitches 5 acres level
grass, sheltered 🔌⊕ No showers £2.50-£5.00

BACTON—see Mundesley

BARFORD, Norfolk   **Map F3**
SEE abbey and market cross at Wymondham 3m S Restaurant: Abbey 3m S at Wyndmondham
☎(01953) 602148

Swans Harbour, Barford Road, Marlingford NR9 4BE ☎(01603) 759658 OS map 144/123086 1m
NE of Barford on left of Marlingford road beyond river bridge Open all year 25 pitches 4 acres
level grass, sheltered 🔌⊕⌀✪ £5.50

BATTLESBRIDGE, Essex   **Map C6**
Restaurant: Barge, Hawk Hill ☎ (01268) 732622

Hayes Farm Caravan Park, Hayes Chase, Burnham Road SS11 7QT ☎ (01245) 320309 OS map 167/788957 2m NE of Battlesbridge off A130 (Chelmsford) on A132 (South Woodham Ferrers) Open Apr-Oct 389 pitches (314 static)–no tents–no adv booking 26 acres level grass, sheltered ▧▧▧▧▧▧▧▧▧▧ club, dancing £8.00-£11.00

BECCLES, Suffolk   **Map G4**
Pop 8.900 EC Wed MD Fri Georgian town on Waveney once busy river port SEE church, East Anglia Transport Museum 5m E ▧ The Quay, Fen Lane ☎ (01502) 713196 Restaurant: Kings Head, New Market ☎ (01502) 712147

Waveney Lodge, Elms Road, Toft Monks NR34 0EJ ☎ Aldeby (01502) 677445 OS map 134/434937 2½m NE of Beccles off A146 (Norwich), A143 (Great Yarmouth) and Aldeby road Open Mar-Oct 15 pitches Level grass, sheltered ▧▧▧▧▧ £7.00

Waveney River Centre, Staithe, Burgh St Peter NR34 0BT ☎ Aldeby (01502) 677343 OS map 134/491934 6m NE of Beccles off A143 (Great Yarmouth) via Burgh St Peter, at Staithe, by river Waveney Open Mar-Oct, 100 pitches (40 static) 20 acres level grass ▧▧▧▧▧▧▧▧▧▧▧ fishing, boating, sauna, solarium, day boat hire, gym, spa bath £8.00-£9.00

BELTON–see Great Yarmouth

BRANDON, Suffolk   **Map D3**
Pop 6,960. EC Wed, MD Thurs, Sat SEE 15c bridge, St Peter's church Restaurant: Brandon House, High St ☎ (01842) 810171

Warren House Caravan Park, Brandon Road, Methwold IP26 4RL ☎ (01366) 728238 OS map 143/46931 4m NW of Brandon on B1112 (Methwold) Open Mar-Oct–must book public holidays 40 pitches *No showers* £3.50

BRENTWOOD, Essex   **Map B6**
Pop 72,800 EC Thurs SEE RC cathedral, old White Hart inn ▧ Old House, Shenfield Rd ☎ (01277) 200300 Restaurant: Post House, Brook St ☎ (01277) 210888

Warren Lane Park (Camping Club), Frog Street, Kelvedon Hatch CM15 0JG ☎ Coxtie Green (01277) 372773 OS map 167/577976 2m N of Brentwood off A128 (Chipping Ongar) Open Mar-Oct 90 pitches 12 acres, level grass and hard standings, sheltered ▧▧▧▧▧▧▧▧ £10.60-£13.90

BRIGHTLINGSEA, Essex   **Map D6**
Modest resort in loop of river Colne a short way from sea Restaurant: Railway Tavern, Station Rd (off B1029 near Waterfront) ☎ (01206) 302581

Lakeside Touring Caravan Park, Promenade Way CO7 0HH ☎ (01206) 303421 OS map 168/082164 ½m SW of Brightlingsea centre off road to Westmarsh Point Open Mar-Oct 270 pitches (240 static) ▧▧▧ £6.00

BUCKDEN, Cambs   **Map B3**
Pop 2,670 SEE church, bishop's palace, old posting inns, Grafham Water 1m W Restaurant: Lion, High Street ☎ (01480) 810313

Old Manor Caravan Park, Grafham PE18 0BB ☎ Huntingdon (01480) 810264 OS map 153/155695 2m NW of Buckden off B661 (West Perry) Open Mar-Oct 92 pitches (8 static) 6 acres level grass ▧▧▧▧▧▧▧ (heated) ▧▧▧ £10.00-£12.00 (most cards)

BUNGAY, Suffolk   **Map F4**
Pop 4,100. EC Wed, MD Thurs Georgian town in loop of river Waveney SEE castle ruins, churches, market cross, aviation museum 3m SW Restaurant: Green Dragon, Broad St ☎ (01986) 892681

Outney Meadow Caravan Park, Outney Meadow NR35 1HG ☎ Bungay (01986) 892338 OS map 134/333905 ¼m N of Bungay off A143 (Great Yarmouth) on Outney Common Open all year 45 pitches Grass, level, part sheltered ▧▧▧▧▧▧▧▧ boating, canoe hire, fishing £7.50-£12.00

BURGH CASTLE–see Great Yarmouth

BURNHAM MARKET, Norfolk   **Map E1**
Pop 850 SEE St Mary's church, windmill, Burnham Thorpe (birthplace of Nelson) and church 1m SE Restaurant: Fishes, Market Place ☎ (01328) 738588

Burnham Market Caravan Park, Back Lane PE31 8EY ☎ (01485) 570595 OS map 132/832428 ½m N of Burnham Market centre off B1355 (Burnham Norton) Open Apr-Oct – no adv booking 30 pitches Grass, level, sheltered ▧ £5.00

BURNHAM ON CROUCH, Essex   **Map D7**
Pop 6,500, EC Wed SEE St Mary's church Restaurant: Olde White Harte, The Quay ☏(01621)
782106
Creeksea Place Caravan Park, Ferry Road CM0 8PJ ☏(01621) 782387/782675 OS map
168/935962 ½m W of Burnham off B1010 (Althorne) Open Mar-Nov 150 pitches (100 static)
Level grass sheltered 🛆🛆🛆🛆🛆🛆🛆🛆🛆 fishing lake £4.50-£12.00

BURWELL–see Newmarket

BURY ST EDMUNDS, Suffolk   **Map D4**
Pop 30,550, EC Thurs SEE abbey, St Mary church (Angel roof) ⊞6 Angel Hill ☏(01284) 764667
Restaurant: Angel, Angel Hill ☏(01284) 753926
The Dell Caravan Camping Park, Beyton Road, Thurston IP31 3RB ☏(01284) 270121 Fax
(01359) 270121 OS map 155/930650 5m E of Bury St Edmunds off A14 (Ipswich) at Thurston
Open all year 60 pitches 5 acres level grass and hard standing, part sheltered
🛆🛆🛆🛆🛆🛆🛆🛆🛆 £8.50

CAISTER ON SEA, Norfolk   **Map G3**
Pop 6,490, EC Wed SEE ruined Caister castle, motor museum Restaurant: Ship, Victoria St
☏(01493) 728008
California Cliffs Caravan Park, California, Ormesby NR29 3QU ☏(01493) 730584 OS map
134/518148 1½m N of Caister off B1159 (Winterton on Sea) near beach Open Apr-Sept–must
book peak periods 690 pitches 🛆🛆🛆🛆🛆🛆 lic club £2.95-£5.40 + VAT (inc showers)
The Grange Touring Park, Ormesby St Margaret NR29 3QG ☏(01493) 730306 OS map
134/512143 1m N of Caister at junction of A149 (North Walsham) and B1159 (Winterton) Open
Apr-Sept 70 pitches Grass, level, sheltered 🛆🛆🛆🛆🛆🛆🛆🛆 £7.00-£10.00
Grasmere Caravan Park, Bultitudes Loke NR30 5DH ☏(01493) 720382 OS map 134/522117 ½m
S of Caister off A149 (Great Yarmouth) near stadium Open Apr 1-Oct 15, 109 pitches (63 static)
5 acres level grass and hard standing 🛆🛆🛆🛆🛆🛆🛆🛆🛆 £5.85-£8.10 (all cards)
Green Farm Caravan Park, Beach Road, Scratby, California NR29 3NW ☏(01493) 730440 OS
map 134/512155 3m N of Caister off A149 (North Walsham) and B1159 (Hembsby) Open Mar-
Nov 250 pitches Level grass 🛆🛆🛆🛆🛆🛆🛆🛆🛆 (indoor) 🛆🛆🛆🛆 £10.00-£12.00
Long Beach Estate Caravan Park, Hemsby NR29 4JD ☏(01493) 730023 OS map 134/503178
4m NNW of Caister off B1159 (Winterton on Sea) Open Apr-Oct 200 pitches (120 static) Grass,
level, part sheltered 🛆🛆🛆🛆🛆🛆 (£30) 🛆🛆🛆🛆 club room, private beach £6.50-£11.00
Newport Caravan-Camping Park, Hemsby NR29 4NW ☏(01493) 730405 OS map 134/502169
3m N of Caister off B1159) (Hemsby) Open Apr-Oct 270 pitches (180 static) Level grass
sheltered 🛆🛆🛆🛆🛆🛆🛆 lic club £6.50-£9.00
Old Hall Leisure Park, High Street NR30 5JL ☏(01493) 720400 OS map 134/518124 ¼m N of
Caister centre on A149 (North Walsham) Open Apr-Oct 81 pitches Grass, level sheltered
🛆🛆🛆🛆🛆 (heated)🛆🛆 £2.50-£6.50
Scratby Hall Caravan Park, Scratby NR29 3PH ☏(01493) 730283 OS map 134/502155 3m N of
Caister off B1159 (Hemsby) Open Easter-Oct 15, 108 pitches Grass, level, sheltered
🛆🛆🛆🛆🛆🛆🛆🛆🛆🛆 £4.95-£10.50
Sundowner Holiday Park, Newport Road, Hemsby NR29 4NW ☏(01493) 730159/731554 OS map
134/501168 3m N of Caister off A149 (Stalham) and B1159 (Mundesley) on Newport road Open
Apr-Sept 100 pitches Grass, level, part sheltered 🛆🛆🛆🛆🛆🛆🛆🛆🛆🛆🛆 £6.00-£11.00

CAMBRIDGE, Cambs   **Map C4**
Pop 101,000. MD daily Charming university city on river SEE Colleges and garden, bridges,
Fitzwilliam museum, King's College chapel, botanic garden ⊞Wheeler Street ☏Cambridge (01223)
322640 Restaurant: Cambridge Blue, Gwydir St ☏(01223) 361382
Highfield Farm Touring Park, Long Road, Comberton CB3 7DG ☏Cambridge (01223) 262308 OS
map 154/389572 4¼m WSW of Cambridge off A1303-A428 (St Neots) on Comberton road–from
M11 junct 12 via A603 (Sandy) and B1046 (Comberton) Open Apr-Oct 120 pitches 8 acres level
grass and hard standing, sheltered 🛆🛆🛆🛆🛆🛆🛆 battery charging, freezer pack service, cycle
hire £7.75-£9.00
Travellers Rest Caravan Site, Chittering CB5 9PH ☏Cambridge (01223) 860751 OS map
154/700499 8m NE of Cambridge on A10 (Ely) Open Apr-Sept 40 pitches Grass, level, sheltered
🛆🛆🛆🛆 bar meals £6.00

CANVEY ISLAND, Essex   Map C7
Pop 33,840. EC Thurs, MD Sat SEE Dutch Cottage museum, Lobster Smack inn, nature reserve
Restaurant: Pipe of Port 6m E at Southend on Sea ☎(01702) 614606

Kings Park, Hindles Road SS8 8HE ☎Canvey Island (01268) 511555 OS map 178/816835 ½m W
of Canvey Island off B1014 (South Benfleet) Open Mar-Oct 450 pitches (250 static)
⬛✗♀⬛⬛⬛⬛⬛⬛⬛⬛⬛⬛ night club, fishing lake £8.00

CHITTERING—see Cambridge

CLACTON ON SEA, Essex   Map E6
Pop 43,590. EC Wed, MD Tues, Sat SEE Norman church, Martello Tower, St Osyth's Priory 3m W
🅸Pier Avenue ☎(01255) 423400 Restaurant: King's Cliff 1m NE at Holland on Sea ☎(01255)
812343

Ashley Holiday Park, London Rd, Little Clacton CO16 9RN ☎(01255) 860200 OS map
169/165189 2m N of Clacton on left of A133 (Colchester) Open Mar 1-Oct 15 125 pitches
♀⬛⬛⬛⬛⬛⬛ £6.00-£8.00 inc elect

Highfield Holiday Park, London Rd CO16 9QY ☎(01255) 424244 OS map 169/166178 2m N of
Clacton on A133 (Colchester) Open Easter-Oct 725 pitches (400 static)–no tents 45 acres grass,
gentle slope ⬛✗♀⬛⬛⬛⬛⬛⬛⬛⬛⬛⬛⬛⬛⬛⬛ £8.00-£17.00 (most cards)

Silver Dawn Touring Park, Jaywick Lane CO16 8BB ☎Clacton (01255) 421856 OS map
168/150153 3m W of Clacton off B1027 (Colchester) Open Easter-Oct 15–adv booking preferred
86 pitches (56 static)–no tents ♀⬛ paddling pool, lic club £7.00-£10.00

Tower Caravan Park, Jaywick CO15 2LF *Resort's only site by the sea* ☎Clacton (01255) 820372
OS map 168/132136 2½m SW of Clacton at Jaywick Sands Open Apr-Oct 625 pitches (525
static) Grass, level, open ⬛✗♀⬛⬛⬛⬛⬛⬛⬛⬛⬛⬛⬛ lic club, cafe £9.00-£10.00

Weeley Bridge Caravan Park, Weeley CO16 9DH ☎Weeley (01255) 830403 OS map 168/147219
5½m NNW of Clacton on A133 (Weeley) near station Open Mar 27-Oct 11, 90 pitches–no tents
Grass, level, open ⬛⬛⬛⬛ (65) £6.00

See also St Osyth

CLIPPESBY—see Acle

COLCHESTER, Essex   Map D6
Pop 140,000. EC Thurs, MD Tues, Sat Oldest recorded town in England, now thriving regional
centre SEE Colchester and Essex museum, Roman Walls, St Martin's church, oyster fisheries,
Bourne mill 🅸Queen St ☎Colchester (01206) 712920 Restaurant: George, High St ☎(01206)
578494

Colchester Camping Caravan Park, Cymbeline Way CO3 4AG ☎Colchester (01206) 545551 OS
map 168/971255 1m W of Colchester near junction of A12 (Chelmsford) and A133 (town
centre)–signposted Open all year 251 pitches Grass and hard standing, level, part sheltered
⬛⬛⬛⬛⬛⬛⬛⬛⬛⬛⬛ mini golf, caravan/m-home wash £7.00-£12.30 (Mastercard/Visa)

Mill Farm, Harwich Road, Great Bromley CO7 7JQ ☎(01206) 250485 OS map 168/076246 4m E
of Colchester on A604 (Harwich) via Elmstead Market Open Mar-Oct, 40 pitches 4 acres, gentle
slope ⬛ £4.00

Seven Arches Farm, Lexden CO3 5SX ☎(01206) 574896 OS map 168/969255 2m W of
Colchester off A604 on old Halstead road by level crossing Open all year 12 pitches Level grass,
sheltered £6.00

CROMER, Norfolk   **Map G2**
Pop 6,200. EC Wed SEE 14c church, lifeboat museum, Birdland, lighthouse █ Bus Stn, Prince of Wales Rd ☎ Cromer (01263) 512497 Restaurant: Bath House, The Promenade ☎ (01263) 514260

Forest Park Caravan Site, Northrepps Road NR27 0JR ☎ Cromer (01263) 513290 OS map 133/233405 1½m SE of Cromer off B1159 (Mundesley) Open Apr-Oct 801 pitches (325 static) Grass, part level (heated indoor) clubhouse, bar meals, woodland walks £6.50-£10.00

Manor Farm Caravan and Tent Site, East Runton NR27 9PR ☎ Cromer (01263) 512858 OS map 133/198418 1½m W of Cromer off A148 (Holt) on East Runton road Open Easter-Oct–no motor cycles 200 pitches Level/sloping grass, sheltered £7.50-£9.00

Seacroft Camping Park, Runton Road NR27 9NJ ☎ Cromer (01263) 511722 OS map 133/199426 ½m W of Cromer on A149 (Sheringham) near beach Open Easter-Oct 120 pitches 5 acres level grass, pitches screened by shrubs, sheltered £6.50-£10.50

Woodhill Caravan and Camping Park, East Runton NR27 9PX ☎ Cromer (01263) 512242 OS map 133/197428 1m W of Cromer on A149 (Sheringham) Open Easter-Sept 394 pitches (132 static) Grass and hard standings, part level, part open £7.45-£10.35 (most cards)

DEREHAM–see East Dereham

DISS, Norfolk   **Map E4**
Pop 5,690. EC Tues, MD Fri SEE St Mary's church, Diss Mere, 17c Scole Inn 2m E █ Meres Mouth, Mere St ☎ (01379) 650523 Restaurant: Greyhound, Nicholas St ☎ (01379) 651613

Honeypot Camp and Caravan Park, Wortham IP22 1PW ☎ Diss (01379) 783312 OS map 144/086771 3m SW of Diss on A143 (Bury St Edmunds) at Wortham Open Apr-Sept 35 pitches (some at lakeside) Grass, level, sheltered freezer pack service, fishing £8.50 (inc hot water)

Willows Camping Caravan Park, Diss Road, Scole IP21 4DH ☎ Diss (01379) 740271 OS map 144/147788 1½m E of Diss on A1066 (Scole) beside river Waveney Open May-Sept 35 pitches Grass, level, sheltered £7.50 (inc hot water)

See also Harleston

DOCKING, Norfolk   **Map E1**
Restaurant: Pilgrims' Reach ☎ (01485) 518383

Garden Caravan Site, Barmer Hall, Syderstone PE31 8SR *Secluded site in walled garden* ☎ (01485) 578220 OS map 132/810335 3m SE of Docking on B1454 (Fakenham) Open Mar-Nov 33 pitches Level/sloping grass, sheltered TV hook-up £8.00

The Rickells, Bircham Road, Stanhoe PE31 8PU ☎ Docking (01485) 518671 OS map 132/793353 1½m SE of Docking on right of B1454 (Fakenham) near junct with B1155 (Stanhoe-Great Bircham) Open Mar 15-Oct 31, 30 pitches Level/sloping grass, sheltered £7.00-£8.50

DOWNHAM MARKET, Norfolk   **Map D2**
Pop 4,600. EC Wed, MD Fri, Sat SEE parish church Restaurant: Castle, High St ☎ (01366) 382157

Woodlakes Leisure, Holme Rd, Stowbridge PE34 3PX ☎ (01553) 810414 OS map 143/617075 3m N of Downham Market off A10 (Kings Lynn) and Stowbridge road Open Mar-Oct 100 pitches 66 acres of woods and lakes, level grass, sheltered fishing, woodland walks £8.00-£13.00

DUNWICH, Suffolk   **Map G5**
Pop 800 SEE museum, Minsmere nature reserve, Dunwich forest, Blythburgh church 3m NW Restaurant: Ship Inn, St James' Street ☎ (01728) 648219

Cliff House, Minsmere Road IP17 3DQ ☎ (01728) 648282 OS map 156/477688 1m S of Dunwich centre on coast road adj bird sanctuary Open Apr-Oct 200 pitches (93 static) booking advisable 30 acres, grass and hard standings, sheltered, level woodland beach access £10.00-£14.00 (most cards)

DUXFORD, Cambs   **Map C4**
Pop 1,690 SEE 15c St Peter's church, Duxford chapel, Imperial War museum (RAF) Restaurant: Duxford Lodge, Ickleton Road ☎ (01223) 836444

Appleacre Park, London Road, Fowlmere SG8 7RU ☎ (01763) 208354/208229 OS map 154/422452 3m W of Duxford off A505 (Royston) on Fowlmere read near junct 10 of M11 Open all year 20 pitches 3 acres level grass, sheltered £4.50-£7.00

Westview Marina

High Street, Earith, Cambs PE17 3PN
☎ 01487 841627

*A rural site with lovely walks along banks of river Ouse,
between St Ives and Ely on Huntingdon road A1123*

EARITH, Cambs   **Map C3**
SEE New Bedford River, dug in 17c at start of reclamation of Fens Restaurant: Slepe Hall 3m W at
St Ives ☎(01480) 463122
Westview Marina, High Street, Earith PE17 3PN ☎(01487) 841627 OS map 142/143/382750 ¼m
  W of Earith centre on left of A1123 (Huntingdon) by river Great Ouse Open Apr-Oct, 28 pitches
  Level grass, sheltered ▯◗⊕⊡ £7.00

EAST BERGHOLT–see Hadleigh

EAST RUNTON–see Cromer

ELY, Cambs   **Map C3**
Pop 10,260 EC Tues MD Thurs SEE Cathedral, Bishop's Palace, Ely Porta school, Monks' Granary
(15c), St Mary's church, Museums, Brass Rubbing Centre ▊Oliver Cromwells House, St Mary's St
☎(01353) 662062 Restaurant: Prince Albert, Silver St ☎(01353) 663494
Riverside Caravan Camping Park, New River Bank, Littleport CB7 4TA ☎(01353) 860255 OS
  map 143/577858 3m N of Ely off A10 (Littleport) near river Great Ouse Open Mar-Oct, 64 pitches
  (24 static) 2½ acres, mainly level ▮◗⊕▣ boating, fishing £5.00-£6.00

FAKENHAM, Norfolk   **Map F2**
Pop 5,800. EC Wed, MD Thurs SEE parish church, ruins of Walsingham Abbey 4m N ▊Red Lion
House, Market Place ☎(01328) 851981 Restaurant: Crown, Market Pl ☎(01328) 872010
Little Snoring Caravan Camping Park, Holt Road, Little Snoring NR21 0AX ☎Thursford (01328)
  878335 OS map 132/962322 3m NE of Fakenham on A148 (Cromer) Open all year 30 pitches
  Hard standings and grass, level, sheltered ▚▯▣◗⊕∅▣ (25), sauna, spa bath, sunbed £6.00-
  £9.50
Fakenham Racecourse NR21 7NY ☎Fakenham (01328) 862388 OS map 132/916287 1m SE of
  Fakenham on A1065 (Swaffham) Open all year 100 pitches Grass and hard standings, level,
  sheltered ▚✕⬥↗▯▣◗⊕∅◻▣& mothercare unit, table tennis, squash, tennis, bowls, golf
  £10.00-£12.50 (most cards)
Old Brick Kilns Caravan Camping Park, Little Barney NR21 0NL ☎(01328) 878305 OS map
  132/133/004332 6m NE of Fakenham off B1354 (Aylsham) Open Mar-Oct 60 pitches Grass and
  hard standings, level, part sheltered ▚✕⬥⟋↗▯▣◗⊕∅⊕⟲◻▣& first aid, battery
  charging £9.00-£11.50 (most cards)

FELIXSTOWE, Suffolk   **Map E6**
Pop 20,850. EC Wed, MD Thurs SEE St Andrew's church, St Peter's church ▊19 Undercliff Road
West ☎Felixstowe (01394) 276770 Restaurant: Ferryboat, Felixstowe Ferry ☎(01394) 284203
Peewit Caravan Park, Walton Avenue IP11 8HB ☎Felixstowe (01394) 284511 OS map
  169/289337 ½m SW of Felixstowe off A45 to port Open Easter-Oct 280 pitches (200 static)
  Grass, level, sheltered ▚↗▯▣◗∅⟲& £5.00-£8.00
Suffolk Sands Holiday Park, Carr Rd, Landguard Common IP11 8TS ☎(01394) 273434 OS map
  169/292340 1m W of Felixstowe centre off A45 Open Mar-Nov 400 pitches (350 static)–no tents
  ▚✕▯▮◗⊕∅⟲⊡ £10.00

FENSTANTON, Cambs   **Map B3**
Pop 540 SEE river Great Ouse N Restaurant: King William, High St (off A604) ☎(01480) 462467
Crystal Lakes Touring Caravan Park, Low Rd PE18 9VV ☎(01480) 497728 OS map 153/314687
  ¼m NW of Fenstanton on St Ives road Open all year 72 pitches 40 acres level grass and lakes,
  sheltered ▚✕⬥▯▣◗⊕∅⊕⟲◻▣& fishing £8.50

GISLEHAM–see Kessingland

FAKENHAM RACECOURSE

Tel (01328) 862388   Fax (01328) 855908

An excellent centre for touring, only 10 miles from
the coast, with modern, well-maintained facilities.
All pitches have 15amp electric hook-up.

GOSFIELD–see Halstead

GRAFHAM–see Buckden

GREAT SHELFORD, Cambs   Map C4
Pop 3,960. EC Wed SEE parish church, Imperial War Museum (RAF) 3m S at Duxford Restaurant:
Duxford Lodge 3m S at Duxford ☎(01223) 832271

Great Shelford Park (Camping Club), Cambridge Road CB2 5NB ☎Cambridge (01223) 841185
OS map 154/455539 1m NW of Great Shelford on A1301 (Cambridge) Open Mar 20-Oct 30
120 pitches 12 acres, level, grass 🛒🗃🛒🔥⊕∅↩🛒♿ £11.80-£14.90 (Mastercard/Visa)

GREAT YARMOUTH, Norfolk   Map G4
Pop 52,000. EC Thurs, MD Wed, Sat SEE The Rows, 17c Fisherman's Hospital, Nelson monument,
parish church, medieval tollhouse 🅸Marine Parade ☎(01493) 842195 Restaurant: Clipper
Schooner, Friars Lane (off South Quay) ☎(01493) 854926

Burgh Castle Marina, Butt Lane NR31 9PZ ☎Great Yarmouth (01493) 780331 OS map
134/474042 5m W of Great Yarmouth off A143 (Bungay) near south shore of Breydon Water
Open all year 200 pitches (180 static) Hard standing and grass, level, sheltered
🛒✕🍽↩🏹🗃🛒🔥⊕∅🖳↩♞♿ harbour and slipway, fishing £8.00-£14.00

Liffens Holiday Park, Burgh Castle NR31 9QB ☎(01493) 780357 OS map 134/489036 3m SW
of Great Yarmouth off A143 (Bungay) at Belton–signposted Open Apr-Oct 300 pitches (150 static)
22 acres level grass 🛒✕🍽↩🏹🗃🛒🔥⊕∅🖳🖼🔥↩🗄🖳🏤 post office, tennis court £8.00-
£15.00

Rose Farm Touring Park, Stepshort, Belton NR31 9JS ☎Great Yarmouth (01493) 780896 OS
map 134/488035 4m SW of Great Yarmouth off A143 (Beccles) and Belton road Open all year 80
pitches 7 acres level grass sheltered 🗃🛒🔥⊕∅↩🗄♿ £5.00-£7.00

Seashore Caravan Holiday Village, North Denes NR30 4HG ☎Great Yarmouth (01493) 851131
(bookings) OS map 134/525103 1m N of Great Yarmouth on A149 (North Walsham) Open
Easter-Sept 198 pitches Grass, level 🛒✕🗃🔥🖳🖼 lic club, hairdressing £3.15-£5.25

Sunfield Holiday Park, Station Road, Belton NR31 9NB ☎Great Yarmouth (01493) 781144 OS
map 134/478026 4m SW of Great Yarmouth off A143 (Diss) via Belton Open Easter-Sept–no adv
booking in peak season 400 pitches (250 static) Level/sloping grass, sheltered
🛒✕🍽↩🏹🗃🛒🔥⊕∅🖳 (heated) ↩🗄🖳♿ lic club, bowling/putting greens £5.50-£9.00

Yarmouth Racecourse, Jellicoe Road NR30 4AU ☎Great Yarmouth (01493) 855223 (0800-2000
hrs) OS map 134/526103 1m N of Great Yarmouth off A149 (Caister) Open Apr-Mid Oct, 122
pitches 🗃🛒🔥⊕∅ £8.40-£9.50

HADLEIGH, Suffolk   Map D5
Pop 5,980. MD Fri SEE Deanery Tower, Guildhall, 15c almshouses, ancient church 🅸Toppesfield
Hall ☎(01473) 822922 Restaurant: Weavers, High St ☎(01473) 827247

Grange Country Park, East Bergholt CO7 6UX ☎(01206) 298567 OS map 155/097352 6m SE of
Hadleigh on B1070 (East Bergholt) Open Feb 1-Jan 3 180 pitches (55 static) 🛒🍽🗃🛒🔥⊕🖳↩
sauna, snacks, games room £9.00-£13.00

HALSTEAD, Essex   Map D5
Pop 9,380. EC Wed SEE St Andrew's church, Gosfield Hall 2m SW Restaurant: Dog Inn,
Hedingham Rd ☎ (01787) 477774

Gosfield Leisure Park, Church Road, Gosfield CO9 1YD ☎ Halstead (01787) 475043 OS map
167/778295 2½m SW of Halstead off A131 (Braintree) Open all year 25 pitches Level grass,
sheltered ✗ (lic), ♀☎❸ fishing in adjoining lake, water skiing £10.00-£12.00 (Mastercard/Visa)

HARLESTON, Norfolk   Map F4
SEE Waveney valley NE/SW, pretty valley of Mendham E Restaurant: Swan, The Thoroughfare
☎ (01379) 852221

Little Lakeland Caravan Park, Wortwell IP20 0EL ☎ and Fax (01986) 788646 OS map
156/280850 2m NE of Harleston off A143 (Bungay) Open Mar-Oct 58 pitches Level grass,
sheltered ⬛❻☎⬀❸⤳⛆⛫ library, fishing £7.80-£9.80 inc awning

Waveney Valley Holiday Park, Airstation Farm, Pulham St Mary IP21 4QF ☎ (01379) 741228 OS
map 156/198831 3m W of Harleston off B1134 (Pulham Market) on Rushall road Open Apr-Oct,
45 pitches Level grass, sheltered ⬛✗♀❻☎⬀❸∅⛫❺ lic club, horse riding £9.00-£11.00

WAVENEY VALLEY HOLIDAY PARK

* Touring Caravan and Camping Park   * Licensed Bar
* Self Catering Stationary Caravans   * Restaurant, Shop, Laundry
* Electric Hook-ups   * Swimming Pool
* Horse Riding, Horse Drawn Caravans   * Good Fishing in locality

Good access to large, level site, 2 miles east of Dickleburgh.

Air Station Farm, Pulham St. Mary, Diss, Norfolk IP21 4QF
Telephone: (01379) 741228/741690

HARLOW, Essex   Map B5
Pop 79,000. EC Wed, MD Tues, Thurs, Fri, Sat Designed as new town in 1947 around village of Old
Harlow SEE museum housed in Georgian manor house Restaurant: Churchgate Manor, Old Harlow
☎ (01279) 420246

Roydon Mill Caravan Park, Roydon CM19 5EJ ☎ (01279) 792777 OS map 167/405095 3m W of
Harlow on B181 (Roydon) near River Stort Open all year 217 pitches (106 static)–adv booking
advisable Hard standings and grass, level, open ⬛✗♀⬀❻☎⬀❸∅⤳⛫❺⛆ club, fishing,
water ski school £10.00-£11.00 (Mastercard/Visa)

HARWICH, Essex   Map E6
Pop 15,000. EC Wed, MD Fri Seafaring town on N tip of Essex coast and ferry port to Holland SEE
old houses, Guildhall, Redoubt Fort, Treadmill crane on green 🅸 Parkeston Quay ☎ Harwich
(01255) 506139 Restaurant: Pier at Harwich, The Quay ☎ (01255) 503363

Dovercourt Haven Caravan Park, Low Road, Dovercourt CO12 3TZ ☎ Harwich (01255) 243433
OS map 169/242301 2m SW of Harwich off A120 (Colchester) near memorial in Upper Dovercourt
Open Mar-Oct 700 pitches (640 static) Grass, level, open ⬛✗❻⬀⛫⤳❺ (50) ⛆ lic club
£6.50-£14.00 inc elect (Mastercard/Visa)

HEACHAM–see Hunstanton

HEMSBY–see Caister

HOPTON ON SEA–see Great Yarmouth

The restaurants recommended in this guide are of three kinds – inns and pubs, restaurants
proper and those forming part of hotels and motels. They all serve lunch and dinner – at a
reasonable price – say under £10 a head. We shall be glad to have your comments on any
you use this season and if you think they are not up to standard to have your suggestions for
alternatives.

HUNSTANTON, Norfolk   Map E1
Pop 3,990. EC Thurs, MD Wed SEE ruined St Edmund's chapel, lighthouse, church of St Mary
⚹ The Green ☎(01485) 532610 Restaurant: Lodge, Cromer Rd ☎(01485) 523896

Chequers Inn, Main Road, Thornham PE36 6LY ☎(01485) 512229 OS map 132/735436 5m NE of Hunstanton on A149 (Wells) Open all year 8 pitches–no tents Grass, level, sheltered ✗ ⚬ ✪
No showers £5.00

Heacham Beach Holiday Park, South Beach Rd, Heacham PE31 7DD ☎(01485) 570270 OS map 132/663369 3m S of Hunstanton off A149 (Kings Lynn) at Heacham South Beach Open Easter-Oct 250 pitches (200 static) ⚏ ⚐ ▣ ⚒ ⚪ ✪ ∅ ↩ £8.00-£10.00

Manor Park Holiday Village, Manor Road PE36 5AZ ☎Hunstanton (01485) 532300 OS map 132/670398 ½m S of Hunstanton off A149 (King's Lynn) Open Apr-Oct 536 pitches (470 static) –no tents Grass, level ⚏ ⚬ ▣ ⚒ ⚪ ✪ ∅ ▭ ↩ ⊡ ⊏ 🏠 lic club, entertainment £10.00-£17.00 (most cards)

Orchards Caravan Park, Station Road, Heacham PE31 7HG ☎Heacham (01485) 570327 OS map 132/677377 2m S of Hunstanton off A149 (Kings Lynn) in Heacham village Open all year 18 pitches–motor caravans only Grass and hard standing, level, sheltered ⚒ ∅ ✪ ⊏ £5.00

Riverside Caravan Park, Jubilee Rd, Heacham PE31 0BB ☎(01485) 570676/572206 OS map 132/664373 3m S of Hunstanton off A149 (Kings Lynn) near Heacham North beach Open Mar-Oct 175 pitches (155 static) booking advisable–no tents 15 acres level grass and hard standings ▣ ⚒ ∅ ✪ ∅ £6.00-£10.00

Searles Holiday Centre, South Beach Road PE36 5BB ☎Hunstanton (01485) 534211 OS map 132/678422 ¼m S of of Hunstanton off A149 (King's Lynn) near South Beach Open Mar 14-Oct 7 800 pitches (450 static) Grass, level, open ⚏ ▣ ∅ ⊏ (heated) ⊡ lic club, barbecue £8.00-£20.00

HUNTINGDON, Cambs   Map B3
Pop 18,150. EC Wed, MD Sat SEE Cromwell museum, old inns, town hall, 14c bridge, Cowpers House, Pepys's House 1m SW at Brampton ⚹ The Library, Princes St ☎(01480) 425831 Restaurant: George, George St ☎(01480) 453096

Hartford Marina, Banks End, Wyton PE17 2AA ☎Huntingdon (01480) 454677 OS map 153/267725 2m E of Huntingdon on A1123 (St Ives) Open Mar-Oct 30 pitches Level grass, sheltered ⚏ ✗ ⚐ ⌁ ▣ ⚒ ✪ ∅ £8.00-£11.00

Houghton Mill Camping Park, Mill Street, Houghton PE17 2BJ ☎St Ives-Cambs (01480) 462413 OS map153/284720 4m E of Huntingdon off A1123 (St Ives) by river Great Ouse Open Easter-Sept 65 pitches Grass, level, sheltered ⚒ ∅ ✪ ∅ ♿ river fishing £9.00-£9.50

Park Lane Touring Park, Park Lane, Godmanchester PE18 8AF ☎Huntingdon (01480) 453740 Fax (01480) 453740 OS map 153/245709 2m SE of Huntingdon off B1043 (Godmanchester) at Black Bull Inn Open Mar-Oct 50 pitches Grass and hard standing, level, part sheltered ⚏ ✗ ▣ ⚒ ⚪ ✪ ∅ ⚐ ♿ £8.50

Quiet Waters Caravan Park, Hemingford Abbots PE28 9AJ ☎St Ives (01480) 463405 OS map153/283710 3m E of Huntingdon off A14 (Cambridge) Open Apr-Oct 20 pitches (9 static) Grass, level, sheltered ▣ ⚒ ∅ ✪ ∅ ⊏ 🏠 boating, angling £9.00-£11.00 (all cards exc Access and Amex)

Willows Caravan Park, Bromholme Lane, Brampton PE18 8NE ☎(01480) 437566 OS map 153/212705 2m SW of Huntingdon off A14 (St Neots) on B1514 (Brampton) Open all year 55 pitches 4 acres level grass ✗ ⚒ ∅ ✪ ♿ £9.00-£11.00

See also Fenstanton

THE BROADS

A low-lying area east of Norwich laced by a network of rivers is notable for its wide shallow lakes fringed by reeds. The Broads as these stretches of water are called are the home of many rare birds, animals and plants, including the marsh harrier, the otter, the royal fern and water parsnip. To anglers these lakes mean pike, some of the largest found anywhere, but fishing on a wider scale is freely available. There are three important nature reserves in the Broads. The Bure Marshes between Wroxham and Ranworth take in Hoveton Great Broad and Ranworth Broad, with several heronries and roosts of cormorants. There is a nature trail open May to September at Hoveton, accessible only by boat. A half-day water trail visiting seven hides is organised by the Norfolk Wildlife Trust (contact the warden at Stubb Road, Hickling NR12 0BW – (01692) 598276).
Horsey Mere, the third reserve and a famous haunt of birds lies near the coast and is owned by the National Trust. Access is only by boat.

IPSWICH, Suffolk   Map E5
Pop 123,000. MD Tues, Wed, Fri, Sat County town of Suffolk and one of oldest settlements in England SEE Christchurch mansion, Great White Horse Hotel (assoc with Dickens), old churches ⚏ Town Hall, Princes Street ☏ Ipswich (01473) 258070 Restaurant: County, St Helens St ☏ (01473) 255153

Low House Touring Caravan Centre, Bucklesham Road, Foxhall IP10 0AU ☏ (01473) 659437 Fax (01473) 659880 OS map 169/222423 3½m SE of Ipswich off A14 ring road (south) and A1156 (East Ipswich) on Bucklesham road Open all year 30 pitches 3½ acres level grass sheltered ▯▱✦↲ pets corner £7.50-£9.00

Orwell Meadows Leisure Park, Priory Farm, Nacton IP10 0JS ☏ Ipswich (01473) 726666 OS map 169/192402 2m SE of Ipswich off southern bypass via Ransomes Europark exit Open Mar-Jan 120 pitches (40 static) 30 acres level grass, sheltered ▮✗♀▯▱▱✦⊘▭↲▮⊟᷂ family room £9.50-£11.00 (Mastercard/Visa)

Priory Park, IP10 0JT ☏ Ipswich (01473) 727393 OS map 169/195405 2m SE of Ipswich off A12/A45 Southern bypass Open all year 280 pitches (160 static) Grass and hard standing, level/sloping, sheltered ✗♀▯▱▱✦⊘▭ (heated) ↲▭☎ lic club, golf course (9-hole), beach frontage, hard tennis courts, nature trails, tidal boat launching £14.00-£20.00

See also Manningtree and Woodbridge

KESSINGLAND, Suffolk   Map G4
Pop 3,500. EC Thurs SEE 17c church, wildlife park and marshlands S, Benacre Broad, Kessingland Cliffs N Restaurant: Pier Avenue 3m S at Southwold ☏ (01502) 722632

Chestnut Farm, Gisleham NR33 8EE ☏ (01502) 740227 OS map 156/510875 1m W of Kessingland on Mutford-Rushmere road Open Apr-Oct 40 pitches Grass, level, sheltered ▯✦ fishing £6.00-£7.00

Heathland Beach Caravan Park, London Road NR33 7PJ ☏ (01502) 740337 OS map 156/533878 1m N of Kessingland off A12 (Lowestoft) Open Apr-Oct 280 pitches (180 static) 30 acres level grass ▮✗♀▯▱✦⊟ (heated) ↲▮᷂᷂ tennis, beach access £11.00-£15.50

White House Farm, Gisleham NR33 8DX ☏ (01502) 740248 OS map 156/517880 1m NW of Kessingland on Carlton Colville road Open Apr-Oct 40 pitches Grass, level, open ▯▱✦⊘↲ ▮ (40), fishing £7.00-£8.00

See also Lowestoft

KINGS LYNN, Norfolk   Map D2
Pop 33,340 EC Wed MD Tues, Fri, Sat Ancient port on river Ouse rich in medieval architecture SEE Guildhall, Customs House, Museum, Walsingham Shrine (RC church), Castle Rising 4m NE, four Wiggenhall villages by river Ouse S ⚏ Old Gaol House, Saturday Market ☏ Kings Lynn (01553) 763044 Restaurant: Dukes Head, The Market Place ☏ (01553) 774996

Gatton Waters Caravan Park, Hillington PE31 6BJ ☏ Hillington (01485) 600643 OS map 132/705255 4m NE of Kings Lynn off A148 (Cromer) Open Easter-Oct 90 pitches level grass ✗♀▯▱✦⊘✦ fishing (lake) £6.50-£7.50

King's Lynn Caravan Park, Parkside House, New Rd, North Runcton PE33 0QR ☏ (01553) 840004 OS map 132/646165 2m SE of Kings Lynn off A47 (Norwich) Open all year 35 pitches 5 acres grass and hard standings, sheltered parkland ▯✦ £5.00-£8.00 (all major cards)

LEISTON, Suffolk   Map F5
Pop 5,130. EC Wed SEE ruins of St Mary's Abbey, Minsmere bird sanctuary, Long Shop museum Restaurant: White Horse, Station Rd ☏ (01728) 830694

Cakes and Ale Camping Park IP16 4TE ☏ (01728) 831655 Fax (01473) 736270 OS map 156/432637 1m W of Leiston off B1119 (Saxmundham) Open Easter-Oct 250 pitches (200 static) Grass, some hard standings, level, part sheltered ▮♀▯▱▱✦⊘✦↲▭▮☎ tennis, clubhouse £15.00-£16.00

LITTLEPORT–see Ely

LOUGHTON, Essex   Map B6
Pop 19,100. EC Thurs Restaurant: Post House 6m N at Epping ☏ (01992) 573137

Debden House Camping, Debden Green IG10 2PA ☏ (0181) 508 3008 OS map 167/438982 1½m N of Loughton off road to Theydon Bois near golf course and junct 26 of M25 Open Apr-Oct 225 pitches Grass, part level ▮▱✦↲᷂ £6.00

Elms Caravan Park, Lippits Hill, High Beach IG10 4AW *Family run park within easy reach of London* ☏ (0208) 508 3749 OS map 177/399971 3m NW of Loughton off A112 (Waltham Abbey-Chingford) at Lippitts Hill Open Mar-Oct 50 pitches 3 acres level grass and hard standings, sheltered ▮✗▯▱▱✦⊘☎ £9.00

LOWESTOFT, Suffolk   **Map G4**
Pop 58,000. EC Thurs, MD Fri, Sat, Sun SEE lighthouse, St Margaret's church, Somerleyton Hall
4m NW ⓘEast Point Pavilion, Royal Plain ✆(01502) 539023 Restaurant: Victoria, Kirkley Cliff
✆(01502) 734433

Azure Seas Caravan Park, The Street, Corton NR32 5HN ✆Lowestoft (01502) 731403 OS map
134/546968 3m N of Lowestoft off A12 (Great Yarmouth) on B1358 (Corton) Open Apr-Oct 100
pitches 10 acres, level, wooded ▣🏕◿ beach adjoining £6.00-£11.50

Beach Farm, Arbor Lane, Pakefield NR33 7BD ✆Lowestoft (01502) 572794 OS map 156/537898
2m S of Lowestoft off A12 (Kessingland) at junction with A1117 (Great Yarmouth) Open Apr-Oct,
112 pitches (80 static) Level grass, sheltered ✗♀↩▣🏕◿⊛∅◻ (heated) ↲▢🏕🗟↧☺
£7.00-£10.00 (all main cards)

Broad View Caravans, Marsh Road, Oulton Broad NR33 9JY ✆Lowestoft (01502) 565587 OS
map 134/516922 2m SW of Lowestoft off A146 (Beccles) near Oulton Broad South station, by
Oulton Broad Open Apr-Oct 68 pitches (53 static)–must book 5 acres level grass, sheltered
▣🏕◿⊛∅☺🏕🗟 fishing £8.00-£9.00

Carlton Manor, Chapel Road, Carlton Colville NR33 8BL ✆Lowestoft (01502) 566511 OS map
156/521903 2m SW of Lowestoft off A146 (Beccles) Open Apr-Oct 90 pitches Grass, level
✗♀↩⤳▣🏕◿∅☺↲▢🏕↧ putting green £6.50-£11.75

See also Kessingland

MALDON, Essex   **Map C6**
Pop 15,500. EC Wed, MD Thurs, Sat SEE old inns, Moot Hall, Plume library, Chelmer and
Blackwater Navigation ⓘCoach Lane ✆Maldon (01621) 856503 Restaurant: Swan, High St
✆(01621) 853170

Beacon Hill Leisure Park, St Lawrence Bay, Southminster CM0 7LS ✆Maldon (01621) 779248
(24 hrs) OS map 168/964050 9m E of Maldon off A1010 (Bradwell) Open Apr-Oct 250 pitches
(120 static) 25 acres level grass 🏕♀⤳▣🏕◿⊛∅◻↲ (40) slipway, battery charging, club
house, leisure complex, sauna, bubble spa £6.50-£11.50 (Mastercard/Visa)

MANNINGTREE, Essex   **Map E6**
Pop 340. EC Wed, MD Sat SEE Swannery, Mistley Towers, Constable country (Dedham Vale) 3m W
Restaurant: Station Buffet ✆(01206) 564777

Strangers Home Inn, Bradfield CO11 2US ✆(01255) 870304 OS map 168/142308 3m E of
Manningtree off B1352 (Harwich) Open Mar-Oct 70 pitches 2 acres level grass 🏕✗♀🏕◿∅↲
£7.50

See also Hadleigh

MARLINGFORD–see Barford

MUNDESLEY ON SEA, Norfolk   **Map G2**
Pop 1,550. EC Wed Quiet holiday village with sands and safe bathing SEE Paston windmill, St
Margaret's church, 16c barn ⓘStation Rd ✆(01263) 721070 Restaurant: Royal, Paston Rd
✆(01263) 720096

Sandy Gulls Clifftop Touring Park, Cromer Road NR11 8DF ✆Mundesley (01263) 720513 OS
map 133/303376 1m NW of Mundesley on B1159 (Cromer) coast road Open Mar-Nov
140 pitches (100 static) 16 acres level grass sheltered 🏕🏕◿⊛∅🗟 £7.00-£14.00

Woodlands Caravan Park, Trimingham NR11 8AL ✆(01263) 579208 Fax (01263) 833144 OS
map 133/274388 3m NW of Mundesley on B1159 (Cromer) Open Apr-Oct 300 pitches (190
static)–no tents Grass, level, sheltered 🏕✗♀⤳▣🏕◿⊛∅☺🏕↧ £10.45-£13.45

NEWMARKET, Suffolk   **Map C4**
Pop 16,650. EC Wed, MD Tues, Sat SEE Devil's Dyke prehistoric earthworks, Nell Gwynne's
House, racecourse ⓘ The Rookery ✆(01638) 667200 Restaurant: White Hart, High St ✆(01638)
663051

Stanford Park, Weirs Drove, Burwell CB5 0BP ✆(01638) 741547 OS map 154/585661 3m NW of
Newmarket off B1103 (Burwell) Open all year 150 pitches Grass and hard standing, level,
sheltered ▣🏕◿⊛∅☺↲🏕🗟↧☺ £8.00-£10.00

Some site operators make it a rule that cars must be left in a separate parking area away from
caravans and tents, which can be inconvenient when shopping by car. But it does minimise
traffic noise and the risk to children.

NORFOLK BROADS
Causeway Cottage Caravan Park, Potter Heigham

Off Gt Yarmouth road near river

Modern facilities, shops and pubs 250 yards. Open Mar 27-Oct 2.

See listing under Potter Heigham

NORTH WALSHAM, Norfolk   **Map G2**
Pop 8,290. EC Wed, MD Thurs SEE church, market cross, Paston school Restaurant: Scarborough
Hill House, Yarmouth Rd ☎(01692) 402151

Two Mills Touring Park, Old Yarmouth Road NR28 9NA ☎North Walsham (01692) 405829 Fax
(01692) 405829 OS map 133/134/291286 1m SE of North Walsham on Old Yarmouth Road
(former A149) opposite Scarborough Hill Hotel Open Mar 1-Jan 3 55 pitches (adults only)–no
tents exc trailer tents 6 acres level grass, sheltered ☎️📦🔌⊕∅📦⛟ £7.50-£10.50 (most
cards)

NORWICH, Norfolk   **Map F3**
Pop 121,000. EC Thurs, MD daily SEE cathedral, city churches, Erpingham gate, old buildings and
streets ℹ️The Guildhall, Gaol Hill ☎(01603) 666071 Restaurant: Maid's Head, Tombland
☎(01603) 628821

Buck Inn, Honingham NR9 5BL ☎Norwich (01603) 880393 OS map 133/103118 7½m NW of
Norwich off A47 (East Dereham) Open Mar-Oct 6 pitches Grass, part level, sheltered 🔌⛟ *No
showers*, bar meals £3.50-£6.00

Royal Norfolk Showground, Long Lane, Bawburgh NR9 3LX ☎(01603) 742708 (0800-2000 hrs)
OS map 134/150102 3m W of Norwich off A47 (East Dereham) at Roundwell Inn on Bawburgh
road Open Apr-mid Oct, 60 pitches–must book Jul-Aug 5 acres, level ⊘∅ £3.70-£4.30

OBY–see Acle

PETERBOROUGH, Cambs   **Map B2**
Pop 110,0000 EC Thurs, MD Wed, Fri, Sat On W edge of Fens, an important settlement since
Bronze Age SEE cathedral, Bishop's Palace, Museum, St John's church, Nene Valley steam railway,
Crowland Abbey 6m N, Peakirk Waterfowl Gardens 7m N ℹ️Bridge Street ☎Peterborough (01733)
317336 Restaurant: Bogarts, North St ☎(01733) 349995

Ferry Meadows Country Park, Ham Lane, Orton Waterville PE2 0UU ☎Peterborough (01733)
233526 (0800-2000 hrs) OS map 142/151975 1m W of Peterborough off A605 (Corby) Open
Apr-Dec, 254 pitches–must book Jul-Aug Level grass and hard standings, sheltered ⊘∅⛟ milk,
eggs £8.00-£12.00

POLSTEAD, Suffolk   **Map D5**
Village centred on its green in heart of Constable country. Restaurant: Cock Inn, The Green
☎(01206) 263150

Polstead Touring Park, Holt Rd CO6 5BZ ☎ and Fax (01787) 211969 OS map 155/987404 2m N
of Polstead off A1071 (Hadleigh-Sudbury) near water tower Open Mar-Oct 30 pitches 3½ acres
grass and hard standings–no tents ☎️📦🔌⊕∅⊕⛟⛟ £7.50-£10.50

Sandy Gulls Clifftop Touring Park

Mundesley, Norfolk NR11 8DF   Tel (01263) 720513

*The area's only clifftop touring park
Clean beaches and panoramic sea views*

POTTER HEIGHAM, Norfolk   Map G3
Holiday village between river Thurne and Hickling Broad SEE 13c bridge, St Nicholas church,
boatyard, Countryside Collection 2m E at Martham Restaurant: Swan 3m W at Horning ☏(01692)
630316

Causeway Cottage, Bridge Road NR29 5JB ☏Potter Heigham (01692) 670238 OS map
134/416187 ½m S of Potter Heigham centre off A149 (Gt Yarmouth) near river Open Mar 27-Oct
2, 14 pitches (no pets) Level grass, sheltered ▨⌀⊕⊖↲🅿✿⊑⅏ £7.00-£9.00

Willowcroft, Staithe Road, Repps with Bastwick NR29 5JU ☏Potter Heigham (01692) 670380 OS
map 134/414173 2m S of Potter Heigham off A149 (Great Yarmouth) on Thurne road Open
Easter-Oct, 40 pitches 2 acres, level grass, sheltered ▨⌀⊕ boating, fishing £8.00

REEDHAM, Norfolk   Map G4
Marshland village at only crossing of river Yare between Norwich and coast at Great Yarmouth (£2
per car) SEE chain ferry across river Yare, church of St John the Baptist, Berney Arms Mill 3m NE
Restaurant: Ferry ☏(01493) 700429

Pampas Lodge, The Street, Haddiscoe NR14 6AA ☏(01502) 677265 OS map 134/447971 4m SE
of Reedham on A143 (Great Yarmouth-Beccles) at Haddiscoe Open Apr-Oct 50 pitches Grass
and hard standing ⌖▤▨⌀⌀⊑ £6.00-£7.00

Reedham Ferry Camping and Caravan Park, NR13 3HA ☏(01493) 700429 OS map 134/407015
½m SW of Reedham on B1140 (Beccles) adjoining Ferry Inn Open Easter-Oct 20 pitches Grass,
level, part sheltered ✗⌖↲▨⌀ fishing, boating, slipway £6.50-£11.00 (Mastercard/Visa)

ST NEOTS, Cambs   Map B3
Pop 12,460 SEE medieval St Mary's church, old inns, Longsands museum of local history, leisure
centre Restaurant: Old Falcon, Market Sq ☏(01480) 472749

St Neots Park (Camping Club), PE19 2UD ☏(01480) 474404 OS map 153/182598 ¼m S of St
Neots centre off Great Gransden road adj riverside park Open Mar 20-Oct 30 180 pitches 10
acres, level grass and hard standing ▤▨⌀⊕⌀⅏ fishing £11.80-£14.90

ST OSYTH, Essex   Map D6
Pop 1,500 SEE priory ruins and gatehouse, parish church with 16c beamed roof Restaurant: White
Hart, Mill St ☏(01255) 820318

Hutley's Caravan Park, St Osyth Beach, St Osyth CO16 8TB ☏St Osyth (01255) 820712 OS
map 168/122155 On W edge of St Osyth on road to beach Open Easter-Oct 750 pitches (730
static)—no tents Grass, level, open ▤✗⌖↲⤳▤▨⌀⊕⌀⊖↲▨ children's room, naturist
beach £13.00 (all major cards)

Orchards Holiday Village, Point Clear CO16 8LJ ☏(01255) 820651 OS map 168/093153 2m W
of St Osyth at Point Clear Open Mar-Oct 1360 pitches (1320 static)
▤✗⌖↲▤▨⌀⊕⌀▢⊖↲⊑ bowling £10.00-£12.00

SAXMUNDHAM, Suffolk   Map F5
Pop 2,370. EC Wed, MD Thurs SEE church Restaurant: Queens Head, High St ☏(01728) 602856

Lakeside Leisure Park, IP17 2QP ☏Saxmundham (01728) 603344 OS map 156/366651 1½m
NW of Saxmundham off B1119 (Framlingham) Open Apr-Oct 275 pitches (151 static) Grass and
hard standing ✗⌖↲▤▨⌀⊕⌀▢ (heated) ↲▢▨⅏ fishing £9.00-£11.00 (most cards)

Marsh Farm, Sternfield IP17 1HW ☏(01728) 602168 OS map 156/387607 1m S of Saxmundham
off A12-B1121 (Aldeburgh) at Sternfield—signposted Open all year 130 pitches (100 static) 6
acres level grass ▨⊕ £5.00

Whitearch, Main Road, Benhall IP17 1NA ☏(01728) 604646 OS map 156/385615 1m S of
Saxmundham near junction of A12 (Woodbridge) and B1121 (Aldeburgh)—signposted Open Apr-
Oct 40 pitches 14 acres level/sloping grass and hard standings ▤▤▨⌀⊕⌀↲⅏ fishing,
tennis, TV hook-ups £8.50-£10.50

See also Yoxford

CHECK BEFORE ENTERING

Beware less-than-honest site operators who give us one price for the following year and then
increase it once the season gets underway. So note the charges for any site featured in this
guide and before pulling in verify how much you will have to pay, and for what. If on leaving
the charges turn out to be higher, ask why the difference.
The outdoor holidaymaker gets a better deal in France. There site charges are governed by
law and must be displayed at the site entrance.

SEA PALLING, Norfolk   Map G3
Restaurant: Fisherman's Return 3m SE at Winterton on Sea ☎(01493) 393305
Golden Beach Holiday Centre, Beach Road NR12 0AL ☎(01692) 598269 OS map 134/430272
¼m N of Sea Palling off road to beach Open Mar 21-Oct 31, 162 pitches (102 static) Grass, level,
some hard standings £7.00-£10.00

SHERINGHAM, Norfolk   Map G2
Pop 5,260. EC Wed, MD Sat SEE priory ruins at Beeston Regis, North Norfolk steam railway
▮Station Approach ☎Sheringham (01263) 824329 Restaurant: Two Lifeboats, High St ☎(01263)
822401
Beeston Regis Caravan Park, West Runton NR27 9NG ☎Sheringham (01263) 823614 OS map
133/175432 1m E of Sheringham off A149 (Cromer) Open Mar-Oct 740 pitches (300 static)–adv
booking advisable 15 acres level grass, clifftop location beach access, coarse fishing
£7.95-£15.00 (Visa/Switch/Delta)
Kelling Heath Holiday Park, Weybourne NR25 7HW ☎(01263) 588181 OS map 133/118415
3½m W of Sheringham off A149 (Wells) near Weybourne church Open Mar 20-Oct 31, 685
pitches (385 static) Grass, level, sheltered (heated fun pool)
tennis courts, adventure playground, nature trail £10.75-£14.95 (most cards)
Laburnum Caravan Park, Water Lane, West Runton NR27 9QB ☎(01263) 837473 OS map
133/180433 1½m E of Sheringham off A149 (Cromer) on clifftop Open Apr-Oct 180 pitches (172
static)–no tents 13 acres level grass, sloping £5.50-£6.50
Roman Camp Caravan Park, West Runton NR27 9ND ☎(01263) 837256 OS map 133/184414
1½m SE of Sheringham off A149 (Cromer) on Aylmerton road Open Apr-Oct 86 pitches (75 static)
4 acres, level, some hard standings ✗ (snack) £5.00
Woodlands Caravan Park, Holt Road, Upper Sheringham NR26 8TU ☎Sheringham (01263)
823802 OS map 133/136408 1½m S of Sheringham on A148 (Cromer-Fakenham) Open Mar 15-
Oct 31 376 pitches (151 static) 21 acres, level grass, sheltered (indoor)
fishing £8.00-£11.85 (all main cards)

SHOEBURYNESS–see Southend

SNETTISHAM–see Hunstanton

SOUTHEND ON SEA, Essex   Map C7
Pop 157,600. MD Thurs, Fri, Sat SEE 13c South church Hall, Civic House, Pier, 12c Prittlewall
Priory and museum, Planetarium ▮High Street Precinct ☎(01702) 215120 Restaurant: Bakers Bar,
Alexandra St (off High St) ☎(01702) 390403
East Beach Caravan Park, Shoeburyness SS3 9SG ☎(01702) 292466 OS map 178/943842 3m
E of Southend off A13 near Shoeburyness station and beach–signposted Open Mar-Oct 160
pitches (75 static) £7.50-£8.50
Riverside Village Holiday Park, Creeksea Ferry Rd, Wallasea Island, Rochford SS4 2EY
☎(01702) 258297 OS map 178/932952 6m NE of Southend off A127 (Romford) and B1013
(Rochford) via Ashingdon Open Mar-Oct, 220 pitches (160 static) Level grass, part sheltered
boules £4.00-£10.00

SOUTHMINSTER, Essex   Map 7D
Pop 650 Restaurant: Station Arms, Station Rd ☎(01621) 772225
Steeple Bay Caravan Park, Steeple CM0 7RS ☎(01621) 773991 OS map 168/933050 3m N of
Southminster at Steeple Bay via Steeple Open Apr-Oct 360 pitches (300 static) Level grass and
hard standing launching facs £7.00-£21.00 (all cards)
See also Maldon

**The distance and direction of a campsite is given from the centre of the key town under
which it appears, the place name in parentheses following the road number indicating which
route to take.**

SOUTHWOLD, Suffolk   **Map G5**
Pop 1,790. EC Wed, MD Mon, Thurs SEE town hall, St Edmund's church, museum, lighthouse
☒ Town Hall, Market Place ☎ Southwold (01502) 724729 Restaurant: Crown, High St ☎ (01502) 722275

Harbour Caravan and Camping Park, Ferry Road IP18 6ND ☎ Southwold (01502) 722486 OS map 156/504750 ½m S of Southwold off A1095 (Blythburgh) on harbour road Open Apr-Oct 150 pitches Grass, level, part open ⏷⏷⚹ £8.45-£10.35

SUDBURY, Suffolk   **Map D5**
Pop 10,060. EC Wed, MD Thurs, Sat SEE churches, Corn Exchange, Gainsborough's house, Old Moot Hall, Salter's Hall ☒ Town Hall, Market Hill ☎ Sudbury (01787) 881320 Restaurant: Fords Bistro, Gainsborough St ☎ (01787) 374298

Willowmere Caravan Park, Bures Road, Little Cornard CO10 0NN ☎ Sudbury (01787) 375559 Fax (01787) 375559 OS map 155/886390 1½m S of Sudbury on B1508 (Colchester) Open Apr-Oct 40 pitches Grass, level, sheltered ⏷⏷⚹⏷ £7.00-£10.00

SWAFFHAM, Norfolk   **Map E2**
Pop 4,770. EC Thurs, MD Sat SEE church, market cross, Pedlar Sign Restaurant: George, Station St ☎ (01760) 721238

Breckland Meadows Touring Park, Lynn Road PE37 7PT ☎ Swaffham (01760) 721246 OS map 144/808095 ¾m W of Swaffham centre on old King's Lynn road Open Mar-Oct 45 pitches 3½ acres level grass ⏷⏷⚹⚹⚹ £6.00-£8.00

Pentney Park, Pentney PE32 1HU ☎ (01760) 337479 OS map 132/743142 7m NW of Swaffham off A47 (King's Lynn) at junction with B1153 (Gayton) Open all year 200 pitches Grass, level, sheltered ⚹✗⚹⚹⚹⚹⚹⚹⚹ (heated) ⚹⚹⚹ (40), gym, miniature railway £8.00-£10.50

THETFORD, Norfolk   **Map E3**
Pop 20,000. EC Wed, MD Tues, Sat SEE churches, King's House, Old Bell Hotel, Ancient House (museum), Euston Hall 3m SE ☒ Ancient House Museum, White Hart Street ☎ Thetford (01842) 712599 Restaurant: Bell, King St ☎ (01842) 754455

Dower House, East Harling NR16 2SE ☎ (01953) 717314 OS map 144/969852 8m E of Thetford off A1066 (Diss) Open Mar-Oct 160 pitches Grass, level, part sheltered ⚹✗⚹⚹⚹⚹⚹⚹⚹ ⚹⚹⚹⚹⚹⚹ £8.50-£10.80 (Mastercard/Visa/Switch/Solo)

TRIMINGHAM–see Mundesley

WANSFORD, Cambs   **Map B1**
Pop 410 SEE packhorse bridge, church Restaurant: Falcon Inn 3m S at Fotheringhay ☎ (01832) 226254

Yarwell Mill Caravan Park, Yarwell PE8 6PS ☎ (01780) 782344 OS map 142/074973 1m S of Wansford off Fotheringhay road by river Nene Open Mar-Oct 148 pitches (24 static)–no tents Level grass, sheltered ⏷⏷⚹⚹⚹ fishing, boating, 9 hole pitch and putt £8.50-£9.50

WATTON, Norfolk   **Map E3**
Pop 4,800 EC Thurs MD Wed SEE Wayland Wood 1m S poss site of `Babes in Wood' Restaurant: Clarence House, High St ☎ (01953) 884252

Puddledock Farm, Great Hockham IP24 1PA ☎ (01953) 882455 OS map 144/942925 5m S of Watton on A1075 (Thetford) Open all year 24 pitches ⚹⚹ fishing £2.50

WELLS NEXT THE SEA, Norfolk   **Map F1**
Pop 2,520. EC Thurs Old-world fishing port of flint cottages and Georgian houses SEE Quay, miniature railways, Holkham Hall 2m W ☒ Staithe St ☎ (01328) 710885 Restaurant: Crown, The Buttlands ☎ (01328) 710209

High Sandcreek Camping, Stiffkey NR23 1QP ☎ (01328) 710479 OS map 132/965438 3m E of Wells off A149 (Sheringham) at Warborough Hill Open Apr-Oct 80 pitches 2 acres, gentle slope ⚹⏷⏷ boating, fishing, bird watching £5.00-£8.00

Pinewoods Holiday Park, Beach Road NR23 1DR ☎ (01328) 710439 OS map 132/914453 1m N of Wells on road to beach Open Mar 15-Oct 31 900 pitches (530 static) 75 acres, level grass and hard standing ⚹✗ (snack) ⚹⚹⚹⚹⚹⚹⚹⚹⚹⚹⚹⚹⚹ boating, fishing, pitch and putt, miniature railway, trampolines £7.50-£16.50 (Mastercard/Visa/Switch)

*deposit £9 , £11.00 per nig
full pay 28 days before arrive.*

Dogs are usually allowed but must be kept on a lead. Sometimes they have to be paid for.

WEST MERSEA, Essex   Map D6
SEE Georgian cottages, fishing museum Restaurant: Blackwater, Church Rd ☎(01206) 383338

Fen Farm, East Mersea CO5 8UA ☎West Mersea (01206) 383275 OS map 168/058144 4m E of West Mersea off B1025 (Colchester) and East Mersea road Open Apr-Sept 130 pitches (85 static) 10 acres level grass ▨▨▨▨▨▨▨ mobile shop £10.00-£15.00

Seaview Holiday Park, Seaview Avenue CO5 8DA ☎West Mersea (01206) 382534 OS map 168/020148 1m N of West Mersea off B1025 (Colchester) by sea Open Mar-Oct 370 pitches (250 static) Level/sloping grass adj beach ▨▨▨▨▨▨▨ £7.00-£8.50

Waldegraves Farm, CO5 8SE ☎(01206) 382898 OS map 168/033128 1m E of West Mersea off B1025 (Colchester) by sea Open Mar-Nov 265 pitches (205 static) Grass, level, part sheltered ▨▨▨▨▨▨▨▨▨▨▨▨ (50) ▨ boating and fishing lakes, satellite TV, golf range, pitch and putt £9.00-£15.00 (all cards)

WEST RUNTON–see Sheringham

WILLINGHAM, Cambs   Map C3
Restaurant: Three Tuns, Church St ☎(01954) 260437

Alwyn Camping Caravan Site, Over Road CB4 5EV ☎Willingham (01954) 260977 OS map 154/396701 ¼m W of Willingham on Over road Open Mar-Oct 90 pitches 5 acres level grass, sheltered ▨▨▨▨▨▨▨▨▨▨ £7.00

Roseberry Tourist Park, Earith Road CB4 5LT ☎Willingham (01954) 260346 OS map 154/407723 1m N of Willingham on B1050 (Chatteris) Open Mar-Oct 80 pitches Grass, level, sheltered ▨▨▨▨▨▨▨▨▨▨ £8.00

WINFARTHING, Norfolk   Map E4
Pop 800 Restaurant: Bunwell Manor 5m N at Bunwell ☎(01953) 788304

The Greyhound, Tibenham NR16 1PZ ☎(01379) 677676 OS map 144/136895 3m NE of Winfarthing off Bunwell road in Tibenham Open Mar-Oct 10 pitches ½ acre, level grass ▨ *No showers* £5.00

WISBECH, Cambs   Map D2
Pop 17,740. EC Wed, MD Thurs, Sat SEE North and South Brinks (Georgian houses), Peckover House, Wisbech and Fenland museum ▨Library, Ely Place ☎Wisbech (01945) 583263 Restaurant: Rose Tavern, North Brink ☎(01945) 588335

Friday Bridge International Farm Camp, March Road PE14 0LR ☎Wisbech (01945) 860255 OS map 143/455040 3m S of Wisbech on B1101 (March) beyond Friday Bridge Open May-Oct 20 pitches Grass, level, sheltered ▨▨ lic club, disco, tennis, pool, volley ball, Sky TV £5.00

WOODBRIDGE, Suffolk   Map E5
Pop 7,220. EC Wed, MD Thurs SEE St Mary's church, Shire Hall, tide mill, marina, old houses and inns Restaurant: Seckford Arms, Seckford St ☎(01394) 384446

Forest Camping, Tangham Camp Site, Butley IP12 3NF ☎(01394) 450707 OS map 169/355485 7½m E of Woodbridge off B1084 (Orford) on forest road via Butley Open Apr-Oct 90 pitches Grass, level, open ▨▨▨▨▨▨▨ forest walks £9.00

Moat Barn Touring, Dallinghoo Rd, Bredfield IP13 6BD ☎(01473) 737520 OS map 156/270535 2m N of Woodbridge off A12 (Lowestoft) Open Easter-Oct 15 pitches 2 acres level grass ▨▨▨▨▨ £9.00

Moon and Sixpence, Waldringfield IP12 4PP ☎(01473) 736650 Fax (01473) 736270 OS map 169/262456 2m S of Woodbridge off A12 (Ipswich) eastern bypass on Newbourn road Open Apr-Oct 250 pitches (175 static) Grass, level, terraced, sheltered ▨▨▨▨▨▨▨▨▨▨▨▨ tennis courts, basketball, petanque, volley ball, lic club, 2 acre lake with beach, woodland walks £11.00-£18.00 (Mastercard/Visa)

St Margaret's House, Shottisham IP12 3HD ☎(01394) 411247 OS map 169/322446 6m SE of Woodbridge off B1083 (Shottisham) Open Apr-Oct 30 pitches Grass, level, sheltered ▨▨▨▨ £5.00-£6.50

The Sandlings Centre, Lodge Road, Hollesley IP12 3RR ☎(01394) 411202 OS map 169/338434 6m SE of Woodbridge off B1083 (Shottisham) Open Mar-Jan 61 pitches (36 static)–no caravans Grass, level, sheltered ▨▨▨▨▨▨▨▨▨ £9.00-£11.00

YOXFORD, Suffolk   Map F5
Pop 450 SEE Minsmere bird reserve and Ipswich forest E, Sibton Park W Restaurant: Crown on B1125 2m E at Westleton ☎(01728) 660777

Haw Wood Caravan Park, Haw Wood, Darsham IP17 3QT ☎(01986) 784248 OS map 156/424717 2m NE of Yoxford off A12 (Lowestoft) Open Apr-Oct 90 pitches (25 static) Grass, level, sheltered ▨▨▨▨▨▨ £7.00-£10.00

See also Saxmundham

8 London and Home Counties

Adjoining Greater London on the north and west, the five Home Counties of Hertford, Bedford, Buckingham, Oxford and Berkshire have withstood population pressures enough to retain a fair share of unspoiled scenery.

Hertfordshire occupies the northern part of the Thames basin which slopes gently up to the Chiltern escarpment extending from Royston to Tring. The main sights are the Roman relics at St Albans, the castle at Hertford and the stately homes of Gorhambury, Hatfield and Knebworth.

Adjoining Hertfordshire on the north, Bedfordshire is best known for the broad scenic valley of the Ouse, for which Bedford is a good centre. There are notable churches at Dunstable, Leighton Buzzard and Eaton, the country houses of Woburn and Luton Hoo and the pretty villages of Chalgrave near Dunstable and Upper Dean near Bedford.

Ivinghoe Beacon, at 904ft the highest point in the Chilterns, is in the southern half of Buckinghamshire. Famed for the beauty of their beech woods, the Chilterns are crossed by two routes for walkers. The North Bucks Way begins near Princes Risborough and ends at Wolverton, and the Ridgeway, which

starts at Ivinghoe Beacon, follows the escarpment all the way to Avebury in Wiltshire. In the north is the Vale of Aylesbury, patterned with rivers and streams. Wendover is a pleasant town, and Haddenham, Hambledon and Latimer are attractive villages. Hughenden Manor is one of several interesting country houses to visit.

Buckinghamshire's neighbour is Berkshire, still threequarters pasture, farmland and woods. Where the Thames flows through the gap at Goring the lush beauty of its valley contrasts with the austerity of the Berkshire Downs on one side and the Chilterns on the other. The Berkshire Ridgeway can still be followed the twenty miles between Thameside Streatley and Ashbury. Windsor Castle is probably the most important building in the county.

Wedged in between Berkshire and Buckinghamshire, Oxfordshire is centred on the Thames basin between the Chilterns on the north and the Cotswolds on the west, where the river flows through remote and peaceful water meadows and past riverside pubs— most inviting between Oxford and Lechlade. Other sights in the county are the university buildings of Oxford, the pretty town of Abingdon, the stately home of Blenheim and the delightful villages of Stanton Harcourt, Minster Lovell and Ewelme.

Although it is no longer the largest city in the world, London covers a vast area. The most important buildings are St Paul's Cathedral, Westminster Abbey, the Tower of London, Westminster Hall, the Royal Hospital, the fine house of Syon Park and the Tudor palace of Hampton Court.

Campsites in the region are few. The only ones in London itself are invariably crowded and campers and caravanners visiting the capital do so more easily by staying at a campsite on the perimeter and travelling to and in the central area by public transport. Campsites exist at several places along the Thames but there are few elsewhere.

ABINGDON, Oxon   **Map B5**
Pop 22,000 EC Thurs MD Mon Attractive market town on loop of river Thames (Isis) SEE 17c
county hall (museum), guildhall (portraits, plate), abbey ruins, St Helens and St Nicholas churches,
river Thames from towpath ⬛Abbey House, Abbey Close ✆(01235) 522711 Restaurant: Old
Anchor, St Helens Wharf ✆(01235) 521726

> **Bridge House**, Clifton Hampden OX14 3EH ✆(01865) 407725 OS map 164/547953 3m E of
> Abingdon off A415 (Henley) at Clifton Hampden on Long Wittenham road by river Thames Open
> Apr-Oct 40 pitches 3½ acres level grass, sheltered ⬛🔧⊕🔩🖵 £8.00-£10.00

AMPTHILL, Beds   **Map E5**
SEE Georgian houses, St Andrew's church, White Hart Hotel (18c) ⬛12 Dunstable St ✆(01525)
402051 Restaurant: Upstairs Downstairs, King's Arms Yd ✆(01525) 404303

> **Rose and Crown**, Ridgmont MK43 0TY ✆Ridgmont (01525) 280245 OS map 153/977363 4m W
> of Ampthill on right of A507 (Woburn) Open all year 15 pitches Level grass, sheltered
> ⬛✗⌂⤸⚲🔧⊕⊘⊕ No showers £5.00-£7.50 (all cards)

BALDOCK, Herts   **Map F3**
Pop 6700 EC Thurs Ancient town with Georgian houses lining High St SEE Wynn almshouses,
Ashwell village 4m NE Restaurant: Forte Travelodge on A1 southbound ✆(01462) 835329

> **Radwell Mill Lake**, Radwell Mill SG7 5ET *Quiet orchard site with easy access to A1(M)* ✆(01462)
> 730253 OS map 153/229358 2m NW of Baldock off A507 (Ampthill) via Radwell (beyond village)
> near junct 10 of A1(M) Open Easter-Nov 10 pitches Level grass, sheltered ⊕🔩 lake £5.00

BANBURY, Oxon   **Map B3**
Pop 38,170. EC Tues, MD Thurs, Sat SEE church, Calthorpe Manor, Broughton castle and church
3m SW, Wroxton cottages 3m NW ⬛ Banbury Museum, 8 Horsefair ✆Banbury (01295) 259855
Restaurant: Cromwell Lodge, North Bar ✆(01295) 259781

> **Barnstones Caravan Park**, Great Bourton OX17 1QU ✆Banbury (01295) 750289 OS map
> 151/455453 3m N of Banbury off A423 (Coventry) on Great Bourton road Open all year 49
> pitches with mains electricity (20 with all mains services) 4 acres, level grass and hard standing,
> sheltered ⌂⬛🔧⊘⊕⊘⊕⤸🔧⚲ heated toilet block £5.50

> **Bo Peep Farm (Caravan Club)**, Adderbury OX17 3NP ✆(01295) 810605 OS map 151/482348 3m
> S of Banbury off A4260 (Oxford) on right of B4100 (Aynho) Open Easter-Oct 82 pitches 9 acres
> level/sloping grass, part sheltered ⬛⬛🔧⊘⊕⊘⊕🔩 £10.00-£14.00

> **Mollington Touring Caravan Park**, The Yews, Mollington OX17 1AZ *Central for touring Cotswolds*
> ✆(01295) 750731 OS map 151/440475 4m N of Banbury on A423 (Coventry) near junct 11 of
> M40 Open all year 24 pitches 2 acres level/sloping grass and hard standings, sheltered 🔩⊕⚲
> £6.00

BEACONSFIELD, Bucks   **Map E5**
Pop 13,400 EC Wed, Sat Busy town on wide main street (A40) in lovely wooded countryside SEE
Model Village, Friends' Meeting House at Jordans, Milton's Cottage at Chalfont St Giles, Chiltern
Hills Restaurant: Greyhound, Windsor End (off A40 roundabout) ✆(01494) 673823

> **Highclere Farm Country Touring Park**, New Barn Lane, Seer Green HP9 2QZ ✆(01494) 874505
> OS map 176/976928 3m E of Beaconsfield off A335 (Amersham) on Seer Green road
> (signposted) at Butlers Cross (M40 junct 2) Open Mar-Jan 60 pitches 3 acres level grass and
> hard standing sheltered ⬛⬛🔧⊘⊕⊘⤸⚲ £9.50-£12.00 (most cards exc Diners)

BICESTER, Oxon   **Map C4**
Pop 7300 Noted fox-hunting centre enclosing wide market square Restaurant: Greyhound Inn 4m E
at Marsh Gibbon ✆(01869) 277365

> **Heyford Leys Farm**, Upper Heyford OX6 3LU ✆(01869) 232048 OS map 164/513245 3m NW of
> Bicester off B4030 (Chipping Norton) between junct 9 and 10 of M40 Open Mar-Oct 100 pitches
> (55 static) ⬛⬛🔧⊘⤸⊕⚲ £6.00

FOLLOW THE COUNTRY CODE

**Guard against all risk of fire. Fasten all gates. Keep dogs under proper control. Keep to the
paths across farmland. Avoid damaging fences, hedges and walls. Leave no litter. Safeguard
water supplies. Protect wildlife, plants and trees. Go carefully on country roads and be
prepared for slow-moving vehicles like tractors. Respect the life of the countryside.**

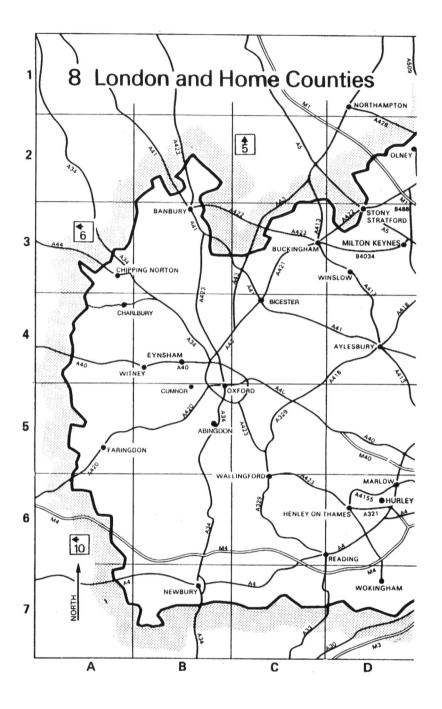

8 London and Home Counties

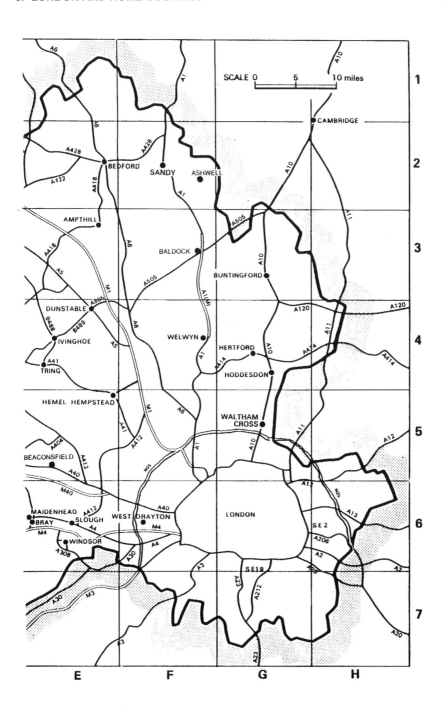

BUCKINGHAM, Bucks   **Map C3**
Pop 8,000. EC Thurs, MD Tues, Sat SEE Stowe School (via Brackley road), Claydon House 8m SE
🛈 Old Gaol Museum, Market Hill ☏ (01280) 823020 Restaurant: White Hart, Market Sq ☏ (01280)
815151
Treefields Caravan Park, Bourton Road MK18 1BE ☏ (01280) 822100 OS map 152/715333 ½m E
  of Buckingham on A421 (Milton Keynes) near river Ouse Open Mar-Sept 20 pitches (10 static)
  Level grass and hard standing, sheltered *No showers* £3.00-£5.00

BURCHFIELD—see Reading

CHARLBURY, Oxon   **Map A4**
Pop 2,630. EC Wed or Thurs Restaurant: Bell, Church St ☏ (01608) 810278
Cotswold View Caravan and Camping Site, OX7 3JH ☏ Charlbury (01608) 810314 Fax (01608)
  811891 OS map 164/363209 1m NNW of Charlbury on B4022 (Enstone) Open Easter-Oct 125
  pitches Grass, part level 🐾 ⚓ 🗑 🔌 ⊕ ⚌ 🛢 🏪 ♿ hard tennis court, bike hire £8.00-£11.00 (inc
  showers)

CHIPPING NORTON, Oxon   **Map A3**
Pop 5,200. EC Thurs, MD Wed Small Cotswold town still with several old inns, the relics of coaching
days SEE church, almshouses, Guildhall, White Hart Inn (17c) 🛈 Guildhall ☏ Chipping Norton
(01608) 642572 Restaurant: White Hart, High St ☏ (01608) 642572
Chipping Norton Park (Camping Club), Chadlington OX7 3PN ☏ Chadlington (01608) 641993 OS
  map 164/315244 2m S of Chipping Norton off A361 (Burford) on right of Chadlington road Open
  Mar-Oct 105 pitches 4½ acres, level grass, sheltered 🗑 🔌 🔌 ⊕ ⊘ ⚌ £13.80-£14.90
Churchill Heath Caravan Site, Kingham OX7 6UJ ☏ Kingham (01608) 658317 OS map
  163/256227 4½m SW of Chipping Norton on left of B4450 (Stow on the Wold) Open all year 50
  pitches Grass and hard standing, level, sheltered 🐾 ↦ ⚓ 🗑 🔌 🔌 ⊕ ⊘ ⚌ 🛢 £10.50-£15.00

CUMNOR, Oxon   **Map B5**
Pop 820 SEE view from summit of Hurst Hill, church (interior) Restaurant: Bear and Ragged Staff,
Appleton Rd ☏ (01865) 862329
Spring Farm, Faringdon Rd OX2 9QY ☏ (01865) 863028 OS map 164/462032 ½m SW of Cumnor
  on right of A420 (Faringdon)—signposted Open Apr-Oct 20 pitches—booking advisable
  Level/sloping grass, sheltered ⊕ ✿ £3.50-£4.50

FARINGDON, Oxon   **Map A5**
Pop 5,100 EC Thurs, MD Tues SEE church, arcaded library, Folly Tower, Great Barn (NT) at Great
Coxwell 2m SE, Buscot House 3m NW 🛈 Pump House, Market Place ☏ Faringdon (01367) 242191
Restaurant: Bell, Market Pl ☏ (01367) 240534
Swan Hotel, Radcot Bridge, Clanfield OX8 2SX ☏ (01367) 810220 OS map 163/286995 2m N of
  Faringdon on A4095 (Witney) by river Thames Open all year, 25 pitches 2 acres, level ✘
  (snack), 🍷 fishing, boating, B & B *No showers* £3.00-£4.00

HEMEL HEMPSTEAD, Herts   **Map E5**
Pop 79,580 EC Wed, MD Thurs SEE civic centre, St Mary's church, water gardens 🛈 Dacorum
Centre, Marlowes ☏ Hemel Hempstead (01442) 234222 Restaurant: Moat House 3m W on A41 at
Bourne End ☏ (01442) 877241
Breakspear Way (Caravan Club), Buncefield Lane, Breakspear Way HP2 4TZ ☏ Hemel
  Hempstead (01442) 68286 (0800-2000 hrs) OS map 166/085076 1m E of Hemel Hempstead off
  A414 (M1/M10) Open Mar 27-Dec 2, 60 pitches 4½ acres, level 🗑 🔌 🔌 ⊕ ⊘ restaurant adj
  £7.00-£8.00

HENLEY ON THAMES, Oxon   **Map D6**
Pop 12,000. EC Wed, MD Thurs SEE Thames bridge, church, Kenton Theatre, royal regatta (Jun-
Jul) 🛈 Town Hall, Market Place ☏ Henley on Thames (01491) 578034 Restaurant: Red Lion, Hart
St ☏ (01491) 572161
Swiss Farm International Caravan Park, Marlow Road RG9 2HY ☏ Henley on Thames (01491)
  573419 OS map 175/760834 ¼m N of Henley on Thames on left of A4155 (Marlow) Open Mar-
  Oct 180 pitches Grass level, sloping, sheltered 🍷 ↦ 🗑 🔌 🔌 ⊕ ⊘ 🖼 ⊕ ⚌ ▭ 🚲 fishing, social club
  £9.00-£11.00

HERTFORD, Herts   Map G4
Pop 25,000 EC Thurs MD Sat SEE St Leonard's church, museum, old houses and inns ⓘ The
Castle ☏ (01992) 584322 Restaurant: Marquee, Bircherley Green ☏ (01992) 558999

Mangrove Road Park (Camping Club), Mangrove Road SG13 8QL ☏ Hertford (01992) 586696
OS map 166/334113 1m S of Hertford off A414 (Chelmsford) Open Mar 24-Nov 3 250 pitches 32
acres, level grass and hard standings, sheltered 🔌🏕️⊕∅🥤 £10.00-£17.00 (Mastercard/Visa)

HODDESDON, Herts   Map G4
Pop 30,130. EC Thurs, MD Wed Restaurant: New Rose and Crown 3m N at Ware ☏ (01920)
462572

Lee Valley Caravan Park, Essex Road EN11 0AS ☏ Hoddesdon (01992) 462090 OS map
166/383082 1m SE of Hoddesdon off A1107 (Cheshunt) near weir pool in Lee Valley Regional
Park Open Easter-Oct 200 pitches (100 static) 24 acres, level grass 🔌🏕️🚿⊕∅🥤♿ boating,
fishing, model railway club £9.90

HURLEY, Berks   Map D6
Pop 700, EC Wed SEE Thames (islands, lock, weir), parish church, ruined priory, cottages
Restaurant: Dew Drop off A423 ☏ (01628) 824327

Hurley Caravan Camping Park, Shepherds Lane, SL6 5NE *Riverside working farm with forest
walks nearby* ☏ (01628) 823501 and 824493 OS map 175/815840 ¾m W of Hurley centre off
A4130 (Henley) by river Thames Open Mar-Oct 650 pitches (450 static) 80 acres grass, level,
part sheltered 🚿 (peak periods) 🔌🏕️⊕∅🚻🍴🚐♿ multi-service hookups, river fishing,
launching ramp £6.50-£11.50 (Mastercard/Visa)

IVINGHOE, Bucks   Map E4
Restaurant: King's Head, Station Rd ☏ (01296) 668388

Silver Birch Cafe, Dunstable Road, Pitstone LU7 9EN ☏ (01296) 668348 OS map 165/947152
1½m SW of Ivinghoe on B488 (Tring) Open Mar-Nov 18 pitches Grass and hard standing,
sheltered ✗ *No showers* £4.50-£5.50

LONDON E4

Lee Valley Campsite, Sewardstone Road, Chingford E4 7RA ✆(0208) 529 5689 OS map
177/380970 10m N of central London on A112 (Waltham Abbey) Open Apr–Oct, 200 pitches 12½
acres, level grass and hard standing 🔋 ⚒ 🗓 🖭 ⊘ ⊕ Ø ⌲ ᕹ ironing room
£11.00 (Mastercard/Visa/Switch)

LONDON E15

Lee Valley Park, Eastway Camping Caravan Park, Temple Mills Lane, Stratford E15 2EN ✆(0208)
534 6085 OS map 177/372852 6 m NE of Central London off A112 (Stratford) Open Apr–Sept 80
pitches Grass, level ✗ 🗓 🖭 ⊕ Ø ❸ tennis, squash, cycle hire £11.00

LONDON N9

Lee Valley Leisure Centre, Meridian Way, Edmonton N9 0AS ✆(0208) 345 6666 OS map
177/360944 8m N of Central London off A406 (North Circular) near junct 25 of M25 Open all year
160 pitches 4½ acres grass (tents) hard standing (caravans), level 🔋 ✗ 🍷 🗓 🖭 🖭 ⊕ Ø ⌲ ᕹ
creche, sauna, golf, tennis, badminton, squash, cinema £11.20 (Mastercard/Visa/Euro)

LONDON SE2

Cooperative Woods (Caravan Club) Federation Road, Abbey Wood SE2 0LS ✆(0208) 310 2233
OS map 177/473785 10m SE of Central London off A206 (Erith) Open all year–must book
(caravans) 180 pitches 9 acres, grass, level/sloping 🔋 ⚒ 🗓 🖭 🖭 ⊕ Ø £6.10–£6.80

KEY: (1) Hemel Hempstead   (2) Sewardstone   (3) Pickets Lock
(4) Eastway   (5) Loughton p**103**   (6) Hackney   (7) Crystal Palace
(8) Chertsey p**126**   (9) West Drayton   (10) Acton

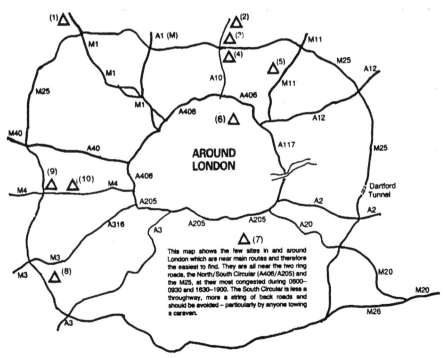

This map shows the few sites in and around
London which are near main routes and therefore
the easiest to find. They are all near the two ring
roads, the North/South Circular (A406/A205) and
the M25, at their most congested during 0800–
0930 and 1630–1900. The South Circular is less a
throughway, more a string of back roads and
should be avoided – particularly by anyone towing
a caravan.

LONDON SE19

Crystal Palace Park (Caravan Club), Crystal Palace Parade SE19 1UF ☎(0208) 778 7155 Fax (0181) 636 0980 OS map 176/177/338712 5½m S of Central London off A212 (Croydon) adj Crystal Palace sports centre Open all year 150 pitches 6 acres, hard standings and grass, level, terraced Late arrivals area open all night ▯◻▯▯▯▯▯ £11.00-£18.00

MAIDENHEAD, Berks   **Map E6**
Pop 50,000. EC Thurs, MD Fri, Sat SEE Oldfield House, river Thames, 18c bridge, Courage Shire Horse Centre 2m W on A4 ▯ Central Library, St Ives Road ☎Maidenhead (01628) 278111 Restaurant: Jack of Both Sides, Queen St ☎(01628) 220870

Amerden Camping Site, Old Marsh Lane, Dorney Reach SL6 0EE ☎Maidenhead (01628) 627461 OS map 175/918797 4m SE of Maidenhead off A4 (Slough) adjoining Bray Lock Open Apr-Oct 40 pitches level grass ▯▯▯▯▯▯▯▯▯ £8.00-£12.00 inc elect

---

NEWBURY, Berks   **Map B7**
Pop 29,000. EC Wed, MD Thurs, Sat SEE 16c church, 16c Cloth Hall, St Bartholomew's Hospital (almshouses) Kennet and Avon Canal (barge trips), racecourse ▯ The Wharf ☎(01635) 430267 Restaurant: Coopers Arms, Bartholomew St ☎(01635) 247469

Oakley Farm Caravan Camping Park, Oakley Farm House, Wash Water RG20 0LP ☎Newbury (01635) 36581 OS map 174/455630 2½m SW of Newbury off A34 (Winchester) on Highclere/Wash Common road Open Mar-Oct 30 pitches 3 acres level grass and hard standing ▯▯▯▯▯▯▯▯ £6.50

OLNEY, Bucks   **Map D2**
Pop 3,470. EC Wed, MD Thurs Small town famous for pancake race and as place where Cowper and Newton published the 300 Olney hymns Restaurant: Bull, Market Pl ☎(01234) 355719

Emberton Country Park, MK46 5DB ☎(01234) 711575 OS map 152/886505 1m S of Olney on A509 (Newport Pagnell) beside river Ouse Open Apr-Oct—must book peak periods 315 pitches (115 static) Grass, level, sheltered ▯▯▯▯▯▯▯ fishing, boating (40 acres of lakes), nature trail £8.25-£14.00 (most cards)

OXFORD, Oxon   **Map B4**
Pop 116,400. MD Wed Industrial and university city where teaching began in 12c SEE colleges, High Street, Bodleian library, Ashmolean museum, All Souls College chapel, Radcliffe camera, churches, old inns, towpath walks ▯ St Aldates ☎(01865) 726871 Restaurant: Turf Tavern, Bath Place via St Helens Passage ☎(01865) 243235

Cassington Mill Caravan Park, Eynsham Road, Cassington OX8 1DB ☎Oxford (01865) 881081 OS map 164/449099 2½m NW of Oxford off A40 (Witney) on Eynsham road Open Apr-Oct 135 pitches (50 static) Grass, hard standing, level ▯▯▯▯▯▯▯▯▯ river swimming, fishing, canoeing £8.00-£9.50 (inc hot water) (1999)

Diamond Farm Caravan Camping Park, Bletchingdon OX5 3DR ☎Bletchingdon (01869) 350909 OS map 164/513169 5m N of Oxford off A423 (Banbury) and A34 (Bicester) on B4027 (Bletchingdon) Open all year 37 pitches 4 acres, level grass, sheltered, some hard standing ▯▯▯▯▯▯▯▯ (heated) ▯▯▯▯ £7.00-£10.00

Oxford Camping (Camping Club), 426 Abingdon Road OX1 4XN ☎Oxford (01865) 244088 OS map 164/519039 1½m S of Oxford centre on A4144 (Abingdon) near junction with ring road, at rear of Touchwood's outdoor life centre Open all year 84 pitches Grass, level, open ▯▯▯▯▯▯ £13.80-£14.90 (Mastercard/Visa)

Slipway Tourist Park, Meadow Lane, Donnington Bridge OX4 4BL ☎Oxford (01865) 243421 OS map 164/526043 2m S of Oxford off A423 (Maidenhead) and A4144 Open Apr-Oct 15 pitches 3 acres level grass fishing and boating near £5.00 (1999)

READING, Berks   **Map D6**
Pop 138,000. MD Mon, Wed, Fri, Sat Major county town on river Kennet where ancient centre still
stands SEE art gallery and museum, churches, Mapledurham House 3m NW, Stratfield Saye House
7m S ◪ Town Hall, Blagrave St ☏ (01734) 566226 Restaurant: Mama Mia, St Mary's Butts
☏ (01734) 581357

Loddon Court Farm, Beech Hill Road, Spencers Wood RG7 1HT ☏ (0118) 988 3153 OS map
175/710653 4½m S of Reading off A33 (Basingstoke) at Doubles Garage near junction 11 of M4
Open all year 100 pitches (60 static) Grass, level, part sheltered ▤⊘⊕⊘⊕▣ £6.00

Rose Lawn, Burghfield RG3 3RU ☏ (01734) 833707 Fax (01734) 832447 OS map 175/667677 3m
SW of Reading off Newbury road near Junction 12 of M4 Open May-Oct 11 pitches Grass and
hard standings, level, open ✕⊻⊘▭▣❖ golf course £5.00

Wellington Country Park, Riseley GU17 7TA ☏ (0118) 9326444 OS map 175/724626 6m S of
Reading off A33 (Basingstoke) on A32 (Alton) Open Mar-Oct 58 pitches Grass, level, part
sheltered ✕▤▣⊘⊕⊘⤳ £7.00-£13.00

STANDLAKE–see Witney

STONY STRATFORD, Bucks   **Map D3**
Pop 5,270. EC Thurs SEE Georgian High Street, Cock inn, Grand Union Canal Restaurant:
Stratford, St Paul's Court, High St ☏ (01908) 566577

Cosgrove Lodge Park, Cosgrove MK19 7JP ☏ (01908) 563360 and 562846 OS map 152/798424
2m N of Stony Stratford off A5-A508 (Northampton) via Cosgrove Open Apr-Oct 900 pitches (300
static) ▤⤳▤▣⊘⊕⊘▭⊕⤳▣ boating, water skiing £9.00-£10.00

WALLINGFORD, Oxon   **Map C6**
Pop 6,500. EC Wed, MD Fri SEE churches, Thames bridge, town hall, old houses and inns, Flint
House museum ◪ Town Hall, St Martins St ☏ Wallingford (01491) 826972 Restaurant: The George,
High St ☏ (01491) 836665

Benson Waterfront, Benson OX10 6SJ ☏ Wallingford (01491) 838304 OS map 164/175/613916
1½m N of Wallingford off A423 (Oxford) by river Thames Open Apr-Oct 50 pitches (25 static) 4
acres, level grass, sheltered ▤✕⊻⤳▤▣⊘⊕⊘ boating, fishing £10.00-£14.00
(Mastercard/Visa)

Bridge Villa International, Crowmarsh Gifford OX10 8HB ☏ Wallingford (01491) 836860 OS map
175/612895 ½m E of Wallingford by bridge over river Thames Open Feb-Dec–must book peak
periods 111 pitches Grass, level, sheltered ▤▣⊘⊕⊘▣ £6.00-£8.00 (Mastercard/Visa/Delta/
Switch)

Riverside Park OX10 8EB ☏ Wallingford (01491) 835232 and (01865) 341035 OS map
175/612895 ¼m E of Wallingford on A4130 (Henley) by river Thames–best approached from E
Open May-Sept–must book 28 pitches Grass, level ⊘▭❖⟁ boating, fishing £7.20-£9.50
(1999)

WALTHAM CROSS, Herts   **Map G5**
SEE King and Tinker Inn (16c), Eleanor Cross, Temple Bar, Waltham Abbey 2m E ◪ Sun St,
Waltham Abbey ☏ (01992) 652295 Restaurant: Royal Chase 2m SW at Enfield ☏ 0181-366 6500

Theobalds Park (Camping Club), Bulls Cross Ride EN7 5HS ☏ Waltham Cross (01992) 620604
OS map 166/344005 2m W of Waltham Cross off Crews Hill road at Bulls Cross Open Mar 20-
Oct 30 150 pitches 14 acres, level grass, sheltered ▤▣⊘⊕⊘⊕ recreation room £9.80-£12.40
(Mastercard/Visa)

Vintage France

192pp ISBN 1-870009-04-5

Tours of the major vineyard areas make a celebratory start with Champagne in the north and end
with Cognac and the Loire in the west. In between come Alsace, the Jura, Burgundy, Beaujolais, the
Rhone Valley, Provence, Armagnac and the world-famous Bordelais around Bordeaux. Each
vineyard area is described in terms of its history and landscape with individual wines related to the
places where they are made and can be tasted. Most of these areas still provide quiet roads, fine
scenery and local restaurant meals at local prices. **For details of publication and possible
reductions on cover price write to Frederick Tingey at Hillsboro, How Caple HR1 4TE.**

WITNEY, Oxon   **Map B4**
Pop 17,500. EC Wed, MD Thurs, Sat SEE Blanket Hall, Butter cross, church ⓘ Town Hall, Market Square ☏ Witney (01993) 775802 Restaurant: Marlborough, Market Sq ☏ (01993) 776353

Hardwick Park, Downs Road, Standlake OX8 7PZ ☏ Standlake (01865) 300501 OS map 164/392045 4m SE of Witney off A415 (Abingdon) by lake Open Apr-Oct 250 pitches (116 static) level grass 🛠♀↗🚐🚿🅿⊕∅↙🚮♿ lake fishing, swimming, windsurfing £7.80-£9.80 (1999) (Mastercard/Visa/Switch)

Lincoln Farm Park, High Street, Standlake OX8 7RH ☏ Standlake (01865) 300239 OS map 164/394028 5m SE of Witney near junction of A415 (Abingdon) and B4449 (Bampton) Open Mar-Nov 90 pitches (21 static) Grass and hard standing, level, sheltered 🛠🚐🚿🅿⊕∅◺↙🚮🏪🏠 fishing, pitch and putt, leisure centre with pool, spa and sauna £5.50-£12.95 (Mastercard/Visa)

WOKINGHAM, Berks   **Map D7**
Pop 27,000. EC Wed, MD Tues, Thurs, Fri, Sat Restaurant: Crooked Billet, Honey Hill (off B3430 2m SE) ☏ (0118) 9733928

California Chalet and Touring Park, Finchampstead RG40 4HU ☏ (01734) 733928 OS map 175/785650 3½m SW of Wokingham off A321 (Sandhurst) and B3016 (Finchampstead) Open Mar-Oct 35 pitches Grass and hard standings, level, sheltered 🛠🚐↙🏠 lake fishing, paddling pool, nature trail £9.00-£10.50

120

9 Southern England

ISLE OF WIGHT

Kent, Surrey, Sussex, Hampshire and the Isle of Wight form the extensive region of Southern England.

The most striking geographical feature of Kent is the North Downs, extending from Greater London to the white cliffs of Dover and broken only by the rivers Medway, Darent and the Stour. The silted-up shore of the Thames Estuary on the north gives way to the sandy beaches of North Foreland, fronted on one side by Margate and on the other by Ramsgate. Along the south coast, high cliffs alternate with sandbanks and reclaimed saltings like flat and secretive Romney Marsh. Places of interest include the walled city of Canterbury, historic Rochester, the stately home of Knole, Dover Castle and the smugglers' prison of Dymchurch, from which a miniature railway operates as far as Romney.

Romney Marsh crosses the boundary into East Sussex, where the coast is strung with resorts. Stretching across the northern part of the county is the Weald, covered by the great Ashdown Forest southwest of East Grinstead. Backing the western half of the coast between Eastbourne and Brighton are the South Downs, cut by the sea into tall cliffs.

An unusual feature of the coast of West Sussex is the headland of Selsey Bill, south of Chichester. At this point the South Downs are well inland, the coast west of Chichester being indented by tidal creeks and inlets forming a natural harbour. Near Chichester is the Weald and Downland Museum at Singleton, the Roman palace of Fishbourne and the Kingsley Vale Nature Reserve. Historical buildings include the castles of Arundel, Bodiam and ruined Pevensey and the fanciful Regency Pavilion at Brighton.

Green belt Surrey retains miles of chalk downs and woodlands cut by rich valleys. The North Downs extend east and west, with Box Hill and Leith Hill and the Hog's Back forming the heights. Some of Surrey's most charming villages are Ripley, Shere, Farnham and Brockham Green. Other important sights are the gardens of Wisley, and Polesden Lacey.

The best known natural feature of Hampshire is the New Forest, centred on Lyndhurst, with its chalk uplands, deep woods and sandy wastelands. Guarding the entrance to Southampton Water is the Isle of Wight, twenty-two miles wide and thirteen miles from north to south, wooded down to the water's edge in many places and rising to an east–west ridge of chalk downs. The rural west around Freshwater is probably the most inviting, being less populated. Ferries carrying passengers operate from Portsmouth to Ryde, and carrying cars and passengers from Portsmouth to Fishbourne, Lymington to Yarmouth and Southampton to Cowes. Bus services are comprehensive but the only railway runs between Ryde and Shanklin. Major sights in Hampshire include Osborne House on the Isle of Wight, the castle and magnificent cathedral of Winchester, the maritime museum at Buckler's Hard and Nelson's *Victory* in Portsmouth Dockyard.

Campsites in Southern England are usually well equipped. Biggest concentrations are around Chichester, Lymington and Sandown in the south and Whitstable in the north. Many cater for campers and caravanners going to and from the cross-Channel ports, though few exist at the ports themselves.

ANDOVER, Hants   **Map B4**
Pop 29,840. EC Wed, MD Thurs, Sat SEE Guildhall, church ▊Town Mill House, Bridge St
☎(01264) 324320 Restaurant: Globe, High St ☎(01264) 323415

Wyke Down Touring Caravan Camping Park, Picket Piece SP11 6LX ☎Andover (01264) 352048
OS map 185/403476 3m E of Andover off A303 (signposted) Open all year 200 pitches Part hard
standing, level grass, part sheltered ✗⚲⇆⚲⊹🔷⊕⌀⬜⚲⊐ golf driving range £9.00
(Mastercard/Visa)

ARUNDEL, W Sussex   **Map D6**
Pop 2,160. EC Wed SEE castle, Swanbourne Lake, St Nicholas church, museum, Wildfowl Trust ▊
61 High Street ☎(01903) 882268 Restaurant: White Hart, Queen St ☎(01903) 882374

Maynards Caravan Camping Park, Crossbush BN18 9PQ ☎(01903) 882075 Fax (01903) 885547
Busy site with good access to A27 OS map 197/035065 ¾m E of Arundel off A27 (Worthing) at
Beefeater restaurant car park Open all year 70 pitches 2½ acres level grass, sheltered
🛒✗⚲⇆🔷⊕⌀⊕⚲⚲& £8.00-£10.00 (inc showers)

Ship and Anchor Marina, Station Road, Ford BN18 0BJ ☎(01243) 551262 OS map 197/002040
2½m S of Arundel on Ford road by river Open Mar-Oct 160 pitches 12 acres, level grass,
sheltered 🛒✗⚲⇆🔷⊕⌀⚲& lic premises £9.50-£11.00

ASHFORD, Kent   **Map G4**
Pop 47,000. EC Wed, MD Tues, Wed, Sat SEE St Mary church, Windmill, memorial gardens ▊The
Churchyard ☎(01233) 629165 Restaurant: Hare and Hounds, Maidstone Rd, Potters Cnr (A20)
☎(01233) 621760

Broadhembury Farm, Steeds Lane, Kingsnorth TN26 1NQ ☎Ashford (01233) 620859 OS map
189/012381 3m S of Ashford off A2070 (New Romney) in Kingsnorth (M20 junct 10) Open all
year 60 pitches (25 static) 5 acres, level grass and hard standing, sheltered
🛒⚲🔷⚲🔷⊕⌀⊕⚲⊐⚲& first aid £10.00-£13.00 (Mastercard/Visa)

BARHAM, Kent   **Map G4**
Pop 4,240. EC Wed SEE church, Downs Restaurant: Dolls House, on Elham Valley Rd (B2065)
☎(01227) 831241

Ropersole Farm, Dover Road CT4 6SA ☎(01227) 831352 OS map 179/228486 1m SE of
Barham on southbound carriageway of A2 (Canterbury\-Dover) Open Mar-Oct, 85 pitches 5
acres, level, woodland setting 🛒✗ (snack), ⚲🔷⌀ £5.00

BARTON ON SEA, Hants   **Map A6**
Pop 3620 EC Wed Modern resort noted for its low cliffs (haunt of fossil hunters) and sand/shingle
beach Restaurant: Old Coastguard, Marine Drive East ☎(01425) 612987

Bunny Creek Caravan Park, Milford Rd, Barton Common BH25 5PB ☎(01425) 612270 OS map
195/252936 1m E of Barton on Sea on B3058 (Milford on Sea) Open all year 10 pitches 1½
acres level grass £6.00-£10.50

BASINGSTOKE, Hants   **Map B4**
Pop 81,000 EC Thurs MD Wed, Sat One-time market town massively expanded by London
overspill SEE 15c church, museum, war memorial park, the Vyne (NT) 3m N, Old Basing 3m E,
Steventon (birthplace of Jane Austen) 5m SW ▊Willis Museum, Old Town Hall, Market Place
☎(01256) 817618 Restaurant: Bounty, Bounty Rd ☎(01256) 820071

Jolly Farmer Inn, Cliddesden RG25 2JL ☎(01256) 473073 OS map 185/632493 2m S of
Basingstoke off A339 (Alton) on right of B3046 (Alresford) in Cliddesden, near junct 6 of M3 Open
all year 6 pitches 7 acres level/sloping grass ✗⚲⊕⌀⚲ £3.00

Kloofs Caravan Park

Sandhurst Lane, Whydown TN39 4RG

2m W of Bexhill off A259 (Eastbourne) at little Common – signposted

Open Mar-Jan, sloping grass and hard standings, sheltered

See listing under Bexhill

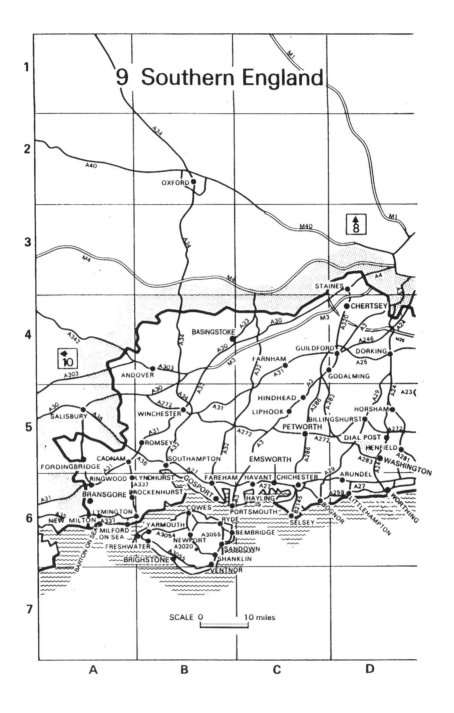

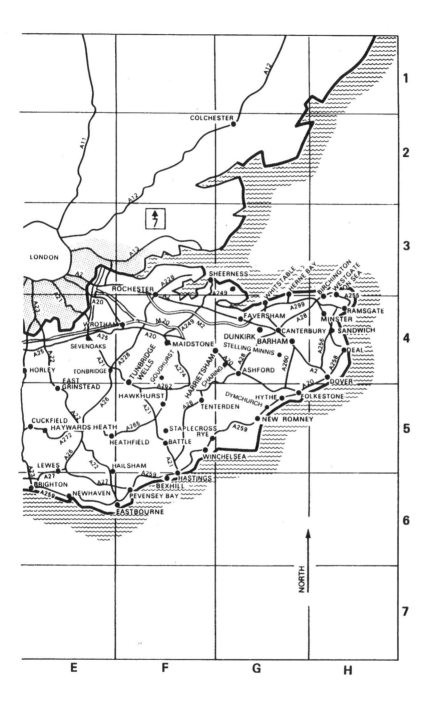

E   F   G   H

BATTLE, E Sussex   **Map F5**
Pop 5,000. EC Wed, MD Fri SEE Abbey ruins, Deanery, Bull Ring, Langton House museum ⓘ 88
High Street ✆(01424) 773721 Restaurant: George, High St ✆(01424) 774466

Brakes Coppice Park, Forewood Lane, Crowhurst TN33 9AB ✆(01424) 830322 OS map
199/765134 2m SE of Battle off A2100 (Hastings) and Crowhurst road Open Mar-Oct 30
pitches—must book 4 acres, level/gentle slope on woodland estate, grass and hard standing
🐾📶🔌🔋✚⊘🔆⏚🚻 fishing £6.00-£7.00

Crazy Lane Tourist Park, Whydown Farm, Crazy Lane, Sedlescombe TN33 0QT ✆(01424) 870147
OS map 199/782170 2½m NE of Battle near junction of A21 (Hastings–Hurst Green) and B2244
(Maidstone) Open Mar-Oct, 36 pitches 3 acres, grass, level, sheltered 🐾🔌📶🔋✚⊘🚻♿
£8.00-£9.00

Normanhurst Court (Caravan Club), Stevens Crouch TN33 9LR ✆Battle (01424) 773808 (0800-
2000 hrs) OS map 199/711148 3m SW of Battle on A271 (Hurstmonceux) Open Apr-Oct, 155
pitches—no tents 18 acres, terraced parkland level/sloping grass and hard standing, sheltered
🔌📶✚⊘🔋⏚♿ £11.20-£13.80 (Mastercard/Visa/Switch)

Senlac Park, Main Road, Catsfield TN33 9DU ✆(01424) 773969 OS map 199/719151 2m W of
Battle off A269 (Bexhill) on B2204 (Ninfield) Open Mar-Oct 32 pitches Level grass and hard
standings, sheltered by secluded woodland 📶⊘✚ heated toilet block £7.50 (Mastercard/Visa)

Tellis Coppice Touring Caravan Park, Catsfield TN33 9LP ✆(01424) 773969 OS map
199/719151 2m W of Battle on A269 (Bexhill) Open Mar-Nov 32 pitches Grass, level, sheltered
⊘✚ sep pitches, woodland £6.00

BEMBRIDGE, Isle of Wight   **Map C6**
Pop 3,180. EC Thurs SEE harbour, windmill Restaurant: Row Barge, Station Rd ✆(01983) 872874

Carpenters Farm, St Helens PO33 1YL ✆Isle of Wight (01983) 872450 OS map 196/618886 3m
W of Bembridge off B3330 (Ryde) Open May-Oct 70 pitches Grass, sloping, sheltered
🔌📶⊘✚⊘ £6.00

Guildford Park Holiday Camping and Caravan Site, Guildford Road, St Helens PO33 1UH ✆Isle
of Wight (01983) 872821 OS map 196/627893 3m NW of Bembridge off B3330 (Ryde) Open
Easter-Sept 130 pitches 5 acres, level 🐾⊘✚⏚ £4.60

Nodes Point Holiday Village, St Helens PO33 1YA ✆Isle of Wight (01983) 872401 OS map
196/637899 2m NW of Bembridge off B3395–B3340 (Ryde) Open May-Oct, 500 pitches (211
static) Grass, sloping 🐾✕🍽🔌📶✚⊘🔋🔆🏨 £10.00-£14.00

Whitecliff Bay Holiday Park PO35 5PL ✆Isle of Wight (01983) 872671 OS map 196/637867
1½m S of Bembridge off B3395 (Sandown) Open Easter-Oct, 400 pitches (224 static) Grass, part
level hard standings 🐾✕🍽⏚🏹🔌📶⊘✚⊘🔋🔆⏚🏨♿ lic club, leisure centre £4.00-
£6.00

BEXHILL ON SEA, E Sussex   **Map F6**
Pop 35,000. EC Wed SEE St Peter's church, De la Warr Pavilion, Manor House gardens in Old
Town ⓘ De La Warr Pavillion, Marina ✆Bexhill on Sea (01424) 212023 Restaurant: Southlands
Court, Hastings Rd ✆(01424) 210628

Cobbs Hill Farm, Watermill Lane, Sidley TN39 5JA ✆Bexhill on Sea (01424) 213460 OS map
199/735107 1m N of Bexhill off A269 (Ninfield) on Watermill Lane Open Apr-Oct—must book
public holidays 45 pitches Level grass and hard standing, sheltered 🐾📶⊘✚⊘🔋⏚🔆 £4.60-
£5.30

Kloofs Caravan Park, Sandhurst Lane, Whydown TN39 4RG ✆(01424) 842839 OS map
199/708091 2m W of Bexhill off A259 (Eastbourne) at Little Common—signposted Open Mar-Jan
125 pitches (75 static) 3 acres level/sloping grass and hard standing, sheltered
🐾📶⊘✚⊘🔋⏚🅿 £5.00

BIDDENDEN—see Tenterden

BILLINGSHURST, W Sussex   **Map D5**
Pop 5,570. EC Wed SEE church Restaurant: The Olde Six Bells, High St ✆(01403) 782124

Limeburners Camping, Newbridge RH14 9JA ✆Billingshurst (01403) 782311 OS map 197/074255
1½ W of Billingshurst off A272 (Petworth) on B2133 (Ashington) Open Apr-Oct 42 pitches Grass,
level, sheltered ✕🍽📶⊘✚⊘🔋 (£15/mth) £8.00 (Mastercard/Visa/Switch)

BIRCHINGTON, Kent   **Map H3**
Pop 7,920. EC Wed SEE DG Rossetti's grave, Quex Park Restaurant: Seaview, Station Rd
☎(01843) 841702

Quex Caravan Park, Park Road CT7 0BL ☎(01843) 841273 OS map 179/310683 1m SE of
Birchington off A28 (Margate) Open Mar-Oct, 208 pitches (120 static) 13½ acres, level grass
🏕🗄🚿🅰️💧🅿️🔌🅱️↩ £9.50-£11.50 (Mastercard/Visa)

St Nicholas at Wade Camping, Court Road, St Nicholas at Wade CT7 0NH ☎Thanet (01843)
847245 OS map 179/263667 2½m SW of Birchington off A28/A299 (Canterbury) Open Apr-Oct
75 pitches Grass, level, sheltered 🏕🚿🅰️💧↩ £9.00-£11.00

Thanet Way Caravan Park, Frost Farm, St Nicholas at Wade CT7 0NA ☎Thanet (01843) 847219
OS map 179/269671 2m SW of Birchington on A299 (Herne Bay) Open Mar-Oct 60 pitches (48
static)–no tents Grass, part level, open 🗄🚿🅰️💧🅱️🅿️ £6.50-£8.50

Two Chimneys Caravan Park, Shottendane Road, CT7 0HD ☎Thanet (01843) 841068/843157
OS map 179/320684 2m SE of Birchington off Manston road near Two Chimneys adj garden
centre Open Mar-Oct 140 pitches (59 static) Grass, level, sheltered 🏕✖
(snacks)🍷↩🗄🚿🅰️💧🅿️🚿🅾️🔲↩🅱️🔌🏪⚓🏧 club house, amusements, solarium, sauna, spa bath,
tennis court £9.00-£16.00 (Mastercard/Visa/Eurocard)

BODIAM–see Staplecross

BOGNOR REGIS, W Sussex   **Map C6**
Pop 36,960. EC Wed, MD Fri SEE Hotham Park arboretum, Dome House ℹ️ Place St Maur des
Fosses, Belmont Street ☎(01243) 823140 Restaurant: Royal Norfolk, Esplanade ☎(01243)
826222

Copthorne Caravan Park, Rose Green Rd PO21 3ER ☎(01243) 262408 OS map 197/909996 2m
NW of Bognor Regis off B2166 (Chichester) on right of Rose Green road Open Apr-Oct 94 pitches
(90 static)–no tents 6 acres level grass, sheltered 🗄🚿🅰️💧🅾️↩🅱️🔌🏪⚓ £7.00-£10.00

Rowan Way Park (Caravan Club), Rowan Way PO22 9RP ☎(01243) 828515 (0800-2000 hrs) OS
map 197/939014 1½m N of Bognor off A29 (Dorking) Open Mar 27-Oct 22, 120 pitches Level
grass 🗄🚿🅰️💧🅾️↩ £10.20-£12.80

The Lillies Nursery and Caravan Site, Yapton Rd, Barnham PO22 0AY ☎and Fax (01243) 552081
OS map 197/960040 4m N of Bognor Regis on B2233 (Eastergate-Climping) in Barnham Open
all year 40 pitches Level grass, sheltered 🏕🗄🚿🅰️💧🅾️🅿️🔲↩🏧 £8.00-£10.00 (most cards)

BOLNEY–see Haywards Heath

BRANSGORE, Hants   **Map A6**
Pop 4,700 SEE church, New Forest Restaurant: Three Tuns, Ringwood Rd ☎(01425) 672232

Harrow Wood Farm, Poplar Lane BH23 8JE ☎Bransgore (01425) 672487 OS map 195/193978
¼m SE of Bransgore off Hinton Admiral road Open Mar-Dec, 60 pitches 6 acres, hard standings
🗄🚿🅰️💧🅾️🅿️🔌 £9.50-£13.75 (Mastercard/Visa)

Heathfield Caravan Park BH23 8LA ☎Bransgore (01425) 672397 OS map 195/208895 1½m E of
Bransgore off Hinton Admiral road Open Mar-Oct 200 pitches–must book peak periods 14 acres,
level grass and hard standings 🏕🚿🅰️💧🅾️💧↩🏧 farm produce £8.00-£10.50

Holmsley Campsite (Forestry Commission), Forest Road, Thorney Hill, BH23 7EQ ☎(0131) 314
6505 OS map 195/215991 2m E of Bransgore on A35 (Southampton-Christchurch) Open Mar
20-Nov 2 700 pitches 89 acres level mainly open 🏕↩🗄🚿🅰️💧🅾️🅿️↩🏧 £6.50-£10.40 (1998)
(Mastercard/Visa)

BRIGHSTONE, Isle of Wight   **Map B6**
Restaurant: Wight Mouse Inn 6m SE at Chale ☎(01983) 730431
Chine Farm Camping, Military Road, Atherfield Bay PO38 2JH ☎Isle of Wight (01983) 740228
   OS map 196/445804 2m SE of Brighstone on A3055 (Ventnor) Open May-Sept 80 pitches
   Grass, level, open ⚲⊕❸↩☎ beach £5.50-£6.00
Grange Farm Brighstone Bay PO30 4DA ☎Isle of Wight (01983) 740296 OS map 196/420820
   1m SW of Brighstone on A3055 (Freshwater–Ventnor) Open Mar-Oct 60 pitches Grass, level,
   open ▲🗑☎⚲⊕∅❸↩🖳☎🏠 £8.50-£10.00 (most cards)

BROCKENHURST, Hants   **Map A6**
Pop 3,300. EC Wed SEE parish church, New Forest Restaurant: Snakecatcher, Lyndhurst Rd
☎(01590) 622348
Hollands Wood Campsite (Forestry Commission), Lyndhurst Road SO42 7QH ☎(01703) 283771
   OS map 196/303034 ½m N of Brockenhurst on A337 (Lyndhurst) near Balmer Lawn Hotel Open
   Mar 21-Sept 29, 600 pitches 168 acres level oak woodland 🗑⊕∅ £7.50-£11.50
Roundhill Camping, Beaulieu Road SQ42 7QL ☎(01703) 283771 OS map 196/335019 2m E of
   Brockenhurst on B3055 (Beaulieu) Open Easter-Sept, 500 pitches Heathland with areas of pine
   ⚲⊕∅ No showers £6.00-£8.50

CADNAM, Hants   **Map A5**
Pop 1,880 EC Wed SEE Rufus Stone Restaurant: Bell Inn 1m W at Brook ☎(01703) 812214
Ocknell Camping, Fritham SO43 7HH ☎(01703) 813771 OS map 195/255127 3m SW of Cadnam
   off A31 (Ringwood) at Stoney Cross–access for westbound traffic only via A3078 (Fordingbridge)
   and Brook Open Easter-Sept, 300 pitches ⚲⊕∅ £5.50-£7.60

CAMBER SANDS–see Rye

CANTERBURY, Kent   **Map G4**
Pop 39,000. EC Thurs, MD Wed, (cattle Mon) SEE Cathedral, churches, King's School, Eastbridge
Hospital (almshouses), city walls, Dane John gardens, castle keep, museum 🅸 34 St Margaret's St
☎(01227) 766567 Restaurant: Canterbury Tales, The Friars (opp Marlowe Theatre) ☎(01227)
768594
Bekesbourne Park (Camping Club), Bekesbourne Lane CT3 4AB ☎Canterbury (01227) 463216
   OS map 179/172577 1½m E of Canterbury off A257 (Sandwich) on right of Bekesbourne road
   Open Easter-Nov 260 pitches Grass, sheltered ▲↗🗑☎⚲⊕↩🖳 first aid £8.80-£9.60
Yew Tree Park, Stone Street, Petham CT4 5PL ☎(01227) 700306 OS map 179/137508 5 m S of
   Canterbury off B2068 (Hythe) by Chequers Inn Open Mar-Oct, 45 pitches 4 acres, grass,
   level/sloping ▲🗑☎⚲⊕∅🖂❸↩✿🖳🏠👤 £7.00-£11.50 (Mastercard/Visa)

CAPEL LE FERNE–see Folkestone

CHARING, Kent   **Map G4**
Pop 750 SEE North Downs Way SE Restaurant: Red Lion 1m W at Charing Heath ☎(01233)
712418
Dean Court Farm, Westwell TN25 4NH ☎(01233) 712924 OS map 189/950489 2m E of Charing
   off A252 (Canterbury) at Challock on Westwell Lane Open all year 20 pitches Level/sloping grass
   ⊕ no showers £7.00

CHERTSEY, Surrey   **Map D4**
Pop 11,620 EC Wed MD Sat SEE St Peter's church, 18c river bridge, museum Restaurant: Bridge,
Chertsey Bridge ☎(01932) 564408
Chertsey International (Camping Club), Bridge Road KT16 8JX ☎Chertsey (01932) 562405
   (0800-2000 hrs) OS map 176/052667 ½m NE of Chertsey on left of B375 (Shepperton) by river
   Thames near junction 11 of M25 Open all year, 250 pitches–adv booking min 3 nights Camping
   carnet or temporary membership required in peak season 12 acres, level grass and hard
   standings, woodland ✘ (snack), 🗑☎↩👤 recreation room £9.20-£12.05

CHICHESTER, W Sussex Map C6
Pop 24,000. EC Thurs, MD Wed, Sat One-time Roman town, still with its ancient street pattern SEE cathedral, market cross, city walls, Council House (corporation plate), Greyfriars monastery ruins, Festival Theatre, Roman Palace and Theatre at Fishbourne ⓘ 29a South St ✆ Chichester (01243) 775888 Restaurant: Crown and Anchor, Dell Quay ✆ (01243) 781712

Bell Caravan Park, Bell Lane, Birdham PO20 7HY ✆ (01243) 512264 OS map 197/819992 4½m SW of Chichester off A268 (West Wittering) on B2198 (Bracklesham) Open Mar-Oct 75 pitches (60 static) Level grass, sheltered £9.00

Gees Camp, Stocks Lane, East Wittering PO20 8NY ✆ (01243) 670223 6m SW of Chichester on A286/B2198 (Bracklesham) Open Mar-Oct, 25 pitches 1 acre, level grass, sheltered £8.00-£8.50

Nunnington Farm, West Wittering PO20 8LZ OS map 197/787988 6m SW of Chichester off A286 (West Wittering) Open Easter-Oct–no adv booking 112 pitches–couples and families only Grass, level, part sheltered £6.50-£8.25

Red House Farm Camping Site, Bookers Lane, Earnley PO20 7JG ✆ (01243) 512959 OS map 197/815979 5m SW of Chichester off B2198 (Bracklesham Bay) Open Easter-Oct 80 pitches Grass, level, open £8.00-£10.00

Southern Leisure Centre, Vinnetrow Road PO19 6LB *Big touring site in rural setting surrounded by several lakes* ✆ Chichester (01243) 787715 OS map 197/878039 1½m SE of Chichester off junction of A259 (Bognor) and A27 on Pagham road Open Mar-Oct 1500 pitches Grass, level, sheltered (heated) (55) fishing, water skiing £8.00-£14.00

Wicks Farm Camping Park, Redlands Lane, West Wittering PO20 8QD ✆ (01243) 513116 OS map 197/797996 5m SW of Chichester off A286/B2179 (West Wittering) Open Mar-Oct 119 pitches (79 static) Grass, level, sheltered tennis court, bike hire £10.00-£12.00 (most cards)

COWES, Isle of Wight Map B6
Pop 16,250. EC Wed SEE Osborne House (royal apartments), Cowes Castle, Whippingham church 2m SE ⓘ The Arcade, Fountain Quay ✆ (01983) 291914 Restaurant: Fountain, High St ✆ (01983) 292397

Comforts Farm, Pallance Road, Northwood PO31 8LS ✆ Isle of Wight (01983) 293888 OS map 196/478938 1m SW of Cowes off A3020 (Newport) Open Mar-Oct 55 pitches Grass, part level, part sheltered horse riding school £5.30-£6.30

Gurnard Pines Holiday Village, Cockleton Lane, Gurnard PO31 8QE ✆ Cowes (01983) 292395 OS map 196/470950 1m SW of Cowes off B3325 (Northwood) Open Mar-Nov (camping), all year (village), 155 pitches lic club/bar £12.00

Thorness Bay Holiday Park, Thorness PO31 8NJ ✆ Isle of Wight (01983) 523109 OS map 196/452927 1m SW of Cowes off A3020 (Newport) on Thorness road Open Easter-Oct 458 pitches (258 static) lic club, riding school, beach access £8.00-£15.00

Waverley Park, Old Road, East Cowes PO32 6AW ✆ Cowes (01983) 293452 OS map 196/505958 ½m E of Cowes off A3021 (Newport) Open Mar-Oct 131 pitches (81 static) 12 acres sloping grass club house £6.50-£11.00 (Mastercard/Visa)

CROWBOROUGH–see Tunbridge Wells

CROWHURST–see Battle

DEAL, Kent Map H4
Pop 26,100. EC Thurs, MD Sat SEE churches, lifeboat station, Deal castle, Walmer castle ⓘ Town Hall, High St ✆ (01304) 369576 Restaurant: Trogs, 114 High St ✆ (01304) 374089

Clifford Park, Thompson Close, Walmer CT14 7PB ✆ Deal (01304) 373373 OS map 179/366499 2m S of Deal on right of A258 (Dover) Open Mar-Oct 174 pitches (161 static) 9 acres level grass and hard standings sheltered £8.50

Leisurescope Caravan Park, Golf Road CT14 6RG ✆ Deal (01304) 363332 OS map 179/368558 1½m N of Deal off coast road opposite Chequers Inn Open Mar-Oct 55 pitches (25 static)–no tents 2½ acres level grass £7.00-£9.00

Sutton Vale Caravan Park, Sutton CT15 5DH ✆ Deal (01304) 374155 OS map 179/339496 3m SW of Deal off A258 (Dover) Open Mar-Jan–must book peak periods 121 pitches–no tents Level grass and hard standings, sheltered lic club £11.50-£18.50 (Mastercard/Delta/Switch)

DENSOLE–see Folkestone

> ### FOLKESTONE -- *Last site before Channel Tunnel*
> # Folkestone Racecourse
> *2m NW of Hythe off A20 and B2068*   Open mid-March to mid-October

DIAL POST, W Sussex   **Map D5**
Restaurant: Red Lion 2m S at Ashington ☎(01903) 892226

Honeybridge Park, Honeybridge Lane RH13 8NX ☎(01403) 710923 OS map 198/153184 ¼m SE
   of Dial Post off A24 (Worthing) on Ashurst road Open all year 100 pitches 15 acres level grass
   and hard standing, sheltered 🛉🗎🔌🅿⊕∅🔄☂🚿🏧 £7.50-£11.50 (2000) (Mastercard/Visa)

DOVER, Kent   **Map H4**
Pop 33,000. EC Wed, MD Sat SEE castle, Roman lighthouse, church, town hall, museum 🛈
Townwall Street ☎Dover (01304) 205108 Restaurant: Blakes, Castle St (near market square)
☎(01304) 202194

Hawthorn Farm International, Martin Mill CT15 5LA ☎Dover (01304) 852658 OS map
   179/341465 4m NNE of Dover off A258 (Deal) near Martin Mill station Open Mar-Oct–no adv
   booking 410 pitches (160 static) Grass, sheltered 🛉⊸🏹🗎🔌⊘⊕∅ rose garden £9.00-£12.00
   (Mastercard/Visa)
For other sites near Dover see Folkestone and Hythe

DUNKIRK, Kent   **Map G4**
Restaurant: White Horse 1½m W at Boughton Street ☎(01227) 751343

Red Lion, Old London Road ME13 9LL ☎(01227) 750661 OS map 179/084489 ½m E of Dunkirk
   on left of old A2 (Canterbury)–access via A2 Open Mar-Oct 25 pitches–no tents 1 acre, level
   grass, sheltered ✗ (snack), ⏃🔌⊕🚿 farm shop £7.00-£9.50

DYMCHURCH, Kent   **Map G5**
Pop 5,600 EC Wed Modest family resort backing sandy beach SEE 12c church, Smugglers Inn,
Martello Towers, Romney, Hythe and Dymchurch railway Restaurant: Ship Inn, High St ☎(01303)
872122

New Beach Touring Park, Hythe Rd TN29 0JX ☎(01303) 872234 OS map 189/110303 ½m NE of
   Dymchurch on right of A259 (Hythe) near beach Open Mar 1-Jan 11 250 pitches Level grass
   🛉✗⏃⊸🗎🔌∅⊕∅ ▭ (indoor) 🔄 £6.00-£11.00

EASTBOURNE–see Pevensey Bay

EAST GRINSTEAD, W Sussex   **Map E5**
Pop 22,400. EC Wed, MD Sat SEE Sackville College (17c almshouses) museum, High Street, St
Swithin's church Restaurant: The Old Cage 3m N at Lingfield ☎(01342) 834271

Long Acres Farm Caravan Park, Newchapel Road, Lingfield RH7 6LE ☎(01342) 833205 OS map
   187/368425 3m NW of East Grinstead off A22 (Croydon) on B2028 (Lingfield) Open all year 60
   pitches 20 acres level grass and hard standings sheltered 🛉⊸🗎🔌⊘⊕∅🔄🚿 fishing £9.50

EMSWORTH, Hants   **Map C6**
Pop 9,000. EC Wed Restaurant: Coal Exchange, South St ☎(01243) 375566

Chichester Camping (Camping Club), 343 Main Road, Southbourne PO10 8JH ☎Emsworth
   (01243) 373202 OS map 197/773055 1m E of Emsworth on A259 (Chichester) Open all year 60
   pitches 🗎🔌⊕♿ £13.90-£14.90

FAREHAM, Hants   **Map B6**
Pop 84,200. MD Mon SEE Titchfield Abbey 2m W, Portchester Castle, church and Roman fort 3m E
🛈 Westbury Manor, West St ☎Fareham (01329) 221342 Restaurant: Castle in the Air, Old Gosport
Rd ☎(01329) 280320

Dibles Park, Dibles Road, Warsash SO31 9SA ☎Locks Heath (01489) 575232 OS map
   196/505060 5m W of Fareham off A27 (Southampton) and Warsash road Open Easter-Oct 63
   pitches (41 static) Grass, level 🗎🔌∅⊕∅▭🚿 £7.00-£10.00

FARNHAM, Surrey **Map C4**
Pop 34,540 EC Wed SEE castle keep, 14c church, Birdworld 4m SW, Frensham Ponds 3m SE ℹ
Vernon House, 28 West St ☏(01252) 715109 Restaurant: Duke of Cambridge 3m SE at Tilford
☏(01252) 792236

Tilford Touring, Tilford GU10 2DF ☏(01252) 792199 OS map 186/878424 3m SE of Farnham off
  B3001 (Milford) Open all year, 75 pitches 2 acres, level grass, sheltered ✗♀☏⊕∅ £5.00-
  £10.00

FAVERSHAM, Kent **Map G4**
Pop 16,000. EC Thurs, MD Wed, Fri, Sat SEE town hall, houses in Abbey Street, Globe House ℹ
Fleur de Lis Heritage Centre, Preston Street ☏(01795) 534542 Restaurant: Read 2m S at Painters
Forstal ☏(01795) 535344

Painters Farm Caravan Camping Park, Painters Farm, Painters Forstal ME13 0EG ☏Faversham
  (01795) 532995 OS map 178/990591 2m SW of Faversham off A2 (London–Canterbury) on
  Painters Forstal road Open Mar-Oct 50 pitches Grass, level, part sheltered ☏❺∅⊕ £6.80-
  £8.80

FOLKESTONE, Kent **Map G5**
Pop 46,500. EC Wed, MD Thurs, Sun SEE church of St Mary, Kingsworth gardens, The Leas, New
Metropole arts centre ℹ Harbour Street ☏(01303) 258594 Restaurant: Paul's, Bouverie Rd West
☏(01303) 259697

Black Horse Farm, Densole, Swingfield CT18 7BG ☏Hawkinge (01303) 892665 OS map
  179/211418 4m N of Folkestone on left of A260 (Canterbury) in Densole near Black Horse Inn
  Open all year 126 pitches Grass and hard standing, level, part open ☒⌁☏❺∅⊕∅❿⅍
  £12.50-£15.00 (Mastercard/Visa/Switch/Delta)

Little Satmar Holiday Park, Winehouse Lane, Capel le Ferne CT18 7JF ☏Folkestone (01303)
  251188 OS map 179/256392 2½m NE of Folkestone off B2011 (Dover) just past Capel le Ferne
  Open Mar-Oct, 110 pitches (70 static) level grass ☒⌁☏❺∅⊕∅❸⌲❿⅏ games room £9.00-
  £12.00

Little Switzerland Camping Caravan Park, off Wear Bay Road CT19 6PS ☏Folkestone (01303)
  252168 OS map 179/243375 1m E of Folkestone off A20 (Dover) via Wear Bay road Open Mar-
  Oct–must book peak periods 32 pitches Grass, level, sheltered ✗♀⌁☏❺∅⊕ £8.00-£10.00

Varne Ridge Caravan Park, 145 Old Dover Road, Capel le Ferne CT18 7HX ☏Folkestone (01303)
  251765 OS map 179/260390 4m E of Folkestone off B2011 (Dover) Open Mar-Nov 18 pitches
  (12 static)–no tents Level grass ☏❺∅⊕∅⌲ £9.00-£13.00

Warren Camping Site, The Warren CT19 6PT ☏Folkestone (01303) 255093 OS map 179/246376
  1m E of Folkestone off A20 (Dover) and road to harbour Open Apr-Sept 82 pitches–no trailer
  caravans ☒☏∅⊕ £8.10-£9.00

White Cliffs Park, New Dover Road, Capel le Ferne CT18 7JA ☏Folkestone (01303) 250192 OS
  map 179/245383 3m NE of Folkestone on A20 (Dover) Open Feb-Jan 289 pitches (138 static)
  Level/sloping grass, hard standings, sheltered ☒☏❺∅⊕∅❿ £10.00
See also Hythe

FORDINGBRIDGE, Hants **Map A5**
Pop 5,070. EC Thurs SEE Augustus John statue, Breamore House 3m N ℹ Salisbury St
☏(01425) 654560 Restaurant: Ashburn, Station Rd ☏(01725) 652060

Sandy Balls Holiday Centre, Godshill SP6 2JZ *Mainly wooded site central for walking and touring*
  ☏Fordingbridge (01425) 653042 OS map 195/169146 2m NE of Fordingbridge off B3078
  (Cadnam) Open all year–booking public and school holidays 630 pitches (200 static) Hard
  standing, level, sheltered ☒✗♀⌁⌁☏❺∅⊕∅⌑ (indoor/outdoor) ⊕⅍⌲🏠⅊ fishing, horse
  riding £11.25-£24.00 (Mastercard/Visa)

GODALMING, Surrey **Map D4**
Pop 18,200 EC Wed, MD Fri SEE Charterhouse School, church, local interest museum, Winkworth
Arboretum 2m SE Restaurant: Inn on the Lake on A3100 ☏(01428) 685575

The Merry Harriers Camping and Caravan Site, Hambledon GU8 4DR ☏(01428) 682883 OS
  map 186/965380 4m S of Godalming off B3100 (Milford) via Milford Station and Hydestile Open
  all year 20 pitches 1 acre level grass ♀⊕∅⅍ pub food £4.00-£6.00

**Except where marked, all sites in this guide have flush lavatories and showers. Symbols for
these amenities have therefore been omitted from site entries.**

GOSPORT, Hants   **Map B6**
Pop 80,000 EC Wed MD Tues SEE 17c Holy Trinity church, Submarine Museum 🛈 Museum,
Walpole Rd ☎(01705) 522944 Restaurant: Old Lodge near sea at Alverstoke ☎(01705) 581865

Kingfisher Park, Browndown Road, Stokes Bay PO13 9BE ☎(02392) 502611 OS map
196/585993 2m W of Gosport centre off B3333 (Lee on Solent) Open all year 220 pitches (100
static) level grass and hard standing 🛇✕♀⊶↗⊡🔌⊘⊕∅⊕❸⤴⧠🔲♿ £6.00-£16.00
(Mastercard/Visa)

GOUDHURST, Kent   **Map F5**
Pop 2,660. EC Wed SEE parish church, Bedgebury Nat Pinetum 2½m S Restaurant: Star and
Eagle, High St ☎(01580) 211512

Tanner Farm Park, Goudhurst Road, Marden TN12 9ND ☎(01622) 832399 OS map 188/734414
3m N of Goudhurst on left of B2079 (Marden) Open all year 100 pitches–must book Jun-Sept 15
acres, grass and hard standing, level/sloping, part sheltered 🛇⊡🔌∅⊕∅⤴♿ £6.50-£11.00
(Mastercard/Visa/Delta/Switch)

HAILSHAM, E Sussex   **Map E5**
Pop 17,000. EC Thurs, MD Wed SEE church, Michelham Priory 2m SW 🛈 Area Library, Western
Road ☎Hailsham (01323) 844426 Restaurant: Olde Forge 1m E at Magham Down ☎(01323)
842893

Old Mill Caravan Park, Chalvington Road, Golden Cross BN27 3SS ☎(01825) 872532 OS map
199/541139 4m NW of Hailsham off A22 (East Grinstead) before Golden Cross Inn Open Apr-Oct
26 pitches Grass, sheltered 🔌∅⊕🔲🏠 £6.50

Peel House Farm Caravan Park, Polegate BN26 6QX ☎(01323) 845629 OS map 199/592070 1m
S of Hailsham on B2104 (Friday Street) Open Mar-Oct, 20 pitches Level grass, sheltered
🛇🔌∅⊕∅ garden produce £7.50-£11.00

HAMBLE–see Southampton

HARRIETSHAM, Kent   **Map G4**
Restaurant: Harrow Inn 4m SE at Lenham ☎(01622) 858727

Hogbarn Caravan Park, Hogbarn Lane ME17 1NZ ☎(01622) 859648 OS map 189/884550 2m
NE of Harrietsham on right of Frinsted road Open Apr-mid Oct, 200 pitches (80 static) Grass and
hard standing, level, sheltered ⊡🔌∅⊕🔲 (indoor), ◉ lounge £7.50

HASTINGS, E Sussex   **Map F5**
Pop 73,620. EC Wed, MD Wed, Sat SEE castle ruins, museum, St Clement's caves, Fisherman's
church, Hastings Historical Embroidery, Fishermen's museum, country park 🛈 4 Robertson Terrace
☎(01424) 718888 Restaurant: Roser's, Eversfield Pl ☎(01424) 712218

Carters Farm, Pett TN35 4JD ☎(01424) 813206 OS map 199/884144 5½m E of Hastings off
A259 (Rye) via Pett Open Mar-Oct 100 pitches–no adv booking Grass, part level, part sheltered
🛇🔌∅⊕∅ £8.00-£10.00

Shear Barn Holiday Park, Barley Lane TN35 5DX ☎Hastings (01424) 423583 OS map
199/842107 1½m E of Hastings off A259 (Rye) Open Mar-Jan 750 pitches (200 static) Grass,
part level 🛇⊶↗⊡🔌∅⊕∅⤴◉ (£2/wk) 🔲 lic club £6.50-£17.50 (Mastercard/Visa)

Spindlewood Country Holiday Park, Rock Lane, Ore TN35 4JN ☎(01424) 720825 OS map
199/835120 1½m NE of Hastings off A259 (Rye) on left of Three Oaks road (Rock Lane) Open
Mar-Oct 125 pitches (75 static) 14 acres level grass, sheltered ✕♀⊡🔌⊕∅🔲 fishing lake
£8.00-£14.00 (Mastercard/Visa)

Stalkhurst Camping, Stalkhurst Cottage, Ivyhouse Lane TN35 4NN ☎Hastings (01424) 439015
OS map 199/829123 1½m NE of Hastings off A259 (Rye) and B2093 (Baldslow) Open Mar 1-Jan
15–booking advised 33 pitches Grass, sloping, sheltered 🛇♀↗⊡∅⊕∅🔲❸◉🔲 £6.50-
£9.00

See listing under Gosport

HAVANT, Hants   **Map C6**
Pop 115,900. EC Wed, MD Tues, Sat SEE parish church, old houses ⓘ 1 Park Road South
☏ (01705) 480024 Restaurant: Bear, East St ☏ (01705) 486501

Fishery Creek Park, Fishery Lane, Hayling Island PO11 9NR ☏ (02392) 462164 OS map
  197/736987 5m S of Havant off A3023 (Hayling Island) via Church Road Open Mar-Oct 165
  pitches–families only 7½ acres level grass boat storage, tidal slipway,
  games room £8.50-£11.00 (£11 BH)

Fleet Farm, Yewtree Road, Hayling Island PO11 0QE ☏ (02392) 463684 OS map 197/727017 4m
  S of Havant off A3023 at Yew Tree Inn Open Mar-Oct 75 pitches Hard standings and grass, level,
  part sheltered, boat launch £8.00-£10.00

Lower Tye Family Campsite, Copse Lane, Hayling Island PO11 0RQ ☏ (02392) 462479 OS map
  197/731020 4m S of Havant off A3023 Open Mar-Nov 150 pitches Grass, level, sheltered
  £10.00

Oven Camping Site, Manor Road, South Hayling PO11 0QX ☏ (02392) 464695 OS map
  197/719005 4½m S of Havant off A3023 at Mill Rythe roundabout Open Mar-Jan 300 pitches
  Grass level, part sheltered games room £10.00

HAYLING ISLAND–see Havant

HEATHFIELD, E Sussex   **Map E5**
SEE Gibraltar Tower, parish church Restaurant: Star Inn 1m E (off B2096) at Old Heathfield
☏ (01435) 863570

Greenviews Caravan Park, Broad Oak TN21 8RT ☏ Heathfield (01435) 863531 OS map
  199/597219 1m E of Heathfield on A265 (Hawkhurst) Open Apr-Oct 60 pitches (50 static) Grass,
  level, open club house £6.50

Horam Manor Touring Park, Horam TN21 0YD ☏ (01435) 813662 OS map 199/576173 3m S of
  Heathfield on A267 (Eastbourne) Open Mar-Oct 90 pitches–booking advisable 7 acres
  level/sloping grass, sheltered £11.85

HENFIELD, W Sussex   **Map D5**
Restaurant: Shepherd and Dog 4m SE via A281 at Fulking ☏ (01273) 857382

Downsview Caravan Park, Bramlands Lane, Woodmancote, BN5 9TG ☏ (01273) 492801 Fax
  (01273) 495214 OS map 198/238138 2m SE of Henfield off A281 (Brighton) Open Apr-Oct
  40 pitches–no facs for children Grass and hard standing, level, part sheltered
  £7.50-£15.00 inc elect

HERNE BAY, Kent   **Map G3**
Pop 26,050. EC Thurs, MD Sat SEE remains of Roman fort at Reculver, clock tower, windmill ⓘ
Council Offices, William Street ☏ (01227) 361911 Restaurant: L'Escargot, High St ☏ (01227)
372876

Hillborough Park, Reculver Road CT6 6SR ☏ Herne Bay (01227) 374618 OS map 179/208680
  2m E of Herne Bay off A299 (Thanet Way) Open Apr-Oct 430 pitches (400 static)
  £10.00

Southview Caravan Park, Maypole Lane, Hoath CT3 4LL ☏ (01227) 860280 OS map 179/203647
  2½m SE of Herne Bay off A299 (Thanet Way) via Maypole Open all year 45 pitches Grass and
  hard standing, level, sheltered (Jul-Aug) £11.00

HINDHEAD, Surrey   **Map C5**
Pop 3,000. SEE Devil's Punchbowl 1m E Waggoners Wells (NT) 2m SW, Frensham Common 3m N
Restaurant: Devil's Punchbowl, London Road ☏ (01428) 606565

Symondstone Farm, Churt GU10 2QL ☏ Headley Down (01428) 712090 OS map 186/844389
  2½m NW of Hindhead off A287 (Farnham) Open Apr-Oct 70 pitches 8 acres, part sloping No
  showers £4.00

HOLLINGBOURNE–see Maidstone

HORSHAM, W Sussex   **Map D5**
Pop 26,000. EC Thurs SEE St Mary's church, North chapel, museum, Leonardslee gardens 4m SE
ⓘ Causeway ☏ (01403) 211661 Restaurant: Olde King's Head, Carfax ☏ (01403) 753126

Raylands Caravan Park, Jackrells Lane, Southwater RH13 7DH ☏ Southwater (01403) 731822 and
  730218 OS map 198/170265 3m S of Horsham off A24 (Worthing) and Copsale road Open Mar-
  Oct 145 pitches (65 static) Grass, level, sheltered tennis, bar/clubhouse at
  weekends £10.00-£11.50 (Mastercard/Visa)

HYTHE, Kent   **Map G5**
Pop 12,200 EC Wed SEE St Leonard's church and crypt, Romney, Hythe and Dymchurch light
railway, military canal, zoo park and gardens at Lympne 2m W ⓘ Prospect Road Car Park
☎ (01303) 267799 Restaurant: Stade Court, West Par ☎ (01303) 268263

Folkestone Racecourse, Westenhanger CT21 4HX ☎ (01303) 261761 (0800-2000 hrs) OS map
179/128370 2m NW of Hythe off A20 (Maidstone\-Dover) and B2068 (Canterbury) Open Mar 26-
Oct 4 50 pitches Level grass, open 🅿🅰🅾 free access to racing £6.20-£12.50
(Mastercard/Visa)

**ISLE OF WIGHT–see Bembridge, Cowes, Freshwater, Newport, Ryde, Sandown, Shanklin,
Ventnor, Yarmouth**

LEWES, E Sussex   **Map E5/6**
Pop 14,800 EC Wed MD Mon SEE castle and museum, Anne of Cleeve's House, Southover
Grange, town walls, Glynde Place 3m E, Firle Place 4m SE ⓘ 187 High Street ☎ Lewes (01273)
483448 Restaurant: Juggs 1m S off A27 at Kingston (The Street) ☎ (01273) 472523

Bluebell Holiday Park, Shortgate BN8 6PJ ☎ (01825) 840407 OS map 199/493151 6m NE of
Lewes on B2192 (Ringmer) at rear of Bluebell Inn Open Apr-Oct 40 pitches (20 static)–no children
2½ acres level grass, sheltered 🅿🅰🅾🅾 ⛽ £7.50-£10.00

LEYSDOWN–see Sheerness

LINGFIELD–see East Grinstead

LITTLEHAMPTON, W Sussex   **Map D6**
Pop 21,970. EC Wed, MD Fri, Sat SEE museum, miniature railway, mill and church at Clymping 2m
W ⓘ Windmill Complex, The Green ☎ Littlehampton (01903) 713480 Restaurant: Beach, Seafront
☎ (01903) 717277

Rutherfords Touring Park, Cornfield Close, Worthing Road BN17 6LD *Central site with clean safe
beach for children* ☎ and Fax (01903) 714240 OS map 197/043030 In Littlehampton on A259
(Worthing) 80 pitches Open Feb-Oct 6 acres level grass 🅿🅰🅾🅾🅾 🅿 tennis,
badminton £8.00-£10.00

White Rose Touring Park, Mill Lane, Wick BN17 7PH ☎ Littlehampton (01903) 716176 OS map
197/043029 1½m N of Littlehampton on A284 (Arundel) Open Mar-Jan–booking public holidays
essential 140 pitches 6 acres, level grass and hard standing 🅿🅰🅾🅾🅾🅾🅾 & serviced
pitches (1000 sq ft) £8.00-£16.50 (Mastercard/Visa)

LYNDHURST, Hants   **Map A6**
Pop 2,900. EC Wed SEE church, Queen's House, New Forest ⓘ New Forest Museum, Main Car
Park ☎ (01703) 282269 Restaurant: Mailmans Arms, High St ☎ (01703) 284196

Ashurst Campsite, Lyndhurst Road, Ashurst SO42 2AA ☎ (01703) 283771 OS map 196/332102 2
NE of Lyndhurst on A35 (Southampton) Open Easter-Oct–booking public holidays advisable 280
pitches Level, part sheltered 🅰🅾🅾🅾 (exc Oct) & £6.50-£10.00

Decoy Pond Farm, Beaulieu Rd SO4 7YQ *Simple site in heart of New Forest* ☎ (01703) 292652
OS map 196/356073 3m E of Lyndhurst off B3056 (Beaulieu) after level crossing Open Mar-Oct
10 pitches ½ acre level grass 🅿🅾 £9.00

MAIDSTONE, Kent   **Map F4**
Pop 86,050 EC Wed, MD Mon, Tues SEE All Saints church, Carriage Museum, Leeds castle 1m
SW ⓘ The Gatehouse, Old Palace Gardens ☎ (01622) 673581 Restaurant: Grange Moor, St
Michael's Road ☎ (01622) 677623

Cold Blow Camping, Cold Blow Lane, Thurnham ME15 3LR ☎ (01622) 735038 OS map
188/805578 2m NE of Maidstone off A249 (Sittingbourne) near junct 7 of M20 adj North Downs
Way Open all year 10 pitches 🅾🅿🅰🅾🅾🅾 B&B camping barn £6.50

Pine Lodge Caravan Park, Ashford Road, Hollingbourne ME17 1XH ☎ Maidstone (01622) 730018
OS map 188/818549 5m SE of Maidstone on A20 (Ashford) near junct 8 of M20 Open all year
100 pitches Level grass and hard standings 🅿🅾🅿🅰🅾🅾🅾🅾🅾🅾& £9.00-£11.00
(Mastercard/Visa)

Riverside Caravan Park, Farleigh Lane, Barming ME16 9ND *South facing site on river Medway adj
rail station* ☎ (01622) 726647 OS map 188/733534 2m W of Maidstone off A26 (Tonbridge) opp
Fountain Inn into Farleigh Lane beyond level crossing Open Mar-Oct 40 pitches (30 static) 4
acres level grass and hard standings, sheltered 🅿🅰🅾🅾🅾🅾🅾🅾 £8.00

MAYPOLE–see Herne Bay

NEW FOREST–see Bransgore, Brockenhurst, Cadnam, Fordingbridge, Lymington, Lyndhurst, Milford on Sea, New Milton, Ringwood

NEWHAVEN, E Sussex   Map E6
Pop 11,000 EC Wed SEE St Michael's church, Fort Museum, cliffs Restaurant: Hope Inn, West Pier
☎(01273) 515389

Buckle Caravan Camping Park, Marine Parade, Seaford BN25 2QR ☎(01323) 897801 OS map
   198/467998 1½m SE of Newhaven off A259 (Eastbourne) at Abbots Lodge Motel adj beach
   Open Mar 1-Jan 2 150 pitches 9 acres, level grass and hard standings ⬛🔲🔲🔲🔲🔲🔲 £7.00-
   £9.00

Hampden Vale Caravan Centre, South Heighton BN9 0HU ☎(01273) 513530 OS map
   198/447030 1m N of Newhaven on A26 (Lewes) Open Mar-Oct 170 piches (155 static) 14 acres
   level grass 🔲🔲🔲🔲🔲🔲🔲🔲🔲🔲 fishing £7.00-£10.00

Rushey Hill Caravan Park, The Highway BN9 8XH ☎(01273) 582344 OS map 198/425007 1½m
   W of Newhaven centre off A259 (Brighton) at Brighton Motel Open Mar-Oct, 297 pitches (250
   static)–no trailer caravans 15 acres, grass, sloping 🔲🔲🔲 £5.00

NEW MILTON, Hants   Map A6
Pop 18,300. EC Wed SEE parish church Restaurant: Cliff House 2m S at Barton on Sea ☎(01425)
619333

Bashley Park, Sway Road BH25 5QR ☎New Milton (01425) 612340 OS map 195/249969 1½m N
   of New Milton off B3058 (Wootton) on B3055 (Sway) Open Mar-Oct–must book 420 pitches (350
   static) Hard standing, level, sheltered 🔲🔲🔲🔲🔲🔲🔲🔲🔲🔲🔲🔲🔲 lic club/bar, golf,
   snooker/pool, table tennis, indoor leisure complex and outdoor pool £9.00-£25.50 inc hot water
   and elec

See also Barton on Sea

NEW ROMNEY, Kent   Map G5
Pop 4,100. EC Wed SEE church, ruined priory, Romney, Hythe and Dymchurch Light Railway
Restaurant: Blue Dolphins, Dymchurch Rd ☎(01797) 363224

Marlie Farm Holiday Village, Dymchurch Road TN28 8UE ☎New Romney (01797) 363060 OS
   map 189/075263 ¼m E of New Romney on A259 (Hythe) Open Mar-Oct 450 pitches (250 static)
   Grass and hard standing, level, part sheltered 🔲🔲🔲🔲🔲🔲🔲🔲🔲🔲🔲🔲🔲🔲🔲🔲 snack bar
   £7.00-£8.80

New Romney Caravan Site, Coast Drive, Greatstone TN28 8PE ☎(01797) 362247 OS map
   189/082239 1m E of New Romney on Greatstone road Open Apr-Oct–no adv booking 225
   pitches (175 static) 🔲🔲🔲🔲🔲🔲🔲🔲 £6.00-£10.00

OWER–see Romsey

PETT–see Hastings

PETWORTH, W Sussex   Map D5
Pop 2,000 EC Wed Charming market town in idyllic country with splendid walks on South Downs 4m
S SEE church, Petworth House and Deer Park (NT), Roman villa at Bignor 5m S Restaurant:
Angel, Angel St ☎(01798) 342153

Great Bury Park (Camping Club), Graffham GU28 0QJ ☎(01798) 867476 OS map 197/941187
   3m SW of Petworth off A285 (Chichester) on Graffham road Open Mar 20-Oct 30 90 pitches–adv
   booking min 2 nights 🔲🔲🔲🔲🔲🔲 £11.80-£14.90 plus £4.20 non-member pitch fee (Mastercard/
   Visa)

See listing under Barton on Sea

SANDOWN, ISLE OF WIGHT
Village Way
at Apse Heath on Newport Road PO36 9PJ

Telephone (01983) 863279

PEVENSEY BAY, E Sussex   **Map F6**
Pop 2,650. EC Thurs SEE parish church, Old Court House, Martello Towers, ruined Normal castle
🅘 Castle Car Park, High Street ☎(01323) 761444 Restaurant: Priory Court opp castle ☎(01323)
763150

Bay View Camping Caravan Park, Old Martello Road BN24 6DX ☎(01323) 768688 OS map
   199/649027 1m S of Pevensey Bay on private road off A259 (Eastbourne)–signposted Open Apr
   1-Oct 7 100 pitches 3½ acres level grass and hard standings 🅛🖸🗗🖉🟤🗸🗗🖾 £8.70-£10.30

Castle View Caravan-Camping Park, Eastbourne Road BN24 6DT ☎(01323) 763038 OS map
   199/646032 1¼m W of Pevensey Bay on A259 (Eastbourne) Open Mar-Nov–must book peak
   periods 146 pitches 🅛🡒🗡🖸🗗🖉🟤🖉🟤🗗🖾 baths £7.20

Fairfields Farm, Eastbourne Road, Westham BN24 5NG ☎(01323) 763165 OS map 199/639039
   1½m SW of Pevensey Bay on B2191 (Langney) Open Apr-Oct 60 pitches 3 acres, level grass,
   sheltered 🖸🗗🖉🟤🖾 fishing £6.50-£7.00

Martello Beach Caravan Park BN24 6DH ☎(01323) 761424 OS map 199/649035 1m SW of
   Pevensey Bay on A259 (Eastbourne) Open Mar-Oct–must book peak periods 360 pitches (320
   static) 🅛✖🡒🖸🗗🖉🟤 lic club, private beach £5.00-£9.50

PORTSMOUTH, Hants   **Map C6**
Pop 175,380. MD Thurs, Fri, Sat SEE Dicken's birthplace, Nelson's flagship Victory in dockyard,
cathedral, Cumberland House Museum, garrison church, Point Battery and Round Tower, Royal
Naval Museum, Royal Marines Museum 🅘 The Hard ☎(02392) 826722 Restaurant: Still and
West, Bath Sq (near Isle of Wight ferry) ☎(02392) 821567

Harbourside Caravan Park, Eastern Road PO3 6QB ☎Portsmouth (02392) 834165 and 663867
   OS map 196/675025 1½m E of Portsmouth on A2030 (Southsea) near golf course Open Mar-Oct
   198 pitches (74 static) Grass, level, open 🖸🗗🖉🟤🖉🟤🖾 £6.65-£8.50

Southsea Caravan Park, Melville Road, Southsea PO4 9TB ☎Portsmouth (02392) 735070 OS
   map 196/677990 3m E of Portsmouth off A2030 (Southsea) and A288, on seafront Open all year
   188 pitches (22 static) Grass, level, sheltered 🅛✖🍴🡒🖸🗗🖉🟤🖉🟤🗗🗗🗸🖾🖾& £7.00-£12.00
   (inc showers)

RAMSGATE, Kent   **Map H4**
Pop 39,560. EC Thurs, MD Fri SEE churches, model Tudor village, replica of Viking ship, harbour,
and yacht marina 🅘 Argyle Centre, Queen Street ☎Thanet (01843) 591086 Restaurant: Churchill
Tavern, The Paragon (by Royal Harbour) ☎(01843) 587862

Manston Caravan Camping Park, Manston Court Road, Manston CT12 5AU ☎Thanet (01843)
   823442 OS map 179/345665 2m NW of Ramsgate off A253 (Sarre) on B2050 (Birchington) near
   airfield Open Easter-Oct 130 pitches (46 static) level grass 🅛🖸🗗🖉🟤🖉🟤🗸🖾 dog walk
   £8.00-£12.00 (Mastercard/Visa/Delta/Switch)

Nethercourt Park, Nethercourt Hill CT11 0RZ ☎Thanet (01843) 595485 OS map 179/363650 ¾m
   W of Ramsgate off A253 (Sarre) Open Apr-Oct 51 pitches Grass, level/sloping, hard standings
   sheltered 🅛🡒🖸🗗🖉🟤🗸🗗& £7.00-£9.00

Pine Meadow Touring Park, Spratling Court Farm, Manston CT12 5AN ☎Thanet (01843) 587770
   OS map 179/356663 1½m W of Ramsgate off A253 (Canterbury) on B2050 (Manston) Open Apr-
   Sept, 40 pitches 2 acres, level grass, sheltered 🗗🟤🖉🟤🗸🖾🏌 golf practice centre £8.00-
   £11.20

RINGWOOD, Hants   **Map A6**
Pop 11,900. EC Thurs, MD Wed SEE parish church, old cottages, New Forest ⓘ The Furlong
☎(01425) 470896 Restaurant: Inn on the Furlong, Meeting House Lane ☎(01425) 475139

Red Shoot Camping Park, Linwood BH24 3QT ☎Ringwood (01425) 473789 OS map 195/188094
    4m N of Ringwood off A338 (Salisbury) via Moyles Court Open Mar-Oct 105 pitches Grass, level,
    part sheltered ☚✗⚊♪🗟🖳⊘❀∅🕀↩♿ mountain bike hire £8.60-£11.80

ROCHESTER, Kent   **Map F3**
Pop 144,000. EC Wed, MD Fri SEE castle, cathedral, Guildhall, Eastgate House museum, 16c
blockhouse, Upnor castle ⓘ Eastgate Cottage, Eastgate High Street ☎Medway (01634) 843666
Restaurant: Royal Victoria and Bull, High St ☎(01634) 846266

Woolmans Wood Tourist Caravan Park, Bridgewood ME5 9SB ☎(01634) 867685 OS map
    178/188/745640 3m S of Rochester off junct 3 of M2 on B2097 near airfield Open all year 60
    pitches 5 acres level grass and hard standings ☚⊷🗟🖳⊘❀∅🕀🖳 £8.00-£9.50 (Mastercard)

ROMSEY, Hants   **Map B5**
Pop 13,150. EC Wed SEE abbey church, King John's House, White Horse Hotel (16c), Broadlands
(home of late Earl Mountbatten) ⓘ Bus Station Car Park, Broadwater Rd ☎(01794) 512987
Restaurant: Tudor Rose, Cornmarket ☎(01794) 512126

Green Pastures Farm, Ower SO51 6AJ ☎(02380) 814444 OS map 185/323158 4m SW of
    Romsey off A3090 (Ringwood) near Junction 2 of M27–signposted near Paultons Park Open Mar
    15-Oct 31 45 pitches Grass, level, part sheltered ☚🗟🖳⊘❀∅🕀♿ £9.00

Hill Farm Caravan Park, Sherfield English SO51 6FH ☎(01794) 340402 OS map 185/295225 4m
    W of Romsey off A27 (Salisbury) on Lockerley road Open Mar-Oct 140 pitches Grass, level, open
    ☚♪🗟🖳⊘❀↩♿🖳🖵 ice pack service £8.00-£12.00

RYDE, Isle of Wight   **Map B6**
Pop 22,950. EC Thurs SEE pier, Shell museum, bird sanctuary, I of Wight Steam Railway at Haven
Street, Spithead ⓘ Western Esplanade ☎(01983) 562905 Restaurant: Yelfs Hotel, Union St
☎(01983) 564062

Pondwell Holidays, Seaview PO34 5AQ ☎Isle of Wight (01983) 612330 OS map 196/623913 2m
    E of Ryde on B3330 (St Helens) Open May-Sept 200 pitches (36 static) Grass, part level,
    sheltered ☚🗟🖳⊘❀∅🕀↩🗖✇🏠 £6.00-£8.00 (Mastercard/Visa)

RYE, E Sussex   **Map F5**
Pop 5,000. EC Tues, MD Thurs SEE Ypres Tower Museum, Cinque Port, Flushing Inn (15c), St
Mary's church, George Hotel, Royal Military Canal, The Salts, Martello Tower at harbour ⓘ Heritage
Centre, Strand Quay ☎(01797) 226696 Restaurant: Ypres Castle, Gun Gardens ☎(01797) 223248

Cock Horse Inn, Peasmarsh TN31 6YD ☎(01797) 230281 OS map 189/896229 3m NW of Rye
    on A268 (Tonbridge) Open Mar-Oct 6 pitches–caravans only 1½ acres, grass, level
    ☚✗⚊🖳❀∅🕀 £10.00-£12.00

Camber Sands Leisure Park, Lydd Road, Camber Sands TN31 7RX ☎Rye (01797) 225282 OS
    map 189/975186 3½m SE of Rye off A259 (New Romney) in Camber near beach Open Mar-Oct
    860 pitches (800 static) ☚✗⚊ (5) 🗟🖳⊘🖵 £15.00-£20.00

ST HELENS–see Bembridge

ST NICHOLAS AT WADE–see Birchington

The
**Open Air
Cook Book**
for boat, tent or caravan
or barbecues at home

£3.95 post-free from Frederick
Tingey, Hillsboro, How
Caple, Hereford HR1 4TE
(cheque or PO with order
please)

SANDOWN, Isle of Wight   **Map B6**
Pop 3,940. EC Wed, MD Mon Coast resort on SE of island noted for safe bathing from fine sandy beaches SEE Snake and Reptile Centre, Yaverland church, Geological museum ℹ️ Esplanade ☎ (01983) 403886 Restaurant: Melville Hall, Melville St ☎ (01983) 406526

Adgestone Camping Park, Adgestone PO36 0HL ☎ Sandown (01983) 403432/403989 OS map 196/591855 1½m N of Sandown off A3055 (Lake) at Manor House pub Open Easter-Sept 200 pitches 15 acres, level grass 🏪 ⇥ ⚓ 🗄 🚿 🅿 ⊘ 🛁 ⊡ (heated) 🌣 ⏀ ♿ picnic garden, river and pond fishing, table tennis, petanque, volley ball, accessory shop £7.60-£11.00

Cheverton Copse Holiday Park, PO36 0JP ☎ Sandown (01983) 403161 OS map 196/5768 1½m SW of Sandown on A3056 (Newport) Open Apr-Oct 83 pitches (57 static) 4½ acres, part level 🏪 🗄 🚿 🅿 ⊘ 🛁 ⏀ ⚘ 🔲 🏠 lic club £7.00-£9.00 (Mastercard/Visa)

Fairway Caravan-Camping Park, Fairway PO36 9PS ☎ Sandown (01983) 403462 OS map 196/589842 1m N of Sandown off A3055 (Ryde) at railway bridge Open Mar-Oct 150 pitches (117 static) Grass, level, sheltered 🏪 ⇥ 🗄 🚿 🅿 ⊘ ⏀ 🔲 lic club £6.00-£7.00 (Mastercard/Visa/Switch)

Old Barn Touring Park, Cheverton Farm, Newport Road PO36 9PJ ☎ Isle of Wight (01983) 866414 OS map 196/573833 1½m W of Sandown on A3056 (Newport) Open Mar-Sept 60 pitches Grass, part level hard standings, sheltered 🗄 🚿 🅿 ⊘ 🛁 ⊡ ♿ games room £7.30-£10.40

Queen Bower Dairy, Alverstone Road, Queen Bower PO36 0NZ ☎ Isle of Wight (01983) 403840 OS map 196/569846 3m W of Sandown off A3056 (Newport) at Apse Heath Open May-Oct, 20 pitches\-no tents 2½ acres, level grass, sheltered 🚿 🌣 farm produce £4.00-£6.00

Southland Camping Park, Newchurch PO36 0LZ *Secluded site on outskirts of rural village with good access* ☎ Isle of Wight (01983) 865385 OS map 196/558847 2m W of Sandown off A3056 (Newport) on Newchurch road Open Apr-Sept 100 pitches Level grass, sheltered 🏪 🗄 🚿 🅿 ⊘ 🌣 ⏀ ♿ sep pitches £7.20-£11.00 (Mastercard/Visa)

Village Way, Newport Road PO36 9PJ ☎ Sandown (01983) 863279 OS map 196/573833 1½m W of Sandown on A3056 (Newport) Open Apr-Oct 28 pitches Level grass 🗄 🚿 🅿 ⊘ ⚘ 🔲 🏠 free coarse fishing £6.00-£7.00

SANDWICH, Kent   **Map H4**
Pop 4,500. EC Wed, MD Thurs SEE port, Barbican, Guildhall, old houses, town walls ℹ️ The Guildhall, Cattle Market ☎ (01304) 613565 Restaurant: Bell, The Quay ☎ (01304) 613388

Sandwich Leisure Park, Woodnesborough Road CT13 0AA ☎ Sandwich (01304) 612681 OS map 179/332574 ½m S of Sandwich centre on A258 (Deal) near level crossing Open Mar-Oct 200 pitches (100 static) 11 acres, level grass and hard standings 🗄 🚿 🅿 ⊘ 🌣 ⏀ ⚘ 🔲 £6.60-£9.50

SEAFORD–see Newhaven

SEDLESCOMBE–see Battle

SELSEY, W Sussex   **Map C6**
Pop 2,400 Quiet holiday resort with sandy beach SEE Selsey Bill S Restaurant: Crab and Lobster on B2145 3m N at Sidlesham ☎ (01243) 641233

Warner Farm Touring Park, Warner Lane PO20 9EL ☎ (01243) 604121 OS map 197/845939 ½m NW of Selsey centre off B2145–signposted Open Mar-Oct 200 pitches (150 static) Level grass and hard standings, part sheltered 🏪 ✗ ⚓ 🗄 🚿 🅿 ⊘ 🛁 ⊡ ⏀ 🔲 sun beds, steam room £6.00-£17.50

SEVENOAKS, Kent   **Map E4**
Pop 20,000. EC Wed, MD Mon, Wed SEE church, Knole (NT) ℹ️ Buckhurst Lane ☎ Sevenoaks (01732) 450305 Restaurant: Royal Oak, Upper High St ☎ (01732) 451109

East Hill Farm, East Hill Rd, Kemsing TN15 6YD ☎ (01959) 522347 OS map 188/560623 4m N of Sevenoaks off A225 (Dartford) via Otford Mount–phone for directions Open Apr-Oct 110 pitches (80 static) 8 acres level grass 🅿 🌣 ⏀ £5.00-£6.00

Except where marked, all sites in this guide have flush lavatories and showers. Symbols for these amenities have therefore been omitted from site entries.

SHANKLIN, Isle of Wight   Map B6
Pop 7,430. EC Wed SEE The Chine, old cottages, church, Crab Inn, Luccombe Common, Roman villa 3m N at Brading ▪67 High Street ☎Isle of Wight (01983) 862942 Restaurant: Fishermans Cottage, Shanklin Chine ☎(01983) 863882

Landguard Camping, Landguard Manor Road PO37 7PH ☎Isle of Wight (01983) 867028 OS map 196/581826 ½m NW of Shanklin off A3056 (Newport) Open May-Sept 150 pitches 7 acres, level grass and hard standing, sheltered ▨ (heated) clubhouse, horse riding £7.30-£11.50 (Mastercard/Visa/Delta/Switch)

Lower Hyde Leisure Park PO37 7LL ☎Isle of Wight (01983) 866131 OS map 196/575819 1m W of Shanklin via Landguard road Open Easter-Oct 26, 365 pitches (237 static)–families only 50 acres, grass, level/sloping and hard standings ▨ (snack), (heated), tennis, cabaret £5.17-£11.48

Ninham Country Holidays, Ninham PO37 7PL ☎Isle of Wight (01983) 864243 Fax (01983) 868881 OS map 196/572827 1m NW of Shanklin off A3056 (Newport) Open Easter-Oct 98 pitches (families and couples only) 18 acres, grass, level/gentle slope, sheltered ▨ (outdoor heated) baby care cubicles, barbecues, games room, water sports, mountain biking £5.70-£9.80

See also Ventnor

SHEERNESS, Kent   Map F3
Pop 13,140. EC Wed, MD Tues SEE promenade, pier (view), Minster abbey church 1m S ▪ Bridge Road Car Park ☎Sheerness (01795) 665324 Restaurant: Royal, The Broadway ☎(01795) 662626

The Plough Inn Caravan Park, Plough Road, Minster in Sheppey ME12 4JF ☎(01795) 872419 OS map 178/972725 1½m E of Sheerness off Eastchurch road Open Mar-Oct 105 pitches (85 static) ▨ £4.00-£4.75

Priory Hill Holiday Park, Wing Road, Leysdown on Sea ME12 4QT ☎(01795) 510267 OS map 178/039702 8m E of Sheerness via Eastchurch and B2231 (Leysdown) on left of Wing Road by sea Open Mar 15-Oct 31 55 pitches 1½ acres level grass ▨ (heated, indoor) clubhouse £5.50-£16.00 (Mastercard/Visa)

Riverbank Park, The Broadway, Minster on Sea ME12 2DB ☎(01795) 870300 OS map 178/960735 2m E of Sheerness in Minster by sea Open Mar-Oct 200 pitches (120 static) 12 acres level grass ▨ £9.50

Sheerness Holiday Park, Halfway Rd ME12 3AA ☎(01795) 662638 OS map 178/927736 ½m SE of Sheerness on A250 (Halfway Houses) Open Easter-Oct 330 pitches (250 static) Level grass ▨ games room £9.50-£17.00 (Mastercard/Visa/Switch/Solo)

Warden Springs Caravan Park, Warden Point, Eastchurch ME12 4HF ☎Eastchurch (01795) 880216 OS map 178/017722 6m E of Sheerness off A249 (Maidstone) and B2231 (Leysdown) Open Mar-Oct 298 pitches (250 static) Grass, part level, open ▨ (heated) pitch and putt £9.00-£13.00 (Mastercard/Visa)

SOUTHAMPTON, Hants   Map B5
Pop 204,400. MD Thurs, Fri, Sat One-time transatlantic port on harbour noted for its double tide SEE docks, Tudor House Museum, God's House Tower, Netley abbey 3m SE ▪ Above Bar Precinct ☎Southampton (02380) 221106 Restaurant: Dolphin, High St ☎(02380) 226178

Riverside Caravan Park, Satchell Lane, Hamble SO3 4HR ☎Southampton (02380) 453220 OS map 196/483082 7m SE of Southampton off A27 (Fareham) and B3397 (Hamble) near junct 8 of M27 Open Mar-Oct, 100 pitches (50 static)–adv booking advisable Grass, level, sheltered ▨ £8.00-£10.00

SOUTHSEA–see Portsmouth

STANSTED–see Wrotham

Down with hi-de-hi

A number of large holiday parks have been deleted from this year's edition to make room for more sites – happily on the increase – geared to the needs of the touring camper and caravanner, which is what this guide is all about. But many static sites have been retained for want of any adequate alternatives nearby.

STAPLECROSS, E Sussex   **Map F5**
SEE Bodiam Castle 2m N Restaurant: Curlew 3m N at Bodiam ✆ (01424) 214214

Lordine Court Caravan Camping Park, TN32 5TS ✆ Staplecross (01580) 830209 OS map
199/802227 1½m E of Staplecross off B2165 (Horns Cross/Clayhill) Open Apr-Oct 200 pitches
(150 static) Grass, part level, hard standings, part sheltered ⚐✕♀⚘☉⚑⚐⚙◲⛭☉⚛⚐⚏ lic
club/bars £5.00-£11.00

Park Farm, Bodiam TN32 5XA ✆ Staplecross (01580) 830514 OS map 199/766245 3m N of
Staplecross off B2165 (Cripps Corner) on B2244 (Maidstone) Open Easter-Oct 50 pitches Grass,
level, part sheltered, some hard standing ☉⚛⚐ fishing, riverside walks £8.00

STELLING MINNIS, Kent   **Map G4**
Pop 400 Restaurant: Rose and Crown ✆ (01227) 709265

Rose and Crown CT4 6AS ✆ Stelling Minnis (01227) 709265 OS map 179/142469 ¼m W of
Stelling Minnis centre adj common Open Mar-Oct 30 pitches 2 acres level grass ✕♀⚘∅ *No
showers* £3.00-£5.00

STORRINGTON, W Sussex   **Map D5**
Pop 6915 EC Wed SEE Parham House W 1½m Restaurant Manleys, Manleys Hill ✆ (01903)
742331

Greenacres Farm Caravan and Camping, Washington Road, RH20 4AF ✆ (01903) 742538 OS
map 198/104137 1m SE of Storrington on right of A283 (Hove) Open Easter-Oct 15 pitches 1¾
acres level grass sheltered ⚐⚐☉⚛⚏ £10.00-£12.50

TENTERDEN, Kent   **Map F5**
Pop 6,250. EC Wed, MD Fri SEE St Mildred's church, steam railway, Smallhythe Place 2m S ⛨
Town Hall, High Street ✆ (01580) 763572 Restaurant: White Lion, High St ✆ (01580) 292921

Spill Land Caravan Park, Biddenden TN27 8BX ✆ (01580) 291379 OS map 188/849369 4m NW
of Tenterden off A262 (Biddenden) on Benenden hospital road Open Apr-Sept 130 pitches (65
static)–last arrival 8pm–no motorvans Grass, sloping, sheltered ⚐⚙☉∅⚐ £8.00-£10.00

Woodlands Caravan-Camping Park, Tenterden Road, Biddenden TN27 8BT ✆ (01580) 291216
OS map 189/865371 3m NW of Tenterden on A262 (Biddenden) Open Mar-Oct 200 pitches
Grass, level, part sheltered ⚐☉⚐⚙☉∅⚛⚐& lic club £8.50-£10.00

TUNBRIDGE WELLS, Kent   **Map F4/5**
Pop 44,820 EC Wed MD Wed SEE Pantiles promenade, King Charles the Martyr Church, Town Hall
Museum, Mount Ephraim, Penshurst Place 4m NW ⛨ Old Fish Market, The Pantiles ✆ (01892)
515675 Restaurant: Sankeys, Mount Ephraim (A26 near junct with A267) ✆ (01892) 511422

Goldsmiths Leisure Centre (Camping Club), Eridge Road, Crowborough TN6 2TN ✆ (01892)
664827 OS map 188/520315 4m SE of Tunbridge Wells on right of A26 (Lewes) Open Feb 1-
Dec 20 60 pitches–adv booking min 3 nights 13 acres, level grass and hard standings
⚐⚐∅☉∅⚛& £7.30-£14.60 (Mastercard/Visa)

UCKFIELD, E Sussex   **Map E5**
Pop 9,200. EC Wed Restaurant: Ye Maiden's Head, High St ✆ (01825) 762019

Honeys Green Farm, Easons Green, Framfield TN22 5RE ✆ Halland (01825) 840334 OS map
199/504177 3m SE of Uckfield off A22 (Eastbourne) at Halland Open Easter-Oct 22 pitches 2
acres level grass, sheltered ⚐☉∅⚏ coarse fishing, walks £8.00-£9.00

Planning a tour in Europe?

Then choose one of the itineraries mapped and described in *Tour Europe* and have the homework
done for you. Each chapter presents a complete holiday – a step by step account of how to enjoy
touring for a fortnight through one of ten chosen regions in seven countries, each rewarding in
itself, from the scenic splendour of the Austrian lake district adjoining Mozart's Salzburg to the
wooded wonderland of the Ardennes/Eifel, from the castle-studded Loire valley to the sun-baked
Italian Marches, and much more. Linking all the local information are touring directions and a
sketch map, with each route forming a circuit so that it can be left and picked up again at any point.

**Reserve your copy at a special pre-publication price by writing to Frederick Tingey (TE),
Hillsboro, How Caple HR1 4TE.**

WARSASH–see Fareham

WASHINGTON, W Sussex   **Map D5**
SEE Chanctonbury Ring 1m SE on South Downs Restaurant: Mill House 2m N at Ashington
✆(01903) 892426
Washington Caravan Camping Park RH20 4AJ ✆(01903) 892869 Fax (01903) 893252 OS map
198/123135 ½m N of Washington on A283 (Shoreham–Petersfield) near junction with A24
(Dorking–Worthing) Open all year, 80 pitches 4 acres, level grass and hard standing
⬛🗐🗩⌀⊛∅🗓 riding stables £9.00

WESTHAM–see Pevensey Bay

WEST WITTERING–see Chichester

WHITSTABLE, Kent   **Map G4**
Pop 25,850. EC Wed, MD Thurs SEE castle, All Saints church 🄸 The Horsebridge ✆(01227)
275482 Restaurant: Tankerton Arms, Tower Hill ✆(01227) 272024
Limberlost Caravan Park, Church Lane, Seasalter CT5 4BU ✆Whitstable (01227) 272270 OS
map 179/096645 2m SW of Whitstable on right of A290/A299 (Boughton Street) Open all year 80
pitches Level grass, sheltered ⚲🗐🗩⊛⌀🗩 £7.00
Primrose Cottage Caravan Park, Golden Hill CT5 3AR ✆Whitstable (01227) 273694 OS map
179/118653 1m S of Whitstable on A299 (Faversham–Herne Bay) Open Mar-Oct 66 pitches (48
static)–no adv booking Grass, level, sheltered ⬛🗐🗩⌀⊛∅🗩🄿🖴 £8.00-£10.50

WINCHELSEA, E Sussex   **Map F5**
SEE church, town walls, old houses Restaurant: New Inn off A259 ✆(01797) 226252
Rye Bay Caravan Park, Pett Level Road TN36 4NE ✆(01797) 226340 OS map 189/913157 2m S
of Winchelsea off A259 (Rye) at Winchelsea beach Open Mar-Oct 335 pitches (265 static)
✗⚲🗐⌀⊛∅⊛🖴 £11.00

WINCHESTER, Hants   **Map B5**
Pop 33,220. MD Mon, Wed, Fri, Sat SEE cathedral, Guildhall, college, Great Hall in castle, West
gate museum, Greenjackets museum 🄸 Guildhall, The Broadway ✆(01962) 840500 Restaurant:
Wykeham Arms, Kingsgate St ✆(01962) 853834
Morn Hill Park (Caravan Club) SO21 1HL ✆(01962) 869877 OS map 185/522295 3m E of
Winchester at junction of A31 (London) and B3404 Open Mar 27-Oct 12, 150 pitches Level
grass, sheltered 🗐🗩⌀⊛∅ £6.20-£13.80

WITTERING, E and W–see Chichester

WORTHING, W Sussex   **Map D6**
Pop 93,400. EC Wed, MD Sat SEE cottages at West Tarring, Cissbury Ring, Salvington Mill 🄸
Town Hall, Chapel Road ✆(01903) 210022 and Marine Parade ✆(01903) 210022 Restaurant:
Rose and Crown, Montague St ✆(01903) 201623
Brook Lane Caravan Park, Brook Lane, Ferring BN12 5JD *Peaceful site for mid- to upper age
group* ✆(01903) 242802 OS map 198/090025 4m W of Worthing off A259 (Littlehampton) and
road to South Ferring Open Mar-Oct 82 pitches (76 static)–no tents or awnings Hard standings,
sheltered 🗐🗩⌀⊛∅ £10.00-£12.00
Northbrook Farm (Caravan Club), Titnore Way BN13 3RT ✆Worthing (01903) 502962 OS map
198/106046 2½m NW of Worthing off A259 (Littlehampton) Open Mar 25-Nov 2, 122 pitches
Level grass 🗐🗩⌀⊛∅⊛ £6.20-£13.80 (Mastercard/Visa)
Onslow Caravan Park, Onslow Drive, Ferring BN12 5RX ✆Worthing (01903) 243170 OS map
198/092029 4m W of Worthing off A259 (Littlehampton) Open Mar-Oct 133 pitches (129
static)–no tents Grass and hard standing, level, sheltered 🗐🗩⌀⊛∅ £8.00-£10.00

CHECK BEFORE ENTERING

Beware less-than-honest site operators who give us one price for the following year and then
increase it once the season gets underway. So note the charges for any site featured in this
guide and before pulling in verify how much you will have to pay, and for what. If on leaving
the charges turn out to be higher, ask why the difference.
The outdoor holidaymaker gets a better deal in France. There site charges are governed by
law and must be displayed at the site entrance.

WROTHAM, Kent Map F4

Pop 1,700 Restaurant: Bull ✆ (01732) 883092

Thriftwood Caravan Camping Park, Plaxdale Green Road, Stansted TN15 7PB ✆ (01732)
822261 Fax (01732) 824636 OS map 188/598608 1½m NNW of Wrotham off A20 (London) on
Stansted road Open Mar-Feb 170 pitches 20 acres, level/gentle slope, grass and hard standing,
sheltered 🛒🍷🏹🗄🔌🌀⊕∅◻↩🚲🏠🚻 cooking facs for campers £8.00-£11.00 (all cards)

To the Woods Camping, Botsham Lane, West Kingsdown TN15 6BN ✆ (01322) 863751 OS map
188/567637 2m NW of Wrotham off A20 (London) at Clearways Café Open all year 40
pitches–no adv booking Grass, part level, sheltered 🛒✖ (snack), 🌀◻🚲 tennis £5.00

YARMOUTH, Isle of Wight Map B6

Pop 890. EC Wed Resort on estuary of Yar with sandy beach accessible only at low tide SEE
castle, old inns 🅿 The Quay ✆ (01983) 760015 Restaurant: Wheatsheaf, Bridge Rd ✆ (01983)
760456

Orchard Park, Newbridge PO41 0TS ✆ (01983) 531331 Fax (01983) 531666 OS map 196/411878
4m E of Yarmouth on B3041 (Newport) Open Feb 17-Jan 2 240 pitches (65 static) Grass, part
level, sheltered, some hard standings 🛒➡🏹🗄🔌🌀⊕∅◻ (indoor and outdoor) ⊕↩◻🚐🚻
battery charging, coarse fishing, pool, tennis £7.95-£11.55 (Mastercard/Visa)

10   Southwest

Four counties between the two coasts facing the Bristol and English Channels make up the Southwest. They include the old counties of Somerset, Dorset and Wiltshire and the new Avon, cobbled together from south Gloucestershire and north Somerset around the triangle of Bath, Bristol and Weston super Mare. Also new is the eastern realignment of the Dorset border to take in Bournemouth.

The widest open space in the region is the breezy plateau of Salisbury Plain in lonely Wiltshire, centred on the 4000 years old stone circle of Stonehenge and bordered on the south by the valley of the Wylye which flows into Salisbury; the city is dominated by the 400ft spire of its ancient cathedral. Beyond the Vale of Pewsey in the north are the Marlborough Downs, covered on the southwest by the Savernake Forest, patterned with ancient tracks and earthworks and dominated by the great Avebury circle. Other sights in the county are the artificial mound of Silbury Hill, the Saxon-Norman site of Old Sarum and the stately home of Wilton House.

Sandwiched between Wiltshire and the Bristol Channel is the ancient seaport of Bristol, with the beautiful Avon Gorge spanned by Brunel's famous suspension bridge to the northwest. A notable sight in Bristol is SS *Great Britain*, the first ocean going iron ship. There are pleasant valleys in the Cotswold escarpment in the north; Georgian Bath is on the east and the vast sands of Weston super Mare on the west. Worth a detour are the three great houses of Badminton, Dodington and Dyrham.

The rolling green hills of Somerset south of Avon rise up to the heathlands of the Mendip Hills near the stalactite caves of Cheddar. Between Taunton and the coast, which is at its best between Minehead and Porlock, are the wooded Quantocks. Below them is Exmoor, bounded on the north by great cliffs. Other sights are the charming old town of Dunster, the cathedral at Wells and the ruined Glastonbury Abbey in the Vale of Avalon.

Rural England remains much as it ever was in Dorset, the southernmost county in the region. The chalk downs extending southeast of Shaftesbury are cut by deep valleys and topped by prehistoric earthworks, most important of which is Maiden Castle, covering 115 acres. The coastline stretches from the vast natural harbour of Poole to Chesil Bank, a seventeen miles long line of pebbles which forms a causeway leading to the Isle of Portland, ending in the rock mass of Portland Bill.

All the major centres in the region possess several campsites, the highest densities being along the Dorset coast and the lowest in Wiltshire. Most coastal campsites cater for static as well as mobile caravanners and campers; many of those inland are on farms.

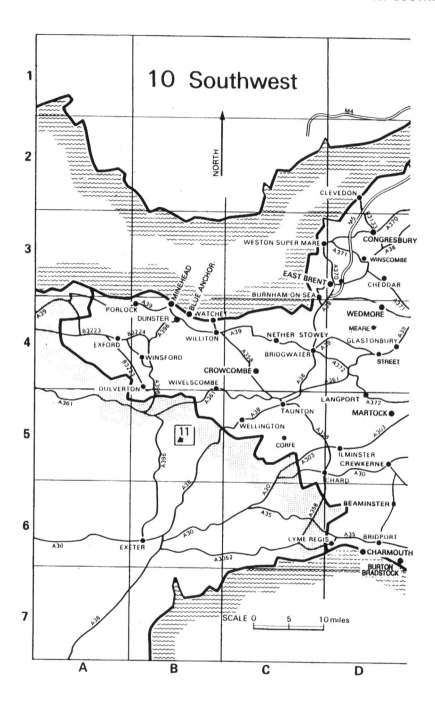

10 Southwest

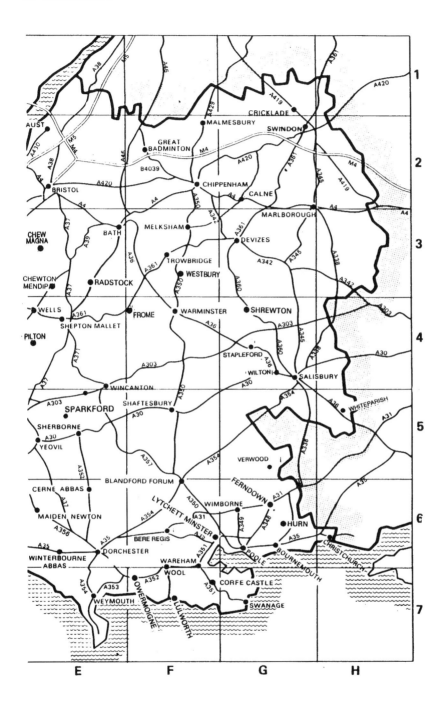

AUST, Avon   Map E2
For those travelling by motorway between Wales and England, a popular place to stop, only ½m
from junct 21 of M4 SEE Severn Bridge Restaurant: Boar's Head ☎(01454) 632278
Boar's Head Campsite, BS12 3AX ☎Pilning (01454) 632278 OS map 172/575890 ¼m SE of Aust
off A403 (Avonmouth) by inn Open Mar-Oct 20 pitches Grass level/sloping ✗ (snack), ⟨symbols⟩
£5.00-£5.50

BADMINTON, Avon   Map F2
SEE Badminton House and Kennels, old Beaufort Arms inn Restaurant: Petty France 3m NW on
A46 ☎(01454) 238361
Petty France Farm, Dunkirk GL9 1AF ☎(01454) 238665 OS map 172/787855 4m NW of
Badminton on A46 (Stroud-Bath) near junct 18 of M4 Open Easter-Sept 12 pitches Grass, level,
part sheltered ⊛ £7.00-£8.00

BATH, Avon   Map E3
Pop 85,000. MD Mon, Wed Elegant city and spa since Roman times, famous for its Regency
architecture SEE Pump Room and Hot Springs, Roman Baths, Assembly Rooms and Museum of
Costume, Royal Crescent, Pulteney Bridge, Claverton Manor (American Museum) 2m E ⓘ 11-13
Bath St ☎Bath (01225) 462831 Restaurant: Crystal Palace, Abbey Green (via Church St)
☎(01225) 423944
Bath Marina and Caravan Park, Brassmill Lane BA1 3JT ☎Bath (01225) 428778 OS map
172/720655 1½m W of Bath off A4 (Bristol) by river Avon Open all year, 88 pitches–no tents
Hard standings ⟨symbols⟩ £12.00-£13.00 (all cards exc Amex)
Bury View Farm, Corston Fields BA2 9HD ☎Bath (01225) 873672 OS map 172/670643 4m W of
Bath on right of A39 (Weston super Mare) Open all year 21 pitches 2 acres level grass ⟨symbols⟩
£9.00
Newton Mill Touring Centre, Newton St Loe BA2 9JF ☎Bath (01225) 333909 OS map
172/715645 3m W of Bath off A4 (Bristol) at Globe Inn Open all year 195 pitches 43 acres,
terraced, grass and hard standing, sheltered ⟨symbols⟩ satellite TV, fishing
£4.20-£8.00

BAYFORD–see Wincanton

BERE REGIS, Dorset   Map F6
Pleasant village in Thomas Hardy country SEE view from Woodbury Hill E, Clouds Hill (NT) former
home of Lawrence of Arabia 3m SW Restaurant: Royal Oak, West St ☎(01929) 471203
Rowlands Wait Touring Park, Rye Hill BH20 7LP ☎Bere Regis (01929) 472727 OS map
194/844930 1m S of Bere Regis off Wool/Bovington road Open Mar-Oct and winter by
arrangement 71 pitches 8 acres, level/sloping grass and hard standing ⟨symbols⟩
games room, crazy golf, bike hire, woodland walks £6.60-£9.60 (all cards exc Amex)

BLANDFORD FORUM, Dorset   Map F6
Pop 7,300. EC Wed, MD Thurs, Sat SEE parish church, Georgian houses ⓘ West Street
☎Blandford (01258) 454770 Restaurant: Crown, West St ☎(01258) 456626
The Inside Park, Down House Estate DT11 9AD ☎Blandford (01258) 453719 OS map 194/864052
1½m SW of Blandford Forum off A354 (Dorchester) on Winterborne Stickland road Open Easter-
Oct 125 pitches 12 acres secluded park and woodland ⟨symbols⟩ games room,
farm tours, woodland walks, dog kennels £7.90-£12.70 (Mastercard/Visa)
Lady Bailey Caravan Park, Winterborne Whitechurch DT11 0HS ☎Milton Abbas (01258) 880786
OS map 194/838001 4½m SW of Blandford Forum on A354 (Puddletown) Open Mar-Oct 121
pitches (32 static) 17 acres, grass, part sloping ⟨symbols⟩ £4.25-£5.50

Bath Marina and Caravan Park

Brassmill Lane, Bath BA1 3JT   Tel (01225) 428778

*Beautifully landscaped site above river Avon catering for caravans only
(hard standings) off A4 (Bristol) 1½m west of Bath.*

Boat hire, touring information, on-site shop. Open all year.

TRAVELLERS REST INN, BRIDPORT

Popular camping park on Dorchester road A35. Level grass and hard standings, sheltered. Bar, restaurant, games room, children's room

Open March-October   **Tel (01308) 458538**

BLUE ANCHOR, Som   **Map B4**
SEE West Somerset Railway, Cleeve Abbey 2m SE, Dunster Castle 3m W Restaurant: Luttrell Arms 3m W at Dunster ☎(01643) 821555

Beeches Holiday Park, TA24 6JW ☎Washford (01984) 840391 OS map 181/035435 1m E of Blue Anchor off B3191 (Watchet) on Old Cleeve road Open Mar 27-Oct 31, 285 pitches (215 static) 🏕🗑🚿🖵 (heated outdoor) 🔧 £4.00-£6.00

Blue Anchor Park, TA24 6JT ☎(01643) 821360 OS map 181/024435 ½m E of Blue Anchor on right of B3191 (Watchet) Open Mar-Oct 426 pitches (321 static) 29 acres, hard standings and level grass 🏕🗑🚿🔧🚿🖵 (indoor) 🔧🎣🛒 £5.50-£13.50 inc elect and awning

BOURNEMOUTH, Dorset   **Map G6**
Pop 144,800. SEE Winter gardens, chines, Pavilion, Hengistbury Head, Compton Acres gardens 2m SW 🅸 Westover Road ☎(01202) 291715 Restaurant: Crust, Bourne Ave, The Square ☎(01202) 421430

Cara Touring Park, Old Bridge Road, Iford BH6 5RQ ☎(01202) 482121 OS map 195/138937 3m E of Bournemouth on right of A35 (Christchurch) Open all year–must book 120 pitches (83 static)–no tents 6 acres level grass and hard standing 🏕🗑🚿🔧🚿🛒 £6.65-£11.75

BREAN–see Burnham

BRIDGWATER, Som   **Map C4**
Pop 27,000. EC Thurs, MD Wed, Sat SEE Town Hall (tapestry, portraits), Admiral Blake House, Sedgemoor Battlefield 4m E 🅸 High St ☎Bridgwater (01278) 427652 Restaurant: Watergate, West Quay ☎(01278) 423847

Fairways International Touring Park, Bath Road, Bawdrip TA7 8PP ☎Bridgwater (01278) 685569 OS map 182/348403 3½m NE of Bridgwater off A39 (Glastonbury) on right of B3141 (Woolavington) Open Mar 1-Nov 15, 200 pitches 6 acres level grass 🏕🥾🗑🚿🔧🚿🔧🛒🛖⛱ games room £6.00-£9.00

BRIDPORT, Dorset   **Map D6**
Pop 6,800. EC Thurs, MD Wed, Sat SEE almshouses, museum, Golden Cap cliffs SW 🅸 32 South Street ☎(01308) 424901 Restaurant: New Inn 3m SE at Shipton Gorge ☎(01308) 897302

Binghams Farm Touring Caravan Park, Melplash DT6 3TT ☎Bridport (01308) 488234 OS map 193/478963 1½m N of Bridport on A3066 (Beaminster) Open all year 60 pitches–adults only 5 acres level grass and hard standing, sheltered 🏕🗑🚿🔧🚿🛖⛱ £8.50-£12.00

Eype House Caravan Camping Park, Eype DT6 6AL ☎Bridport (01308) 424903 OS map 193/446911 2m SW of Bridport off A35 (Charmouth) Open Apr-Oct 55 pitches (35 static)–no touring caravans 4 acres, level grass 🏕🗑🚿🔧🚿🛒 £7.50-£11.50

Golden Cap Caravan Park, Seatown, Chideock DT6 6JX ☎(01297) 489341 OS map 193/422918 3m W of Bridport off A35 (Chideock) on Seatown road Open Mar-Oct 350 pitches (200 static) 28 acres level/sloping grass and hard standings 🏕🥾🗑🔧🛒🛖⛱ farm produce, fishing lake £8.00-£12.50 (Mastercard/Visa)

Highlands End Farm Caravan Park, Eype DT6 6AR ☎Bridport (01308) 422139 OS map 193/453915 1m W of Bridport off A35 (Charmouth) on Eype Mouth road Open Mar-Oct 355 pitches (160 static) 28 acres, level grass and hard standings 🏕✖🍺🔧🥾🗑🚿🔧🚿🖵 (indoor, heated) 🚿🔧🛒🛖⛱ farm produce, tennis court, pitch and putt £8.00-£12.50 (inc showers) (Mastercard/Visa)

Travellers' Rest Inn, Dorchester Road DT6 4PJ ☎Bridport (01308) 458538 OS map 194/515926 3m E of Bridport on A35 (Dorchester) Open Mar-Oct 26 pitches Level/sloping grass and hard standing, sheltered ✖ (snack) 🍺🚿🔧 games room, children's room £6.00 (most cards)

See also Burton Bradstock

BRISTOL, Avon   **Map E2**
Pop 399,300. EC Wed, MD Sun SEE Merchant Venturer's almshouses, cathedral, Temple church, old Vandodger Trow Inn, Theatre Royal, Clifton suspension bridge, SS Great Britain at Great Western Dock, Maritime Heritage Centre ▨ St Nicholas Church, St Nicholas St ✆Bristol (01179) 260767 Restaurant: Barbizon, Corn St ✆(01272) 222658

Baltic Wharf (Caravan Club), Cumberland Road BS1 6XG ✆(0117) 926 8080 OS map 172/573722 ½m W of Bristol centre off A370 (Weston super Mare) Open all year, 58 pitches–booking advisable 2½ acres, hard standings and level grass ▱❂∅ £7.50-£14.00

Brook Lodge Country Touring and Camping Park, Cowslip Green, Redhill BS40 5RD ✆(01934) 862311 OS map 172/485620 8m SW of Bristol off A38 (Bridgwater) Open Mar-Oct 29 pitches Level grass and hard standings, sheltered ▰▱▱❂∅▱ (Jun 15-Aug) ✦▰▱ £8.00-£13.50

BRUTON, Som   **Map E4**
Pop 1,740 EC Thurs SEE church, packhorse bridge, 16c dovecote (NT), 17c Sexeys hospital (almshouses) Restaurant: Three Horseshoes 2m NE at Batcombe ✆(01749) 850359

Batcombe Vale Caravan Park, Batcombe BA4 6BW ✆(01749) 830246 OS map 183/681379 2m N of Bruton off B3081 (Shepton Mallet) Open Apr-Sept 32 pitches Level grass, sheltered ▰▱❂∅❸▱ fishing £9.00

BUCKNOWLE–see Corfe Castle

BURNHAM ON SEA, Som   **Map C3**
Pop 15,000. EC Wed, MD Mon SEE St Andrew's church, Gore Sands, Brean Down bird sanctuary ▨ South Esplanade ✆(01278) 787852 Restaurant: Royal Clarence, Esplanade ✆(01278) 783138

Burnham Association of Sports Clubs, Stoddens Road TA8 2NZ ✆Burnham (01278) 788355 OS map 182/315502 1m NE of Burnham centre off B3140 (East Brent) at Middle Burnham–signposted Open all year 20 pitches–must book 23 acres sportsground, level grass ▱❂✿ lic club (evenings) £6.00

Channel View Camping Caravan Park, Brean Down TA8 2RR ✆Brean Down (01278) 751241/760485 OS map 182/297554 2½m N of Burnham off B3140 (Berrow) on coast road beyond Brean Open Easter-Oct 90 pitches ▱❂ £5.50-£10.75

Diamond Farm Caravan Touring Park, Diamond Farm, Weston Rd, Brean TA8 2RL ✆Burnham (01278) 751041 OS map 182/308560 4m N of Burnham on Sea on Lympsham road via Brean Open Mar-Oct 175 pitches 6 acres level grass ▰✕▱▱▱❂✦▱▱▱ᕦ fishing, caravan spares £3.50-£9.00

Edithmead Leisure and Park Homes, Highbridge TA9 4HE ✆Burnham on Sea (01278) 783475 OS map 182/337492 1½m E of Burnham on A38 (Bristol) near Junction 22 of M5 Open Feb 10-Jan 10 280 pitches (80 static) 15 acres level grass and hard standings, sheltered ▰▱▱▱ clubroom, amusements £5.00-£10.00

Home Farm Touring Caravan and Camping Park,Edithmead TA9 2HD ✆Burnham on Sea (01278) 788888 OS map 182/328492 1m E of Burnham off A38 (Bristol) on Edithmead road near junct 22 of M5 Open all year 400 pitches 40 acres, level grass, sheltered ▰✕▱▱◭▱▱▱❂❸✦ ▰▱ᕦ lic club, cycle hire, fishing, amusements, nightly entertainment, BMX track, ten-pin bowling £3.00-£14.00

New House Farm, Mark Road, Highbridge TA9 4RA ✆Burnham on Sea (01278) 782218 OS map 182/327473 3m SE of Burnham on right of B3139 (Wedmore) near motorway bridge Open Mar-Oct 30 pitches 4 acres level grass ▰▱▱▱▱❂✦ £4.00-£5.50

Northam Farm Caravan Park, Brean TA8 2SE ✆Brean Down (01278) 751244 OS map 182/297561 4m N of Burnham off B3140 (Berrow) on coast road to Brean Open Easter-Oct 350 pitches Level grass ▰✕▱◭▱▱▱❂∅✦▱ᕦ fishing lake £4.00 (Mastercard/Visa)

Southfield Farm Camp Site, Brean TA8 2RL ✆Brean Down (01278) 751233 OS map 182/295561 4m N of Burnham off B3140 (Berrow) on coast road in Brean by sandy beach Open Spring Holiday-Oct 550 pitches (245 static) Level grass part, sheltered ▰▱▱▱❂❸ᕦ £5.50-£7.00

Unity Farm Holiday Centre, Coast Road, Brean Sands TA8 2RB ✆Brean Down (01278) 751235 OS map 182/294540 3m N of Burnham off B3140 (Berrow) on coast road to Brean Open Mar-Oct 1350 pitches (550 static) Grass and hard standings ▰✕▱◭▱▱▱❂∅▱ (indoor and outdoor) ❸✦❑▰▱ lic club, children's entertainment, 18 hole golf course, fishing, nightclub, fun fair, pony trekking, ten-pin bowling £6.00-£14.00 (inc electricity)

Warren Farm Holiday Park, Warren Road, Brean Sands TA8 2RP ✆Brean Down (01278) 751227 OS map 182/297564 4m N of Burnham off B3140 (Berrow) and coast road to Brean Down–M5 junction 22 Open Apr-Oct 15 500 pitches 40 acres, level grass ▰✕▱◭▱▱▱❂∅❸✦ ❑▱ᕦ lic club £5.50-£9.50 (Mastercard/Visa)

BURTON BRADSTOCK, Dorset   Map D6
Pop 750 Village noted for its thatched houses and banded cliffs on E Restaurant: Three
Horseshoes, Mill St ☎(01308) 897259

Coastal Caravans, Annings Lane DT6 4QP ☎(01308) 897361 OS map 193/494898 On E edge of
Burton Bradstock in Annings Lane Open Easter-Oct 110 pitches (90 static) 10 acres level grass,
sheltered ▨❂⌸ £7.50-£11.75

Freshwater Beach Holiday Park, Burton Bradstock DT6 4PT ☎Burton Bradstock (01308) 897317
OS map 193/491883 ½m W of Burton Bradstock on left of B3157 (Bridport) Open mid Mar-mid
Oct 550 pitches (289 static) Level/sloping grass, sheltered ▨✕♀⊸↗▨▨❂⊕∅⊡ (heated)
❂⌄⌸🏠 lic club, private beach, horse riding £8.50-£18.00 (Mastercard/Visa)

CALNE, Wilts   Map G2
Pop 11,000. EC Wed, MD Fri SEE almshouses, Adam church 🅸 Lansdowne Strand Hotel ☎Calne
(01249) 812488 Restaurant: Lansdowne Strand, The Strand ☎(01249) 812488

Blackland Lakes Holiday Centre, Knights Marsh Farm, Stockley Lane SN11 0NQ ☎Calne (01249)
813672 OS map 173/005689 1½m SSE of Calne off A4 (Marlborough) on Heddington road
(signposted) Open all year–adv booking preferable 180 pitches 17 acres, grass and hard
standing, level/sloping, sheltered ▨↗▨▨❂⊕∅⊡ (indoor) ⌄⌖ lake fishing, bird sanctuary,
'super' pitches £7.75-£9.70

CANNARDS GRAVE–see Shepton Mallet

CERNE ABBAS, Dorset   Map E6
SEE Cerne Abbas Giant N Restaurant: Red Lion, Long St ☎(01300) 341441

Giants Head Farm, Old Sherborne Road DT2 7TR ☎Cerne Abbas (01300) 341242 OS map
194/675029 2m NE of Cerne Abbas on Buckland Newton road Open Easter-Oct 50 pitches 3½
acres, level grass, sheltered ▨▨❂⊕⌸▨🅿🏠 £6.00-£8.50

Lyons Gate Caravan Park, Lyons Gate DT2 7AZ ☎(01300) 341260 OS map 194/662060 3m N of
Cerne Abbas on A352 (Sherborne) Open Mar-Oct 60 pitches ▨♀▨▨▨❂⊕∅⊡ (indoor) ❂⌄▨
(70) ⌸ (1) lake fishing, golf course £4.00-£5.00

CHARD, Som   Map B5
Pop 9,380. EC Wed, MD Sat Market town of Saxon origin SEE Choughs Inn, Manor House, wildlife
park 3m E at Cricket St Thomas 🅸 The Guildhall, Fore St ☎(01460) 67463 Restaurant: George,
Fore St ☎(01460) 63413

Alpine Grove, Forton TA20 4HD ☎Chard (01460) 63479 OS map 193/342070 1½m SE of Chard
off B3167 (Axminster-Crewkerne)–signposted Open Easter-Sept, 40 pitches 7½ acres, level, oak
woodland Grass and hard standings ▨▨▨▨❂⊕∅⊡ (heated) ❂⌄ £5.50-£7.50

South Somerset Holiday Park, Exeter Road, Howley TA20 3EA ☎Chard (01460) 62221/66036
OS map 193/275095 2½m W of Chard on A30 (Honiton) Open all year, 140 pitches Level grass
and hard standing, sheltered ⊸▨▨▨❂⊕∅⌄⌖ lic club £6.00-£8.50

CHARMOUTH, Dorset   Map D6
Pop 1,120 EC Thurs SEE 16c Queen's Armes, fossil exhibition, Blue Lias cliffs Restaurant: Queen's
Armes, The Street ☎(01297) 560339

Monkton Wylde Farm Touring Caravan Park, DT6 6DB ☎Charmouth (01297) 34525 OS map
193/328967 3m NW of Charmouth off A35 (Axminster) on left of B3165 (Marshwood) Open
Easter-Nov 14 60 pitches 6 acres level grass sheltered–some hard standing ▨▨▨▨❂⊕∅⌄▨
£6.50-£11.50

Newlands Caravan and Camping Park, DT6 6RB ☎Charmouth (01297) 560259 OS map
193/375936 ½m E of Charmouth centre on right of A35 (Bridport) Open Mar 16-Oct 16, 280
pitches (80 static) Level grass and hard standing ▨✕♀⊸▨▨▨❂⊕∅⊡ (indoor)
❂⌄⌸🏠⌖ club bar, fish and chip bar £8.00-£16.00

Wood Farm Caravan and Camping Park, Axminster Road DT6 6BT ☎Charmouth (01297) 560697
(in season) OS map 193/355940 1m NW of Charmouth centre on right of A35 (Axminster) Open
Apr-Oct 216 pitches (80 static) Level/sloping grass and hard standing, sheltered ▨⊸▨∅⊡
(heated indoor) ❂⌄ tennis, fishing lake £7.00-£11.00

Froglands Farm
Caravan and Camping Park

CHEDDAR, SOMERSET BS27 3RH

Telephone Cheddar (01934) 742058 or 743304

CC/AA 3 pennant/BTA listed for TOURING CARAVANS, MOTOR CARAVANS AND TENTS

68 touring pitches

Froglands farm is a small family site situated in a designated area of outstanding natural beauty on A371 Wells/Weston-super-Mare road, close to church, shops, banks, post office, library and leisure centre. Within walking distance of Cheddar Gorge and Caves.

Open Easter to October. Bookings taken. Adjoining field available for rallies. S.A.E. for charges.

CHEDDAR, Som   **Map D3**
Pop 6,000. EC & MD Wed SEE gorge, caves, Jacob's Ladder ⬛ The Gorge ✆(01934) 744071
Restaurant: Poacher's Table, Cliff St ✆(01934) 742271

Broadway House Caravan and Camping Park BS27 3DB ✆Cheddar (01934) 742610 OS map 182/448546 1m NW of Cheddar on A371 (Axbridge) Open Mar-Nov 200 pitches (35 static) Level/sloping grass, some hard standings, sheltered ⬛♀↩↗⬛🔌🅿◉∅⬛➌↲▭🛒♿ babies' room, table tennis, crazy golf, activity programme, bicycle hire, nature trail £5.50-£13.50 (all cards)

Bucklegrove Caravan Park, Rodney Stoke BS27 3UZ ✆(01749) 870261 OS map 182/488502 3½m SE of Cheddar on A371 (Wells) Open Mar-Oct—must book peak periods 170 pitches (35 static) Level/sloping grass and hard standings, sheltered ⬛♀↩↗⬛🔌🅿◉∅⬛➌↲▭🖤 (50) ✿🛒♿ £5.00-£10.50 (Mastercard/Visa/Switch/Delta)

Church Farm Caravan and Camping Site, BS27 3RF ✆Cheddar (01934) 743048 OS map 182/460530 ¼m S of Cheddar off A371 (Wells) Open Easter-Oct 155 pitches 5 acres, level grass and hard standings, sheltered ⬛🔌🅿◉∅◉🛒♿ £6.50-£10.00

Froglands Farm, Draycott Road BS27 3RH ✆Cheddar (01934) 742058 OS map 182/463530 ½m SE edge of Cheddar on A371 (Wells) Open Apr-Oct 68 pitches Level grass and hard standings, sheltered 🔌🅿◉◉∅ farm shop £5.50-£8.50 inc awning

Longbottom Farm, Shipham BS25 1RW ✆Cheddar (01934) 743166 OS map 182/459567 3m N of Cheddar off A371 (Axbridge) and Shipham road Open all year, 15 pitches Level/sloping grass, sheltered *No showers* £6.00

Ragwood Farm, Clewer BS28 4JG ✆Cheddar (01934) 742254 OS map 182/442510 2m SW of Cheddar on B3151 (Wedmore) Open Whitsun-Aug, 60 pitches ⬛🔌◉➌↲🖤 £5.00

Rodney Stoke Inn, Rodney Stoke BS27 3XB ✆(01749) 870209 OS map 182/483502 2m SE of Cheddar on right of A371 (Wells) in Rodney Stoke Open all year 41 pitches 2½ acres level grass sheltered ✗♀↩↗🔌🅿◉∅➌↲ £3.50-£7.50

CHEW MAGNA, Avon   **Map E3**
Pop 450 SEE 15c church and adj ale house, Tun bridge over river Chew, Chew Valley lake 1m S (bird watching, sailing) Restaurant: Pony and Trap ✆(01275) 332627

Bath Chew Valley Caravan Park, Ham Lane, Bishop Sutton BS39 5TZ ✆(01275) 332127 (0800-2000 hrs) OS map 172/585599 2m SE of Chew Magna on Bishop Sutton road Open Mar-Oct 35 pitches—no children—must book 🔌🅿◉◉∅▭♿ £12.00-£15.00 inc elect, awning, pets, TV hook-up

---

CHEWTON MENDIP, Som   **Map E3**
Pop 750 SEE Cheddar being made at cheese dairy, tower of parish church, Mendips SW Restaurant: Old Down Inn 2m SE at junct of A37 and B3139 ✆(01761) 232398

Chewton Cheese Dairy, Priory Farm, BA3 4NT *Quiet level site at edge of Mendips* ✆(01761) 241666 OS map 183/591525 ½m S of Chewton Mendip off A39 (Wells) at Bathway Open all year 25 pitches 5 acres level grass and hard standing, sheltered ⬛✗🔌◉∅↲ £7.00-£8.50 (most cards)

CHIDEOCK–see Bridport

Help us make CARAVAN AND CAMP IN BRITAIN better known to site operators – and thereby more informative – by showing them your copy when booking in.

CHIPPENHAM, Wilts   Map F2
Pop 21,000. EC Wed, MD Fri, Sat SEE Maud Heath's Causeway, Yelde Hall museum, parish
church, Lacock Abbey 3m S ▪ The Citadel, Bath Rd ☏(01249) 657733 Restaurant: Angel, Market
Pl ☏(01249) 652615

Piccadilly Caravan Park, Folly Lane West, Lacock SN15 2LP *Family site above Lacock village*
☏Lacock (01249) 730260 OS map 173/912682 3½m S of Chippenham off A350 (Melksham) on
Gastard road Open Apr-Oct 40 pitches 2½ acres, grass, level/sloping, some hard standings
🔲🔲🔲🔲 £8.50-£10.50

CHRISTCHURCH, Dorset   Map H6
Pop 29,000. EC Wed, MD Mon SEE priory church, Red House museum, Hengistbury Head,
Tucktonia model village Restaurant: King's Arms, Castle St ☏(01202) 484117

Grove Farm Meadow Holiday Park, Stour Way BH23 2PQ *Well-run site by river Stour*
☏Christchurch (01202) 483597 OS map 195/136947 2m NW of Christchurch off A35
(Bournemouth) on Hurn road Open Mar-Oct 250 pitches (193 static)–no tents 10 acres, level
grass, sheltered 🔲🔲🔲🔲 first aid, fishing, games room £4.50-£11.00

Hoburne Park, Hoburne Lane BH23 4HU ☏(01425) 273379 OS map 195/192935 2m E of
Christchurch on A337 (Lymington) Open Mar-Oct–min booking 7 nights (Jul-Aug) 581 pitches (285
static) Hard standing, part level/sloping, part sheltered 🔲🔲🔲🔲 (heated indoor
and outdoor) 🔲🔲 baths, tennis, lic club £9.00-£22.50 (inc elect and showers)

CLEVEDON, Avon   Map D2
Pop 20,980. EC Wed SEE church, Clevedon Court Manor 1m E Restaurant: Walton Park,
Wellington Terr ☏(01272) 874253

Warrens Holiday Park, Lake Farm, Colehouse Lane, Kenn BS21 6TQ ☏(01275) 871666 OS map
171/172/405695 1m S of Clevedon off B3133 (Yatton) Open Mar-Jan 100 pitches (53 static) 13
acres, level grass and hard standings, sheltered 🔲🔲🔲🔲 club house, fishing £8.00-
£10.00

CONGRESBURY, Avon   Map D3
SEE Yatton church 1m N, Cadbury Hill (views) 1m N Restaurant: Old Inn, St Paul's Causeway
☏(01934) 832270

Oak Farm Touring Park, Weston Road BS49 5EB ☏(01934) 833246 OS map 182/433640 ½m W
of Congresbury on A370 (Weston super Mare)–M5 junct 21 Open Mar-Oct, 27 pitches 2 acres,
level grass, sheltered 🔲🔲🔲 £9.00

CORFE, Som   Map C5
Pop 260 SEE Widcombe bird gardens Restaurant: Greyhound Inn 3m SE at Staple Fitzpaine
☏(01823) 480227

Holly Bush Park, Culmhead TA3 7EA *Homely site in lovely country* ☏(01823) 421515 OS map
193/220162 3m S of Corfe off B3170 (Honiton) Open all year 40 pitches 2 acres level grass and
hard standings, sheltered 🔲🔲🔲🔲 £6.00-£7.50

CORFE CASTLE, Dorset   Map F7
SEE castle ruins, model village Restaurant: Fox Inn, West St ☏(01929) 480449

Burnbake Campsite, Rempstone BH20 5JH ☏Corfe Castle (01929) 480570 OS map 195/993832
2m E of Corfe Castle off B3351 (Studland) Open Apr-Sept–no adv booking 130 pitches–no
caravans Level grass sheltered 🔲🔲🔲🔲 £8.00-£9.00

East Creech Farm BH20 5AP ☏Corfe Castle (01929) 480519 OS map 195/928827 2m W of
Corfe Castle off A351 (Wareham) on Blue Pool road Open Apr-Oct 60 pitches 2 acres, grass,
level/sloping, part sheltered £6.50-£9.00

Woodlands Camping Caravan Park, Glebe Farm, Bucknowle BH20 5NG ☏Corfe Castle (01929)
480280 OS map 195/948817 1m W of Corfe Castle off Church Knowle road Open Easter-Oct
(preferred stay 5 nights or multiples in peak periods) 65 pitches–no adv booking 7 acres, grass,
level/sloping, sheltered 🔲🔲🔲🔲 £10.00

Woodhyde Farm BH20 5HT ☏Corfe Castle (01929) 480274 OS map 195/973804 ½m S of Corfe
Castle on right of A351 (Swanage) Open Easter-Oct, 150 pitches 15 acres, level 🔲🔲 £5.00

CORFE MULLEN–see Wimborne

The restaurants recommended in this guide are of three kinds – inns and pubs, restaurants
proper and those forming part of hotels and motels. They all serve lunch and dinner – at a
reasonable price – say under £10 a head. We shall be glad to have your comments on any
you use this season and if you think they are not up to standard to have your suggestions for
alternatives.

CRICKLADE, Wilts　　　　　　　　　　　　　　　　　　　　　　**Map G1**
Pop 4,000. EC Wed, Sat　SEE Inglesham church, North Meadow nature reserve　Restaurant: White Hart, High St　☎(01793) 750206

Second Chance Touring Park, Marston Meysey SN6 6SZ　☎Kempsford (01285) 810675　OS map 163/140960　3m NE of Cricklade off A419 (Swindon) on Kempsford road via Castle Eaton　Open Mar-Nov, 26 pitches　2 acres mainly level grass and hard standings, sheltered　🖵🅰🅰🅰 fishing, canoeing　£7.00

CROWCOMBE, Som　　　　　　　　　　　　　　　　　　　　　　**Map C4**
Pop 350　SEE church, Church House, Quantock Forest 2m E　Restaurant: White Horse Inn 3m W at Stogumber　☎(01984) 656277

Quantock Orchard Caravan Park TA4 4AW　☎(01984) 618618　OS map 181/142350　1m S of Crowcombe on A358 (Taunton-Minehead) by Flaxpool Garage　Open all year, 75 pitches　4 acres, level grass, some hard standings, sheltered　🖵🖵🅰🅰🅰🅰🅰 (heated) 🅰🅰🅰 games room, mountain bike hire　£6.90-£9.95

DEVIZES, Wilts　　　　　　　　　　　　　　　　　　　　　　**Map G3**
Pop 11,000. EC Wed, MD Thurs, Sat　Pleasant old market town in fertile countryside　SEE market cross, museum, St Mary's church, St John's Alley　⬛ St John's St　☎Devizes (01380) 729408　Restaurant: Bear, Market Pl　☎(01380) 722444

Bell Caravan and Camp Site, Lydeway SN10 3PS　☎Devizes (01380) 840230　OS map 173/050583　3m SE of Devizes on A342 (Andover)　Open Apr-Sept 30 pitches　Level grass, sheltered　🖵🖵🅰🅰🅰🅰🅰🅰 (heated) 🅰🅰 table tennis, covered barbecue area　£6.75-£8.25

Lower Foxhanger Farm, Rowde SN10 1SS　☎Devizes (01380) 828254　OS map 173/969613　2m W of Devizes on A361 (Trowbridge) adj Kennet and Avon canal　Open Apr-Oct, 10 pitches　Grass, sloping, sheltered　🖵🅰🅰🅰🅰 £7.00-£8.00

DULVERTON, Som　　　　　　　　　　　　　　　　　　　　　　**Map B4**
Pop 1,290. EC Thurs　Tourist resort beautifully set on river Barle at edge of Exmoor　SEE church tower, earthworks, Tarr steps 5m NW　Restaurant: Anchor Inn 2m S at Exebridge　☎(01398) 323433

Exe Valley Park, Mill House, Bridgetown TA22 9JR　☎(01643) 851432　OS map 181/923333　7m N of Dulverton off A396 (Dunster) by river Exe　Open Mar-Oct 30 pitches　Grass, level, hard standings, sheltered　🅰🖵🅰🅰 fly fishing　£7.00-£10.00

Lakeside Touring Caravan Park, Higher Grants, Exebridge TA22 9BE　☎Dulverton (01398) 324068　OS map 181/932241　3m S of Dulverton on A396 (Dunster-Tiverton)　Open Mar-Oct　50 pitches　4 acres grass and hard standing, level/sloping, sheltered　✕🖵🅰🖵🅰🅰🅰🅰 dog walk　£7.50-£10.00

Zeacombe House (Caravan Club), Anstey Mills EX16 9JU　☎Anstey Mills (01398) 341279 (0800-2000 hrs)　OS map 181/862241　3m SW of Dulverton on B3227 (old A361: Bampton-South Molton)　Open mid Mar-Oct　50 pitches　4½ acres level grass and hard standings, sheltered　🖵🖵🅰🅰🅰🅰 dog walk　£10.00-£15.00 (Mastercard/Visa)

DUNKIRK–see Badminton

EXFORD, Somerset

—— Downscombe Farm ——
by River Exe

Open May-October for tents only.   6 acres level grass, sheltered.

£9.00 per night for two.

DUNSTER, Som   **Map B4**
Pop 800 EC Wed Ancient village dominated by Conygar Hill, a landmark for shipping. SEE historic
castle, Yarn Market, church, dovecote, nunnery, grist mill, Cleeve abbey 4m SE Restaurant: Luttrell
Arms ✆ (01643) 821555

Totterdown Farm, Timberscombe TA24 7TA ✆ (01643) 841317 OS map 181/957424 2m SW of
Dunster on left of A396 (Tiverton) Open Jul 15-Sept 15 22 pitches Level grass £4.00-£5.00

EAST BRENT, Som   **Map D3**
Restaurant: Brent House ✆ (01278) 760246

Dulhorn Farm, Weston Road, Lympsham BS24 0JQ ✆ Edingworth (01934) 750298 OS map
182/349534 1m N of East Brent on left of A370 (Weston super Mare) Open Mar-Oct 43 pitches
2 acres, level grass 🔌🅿⊕↩🚻🏠 £7.00-£8.50

EAST STOKE–see Wool

EXEBRIDGE–see Dulverton

EXFORD, Som   **Map A4**
At heart of Exmoor, unspoiled moorland village in hollow by river Exe Restaurant: Crown ✆ (01643)
831554

Downscombe Farm TA24 7NP ✆ (01643) 831239/831141 OS map 181/844395 1m N of Exford off
Porlock road by river Exe Open May-Oct, 60 pitches–tents only–no children 6 acres level grass
sheltered 🅿⊕∅ £9.00

Westermill Farm TA24 7NJ ✆ (01643) 831238 OS map 181/824398 2½m W of Exford off Porlock
road, by river–signposted Open all year 60 pitches–unsuitable for trailer caravans 6 acres, level
grass, sheltered 🛒🅿∅⊕∅🏠 bathing, fishing, waymarked walks £8.00

FERNDOWN, Dorset   **Map G6**
Pop 23,470. EC Wed SEE church Restaurant: Bridge House 1m SW on A348 at Longham
✆ (01202) 578828

Camping International, Athol Lodge, 229 Ringwood Road, St Leonards BH24 2SD ✆ Ferndown
(01202) 872817 OS map 195/104023 2m NE of Ferndown on A31 (Ringwood) Open Mar-Oct
205 pitches 9 acres, level grass and hard standing, sheltered 🛒✕🍴↩🏹🅿🔌∅⊕∅▱ (heated
outdoor) ⊕↩🚻🎣 £8.30-£12.50 (Mastercard/Visa)

Oakdene Forest Park, St Leonards BH24 2RZ ✆ Ferndown (01202) 875422 OS map 195/105030
2m E of Ferndown off A31 (Ringwood) Open Feb 1-Jan 5 405 pitches (205 static) 55 acres level
grass 🛒✕🏹🅿∅⊕∅▱ (indoor and outdoor) ⊕ paddling pools, pony trekking, disco, lic club,
mini gym, sauna, solarium, adventure playground £5.00-£18.00

Oak Hill Farm Caravan Park, St Leonards BH24 2SB ✆ Ferndown (01202) 876968 OS map
195/107021 3m NE of Ferndown off A31 (Ringwood) Open Easter-Oct 80 pitches 10 acres level
grass, sheltered 🔌🅿∅∅🎣 £7.00-£10.00 (Mastercard/Visa)

Redcote Holiday Park, Boundary Lane, St Leonards BH24 2SE ✆ Ferndown (01202) 872817 OS
map 195/105023 3m NE of Ferndown off A31 (Ringwood) on Matchams road Open Apr-Sept 145
pitches Level grass 🛒🏹🔌🅿∅⊕∅▱⊕↩🚻🎣 £5.80-£7.80

St Leonards Farm Caravan and Camping Park, West Moors BH22 0AQ ✆ Ferndown (01202)
872637 OS map 195/095020 2m NE of Ferndown on A31 (Ringwood) Open Apr-Sept 175
pitches Level grass, sheltered 🔌🅿∅⊕∅↩& £7.00-£10.00

Shamba Tourist Park, St Leonards BH20 2SB ✆ Ferndown (01202) 873302 OS map 195/104026
2m NE of Ferndown off A31 (Ringwood) on East Moors Farm lane Open Easter-Sept, 150 pitches
6 acres, level grass and hard standings 🛒✕ (snack) 🍴↩🏹🔌🅿∅⊕∅▱↩🚻 £8.00-£12.00

GLASTONBURY, Som   **Map D4**
Pop 7,360. EC Wed, MD Tues SEE Benedictine abbey ruins (oldest religious foundation in Britain), almshouses, St Michael's Tower on Glastonbury Tor, Tribunal House with relics of prehistoric lake village ◪ The Tribunal, High St ☏ Glastonbury (01458) 832954 Restaurant: George and Pilgrims, High St ☏ (01458) 831146

Ashwell Farm House, Ashwell Lane, Edgarley BA6 8LB ☏ Glastonbury (01458) 832313 OS map 182/514382 ¾m E of Glastonbury on A361 (Shepton Mallet) Open all year, 80 pitches (15 static) 2 acres, gentle slope/level grass ▣⌀⊛⌀ £6.00-£8.00

Isle of Avalon Touring Caravan Park, Godney Road BA6 9AF ☏ Glastonbury (01458) 833618 OS map 182/493396 ½m W of Glastonbury centre off B3151 (Wedmore) Open all year 120 pitches 8 acres, level grass and hard standings, sheltered ▤▣▣⌀⊛⌀⊕⤳▣⌖ bike hire £8.85-£9.85 (inc showers) (1999)

The Old Oaks Touring Caravan Camping Park, Wick Farm, Wick BA6 8JS ☏ Glastonbury (01458) 831437 OS map 182/522394 2m NE of Glastonbury off A361 (Shepton Mallet) and A39 (Wells) Open Mar-Oct 40 pitches 4 acres, grass and hard standings, level/sloping, sheltered ▤⤳▣▣⌀⊛⌀⊕⌖ fishing £7.50-£10.00 (Mastercard/Visa)

For other sites near Glastonbury see also Street

HARMANS CROSS–see Swanage

HIGHBRIDGE–see Burnham

HURN, Dorset   **Map G6**
Restaurant: Avon Causeway ☏ (01202) 482714

Longfield Caravan Park, Matchams Lane, BH23 6AW ☏ (01202) 485214 OS map 195/128997 2m N of Hurn on left of Matchams Lane Open all year–must book peak periods 29 pitches 2 acres, level grass and hard standings ▣⌀▣ (all pitches) ⊛▱ farm produce £7.50-£9.50

Mount Pleasant Touring Park, Matchams Lane, BH23 6AW ☏ (01202) 475474 OS map 195/130990 1m N of Hurn on right of Matchams Lane Open Mar-Oct 170 pitches 7 acres grass, part sloping ▤⤳▣▣⌀⊛⌀⊕⤳⌖ £5.00-£11.00

Port View, Matchams Lane, BH23 6AW ☏ (01202) 474214 OS map 195/129991 1½m N of Hurn on right of Matchams Lane Open Easter-Oct 35 pitches Grass, part level, part sheltered ▣⌀▣ (£2.50/wk) £4.00-£5.00

ILMINSTER, Som   **Map D5**
Pop 3725 EC Thurs MD alt Wed SEE Barrington Court 3m N (NT) Restaurant: Shrubbery ☏ (01460) 52108

Stewley Cross Caravan Park, Stewley Cross, Ashill TA19 9NP ☏ (01823) 480314 OS map 193/312180 3m NW of Ilminster off A303 (Honiton) on left of A358 (Taunton) at Stewley Cross Open Apr-Oct, 20 pitches ½ acre level grass £5.00

Thornleigh Caravan Park, Thornleigh, Horton TA19 9QH ☏ Ilminster (01460) 53450 OS map 193/329151 2m W of Ilminster on A303 (Honiton) Open Mar-Oct 20 pitches 1½ acres level grass ▣⊛▥⌖ sauna, sunbed £6.00

LACOCK–see Chippenham

LANGPORT, Som   **Map D5**
Pop 940. EC Wed SEE parish church, Hanging Chapel Restaurant: Langport Arms, Cheapside ☏ (01458) 250530

Bowdens Crest Caravan Camping Park, Bowdens TA10 0DD ☏ Langport (01458) 250553 OS map 193/413289 1½m N of Langport off A372 (Bridgwater) on Bowdens road Open Mar-Nov 60 pitches (30 static) 6 acres level grass sheltered ▤♟⤳⤳▣⌀⊛⌀⊕⤳▣▱ lic clubhouse £9.00 (Mastercard/Visa)

Thorney Lakes Caravan Park, Muchelney TA10 0DW ☏ Langport (01458) 250811 OS map 193/429228 2m S of Langport on Kingsbury Episcopi road by river Parrett Open Mar-Jan 40 pitches Level grass, sheltered ▣⊛ fishing lakes £6.00

LANGTON MATRAVERS–see Swanage

LONGLEAT–see Warminster

LULWORTH, Dorset   **Map F7**
SEE cove, Durdle Door (natural cliff arch), Fossil Forest (access at certain times), Lulworth Castle, church, Dorset coast path Restaurant: Castle on B3070 ☎(01929) 400311

Durdle Door Holiday Park, West Lulworth BH20 5PU ☎West Lulworth (01929) 400200 Fax (01929) 400260 OS map 194/812809 1m W of Lulworth on Daggers Gate road Open Mar-Oct 555 pitches (380 static) 45 acres grass, level/sloping, sheltered ☚✗ (snack) ♇⊷🗗🖳⊘⊛∅🕄 ↵🖳🗁 mountain bike hire £10.00-£17.00 (all cards)

LYME REGIS, Dorset   **Map D6**
Pop 3,500. EC Thurs SEE harbour (The Cobb), museum, Umbrella Cottage, Dorset coast path, Landslip 3m W ☑ Guildhall Cottage, Church St ☎Lyme Regis (01297) 442138 Restaurant: Royal Standard, Marine Parade ☎(01297) 442637 Nearest sites 3m W at Uplyme

---

ORGANFORD MANOR near Poole

The Lodge, Organford BH16 6ES   Tel (01202) 622202/623278

Secluded site in manor grounds off A35 beyond junction with A351.
All main facilities including shop in season.

£7.50 - £9.00 per night for two

See listing under Lytchett Minster

LYTCHETT MINSTER, Dorset   **Map F6**
Village close by Poole harbour Restaurant: Chequers 1½m NW at Lytchett Matravers ☎(01202) 622215

Beacon Hill Touring Park, Blandford Road North, BH16 6AB *Well equipped and quiet site in woodland setting* ☎(01202) 631631 OS map 195/975940 1½m NE of Lytchett Minster on A350 (Poole–Blandford) just N of junction with A35 Open Easter-Sept 170 pitches 30 acres, mainly level grass, some hard standings, sheltered ☚♇⊷↗🗗🖳⊘⊛∅🖳 (heated) ⊛↵🗆☖ tennis, fishing £8.50-£17.00

Huntick Farm, Lytchett Matravers BH16 6BB ☎Lytchett Minster (01202) 622222 OS map 195/957949 1m N of Lytchett Minster off Lytchett Matravers road at Rose and Crown Open Apr-Oct 30 pitches Level grass, sheltered 🖳∅⊛∅↵🖳 boat storage £4.50-£6.00

Organford Manor, Organford BH16 6ES *Secluded site in grounds of manor* ☎Lytchett Minster (01202) 622202 OS map 195/945925 2m SW of Lytchett Minster off B3067/A35 (Dorchester) on right of Organford road Open Mar 15-Oct 31, 120 pitches (45 static) 8 acres, level grass, sheltered ☚ (high season) 🗗🖳∅⊛∅🗁☖♙ £7.50-£9.00

Pear Tree Touring Park, Organford BH16 6LA ☎Lytchett Minster (01202) 622434 OS map 195/940915 1½m SW of Lytchett Minster off A3067/A351 (Wareham) on left of Organford road Open Apr-Oct 15, 125 pitches 7½ acres, level grass and hard standings ☚🗗🖳∅⊛∅↵🖳☖ riding stables £6.50-£9.00 (all cards)

Sandford Park, Holton Heath BH16 6JZ *Family site with lots of entertainment with direct access to A351* ☎Lytchett Minster (01202) 631600 OS map 195/941912 1½m SW of Lytchett Minster on right of A351 (Wareham) Open Easter-Jan 447 pitches (268 static)–adv booking advisable 60 acres, level grass, sheltered ☚✗♇⊷↗🗗🖳∅⊛∅🖳 (indoor, heated) ⊛↵🗆🗁☎ crazy golf, tennis, barbecues, paddling pool, ballroom, ladies hairdresser £8.50-£14.25

South Lytchett Manor Caravan Park, Lytchett Minster BH16 6JB ☎Lytchett Minster (01202) 622577 OS map 195/964932 ¼m NE of Lytchett Minster on B3067 (Upton) Open Apr-Oct 15–must book peak periods 150 pitches Level/sloping grass, sheltered ☚🗗🖳∅⊛∅↵🗆🖳☖ £7.40-£9.00

MAIDEN NEWTON, Dorset   **Map E6**
Pop 760. SEE church with Norman chancel Restaurant: Old Market House 4m NE at Cerne Abbas ☎(01300) 341680
Clay Pigeon Tourist Park, Wardon Hill DT2 9PW ☎(01935) 83492 OS map 194/610023 3m N of Maiden Newton on A37 (Dorchester–Yeovil) Open all year 60 pitches 3½ acres, level grass and hard standing ☚🗗🖳∅⊛∅⊛↵ £6.00-£9.00

MALMESBURY, Wilts   Map F2
Pop 2,590. EC Thurs SEE abbey, market cross, almshouses, Old Bell Museum ⚹ Town Hall,
Market Lane ☏Malmesbury (01666) 823748 Restaurant: Suffolk Arms on B4014 (Tetbury)
☏(01666) 824323

Burton Hill Caravan and Camping Park, Arches Lane SN16 0EJ ☏Malmesbury (01666) 826880
   OS map 173/933872 ¼m S of Malmesbury off A429 (Chippenham) opposite hospital Open Apr-
   Nov, 30 pitches 2 acres, level grass, sheltered 🔲🔲⊘⊛🔲 £7.00

MARLBOROUGH, Wilts   Map G2
Pop 7,000. EC Wed, MD Wed, Sat SEE college, old houses and inns, White Horse, Savernake
Forest ⚹ Car Park, George Lane ☏Marlborough (01672) 513989 Restaurant: Castle and Ball,
High St ☏(01672) 515201

Hill View Caravan Park, Oare SN8 4JE ☏Marlborough (01672) 563151 OS map 173/156623 6m
   SW of Marlborough on A345 (Pewsey) Open Apr-Sept 46 pitches (36 static) 4 acres level grass,
   sheltered 🔲⊛ £7.50-£10.50 (inc hot water)

Postern Hill, (Forest Enterprise) SN8 4ND ☏(01672) 515195 OS map 173/197680 1m S of
   Marlborough on left of A346 (Andover) Open Mar 15-Oct 15 170 pitches–no adv booking 20
   acres level grass, sheltered 🔲⊘⊛∅ £6.00-£8.20 (Mastercard/Visa)

MARTOCK, Som   Map D5
Pop 3,720 EC Thurs SEE 15-16c church (interior), Treasurer's House (NT), 17c Church House, East
Lambrook Manor 2m W Restaurant: White Hart, East St ☏(01935) 822005

Southfork Caravan Park, Parrett Works TA12 6AE ☏Martock (01935) 825661 OS map
   193/443190 ½m W of Martock off South Petherton road by river Parrett Open all year, 30 pitches
   2 acres level grass 🔲⚲🔲🔲⊘⊛∅⊗⤳🔲 fishing, caravan spares and service £6.00-£9.00
   (Mastercard/Visa)

MEARE, Som   Map D3
Pop 750 SEE peat moors visitor centre, nature reserve, Fish House (enq at Manor Farm)
Restaurant: Ye Olde Burtle Inn 2m W at Burtle ☏(01278) 722269

Orchard Camping, Ye Olde Burtle Inn, Burtle TA7 8NG ☏(01278) 722269 OS map 182/402429
   2m W of Meare off Shapwick road Open all year 30 pitches 1 acre level grass ✕⚲⤳⊛∅⤳
   skittle alley £4.95-£5.95 (all cards)

MINEHEAD, Som   Map B4
Pop 8,720. EC Wed SEE old houses, model village, Dunster village and castle 2m SE, West
Somerset Railway, Exmoor ⚹ 17 Friday St ☏(01643) 702624 Restaurant: Luttrell Arms 2m SE at
Dunster ☏(01643) 821555

Hill Road Park (Camping Club), North Hill TA24 5SF ☏Minehead (01643) 704138 OS map
   181/958471 1½m NW of Minehead centre on North Hill road Open Apr-Sept, 60 pitches–no
   caravans–adv booking min 2 nights 4 acres sloping grass, sheltered 🔲🔲⊛∅ £8.20-£10.40

Minehead and Exmoor Caravan and Camping Park, Porlock Road TA24 8SN ☏Minehead
   (01643) 703074 OS map 181/951458 1m W of Minehead centre on right of A39 (Porlock) Open
   Mar-Oct 50 pitches Grass and hard standing, level, part sheltered 🔲🔲⊛∅⤳🔲⚷ £10.00

See also Dunster

BURTON HILL
CARAVAN & CAMPING PARK

Burton Hill, Malmesbury SN16 0EJ

Off Chippenham road in quiet location opposite hospital
River walks to historic town of Malmesbury
Excellent base for touring the Cotswolds

Telephone: 01666 826880

NETHER STOWEY, Som   Map C4
SEE Coleridge's cottage Restaurant: Cottage Inn at Keenthorne on A39 (Cannington) ☎ (01278) 732355

Currypool Mills, Cannington TA5 2NH ☎ (01278) 653215 OS map 182/231383 2m E of Nether Stowey off A39 (Bridgwater) on Spaxton road Open Easter-Oct 35 pitches 1½ acres level grass sheltered ▨▨◪◕⊘⊡ (indoor), ☎ £2.00-£3.50

Mill Farm Caravan Camping Park, Fiddington TA5 1JQ ☎ Nether Stowey (01278) 732286 OS map 182/218407 2½m E of Nether Stowey off A39 (Bridgwater) Open all year 125 pitches 15 acres level grass and hard standings, sheltered ▨⊸↗▨▨◪◕⊘⊡ (heated) ◕↩□▨▥ farm produce, canoe hire, pony rides, pets corner, free boating, £8.00-£10.00

NORTH WOOTTON–see Pilton

ORCHESTON–see Shrewton

ORGANFORD–see Lytchett Minster

OWERMOIGNE, Dorset   Map F7
Restaurant: Streamside 4m SW on A353 at Overcombe ☎ (01305) 833121

Moreton Glade Touring Park, Station Road, Moreton DT2 8BB ☎ Warmwell (01305) 853801 OS map 194/782892 3m N of Owermoigne on B3390 (Warmwell–Affpuddle) adj Moreton station Open Mar 16-Nov 30, 140 pitches Level grass and hard standings ▨⊸▨▨◪◕⊘↩▨◔ £4.50-£7.50 (OAP concession)

Sandyholme Holiday Park, Moreton Road, DT2 8HZ ☎ Warmwell (01305) 852677 OS map 194/768867 1m N of Owermoigne on Moreton road Open Apr 1-Oct 31, 105 pitches (45 static) 5 acres level grass ▨✗⊻⊸↗▨▨◪◕⊘↩▨⊡◔ bar meals £6.50-£12.00 (Mastercard/Visa/Switch)

Warmwell Touring Park, Warmwell DT2 8JD ☎ Warmwell (01305) 852313 OS map 194/735871 2m W of Owermoigne on B3390 (Warmwell-Affpuddle) near Warmwell Open Mar 15-Jan 15, 190 pitches Grass and hard standing, level/sloping, sheltered ▨⊻⊸↗▨▨◪◕⊘↩□▨ lic club £5.00-£13.00 (Mastercard/Visa)

PILTON, Som   Map E4
Pop 450 SEE church (roof, screen), tithe barn, Pilton Manor Vineyards Restaurant: Crossways 1½m W at North Wootton ☎ (01749) 890237

Greenacres Camping, Barrow Lane, North Wootton BA4 4HL ☎ (01749) 890497 OS map 182/183/553416 2m W of Pilton via North Wootton Open Apr-Oct 30 pitches–tents, trailer tents and motorhomes only 4½ acres level grass ◪◕↩◔ £9.00

POOLE, Dorset   Map G6
Pop 123,000. EC Wed, MD Tues, Sat SEE Guildhall museum, park and zoo, largest natural harbour in Britain with Brownsea Island (NT) ⓘ Poole Quay ☎ Poole (01202) 673322 and Dolphin Centre Restaurant: Dolphin, High St ☎ (01202) 673612

Rockley Park, Hamworthy BH15 4LZ ☎ Poole (01202) 679393 OS map 195/976910 2m W of Poole off Blandford road Open Apr-Oct, 1178 pitches (1077 static) ▨✗⊻⊸↗▨▨◪◕⊘⊡◕↩⊡ club, dancing £9.00-£20.00

See also Lytchett Minster

PORLOCK, Som   Map B4
Pop 1,370. EC Wed SEE church, Porlock Weir, Porlock Hill (one of steepest in Britain) Restaurant: Anchor and Ship 1m NW at Porlock Weir ☎ (01643) 862636

Burrowhayes Farm Caravan and Camping Site, West Luccombe TA24 8HT ☎ Porlock (01643) 862463 OS map 181/898459 1m E of Porlock off A39 (Minehead) Open Mar-Oct–booking advisable in peak periods 140 pitches (20 static) 8 acres, grass, level/sloping, sheltered ▨▨▨◪◕⊘⊡ horses and ponies for hire £6.00-£8.50 (Mastercard/Visa)

Porlock Caravan Park TA24 8ND ☎ Porlock (01643) 862239 Fax (01643) 862269 OS map 181/885470 ½m N of Porlock on B3225 (Porlock Weir) Open Apr-Oct 96 pitches (56 static) Level grass, sheltered ▨▨▨◪◕⊘▨⊡ £8.00

RADSTOCK, Som   Map E3
SEE Ammerdown Park yew gardens 2m SE Restaurant: Old Malt House 2m NW at Timsbury ☎ (01761) 470106

Pitcote Farm, Stratton on the Fosse BA3 4SX ☎ Mendip (01761) 232265 OS map 183/656494 3m S of Radstock off A367 (Shepton Mallett) Open all year, 30 pitches 2 acres, level *No showers* £3.00

RODNEY STOKE–see Wells

ROWDE–see Devizes

ST LEONARDS–see Ferndown

SALISBURY, Wilts   **Map G4**
Pop 36,000. EC Wed, MD Tues, Sat SEE cathedral with 404ft spire, Salisbury and S Wilts museum, Joiners' Hall, old inns, Old Sarum (pre-Roman settlement) 2m N 🄸 Fish Row ☎Salisbury (01722) 334956 Restaurant: Kings Arms, St John's St ☎(01722) 327629

Alderbury Caravan Camping Park, Old Southampton Rd, Whaddon SP5 3HB ☎Salisbury (01722) 710125 OS map 184/198264 3m SE of Salisbury off A36 (Southampton) in Whaddon Open all year 40 pitches 1½ acres level grass and hard standings, sheltered 🖬🟦♿ £7.50-£9.40 inc elect

Coombe Touring Park, Combe Nurseries, Race Plain, Netherhampton SP2 8PN ☎Salisbury (01722) 328451 OS map 184/093283 4m W of Salisbury off A36 (Warminster) and A3094 (Netherhampton) Open all year 50 pitches 3 acres, level grass, part sheltered 🛒🔲🟦◎🟦◎∅➷ battery charging, freezer pack service £8.00-£10.00

Hudson's Field (Camping Club), Castle Road SP1 3RR ☎Salisbury (01722) 320713 OS map 184/140320 1m N of Salisbury centre on left of A345 (Marlborough) near Old Sarum Open Mar-Oct 150 pitches–adv booking min 2 nights 4½ acres, level grass 🟦◎∅ £7.30-£10.40 plus £4.20 non-member pitch fee
See also Whiteparish

SEVERN BRIDGE–see Aust

SHAFTESBURY, Dorset   **Map F5**
Pop 5,300 EC Wed MD Thurs Only hilltop town in Dorset, perched above Blackmore Vale SEE abbey ruins, museum, Castle Hill, cobbled and much photographed Gold Hill 🄸 Bell St ☎(01747) 853514 Restaurant: Ship, Bleke St ☎(01747) 853219

Blackmore Vale Caravan Park, Sherborne Causeway SP7 9PX ☎(01747) 851523 OS map 183/836230 1m W of Shaftesbury on A30 (Yeovil) Open all year 50 pitches Level grass and hard standing, sheltered 🛒🟦∅◎∅ £6.00-£8.00 (Mastercard/Visa)

SHEPTON MALLET, Som   **Map E4**
Pop 6,600. EC Wed, MD Fri SEE market cross, almshouses, church, museum 🄸 The Centre ☎(01749) 845258 Restaurant: Oakhill House 3m NE at Oakhill ☎(01749) 840180

Manleaze Caravan Park, Cannards Grave BA4 4LY ☎Shepton Mallet (01749) 342404 OS map 183/626423 1m S of Shepton Mallett on A371 (Castle Cary) Open all year 25 pitches 3 acres, level grass 🛒➷🔲🟦∅◎🗔 £5.00

Old Down Touring Park, Emborough BA3 4SA ☎Mendip (01761) 232355 Fax (01761) 232619 OS map 183/626513 6m N of Shepton Mallet at junction of A37 (Bristol) and B3139 (Radstock-Wells) opp Old Down Inn Open Mar-Nov 35 pitches 5 acres, level grass and hard standings 🛒🔲🟦∅◎∅🟢🟦🔆 £8.00-£9.50

Phippens Farm, Stoke St Michael, Oakhill BA3 5JH ☎Shepton Mallet (01749) 840395 OS map 183/649472 2m N of Shepton Mallet off A367 (Bath) on right of Stoke St Michael road Open Apr-Oct 25 pitches 7 acres level grass 🟦◎🟦🗔 *No showers* £3.50
See also Chewton Mendip and Pilton

SHREWTON, Wilts   **Map G4**
Restaurant: George Inn, London Rd ☎(01980) 620341

Brades Acre Camping Park, Tilshead, SP3 4RX ☎Shrewton (01980) 620402 OS map 184/034470 3m NW of Shrewton on left of A360 (Devizes) Open Apr-Nov 26 pitches Level grass, sheltered 🛒🟢🔲🟦∅∅◎🟦 £8.00-£9.50

Stonehenge Touring Park, Orcheston SP3 4SH ☎(01980) 620304 Fax (01980) 621121 OS map 184/060455 1m NW of Shrewton off A360 (Devizes) on Orcheston road adj Crown Inn Open all year 30 pitches 2 acres level grass and hard standing, sheltered 🛒✖🟢➷🔲🟦∅◎∅🟢➷ £6.00-£10.00

 Long Hazel International Caravan Camping Park

on Yeovil road out of Sparkford

Modern facilities, level grass and hard standings. Open Mar-Dec.

SPARKFORD, Som   Map E5
Pop 360 Restaurant: George N 4m at Castle Cary ☏(01963) 450761

Long Hazel International Caravan and Camping Park, High Street BA22 7JH ☏(01963) 440002
OS map 183/602262 ¼m SW of Sparkford on A359 (Yeovil) Open Mar-Dec 75 pitches Level
grass and hard standing, sheltered ▣⌀⊛⌀⌀⌀⊛⛒⛬ £10.00-£12.00

STREET, Som   Map D4
Pop 9,550. EC Wed Shoe-making town within reach of several viewpoints–Windmill Hill SE, Ivythorn
and Walton Hills S Restaurant: Bear, High St ☏(01458) 442021

Bramble Hill Camping Park, Walton BA16 9RQ ☏Street (01458) 442548 OS map 182/454362
1m W of Street on A361-A39 (Taunton) Open Mar-Oct 45 pitches 3½ acres, level grass,
sheltered ▣⊛ £8.00-£10.00

SWANAGE, Dorset   Map G7
Pop 8,640. EC Thurs (winter) Quiet family resort on Isle of Purbeck with good sandy beaches SEE
parish church and mill pond, clock tower, town hall, Tilly Whim caves 🄸 The White House, Shore
Road ☏Swanage (01929) 422885 Restaurant: Pines, Burlington Rd ☏(01929) 425211

Flower Meadow Caravan Park, Haycrafts Lane, Harmans Cross BH19 3EB ☏(01929) 480035 OS
map 195/984800 2½m W of Swanage off A351 (Wareham) at Harmans Cross on left of Haycrafts
Lane Open Apr-Oct 28 pitches Level/sloping grass and hard standing ▣⌀⌀⊛ℙ⌀ (Jul-Aug)
£6.50

Haycrafts Farm, Haycrafts Lane, Harmans Cross BH19 3EB ☏(01929) 480572 OS map
195/965798 3m W of Swanage off A351 (Wareham) at Harmans Cross Open Easter-Sept–must
book peak periods 50 pitches–*families and couples only* 5 acres, grass, level/sloping, some hard
standings ▣⊛⌀⌀ £6.80-£11.50

Herston Yards Farm, Washpond Lane BH19 3DJ ☏(01929) 422932 OS map 195/015796 1½m W
of Swanage off A351 (Wareham) at Herston Cross Open Apr-Oct 80 pitches Level grass,
sheltered ⌁▣⌀⊛ £5.50

Ponderosa Camping Caravan Park, Valley Rd BH19 3DX ☏(01929) 426130/480258 OS map
195/002795 2m W of Swanage on A351 (Wareham) Open Jul-Sept 70 pitches–no adv booking 6
acres level/sloping grass, sheltered ⌀ £8.00-£10.00

Priest's Way Holiday Park, off Steer Road BH19 2RS ☏Swanage (01929) 422747 OS map
195/018785 1m W of Swanage off A351 (Wareham) Open Apr-Sept 170 pitches (108 static) 12
acres level/sloping grass and hard standing, sheltered ⌁▣▣⌀⊛⌀ £7.00-£12.50

Tom's Field Camping Site, Tom's Field Road, Langton Matravers BH19 3HN OS map 195/995788
2½m W of Swanage off A351 (Wareham) and B3069 (Kingston) Open Easter-Oct–100 pitches–*no
trailer caravans* 4 acres, grass, level/sloping, sheltered ⌁⌀⊛⌀⛬ £7.00-£8.00

Ulwell Cottage Caravan Park, Ulwell BH19 3DG ☏(01929) 422823 Fax (01929) 421500 OS map
195/022808 1½m NW of Swanage off A351 (Wareham) Open Mar 1-Jan 7 217 pitches (140
static) 13 acres, hard standings and grass, level/sloping, sheltered ⌁✗⏦⏦🄱▣▣⌀⊛⌀⛒
⊛⌀⛒⛬ snacks £10.50-£23.00 (Mastercard/Visa)

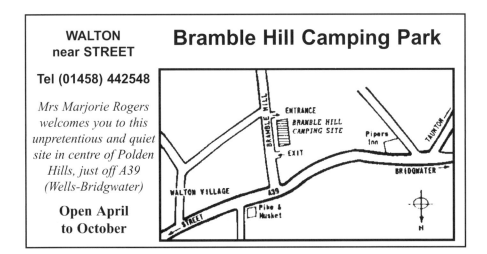

WALTON
near STREET

Tel (01458) 442548

Mrs Marjorie Rogers
welcomes you to this
unpretentious and quiet
site in centre of Polden
Hills, just off A39
(Wells-Bridgwater)

Open April
to October

Bramble Hill Camping Park

TAUNTON, Som   Map C5
Pop 36,140 Cider-making town in Tone valley SEE castle, county museum, public school, Priory
gatehouse, West Somerset Railway ℤ Library, Corporation Street ☏ Taunton (01823) 274785
Restaurant: County, East St ☏ (01823) 287651

Ashe Farm, Thornfalcon TA3 5NW ☏ Henlade (01823) 442567 OS map 193/280224 4m SE of
   Taunton off A358 (Chard) Open Apr-Oct 40 pitches 7 acres, level grass and hard standing,
   sheltered 🆘 ▣ ▣ ▱ ✿ ⊘ ✪ ↵ ▣ ▭ games room, tennis court, dog walk £6.50-£8.00

Tanpits Cider Farm, Dyers Lane, Bathpool TA2 8BZ ☏ (01823) 270663 OS map 193/254258 2m
   NE of Taunton off A38 (Bridgwater)–signposted Open Mar-Nov 20 pitches 1 acre level grass and
   hard standings, sheltered ▣ ▣ ▱ ✿ £4.00-£6.00

THREE LEGGED CROSS–see Verwood

TILSHEAD–see Shrewton

TROWBRIDGE, Wilts   Map F3
Pop 24,000. EC Wed, MD Tues, Fri, Sat SEE 18c lock up, town hall, The Courts at Holt 3m N,
Tropical Bird Gardens at Rode 4m W ℤ St Stephen's Place ☏ (01225) 777054 Restaurant:
Polebarn, Polebarn Rd ☏ (01225) 777006

Stowford Mill Caravan Park, Wingfield BA14 9LH ☏ Trowbridge (01225) 752253 OS map
   173/810576 3m W of Trowbridge on left of A366 (Radstock) past junct with B3109 Open Apr-Oct
   20 pitches Level grass, sheltered ▣ fishing £6.00

VERWOOD, Dorset   Map G5
Pop 2,500 SEE Ringwood Forest, Moors Valley country park Restaurant: Albion Inn, Station Rd
☏ (01202) 825267

Woolsbridge Manor Farm Caravan Park, Three Legged Cross BH21 6RA ☏ Verwood (01202)
   826369 OS map 195/102049 3m S of Verwood off B3072 (West Moors) on left of Ashley Heath
   road Open Easter-Oct 60 pitches 7 acres level grass, part sheltered 🆘 ▣ ▣ ▱ ✿ ⊘ ↵ ⅋ £6.00-
   £8.00

WAREHAM, Dorset   Map F6
Pop 7,940. EC Wed (winter), MD Thurs Old town on river Frome ringed by Anglo-Saxon earthworks SEE St Martin's church (Lawrence of Arabia associations) ◩ Town Hall, East St ☏(01929) 552740 Restaurant: Quay, South St ☏(01929) 552735

Birchwood Tourist Park, North Trigon BH20 4DD ☏Wareham (01929) 554763 OS map 195/899902 2m NW of Wareham on right of Bere Regis road Open Mar-Oct 175 pitches Grass, level, sheltered putting, tennis, mountain bike hire £6.00-£9.50

Hunter's Moon Caravan Camping Park, Cold Harbour BH20 7PA ☏Wareham (01929) 556605 OS map 195/899902 2½m NW of Wareham on Bere Regis road Open Easter-Oct 90 pitches 5 acres, level grass, sheltered £7.50-£14.00

Lookout Park, Stoborough BH20 5AZ ☏Wareham (01929) 552546 OS map 195/927856 1m S of Wareham on left of A351 (Swanage) Open Feb-Nov 240 pitches (90 static) Grass and hard standing, level, sheltered games room £9.00-£11.00

Redcliffe Farm, Ridge BH20 5BE ☏Wareham (01929) 552225 OS map 195/931867 2m SE of Wareham off A351 (Swanage) by river Frome Open Easter-Oct 154 pitches 8 acres gentle slope, grass, sheltered slipway to river Frome and Poole harbour £9.00-£10.00

Ridge Farm Camping and Caravan Park, Barnhill Rd, Ridge BH20 5BG ☏Wareham (01929) 556444 OS map 195/938866 2m SE of Wareham off A351 (Swanage) in Ridge Open Easter-Oct 60 pitches 4 acres, level grass, sheltered £7.00-£9.00 (1999)

Wareham Forest Tourist Park, North Trigon BH20 7NZ ☏and Fax (01929) 551393 OS map 195/895912 3m N of Wareham on Bere Regis road Open all year 200 pitches–some with all mains services 43 acres, level grass and hard standings, sheltered forest walks £7.60-£12.00 (Mastercard/Visa)

See also Corfe Castle and Wool

WARMINSTER, Wilts   Map F4
Pop 16,000 EC Wed MD Fri At heart of Upper Wylye valley, ancient town still with many old houses and inns SEE church, old inns, Longleat House 4m W, Bratton Castle 6m NE, White Horse on Westbury Hill 8m N ◩ Central Car Park ☏(01985) 218548 Restaurant: Old Bell, Market Place ☏(01985) 216611

Longleat Estate (Caravan Club), BA12 7NL ☏Warminster (01985) 844663 (0800-2000 hrs) OS map 183/806434 3m W of Warminster off A362 (Frome)–signposted Open Mar-Oct 150 pitches Level grass, sheltered £6.00-£8.00

WARMWELL–see Owermoigne

WATCHET, Som   Map B4
Pop 3,050. EC Wed Bristol Channel port and resort with rock and sand beach, handy base for exploring Quantock Hills to SE SEE St Decuman's Well and church, West Somerset Steam Railway Restaurant: West Somerset Hotel, Swain St ☏(01984) 634434

Warren Farm TA23 0JP ☏Watchet (01984) 631220 OS map 181/048432 1½m W of Watchet on right of B3191 (Blue Anchor) near beach Open Easter-Sept, 100 pitches 13 acres, grass, level/sloping, sheltered £5.50-£6.50

For other sites near Watchet see also Blue Anchor and Williton

WEDMORE, Som   **Map D4**
Pop 780 Village on N edge of Sedgemoor, a wilderness once, lush country now SEE church
(Jacobean pulpit), stone-built Ashton windmill Restaurant: The George, Church St ☎(01934)
712124

Splott Farm, Blackford BS28 4PD ☎(01278) 641522 OS map 182/410480 1m W of Wedmore on
   B3139 (Highbridge) Open Mar-Nov 32 pitches enclosed by hedges 4½ acres level/sloping grass,
   hedged ▣➋✲➌➍➎ £5.00

See also Wells and Burnham

WELLINGTON, Som   **Map C5**
Pop 10,535 EC Thurs Wool town from which the Iron Duke took his title SEE 15c church (stair
turret, tombs), Wellington School, Wellington monument built 1817 on crest of Blackdown Hills 2m S
Restaurant: Kings Arms, High St ☎(01823) 662809

Gamlins Farm, Greenham TA21 0LZ ☎Greenham (01823) 672596 OS map 181/080197 3m W of
   Wellington off A38 (Exeter) and Greenham road (junct 26 of M5) Open Easter-Sept 25 pitches 3
   acres terraced, part hard standing ▣➋✲ £5.00-£8.00

WELLS, Som   **MapE4**
Pop 9,120. EC Wed, MD Wed, Sat SEE cathedral, bishop's palace, town hall, tithe barn, museum,
Wookey Hole caves 1½m NW ℹ Town Hall, Market Square ☎Wells (01749) 672552 Restaurant:
Crown, Market Pl ☎(01749) 673457

Ebborlands Farm and Riding Centre, Wookey Hole BA5 1AY ☎Wells (01749) 672550 OS map
   182/525478 2m NW of Wells off A371 (Cheddar) at Easton or Haybridge Open May-Oct 20
   pitches−no adv booking 2 acres gentle slope, sheltered *No showers*, riding lessons, hacking
   £4.00-£5.00

Haybridge Farm, Haybridge BA5 1AJ ☎Wells (01749) 673681 OS map 183/531460 1m W of
   Wells on left of A371 (Cheddar) past junct with B3139 (Burnham) Open all year 35 pitches 4
   acres hard standings and part sloping part level grass ➋✲➍➏⅃ £5.50

Homestead Park, Wookey Hole BA5 1BW ☎Wells (01749) 673022 OS map 181/532475 1½m
   NW of Wells off A371 (Cheddar) Open Easter-Oct, 50 pitches 4 acres, level grass, sheltered
   ➋⌀✲ £9.00

Mendip Heights Caravan Camping Park, Townsend, Priddy BA5 3BP ☎Wells (01749) 870241
   OS map 182/523518 4m N of Wells off A39 (Bath) on B3135 (Cheddar) Open Mar 1-Nov 15 90
   pitches Grass and hard standing, level/sloping, sheltered ▦⚲▣➋⌀✲Ø⅃⊟ £6.50-£7.90

WESTBURY, Wilts   **Map F3**
Pop 8000 EC Wed, MD Fri SEE parish church, White Horse on Downs, Brokerswood Countryside
Museum ℹ The Library, Edwards St ☎(01373) 827158 Restaurant: Oak Inn, Warminster Rd
☎(01373) 823169

Woodland Park, Brokerswood, Westbury BA13 4EH ☎Westbury (01373) 822238 OS map
   183/838525 2m SW of Westbury off A3098 (Frome) at Penknap adj forest park Open all
   year−must book peak periods 69 pitches Grass and hard standing, level, sheltered
   ▦⌁➋✲Ø⅃ narrow gauge rlwy £8.00-£12.00

WESTHAY−see Meare

WEST LULWORTH−see Lulworth

WESTON SUPER MARE, Avon   **Map C3**
Pop 59,610. EC Thurs, MD Sun SEE Winter gardens, Floral clock, model village, British Camp on
Worlebury Hill, St Kew steps, church and woods at Kewstoke, Steepholm and Flatholm islands ℹ
Beach Lawns ☎Weston super Mare (01934) 626838 Restaurant: Claremont Vaults on seafront (N
end) ☎(01934) 629503

Airport View Caravan Park, Moor Lane, Worle BS24 7LA ☎Weston super Mare (01934) 622168
   OS map 182/351611 2½m NE of Weston super Mare off A370 (Congresbury) on A371 (Cheddar)
   Open Mar-Oct 135 pitches ▦✗ (snack) ⚲⌁➋⌀✲Ø⅃➍⊟⅃ children's room, club house
   £5.50-£7.50

Ardnave Caravan Park, Kewstoke BS22 9XJ ☎Weston super Mare (01934) 622319 OS map
   182/335635 2m N of Weston super Mare off A370 (Worle) near junction 21 of M5 Open Mar-Oct
   120 pitches (110 static) Level grass ▦▣➋⌀✲Ø⊟ £7.50-£11.50 (Mastercard/Visa)

Country View Caravan Park, Sand Road, Sand Bay BS22 9UJ ☎Weston super Mare (01934)
   627595 OS map 182/334646 4m N of Weston super Mare off A370 (Bristol) via Kewstoke Open
   Apr-Oct 120 pitches (66 static) Grass and hard standing, level ▦⚲▣➋⌀✲Ø⊡ (heated)
   ⅃➍⊟⅃ £4.50-£7.00

Manor Farm, Grange Road, Uphill BS23 4TU ☎Weston super Mare (01934) 627873 OS map
   182/362585 1m S of Weston super Mare off A370 (East Brent) Open Apr 1-Oct 20, 60 pitches
   Grass, level ▣⌀ £4.00

Continued on facing page

Purn International Holiday Park, Bleadon BS24 0AN ☎Weston super Mare (01934) 812342 OS map 182/330570 2m S of Weston super Mare on A370 (Bridgwater) adj Anchor Inn Open Mar-Nov, 280 pitches (120 static) 11 acres level grass and hard standing, sheltered lic club, entertainment, children's club £6.50-£10.50

Sunny Bank Caravan Park, Summer Lane, West Wick BS24 7TB ☎(01934) 512088 OS map 182/351611 2m E of Weston super Mare off A370 (Bristol) on left of B3368 (Banwell) near junct 21 of M5 Open Apr-Sept 25 pitches (no facs for children) 1½ acres level grass, sheltered £6.00-£7.00

West End Farm Touring Park, Locking BS24 8RH ☎(01934) 822529 OS map 182/354600 2m E of Weston super Mare off A371 (Cheddar) near helicopter museum Open all year 75 pitches Level grass and hard standing, sheltered (snack) £7.50-£10.50 (all cards)

Weston Gateway Tourist Caravan Park, West Wick BS24 7TF ☎(01934) 510344 OS map 182/370621 3m NE of Weston super Mare off A370 (West Wick) Open all year 180 pitches Level grass and hard standing, sheltered lic club, children's room £7.00-£10.00

WEYMOUTH, Dorset　　　　　　　　　　　　　　　　　　　　Map E7
Pop 45,000. EC Wed, MD Thurs Ferry port (Channel Islands and France) and resort occupying the area between Weymouth Bay and Portland. The town is noted for its fine Georgian houses. SEE houses in Trinity St (17c), Chesil Beach pebble breakwater 11m long W ☑ The Esplanade ☎Weymouth (01305) 765221 Restaurant: Glenburn 2m NE at Overcombe ☎(01305) 832353

Bagwell Farm Touring Park, Chickerell DT3 4EA ☎Weymouth (01305) 782575 OS map 194/625816 4m NW of Weymouth on B3157 (Abbotsbury) Open Mar 16-Oct 31, 320 pitches 14 acres, level grass and hard standing, sheltered pets' corner, barbecue area, games room, camper's shelter £6.00-£11.50 (Mastercard/Visa)

East Fleet Touring Park, Fleet DT3 4DW ☎Weymouth (01305) 785768 OS map 194/636800 3m NW of Weymouth off B3157 (Bridport) at Chickerell Open Mar 15-Jan 15, 210 pitches–booking advisable 20 acres grass and hard standing, level/gentle slope £4.50-£10.50 (Mastercard/Visa)

Littlesea Holiday Park, Lynch Lane DT4 9DT ☎Weymouth (01305) 774414 OS map 194/639822 1½m W of Weymouth off B3157 (Abbotsbury) Open Apr-Oct 900 pitches (690 static) Grass, part level bowling, lic club, amusements £7.50-£14.00 (inc showers)

Osmington Mills Holidays, East Farm Dairy, Osmington Mills DT3 6HB ☎Weymouth (01305) 832311 OS map 194/733822 5m E of Weymouth off A353 (Wareham) Open Easter-Oct 225 pitches–tents only Grass, part level, sheltered (heated) club house, bar food, horse riding, fishing £8.00-£15.00 (Mastercard/Visa/Switch)

Pebble Bank Caravan Park, Camp Road, Wyke Regis DT4 9HF ☎Weymouth (01305) 774844 OS map 194/655775 2m W of Weymouth centre off A354 (Portland) Open Apr 1-Oct 10, 180 pitches (90 static) 7 acres level/sloping grass sheltered £6.75-£14.00 (Delta/Switch)

Portesham Dairy Farm, Bramdon Lane, Portesham DT3 4HG ☎Weymouth (01305) 871297 OS map 194/604855 6m NW of Weymouth on left of B3157 (Bridport) Open mid Mar-Oct, 60 pitches 3 acres, level grass, sheltered £6.50-£9.00

Sea Barn Farm, Fleet DT3 4EF ☎Weymouth (01305) 782218 OS map 194/626815 3m W of Weymouth off B3157 (Abbotsbury) Open Easter-Nov 250 pitches Grass, level, open £7.00-£10.50

Seaview Holiday Village, Preston DT3 6XZ ☎(01305) 833037 OS map 194/710830 3m NE of Weymouth on right of A353 (Bere Regis) beyond Preston Open May 1-Sept 15 300 pitches (250 static) Level/sloping grass and woodland £7.00-£13.00

Waterside Holiday Park, Bowleaze Cove DT3 6PP ☎(01305) 833103 OS map 194/704825 2m NE of Weymouth off A353 (Bere Regis) at Bowleaze cove near beach Open Apr-Nov 123 pitches–booking advisable 35 acres level/sloping grass £10.00-£19.00 (Mastercard/Visa)

West Fleet Holiday Farm DT3 4ED ☎Weymouth (01305) 782218 OS map 194/625812 3m W of Weymouth off B3157 (Fleet) Open Easter-Oct 250 pitches–tents only 12 acres, grass, level, sheltered (heated) club house £8.00-£12.00

FACTS CAN CHANGE

We do our best to check the accuracy of the entries in this guide but changes can and do occur after publication. So if you plan to stay at a site some distance from home it makes sense to ring the manager or owner before setting off.

WHITEPARISH, Wilts   **Map H5**
Pop 300 SEE Newhouse 2m W, rare example of country house built in form of Y, with Jacobean
centre and Georgian wings Restaurant: Kings Head ☎(01794) 884287

Hillcrest, Southampton Road SP5 2QW ☎(01794) 884471 Fax (01794) 884707 OS Map
   184/240223 1m SW of Whiteparish on A36 (Southampton-Salisbury) near Newton Open all year
   35 pitches Grass, level/sloping, sheltered ▣➍⊘⊛∅ £7.70-£8.00

WICK–see Glastonbury

WILLITON, Som   **Map B4**
Pop 2,460. EC Sat Restaurant: Foresters Arms ☎(01984) 632508

Home Farm Holiday Park, St Audries Bay TA4 4DP ☎Williton (01984) 632487 OS map
   181/105430 3m NE of Williton off A39 (W. Quantoxhead) Open all year 270 pitches (230 static)
   Level/sloping grass and hard standing, sheltered ▤♀▣➍⊘⊛∅◳ (indoor) ◢ ⌸🖾 lic club,
   private beach £8.00-£10.00

WIMBORNE, Dorset   **Map G6**
Pop 5,530. EC Wed, MD Fri SEE Minster, St Margaret's chapel and hospital, museum, Badbury
Rings 3m NW ❻ 6 Cook Row ☎Wimborne (01202) 886116 Restaurant: Cricketers Arms, Park
Lane ☎(01202) 882846

Charris Camping Caravan Park, Candys Lane, Corfe Mullen BH21 3EF ☎Wimborne (01202)
   885970 OS map 195/995990 1m WSW of Wimborne on A31 (Dorchester) Open Mar-Oct 45
   pitches 3 acres, grass level/sloping, sheltered ▤▣➍⊘⊛∅➊ £7.00-£8.00

Merley Court Touring Park, Merley BH21 3AA ☎Wimborne (01202) 881488 OS map 195/013984
   2m S of Wimborne off A31 bypass Open Mar-Jan–booking essential 160 pitches 20 acres, level
   grass and hard standings, sheltered ▤♀⌐➚▣➍⊘⊛∅🖾 (heated) ⊕◢✿ (Jul-Aug) ঌ tennis
   court, woodland walk, crazy golf, croquet, table tennis, mini-football, games room £7.50-£12.50
   (Mastercard/Visa)

Springfield Touring Park, Candys Lane, Corfe Mullen BH21 3EF ☎Wimborne (01202) 881719 OS
   map 195/993989 1¼m SW of Wimborne on left of A31 (Dorchester) Open Mar 15-Oct 31, 45
   pitches 3½ acres, level/sloping grass and hard standing ▤▣➍⊘⊛∅◢ঌ £6.50-£8.50

Wilksworth Farm Caravan Park, Cranborne Road BH21 4HW ☎Wimborne (01202) 885467 OS
   map 195/008019 1m N of Wimborne on B3078 (Cranborne) Open Mar-Oct 162 pitches (77 static)
   11 acres, level grass and hard standings, sheltered ▤▣➍⊘⊛∅🖾 (heated) ⊕◢⌸ঌ serviced
   pitches, tennis £6.00-£10.00

Wincanton Racecourse

Well-kept level grassy site on downs one mile from town centre off A303 at
Hunter's Lodge on Bruton road. Wide range of modern facilities in quiet location.

Tel (01963) 32344   Fax (01963) 34668

WINCANTON, Som   **Map E4**
Pop 3,800. EC Thurs, MD Tues Thriving market town, major staging post in coaching days ❻ The
Library, 7 Carrington Way ☎Wincanton (01963) 32173 Restaurant: Dolphin, High St ☎(01963)
32215

Sunny Hill Caravan Park, Sunny Hill Farm, Riding Gate, Bayford BA9 8NG ☎Wincanton (01963)
   33281 OS map 183/733303 2m NE of Wincanton on old A303 (Bayford) Open Apr-Oct 20
   pitches 2 acres level grass ➍⊛ table tennis, pool £5.50

Wincanton Racecourse, BA9 8BJ ☎(01963) 32344 OS map 183/711294 ½m N of Wincanton on
   B3081 (Bruton) Open Apr 18-Sept 29 50 pitches Level grass ▣➍⊘⊛∅⊕⊡ঌ golf £6.20-
   £7.50 (Mastercard/Visa)

WINSCOMBE, Avon   **Map D3**
Pop 3,900 Restaurant: Penscot Farmhouse ☎(01934) 842659

Netherdale Caravan and Camping Site, Bridgwater Road, Sidcot BS25 1NH ☎(01934)
   843481/843007 OS map 182/426567 1m SE of Winscombe on left of A38 (Bridgwater) Open
   Mar-Oct 61 pitches (36 static) 4 acres, level grass, sheltered ▣➍⊘⊛⊕◢◳ £8.00-£9.00

WINSFORD, Som   Map B4
Pop 340. SEE Devil's Punchbowl Restaurant: Royal Oak ☎(01643) 851455
Halse Farm Camping Caravan Park, TA24 7JL ☎(01643) 851259 Fax (01643) 851592 OS map
    181/898342 1½m SW of Winsford off B3223 at Royal Oak pub in Halse Lane Open Mar 21-
    Oct 31 44 pitches 3 acres level grass and hard standing 🗑🔌🗑⊗∅↩️♿ £6.00-£8.00
See also Dulverton

WIVELISCOMBE, Som   Map B4
Pop 1320 EC Thurs SEE Brendon Hills and lakes NW Restaurant: Rock Inn 2m SW on B3227 at
Waterrow ☎(01984) 623293
Waterrow Touring Park, Bouchers Farm, Waterrow TA4 2AZ ☎(01984) 623464 OS map
    181/053248 3m SW of Wiveliscombe on left of B3227 (Bampton) after Waterrow, by river Tone
    Open all year 90 pitches 4 acres level grass 🔌⊗🗑🗑 £5.50

WOOKEY HOLE–see Wells

WOOL, Dorset   Map F6
Pop 5,190 Old town on S bank of river Frome. SEE Bindon Abbey ruins, Clouds Hill (Lawrence of
Arabia cottage) 4m NW, Bovington tank museum 2m NW Restaurant: Lulworth 3m S at West
Lulworth ☎(01929) 400230
Manor Farm, East Stoke BH20 6AW ☎(01929) 462870 OS map 194/875864 2m E of Wool off
    A352 East Stoke road Open Easter-Sept 50 pitches 2½ acres level grass, sheltered
    🗑🔌⊘⊗∅⊗↩️🗑 £7.00-£9.00
Whitemead Caravan Park, East Burton Road BH20 6HG ☎Bindon Abbey (01929) 462241 OS
    map 194/842868 ½m W of Wool on East Burton road Open Apr-Oct 95 pitches Level grass,
    sheltered, some hard standings 🗑↩️🗑🔌⊘⊗∅⊗↩️🗑 £6.25-£10.25
Woodlands Camping Park, Bindon Lane, East Stoke BH20 6AS ☎Bindon Abbey (01929) 462327
    OS map 194/862863 2m E of Wool on East Stoke road via Bindon Abbey Open all year 40
    pitches 2 acres level grass, sheltered 🗑♿ £6.00-£8.50

11 West Country

Most popular holiday region in England, the West Country of Devon and Cornwall is overrun in July and August. The region's main attractions are its coasts, lined with sandy beaches, and its mild climate, May and June often being sunnier than mid-season.

Inland Devon retains great tracts of peaceful country crossed by wooded valleys and high-banked lanes. Tall headlands and forested river mouths line the north coast, more gentle scenery the south—the highlight of which is the lovely Dart Estuary from which steamers regularly sail upstream to Totnes. The largest city on the south coast is Plymouth, more a port than a resort, but to the east on either side of the Salcombe headland are many unspoilt bays. Farther east is Torbay, some twenty miles round, with a climate mild enough for palm trees to flourish and its three big resorts of Torquay, Paignton and Brixham.

The granite mass of Dartmoor, a 1000ft high plateau bounded by Okehamptom, Plymouth, Tavistock and Bovey Tracey, is relatively uncrowded. The same goes for that part of Exmoor spilling over into North Devon from Somerset, for which South Molton is a handy base. The coast on either side of nearby Ilfracombe is one of the most attractive in the county. Between Dartmoor and Exmoor is a little-visited region centred on the Torridge and Taw Valleys. Two interesting sights in Devon are the country houses of Saltram and Buckland Abbey.

Despite the influx of tourists, Cornwall retains a secretive charm symbolised by unfamiliar place names, Celtic crosses and holy wells. For touring, the short distance between the north and south coasts, the north bold and rugged, the south sheltered and with more luxuriant vegetation, is an advantage. The long rollers of the Atlantic coast on the north are ideal for experienced surfers, but their undertow can trap the unwary. Lining both coasts are wooded creeks and quaint fishing ports with a charm now more theatrical than real. The largest resort on the north coast is Newquay, and on the south the deepwater harbour of Falmouth.

Confirmation of the region's popularity are the number of campsites (over 300), though most of these are well distributed. Main concentrations are at Newquay, St Austell, Lynton, Ilfracombe, Looe and Paignton on the coast and at Okehampton, Newton Abbot and Helston inland. Some of the coastal campsites—full to overflowing in season—are the equal of holiday villages, but most of those inland are small and with only basic facilities.

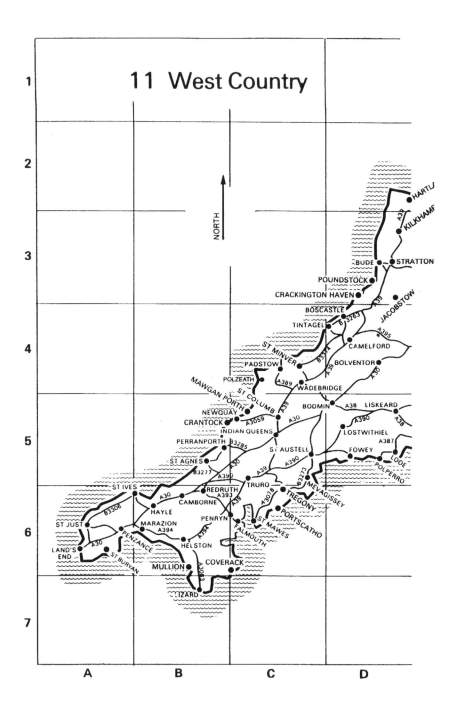

11 West Country

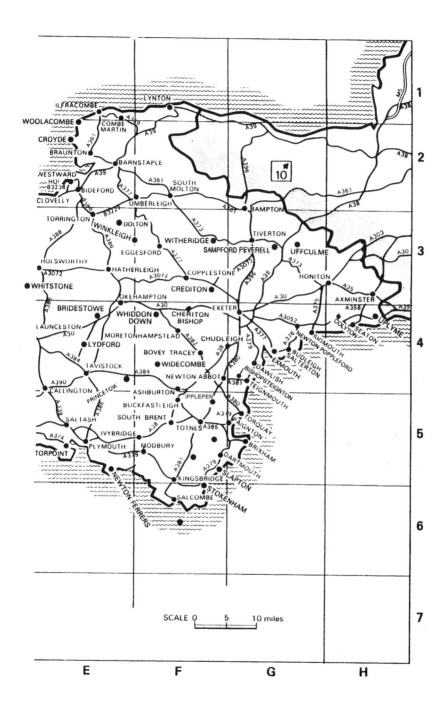

ASHBURTON, Devon   Map F4
Pop 3,550. EC Wed SEE Little House museum, St Andrew's church, Buckfast Abbey 3m SW
Restaurant: London Hotel, West St ✆(01364) 652478
Ashburton Caravan Park, Waterleat TQ13 7HU ✆Ashburton (01364) 652552 OS map
    202/752721 1½m NE of Ashburton off A38 (Exeter) Open Mar-Sept 75 pitches (40 static) Grass,
    level, sheltered 🏕️🛁🌊🔥⊘🚻♿ £7.00-£10.00
Lemonford Caravan Park, Bickington TQ12 6JR ✆Bickington (01626) 821242 OS map
    191/794724 2m NE of Ashburton off A38/A383 (Newton Abbot) Open Mar 15-Oct 90 pitches
    Level grass and hard standing, sheltered 🛒🛁🌊🔥⊘🚿🔆↩️🚻 £5.00-£9.00
Lower Aish Guest House, Poundsgate TQ13 7NY ✆(01364) 631229 OS map 191/705725 4m
    NW of Ashburton on B3357 (Tavistock) Open Mar-Oct 50 pitches (35 static) Level/sloping grass,
    sheltered ✖ (snack), ⊘ guided walks £3.00 (inc showers)
River Dart Country Park, Holne Park TQ13 7NP ✆Ashburton (01364) 652511 OS map
    202/732700 2m W of Ashburton off Two Bridges road Open Apr-Sept–must book peak periods
    170 pitches Level grass, sheltered 🛒✖🍴🛁🌊🔥⊘🚿🚻↩️🚻 nature and forest trails £9.40-
    £12.50 (2000) (most cards)

AXMINSTER, Devon   Map H3
Pop 4,900. EC Wed, MD Thurs SEE parish church ℹ️ Old Courthouse Complex, Church Street
✆Axminster (01297) 834386 Restaurant: George, Trinity Sq ✆(01297) 832209
Andrewshayes Caravan Park, EX13 7DY ✆(01404) 831225 OS map 192/247988 3m W of
    Axminster off A35 (Honiton) on Dalwood-Stockland road Open Mar-Jan, 170 pitches (80 static)
    12 acres, grass and hard standings, sloping, sheltered 🛒✖⛽🥾🛁🌊🔥⊘🚿 (heated)
    🔥↩️🚻♿ bike hire £7.50-£9.50 (most cards)
Hunters Moon Holiday Park, Hawkchurch EX13 5UL ✆(01297) 678402 OS map 193/347989
    3m E of Axminster off B3165 (Crewkerne) Open Mar 15-Nov 14 179 pitches 11 acres, level
    grass, hard standings 🛒✖🍴🔆🛁🌊🔥🚿↩️ club, games room and putting green £4.50-£10.00

BAMPTON, Devon   Map G2
Pop 1,440. SEE 13c church, castle mound, town hall, Exmoor Pony Fair last Thurs in Oct
Restaurant: Exeter Inn, Tiverton Rd ✆(01398) 331345
Lowtrow Cross Inn, Upton TA4 2DB ✆(01398) 371220 OS map 181/006292 6m NE of Bampton
    on B3190 (Watchet) at Lowtrow Cross Open Apr-Oct, 23 pitches 4½ acres, part level grass
    ✖ (snack) 🍴🔆🛁🌊⊘🍴 £7.00-£9.75

BARNSTAPLE, Devon   Map E2
Pop 18,500. EC Wed, MD Tues, Fri SEE arched bridge, almshouses, Queen Anne's Walk, museum,
new civic centre ℹ️ North Devon Library, Tuly St ✆(01271) 388583/4 Restaurant: Imperial, Taw
Vale Parade ✆(01271) 845861
Midland Holiday Park, Braunton Road EX31 4AU ✆(01271) 343691 Fax (01271) 326355 OS map
    180/540347 1½m W of Barnstaple on right of A361 (Ilfracombe) Open Easter-mid Nov 100
    pitches (62 static) Level grass and hard standing, sheltered 🛒✖🍴🔆🛁🌊🔥⊘🚿🚻↩️🚻🐕🚻
    dog exercise area £7.00-£12.00 (1999) (Mastercard/Visa)

BERRYNARBOR–see Combe Martin

BIDEFORD, Devon   Map E2
Pop 12,210. EC Wed, MD Tues SEE Victoria Park (Armada guns), St Mary's Church, Chudleigh Fort
ℹ️ The Quay ✆(01237) 477676 Restaurant: Kings Arms, The Quay ✆(01237) 472675
Knapp House, Churchill Way, Northam EX39 1NT ✆Bideford (01237) 474804 OS map 180/458294
    2m N of Bideford off A386 (Appledore) Open Mar-Oct 70 pitches 70 acres level/sloping grass
    🛒🛁🌊🔥⊘🚻↩️🚻 tennis, assault course £9.00 (1999)

BISHOPSTEIGNTON, Devon   Map G4
Pop 2025 EC Thurs SEE church, remains of bishops' palace Restaurant: Old Rydon 1½m W at
Kingsteignton (Rydon Rd) ✆(01626) 54626
Bishopsbrook Camping Park, TQ14 9PT *Site in area designated AONB* ✆(01626) 775249 OS
    map 192/909730 ¼m S of Bishopsteignton on A381 (Teignmouth-Newton Abbot) near sea Open
    Easter-Oct 77 pitches–no caravans 2 acres level/sloping grass £3.50

BLACKWATER–see St Agnes

BODMIN, Cornwall   **Map D5**
Pop 15,000. EC Wed, MD Sat SEE St Petroc's church, chantry chapel ruins, regimental museum, Bodmin Beacon, Lanhydrock House (NT) 2m SE 🄸 Shire House, Mount Folly Square ✆ Bodmin (01208) 76616 Restaurant: Hole in the Wall, Crockwell St (A389) ✆ (01208) 72379

Old Callywith Road Park (Camping Club) PL31 2DZ ✆ Bodmin (01208) 73834 OS map 200/081676 ½m NE of Bodmin off Launceston road Open Apr 1-Sept 28, 200 pitches 10½ acres, level grass, sheltered ⊟🄀⊕∅↩ £3.70-£4.30

Ruthern Valley Holidays, Ruthern Bridge PL30 5LU ✆ Bodmin (01208) 831395 OS map 200/031666 4m W of Bodmin off A389 (St Austell) via Nanstallon Open Apr-Oct 30 pitches 7½ acres level grass, sheltered 🛒⤳🄀⊟🄀⊕∅↩⊡🏠 £7.75-£11.25

Glenmorris Park, Longstone Road, St Mabyn PL30 3BY ✆ (01208) 841677 OS map 200/055734 4m N of Bodmin off B3266 (Camelford) at Longstone Open Easter-Oct—must book peak periods 80 pitches Level grass and hard standing, sheltered 🛒⤳🄀⊟🄀⊕∅▢ (heated) ⊕↩⊡🔌⊡🏠 £5.00-£7.50 (Mastercard/Visa)

See also Bolventor

BOLVENTOR, Cornwall   **Map D4**
Restaurant: Jamaica Inn ✆ (01566) 86250

Colliford Tavern, PL14 6PZ ✆ Cardinham (01208) 821335 OS map 201/172740 2m W of Bolventor off A30 (Bodmin) and St Neot road Open Apr-Oct 40 pitches—must book in peak season 3 acres, level grass, sheltered 🛒✕⤴🄀⊟🄀⊕∅♿ sep pitches, free house inn, accommodation £8.00-£10.00

BOSCASTLE, Cornwall   **Map D4**
Pop 750. SEE harbour, witchcraft museum Restaurant: Cobweb Just E of harbour ✆ (01840) 250278

Lower Pennycrocker Farm, St Juliot PL35 0BY ✆ Boscastle (01840) 250257 OS map 190/125929 2½m NE of Boscastle off B3263 (Bude) Open Easter-Sept, 40 pitches 4 acres, level/gentle slope, sheltered dairy produce £6.00

BRAUNTON, Devon   **Map E2**
Pop 8,000. EC Wed SEE museum, Saunton Sands 2m W Restaurant: Otters, Caen St ✆ (01271) 813633

Chivenor Caravan Park, Chivenor EX31 4BN ✆ Braunton (01271) 812217 OS map 180/508350 2m SE of Braunton on A361 (Barnstaple) Open Mar-Nov 35 pitches 🛒⤳🄀⊟🄀⊕∅⊕↩ bar/club £6.00-£11.00 (most cards)

Hidden Valley Touring and Camping Park, West Down EX34 8NU ✆ Braunton (01271) 813837 OS map 180/497406 2m N of Braunton on left of A361 (Ilfracombe) Open all year 135 pitches 25 acres, level grass and hard standings, sheltered 🛒✕🄀⊟🄀⊕∅♿ lounge, children's room, baby changing room, TV hook-ups £3.50-£14.00 (all cards exc Amex)

Lobb Fields Caravan and Camping Park, Saunton Road EX33 1EB ✆ Braunton (01271) 812090 OS map 180/473371 1m W of Braunton on right of B3231 (Croyde) Open Easter-Sept 180 pitches 14 acres level grass 🛒🄀⊟🄀⊕∅⊕↩ £5.00-£8.50

For other sites near Braunton see Barnstaple and Croyde

BRIDESTOWE, Devon   **Map E4**
Pop 400 SEE parish church Restaurant: White Hart Inn ✆ (01837) 861318

Bridestowe Caravan Park EX20 4ER ✆ (01837) 861261 OS map 191/517892 ½m E of Bridestowe centre on Lake road Open Mar-Dec, 53 pitches (36 static) 5 acres, level grass, sheltered 🛒🄀⊟🄀⊕⊕↩🔌⊡ £6.50

Bundu Caravan Camping Park, Sourton Cross EX20 4HT ✆ Bridestowe (01837) 861611 OS map 191/547916 2m NE of Bridestowe off junction of A30 (Okehampton) and A386 (Tavistock) Open Mar 15-Nov, 38 pitches 4½ acres, level grass and hard standing, sheltered 🄀⊟🄀⊕∅⊕↩ £6.00-£10.30 inc elect

---

DARTMOOR

The largest and wildest open space in southern England, Dartmoor consists of two high, boggy plateaux divided by the river Dart and its tributaries. Surrounding them is rocky land where dramatic outcrops, called tors, form a spectacular backdrop. Walking is the most popular outdoor recreation on Dartmoor, offering routes both on the High Moor and along the wooded valleys. *Dartmoor National Park, Haytor Road, Bovey Tracey TQ13 9JQ - (01626) 832093.*

BRIXHAM, Devon   Map G5
Pop 11,900. EC Wed SEE aquarium, Golden Hind replica, parish church, Berry Head fortifications, lighthouse 🄸 Old Market House, The Quay ☎(01803) 852861 Restaurant: Blue Anchor, Fore St ☎(01803) 859373

Centry Touring Caravans and Tents, Gillard Road TQ5 9EY ☎Brixham (01803) 853215 OS map 202/932558 1½m E of Brixham centre on right of Berry Head road Open Apr-Sept 80 pitches 8 acres level grass sheltered 🛉🛉🛉🛉 £8.00-£9.00

Galmpton Touring Park, Greenway Road, Galmpton TQ5 0EP ☎(01803) 842066 OS map 202/885558 2m W of Brixham off A379 (Torbay) and road to Dittisham ferry Open Apr-Oct 120 pitches 10 acres level/sloping grass, terraced, sheltered 🛉🛉🛉🛉🛉🛉🛉 (peak) 🛉🛉 £6.50-£11.00

Hillhead Camp, TQ5 0HH ☎Brixham (01803) 853204 OS map 202/903538 2m W of Brixham on B3205 (Kingswear) Open Easter-Oct 330 pitches 20 acres level grass, sheltered 🛉🛉🛉🛉🛉🛉🛉🛉🛉 (heated) 🛉🛉🛉🛉 amusements, live entertainment in season £6.00-£11.00 (inc showers)

Upton Manor Farm Camping Park, St Mary's Road TQ5 9QH ☎Brixham (01803) 882384 OS map 202/925548 1m SW of Brixham off B3205 (Kingswear) Open Spring BH-Sept 15, 250 pitches Grass, level, sheltered 🛉🛉🛉🛉🛉🛉 £6.50-£9.00

BUCKFASTLEIGH, Devon   Map F5
Pop 3,000. EC Wed SEE Buckfast Abbey, church, caves, farm museum, Dart Valley Railway to Totnes Restaurant: Dartbridge Inn ☎(01364) 642214

Beara Farm, Colston Road TQ11 0LW ☎Buckfastleigh (01364) 642234 OS map 202/751645 1m SE of Buckfastleigh off A384 (Totnes) on Colston road near river Dart Open all year 25 pitches –no touring caravans 3½ acres, level grass and hard standing 🛉🛉 £6.00-£7.00

Churchill Farm TQ11 0EZ ☎(01364) 642844 OS map 202/743665 ½m NE of Buckfastleigh off Buckfast road–access opp church Open Mar-Nov, 25 pitches 2 acres level/sloping grass, sheltered 🛉🛉 £6.00-£10.00

BUDE, Cornwall   Map D3
Pop 4,620. EC Thurs SEE Compass Hill, Poughill church 1½m NE ■ Visitor Centre, The Crescent
☎Bude (01288) 354240 Restaurant: Falcon, Falcon Terrace ☎(01288) 352005

Bude Holiday Park, Maer Lane EX23 9EE ☎Bude (01288) 355955 OS map 190/205072 1m N of
Bude on Maer road Open May-Sept–adv booking advisable 250 pitches (131 static) Grass and
hard standing ⬛✕⬤↩↗⬤⬤⬤⬤⬤⬤⬤⬤⬤↩⬤⬤ lic club/bar £5.95-£11.95 (Mastercard/Visa)

Upper Lynstone Caravan and Camping Site EX23 0LP ☎Bude (01288) 352017 OS map
190/205054 ½m S of Bude on coast road (Widemouth Bay) Open Easter-Sept 132 pitches (42
static) Level/sloping grass ⬛⬤⬤⬤⬤⬤⬤⬤↩⬤ £7.00-£10.50 (most cards)

See also Kilkhampton, Poundstock and Stratton

BUDLEIGH SALTERTON, Devon   Map G4
Pop 4,340. EC Thurs SEE Octagon, Raleigh's birth place at Ware Barton 2m NW, Bicton gardens at
East Budleigh ■ Rolle Mews car park, Fore Street ☎(01395) 445275 Restaurant: Salterton Arms,
Chapel St ☎(01395) 445048

Ladram Bay Caravan Site, Otterton EX9 7BX ☎(01395) 568398 OS map 192/096851 4m N of
Budleigh Salterton off B3178 (Newton Poppleford) via Otterton Open Apr-Sept–must book peak
periods 309 pitches (120 static) Level/sloping grass ⬛⬤↩↗⬤⬤⬤⬤⬤⬤↩⬤ fishing,
boating, surgery £7.00-£15.00

CAMBORNE, Cornwall   Map B6
Pop 13,000. EC Thurs, MD Fri SEE 15c church, School of Mines, Restaurant: Tyacks Hotel,
Commerical St ☎(01209) 612424

Magor Farm, Tehidy TR14 0JF ☎Camborne (01209) 713367 OS map 203/635425 1½m NNW of
Camborne off A30 (Hayle) via Coombe Open Mar-Oct 168 pitches ⬤⬤⬤ £4.50

Lakefield Caravan Park and Equestrian Centre
Lower Pendavy Farm, Camelford, Cornwall PL32 9TX
Tel (01840) 213279

A quiet secluded site with its own lake and valley views set in five acres on a 25
acre farm. Site shop, toilet/shower block, play area and dog walk. Full equestrian
facilities are available. Sand menage, show jumping paddock and beginners' cross-
country course. All abilities catered for. Children and novice riders our speciality.
BHS approved riding school with BHS qualified instruction. Close to Tintagel,
Boscastle and Bodmin Moor.

CAMELFORD, Cornwall   Map D4
Pop 1,800. EC Wed SEE St Thomas's church, Brown Willy Hill ■ North Cornwall Museum, The
Cleese ☎Camelford (01840) 212954 Restaurant: Poldark Inn 2m W at Delabole ☎(01840) 212565

Juliot's Well Holiday Park PL32 9RF ☎Camelford (01840) 213302 OS map 200/095829 2m S of
Camelford off B3266 (Tintagel) Open Mar-Oct 80 pitches (50 static) 8½ acres level/sloping grass
and hard standings, sheltered ⬛✕⬤↩⬤⬤⬤⬤⬤⬤ tennis £6.00-£11.00

Lakefield Caravan Camping Park, Lower Pendavey PL32 9TX ☎Camelford (01840) 213279 OS
map 200/097853 1m N of Camelford on left of B3266 (Boscastle) Open Mar-Oct 40 pitches
5 acres, level grass ⬛⬤⬤⬤⬤⬤⬤⬤↩ dog walk, farm animal corner, riding school, tea room
£6.00-£10.50

Otterham Station Park, Otterham PL32 9SW ☎(01840) 213229 OS map 190/155895 4m N of
Camelford on A39 (Stratton) Open all year 55 pitches Level grass and hard standing, sheltered
⬤⬤↩ games room, dog walk £4.00-£5.00 (inc showers)

Planet Caravan Park, Delabole PL33 9DT ☎Camelford (01840) 213361 OS map 200/064834 3m
NW of Camelford on B3314 (Delabole) Open all year 40 pitches 3 acres level grass
⬤⬤⬤⬤⬤⬤⬤⬤↩⬤⬤⬤ £4.50-£6.50

CARLYON BAY–see St Austell

CHERITON BISHOP, Devon   **Map F4**
Pop 600. SEE 13c church, old well Restaurant: Old Thatch Inn ☎(01647) 224204
Barley Meadow Caravan and Camping Park, Crockernwell EX6 6NR ☎(01647) 281629 OS map
191/755935 1½m W of Cheriton Bishop on old A30 (Okehampton) by Bay Tree Motel Open Mar
15-Nov 15 40 pitches Grass, level 🐾🗎🏢🗑⊘🛇➦↵🏁🖵🚽🏧⛽ £7.50-£8.50
Springfield Holiday Park, Tedburn St Mary EX6 6EW ☎Cheriton Bishop (01647) 24242 OS map
191/792936 1m ENE of Cheriton Bishop on old A30 (Tedburn St Mary) Open Mar 15-Nov 15
100 pitches Grass and hard standing, level, part sheltered
🐾✗♀↵↗🗎🏢🗑⊘🛇🗂🌐↵🏁🖵🚽 £7.50-£10.00 (Mastercard/Visa)

CHUDLEIGH, Devon   **Map G4**
Restaurant: Riverside 3m SW at Bovey Tracey ☎(01626) 832422
Finlake Holiday Park, TQ13 0EJ ☎Chudleigh (01626) 853833 OS map 191/855786 1m SW of
Chudleigh near junct of B3344 (Chudleigh Knighton) and B3193 (Dunsford-Kingsteignton) Open
Easter-Oct 450 pitches–no single sex groups 130 acres grass and hard standing, sheltered
🐾✗♀🗎🏢🗑🗂 (heated) ➦🏧 lic club, games room, 9-hole golf, fishing, boating, horse riding
£6.00-£16.50
Holmans Wood Caravan Park, Harcombe Cross TQ13 0DZ ☎Chudleigh (01626) 853785 OS
map 192/883812 2m NE of Chudleigh on right of B3344 (Exeter) Open Mar-Oct 144 pitches
Hard standings and level grass, sheltered 🐾↗🗎🏢🗑⊘🛇➦🏁 (£3/wk) 🚽⛽ forest walks,
tennis, badminton £6.00-£9.75 (1998)

CHUDLEIGH KNIGHTON–see Bovey Tracey

COLYTON, Devon   **Map H4**
Pop 2980 EC Wed Market town of medieval charm in Coly valley 1m inland from coastal resort of
Seaton, with picturesque winding streets and 14c river bridge SEE church (monuments), Great
House in South St Restaurant: Kingfisher, Dolphin St ☎(01297) 552471
Leacroft Touring Park EX24 6HY ☎(01297) 552823 OS map 192/219923 2m SW of Colyton on
Branscombe/Beer road via Colyton Hill Open Apr-Oct 138 pitches 10 acres level/sloping grass
and hard standings 🐾↗🗎🏢🗑⊘🛇➦🏁 £6.00-£11.00

COMBE MARTIN, Devon   **Map E1**
Pop 2,500. EC Wed SEE church, Pack of Cards Inn 🖾 Sea Cottage, Cross Street ☎Combe Martin
(01271) 883319 Restaurant: Campo Casana at Berrynarbor ☎(01271) 882557
Berrynarbor Caravan Park, Sterridge Valley EX34 9TB ☎Combe Martin (01271) 882631/882890
OS map 180/558463 1m W of Combe Martin off A399 (Ilfracombe) Open Apr-Sept 100 pitches
(45 static)–no tents 9 acres level grass, sheltered 🗎🏢🗑⊘🛇🚽⛽ £8.00-£10.00
Mill Park Touring Site, Berrynarbor EX34 9SH ☎Combe Martin (01271) 882647 OS map
189/565472 1½m W of Combe Martin off A399 (Ilfracombe) Open Mar-Nov 160 pitches Grass,
level, sheltered 🐾↵↗🗎🏢🗑⊘🛇🌐➦🏁 fishing £5.00-£10.00 (Mastercard/Visa)
Napps Camping Site, Old Coast Road, Berrynarbor EX34 9SW ☎Combe Martin (01271) 882557
OS map 180/561476 2m W of Combe Martin on A399 (Ilfracombe) Open Easter-Oct 200 pitches
Level grass and hard standings 🐾✗♀↵↗🗎🏢🗑⊘🛇🗂🌐➦🏁🖵🚽⛽ tennis court £5.00-
£11.00 (all cards)
Newberry Farm Caravan Site, Woodlands EX34 0AT ☎Combe Martin (01271) 882334 OS map
180/574470 ½m W of Combe Martin on A399 (Ilfracombe) Open Easter-Oct 110 pitches
30 acres level grass sheltered 🗎🏢🗑⊘➦❀🏧 coarse fishing, woodland walks £6.50-£9.00
Sandaway Holiday Park, Berrynarbor EX34 9ST ☎Combe Martin (01271) 866666 OS map
180/568473 ¼m W of Combe Martin off A399 (Ilfracombe) Open Mar 15-Oct 31, 125 pitches (102
static) 🐾↵🗎🏢🗑⊘🗂 (heated) 🌐🖵⛽🏧 lic club, own beach £5.00-£15.00
Stowford Farm Meadows, EX34 0PW ☎(01271) 882476 Fax (01271) 883053 OS map
180/560426 4m SW of Combe Martin off A3123 (Ilfracombe) Open Easter-Oct 570 pitches
Grass, level/sloping 🐾✗♀ (café) ↵🗎🏢🗑⊘🛇🗂🌐➦🏁♀⛽ £4.00-£9.40 (Mastercard/Visa)
Watermouth Cove Holiday Park, Berrynarbor EX34 9SJ ☎(01271) 862504 OS map 180/550480
2m W of Combe Martin on A399 (Ilfracombe) Open Easter-Oct 90 pitches Level grass and hard
standings, sheltered 🐾✗♀↵🗎🏢🗑⊘🗂🌐➦🏁🏧 lic club, beach, fishing £7.00-£17.00
(Mastercard/Visa/Switch)

COPPLESTONE, Devon   **Map F3**
Restaurant: Crediton Inn 4m SE at Crediton ☎(01363) 772882

Nichols Nymett Holiday Park, North Tawton EX20 2BP ☎(01837) 82484 OS map 191/693023
5m W of Copplestone off A3072 (Sampford Courtenay) Open Mar-Oct 25 pitches

---

COVERACK, Cornwall   **Map B6**
Pop 375 SEE cliffs, Goonhilly Downs 3m W, `raised beach' at Lowland Point 1½m NE Restaurant:
White Hart 3m E at St Keverne ☎(01326) 280325

Little Trevothen Caravan Park, TR12 6SD ☎St Keverne (01326) 280260 OS map 203/775179
¾m W of Coverack on Ponsongath road Open Easter-Oct 72 pitches (25 static) Grass, level
£5.00-£6.50 inc hot water

Penmarth Campsite, Penmarth Farm TR12 6SB ☎St Keverne (01326) 280389 OS map
205/775179 ¼m W of Coverack on Ponsongath road Open Easter-Oct, 35 pitches 2 acres, level
grass £6.50

For other sites near Coverack see Mullion and Lizard

CRACKINGTON HAVEN, Cornwall   **Map D3**
Pop 1,800 SEE cliffs, surfing beaches Restaurant: Coombe Barton ☎(01840) 230345

Hentervene Caravan Camping Park EX23 0LF ☎(01840) 230365 Fax (01840) 230514 OS map
190/155944 1m SE of Crackington Haven off A39 (Wadebridge-Bude) at Otterham
Garage–signposted Open all year, 57 pitches (22 static) 8½ acres, level grass and hard
standings, sheltered barbecue, library, video films, babycare
room, solarium £7.20 (Mastercard/Visa)

CRANTOCK, Cornwall   **Map B5**
Pop 910 EC Wed SEE beach and dunes, 12c church, St Ambrose Well Restaurant: Old Albion Inn,
Langurroc Rd ☎(01637) 830243

Cottage Farm Tourist Park, Treworgans, Cubert TR8 5HH ☎Crantock (01637) 831083 OS map
200/786589 1m S of Crantock off Cubert Road Open Easter-Oct 50 pitches Level/sloping grass
and hard standings £7.50-£8.50

Crantock Plains Tourist Park, Crantock Plains Farm TR8 5PH ☎Crantock (01637)
830955/831273 OS map 200/805589 1½m SE of Crantock off Newlyn East road and A3075
(Newquay-Redruth) Open Apr-Sept 40 pitches 6 acres, level grass, sheltered
£5.25-£8.50

Holywell Bay Holiday Park, Holywell Bay TR8 5PR ☎(01637) 871111 OS map 200/600780 2m S
of Crantock on Cubert–Holywell road Open Apr 1-Oct 15 224 pitches (149 static) Grass, level,
sheltered, some hard standings access to sandy beach
£6.80-£14.30

The Meadow, Holywell Bay TR8 5PP *Quiet site 300 yds from sandy beach* ☎(01872) 572752 OS
map 200/768588 3m S of Crantock on Cubert-Holywell road, at Holywell village Open Easter-Oct
22 pitches–no tents 1¼ acres level grass, sheltered £6.00-£12.00

Quarryfield Caravan Camping Park, TR8 5RJ ☎(01637) 872792 OS map 200/793608 ¼m N of
Crantock off road to Newquay Open Apr-Oct–must book (caravans) 145 pitches 10 acres level
grass £6.90

Treago Farm, West Pentire Road, TR8 5QS ☎Crantock (01637) 830277 OS map 200/782601 1m
W of Crantock on West Pantire road Open Apr-Oct 100 pitches 7 acres grass, level/sloping,
sheltered £7.00-£8.50

Trebellan Tourist Park, Trebellan, Cubert TR8 5PY ☎(01637) 830522 OS map 200/790571 2m S
of Crantock via Cubert Open Spring BH-mid Sept, 150 pitches 11 acres, part level grass,
sheltered (heated) fishing lakes £7.00-£10.00

Trevella Caravan Park, TR8 5EW ☎Crantock (01637) 830308 OS map 200/801597 ½m SE of
Crantock off Newlyn East road Open Easter-Nov 1, 320 pitches (270 static) 25 acres level/sloping
grass and hard standings, sheltered snack bar, crazy golf, fishing
£5.95-£9.80

Trevornick Holiday Park, Holywell Bay TR8 5PW ☎(01637) 830531 OS map 200/775587 1½m
SW of Crantock on Cubert–Holywell road Open May-Sept 550 pitches Sloping grass
(heated) children's club, lic club, golf, coarse fishing, pre-
erected tent hire £6.50-£11.50

CROCKERNWELL–see Cheriton Bishop

CROYDE, Devon   **Map E2**
Pop 450 Village of thatched cottages by a stream with sandy beach ½m away SEE Baggy Point
cliffs and rock garden 2m NW, Georgeham village 1m NE, Woolacombe Sands 2m N Restaurant:
Thatched Barn on B3231 ☎(01271) 890349

Bay View Farm, Croyde Bay EX33 1PN ☎Croyde (01271) 890501 OS map 180/443388 ¼m SW
of Croyde on left of B3231 (Braunton) Open May-Sept 70 pitches 10 acres level grass
🛁🔌🍴⊕∅☺⌁🚽♿ £11.00-£12.00

Croyde Bay Holidays, Croyde Bay EX33 1NZ ☎Croyde (01271) 890351 OS map 163/434396
½m W of Croyde on road to beach Open Easter-Nov 162 pitches (50 static)–min stay 2 nights for
tents in season 10 acres level grass adj beach and sand dunes 🛁✗🍺🔌🍴◊⌁✲ tennis, fishing
£4.80-£7.70

Putsborough Sands Caravan Park, Manor Farm, Putsborough EX33 1LB ☎(01271) 890230
Fax (01271) 890208 OS map 180/448409 1m N of Croyde on Putsborough Sands road–narrow
approach Open Easter-Oct 5 22 pitches–must book Whitsun-Sept 15–no tents 2 acres, gentle
slope/terraced 🛁🔌⊕∅☺ adj sandy beach £12.00-£22.00 (most cards)

Ruda Holiday Park, Croyde Bay EX33 1NY ☎Croyde (01271) 890671 OS map 180/438397 ½m
W of Croyde off road to Baggy Point adj beach Open Easter-Oct–must book peak periods 495
pitches (280 static) Level grass 🛁✗ (snack), 🍺🔌🍴◊⊕∅⌑☺⌁🚽🍴✲🚽🏠 lic club,
doctor, free entertainment £6.00-£28.00 (Mastercard/Visa)
For other sites near Croyde see Braunton and Woolacombe

CULLOMPTON–see Honiton

DARTMOUTH, Devon   **Map F5**
Pop 5,540. EC Wed, MD Tues, Fri SEE Butterwalk Museum, Castle, St Saviour church, Mayflower
Stone, borough museum, Newcomen Engine House 🅰 Engine House, Mayor's Avenue ☎(01803)
834224 Restaurant: Royal Castle, The Quay ☎(01803) 832397

Deer Park Holiday Estate, Stoke Fleming TQ6 0RF ☎Stoke Fleming (01803) 770253 OS map
202/864493 2m S of Dartmouth on A379 (Torcross) Open Mar 15-Oct 31–must book 160 pitches
Grass, mainly level, open 🛁✗🍺🔌🍴◊⊕∅⌑☺⌁🍴♿ bar food £6.75-£9.95 (Mastercard/
Visa)

Leonards Cove Holiday Estate, Stoke Fleming TQ6 0NR ☎Stoke Fleming (01803) 770206 OS
map 202/865483 2m S of Dartmouth off A379 (Stoke Fleming) Open Easter-Oct 152 pitches (112
static) 🛁✗🔌⌁🔧🔌🍴◊∅☺✲🚽🏠 £7.75-£12.50

Little Cotton Caravan Park, Little Cotton TQ6 0LB ☎(01803) 832558 OS map 202/860508 2m W
of Dartmouth on A3122 (Halwell) Open Mar-Nov 95 pitches Level/sloping grass, part sheltered
🛁🔌🍴◊⊕∅♿ £5.75-£9.00 (Mastercard/Visa)

Start Bay Caravan Park, Strete TQ6 0RU ☎(01803) 770535 OS map 202/840473 5m SW of
Dartmouth off A379 (Kingsbridge) on Halwell road Open Easter-Oct 25 pitches 1¼ acres level
grass, part sheltered ⌁🔌🍴◊⊕∅⌑ barbecues £6.00-£12.00

Woodland Leisure Park, TQ9 7DQ ☎(01803) 712598 OS map 202/813522 4½m W of Dartmouth
on left of A3122 (Totnes) Open Easter-Nov 5 225 pitches Level grass part sheltered
🛁✗⌁🔌🍴◊⊕∅☺⌁🍴♿ leisure park (free entry) £7.50-£13.95 (Mastercard/Visa)

DAWLISH, Devon Map G4
Pop 10,000. EC Thurs SEE The Lawn, Manor House, Stonelands House, Dawlish Warren peninsula 2m NE The Lawn (01626) 863589 Restaurant: Charlton House, Exeter Rd (01626) 863260

Cofton Country Holiday Park, Starcross EX6 8RP Starcross (01626) 890111 OS map 192/967803 2m N of Dawlish on A379 (Exeter) Open Easter-Oct–must book peak periods 512 pitches (62 static) coarse fishing lake £5.00-£9.50

Golden Sands Holiday Park, Week Lane EX7 0LZ Dawlish (01626) 863099 OS map 192/873783 1m NE of Dawlish off A379 (Exeter) Open Apr-Oct 270 pitches (188 static) Grass, level, sheltered (indoor/outdoor) (season) lic club, amusements, entertainment £6.00-£12.00

Lady's Mile Touring and Camping Park, Shutterton EX7 0LX Dawlish (01626) 863411 OS map 192/968780 1m N of Dawlish on A379 (Exeter) Open Mar-Oct 600 pitches Level/sloping grass, sheltered 9-hole golf, disco £7.00-£11.50 (Mastercard/Visa/Eurocard)

Leadstone Camping, Warren Road, Dawlish Warren EX7 0NG Shaldon (01626) 872239 OS map 192/974783 1m NE of Dawlish off A379 (Exeter) Open Jun 15-Sept 8 160 pitches Grass, part level, some hard standings, sheltered farm produce £7.60-£11.70

Peppermint Park, Warren Road, Dawlish Warren EX7 0PQ Dawlish (01626) 863436 OS map 192/978788 2m NE of Dawlish off A379 (Exeter) Open Mar-Oct 300 pitches 17 acres grass, part level (heated) golf, beach, entertainment £5.50-£11.00 (1999) (Mastercard/Visa)

DOLTON, Devon Map E3
SEE church, Iddesleigh village S Restaurant: Beaford House 2m N at Beaford (01805) 804503

Dolton Caravan Park, EX19 8QF (01805) 804536 OS map 180/5 In Dolton off A3124–access between school and Royal Oak Inn Open Easter-Oct 4, 25 pitches 2 acres level grass, sheltered £6.00-£8.00

DOWNDERRY–see Seaton (Cornwall)

DUNKESWELL–see Honiton

EXETER, Devon Map G4
Pop 98,800. MD daily University city of Roman origin on river Exe and county town of Devon, with England's oldest ship canal (16c) SEE cathedral, city walls, Customs House maritime museum, Northernhay gardens, Rougemont castle Civic Centre, Paris St Exeter (01392) 265700 Restaurant: Exeter and Devon Arts Centre, Bradninch Place, Gandy St (01392) 219741

Exeter Racecourse (Caravan Club), Kennford EX6 7XS (01392) 832107 (0800-2000 hrs) OS map 192/897836 6m SW of Exeter off A38 (Plymouth) on Exeter racecourse road Open Easter-Sept, 100 pitches 10 acres, grass, mainly level £5.00-£7.00

Haldon Lodge Caravan Camping Park, Clapham, Kennford EX6 7YG Exeter (01392) 832312 OS map 192/894868 5m SW of Exeter off A38 (Ashburton) at Kennford services on Dunchideock road (signposted) Open all year 90 pitches 4½ acres level/sloping grass and hard standings, sheltered horse riding, games room £5.00-£8.00

Kennford International Caravan Park, Kennford EX6 7YN (01392) 833046 OS map 192/911586 4m S of Exeter on A38 (Plymouth) opposite Kennford service area ½m from end of M5 Open all year 120 pitches Level grass and hard standings serviced pitches (individually hedged), picnic tables, lounge bar £10.50 (Mastercard/Visa)

EXMOUTH, Devon Map G4
Pop 28,300. EC Wed SEE La Ronde house with shell gallery Alexandra Terrace Exmouth (01395) 263744 Restaurant: Grand, Sea Front (01395) 263278

Castle Brake Holiday Park, Woodbury EX5 1HA (01395) 232431 OS map 192/028879 4m N of Exmouth off B3180 (Ottery St Mary) near Woodbury Castle Open Mar-Oct 80 pitches (38 static) 9 acres level grass, sheltered £6.00-£10.00 (most cards)

Devon Cliffs Holiday Park, Sandy Bay EX8 5BT (01395) 265333 OS map 192/035800 2m E of Exmouth off A376 (Budleigh Salterton) via Littleham, at Sandy Bay, near junct 30 of M5 Open Easter-Oct 775 pitches (575 static) 143 acres terraced £8.00-£15.00

Webbers Farm, Castle Lane, Woodbury EX5 1EA (01395) 232276 Fax (01395) 233389 OS map 192/018874 3m N of Exmouth off B3179 at Woodbury–signposted Open Easter-Sept 115 pitches–must book Grass level/gentle slope freezer pack service £7.50-£10.50 (Mastercard/Visa)

FALMOUTH, Cornwall   **Map C6**
Pop 18,000. SEE 17c church, Pendennis Castle, Jacob's Ladder, Maritime Museum ⚹ Killigrew St
✆ Falmouth (01326) 312300 Restaurant: Bay, Cliff Rd ✆ (01326) 312094

Maen Valley Caravan Park TR11 5BJ ✆ Falmouth (01326) 312190 OS map 204/788312 1½m SW
of Falmouth off A39 (Penryn-Gweek) Open Apr-Oct 200 pitches (70 static) Grass, level, sheltered
🛒✗⟲🗄🏕⊘🛁⊕∅⤳🏕 (40) 🚐🏠 lic club, tennis £6.00-£12.00

Menallack Farm, Treverva TR10 9BP *Rural site with fine views* ✆ Falmouth (01326) 340333 OS
map 204/752312 4m SW of Falmouth on Gweek road Open Apr-Oct 30 pitches Level/sloping
grass 🛒⟲🏕⊘⊕❸ £5.50-£6.00

Pennance Mill Farm, Maen Porth TR11 5HJ ✆ (01326) 312616 Fax (01326) 317431 OS map
204/791307 3m SW of Falmouth on coast road to Maen Porth beach Open May-Sept 55 pitches
4 acres level grass, sheltered 🛒🗄🏕⊘⊕∅❸⤳🏕🏠⚓ farm produce £7.50-£9.00

Tregedna Farm, Maenporth TR11 5HL ✆ Falmouth (01326) 250529 OS map 204/785305 2½m
SW of Falmouth on right of Maenporth road Open May-Sept 40 pitches 10 acres, grass, sloping
🛒🗄🏕⊘⊕∅❸ £7.00-£7.50

Tremorvah Tent Park, Swanpool TR11 5BE ✆ Falmouth (01326) 312103 OS map 204/798312 1m
SW of Falmouth off Mawnan road Open May 15-Sept 30 75 pitches 3 acres, gently
sloping/terraced 🛒🗄🏕∅ £9.00-£11.00

FOWEY, Cornwall   **Map D5**
Pop 2,390. EC Wed On W shore of natural harbour, a major port in medieval times and notorious
centre of piracy SEE church, museum, St Catherine's Point ⚹ The Post Office, Custom House Hill
✆ (01726) 833616 Restaurant: Old Quay House, Fore St ✆ (01726) 833302

Penhale Caravan Camping Park, PL23 1JU ✆ Fowey (01726) 833425 OS map 200/104526 1½m
NW of Fowey on left of A3082 (Par) Open Apr-Oct 56 pitches 9 acres gentle slope, grass
🗄🏕⊘⊕∅🚐 £5.00-£9.00

Polruan Holidays–Camping and Caravanning, Polruan PL23 1QH ✆ (01726) 870263 OS map
200/132507 3m SE of Fowey via Bodinnick (ferry) Open Apr-Oct 43 pitches (11 static) Grass and
hard standings, part level, part sheltered 🛒🗄🏕⊘⊕∅❸🚐 £6.75-£10.25

Yeate Farm Camp and Caravan Site, Bodinnick by Fowey PL23 1LZ ✆ (01726) 870256 OS map
200/133527 1m E of Fowey off Bodinnick road (ferry) Open Apr-Oct 33 pitches 1 acre level
grass, sheltered 🗄🏕⊘⊕🚐 (2) slipway, quay and limited moorings £6.00-£8.50 (2000)

GOON HAVERN–see Perranporth

GORRAN HAVEN–see Mevagissey

HAYLE, Cornwall   **Map B6**
Pop 6,200. EC Thurs Port and market town on estuary in St Ives Bay, with find sands and dunes
SEE St Felicitas church Restaurant: Bird in Hand, Trelissick Rd ✆ (01736) 753974

Atlantic Coast Caravan Park, 53 Upton Towans TR27 5BL ✆ Hayle (01736) 752071 OS map
203/580400 2m NE of Hayle on B3301 (Portreath) Open Apr-Oct 65 pitches (33 static) Grass,
level, part sheltered 🛒⟲⤴🗄🏕⊘⊕∅🚐 games room £7.00-£12.00

Calloose Caravan Camping Park, Leedstown TR27 5ET ✆ (01736) 850431 OS map 203/605353
3½m SE of Hayle off B3302 (Helston) Open Apr-Oct 120 pitches 12 acres, level grass and hard
standings, sheltered 🛒⚻⟲🗄🏕⊘⊕∅🗖 (heated) ❸⤳🏕🚐⚓ crazy golf, skittle alley, tennis
court, sep pitches, snacks £6.50-£12.50

Higher Trevaskis Touring Caravan Camping Park, Gwinear Road, Connor Downs TR27 5JQ
✆ (01209) 831736 OS map 203/610385 3m NE of Hayle off A30 (Camborne) on Carnhell Green
road Open Apr-Oct 82 pitches 5½ acres level grass and hard standings, sheltered
🛒🗄🏕⊘⊕∅❸⤳ £5.00-£10.00

Parbola Holiday Park, Wall, Gwinear TR27 5LE ✆ (01209) 831503 OS map 203/619368 2½m
ESE of Hayle off A30 (Camborne) Open Easter-Sept–must book peak periods 135 pitches
Woodland clearings and level field 🛒⟲⤴🗄🏕⊘⊕∅🗖❸⤳🏕🚐🏠❀ (season) ⚓ baby
room, crazy golf £7.50 (most cards)

St Ives Bay Holiday Park, Upton Towans TR27 5BH *Site on sand dunes adj beach* ✆ Hayle
(01736) 752274 OS map 203/575388 1m NE of Hayle off A30 (Redruth) on B3301 (Portreath) by
beach Open May-Sept 400 pitches (250 static) 🛒⟲🗄🗖 (indoor heated) ⤳ pub, children's
room, beach access, petrol £6.00-£21.75

Sunnymeadow Holiday Caravan Park, Lelant Downs TR27 6LL ✆ Hayle (01736) 752243 OS map
203/528360 2m W of Hayle off A30 (Penzance) Open Mar-Jan 11 pitches Grass, level,
sheltered 🛒🗄🏕⊘⊕🏠🚐 £5.00-£6.50 (Visa)

HELSTON, Cornwall   Map B6
Pop 7,970. EC Wed, MD Mon, Sat Market town on Lizard peninsula SEE museum, St Michael's church, Godolphin House 5m NW, Furry Day festival (May) 🖰 Clodgey Lane ☎(01236) 565431 Restaurant: Angel, Coinagehall St ☎(01326) 572701

Boscrege Caravan Park, Ashton TR13 9TG ☎(01736) 762231 OS map 203/590303 4½m NW of Helston off A394 (Penzance) Open Mar-Oct 50 pitches (26 static) 6 acres, level grass, sheltered 🖸🖳🖉⊛∅☻⤏▢🖭 microwave facs for campers £6.00-£12.50

Gunwalloe Caravan Park TR12 7QP ☎Helston (01326) 572668 OS map 203/658229 3m S of Helston off A3083 (Lizard) Open Apr-Oct 40 pitches 2½ acres, level grass, sheltered 🖳🖉⊛∅ £4.00-£7.00

Lower Polladras Caravan-Camping Site, Carleen TR13 9NX ☎(01736) 762220 OS map 203/617308 3½m NW of Helston off B3302 (Camborne) Open Apr-Oct 60 pitches 4 acres level, grass, part sheltered 🖳🖸🖳🖉⊛⤏🖳 £7.00-£8.00

Pengersick Caravan Site, Praa Sands TR20 9SH ☎(01736) 762201 OS map 203/582285 5m W of Helston on A394 (Penzance) Open all year–no adv booking 286 pitches (86 static) 14 acres, level grass 🖳🖉 £2.50-£5.00

Poldown Caravan Park, Carleen TR13 9NN ☎Helston (01326) 574560 OS map 203/629299 2½m NW of Helston off A394 (Penzance) and B3302 (Hayle) Open Apr-Oct 20 pitches (7 static) 2 acres, level grass, sheltered 🖸🖳🖉⊛∅⤏🖭 £6.00-£9.50

Retanna Holiday Park, Edgcumbe TR13 0EJ ☎(01326) 340643 OS map 203/710327 3½m NE of Helston on A394 (Penryn) Open Apr-Oct 59 pitches (35 static) Level grass and hard standings, sheltered 🖳⤏🖸🖳🖉⊛∅☻⤏▢🖳🖭 £5.00-£7.50 (Mastercard/Visa/Switch)

Trelowaren Chateau Park (Camping Club), Mawgan TR12 6AF ☎(01326) 572637 OS map 203/721239 4m SE of Helston off A3083/B3293 (St Keverne) Open Mid Apr-Sept, 230 pitches–must book 10 acres, level grass, sheltered 🖳✗⤏↗🖸🖳🖉⊛∅☻⤏▢🖳♿ £7.90

HOLSWORTHY, Devon   Map E3
Pop 1,640. EC Tues, MD Wed, Thurs SEE church, museum, St Peter's Fair (Jul) Restaurant: Kings Arms, The Square ☎(01409) 253517

Lufflands Caravan Park, Soldon Cross, Bradworthy Road EX22 7PJ ☎(01409) 253426 OS map 190/324099 4m NW of Holsworthy off A3072 (Bude) on Bradworthy road Open Mar 15-Oct 30, 50 pitches 🖳🖳🖸🖉⊛🖭 £2.50-£5.50

HONITON, Devon   Map H3
Pop 6,490. EC Thurs, MD Tues, Sat SEE Priory museum, Honiton Pottery 🖰 Dowel St, East Car Park ☎Honiton (01404) 843716 Restaurant: Angel, High St ☎(01404) 842829

Fishponds House Campsite, Dunkeswell EX14 0SH ☎Honiton (01404) 891287 OS map 192/154074 5m N of Honiton off A30 (Chard) and Dunkeswell road in wildlife sanctuary Open all year 15 pitches Level/sloping grass and hard standings 🖳✗🖳⊛∅🖭 tennis £5.50

Forest Glade Holiday Park, Cullompton EX15 2DT ☎(01404) 841381 Fax (01404) 841593 OS map 192/100075 6m NW of Honiton off A373 (Cullompton) at Keepers Cottage Inn Grass and hard standings, level, sheltered Open Mar-Nov–must book (caravans) 120 pitches (40 static) 🖳✗ (snack) ⤏↗🖸🖳🖉⊛∅🖭 (heated indoor) ☻⤏▢🖳 🖭♿ first aid, tennis, mother and baby room, sauna £6.00-£11.50 (Mastercard/Visa/Switch)

Honiton Golf Club EX14 9TR ☎Honiton (01404) 844422 OS map 192/173992 2m SE of Honiton off A35 (Wilmington) Open Mar 15-Oct 31–one party member to play golf, no child under 16 unless a competent golfer 10 pitches Hard standings, sheltered ✗🖳⊛∅▢ golf £10.00

Otter Valley Park, (Camping Club), Northcote EX4 8SS ☎Honiton (01404) 844546 OS map 192/176015 1m NE of Honiton off A30 (Yeovil) Open Apr 1-Sept 28, 75 pitches–adv booking min 3 nights 5 acres, level grass 🖳🖸🖉⊛ £4.30-£5.30

ILFRACOMBE, Devon   **Map E1**
Pop 10,000. EC Thurs, MD Sat SEE church, museum, St Nicholas chapel on Lantern Hill, Torrs
Walk, 'Pets Village' at Bicclescombe, viewpoints of Capstone Point N and Hillsborough E ◼ The
Promenade ☎ (01271) 863001 Restaurant: Coach House, Bicclescombe Park Rd (off A361)
☎ (01271) 864160

Big Meadow Camping Park, Watermouth EX34 9SJ ☎ Ilfracombe (01271) 862282 OS map
180/554479 2m E of Ilfracombe on A399 (Combe Martin) Open Easter-Sept–adv booking
advisable 125 pitches Level grass, sheltered ▨ ⇆ ⚲ ▨ ▨ ⊘ ⊛ ⊘ ⤳ ▱ £4.50-£8.50

Hele Valley Holiday Park, Hele Bay EX34 9RD ☎ Ilfracombe (01271) 862460 OS map 180/536474
1½m E of Ilfracombe off A399 (Combe Martin) Open Mar 15-Nov 15 139 pitches (80 static)
Grass and hard standings, level, sheltered ▨ ⚲ ▨ ▨ ⊘ ⊛ ⊘ ⊜ ⤳ ▰ ▱ 🏠 £6.00-£9.00 (all cards)

Little Meadow Camping, Lydford Farm EX34 9SJ ☎ Ilfracombe (01271) 862222 OS map
180/550480 2m E of Ilfracombe off A399 (Combe Martin) at Watermouth, adj golf course Open
Easter-Sept 50 pitches 6 acres level grass ▨ ⊘ ⊘ ⤳ ▰ ▱ £5.00-£8.50

Mullacott Cross Caravan Park, Mullacott Cross EX34 8NB ☎ Ilfracombe (01271) 862212 OS
map 180/512445 2m S of Ilfracombe near junction of A361 (Braunton) and B3343 Open Easter-
Oct 100 pitches (35 static) ✕ ⚲ ▨ ⊘ £5.00-£10.00

See also Woolacombe and Combe Martin

INDIAN QUEENS, Cornwall   **Map C5**
Restaurant: Victoria 3m E at Roche ☎ (01726) 890207

Resparva House Touring Park, Chapel Town, Summercourt TR8 5AH ☎ Mitchell (01872) 510332
OS map 200/881557 3m SW of Indian Queens off A30 (Redruth) on Summercourt road Open
May-Sept 15 pitches–no children 1 acre, level grass ▨ ⊘ ⊛ £5.00-£8.00

Summer Lodge Holiday Park, White Cross TR8 4LW ☎ (01726) 860415 OS map 200/890597 2m
W of Indian Queens on A392 (Newquay) Open Easter-Sept, 166 pitches (116 static) 10 acres
level grass, sheltered ▨ ✕ ⚲ ⇆ ⚲ ▨ ▨ ⊘ ⊛ ⊘ ⊜ ⤳ ▱ 🏠 ♿ £6.00-£11.00 (most cards)

White Acres Holiday Park, White Cross TR8 4LW ☎ (01726) 860220 OS map 200/890600 2m W
of Indian Queens on A392 (Newquay) Open Apr-Sept 350 pitches (100 static) ▨ ✕ ▨ ⊛ ⊘ ⊜ ⤳
(heated) £5.50

IPPLEPEN, Devon   **Map F5**
Restaurant: Court Farm, 2m NE off A381 at Abbotskerswell ☎ (01626) 361866

Dornafield Farm, Two Mile Oak TQ12 6DD ☎ (01803) 812732 OS map 202/838683 1½m N of
Ipplepen off A381 (Newton Abbot-Totnes) at Two Mile Oak Cross, near Denbury road Open
Easter-Oct 12 135 pitches 13 acres, hard standings and level grass, sheltered ▨ ⇆ ⚲ ▨ ▨
⊘ ⊛ ⊘ ⊜ ⤳ ▱ ♿ all-weather tennis court £8.50-£12.50 (Mastercard/Visa)

Ross Park Caravan Park, Park Hill Farm TQ12 5TT ☎ (01803) 812983 OS map 202/845671 1m E
of Ipplepen on A381 (Newton Abbot-Totnes) Open Mar-Jan 110 pitches Level grass and hard
standings, sheltered ▨ ✕ ⚲ ⇆ ⚲ ▨ ▨ ⊘ ⊛ ⊘ ⊜ ⤳ ▱ ♿ £7.90-£12.10

Woodville Park, Totnes Rd TQ12 5TN ☎ (01803) 812240 OS map 202/845674 In village on A381
Open Mar 15-Oct 15 25 pitches–no tents, no facs for children 3½ acres, grass and hard standing,
sheltered ▨ ⊛ ⊘ ▰ ♿ barbecue area, farm shop near £6.00-£7.50

See also Newton Abbot and Totnes

IVYBRIDGE, Devon   **Map F5**
Pop 5,500. EC Wed ◼ South Dartmoor, Leonards Rd ☎ (01752) 897035 Restaurant: Imperial,
Western Rd ☎ (01752) 892269

Smithaleigh Caravan and Camping Park PL7 5AX ☎ Ivybridge (01752) 893194 OS map
202/588554 2½m W of Ivybridge off A38 (Plymouth) Open all year–must book peak periods
90 pitches 7 acres, level grass and hard standings ▨ ▨ ▨ ▨ ⊘ ⊛ ⤳ ▱ ▰ ▱ family room, skittles,
crazy golf £5.00-£6.00

Whiteoaks Caravan Camping Park, Davey's Cross, PL21 0DW ☎ Ivybridge (01752) 892340 OS
map 202/652562 1m E of Ivybridge off B3213 (Bittaford) Open Apr-Oct 16 pitches Grass, level
▨ ▨ ⊘ ⊛ ▰ £6.50

JACOBSTOW, Cornwall   **Map D3**
Pop 300 Quiet village off A39 (Bude-Newquay) SEE church Restaurant: Combe Barton 3m W at
Crackington Haven ☎ (01840) 230345

Edmore Tourist Park, Wainhouse Corner EX23 0BJ ☎ St Gennys (01840) 230467 OS map
190/187955 1m W of Jacobstow at Wainhouse Corner on A39 (Stratton-Newquay) Open Easter-
Oct 30 pitches 3 acres grass, part sloping, part sheltered ▨ ▨ ⊘ ⊛ ⊘ ⊜ ⤳ ▱ ▰ ▱ £6.00-£7.00

KENNACK SANDS–see Lizard

KILKHAMPTON, Cornwall   Map D3
Pop 400 North Cornwall village on A39 (Bideford-Bude) W of Tamar lake SEE church (carved bench ends) Restaurant: New Inn ☎(01288) 352488

Atlantic Leisure Park, Sandymouth Bay EX23 9HW ☎(01288) 352563 OS map 190/210104 2½m SW of Kilkhampton off A39 (Wadebridge) on road to Sandy Mouth Bay via Stibb Open Apr-Oct, 210 pitches (150 static) ▣✕ (snack) ▣⌐⤴▣▣⌀⊕⌀▭⤴▢▦⌐▦ gymnasium, solarium, disco

East Thorne Caravan Park EX23 9RY ☎(01288) 321618 OS map 190/260110 ½m SE of Kilkhampton on right of B3254 (Launceston) Open Apr-Oct, 29 pitches 2 acres, level grass sheltered ▣▣⌀⊕⊕⤴▦⌐ games room £6.60

Tamar Lake Farm, Thurdon EX23 9SA ☎(01288) 321426 OS map 190/287108 3m E of Kilkhampton on Tamar Lakes road Open Apr-Oct, 15 pitches ½ acre, level grass, sheltered ⌐▦ fishing £2.00-£4.00

KINGSBRIDGE, Devon   Map F5
Pop 4,230. EC Thurs, MD Wed, Fri SEE Shambles arcade, Kingsbridge Estuary, annual fair (Jul), Cookworthy porcelain museum, local artists summer exhibition ℹ The Quay ☎(01548) 853195 Restaurant: Ship and Plough, The Promenade ☎(01548) 852485

Island Lodge, Stumpy Post Cross, Ledstone TQ7 4BL ☎(01548) 852956 OS map 202/742470 1½m N of Kingsbridge on A381 (Totnes) Open Easter-Nov 30 pitches Level grass ▣▣⊕⌀⤴▦ £9.25

Mounts Farm Touring Park, The Mounts, East Allington TQ9 7QJ ☎(01548) 521591 OS map 202/753489 3m NE of Kingsbridge on A381 (Totnes) Open Apr-Oct 50 pitches 6 acres level grass, sheltered ▣▣▣⊕⌀ £7.50

Parkland Caravan Site, Sorley Green Cross TQ7 4AF ☎Kingsbridge (01548) 852723 OS map 202/730463 1m N of Kingsbridge on A381 (Totnes) Open all year 35 pitches Grass and hard standing ▣▣⌀⊕⌀⊕⤴▦⊘ barbecue £8.25

KINGSTEINTON–see Newton Abbot

LAND'S END, Cornwall   Map A6
Restaurant: State House (Lands End complex) ☎(01736) 871680

Cardinney Caravan and Camping Park, Crows an Wra TR19 6HJ ☎Sennen (01736) 810880 OS map 203/375273 3m NE of Land's End on A30 (Penzance) Open Feb-Nov 105 pitches 5 acres level grass and hard standings, sheltered ▣✕⌐⤴▣▣⌀⊕⌀⊕⤴▢ games room £5.00-£8.00 (Mastercard/Visa)

Sea View Caravan Park, Sennen TR19 7AD ☎Sennen (01736) 871266 OS map 203/357253 1m E of Land's End on right of A30 (Penzance) Open Apr-Oct 100 pitches (75 static) Level grass ▣✕⌐⤴▣▣⌀⊕⌀▭⤴⌐ £8.00 (Mastercard/Visa)

For other sites near Land's End see St Buryan

LAUNCESTON, Cornwall   Map E4
Pop 5,000. EC Thurs, MD Tues ℹMarket House Arcade ☎Launceston (01566) 772321 Restaurant: Westgate Inn, Westgate St ☎(01566) 772493

Chapmanswell Caravan Park, St Giles on the Heath PL15 9SG ☎(01409) 211382 OS map 190/356932 7m N of Launceston on A388 (Holsworthy) Open Mar 15-Nov 15 81 pitches (25 static) 4 acres, level grass, part hard standings, sheltered by hedges ▣▣▣⌀⊕⌀⊕▦ £8.00-£10.00 (Delta/Switch)

LISKEARD, Cornwall   Map D5
Pop 6,500. EC Wed, MD Mon, Thurs SEE Guildhall, Castle Park, Pipe Well Restaurant: Lord Eliot, Castle St ☎(01579) 342717

Great Trethew Manor Campsite, Horningtops PL14 3PY ☎(01503) 240663 OS map 201/286601 3m SE of Liskeard off A38 (Plymouth) on B3251 (Looe) Open Mar-Sept 55 pitches 30 acres level/sloping grass, sheltered ▣✕▣⊕⊕▭⊕⤴▦ pony rides, tennis £6.00-£8.00

Pine Green Caravan and Camping Park, Doublebois PL14 6LD ☎(01271) 328981 OS map 201/195653 4m W of Liskeard off A38 (Bodmin) on B3360 (East Taphouse) Open Jan-Dec 50 pitches Hard standings and terraced grass ▣⌀⊕⌀▦⌐ £5.00-£9.00

Trenant Caravan Park, St Neot PL14 6RZ ☎Liskeard (01579) 320896 OS map 201/212685 2½m NW of Liskeard off A38 (Bodmin) via Dobwalls and Treverbyn Open Apr-Oct, 12 pitches–phone before arrival 1½ acres, level grass, sheltered ▣▣⊕ £4.00-£5.00

See also Bolventor

LIZARD, Cornwall   Map B7
Pop 810 SEE lighthouse, cliffs, Cadgwith 2m NE Restaurant: Housel Bay, Housel Cove ☎(01326)
290417

Chy-Carne Holiday Park, Kennack Sands, Ruan Minor TR12 7LX ☎(01326) 290200 OS map
204/727164 4m NE of Lizard off A3083 (Helston) Open Apr-Oct 94 pitches Level/sloping grass,
sheltered ▨▣❺❷◍❀❸⌄❀⊡🏠 £3.00-£8.00

Gwendreath Farm Caravan Park, Kennack Sands, Ruan Minor TR12 7LZ ☎Lizard (01326)
290666 OS map 204/730169 3m NNE of Lizard off B3293 (Helston-St Keverne) Open Apr-Oct
40 pitches (30 static) 7 acres level grass, sheltered ▨⋏▣❺❷◍❷❸⌄⊡⊟ £5.30-£6.50
(Mastercard/Visa)

Sea Acres Holiday Park, Kennack Sands TR12 7LT ☎Lizard (01326) 290665 OS map
204/734164 3m NE of Lizard off A3083 (Helston) Open Easter-Sept 150 pitches (100 static) 20
acres, level grass ▨⋇♀⌄▣❺❷◍❷❸⊟⌄⊡⊟ club, beach £6.50-£12.00

Silver Sands Holiday Park, Kennack Sands, Ruan Minor TR12 7LZ *Remote small site with
woodland walk to beach* ☎Lizard (01326) 290631 OS map 204/731169 3m NE of Lizard off
B3293 (St Keverne) Open May-Sept 50 pitches (16 static) 9 acres level grass, sheltered
▣❺❷◍❷❸⌄⊡⊟❹ £6.00-£7.50

LOOE, Cornwall   Map D5
Pop 4,700. EC Thurs SEE West Looe church, Guildhall museum, Cornish Museum, Deep Sea and
Shark Angling Festival 🄸 The Guildhall, Fore Street, East Looe ☎(01503) 262072 Restaurant:
Ship, Fore St, East Looe ☎(01503) 263124

Camping Caradon, Trelawne Gardens, Trelawne PL13 2NA ☎(01503) 272388 OS map
201/219542 2m W of Looe off A387 (Polperro) and B3359 (Pelynt) Open Apr-Oct 85 pitches
Grass, level ▨♀⌄▣❺❷◍❷❸⌄⊡ wet weather facilities for campers £5.00-£8.50

Looe Valley Touring Park, Polperro Road PL13 2SG *Holiday park popular with young families*
☎Looe (01503) 262425 OS map 201/228536 2m SW of Looe off A387 (Polperro) Open mid
May-Sept 550 pitches (40 static) Level grass, sheltered ▨⋇♀⌄⋏▣❺❷◍⊟ (heated)
❸⌄⊡❶⊟🏠 lic club, disco £7.00-£10.90

Polborder House Camping Caravan Park, St Martin's by Looe PL13 1QR *Well run small site
above Looe* ☎(01503) 240265 OS map 201/283555 2m NE of Looe off B3253 (Normansland)
Open Apr-Oct 36 pitches 3 acres, level grass and hard standing, sheltered ▨⋏▣❺❷◍❷❸⌄
⊟🏠♿ baby room £6.00-£9.50 (Mastercard/Visa)

Tencreek Caravan-Camping Park PL13 2JR ☎Looe (01503) 262447/262757 OS map 201/233524
1½m WSW of Looe on A387 (Polperro) Open all year 245 pitches (62 static)–families and couples
only 14 acres, level/part sloping grass ▨⋇♀⌄▣❺❷◍❷❸⊟ (indoor) ⌄⊡❶⊟⊟♿ club room,
solarium £7.50-£13.50

Tregoad Farm Touring Caravan Camping Park, St Martin's PL13 1PB ☎Looe (01503) 262718
OS map 201/272560 1½m NE of Looe off B3253 (Widegates) Open Apr-Oct–no adv booking
150 pitches Level grass, sheltered ▨⋇♀⌄▣❺❷◍❷⌄❶⊟ lic club, fishing £6.50-£10.50
(Mastercard/Visa)

Trelawne Manor Holiday Estate PL13 2NA ☎(01503) 272151 OS map 201/219538 2m W of
Looe off A387 (Polperro) and B3359 (Pelynt) Open Easter, Mar-Oct–must book peak periods 317
pitches (200 static) ▨⋇⌄⋏▣❺❷◍❷⊟ (heated) ❸⌄⊡ lic club/bar, ballroom £3.50-£9.50

Trelay Farm Park, Pelynt PL13 2JX ☎Lanreath (01503) 220900 OS map 201/210545 3m W of
Looe off A387 (Polperro) and B3359 (Pelynt) Open Easter-Oct 75 pitches (20 static)
Level/sloping grass ▣❺❷◍❷❸⊟♿ £7.00-£8.50

LOSTWITHIEL, Cornwall   Map D5
Pop 2,240. EC Wed SEE Duchy Hall, bridge, museum, St Bartholomew's church, Restormel castle
ruins 1m N 🄸 Community Centre, Liddicoat Road ☎(01208) 872207 Restaurant: Royal Oak, Duke
St ☎(01208) 872552

Powderham Castle Tourist Park, Lanlivery PL30 5BU ☎(01208) 872277 OS map 200/083592
1½m SW of Lostwithiel off A390 (St Austell)–signposted Open Apr-Nov 75 pitches 10 acres level
grass and hard standings, sheltered ▣❺❷◍❷❸⌄⊡❶ battery charging, freezer pack service,
paddling pool, indoor badminton, 9-hole putting green £6.90-£10.10

Charges quoted are the minimum and maximum for two people with car and caravan or tent.
They are given only as a guide and should be checked with the owner of any site at which
you plan to stay.
Remember to ask whether hot water or use of the pool (if any) is extra and make sure that
VAT is included.

LYDFORD, Devon   Map E4
Pop 320 SEE St Petroc's church, Lydford Gorge and waterfall, ruined castle Restaurant: Dartmoor Inn ☎(01822) 820221

Lydford Park (Camping Club), The Croft EX20 4BE ☎(01822) 820275 OS map 191/512853 ¼m N of Lydford centre on Bridestowe road Open Mar 23-Nov 2, 70 pitches 4 acres, level grass, sheltered ▯▤◪◉∅❸ £6.20-£9.40 plus £4.20 non-member pitch fee

LYNTON, Devon   Map F1
Pop 1,600. EC Sat (winter) Clifftop village which developed as resort in Victorian-Edwardian times. Linked with tiny harbour of Lynmouth below by steep winding road down wooded hillside and a cliff railway. Good centre for walks on Exmoor. SEE Lyn and Exmoor museum, Watersmeet, Valley of Rocks, Countisbury church 2m E ▣ Lee Road ☎(01598) 752225 Restaurant: Rising Sun by harbour at Lynmouth ☎(01598) 753223

Channel View Caravan Park, Manor Farm, West Lyn EX35 6LD *Easily accessible site with panoramic views* ☎Lynton (01598) 753349 OS map 180/724482 2m SE of Lynton on A39 (Barnstaple) Open Easter-Oct 15, 80 pitches Level grass and hard standings, sheltered ▤⚲▯▤◪◉∅❷⤙▱⬥ parent-baby room £7.00-£10.00 (2000) (Mastercard/Visa/Switch)

Lorna Doone Farm, Parracombe EX31 4RJ ☎(01598) 763576 OS map 180/675446 5m SW of Lynton on A39 (Barnstaple) Open Mar-Oct 40 pitches 2½ acres, level/sloping grass £5.00

Sunny Lyn Holiday Park, Lyn Bridge EX35 6NS ☎Lynton (01598) 753384 OS map 180/721486 ¼m S of Lynton on B3234 (Barbrook) Open Easter-Oct 15–no adv booking 38 pitches Grass and hard standings, level, sheltered ▤✕⚲⤙⚲▯▤◪◉∅❸▱▰⬟ fishing £7.00

MALBOROUGH–see Salcombe

MARAZION, Cornwall   Map B6
Pop 1,380. EC Wed SEE St Michael's Mount, Age of Steam Restaurant: Cutty Sark, The Square ☎(01736) 710334

Kenneggy Cove Holiday Park, Higher Kenneggy, Rosudgeon TR20 9AU ☎(01736) 763453 OS map 203/568288 3m E of Marazion on A394 (Helston) near beach Open Apr-Oct 70 pitches Level/sloping grass, sheltered ▤⤙▯▤◪◉∅❸⤙▱▰ £5.00-£8.50

River Valley Country Park, Relubbus TR20 9ER ☎(01736) 763398 OS map 203/566320 3m NE of Marazion off A394 (Helston) on B3280 (Leedstown) Open Mar 31-Oct 27 150 pitches Grass and hard standing, level, sheltered ▤▯▤◪◉∅▰ fishing, area reserved for adults only £7.50-£12.50 (all cards exc Amex)

Trevair Touring Site, South Treveneague, St Hilary TR20 9BY ☎(01736) 740647 OS map 203/548326 2m NE of Marazion off B3280 (Goldsithney) Open Easter-Oct 40 pitches 3 acres level grass sheltered ▯▤◉▱⬟ £6.00-£8.00

Wayfarers Camping Site, St Hillary TR20 9EF ☎(01736) 763326 OS map 203/551314 2m E of Marazion on B3280 (Goldsithney) Open Mar-Jan 60 pitches 5 acres level grass and hard standings sheltered ▤⤙▯▤◪◉∅⤙▰▱ first aid £6.00-£9.00

Wheal Rodney Carapark TR17 0HL ☎Marazion (01736) 710605 OS map 203/521329 ½m N of Marazion on Crowlas road Open Apr-Oct 45 pitches Level grass, sheltered ▯▤◪◉∅☒ (indoor heated) ▱⬟ spa bath, sauna, solarium £4.70-£7.65

Planning a tour in Europe?

THE LIZARD

A rugged peninsula with a central plateau ablaze with heather from spring to autumn, Lizard Point with its lighthouse is the southernmost place in England and one of the most dangerous for shipping. Along the coast are tall cliffs and caverns with beaches at only a few places, one of the most extensive – and most popular – being Kennack Sands.

MAWGAN PORTH, Cornwall **Map C5**
Pop 1,185 SEE Mawgan Vale SE, Watergate Bay S Restaurant: Tredragon *(01637) 860213

Magic Cove Touring Park, TR8 4BZ *St Mawgan (01637) 860263 OS map 200/852672 ¼m S of Mawgan Porth on B3276 (Newquay-Padstow) near beach Open Easter-Oct–adv booking (minimum 7 nights in season)–25 pitches Level grass, sheltered ⚡❀ £5.00-£10.00

The Marver Site, TR8 4BB *St Mawgan (01637) 860493 OS map 200/855672 ½m E of Mawgan Porth off B3276 (Newquay-Padstow) near beach Open Easter-Sept 25 pitches–no advance booking 1 acre level grass ▣ sauna, solarium, crazy golf £5.00-£6.90

Sun Haven Valley Caravan and Camping Park, Mawgan Porth TR8 4BQ *St Mawgan (01637) 860373 OS map 200/860668 ½m SE of Mawgan Porth on left of St Mawgan road Open Apr-Oct 154 pitches Grass and hard standing ▙↗▣⚡🅰❀∅❁↵⊡🏠 £8.50-£12.50 (Mastercard/Visa)

Treporth Campsite, Porthcothan PL28 8LS *(01841) 520479 OS map 200/860716 2m N of Mawgan Porth on right of B3276 (Padstow) Open Apr-Oct 16 pitches 1 acre grass, gentle slope £5.50-£7.00

Trevarrian Holiday Park, Trevarrian TR8 4AQ *Holiday park overlooking beach* *St Mawgan (01637) 860381 OS map 200/851662 ½m S of Mawgan Porth on B3276 (Newquay) Open Easter-Sept 185 pitches 5 acres level grass, open ▙♟▣⚡🅰❀∅⊡❁↵⊡ paddling pool, live entertainment, tennis, pitch and putt, bar snacks £3.00-£8.40

Watergate Bay Holiday Park, Tregurrian, Watergate Bay TR8 4AD *Well organised touring site* *St Mawgan (01637) 860387 OS map 200/849655 1½m S of Mawgan Porth off B3276 (Newquay) at Tregurrian Open Easter-Oct 171 pitches 30 acres level grass and hard standings ▙✗♟↵▣ ⚡🅰❀∅⊡ (heated) ❁↵⊡⚡⊡🏠⚖ lic club, evening entertainment, free minibus to beach, dog exercise area £7.50-£12.00 (all cards)

See also Newquay and St Columb Major

MEVAGISSEY, Cornwall **Map C5**
Pop 2,270. SEE harbour, museum, aquarium, model railway Restaurant: Fountain Inn *(01726) 842320

Pengrugla Caravan and Camping Park, St Ewe PL26 6EL *Mevagissey (01726) 842714 OS map 204/998470 2m NW of Mevagissey off B3273 (St Austell) on Sticker road Open Mar-Oct 112 pitches Level/sloping grass, hard standing, sheltered ▙▣🅰∅ dairy produce, beach access, slipway £6.00-£14.40 (Mastercard/Visa/Switch)

Penhaven Touring Park, Pentewan PL26 6DL *(01726) 843687 OS map 204/015475 2m N of Mevagissey on right of B3273 (St Austell) Open Apr-Oct 105 marked pitches 13½ acres level grass sheltered, some hard standings ▙↵♟▣⚡🅰❀∅⊡↵⚡⚖ bike hire £8.80-£18.00 (most cards)

Pentewan Sands Holiday Park PL26 6BT *Mevagissey (01726) 843485 OS map 204/017468 1m N of Mevagissey on B3273 (St Austell) Open Apr-Oct–must book peak periods 600 pitches (114 static) 26 acres, hard standings, level grass ▙✗♟↵♟▣🅰❀∅⊡ (heated) ❁↵⊡⚡⊡🏠⚖ tennis, sailing club, private beach £6.50-£15.95 (Mastercard/Visa/Switch)

Sea View International Holiday Park, Boswinger, Gorran Haven PL26 6LL *Landscaped park above Veryan Bay notable for its facilities* *Mevagissey (01726) 843425 Fax (01726) 843358 OS map 204/991412 3m S of Mevagissey off Gorran Haven road Open Easter-Sept–must book peak periods 203 pitches (38 static) Grass and hard standing ▙↵♟▣⚡🅰❀∅⊡ (2 heated) ❁↵⊡🏠⚖ campers' kitchen, badminton, volley ball, tennis, putting, basketball £5.90-£16.90 (Mastercard/Visa)

Sun Valley Holiday Park, Pentewan PL26 6DJ *Mevagissey (01726) 843266 OS map 204/006484 1½m N of Mevagissey on B3273 (St Austell) Open Apr-Oct–must book peak periods 100 pitches (75 static) 20 acres, level grass and hard standings, sheltered ▙✗♟↵♟▣⚡ 🅰❀∅⊡ (heated indoor) ❁↵⊡⊡🏠 children's room, tennis £8.50-£22.00 (Mastercard/Visa)

Tregarton Park, Gorran PL26 6NF *Mevagissey (01726) 843666 OS map 204/985437 2m W of Mevagissey off Gorran Haven road Open Apr-Sept–booking advisable 150 pitches Grass, part sloping, sheltered ▙♟▣⚡🅰❀∅⊡ (heated) ❁↵ £6.00-£12.90 (1999) (Mastercard/Visa/ Switch)

Continued on facing page

Trelispen Caravan and Camping Park, Gorran Haven PL26 6NR ☎ Mevagissey (01726) 843501 OS map 204/008421 2m SW of Mevagissey off Gorran Haven road Open Apr-Oct 40 pitches Level grass, sheltered ▣▣◙◉✦▣ nature reserve £7.00-£15.00

Treveague Farm, Gorran PL26 6NY ☎ Mevagissey (01726) 842295 OS map 204/001410 3m S of Mevagissey off coast road near Gorran Haven: follow signs Penare Open Jul-Aug 30 pitches 8 acres level/sloping grass £4.00-£8.00

Treveor Farm Caravan and Camping, Gorran PL26 6LW ☎ (01726) 842387 OS map 204/988418 2½m SW of Mevagissey via Gorran Open Easter-Oct 50 pitches 4 acres mainly level grass ▣▣◉◙✦ coarse fishing £7.00-£12.00

Treveor Farm

Gorran PL28 6LW

Tel (01726) 842387

Small family run campsite with good facilities forming part of working dairy farm. Close to beaches, coastal walks and the Lost Gardens of Helligan. Open Easter-October.

MODBURY, Devon　　　　　　　　　　　　　　　　　　　　　　　　　　**Map F5**

Pop 1,220. Hilly town in region of South Hams, with Bigbury only feasible access to sea SEE church, Erme valley, Bigbury sands and Burgh Island 4m S ▣ Poundwell Meadow Car Park ☎ (01548) 830159 Restaurant: Modbury Inn, Brownston St ☎ (01548) 830275

Broad Park Touring (Caravan Club) East Leigh PL21 0SH ☎ Modbury (01548) 830256 OS map 202/691524 2m E of Modbury on B3207 (Halwell) Open May 16-Sept 21—must book 135 pitches Grass, part sloping ▣▣▣◙◉◙◙& £5.00-£8.00

California Cross Park (Camping Club) PL21 0SG ☎ (01548) 821297 OS map 202/705530 3m E of Modbury on B3207 (Halwell) near junction with B3196 (South Brent–Kingsbridge) Open Mar-Oct 80 pitches—adv booking min 2 nights 3½ acres, level grass, sheltered ▣✕▣◄▣▣◙◉◙& £6.20-£9.40 plus £4.20 non-member pitch fee

Moor View Touring Caravan Park, California Cross PL21 0SG ☎ (01548) 821485 OS map 202/701523 3m E of Modbury on B3207 (Dartmouth) Open Mar-Oct 68 pitches Level grass and hard standing, sheltered ▣◄▣▣◙◉◙◉✦▣◪ pool table £7.00-£10.00 (Mastercard/Visa)

Pennymoor Camping-Caravan Park PL21 0SB ☎ Modbury (01548) 830542/830269 OS map 202/685516 1½m E of Modbury off A379 (Kingsbridge) at Harraton Cross Open Mar 15-Nov 15, 155 pitches (70 static) 11½ acres grass, level/gentle slope ▣▣▣◙◉◙◉✦▣& £5.00-£9.00 (1999)

South Leigh Caravan and Camping Park, PL21 0SB ☎ Modbury (01548) 830346 OS map 202/689514 1m E of Modbury off A379 (Kingsbridge) at Harraton Cross Open Mar 24-Oct 31, 200 pitches (100 static) Level/sloping grass ▣▣◄▣▣◙◉◙▣◪▣◪& snack bar, live entertainment in season £2.60-£8.60

MORTEHOE–see Woolacombe

Camping Caravanning Through France

160pp ISBN 1-870009-23-1 £6.50 net in UK only

A unique guide which describes and maps main-road routes crossing the country from north to south which start at ports served by tunnel or ferry from Britain. These are backed by link routes leading from and joining up with them so that, for example, those arriving at one port can pick up a route starting from another. Every campsite on or near the routes is pinpointed and historic sights, shopping for food and good-value restaurants noted at places along the way.

Each route leads to or passes near a popular holiday location and in a separate section are featured regions by the sea or inland where outdoor holidaymakers are welcomed and catered for. A brief description of each region is followed by a selection of campsites chosen for their location or amenities.

Publication is planned for Easter 2001 and to reserve your copy write to Frederick Tingey (CCF), Hillsboro, How Caple HR1 4TE. Copies ordered prior to publication cost only £5.00 post-free. Send no money now.

MULLION, Cornwall   **Map B6**
Pop 2,000. EC Wed Remote resort on Lizard Peninsula, one most scenic parts of wild and rocky coastline, the cliffs running S to isolated Predannack Head and N to coves of Polurrian and Poldhu SEE church (carved bench ends), Mullion Cove 1m SW, Poldhu Point and Marconi Memorial 1m NW Restaurant: Old Inn ☎(01326) 240240

Criggan Mill, Mullion Cove, TR12 7EU ☎Mullion (01326) 240496 OS map 203/669179 1m SW of Mullion on B3296 (Mullion Cove) Open Apr-Oct 45 pitches Grass, level, sheltered ✗⬛⬛✦∅❀⌂🏠 first aid £7.50-£12.00 (Mastercard/Visa)

Franchis Park, Cury Cross Lanes TR12 7AZ ☎Mullion (01326) 240301 OS map 203/696204 1m NE of Mullion on A3083 (Helston-Lizard) Open Mar-Oct 70 pitches 17 acres, level grass, sheltered ⬛⤳➚⬛∅✦∅⌂🏠 £8.00-£9.00 (Mastercard/Visa)

The Friendly Camp and Caravan Park, Tregullas Farm, Penhale TR12 7LJ ☎Mullion (01326) 240387 OS map 203/698185 1m SE of Mullion on A3083 (Helston-Lizard) Open Apr-Oct 30 pitches 1½ acres level grass sheltered ∅⌂ £5.00

Mullion Holiday Park, Penhale TR12 7LJ *Family site in lovely setting on Lizard peninsula* ☎Mullion (01326) 240000 OS map 203/698185 1½m SE of Mullion at junction of B3296 (Penhale) and A3083 (Helston-Lizard) Open Easter-Oct 498 pitches (348 static) Grass, level ⬛✗⤳➚⬛⬛∅✦∅⬛ (indoor/outdoor) ✦⤳⬛✦⌂🏠 lic club, solarium, amusements £7.90-£14.50

Teneriffe Farm, Predannack, TR12 7EZ ☎Mullion (01326) 240293 OS map 203/676169 2m S of Mullion off B3296 (Mullion Cove) on Predannack road Open Apr-Oct 20 pitches Grass, part level, open ⬛∅✦∅❦ £5.00-£6.00 (all cards)

CHECK BEFORE ENTERING

Beware less-than-honest site operators who give us one price for the following year and then increase it once the season gets underway. So note the charges for any site featured in this guide and before pulling in verify how much you will have to pay, and for what. If on leaving the charges turn out to be higher, ask why the difference.

NEWQUAY, Cornwall   **Map C5**
Pop 15,460. EC Wed (winter) One-time port and fishing centre on N Cornish coast noted for its fine sands, surfing beaches and impressive cliff scenery N beyond Watergate Bay SEE surfing beaches, zoo, St Columb Minor Church (15c), Trerice Manor 4m S, Kelsey Head 5m SW ▨ Municipal Offices, Marcus Hill ✆ Newquay (01637) 871345 Restaurant: Kilbirnie, Narrowcliff ✆ (01637) 875155

Hendra Holiday Park, Lane TR8 4NY ✆ Newquay (01637) 875778 OS map 200/834606 1½m SE of Newquay on A392 (Indian Queens) Open Apr-Oct 788 pitches (160 static) 46 acres level grass and hard standings, sheltered [symbols] lic club, disco, amuse- ments, crazy golf, children's club £7.60-£11.30

Newquay Holiday Park TR8 4HS ✆ Newquay (01637) 871111 OS map 200/855626 2m E of Newquay on A3059 (St Columb) Open May 12-Sept 16 488 pitches (138 static) 23 acres, grass, part sloping, hard standings, sheltered [symbols] (heated) [symbols] paddling pool, lic club £7.10-£12.90 (Mastercard/Visa)

Porth Beach Tourist Park, Porth TR7 3NH ✆ Newquay (01637) 876531 OS map 200/832629 1½m N of Newquay on B3276 (Padstow) near beach Open Apr-Oct 201 pitches 7 acres level grass, sheltered [symbols] ice packs £5.00-£12.50

Riverside Holiday Park, Lane TR8 4PE ✆ Newquay (01637) 873617 OS map 200/831593 2½m E of Newquay off A3075 (Redruth) and Quintrell Downs road Open Easter-Oct, 150 pitches 14 acres level grass, sheltered [symbols] fishing £6.00-£10.00 (all cards)

Rosecliston Tourist Park, Trevemper TR8 5JT *Well organised pitches for tourists* ✆ (01637) 830326 OS map 200/813593 2m S of Newquay on A3075 (Redruth) Open Apr-Oct, 126 pitches 6 acres, level grass and hard standings [symbols] (heated) [symbols] sauna, solarium £5.60-£10.00

Sunnyside Holiday Park, Quintrell Downs TR8 4PD *In beautiful countryside near coast exclusively for 17-35 age group* ✆ (01637) 873338 OS map 200/850602 2m E of Newquay on left of A392 (St Austell) beyond Quintrell Downs Open Apr-Oct 115 pitches–no trailer caravans 25 acres level grass, sheltered [symbols] lic club with entertainment, whirlpool spa £9.00-£15.00 (Mastercard/Visa)

Trebarber Farm Camping Caravan Site, St Columb Minor TR8 4JT ✆ and Fax (01637) 873007 OS map 200/864626 3m NE of Newquay off A3059 (St Columb Major) Open May-Oct 65 pitches level grass [symbols] £6.00-£11.00

Tregustick Farm Holiday Park, Porth TR8 4AR ✆ Porth (01637) 872478 OS map 200/845631 2m N of Newquay off B3276 (Padstow) Open Apr-Oct, 120 pitches (100 static) 9 acres, part level [symbols] £6.00

Treloy Tourist Park TR8 4JN ✆ Newquay (01637) 872063/876279 OS map 200/860636 3m E of Newquay off A3059 (St Columb) on RAF St Mawgan road Open Apr-Sept 140 pitches 11½ acres, hard standings and grass, level/sloping [symbols] golf course concession £6.00-£10.80 (Mastercard/Visa/Switch)

Trenance Caravan Park, Edgcumbe Avenue TR7 2JY *One of nearest sites to town centre* ✆ Newquay (01637) 873447 OS map 200/816611 ½m S of Newquay on left of A3075 (Redruth) Open Apr-Oct 184 pitches (134 static) 10 acres, grass, sloping, sheltered [symbols] £7.00-£13.00 (Mastercard/Visa/Amex)

Trencreek Holiday Park TR8 4NS *Family park in village setting* ✆ Newquay (01637) 874210 OS map 200/829608 1m SE of Newquay off A392 (Indian Queens) Open Apr-Sept 150 pitches Level grass and hard standings [symbols] children's room, coarse fishing, entertainment, paddling pool £7.30-£11.50

Trethiggey Touring Park, Quintrell Downs TR8 4LG *Peaceful family-run site with country views* ✆ Newquay (01637) 877672 OS map 200/848597 2m E of Newquay on A3058 (St Austell) Open all year–must book peak periods 157 pitches 15 acres, level/sloping grass and hard standing, sheltered [symbols] (all year) [symbols] battery charging £5.95-£8.45

Trevelgue Caravan Park, Porth TR8 4AS ✆ Newquay (01637) 873475/875905 OS map 200/837635 2m NE of Newquay off B3276 (Padstow) on Tregustick road Open Apr-Oct 399 pitches (142 static) 15 acres level grass [symbols] (indoor heated) [symbols] jacuzzi £2.50-£5.90

See also Crantock, Mawgan Porth, Indian Queens and St Columb

CARAVAN STORAGE

Many sites in this guide offer caravan storage in winter but some will also store your caravan in summer, which for those of us able to tour several times a year saves towing over long distances. Sites most conveniently placed for this are those on or near popular routes to the West Country and Scotland.

NEWTON ABBOT, Devon   **Map F4**
Pop 20,500. EC Thurs, MD Wed, Sat Busy market town beside river Teign and popular touring centre on E edge of Dartmoor SEE Forde House, Wolborough church ◪ Bridge House, Courtenay St ☏(01626) 867494 Restaurant: Dartmouth Inn, East St ☏(01626) 853451

Twelveoaks Farm Caravan Park, Teingrace TQ12 6QT *Family-managed rural site in quiet location* ☏(01626) 352979 OS map 191/852735 1½m NW of Newton Abbot off A382 (Moretonhampstead) Open all year 25 pitches–no tents Hard standing and grass, sloping ⚓◉⊟⊘◈⊡◖◨ £6.00-£8.50

Ware Barton, Kingsteignton TQ12 3QQ ☏(01626) 854025 OS map 192/884729 2½m NE of Newton Abbot on A381 (Teignmouth) Open May-Sept 90 pitches (40 static) Level/sloping grass, sheltered £4.00-£7.00

See also Ipplepen

NEWTON POPPLEFORD, Devon   **Map G4**
Restaurant: Coach House at Southerton ☏(01395) 68946

Popplefords, Exeter Road EX10 0DE ☏Colaton Raleigh (01395) 568672 OS map 192/064895 1½m W of Newton Poppleford on right of A3052 (Exeter) Open Mar-Oct 6 pitches 10 acres grass and hard standing, level, sheltered ✖◨◖ £6.00-£8.00

NORTHAM–see Bideford

OKEHAMPTON, Devon   **Map E4**
Pop 4,000. EC Wed, MD Sat SEE town hall (17c) parish church, Fitz Well, Dartmoor (2028ft Yes Tor, 2039ft High Willhays, West Okement Valley) ◪3 West Street ☏Okehampton (01837) 53020 Restaurant: Plume of Feathers, Fore St ☏(01837) 52815

Culverhayes Caravan Site, Sampford Courtenay EX20 2TG ☏North Tawton (01837) 82431 OS map 191/629010 4m NE of Okehampton off B3217 (Exbourne) on A3072 (North Tawton) Open Mar-Oct 75 pitches Hard standings and sloping grass ◨◘◈◔◖◨ farm produce, fishing £6.00 (1998)

Olditch Farm Caravan Park, Sticklepath EX20 2NT ☏Okehampton (01837) 840734 OS map 191/646935 4m E of Okehampton on left of old A30 (Exeter) before Sticklepath Open Mar-Nov 52 pitches (19 static) Level/sloping grass and hard standings, sheltered ⚓✖♟◉◨◘◈⊘◖◻◨ (£2.00/wk) ◖◨ meals £6.00-£8.00

Yertiz Camping Site, Exeter Road EX20 1QF ☏Okehampton (01837) 52281 OS map 191/602954 ½m E of Okehampton on right of B3260-old A30 (Exeter) Open all year 30 pitches 3½ acres, level grass and hard standing, sheltered ◉◨◘◈⊘◖◖◨⚓ £5.00-£7.50

For other sites near Okehampton see Bridestowe and Whiddon Down

---

Travelling to and from the West Country, try to avoid Friday evenings or Saturdays in July, August and September. On Saturdays in July and August there may well be traffic jams on M5 southbound between junctions 14 and 20. If you have to use the motorway on a Saturday during these months try to time your journey to be outside the peak hours of 0600 to 1400. Motorists should also avoid the Tamar Bridge at Saltash on the A38 west of Plymouth at peak times, particularly on Saturdays in July and August between 0900 and 1600.

PADSTOW, Cornwall   **Map C4**
Pop 3,000. EC Wed, MD Thurs Popular resort on Camel estuary with ancient harbour SEE St Petroc's church, Tropical Bird and Butterfly garden, Hobby Horse festival (May Day) ☒ Red Brick Bldg, North Quay ☎(01841) 533449 Restaurant: Old Custom House, South Quay ☎(01841) 532359

Carnevas Farm Holiday Park, St Merryn PL28 8PN *Spacious site in open countryside* ☎Padstow (01841) 520230 OS map 200/862728 3m SW of Padstow off B3276 (Newquay) Open Apr-Oct 198 pitches 8 acres, grass, level/sloping £6.00-£10.00

Dennis Cove Camping PL28 8DR *Site with access to Padstow beach* ☎Padstow (01841) 532349 OS map 200/921744 ¼m S of Padstow off A389 (Wadebridge) by river Open Whitsun-Sept 62 pitches Grass, level, part sheltered (heated) fishing, sailing, slipway £8.60-£12.00

Harlyn Sands Holiday Park, Trevose Head, St Merryn PL28 8SQ ☎Padstow (01841) 520720 OS map 200/869755 3m W of Padstow off B3276 (Newquay) Open Apr-Oct 425 pitches (300 static) Level grass club house, beach near £3.50-£8.00

Higher Harlyn Park, St Merryn PL28 8SG ☎Padstow (01841) 520022 OS map 200/877744 2½m SW of Padstow off B3276 (Newquay) Open Mar-Sept, 325 pitches (70 static)–no adv booking 30 acres, level grass children's room £6.00-£12.00 (Mastercard/Visa/Delta/Switch)

Mother Ivey's Bay Caravan Park, Trevose Head PL28 8SL ☎(01841) 520990 OS map 200/860762 5m W of Padstow off B3276 (Mawgan Porth) on Trevose Head road on clifftop–signposted Open Easter-Oct 350 pitches (250 static)–booking advisable 13 acres level/sloping grass, open £7.00-£25.00 (most cards)

Ponderosa Caravan Park, St Issey PL27 7QA ☎(01841) 540359 OS map 200/927719 2½m S of Padstow on left of A389 (Wadebridge) Open Easter-Oct, 60 pitches 4 acres, level grass dairy produce £3.50-£6.30

Seagull Tourist Park, Treginegar Farm, St Merryn PL28 8PT ☎Padstow (01841) 520117 OS map 200/883713 3½m SW of Padstow off B3276 (Newquay) Open Apr-Oct 86 pitches (36 static) 5 acres, level grass £3.80-£7.00

Tregavone Farm Touring Park, St Merryn PL28 8JZ ☎(01841) 520148 OS map 200/897732 2m S of Padstow off A389 (Wadebridge) and Shop road Open Mar-Oct 40 pitches 4 acres level grass £6.00-£8.00

Tregidier Caravan Park, Trevean Lane, St Merryn PL28 8PR ☎Padstow (01841) 520264 OS map 200/875725 3½m SW of Padstow off B3276 (Trenance) Open Apr-Oct–must book peak periods 18 pitches 1 acre, level grass £3.50-£6.00

Trerethern Touring Park PL28 8LE ☎Padstow (01841) 532061 OS map 200/912739 1m S of Padstow on left of A389 (Wadebridge) Open Apr-Oct 100 pitches 13½ acres level grass and hard standings, sheltered motorhome pumpout £7.00-£10.00

Trethias Farm, St Merryn PL28 8PL ☎Padstow (01841) 520323 OS map 200/865734 4m WSW of Padstow off B3276 (Newquay) on Treyarnon Beach road–signposted Open Apr-Sept 128 pitches (65 static) Level grass £7.25-£8.50

Trevean Farm Caravan and Camping, St Merryn PL28 8PR ☎Padstow (01841) 520772 OS map 200/875724 4m SW of Padstow off B3276 (Newquay) on Rumford road–signposted Open Apr-Oct 39 pitches 2 acres level grass £7.00-£8.00

Trewince Farm Holiday Park, St Issey PL27 7RL ☎(01208) 812830 OS map 200/938714 3m SE of Padstow on right of A389 (Wadebridge) Open Easter-Oct, 120 pitches (30 static) 4½ acres, level and terraced, grass woodland walks £3.50-£4.50

Treyarnon Bay Caravan Park, Treyarnon Bay, St Merryn PL28 8JR ☎Padstow (01841) 520681 OS map 200/860737 3½m W of Padstow off B3276 (Newquay) near Treyarnon beach Open Apr-Sept 260 pitches (200 static) 22 acres grass part level/sloping part sheltered £5.00-£7.00

For other sites near Padstow see St Minver and Wadebridge

The restaurants recommended in this guide are of three kinds – inns and pubs, restaurants proper and those forming part of hotels and motels. They all serve lunch and dinner – at a reasonable price – say under £10 a head. We shall be glad to have your comments on any you use this season and if you think they are not up to standard to have your suggestions for alternatives.

PAIGNTON, Devon   **Map G5**
Pop 35,100. EC Wed SEE zoo, Oldway Mansion, Kirkham House, St John's church, harbour, aquarium ☒ Esplanade ☎(01803) 558383 Restaurant: Inn on the Green, Esplanade Rd ☎(01803) 557841

Barton Pines Inn, Blagdon Road, Higher Blagdon TQ3 3YG *Touring site in wooded grounds of charming inn with extensive views* ☎Paignton (01803) 553350 OS map 202/847612 2½m W of Paignton off A380 (Marldon)–signposted Open Mar-Oct–must book peak periods 33 pitches Level/sloping grass, sheltered (heated) tennis £5.00-£18.75 (Mastercard/Visa)

Beverley Park, Goodrington Road TQ4 7JE ☎(01803) 843887 OS map 202/886576 1½m S of Paignton off A379 (Dartmouth) Open Easter-Oct–must book 391 pitches (197 static) Grass, level, open, hard standings (heated, indoor and outdoor) tennis, ballroom, sauna £9.00-£20.00 (Mastercard/Visa)

Byslades Camping and Touring Park, Totnes Road TQ4 7PY *Well equipped site for tourers two miles from safe beaches* ☎Paignton (01803) 555072 OS map 202/848602 2m W of Paignton on A385 (Totnes) Open Easter-Sept 170 pitches 23 acres, grass and hard standings (heated) children's room, lic clubroom, tennis, crazy golf £5.50-£11.00 (Mastercard/Visa)

Grange Court Holiday Centre, Grange Road, Goodrington TQ4 7JP ☎Paignton (01803) 558010 OS map 202/888588 1½m S of Paignton on A379 (Dartmouth) Open Feb 15-Jan 15 677 pitches (520 static) Level/sloping grass and hard standings sep pitches, lic club/bar, steam room, solarium, snooker, boules £8.00-£19.00 inc showers

Higher Well Farm Holiday Park, Stoke Gabriel TQ9 6RN ☎(01803) 782289 OS map 202/585856 4m W of Paignton off A385 (Totnes) at Parkers Arms Hotel on Stoke Gabriel road Open Easter-Nov 98 pitches Level/sloping grass, sheltered (18) £5.50-£8.50

Holly Gruit Camp, Brixham Road TQ4 7BA ☎Paignton (01803) 550763 OS map 202/876586 2m SW of Paignton on A3022 (Newton Abbot-Brixham) ring road near garden centre Open Easter-Oct 70 pitches snack bar, children's room £7.00-£8.50

Lower Yalberton Caravan and Camping Park, Long Road TQ4 7PH ☎Paignton (01803) 558127 OS map 202/863586 2½m SW of Paignton off A380 (Brixham) ring road Open May-Sept 543 pitches 8 acres level/sloping grass (heated) disco £7.00-£10.50

Marine Park Holiday Centre, Grange Road, Goodrington TQ4 7JR ☎(01803) 843887 OS map 202/888582 1½m SW of Paignton off A3022 (Brixham) ring road Open May-Sept 88 pitches (66 static) Grass, level/sloping, sheltered £9.00-£17.00 (all cards)

Orchard Park, Totnes Road TQ4 7PW ☎Paignton (01803) 550504 OS map 202/854601 1m W of Paignton on right of A385 (Totnes) in grounds of manor house Open mid Mar-Oct, 200 pitches 17 acres, part level (snack), £5.00-£13.00

Paignton Holiday Park, Totnes Road TQ4 7PY ☎Paignton (01803) 550504 OS map 202/855603 2m W of Paignton on right of A385 (Totnes) Open Mar-Oct 250 pitches (82 static)–must book Jul-Aug 14 acres, grass and hard standing (heated) entertainment £6.00-£11.50 (Mastercard/Visa)

Ramslade Touring Park, Stoke Road, Stoke Gabriel TQ9 6QB ☎(01803) 782575 OS map 202/857588 3m SW of Paignton off A385 (Totnes) at Parkers Arms, Collaton Open mid Mar-end Oct 135 pitches 8 acres, grass, level/sloping, hard standings, sheltered (Jul-Aug) paddling pool, serviced pitches £8.80-£12.80 (all major cards)

Whitehill Farm Holiday Park, Stoke Road TQ4 7PF ☎(01803) 782338 Fax (01803) 782722 OS map 202/857588 2m W of Paignton off A385 (Totnes) on Stoke Gabriel road Open May-Sept (families and couples only) 400 pitches (60 static) 20 acres, gentle slope and level grass (heated) £6.50-£10.00

Widend Caravan and Camping Park, Berry Pomeroy Road, Marldon TQ3 1RT ☎Paignton (01803) 550116 2m NW of Paignton on right of Marldon-Berry Pomeroy road Open Easter-Oct, 207 pitches 22 acres, level grass, sheltered, some hard standings (heated) (Jul Aug) £5.50-£10.00 (Mastercard/Visa/Delta/Switch)

PAR–see St Austell

PARRACOMBE–see Lynton

The distance and direction of a campsite is given from the centre of the key town under which it appears, the place name in parentheses following the road number indicating which route to take.

PENRYN, Cornwall **Map C6**
Pop 5,090. EC Thurs SEE St Gluvias church, Seven Stars Inn, museum, town hall Restaurant: Quayside 2m SE at Falmouth (01326) 312113

Calamankey Farm, Longdowns TR10 9DL (01209) 860314 OS map 204/745342 2½m W of Penryn on A394 (Helston) Open Apr-Oct 60 pitches–no trailer caravans 3 acres, gentle slope £8.00

PENZANCE, Cornwall **Map A6**
Pop 19,570. EC Wed, MD Tues, Thurs, Sat SEE nautical museum, geological museum, Gulval church, Penlee memorial park, Chysauster prehistoric village 3m N, Trengwainton gardens 2m NW Station Rd (01736) 62207 Restaurant: Fountain Tavern, St Clare St (01736) 62673

Bone Valley Caravan Camping Park, Heamoor TR20 8UJ Penzance (01736) 360313 OS map 203/463313 1m N of Penzance on B3312 (Madron) Open Mar-Dec–booking advisable Jul-Aug 17 pitches Level grass and hard standing, sheltered battery charging, ice pack service £8.50-£10.50

For other sites near Penzance see Marazion and St Buryan

PERRANARWORTHAL–see Penryn

PERRANPORTH, Cornwall **Map B5**
Pop 1,750. SEE open air theatre, St Agnes Head, Perran Bay Restaurant: Beach Dunes 1m N at Reen Sands (01872) 572263

Monkey Tree Farm Tourist Park, Rejerrah TR8 5QL (01872) 572032 OS map 200/802552 3m NE of Perranporth on A3075 (Redruth–Newquay) Open Apr-Oct 295 pitches Grass and hard standing, level, part sheltered snack bar, sauna, solarium £5.00-£10.00

Newperran Tourist Park, Rejerrah TR8 5QJ (01872) 572407 OS map 200/792543 2½m E of Perranporth off B3285 (Goonhavern) and A3075 (Newquay) Open May-Sept 270 pitches Level grass and hard standing (heated) crazy golf £5.95-£9.20

Penrose Farm Touring Park, Goonhavern TR4 9QF (01872) 573185 OS map 200/795534 2½m E of Perranporth on B3285 (Indian Queens) in Goonhavern Open Apr-Sept 100 pitches–families and couples only 9 acres level grass and hard standing, sheltered £8.00-£12.00 (all cards)

Perranporth Touring Park, Budnick Rd TR6 0DB (01872) 572174 OS map 200/190/758543 ¼ NE of Perranporth on B3285 (Goonhavern) Open Apr 17-Sept 30, 235 pitches–booking advisable Grass and hard standing, level/sloping, sheltered (heated) snack bar, club bar £6.00-£10.00

Perran Quay Tourist Park, Hendra Croft, Rejerrah TR8 5QP (01872) 572561 OS map 200/800550 3m NE of Perranporth on A3075 (Redruth–Newquay) Open Easter-Oct 135 pitches Grass and hard standings, level, sheltered babies' room, lounge, first aid, barbecue, paddling pool, games room £4.50-£9.20

Perran Sands Holiday Park, TR6 0AQ (01872) 573742 OS map 200/768548 ½m NE of Perranporth off B3285 (Goonhavern) Open mid May-Sept 950 pitches (450 static) 500 acres, dunes and grass, mainly level tent hire, entertainment £9.50-£23.50 (all major cards)

Rosehill Farm Tourist Park, Goonhavern TR4 9LA (01872) 572448 OS map 200/786539 2m E of Perranporth on B3285 (Goonhavern) Open Apr-Oct 65 pitches 7 acres level grass, sheltered £5.00-£8.50

Silverbow Park, Goonhavern TR4 9NX (01872) 572347 OS map 200/781531 2m ESE of Perranporth on A3075 (Newquay-Redruth) Open May-Oct 100 pitches 24 acres, level/sloping grass, hard standings, sheltered (heated) sep pitches, badminton, tennis, serviced pitches, short mat bowls £6.00-£14.00

See also St Agnes and Crantock

See listing on page 190

PLYMOUTH, Devon   **Map E5**
Pop 255,200 ⚅ Island House, 9 The Barbican ✆Plymouth (01752) 264849 SEE The Hoe, St
Andrew's church, Smeaton's Tower (aquarium), cathedral (RC), Barbican (maze of alleys), Saltram
House 3m E Restaurant: China House, Sutton Wharf (off Sutton Rd) ✆(01752) 260930

Brixton Camping Site, Venn Farm, Brixton PL8 2AX ✆Plymouth (01752) 880378 OS map
  202/548520 6m SE of Plymouth on A379 (Kingsbridge) Open Easter-Oct 43 pitches Grass, level,
  sheltered ⬛ £4.25-£5.50

Riverside Caravan Park, Longbridge Road, Marshmills, Plympton PL6 8LD ✆Plymouth (01752)
  344122 OS map 201/517576 3m E of Plymouth near junction of A38 (Bodmin-Exeter) and A374
  (Longridge-Plympton) Open all year 292 pitches Hard standings, level grass, sheltered
  ⬛✗⬤↩⬈⬛⬛⬥⬤∅⬜ (heated) ⬤↩⬜⬛ £7.50-£10.00 (Mastercard/Visa)

POLPERRO, Cornwall   **Map D5**
Pop 920. EC Sat SEE museum (of smuggling), `The House on the Props', chapel cliff Restaurant:
Three Pilchards, The Quay ✆(01503) 72233

Killigarth Manor Holiday Estate PL13 2JQ ✆Polperro (01503) 72216 OS map 201/215516 1m N
  of Polperro off A387 (Looe) Open May-Oct 350 pitches (150 static) 6½ acres level grass
  ⬛✗⬤↩⬛⬛⬥⬤∅⬜↩⬜⬛⬜ lic club £8.20

POLRUAN–see Fowey

POLZEATH, Cornwall   **Map C4**
Pop 250 Small resort on Padstow Bay SEE surfing beach, Pentire headland Restaurant: White
Lodge, Old Polzeath ✆(01208) 862370

Southwinds Caravan Camping Park PL27 6QU ✆Polzeath (01208) 863267 OS map 200/948791
  ½m E of Polzeath on St Minver road Open Easter-Oct 100 pitches 10 acres level grass, sheltered
  ⬛⬛⬥⬤∅⬤⬤↩⬥ path to beach £8.00-£15.00

Tristram Caravan Camping Park, Cliff Top PL27 6SR ✆Polzeath (01208) 862215/863267 OS
  map 200/934790 On W outskirts of Polzeath overlooking Hayle Bay Open Mar-Nov 140 pitches
  10 acres level grass, sheltered ⬛✗⬤⬈⬛⬛⬥⬤∅⬤↩⬜ own access to beach £15.00-£30.00
  (Mastercard/Visa)

PORTH–see Newquay

PORTHTOWAN–see Redruth

PORTSCATHO, Cornwall   **Map C6**
Pop 500 Attractive fishing village backed by lovely scenery SEE quay, Porthcurnick beach N, St
Anthony Head 3m SW Restaurant: Plume of Feathers ✆(01872) 580321

Trewince Manor TR2 5ET ✆Portscatho (01872) 580289 OS map 204/868339 ¾m S of Portscatho
  on St Anthony road Open Jul-Aug 54 pitches 6 acres, level/sloping grass ⬛✗⬤↩⬈⬛⬛⬥⬤
  ∅⬤⬜⬛⬥ games room, moorings (own quay and river frontage) £12.00-£18.00 inc elect (most
  cards)

POUNDSTOCK, Cornwall   **Map D3**
Pop 200 SEE church, 14c guildhall (now barn), Penfound Manor 1m E on Longford Barton road
Restaurant: Bideford Inn 5m N at Stratton ✆(01288) 352033

Budemeadows Touring Holiday Park EX23 0NA ✆Widemouth Bay (01288) 361646 OS map
  190/215014 2m NE of Poundstock on right of A39 (Bideford) Open all year, 100 pitches 9½
  acres, grass and hard standings, part level ⬛↩⬛⬛⬥⬤∅⬜⬤⬤↩⬜⬛⬛ barbecues, games
  room £8.40-£12.00 (Mastercard/Visa/Switch)

Cornish Coasts Caravan Camping Park, Middle Penlean EX23 0EE ✆(01288) 361380 OS map
  190/204983 ½m S of Poundstock on right of A39 (Camelford) Open Apr-Oct 45 pitches 4 acres,
  grass, part level, part sheltered, hard standings ⬛⬛⬥⬤∅⬤↩⬜ £4.50-£7.50

Penhalt Farm Holiday Park EX23 0DG ✆Widemouth Bay (01288) 361210 OS map 190/194003
  ½m NW of Poundstock on Millook road Open Easter-Oct, 100 pitches 8 acres, level/gentle slope,
  grass and hard standing ⬛⬛⬥⬤∅⬤⬤↩⬜⬛⬥ £5.00-£11.00

Widemouth Bay Caravan Park, Great Wanson EX23 0DF ✆Widemouth Bay (01288) 361208 OS
  map 190/199008 3m NW of Poundstock on Wanson road via Coppathorne Open Easter-Sept,
  467 pitches (132 static) ⬛✗ (snack), ↩⬛⬛⬥⬤∅⬜ (heated), ↩⬜ games room, lic club,
  entertainment (high season) £5.00-£15.00

See also Bude

PRAA SANDS–see Helston

PRINCETOWN, Devon   Map E4
Pop 1,500 Restaurant: Plume of Feathers ✆ (01822) 890240
Plume of Feathers Inn PL20 6QG ✆ (01822) 890240 OS map 191/587735 100m SE of Princetown centre near junction of B3212 (Yelverton) and Tavistock road Open all year 85 pitches–no trailer caravans 2½ acres level grass and hard standings sheltered £3.00-£4.00

REDRUTH, Cornwall   Map B6
Pop 10,180. EC Thurs, MD Fri SEE Murdoch's House, Carn Brea hill fort Restaurant: Fox and Hounds at Scorrier ✆ (01209) 820205
Cambrose Touring Park, Portreath Road TR16 4HT ✆ (01209) 890747 OS map 203/687455 2m W of Redruth on B3300 (Portreath) Open Mar-Oct 60 pitches Level grass, sheltered (heated) £7.00-£10.50
Chacewater Camping Caravan Park, Cox Hill, Chacewater TR4 8LY ✆ St Day (01209) 820762 OS map 204/738438 3m E of Redruth off A390 (Truro) Open Apr-Oct 100 pitches–adults over 30 only Level grass and hard standing, sheltered £9.00 (most cards)
Lanyon Holiday Park, Loscombe Lane, Four Lanes TR16 6LP ✆ (01209) 313474 OS map 203/685387 3m S of Redruth off B3297 (Helston) at Four Lanes–signposted Open Apr-Oct 75 pitches (50 static) Level grass (heated) pool room £4.50-£12.00 (all cards)
Porthtowan Tourist Park, Mile Hill, Porthtowan TR4 8TY ✆ Porthtowan (01209) 890256 OS map 203/694465 2m N of Redruth off Porthtowan road Open Easter-Oct 60 pitches 5 acres, level grass, sheltered table tennis £5.00-£9.00
Rose Hill Touring Park, Rose Hill, Porthtowan TR4 8AR *Sheltered quiet woodland site 4 mins walk to beach* ✆ Porthtowan (01209) 890802 OS map 203/693473 3½m N of Redruth at Porthtowan near beach Open Mar-Oct 50 pitches Level grass and hard standings, sheltered £7.00-£12.00
Tehidy Holiday Park, Harris Mill, Illogan TR16 4JQ ✆ Redruth (01209) 216489 OS map 203/682434 1½m NW of Redruth off B3300 (Portreath) Open Apr-Oct 38 pitches 4½ acres level/sloping grass, sheltered £6.50-£8.00 (most cards)
Tresaddern Holiday Park, St Day TR16 5JR ✆ St Day (01209) 820459 OS map 204/733422 2m E of Redruth on B3298 (St Day) Open Apr-Oct 32 pitches 2 acres, grass, level/sloping £6.00-£7.00
Wheal Rose Caravan Camping Park, Wheal Rose, Scorrier TR16 5DD *Secluded family-run park with spotless facs central for West Cornwall* ✆ (01209) 891496 OS map 203/715448 1m NE of Redruth off A30 (Truro) on Porthtowan road Open Mar-Dec 50 pitches Level grass and hard standing, sheltered £7.00-£11.00

RUAN MINOR–see Lizard

ST AGNES, Cornwall   Map B5
Pop 2,000. EC Wed SEE church, harbour, St Agnes Head, Trevaunance Cove, Tin mine engine houses, view from St Agnes Beacon (700 ft) accessible by car Restaurant: Railway Inn, Vicarage Rd ✆ (01872) 552310
Beacon Cottage Farm Touring Park, Beacon Drive TR5 0NU ✆ St Agnes (01872) 552347 OS map 203/705501 2m W of St Agnes off Beacon Drive Open May-Oct 50 pitches 2 acres level grass sheltered dog walk £5.00-£14.00
Chiverton Caravan and Touring Park, Blackwater TR4 8HS ✆ (01872) 560667 OS map 204/743468 2½m SE of St Agnes on B3277 (Three Burrows) near junction with A30-A390 Open Apr-Oct 70 pitches (40 static) 2 acres level grass £5.00-£7.00
Presingoll Farm TR5 0PB ✆ (01872) 552333 OS map 204/190/721494 1m S of St Agnes on B3277 (Truro) Open Apr-Oct 90 pitches 3½acres, level grass farm produce £5.00
Trevarth Holiday Park, Blackwater TR4 8HR ✆ (01872) 560266 OS map 204/743469 3m SE of St Agnes off B3277 (Truro) and Chiverton roundabout (A30) on Blackwater road Open Apr-Oct 75 pitches (20 static) 4½ acres level grass, sheltered £5.00-£8.00 (Mastercard/Visa)

ST AUSTELL, Cornwall   **Map C5**
Pop 19,860. EC Thurs SEE old inns, church, china clay quarries (tours), market house Restaurant:
White Hart, Church St ☎(01726) 872100

Carlyon Bay Caravan Camping Park, Cypress Avenue, Carlyon Bay PL25 3RE ☎(01726) 812735
    OS map 200/052527 2½m E of St Austell on A390 (St Blazey) at Britannia Inn roundabout Open
    Easter-Oct—must book peak periods 180 pitches 32 acres, grass, level, sheltered
    ▨➤◨◳◔◈▱ (heated) ◀▢ footpath to beach £7.00-£16.00 (most cards)

Par Sands Holiday Park, Par PL24 2AS *Sheltered site behind Par beach* ☎(01726) 812868 OS
    map 204/084535 4m E of St Austell off A3082 (Par Sands) Open Apr-Sept 375 pitches (210
    static) Level grass ▨➤◨◳◔◈⊘▱ (indoor heated) ◈◀▱♿ café, crazy golf, tennis, bowls,
    cycle hire £6.00-£14.00 (Mastercard/Visa)

Penhaven Touring Park, Pentewan PL26 6DL *Landscaped site in wooded valley* ☎(01726)
    843687 Fax (01726) 843870 OS map 204/015475 2m S of St Austell on left of B3273
    (Mevagissey) Open Apr-Oct, 105 pitches 13½ acres, level grass and hard standings, sheltered
    ▨➤▸◨◳◔◈⊘▱◀◉♿ bike hire £8.40-£17.50 (most cards)

River Valley Holiday Park, London Apprentice PL26 7AP ☎St Austell (01726) 73533 OS map
    204/008504 1½m S of St Austell on B3273 (Mevagissey) Open Apr 12-Oct 31, 60 pitches Level
    grass, sheltered ▨◨◳◔◈⊘▱ (heated) ◈◀◉▱ bike hire, pitch and putt, boules £6.00-
    £12.00

Trencreek Farm Holiday Park, Hewaswater PL26 7JG ☎St Austell (01726) 882540 OS map
    204/965485 3m SW of St Austell on B3287 (Tregony) Open Apr-Oct—must book peak periods
    178 pitches (38 static) Grass, part level, sheltered ▨➤▸◨◳◔◈⊘▱ (heated) ◈◀▢▱
    ⌂♿ fishing, tennis court, pitch and putt, fitness and agility course £5.50-£12.00 (most cards)

Trewhiddle Holiday Estate, Pentewan Road PL26 7AD ☎(01726) 67011 Fax (01726) 67010 OS
    map 204/005512 1m S of St Austell on B3273 (Mevagissey) Open all year 105 pitches (68
    static) 16 acres level/sloping grass and hard standings, sheltered ▨✕◲➤◨◳◔◈⊘▱◈◀▢
    ▱ lic club, games room £6.00-£12.00 (most cards)

See also Mevagissey

ST BURYAN, Cornwall   **Map A6**
Pop 400 SEE granite church, Boscawen stone circle Restaurant: Old Success Inn 3m W at Sennen
Cove ☎(01736) 871232

Boleigh Farm, Lamorna TR19 6BN ☎St Buryan (01736) 810305 OS map 203/434249 1½m SE of
    St Buryan on B3315 (Penzance-Land's End) Open Easter-Oct 30 pitches 1½ acres level grass,
    sheltered ◳◈ £6.00

Lower Treave Caravan Park, Crows an Wra TR19 6HZ ☎St Buryan (01736) 810559 OS map
    203/387273 2m NW of St Buryan on A30 (Penzance-Land's End) Open Apr-Oct 85 pitches 4½
    acres, terraced/level grass ▨◨◳◔◈⊘▱ £6.50-£8.50 (most cards)

Tower Park, TR19 6BZ ☎St Buryan (01736) 810286 OS map 203/405263 ¼m NW of St Buryan
    on right of St Just road Open Easter-Oct 112 pitches 12 acres, level grass, sheltered
    ▨➤◨◳◔◈⊘◀▢▱♿ £6.00-£8.50

Treverven Touring Caravan and Camp Site, TR19 6DL ☎St Buryan (01736) 810221 OS map
    203/413238 1m S of St Buryan on B3315 (Newlyn-Treen) Open Apr-Oct 115 pitches 6 acres
    level grass ▨ (mobile) ◨◳◔◈⊘◀ £5.00-£9.00

See listing under Redruth

Lanyon Holiday Park

REDRUTH TR16 6LP

Good-value family-run park in the heart of beautiful
Cornish countryside, an ideal location for touring
or just staying put. Why not try us?

Tel Mr or Mrs Reilly on 01209 313474

See listing under Redruth

ST COLUMB, Cornwall   Map C5
Pop 2,740. EC Wed, MD Mon Restaurant: Falcon 2½m N at St Mawgan ☎(01637) 860225
Music Water Touring Site, Rumford PL27 7SJ ☎(01841) 540257 OS map 200/906685 3m N of St
  Columb off A39 (Wadebridge) and B3274 (Padstow) Open Apr-Oct, 140 pitches 8 acres, grass,
  level/gentle slope, sheltered 🛒🍷⊶🏹🗄🍴⊘🛢⊕∅⊠✓🛢⊛🏪 £4.00-£7.00
Trekenning Tourist Park, TR8 4JF *Well equipped site in peaceful setting* ☎St Columb (01637)
  880462 OS map 200/907625 ½m S of St Columb at junction of A39 (Truro) and A3059
  (Newquay) Open Apr-Oct 75 pitches Grass and hard standings, level/sloping, sheltered 🛒✖
  (café) 🍷🏹🗄🍴⊘⊕∅⊠⊕✓🛢⊛🚃 £7.50-£10.80 (all cards)

ST DAY–see Redruth

ST ISSEY–see Padstow

ST IVES, Cornwall   Map B6
Pop 13,500. EC Thurs, MD Mon, Fri Old fishing port which became a centre for artists in the 1880s
SEE All Saint's church, stone bridge and chapel, Norris Museum, Porthmeor surfing beach, Barbara
Hepworth museum, Tate Gallery ℹ The Guildhall, Street-an-Pol ☎(01736) 796297 Restaurant:
Chy-an-Drea, The Terrace ☎(01736) 795076
Ayr Holiday Park, Higher Ayr TR26 1EJ *Nearest site to town centre, on cliffside above bay* ☎St
  Ives (01736) 795855 OS map 203/515407 ½m W of St Ives off B3306 (St Just) Open Apr-Oct 80
  pitches (43 static) Level grass and hard standings 🛒🗄🍴⊘⊕∅✓ £6.00-£10.00 (inc showers)
Balnoon Campsite, Halsetown TR26 3JA ☎(01736) 795431 OS map 203/510390 2m SW of St
  Ives off B3311 (Penzance) at Halsetown Open Apr-Oct 25 pitches 1 acre level grass 🛒⊘⊕
  £6.00-£10.00
Hellesveor Caravan and Camping Site, TR26 3AD ☎St Ives (01736) 795738 OS map
  203/503401 1m W of St Ives on right of B3306 (St Just) Open Easter-Oct 20 pitches 1 acre,
  level grass 🛒🗄🍴⊘∅🛢 £6.00-£10.00
Higher Chellew Campsite, Nancledra TR20 8BD ☎(01736) 364532 OS map 203/498351 3m S of
  St Ives on B3311 (Penzance) Open Mar-Oct 30 pitches 1½ acres level grass, sheltered 🗄⊕
  £5.00-£8.50
Penderleath Caravan and Camping Park, Towednack TR26 3AF ☎(01736) 798403 OS map
  203/497375 2m SW of St Ives off B3311 (Penzance) Open Easter-Oct 75 pitches 8 acres level
  and sloping grass 🛒✖🍷⊶🏹🗄🍴⊘⊕∅⊕✓🛢♿ £6.00-£12.00
Polmanter Tourist Park, Halsetown TR26 3LX *Inland site in quiet location* ☎(01736) 795640 OS
  map 203/512388 1½m SW of St Ives off B3311 (Penzance) Open Apr-Oct 240 pitches 12 acres
  level grass and hard standings 🛒✖🍷⊶🏹🗄🍴⊘⊕∅⊠ (heated) ⊕✓🏪 paddling pools,
  tennis £7.00-£13.50
Trevalgan Holiday Farm TR26 3BJ ☎(01736) 796433 OS map 203/490400 1½m W of St Ives off
  B3306 (Land's End) Open May-Sept 120 pitches 5 acres, level grass 🛒⊶🏹🗄🍴⊘⊕∅⊕✓
  🗄🚃 games room, pets corner, picnic area, farm trail, barbecue, crazy golf £7.00-£11.40
  (Mastercard/Visa)

ST JUST IN PENWITH, Cornwall   **Map A6**
Pop 4,020. EC Thurs Quiet resort on cliffs of Penwith peninsula, most westerly in England, along rugged coast of which are sheltered coves accessible only on foot SEE tin mining museum, 15c church, cape Cornwall 1m W, Pendeen Watch (view) Restaurant: Star, Fore St ☎ (01736) 788767

Bosavern House TR19 7RD *Small site in enclosed garden* ☎ (01736) 788301 OS map 203/371305 ½m S of St Just on left of B3306 (Land's End) in grounds of manor house Open Mar-Oct, 12 pitches 1 acre, level grass, sheltered ▯◨▤▯▨▯ £10.75 inc electricity and awning (most cards)

Higher Tregiffian Farm (Camping Club), St Buryan TR19 6JB ☎ (01736) 871588 OS map 203/378276 2m S of St Just on right of B3306 (Land's End) Open Mar 23-Sept 28, 75 pitches–adv booking min 2 nights ▯▤▯◨▯�& £6.00-£9.00 plus £4.00 non-member pitch fee

Kelynack Caravan Camping Park TR19 7RE ☎ (01736) 787633 OS map 203/373301 ¾m S of St Just off B3306 (Land's End) Open Easter-Oct 37 pitches Level grass and hard standing, sheltered ▮▯◨▤◨▯▨▯◻▯& camping barn £6.00

Levant Caravan Camping Park, Levant Road, Pendeen TR19 7SX ☎ (01736) 788795 OS map 203/374337 2½m N of St Just off B3306 (St Ives) Open Apr-Oct 43 pitches Level/sloping grass ▮◨◨◨ £6.00-£7.00

Roselands Caravan Park, Dowran TR19 7RS *Small site in remote rural setting* ☎ St Just (01736) 788571 OS map 203/387305 1m SE of St Just off A3071 (Penzance) on Sancreed road Open Jan-Oct 30 pitches 3 acres level grass, sheltered ▮▯◨◨▤◨▯◨▯◻▯◨▯ £5.00-£8.00

Trevaylor Caravan Park, Truthwall TR19 7PU ☎ (01736) 787016 OS map 203/368325 1m N of St Just on B3306 (St Ives) Open Easter-Oct 55 pitches 6 acres, level grass, sheltered ▮◨↗▯◨▤◨▯◨▯ bar and bar food £6.20-£7.50

ST KEW HIGHWAY–see Wadebridge

ST MABYN–see Bodmin

ST MAWES, Cornwall   **Map C6**
Pop 1,100. SEE castle, waterfront Restaurant: St Mawes, The Seafront ☎ (01326) 270266

Trethem Mill Touring Park, St Just in Roseland TR2 5JF ☎ (01872) 580504 OS map 204/862364 2m N of St Mawes on A3078 (Tregony) Open Apr-Oct 90 pitches Level/sloping grass and hard standings ▮↗▯◨▤◨▯◨▯◻ £7.00-£11.00 (most cards)

ST MERRYN–see Padstow

ST MINVER, Cornwall   **Map C4**
Pop 780 EC Thurs SEE church, beaches of Polzeath (2m NW) and Rock (2m SW) Restaurant: Four Ways ☎ (01208) 862384

Dinham Farm Caravan-Camping Park, PL27 6RH ☎ (01208) 812878 OS map 200/971750 1m S of St Minver off B3314 (Wadebridge) on Treganna road Open Apr-Oct 60 pitches Level/sloping grass, sheltered ▯◨▤◨▯◻ (heated) ◨◻▯◻▦ 7.00-£8.00

Gunvenna Touring Caravan and Camping Park, PL27 6QN ☎ (01208) 862405 OS map 200/968782 ½m N of St Minver on right of B3314 (Port Isaac) Open Apr-Oct (no groups of single persons unless members of a bona fide club) 75 pitches Level grass ▮✕▯◨▯◨▯▤◨▯◻ (heated, indoor) ◨▯▦& £7.00-£12.00

St Minver House Holiday Estate, PL27 6RR ☎ (01208) 862305 OS map 200/965767 1m S of St Minver off B3314 (Delabole–Wadebridge) Open Easter/Apr-Oct 315 pitches (200 static) Level grass ▮▯◨▯◨▤◨◻◨◻▯◻ lic club, snack bar, amusements £8.50-£17.00 (inc showers)
See also Polzeath

ST TUDY–see Camelford

Travelling to and from the West Country, try to avoid Friday evenings or Saturdays in July, August and September. On Saturdays in July and August there may well be traffic jams on M5 southbound between junctions 14 and 20. If you have to use the motorway on a Saturday during these months try to time your journey to be outside the peak hours of 0600 to 1400. Motorists should also avoid the Tamar Bridge at Saltash on the A38 west of Plymouth at peak times, particularly on Saturdays in July and August between 0900 and 1600.

SALCOMBE, Devon   Map F6
Pop 2,450. EC Wed Superb coastal scenery, a gentle climate and good beaches explain this resort's popularity SEE site, maritime museum, Bolt Head cliffs (400ft) 🅸 Council Hall, Market St ✆(01548) 843927/842736 Restaurant: Ferry Inn, Ferry Steps (off High St) ✆(01548) 844000

Alston Farm Caravan and Camping Site, Malborough TQ7 3BJ ✆Kingsbridge (01548) 561260 OS map 202/717407 2m N of Salcombe off A381 (Kingsbridge) Open Easter-Oct 300 pitches (40 static) Level/sloping grass, sheltered ♨🗑🚿🔌⊛∅🔵🅿 £6.00-£10.50

Bolberry House Farm, Bolberry, Malborough TQ7 3DY *Family-run park near sandy beach* ✆(01548) 561251/560926 OS map 202/688394 3m W of Salcombe off A381 (Kingsbridge) at Malborough Open Easter-Oct 70 pitches 5½ acres level grass ♨🗑🚿🔌⊛∅🐕🚐 freezer pack service, dog exercise area £6.50-£9.50

Higher Rew Farm, Malborough TQ7 3DW ✆Salcombe (01548) 842681 OS map 202/714383 3m W of Salcombe off A381 (Kings bridge) and Soar road via Malborough Open Mar-Oct 90 pitches 4 acres, level/gentle slope, grass ♨🗑🚿🔌⊛∅🔵🐕🚐 £6.00-£9.00

Karrageen Caravan and Camping Park, Bolberry, Malborough TQ7 3EN ✆Kingsbridge (01548) 561230 Fax (01548) 560192 OS map 202/689394 3m W of Salcombe off A381 (Kingsbridge) at Malborough on Bolberry road Open Mar 15-Nov 15 95 pitches 7½ acres grass, level/sloping, terraced ♨🚐🏹🗑🚿🔌⊛∅🔵♿ freezer pack service, baby room £7.00-£11.00

Sun Park, Soar TQ7 3DS ✆Kingsbridge (01548) 561378 OS map 202/708378 3m W of Salcombe off A381 (Kingsbridge) at Marlborough on Soar road Open Easter-Oct 98 pitches (33 static) 5 acres, level grass 🗑🚿∅⊛∅🔵🐕🗄🚐 games room £6.00-£9.00

SALCOMBE REGIS–see Sidmouth

SALTASH, Cornwall   Map E5
Pop 13,700. EC Thurs SEE Saltash Quay, Tamar bridge, Ince Castle 4m W Restaurant: Holland Inn, 2m NW at Hatt ✆(01752) 853635

Dolbeare Caravan Camping Park, St Ive Road, Landrake PL12 5AF ✆Landrake (01752) 851332 OS map 201/364615 4m NW of Saltash off A38 (Liskeard) on Blunts road Open all year 60 pitches Level/sloping grass and hard standings, sheltered ♨🗑🚿🔌⊛∅🔵🐕🚐 £5.50-£8.50

Notter Bridge Caravan and Camping Park, Notter Bridge PL12 4RW ✆Saltash (01752) 842318 OS map 201/385609 3½m NW of Saltash on A38 (Liskeard) Open Apr-Sept 56 pitches 5 acres, level grass, sheltered 🗑🚿∅⊛∅🔵🐕🚐🗄 fishing, canoeing £5.00-£7.00

SAMPFORD PEVERELL, Devon   Map G3
Pop 950 EC Wed SEE 12c church Restaurant: Globe, Lower Town ✆(01884) 821214

Minnows Caravan Camping Park EX16 7EN ✆(01884) 821770 OS map 181/040147 ½m E of Sampford Peverell off A361 (Tiverton-Barnstaple) on Holcombe Rogus road by Grand Western canal, near junct 27 of M5 Open Mar-Nov 45 pitches Level hard standings 🚿∅⊛∅🐕♿ service pitches, freezer pack service, fishing, boating £7.65-£12.25 inc elect (most cards)

SEATON, Cornwall   Map D5
Pop 250 Restaurant: Halfway House 3m N on A387 at Polbathic ✆(01503) 250202

Carbeil Holiday Park, Trelidden Lane, Downderry PL11 3LS ✆(01503) 250636 OS map 201/318544 2m E of Seaton off B3247 (Millbrook) on Narkurs road–signposted Open Easter-Oct, 22 pitches–booking advisable 1¼ acres sloping grass and hard standings, sheltered ♨✗🍴🚐🗑🚿🔌⊛∅🗄🐕🚐 £5.50-£13.00

SEATON, Devon   Map H4
Pop 4,890. EC Thurs, MD Mon SEE church 🅸 The Esplanade ✆(01297) 21660 Restaurant: Dolphin, Fore St ✆(01297) 20068

Ashdown Touring Caravan Park EX13 6HY ✆Seaton (01297) 21587 OS map 192/216922 3m NW of Seaton off A3052 (Lyme Regis–Exeter) on Colyton road Open Apr-Oct, 90 pitches 5 acres, level grass ♨🗑🚿⊛∅🐕🚐 £6.00

Manor Farm Camping Site EX12 2JA ✆Seaton (01297) 21524 OS map 192/236917 1m N of Seaton on A3052 (Sidmouth-Lyme Regis) Open Mar-Oct 274 pitches 22 acres, grass, level/sloping ♨🗑🚿🔌⊛∅🐕🚐 £8.50-£10.50

CHECK BEFORE ENTERING

Beware less-than-honest site operators who give us one price for the following year and then increase it once the season gets underway. So note the charges for any site featured in this guide and before pulling in verify how much you will have to pay, and for what. If on leaving the charges turn out to be higher, ask why the difference.

SENNEN–see Land's End

SIDMOUTH, Devon   **Map G4**
Pop 11,820. EC Thurs Once fashionable watering place with wealth of Regency and Victorian architecture backing long pebble beach SEE Esplanade, museum, Beer Head E, High Peak (view) 2m W, Sidbury church 3m N ⓘ The Esplanade ✆(01395) 516441 Restaurant: The Blue Ball at Sidford ✆(01395) 514062

Kings Down Tail Caravan and Camping Park, Salcombe Regis EX10 0PD ✆(01297) 680313 OS map 192/172908 3m NE of Sidmouth on A3052 (Lyme Regis) Open Mar 15-Nov 15, 102 pitches Level grass and hard standings, sheltered ▯▯▯▯▯▯▯▯▯ £5.75-£8.00

Oakdown Touring and Holiday Home Park, Weston EX10 0PH ✆(01297) 680387 Fax (01297) 680541 OS map 192/167903 2½m NE of Sidmouth on right of A3052 (Exeter-Lyme Regis)–signposted Open Easter-Oct 166 pitches (46 static) 13½ acres, level grass and hard standing, sheltered ▯▯▯▯▯▯▯▯▯▯▯ serviced pitches, field trail to donkey sanctuary £7.75-£11.00 (Mastercard/Visa)

Salcombe Regis Caravan and Camping Park, Salcombe Regis EX10 0JH ✆(01395) 514303 OS map 192/150892 1½m E of Sidmouth off A3052 (Lyme Regis) Open Apr-Oct 110 pitches 16 acres, level grass and hard standings ▯▯▯▯▯▯▯▯▯▯ £6.50-£9.50 (Mastercard/Visa)

SOURTON CROSS–see Bridestow

SOUTH BRENT, Devon   **Map F5**
Pop 2,160. EC Wed Restaurant: Royal Oak, Station Rd ✆(01364) 72133

Cheston Caravan Park, Folly Cross, Wrangton Rd TQ10 9HF ✆ and Fax (01364) 72586 OS map 202/683586 1m SW of South Brent off A38 (Plymouth) via Wrangton Cross at Cheston–signposted Open Mar 15-Jan 15 24 pitches 1½ acres level grass, sheltered, some hard standings ▯▯▯▯▯▯▯▯ £6.00-£7.00

Edeswell Farm, Rattery TQ10 9LN ✆South Brent (01364) 72177 OS map 202/732605 2m E of South Brent on right of A385 (Cott) Open Apr-Oct 46 pitches Grass, terraced, sheltered ▯▯▯▯▯▯▯▯▯▯▯ (indoor heated) ▯▯▯▯▯▯▯ badminton £6.00-£10.00

Great Palstone Caravan Park TQ10 9JP ✆(01364) 72227 OS map 202/705601 1m E of South Brent on Exeter road (old A38) Open Mar 15-Nov 15, 50 pitches Level grass, sheltered ▯▯▯▯▯▯▯ guided walks (free) £5.00-£7.00

Webland Farm, Avonwick TQ10 9EX ✆South Brent (01364) 73273 OS map 202/714591 1½m SE of South Brent off A38/A385 junction on Webland Lane Open Mar 15-Nov 15 81 pitches (43 static) 10 acres level grass sheltered ▯▯▯▯▯▯▯ £5.00-£6.50

SOUTH MOLTON, Devon   **Map F2**
Pop 3,600. EC Wed, MD Thurs SEE Guildhall, church ⓘ 1 East Street ✆South Molton (01769) 574122 Restaurant: Stumbles, East St ✆(01769) 554145

Molland Caravan Park, Black Cock Hotel EX36 3NW ✆(01769) 550297 OS map 180/788262 4m E of South Molton off B3227 (Bampton) Open all year 65 pitches 7 acres, level/gentle slope, grass and hard standings ▯▯▯▯▯▯▯▯▯▯ (indoor) ▯▯▯▯▯▯ £8.50-£11.00 (Mastercard/Visa/Amex/Switch)

STICKLEPATH–see Okehampton

STOKE FLEMING–see Dartmouth

STOKENHAM, Devon   **Map F6**
Restaurant: Church House ✆(01548) 580253

Union Inn, Chillington TQ7 2LD ✆(01548) 580241 OS map 202/793427 1m W of Stokenham off A379 (Kingsbridge) in Chillington Open Mar 15-Oct 31, 10 pitches 1 acre level grass and gravel, sheltered ▯ (mobile) ▯▯▯▯▯ £5.00

Old Cotmore Farm, TQ7 2LR ✆(01548) 580240 OS map 202/804415 1m S of Stokenham on Start Point/East Prawle road Open Mar-Nov 30 pitches Grass, sheltered ▯▯▯▯▯▯▯▯▯ ▯▯▯▯ £8.50-£9.00 (Mastercard/Visa)

STOKE GABRIEL–see Paignton

STRATTON, Cornwall   **Map D3**
SEE parish church, Tree Inn, Poughill church (15c wall paintings) 1m NW, Launcells church (15c interior) 1m SE Restaurant: Kings Arms Inn, Howells Rd (A3092) ☎(01288) 352396

Red Post Inn and Holiday Park, Launcells EX23 9NW ☎(01288) 381305 OS map 190/265052
  2m E of Stratton on A3072 (Holsworthy) at junction with B3254 (Kilkhampton–Launceston) Open Mar-Oct, 50 pitches 3½ acres, level grass and hard standings, sheltered £4.00-£8.50

Red Post Meadows Tourist Park, Launcells EX23 9NW ☎(01288) 381306 OS map 190/263051
  2m E of Stratton on right of A3072 (Holsworthy) Open Easter-Oct, 70 pitches 8 acres, level grass, sheltered farm produce, pets corner £4.00-£4.50

Willow Valley Camping Park, Bush EX23 9LB ☎(01288) 353104 OS map 190/236078 1m N of Stratton on left of A39 (Bideford) Open Apr-Oct, 45 pitches 4 acres, level grass, sheltered £5.50-£8.50 (Mastercard/Visa/Delta/Switch)

Wooda Caravan Park, Wooda Farm, Poughill EX23 9HJ ☎(01288) 352069 OS map 190/227079
  1m N of Stratton on right of Stibb/Coombe Valley road Open Apr-Oct, 200 pitches (54 static) 12 acres, grass, part level, some hard standings (£40) fishing, pitch and putt, clay pigeon shooting, archery, pony trekking, woodland walks, pets corner £7.50-£11.00 (Mastercard/Visa/Switch)

For other sites near Stratton see Bude, Kilkhampton and Poundstock

---

SUMMERCOURT–see Indian Queens

TAVISTOCK, Devon   **Map E4**
Pop 9,180. EC Wed, MD Fri SEE Goose fair (Oct), canal port and copper mine at Morwellham 4m SW (tours), Wheal Betsy mine and Gibbet Hill (1,158ft) 5m NE ⓘ Bedford Square ☎Tavistock (01822) 612938 Restaurant: Tavistock Inn, Brook St ☎(01822) 612661

Harford Bridge Holiday Park, Peter Tavy PL19 9LS ☎(01822) 810349 Fax (01822) 810028 OS map 201/505767 2m N of Tavistock off A386 (Okehampton) on Peter Tavy road Open Mar-Nov 200 pitches (80 static) 16 acres level grass fishing, tennis £6.50-£10.50 (Mastercard/Visa)

Higher Longford Caravan Park PL19 9LQ ☎Tavistock (01822) 613360 OS map 201/518745 2m E of Tavistock on B3357 (Princetown) Open all year 80 pitches 6 acres, level grass and hard standings, sheltered £8.00-£9.00 (most cards)

Langstone Manor Caravan Park, Moortown PL19 9JZ ☎Tavistock (01822) 613371 OS map 201/525738 2m E of Tavistock off B3357 (Two Bridges) Open Mar-Nov 42 pitches £7.00-£9.00

Magpie Leisure Park, Bedford Bridge, Horrabridge PL20 7RY ☎(01822) 852651 OS map 201/506704 3m SE of Tavistock on A386 (Plymouth) Open Mar-Jan 48 pitches Level grass, sheltered fishing £5.00-£7.50

Woodovis Hoiday Park, PL19 8NY ☎Tavistock (01822) 832968 OS map 201/432744 4m W of Tavistock off A390 (Liskeard) Open Mar-Dec 84 pitches 14 acres, grass and hard standing, level, sheltered (indoor heated) mini-golf £8.50-£12.50 (Mastercard/ Visa)

TEIGNMOUTH, Devon   **Map G4**
Pop 13,500. EC Thurs Popular resort since early 19c SEE seafront, Teign road bridge (view), Ness headland E ⓘ The Den, seafront ☎(01626) 779769 Restaurant: Ship, Quayside ☎(01626) 772674

Coast View Country Club, Torquay Road, Shaldon TQ14 0BG ☎(01626) 772392 OS map 202/937718 1m S of Teignmouth on A379 (Torquay) over Shaldon Bridge Open Apr-Oct 162 pitches (50 static) 16 acres level/sloping grass and hard standings (heated) club, snack bar £6.50-£8.50

Wear Farm, Bishopsteignton TQ14 9PT ☎Teignmouth (01626) 775249 OS map 192/890732 2½m W of Teignmouth on A381 (Newton Abbot) Open Easter-Oct 247 pitches (100 static) Level grass, sheltered fishing, access to river for boats £5.00-£8.00

See also Bishopsteignton

Travelling to and from the West Country, try to avoid Friday evenings or Saturdays in July, August and September. On Saturdays in July and August there may well be traffic jams on M5 southbound between junctions 14 and 20. If you have to use the motorway on a Saturday during these months try to time your journey to be outside the peak hours of 0600 to 1400. Motorists should also avoid the Tamar Bridge at Saltash on the A38 west of Plymouth at peak times, particularly on Saturdays in July and August between 0900 and 1600.

TINTAGEL, Cornwall   **Map D4**
Pop 1,600. EC Wed, MD Thurs SEE ruined castle on headland, Old Post Office, Bossiney beach
and Rocky Valley NE Restaurant: Tintagel Arms, Fore St ☎(01840) 770780

Bossiney Farm, Bossiney PL34 0AY ☎(01840) 770481 OS map 200/066888 ¼m NE of Tintagel
on B3263 (Boscastle) Open Apr-Oct 60 pitches Level grass, sheltered ▒▯▩◐◉◻▥▦◕
£6.00-£9.00 (Mastercard/Visa)

Headland Caravan and Camping Site, PL34 0DE ☎(01840) 770239 Fax (01840) 770925 OS map
200/058888 ½m N of Tintagel off B3263 (Boscastle)–signposted Open Easter-Oct–no adv
booking 90 pitches (30 static) 5 acres, level/gentle slope, grass and hard standings
▒▯▩◐◉∅◕▥ £7.00-£8.50 (most cards)

Ocean Cove Caravan Park, Bossiney PL34 0AY ☎(01840) 770352 OS map 200/065890 1m NE
of Tintagel on B3263 (Boscastle) Open Apr-Sept 171 pitches (150 static) ▒▮▯◐▭ (heated),
sauna £5.00

Trewethett Farm, Trethevy PL34 0BQ ☎(01840) 770533 OS map 190/200/074895 1½m NE of
Tintagel off B3263 (Boscastle) Open Apr-Oct 75 pitches ▒▮⏚▯▩◐◐◉◕∎▭▦◕ bar meals,
tennis £5.00-£6.00

TORPOINT, Cornwall   **Map E5**
Pop 7,000. EC Wed SEE Antony House, Plymouth Sound Restaurant: Rising Sun on village green
4m S at Kingsand ☎(01752) 822840

Whitsand Bay Holiday Park, Mill Brook PL10 1JZ ☎(01752) 822597 OS map 201/410514 3m S
of Torpoint off A374 and B3247 (Mill Brook) on coast road Open all year 190 pitches (100 static)
Level/sloping grass, sheltered ▒✕▮⏚⏚▱▯◐◉∅ ▭ (heated) ◉◕▭◍◈▦▦ lic club,
bowling green £3.00-£25.00

TORQUAY, Devon   **Map G5**
Pop 120,000. EC Wed, Sat Resort with gentle climate, sandy beaches and favoured location
overlooking Tor Bay which developed in mid 19c after the arrival of the railway. SEE Torre Abbey,
Kent's Cavern (stalagmites and Stalactites), model village, Cockington village, museums, Torbay and
Dartmouth Railway, Compton Castle 4m NW ▮ Vaughan Parade ☎Torquay (01803) 297428
Restaurant: Devon Dumpling Inn, Shiphay Lane, Shiphay ☎(01803) 613465

Manor Farm, Daccombe TQ12 4ST ☎(01803) 328294/862395 OS map 202/903678 2m NE of
Torquay off A380 (Newton Abbot) Open May 20-Sept 20, 75 pitches 3 acres, gentle slope
▒▯◐ farm produce £7.00

Widdicombe Farm, Marldon TQ3 1ST ☎Torquay (01803) 558325 OS map 202/875634 2½m W of
Torquay off A380 (Brixham) Open Mar 15-Nov 15, 200 pitches–families and couples only Level
grass and hard standings ▒✕▮⏚▯▩◐◉◉◕◕∎▭◕ games room, club room, baby
bathroom £6.00-£12.00 (Mastercard/Visa)

TORRINGTON, Devon   **Map E3**
Pop 7,500. Market town on hill above river Torridge, a good centre for touring lovely Taw valley ▮
Town Hall, High Street ☎Torrington (01805) 624324 Restaurant: Black Horse, High St ☎(01805)
622121

Greenways Valley, EX38 7EW ☎Torrington (01805) 622153 Fax (01805) 622320 OS map
180/505185 ½m NE of Torrington off B3227 (South Molton)–signposted Open Mar 15-Oct 31
22 pitches (19 static) Level grass, sheltered ▒⏚▯▩◐◉∅▭ (heated) ◕▭▦ tennis, games
room £4.00-£8.00

Smytham Holiday Park, Little Torrington EX38 8PU ☎Torrington (01805) 622110 OS map
180/485162 2m S of Torrington on right of A386 (Hatherleigh) Open Mar 15-Oct 31, 80 pitches
(40 static) Level/sloping grass, sheltered ▒✕▮⏚▯▩◐◉◉◉▭◉◕▭◍▭▦ £7.50-
£12.50 (Mastercard/Visa)

TOTNES, Devon   **Map F5**
Pop 5,520. EC Thurs MD Tues, Fri Colourful market town on steep hill which grew up where Dart
becomes navigable SEE site, St Mary's church, castle, Butterwalk, Dart Valley Railway ▮ The
Plains, Totnes ☎(01803) 863168 Restaurant: Kingsbridge Inn, Leechwell St ☎(01803) 863324

Steamer Quay Park (Caravan Club), Steamer Quay Road TQ9 5AL ☎Totnes (01803) 862738
(0800-2000 hrs) OS map 202/807601 ½m SE of Totnes off A385 (Torbay) Open Apr-Sept, 40
pitches–must book 3 acres, level, sheltered ▯◐◉ £5.40-£6.20

See also Ipplepen

**Some site operators make it a rule that cars must be left in a separate parking area away from
caravans and tents, which can be inconvenient when shopping by car. But it does minimise
traffic noise and the risk to children.**

TREGONY, Cornwall   Map C6
Pop 550 SEE round houses at Veryan 3m S, Fal valley SW Restaurant: New Inn 2m S at Veryan
✆ (01872) 501362

Tretheake Manor Tourist Park (Camping Club), Veryan TR2 5PP ✆ and Fax (01872) 501658 OS
map 204/934414 2m S of Tregony off A3078 (St Mawes) on Veryan road–signposted Open Mar
24-Sept 29 120 pitches 9 acres, grass, mainly level, sheltered ▯▯◿◉∅ games room, coarse
fishing, serviced pitches (elect, water, drainage), recreation room £8.75-£11.55

TRURO, Cornwall   Map C5
Pop 16,500. MD Wed Georgian town which originated as major river port SEE cathedral, county
and pottery museums, Trelissick gardens 4m S ▯ Municipal Buildings, Boscawen Street ✆ Truro
(01872) 874555 Restaurant: Old Ale House, Quay St ✆ (01872) 871122

Carnon Downs Caravan and Camping Park, Carnon Downs TR3 6JJ *Quiet landscaped site with
good access* ✆ Truro (01872) 862283 OS map 204/805408 3m SW of Truro on A39 (Falmouth)
Open Apr-Oct 150 pitches 10 acres, level grass and hard standings, sheltered
▯▯▯◿∅◉❸✔▯◉▯& £6.25-£12.75 (most cards)

Leverton Place Caravan Camping Park TR4 8QW ✆ Truro (01872) 560462 OS map 204/770451
3m W of Truro off A390 (Redruth) on Chacewater road Open all year 125 pitches 9½ acres level
grass and hard standings, sheltered ▯✕♀↵∕▯▯◿◉∅▭✔ (heated) ❸✔▯◉▯◉▯&
fishing £7.00-£13.00 (inc showers)

Liskey Touring Park, Green Bottom, Chacewater TR4 8QN ✆ Truro (01872) 560274 OS map
204/769451 3½m W of Truro off A390 (Redruth) Open Apr-Sept–booking advisable Jul-Aug
60 pitches 8 acres, grass and hard standings, level/slightly sloping, sheltered ∕▯▯◿◉
∅❸✔▯ bathroom, play barn, serviced pitches £6.50-£10.50 (Mastercard/Visa)

Ringwell Valley Holiday Park, Bissoe Road, Carnon Downs TR3 6LQ ✆ Truro (01872) 862194 OS
map 204/794408 3m SW of Truro off A39 (Falmouth) at Carnon Downs Open Apr-Oct 80 pitches
(44 static) Level/sloping grass, sheltered ▯✕♀▯▯◿◉∅▭✔ pub meals £8.00-£14.00
(Mastercard/Visa)

Summer Valley Touring Park, Shortlanesend TR4 9DW ✆ Truro (01872) 877878 OS map
204/802479 2m NW of Truro on B3284 (Perranporth) Open Apr-Oct 60 pitches 3 acres, grass,
level/gentle slope ▯∕▯▯◿◉∅✔ campers lounge £7.00-£9.00

UFFCULME, Devon   Map G3
SEE Coldharbour working mill museum Restaurant: Racehorse 6m W at Tiverton ✆ (01884) 252606

Old Well Camping Park, Waterloo Cross, EX15 3ES ✆ Craddock (01884) 240873 OS map
181/058139 2m NW of Uffculme on A38 (Tiverton–Wellington) near junction 27 of M5 Open Mar-
Nov 20 pitches ▯✕↵▯◉ £3.75

Waterloo Cross Camping and Caravan Park, Waterloo Inn, Waterloo Cross EX15 3ES
✆ Craddock (01884) 240317 OS map 181/055139 2m NW of Uffculme on B3191 near junction of
A38 (Tiverton–Wellington) Open Mar 15-Nov 15, 50 pitches ▯✕◿ £5.00

UPLYME, Devon   Map H4
Quiet village N of Lyme Regis Restaurant: Pilot Boat 1m SE at Lyme Regis (Bridge St) ✆ (01297)
443157

Cannington Farm, Cannington La DT7 3SW ✆ (01297) 443172 OS map 193/318924 1m SW of
Uplyme (narrow approach) on unclass road Open Mar-Oct, 33 pitches (must book caravans) 4½
acres, level/gentle slope, sheltered £5.50-£6.00

Shrubbery Caravan Park, Rousdon DT7 3XW ✆ (01297) 442227 OS map 193/269914 2m SW of
Uplyme on right of A3052 (Lyme Regis–Colyford) Open Mar-Nov, 120 pitches–must book peak
periods 10½ acres, level grass, sheltered ▯▯◿◉❸✔▯& dairy produce £5.00-£9.00

Uplyme Touring Park, Gore La DT7 3UU *Peaceful family-run site* ✆ (01297) 442801 OS map
193/323930 ½m S of Uplyme on right of Ware road Open all year, 117 pitches 5 acres, grass,
level/sloping, some hard standing, sheltered ▯▯◿◉∅✔▭◉ £6.00-£9.00

Westhayes Caravan Park, Rousdon DT7 3RD ✆ (01297) 23436 OS map 193/287917 3m SW of
Uplyme on right of A3052 (Lyme Regis-Colyford) Open all year, 150 pitches 7 acres level grass,
sheltered ▯♀∕▯▯◿◉∅▭ (heated outdoor) ❸✔▯& £9.30-£12.50 (Mastercard/Visa)

VERYAN–see Tregony

WADEBRIDGE, Cornwall   Map C4
Pop 4,800. EC Wed, MD Mon SEE 15c bridge, Walmsley bird sanctuary 2m N Restaurant: Molesworth Arms, Molesworth St ☎(01208) 812055

Lanarth Hotel Caravan Park, St Kew Highway PL30 3EE ☎(01208) 841215 OS map 200/027749 3m NE of Wadebridge on right of A39 (Camelford) Open Apr-Oct 86 pitches Level grass, sheltered £6.50-£8.50

Laurels Touring, Hals Grave, Whitecross PL27 7JQ ☎Wadebridge (01208) 813341 OS map 200/959716 2m W of Wadebridge near junction of A39 (Truro) and A389 (Padstow) Open Easter-Oct, 30 pitches 3 acres, level grass, sheltered £9.00-£14.00

Little Bodieve Holiday Park, Bodieve PL27 6EG *Well equipped and well run site in quiet rural area* ☎Wadebridge (01208) 812323 OS map 200/990734 1m N of Wadebridge off A39 (Camelford) on B3314 (St Minver) Open Apr-Oct 270 pitches (75 static) 20 acres level grass bar meals, clubhouse, crazy golf £7.00-£10.00 (Mastercard/Visa)
For other sites near Wadebridge see Padstow, St Columb and St Minver

---

WATERGATE BAY–see Mawgan Porth

WATERLOO CROSS–see Uffculme

WESTWARD HO!, Devon   Map E2
Pop 2,090. EC Wed SEE Northam Burrows (1000 acres) Restaurant: Royal George 2m NE at Appledore ☎(01237) 474335

Pusehill Farm, Pusehill EX39 5AH ☎(01237) 474295 OS map 180/427283 ½m SW of Westward Ho! off B3236 (Abbotsham) Open Easter-Sept 60 pitches–tents and m/caravans only Grass, level, sheltered £5.00-£7.00

WHIDDON DOWN, Devon   Map F4
Restaurant: Oxenham Arms 3m W at South Zeal ☎(01837) 840244

Dartmoor View Holiday Park EX20 2QL ☎Whiddon Down (01647) 231545 OS map 191/684928 ¼m W of Whiddon Down on right of old A30 (Okehampton) Open Mar-Oct, 115 pitches (30 static) 5½ acres, part sloping grass and hard standing (heated) £7.50-£9.75 (all cards)

WHITSTONE, Cornwall   Map E3
Pop 300 SEE church, Swannacott Wood W Restaurant: Court Barn 6m E via North Tamerton at Clawton ☎(01409) 27219

Hedley Wood Caravan Camping Park, Bridgerule EX22 7ED ☎(01288) 381404 OS map 190/262015 2m N of Whitstone off B3254 (Kilk-hampton) on Widemouth Bay road Open all year, 120 pitches 16 acres, level, open or woodland, grass and hard standings dog kennelling, dog walk, nature trail £6.00-£8.00

Keywood Caravan Park, Keywood Park EX22 6TW ☎(01288) 381338 (bookings (01752) 707391) OS map 190/253997 2m NW of Whitstone on Whitstone Head road Open Easter-Oct, 75 pitches–must book peak periods 5 acres, level woodland £5.00-£6.00

WIDECOMBE IN THE MOOR, Devon   Map F4
Pop 500 SEE church, Church House (NT), Widecombe Fair (Sept), Grimspound prehistoric village 3m W Restaurant: Olde Inne ☎(01364) 621207

Cockingford Farm TQ13 7TG ☎(01364) 252258 OS map 191/718751 1m S of Widecombe on Buckland road Open May-Oct, 30 pitches–must book (caravans) 2½ acres, gentle slope £3.50-£4.00

WIDEMOUTH BAY–see Poundstock

WINKLEIGH, Devon   Map F3
Pop 1,430 SEE Ashley Countryside Collection NE Restaurant: Kings Arms, The Square ☎(01837) 83384

Wagon Wheels Holiday Park EX19 8DP ☎(01837) 83456 OS map 191/624090 1m N of Winkleigh on left of B3220 (Torrington) Open Mar 17-Oct 26, 120 pitches (100 static) 9½ acres, grass, level (heated) lic club, amusements £6.00-£11.00 inc showers

---

There's usually no objection to your walking onto a site to see if you might like it but always ask permission first. Remember that the person in charge is responsible for safeguarding the property of those staying there.

WITHERIDGE, Devon   Map F3
Pop 700 SEE church, thatched cottages Restaurant: Stag Inn, 4m NE at Rackenford ✆(01884)
881369

West Middlewick Farm, Nomansland, EX16 8NP *Working farm with panoramic views* ✆(01884)
860286/861235 OS map 181/825138 1m E of Witheridge on left of B3137 (Tiverton) Open all
year 15 pitches Level grass, sheltered ▣⊕☺ farm produce £4.30-£6.10

Yeatheridge Farm Caravan Park, East Worlington EX17 4TN ✆(01884) 860330 OS map
191/768110 3m SW of Witheridge off B3042 (Eggesford) Open Easter-mid Sept, 85 pitches–must
book peak periods 9 acres, level/gentle slope, grass, sheltered ▤♀↗⌐⌐🗗▣⌀⊕∅🗔 (indoor
heated), ☺↵⌐▰🗠 fishing, woodland walks, horse riding, skittle alley £6.50-£7.50

WOODBURY–see Exmouth

WOOLACOMBE, Devon   Map E2
Pop 1,170 EC Wed SEE surfing beach, Mortehoe church 1m N, Morte Point cliffs 2m NW, Bull Point
lighthouse 2½m N ▮ Red Barn Café Car Park, Barton Rd ✆(01271) 870553 Restaurant: Little
Beach, Esplanade ✆(01271) 870398

Easewell Farm, Mortehoe EX34 7EH ✆Woolacombe (01271) 870225 OS map 180/465455 1½m
N of Woolacombe centre off North Morte road Open Mar-Oct 250 pitches Hard standings and
grass, part level, part sheltered ▤✗⌐🗗▣⌀⊕∅ 🗔 (heated) ⌐ lic club, 9 hole golf course
£6.50-£13.00 (all cards)

Little Roadway Farm Camping EX34 7HL ✆Woolacombe (01271) 870313 OS map 180/470424
1m SE of Woolacombe near junction of Challacombe Hill and B3231 (Ilfracombe–Croyde) Open
Easter-Oct, 100 pitches 10 acres, level/sloping grass ▤⌐↗▣⌀⊕∅↵▰ sand pit, games
room £6.00

North Morte Farm Caravan and Camping Park, Mortehoe EX34 7EG ✆Woolacombe (01271)
870381 OS map 180/462455 1½m N of Woolacombe centre off North Morte road Open Easter-
Sept–must book (caravans) 248 pitches (73 static) Level/sloping grass
▤↗🗗▣⌀⊕∅↵▰🗠⌖ £8.00-£11.75 (most cards)

Twitchen Parc, Mortehoe EX34 7ES ✆Woolacombe (01271) 870343 OS map 180/465448 1m NE
of Woolacombe centre off Mortehoe–Turnpike Cross road Open Easter-Oct 345 pitches (295
static) Level/sloping grass and hard standing, sheltered ▤✗♀⌐🗗▣⌀⊕∅🗔 (heated)
☺↵⌐🗠 flat rental, lic club £7.90-£32.00 (inc elect and hot showers)

Warcombe Farm Camping Park, Station Road, Mortehoe EX34 7EJ ✆Woolacombe (01271)
870690 Fax (01271) 871070 OS map 180/478455 2m NE of Woolacombe off Mortehoe road
Open Mar-Oct, 100 pitches 19 acres, level grass, sheltered ▤🗗▣⌀⊕∅↵ fishing £3.50-£9.50

Woolacombe Bay Holiday Village, Seymour EX34 7BN ✆Woolacombe (01271) 870221 OS map
180/468442 ½m NE of Woolacombe centre off Mortehoe road Open Easter-Oct 431 pitches (231
static)–tents only Grass, sloping ▤✗♀⌐↗🗗▣⌀⊕∅🗔 (heated) ☺↵⌐🗠 snack bar
£7.90-£21.30 (most cards)

Woolacombe Sands Holiday Park, Station Road EX34 7AF ✆Woolacombe (01271) 870569 OS
map 180/463438 ¼m E of Woolacombe on right of B3343 (Mullacott Cross) Open Easter-Sept,
200 pitches (65 static) 30 acres, level/terraced grass, sheltered
▤♀⌐🗗▣⌀⊕∅🗔☺↵▰🗠🏠 £5.00-£12.00

12 North Wales

North Wales consists of the new counties of Clwyd, named from the vale extending south from Rhyl, and Gwynedd, named from an ancient Welsh kingdom. Clwyd is an amalgamation of Denbigh and Flint, Gwynedd a replacement for Caernarvon and Merioneth. Like regional names, place names in Wales are taking unfamiliar forms too: Wrexham, for example, has now reverted to its original Wrecsam.

The dominant physical feature of Gwynedd is Snowdonia, a range of 3000ft high foldings, bounded on the east by the beautiful Vale of Conway and on the west by the Menai Straits separating Anglesey from the mainland. Betws y Coed is a popular centre for walks and climbs in Snowdonia. For the less energetic, lakeside Bala to the south is another.

Telford's Menai Bridge links Bangor with Anglesey, an island of unspectacular scenery ringed by an attractive coastline of quiet bays enclosing uncrowded beaches. Best known are Amlwch and Benllech in the north, Rhosneigr in the south. Below Anglesey is the long arm of the Lleyn Peninsula, its more hospitable and sandy eastern shore dotted with tiny resorts linked by often ultra-narrow roads. The most crowded place in summer is Abersoch.

West of Edwardian Llandudno modest resorts like Penmaenmawr and Llanfairfechan line the northern mainland coast, but more popular with campers are the long stretches of sand on the west between Porthmadog and the Dovey Estuary below Tywyn, linked to inland Abergynolwyn by a miniature railway.

More low-lying Clwyd forming the eastern half of the region is noted for the fine sands and sophisticated resorts along the coast west of the Dee Estuary and the purple moorlands flanking the picturesque vale from which it takes its name. A large coalfield surrounds Wrecsam, Chirk and Ruabon near the border with England. Guarding the Vale of Llangollen in southeast Clwyd are the Berwyn Mountains, traversed by the northern section of Offa's Dyke Path, one of many routes for walkers in the region. North Wales may be a land of chapels yet it also has fine churches, like that of St Asaph, one of the smallest cathedrals in Britain. The finest castle in Wales is at Caernarfon, but those at Rhuddlan, Beaumaris, Chirk and Harlech are almost as impressive.

Campsite locations are most attractive inland, for example along the Vales of Conwy and Clwyd. Many campsites along the coast are occupied mainly by static caravans and have a holiday camp atmosphere. Others are made noisy by the railway that runs close to the sea at many points. Campsite amenities vary from sophisticated on the coast to primitive inland.

ABERDARON, Gwynedd   **Map B6**
Pop 370. EC Wed SEE Wishing Well, Whistling Sands, Hell's mouth, Bardsey Island Restaurant: Ty Newydd ☎(01758) 760207

Mur Melyn Camping, Mur Melyn LL53 8LW ☎(01758) 760522 OS map 123/176289 2m N of Aberdaron off B4413 (Llanbedrog) on Whistling Sands road–signposted Open Whitsun-Sept 20 pitches– must book touring caravans 5 acres level grass, sheltered ⊕🔌 £3.50

Ty Mawr Caravan Park, Bryncroes, Sarn LL53 8EH ☎(01248) 351537 (enqs) OS map 123/219317 4m NE of Aberdaron off B4413 (Llanbedrog) Open Apr-Oct 25 pitches 2 acres level grass, sheltered 🎫🔌⊕∅⊕⤴⛟♿ £6.00

ABERDOVEY, Gwynedd   **Map D7**
Pop 1,500 EC Wed SEE Happy Valley, Dolgoch Falls, Cader Idris (2,927ft) 🏴The Wharf Gardens, ☎(01654) 767321 Restaurant: Penhelig Arms, Terrace Rd ☎(01654) 767215

Cefn Crib Caravan Park, Pennal SY20 9LB ☎Pennal (01654) 791239 OS map 135/680990 4½m E of Aberdovey on A493 (Machynlleth) Open Mar 15-Sept 30, 52 pitches 4 acres level grass, sheltered 🎫⊕ £4.50

For other sites near Aberdovey see Machynlleth and Tywyn

ABERGELE, Clwyd   **Map E3**
Pop 12,315 EC Thurs, MD Mon SEE Gwrych Castle Restaurant: Oriel House 6m SE at St Asaph ☎(01745) 582716

Gwrych Towers Camping LL22 8ET ☎(01745) 832109 and (01829) 260210 OS map 116/938775 ½m W of Abergele on A547 (Llanddulas) at entrance to Gwrych castle Open Spring BH, Jul-Sept 50 pitches 3 acres level grass, sheltered £4.00-£6.00

Haven Ty-Mar Holiday Park, Towyn Rd LL22 9HG ☎(01745) 832079 OS map 116/965792 2m NE of Abergele on A547 (Rhyl) Open Easter-Oct 450 pitches (400 static) 45 acres level grass and hard standings 🎫✕🍴⤴🏹🎫🎫∅⊕∅⊕🗺⊕⤴🎫♿ £8.00-£14.50

Henllys Farm, Towyn LL22 9HF ☎(01745) 351208 OS map 116/972792 1½m NE of Abergele on A548 (Rhyl) Open Apr-Sept 280 pitches Level grass 🎫🎫∅⊕⊕⤴ £10.00-£13.00

Hunter's Hamlet, Sirior Goch Farm, Betws-yn-Rhos LL22 8PL ☎Abergele (01745) 832237 OS map 116/930736 3m S of Abergele off A548 (Llanrwst) on left of B5381 (Llandudno Junction) Open Mar 21-Oct 31, 23 pitches–no tents 2½ acres grass and hard standings 🎫🎫🎫∅⊕∅⊕⤴🎫♿ games room, flat rental, serviced pitches £8.00-£16.00

ABERSOCH, Gwynedd   **Map B5**
Pop 1,050. EC Wed One most attractive villages on Lleyn peninsula, with fine beaches SEE Llanengan church 2m W, Hell's Mouth 3m W Restaurant: White House ☎(01758) 713427

Beach View Caravan and Camping Site, Bwlchtocyn LL53 7BT ☎Abersoch (01758) 712956 OS map 123/306266 1½m SW of Abersoch on Bwlchtocyn road Open Mar-Oct 50 pitches 5 acres, level grass, sheltered £8.00-£12.00

Bryn Cethin Bach Caravan Park LL53 7UL ☎Abersoch (01758) 712719 OS map 123/304290 1m NW of Abersoch off A499 (Pwllheli) on Lon Garmon road Open Mar-Oct 74 pitches (53 static)–no tents, families only Level grass and hard standings, sheltered 🎫🎫∅⊕∅⊕🗺🏠 fishing £10.00-£12.00

Seaview Camping Caravan Park, Sarn Bach LL53 7ET ☎Abersoch (01758) 712062 OS map 123/305266 1½m SSW of Abersoch off Marchros road via Sarn Bach Open Mar-Oct 66 pitches 4½ acres level/sloping grass, sheltered 🎫🎫∅∅⤴🎫 £7.00-£9.00 (Mastercard/Visa)

Tyn-y-Mur Camping and Touring Park, Lon Garmon LL53 7UL ☎Abersoch (01758) 712328 OS map 123/300290 ½m W of Abersoch on Llangian road Open Mar-Oct 90 pitches 3 acres, level, gentle slope 🎫🎫∅⊕∅⊕⤴ £10.00-£12.00

Warren Touring Park LL53 7AA ☎Abersoch (01758) 712043 OS map 123/318303 2m N of Abersoch on A499 (Pwllheli) Open May-Oct, 90 pitches 4 acres, level/gentle slope, families only 🎫⊕∅⊕⊕ £12.70-£14.00 (Mastercard/Visa)

See also Llanbedrog

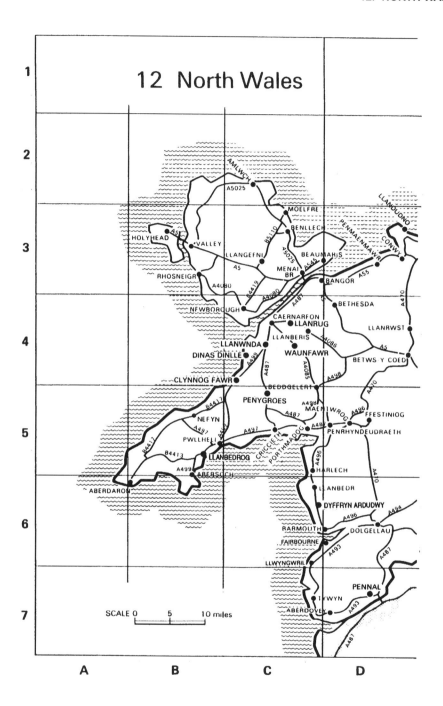

12 North Wales

AMLWCH
A5025
MOELFRE
LLANDUDNO
BENLLECH
PENMAENMAWR
HOLYHEAD
A5
VALLEY
B5110
A5025
CONWY
LLANGEFNI
BEAUMARIS
A5
A545
RHOSNEIGR
MENAI
BR
A4080
BANGOR
A55
A419
A4080
A487
NEWBOROUGH
BETHESDA
A470
CAERNARFON
LLANRUG
LLANBERIS
LLANRWST
WAUNFAWR
A4086
A5
LLANWNDA
DINAS DINLLE
A499
A487
BETWS Y COED
CLYNNOG FAWR
A4085
A498
A470
BEDDGELERT
B4417
PENYGROES
A498
MAENTWROG
NEFYN
A487
A496
FFESTINIOG
A497
A487
PENRHYNDEUDRAETH
B4417
PWLLHELI
A497
CRICCIETH
PORTHMADOG
B4413
LLANBEDROG
A496
A499
ABERSOCH
HARLECH
A470
ABERDARON
LLANBEDR
DYFFRYN ARDUDWY
A496
A494
BARMOUTH
DOLGELLAU
FAIRBOURNE
A493
A487
LLWYNGWRIL
PENNAL
TYWYN
A493
ABERDOVEY
A487

SCALE 0   5   10 miles

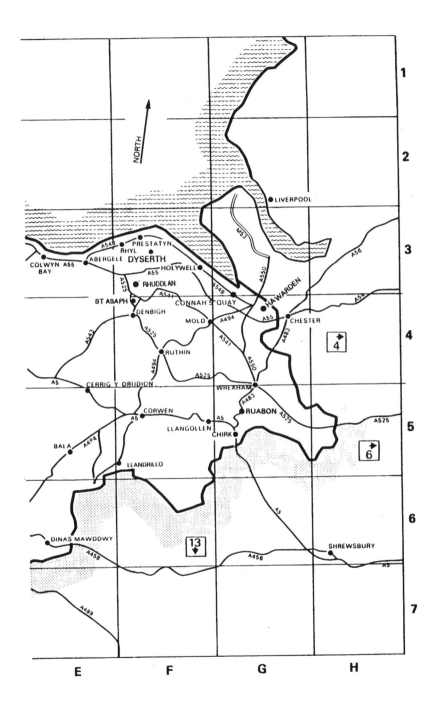

AMLWCH, Anglesey, Gwynedd   **Map C2**
Pop 4,000. EC Wed, MD Fri SEE harbour, Church of our Lady, cliffs Restaurant: Trecastell, Bull
Bay ✆(01407) 830651

Point Lynas Caravan Park, Llaneilian LL67 9LT ✆(01407) 831130 OS map 114/476930 2m E of
   Amlwch off A5025 (Pentraeth) at Twrcelyn Garage on Point Lynas road Open Mar-Oct 50 pitches
   Level grass, part sheltered 🔲🔀🗑❀ adj beach £6.00-£8.00

Tyn-Rhos Farm, Penysarn LL69 9YR ✆Amlwch (01407) 830574 OS map 114/462902 2m SE of
   Amlwch on A5025 (Menai Bridge) at Penysarn Open Easter-Sept 32 pitches 2 acres level grass,
   part sheltered 🍷🏹🔀❀🚏 golf, swimming, fishing £10.00-£15.00
See also Moelfre

BALA, Gwynedd   **Map E5**
Pop 1,850 EC Wed, MD Thurs Attractive market town at head of Bala lake and popular walking
centre SEE Bala lake, Gorsedd circle ℹ️ Leisure Centre ✆Bala (01678) 520367 Restaurant: Eagles
at Llanuwchllyn ✆(01678) 540278

Bryn Gwyn Farm, Llanuwchllyn LL23 7SU ✆(01678) 540687 OS map 124/865308 5m SW of Bala
   off A494 (Dolgellau) Open Easter-Oct 40 pitches 🔀🗑🚭🔀 (£50) ☎ fishing £5.00-£8.00

Bryn Melyn Farm, Llandderfel LL23 7RA ✆(01678) 520212 OS map 125/996363 4m E of Bala on
   B4401 (Corwen) Open Apr-Oct—must book peak periods 139 pitches 🛒🔲🗑❀🔀 farm produce,
   fishing, rough shoot £3.00-£4.50

Crynierth Caravan Park (Camping Club), Cefn-ddwysarn LL23 7IN ✆(01678) 520324 OS map
   125/962391 3m NE of Bala off A494 (Ruthin) Open Mar 20-Oct 30 50 pitches Level grass,
   sheltered 🔲🔀🗑❀🚭🔀♿ £11.80-£14.90

Glanllyn Lakeside Caravan Camping Park LL23 7ST ✆(01678) 540227 OS map 125/892324 3m
   SW of Bala off A494 (Dolgellau) by lake Open Mar 15-Oct 15 150 pitches Level grass, sheltered
   🛒🔲🔀🗑❀ boat launching facs £8.00 (Mastercard/Visa/Switch)

Penybont Touring and Camping Park, Llangynog Road LL23 7PH ✆Bala (01678) 520549 OS
   map 125/932350 ½m SE of Bala on B4391 (Llangynog) Open Apr-Oct—must book peak periods
   85 pitches Level/sloping grass and hard standing, sheltered 🛒🔲🔀🗑🚭❀🔀♿ £8.45-£10.45
   (Mastercard/Visa)

Pen-y-Garth Caravan Camping Park, LL23 7ES ✆Bala (01678) 520485 OS map 125/940349 1m
   NE of Bala off B4391 (Lake Vyrnwy) Open Mar-Oct—must book peak periods 117 pitches (54
   static) 20 acres level grass and hard standings, sheltered 🛒🔲🔀🗑🚭❀🔀🔀🚏 table tennis,
   games room £7.50-£9.50 (most cards)

Ty Isaf Caravan Park, Llangynog Road LL23 7PP ✆Bala (01678) 520574 OS map 125/957355
   2m E of Bala on B4391 (Llangynog) Open Apr-Oct 30 pitches Level grass, part sheltered
   🔲🔀🗑❀🔀🚏 £7.00-£8.00 inc hot water

Tyn Cornel Camping Caravan Park, Frongoch LL23 7NU ✆Bala (01678) 520759 OS map
   125/895400 4m NW of Bala on A4212 (Porthmadog) by river Open Mar-Oct 37 pitches 2 acres
   level grass 🔀❀🚭 cable TV–*No showers* £8.50

Ty Tandderwen LL23 7EP ✆Bala (01678) 520273 OS map 125/951363 2½m SE of Bala off
   B4391 (Llangynog) Open Easter-Oct 125 pitches (60 static) Level grass, sheltered
   🛒🔲🔀🗑🚭❀🔀♿ bathing, fishing £7.00-£8.00 inc hot water

BANGOR, Gwynedd   Map C3
Pop 14,550. EC Wed, MD Fri SEE cathedral, University of Wales, museum, Menai Bridge, Penrhyn
Castle 1m E 🚻 Theatr Gwynedd, Deiniol Rd ☎(01248) 352786 Restaurant: Union Hotel, Garth Rd
☎(01248) 362462
Tros-y-Waen Holiday Farm, Pentir LL57 4EF ☎Bangor (01248) 364448 OS map 114/115/570661
    3½m S of Bangor off A4087 (Caernarfon) and B4547 (Llanberis) Open all year 20 pitches
    🏕🗑⌀↵ £4.00

BARMOUTH, Gwynedd   Map D6
Pop 2,200. EC Wed, MD Thurs Popular seaside resort on N shore of Mawddach estuary SEE Guild
of St George cottages, Fairbourne railway S, Llanaber church 2m NW, Bontddu gold mines 2m NE
🚻 Old Library ☎(01341) 280787 Restaurant: Last Inn, Church St ☎(01341) 280530
Hendre Mynach Touring Caravan and Camping Park LL42 1YR ☎Barmouth (01341) 280262 OS
    map 124/609167 ½m N of Barmouth on A496 (Harlech) Open Mar-Dec—must book peak periods
    (caravans) 220 pitches Level grass and hard standings, sheltered 🏕✗⌫↗🗑🛒⌀⊕⌀⊕↵
    £7.00-£14.00 (Mastercard/Visa/Switch)

See also Llanbedr and Fairboume

BEAUMARIS, Anglesey, Gwynedd   Map D3
Pop 2,500. EC Wed SEE castle ruins, 14c church, old gaol and courthouse Restaurant: Old Bulls
Head, Castle St ☎(01248) 810329
Kingsbridge Caravan Park, Llanfaes LL58 8LR ☎(01248) 490636 OS map 115/607786 2m N of
    Beaumaris off B5109 (Llangoed) on Llanfaes road Open Mar-Oct 77 pitches (29 static) Level
    grass, sheltered 🏕🛒⌀⊕⌀⊕↵🚐 £8.00-£11.00

BEDDGELERT, Gwynedd   Map C4
Pop 320. EC Wed SEE priory church, Gelert's grave, Sygun copper mine, Aberglaslyn pass S,
Gwynant valley NE, Gwynant and Dinas lakes NE Restaurant: Royal Goat ☎(01766) 890224
Beddgellert Camp Site LL55 4UU ☎(01766) 890288 OS map 116/578491 1¼m N of Beddgelert
    on A4085 (Caernarfon) Open all year 300 pitches 🏕✗🗑🛒⌀⊕⌀⊕↵♿ £7.00-£8.00

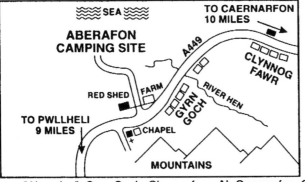

BENLLECH, Anglesey, Gwynedd   **Map C3**
Pop 3,500. EC Thurs SEE Roman village Restaurant: Rhostrefor, Amlwch Rd ☎(01248) 852347

Ad Astra Caravan Site, Brynteg LL78 7JH ☎Tynygongl (01248) 853283 OS map 114/490820 2m
W of Benllech off B5108 (Brynteg) on B5110 (Llangefni) Open Mar-Oct 50 pitches (38 static)
Level grass, sheltered ▯▤▨⊕∅⊕◡▭ £6.00-£10.00

Bodafon Caravan and Camping Site LL74 8RU ☎Tynygongl (01248) 852417 OS map
114/516836 ½m N of Benllech on left of A5025 (Amlwch) Open Mar-Oct 80 pitches 5 acres
level/sloping grass, sheltered ▤▨⊕∅▥▭▣ games room £5.00-£12.00

Bwlch Holiday Park, Bwlch Farm, Tyngongl LL74 8RF ☎Tynygongl (01248) 852914 OS map
114/510820 ½m SW of Benllech off B5108 (Llangefni) Open Mar-Oct 66 pitches (52 static) Hard
standings ▯▤▨∅◡▥✿ games room £6.00-£13.00

Garnedd Touring Park, Brynteg LL78 8QA ☎Tynygongl (01248) 853240 OS map 114/495818
1½m SW of Benllech off B5108 (Llangefni) Open Mar-Oct—must book peak periods 20
pitches—couples preferred, children by arrangement Level/sloping grass, part sheltered
▯▤▨⊕⊕✿▭▣ battery charging £6.00

Glan Gors Caravan Park, Brynteg LL78 8QA ☎Tynygongl (01248) 852334 OS map 114/499819
1m W of Benllech near junction of B5108 (Brynteg) and B5110 (Moelfre-Llangefni) Open Mar-Oct
195 pitches Level grass, sheltered ▨▞▯▨▱ (heated) ✦ £8.00-£10.00

Home Farm Caravan Park, Marianglas LL73 8PH ☎(01248) 410614 OS map 114/496847 2m NW
of Benllech off A5025 (Amlwch) at Llanallgo Open Apr-Oct 133 pitches (72 static) Level grass,
sheltered ▯▤▨⊕∅⊕◡⛨ indoor play area, fully serviced pitches £7.50-£16.75

Nant Newydd Caravan Park, Brynteg LL78 7JH ☎(01248) 852842/852266 OS map 114/484814
3m SW of Benllech off B5108 (Brynteg) on B5110 (Llangefni) Open Mar-Oct—must book peak
periods 113 pitches (83 static) 4 acres grass and hard standings, sloping/level, sheltered
▨▞▯▤▨⊕∅▱⊕◡▥▭⛨ Satellite TV £7.50-£13.00

Plas Uchaf Caravan Camping Park, Benllech Bay LL74 8NU ☎(01407) 763012 (bookings) OS
map 114/509835 ½m NW of Benllech on Marianglas road Open Mar-Oct 100 pitches (25 static)
8 acres level grass sheltered ▤▨⊕∅⊕◡▥▭ £7.00-£9.00

Rhos Farm, Pentraeth LL75 8DZ ☎(01248) 450214 OS map 114/519794 2½m S of Benllech on
A5025 (Menai Bridge) Open Mar-Oct 118 pitches (66 static) 15 acres, level grass, sheltered
▨▯▤▨⊕∅◡▭ £6.50-£8.50

St David's Park, Red Wharf Bay LL75 8RJ ☎(01248) 852341 OS map 114/531819 1½m S of
Benllech off A5025 (Menai Bridge) Open Apr-Sept 100 pitches—must book Level/sloping grass,
sheltered ▨✗▯⟲▞▯▤▨⊕∅⊕✿▣▭ lic club, own beach £10.00-£15.00

Ty Newydd Caravan Park, Llanbedrgoch LL76 8TZ ☎(01248) 450677 OS map 114/115/507812
2m S of Benllech off A5025 (Menai Bridge) on Llanbedrgoch road Open Mar-Oct 100 pitches (60
static) 9 acres level grass and hard standings, sheltered ▨✗▯⟲▞▯▤▨⊕∅▱ (heated)
⊕◡▭▥▭⛨ health centre £7.00-£19.00
See also Moelfre

BETHESDA, Gwynedd   **Map D4**
Restaurant: Ty Uchaf 2½m NW at Tal-y-bont ☎(01248) 352219

Ogwen Bank Caravan Park, Ogwen Bank LL57 3LQ ☎Bethesda (01248) 600486 OS map
115/627661 ½m S of Bethesda on A5 (Betws y Coed) Open Mar-Oct 176 pitches (100
static)—touring pitches with all mains services—no tents Gravel, level, terraced
▨✗▯⟲▯▤▨∅∅▯▥ (£75) ▭⛨ lic club, pony trekking, hill walks £8.00-£14.00

BETWS Y COED, Gwynedd   **Map D4**
Pop 7,000. EC Thurs SEE old church, Conwy Falls, Swallow Falls, Pont-y-Pair bridge, Railway
Museum, Dolwyddelan Castle 5m SW ▣ Royal Oak Stables ☎(01690) 710426 Restaurant: Royal
Oak ☎(01690) 710363

Cwmlanerch Farm LL24 0BG ☎Betws-y-Coed (01690) 710285/710363 OS map 115/800580 1m
N of Betws-y-Coed on right of B5106 (Conwy) Open Mar-Oct 49 pitches (30 static) 3 acres, level,
sheltered, grass and hard standings ▯▤▨⊕∅⊕◡▭ £3.50-£11.50

Hendre Farm LL24 0BN OS map 115/784566 ½m W of Betws y Coed on left of A5 (Bangor) Open
Apr-Oct 56 pitches 2 acres level grass ▯▨∅✿ £4.00

Riverside Caravan and Camping Ground, LL24 0AL ☎Betws y Coed (01690) 710310 OS map
115/797564 In Betws y Coed off A5 adj golf course Open Mar-Oct 120 pitches (75 static) 7 acres
level grass, sheltered ▯▤▨⊕∅▥⛨ farm produce, forest walks £8.00-£10.00

See listing under Waunfawr

BETWS GARMON–see Waunfawr

BRYNCRUG–see Tywyn

BRYNSIENCYN–see Menai Bridge

BRYNTEG–see Benllech

CAERNARFON, Gwynedd   Map C4
Pop 9,260. EC Thurs, MD Sat Town at SW end of Menai Strait dominated by great medieval fortress SEE Castle, town walls, Roman fort, Hafodty gardens 🖼 Oriel Pendeits, Castle St ☎(01286) 672232 Restaurant: Royal, North Rd ☎(01286) 673184

Cadnant Valley Caravan Camping Park, Llanberis Road LL55 2DF ☎Caernarfon (01286) 673196 OS map 114/491628 ½m E of Caernarfon on A4086 (Llanberis) Open Mar 14-Oct–must book peak periods 70 pitches 5 acres level grass and hard standings, sheltered 🔲🛒🔲🔲🔲🔲🔲 £8.00-£11.00

Glan Gwna Holiday Park, Caeathro LL55 2SG ☎Caernarfon (01286) 673456 OS map 114/502622 1m SE of Caernarfon on A4085 (Beddgelert) Open Apr-Oct 100 pitches Level grass and hard standings 🔲✖🔲🔲🔲 (heated) lic club, horse riding, fishing £6.00-£14.00 (inc electricity)

Menai Caravan Park, Coed Helen LL53 7AA ☎Caernarfon (01286) 672852 OS map 114/115/475625 1m W of Caernarfon off A487 (Porthmadog) Open Mar-Oct 50 pitches 🔲🔲🔲 (heated) 🔲🔲 children's room, lic club £4.00

Rhyd-y-Galen Caravan Park, Bethel Road LL55 3PS ☎Caernarfon (01248) 670110 OS map 115/508644 2m NE of Caernarfon on right of B4366 (Bethel) Open Easter-Oct 35 pitches 3 acres grass, mainly sloping 🔲🔲🔲🔲 £9.50

Riverside Camping, Caer Glyddyn, Pontrug LL55 2BB ☎Caernarfon (01286) 678781/672524 OS map 114/505627 2m E of Caernarfon on A4086 (Llanberis) Open Easter-Oct 60 pitches 4½ acres level grass, sheltered 🔲🔲🔲🔲🔲🔲 £5.00-£10.50 inc awning

For other sites near Caernarfon see Dinas Dinlle, Llanrug, Llanwnda and Waunfawr

---

CERRIG-Y-DRUDION, Clwyd   Map E4
Restaurant: Plas Coch 10m S at Bala ☎(01678) 520309

Glan Ceirw Caravan Site, Tynant, Corwen LL21 0RF ☎(01490) 420346 OS map 116/963462 1½m S of Cerrig-y-Drudion off A5 (Corwen) Open Mar-Oct 38 pitches (29 static) Hard standings, level 🔲🔲🔲🔲🔲🔲🔲🔲🔲🔲🔲🔲 £5.50-£8.00

Saracen's Head Hotel, LL21 9SY ☎(01490) 420684 OS map 116/950490 ¼m NW of Cerrig-y-Drudion on A5 (Betws-y-Coed) Open all year 21 pitches Level grass and hard standings ✖🔲🔲 £4.00

CHIRK, Clwyd   Map G5
Pop 4,500. SEE castle Restaurant: Gales 5m NW at Llangollen ☎(01978) 860089

Pontbell Caravan Park, Glyn Ceiriog LL20 7AB ☎(01691) 718320 OS map 126/203378 6m W of Chirk on B4500 (Llanarmon) Open Apr-Sept 12 pitches 1 acre level grass, sheltered 🔲🔲🔲🔲 fishing £5.50

CLYNNOG FAWR, Gwynned   Map C4
Restaurant: Caeau Capel 8m SW at Nefyn ☎(01758) 720240

Aberafon Camping, Gyrn Goch LL54 5PN ☎Clynnog Fawr (01286) 660295 OS map 123/400485
1m S of Clynnog Fawr on A499 (Pwllheli) Open all year 150 pitches 10 acres, part level grass,
sheltered 🏠⛺🔲🔌⊘⊗⊘☐🏠 private beach, pool room £5.50-£6.00

Llyn-y-Gele Farm, Pontllyfni LL54 5EL ☎Clynnog Fawr (01286) 660289 OS map 115/432522 2m
NE of Clynnog Fawr on left of A499 (Caernarfon) by garage in Pontllyfni Open Easter-Oct, 54
pitches (24 static) 2 acres, level grass 🏠🔌⊘⊗ £7.00-£8.00

COLWYN BAY, Clwyd   Map E3
Pop 25,500. EC Wed Seaside resort with 3m long promenade overlooking Colwyn Bay with original
nucleus a short way inland SEE Welsh Mountain Zoo, Puppet Theatre, Bodnant gardens 5m SW 🚹
Station Rd ☎(01492) 530478 Restaurant: Platform 3, Colwyn Bay Station, Princes Drive ☎(01492)
533161

Bron y Wendon Touring Caravan Park, Wern Road, Llanddulas LL22 8HG ☎(01492) 512903 (24
hrs) OS map 116/785903 3m E of Colwyn Bay off A55 (Chester) at Llanddulas–signposted Open
Mar 21-Oct 30, 130 pitches–no tents 8 acres grass and hard standings, level/sloping
🔲🔌⊘⊘⊗⊗☐🔧 £9.00-£11.00

Dinarth Hall, Rhos on Sea LL28 4PX ☎(01492) 548203 OS map 116/825805 2m NW of Colwyn
Bay off A55 (Bangor) on B5115 (Llandudno)–entr opp college Open Mar-Oct 40 pitches on level
grass 🏠🔲🔌⊘⊗⊘⊗↩ £7.00-£8.00

Westwood Caravan Park, Llysfaen LL29 8SW ☎Colwyn Bay (01492) 517410 OS map
116/895775 ½m E of Colwyn Bay off A547 (Llanddulas) on Highlands road Open Apr-Oct 88
pitches 🔲🔌⊘⊗ £5.00-£6.00

CONWY, Gwynedd   Map D3
Pop 13,000. EC Wed, MD Tues, Sat SEE Castle, St Mary's church, Elizabethan mansion of Plas
Mawr, suspension bridge 🚹 Visitor Centre, the Castle ☎(01492) 592248 Restaurant: Castle, High
St ☎(01492) 592324

Conwy Touring Park, Gyffin LL32 8UX ☎Conwy (01492) 592856 OS map 115/775758 1¼m S of
Conwy on B5106 (Betws y Coed) Open Apr-Oct–must book Jul-Aug 400 pitches Level grass and
hard standing, sheltered 🏠🍴🔲🔌⊘⊘⊗⊗↩🔧🔌 £4.85-£10.75 (Mastercard/Visa/Delta/Switch)

Tyn Terfyn Touring Park, Tal-y-Bont LL32 8YX ☎Dolgarrog (01492) 660525 OS map 115/768695
5m S of Conwy on B5106 (Betws-y-Coed) Open Mar 14-Oct 30, 15 pitches 2 acres level grass
and hard standings, sheltered 🔲🔌⊘⊗⊗🏠 £5.30

CORWEN, Clwyd   Map F5
Restaurant: Hand 11m E at Llangollen ☎(01978) 860303

Llaw Bettws Farm Caravan Park, LL21 0HD ☎(01490) 460224 OS map 125/018425 3m W of
Corwen off A494 (Ruthin-Bala) at Glan-yr-Afon Open Mar-Oct 105 pitches Level/sloping grass,
sheltered 🏠🔲🔌⊘⊘⊗⊘⊗↩🔧🔌 £5.00-£6.00

Maerdy Mawr Caravan Park, Gwyddelwern LL21 9SD ☎Corwen (01490) 412187 OS map
116/070474 2½m N of Corwen off A5 (Bangor) on A494 (Ruthin) beyond Gwyddelwern Open
Mar-Oct 30 pitches 🔌⊘⊗

Pleasant View Caravan Park, Llawr Betws LL21 0HD ☎(01490) 412224 OS map 125/018425
3½m W of Corwen off A5 (Bangor) and A494 (Bala) Open Mar 25-Oct 105 pitches (72 static)
🏠🔲⊘🔧 (£40) 🔌 fishing £7.00

See also Llandrillo

BEGINNER'S GUIDE TO DIY OUTDOOR HOLIDAYS

free to buyers of this year's guide –

see order form on p9

CRICCIETH, Gwynedd   **Map C5**
Pop 1,530. EC Wed Modest resort in sheltered position on Tremadoc Bay with sandy beaches on either hand SEE Lloyd George Museum, view of Cardigan Bay from summit of headland, Llanystumdwy castle ruins 1½m W Restaurant: Plas Isa, Porthmadog Rd ☎(01766) 522443

Cae Canol Farm, Caernarfon Road LL52 0NB ☎Criccieth (01766) 522351 OS map 123/485402 1½m NW of Criccieth on B4411 (Caernarfon) Open Mar-Oct 20 pitches Level grass, sheltered ▣◿✤🏠 trout fishing £5.00-£7.50

Eisteddfa Camp Site, Pentrefelin LL52 0PT ☎Criccieth (01766) 522696 OS map 124/520394 1m NE of Criccieth on A497 (Porthmadog) by Plas Gwyn Hotel Open Mar-Oct 140 pitches Level/sloping grass, sheltered ▤▣▣◿✤∅☺⤴ £6.50-£7.50

Gell Farm LL52 0PN ☎Criccieth (01766) 522781 OS map 123/497398 1m NW of Criccieth on right of B4411 (Caernarfon) Open Apr-Oct 58 pitches (50 static) 5 acres, level grass, sheltered ▣◿✤▣▣🏪 £3.00-£4.00

Llwyn-Bugeilydd Farm LL52 0PN *Quiet family site with fine views* ☎Criccieth (01766) 522235 OS map 123/498396 1m N of Criccieth on right of B4411 (Caernarfon)–signposted Open Apr-Oct 45 pitches 6 acres, level grass ▣◿✤ £6.00-£8.50

Maes Meillion, Llwyn Mafon Isaf LL52 0RE ☎(01766) 522642 OS map 124/520417 3½m N of Criccieth on A487 (Porthmadog-Caernarfon) Open Apr-Oct 20 pitches ▣ £3.50

Muriau Bach Touring Park, Rhoslan LL52 0NP ☎(01766) 530642 OS map 123/482420 3m N of Criccieth on B4411 (Caernarfon) Open Mar-Oct 20 pitches Level grass, sheltered ▣◿⤴🏪 £5.00-£7.50

Ocean Heights Caravan Park, Pen-y-Bryn, Chwilog LL53 6NQ ☎(01766) 522519 OS map 123/435380 4m W of Criccieth off A497 (Pwllheli) Open Mar-Oct 94 pitches (74 static) Grass, level, sheltered ▣▣▣ (£60) 🏪 (9) farm produce, sep pitches £3.00-£5.50

Tyddyn Cethin Farm LL52 0NF ☎(01766) 522149 OS map 123/492404 1½m N of Criccieth on B4411 (Caernarfon) by river Dwyfor Open Mar-Oct 80 pitches (40 static) 8 acres level grass ▣◿✤▣ £7.50-£10.00

Tyddyn Morthwyl LL52 0NF ☎Criccieth (01766) 522115 OS map 123/485402 1½m N of Criccieth on B4411 (Caernarfon) Open Mar 14-Oct 30, 32 pitches (22 static)– Level grass, sheltered ▣✤∅☺🏪 £6.00

DENBIGH, Clwyd   **Map F4**
Pop 9,000. EC Thurs SEE castle ruins, St Hilary's Tower, old Bull Inn, old town walls Restaurant: Bull, Hall Sq ☎(01745) 812582

Caer Mynydd Caravan Park, Pentre Saron LL16 4TL ☎(01745) 550302 OS map 116/028607 4½m SW of Denbigh off B4501 (Cerrigydrudion) Open Mar-Oct 29 pitches Level grass, sheltered ▤▣▣◿✤☺⤴▣▣∅🏪 games room £6.50

Station House Caravan Park, Bodfari LL16 4DA ☎Bodfari (01745) 710372 OS map 116/094700 3½m N of Denbigh off A541 (Mold) on B5429 (Tremeirchion) Open Apr-Oct 26 pitches Level grass ▣▣✤⤴▣ games room £5.50-£6.00

Tyn-yr-Eignen Touring Caravan and Camping Park, Mold Road LL16 4BH ☎Denbigh (01745) 813211 OS map 116/070568 ½m SE of Denbigh on A525 (Ruthin) Open Mar-Oct 45 pitches ◿✤ £6.50

DINAS DINLLE, Gwynedd   **Map C4**
SEE Iron Age fort Restaurant: Stables 3m NE at Llanwnda ☎(01286) 830711

Dinlle Caravan Park LL54 5TW ☎(01286) 830324 OS map 115/438568 ½m N of Dinas Dinlle off road to Morfa Dinlle Open Mar-Oct–booking advisable peak periods 388 pitches (138 static) ▤▦⤴▣▣◿✤∅▣☺⤴▣ (£35), 🏪♿ family room, boating, club, fishing £3.50-£7.50

Morfa Lodge Caravan Park LL54 5TP ☎(01286) 830205 Fax (01286) 831329 OS map 115/443587 1½m N of Dinas Dinlle on Foryd Bay road Open Mar-Oct 370 pitches (150 static) Level grass and hard standings ▤▦⤴▣▣◿✤∅▣☺⤴▢▣🏪♿ children's room, clubhouse £3.60-£9.00

DINAS MAWDDWY, Gwynedd   **Map E6**
Pop 350. EC Thurs Restaurant: Red Lion (off A470) ☎(01650) 531247

Tynypwll Camping SY20 9JF ☎Dinas Mawddwy (01650) 531326 OS map 124/862149 ¼m NE of Dinas Mawddwy on Llanymawddwy road Open all year 60 pitches (50 static) Grass, level, sheltered 🏪 fishing, climbing, walks £5.00

DOLGELLAU, Gwynedd   **Map D6**
Pop 2,500. EC Wed, MD Fri SEE Precipice Walk NW, ruins of Cymmer Abbey 1m N, Torrent Walk
NE, Coed-y-Brenin forest 2m N via A470, road S to Cader Idris 🅐 Ty Meirion, Eldon Sq ☎(01341)
422888 Restaurant: Royal Ship, Queens Sq ☎(01341) 422209

Cwmrhwyddfor Caravan Camping Park, Talyllyn LL36 9AJ ☎Corris (01654) 761286/761380 OS
   map 124/737120 3½m S of Dolgellau off A470 (Mallwyd) on A487 (Machynlleth) Open all year 35
   pitches Level/sloping grass and hard standing 🔲⊛

Dolgamedd Caravan Camping Park, Bont Newydd, Brithdir LL40 2DG ☎(01341) 422624 OS map
   124/773202 3m NE of Dolgellau on B4416 (Brithdir) by river Open Mar 27-Oct 31 65 pitches
   Level grass, sheltered 🔲🔲⊛🔲 fishing £6.00-£8.00

Llwyn yr Helm Farm, Brithdir LL40 2SA ☎(01341) 450254 OS map 124/778192 3m NE of
   Dolgellau off A470 (Machynlleth) and B4416 at Brithdir Open Easter-Oct 25 pitches 3 acres level
   grass, sheltered 🔲🔲🔲🔲⊛🔲🔲🔲 £5.00-£5.50

Tan-y-fron Camping Park, Arran Road LL40 2AA ☎Dolgellau (01341) 422638 OS map
   124/735176 ½m E of Dolgellau on A470 (Mallwyd) Open all year 63 pitches Level grass and
   hard standings, sheltered 🔲🔲🔲⊛🔲🔲🔲🔲 £10.00-£15.00

Vanner Abbey Farm, Llanelltyd LL40 2HE ☎Dolgellau (01341) 422854 OS map 124/725194 1½m
   NW of Dolgellau off A470 (Barmouth) Open Apr-Oct 15, 50 pitches—no adv booking 🔲⊛🔲🔲
   fishing, B and B £5.50-£8.50

DULAS—see Moelfre

DYFFRYN ARDUDWY, Gwynedd   **Map C6**
Pop 1200 Modest resort close to wide sandy beaches of Barmouth Bay Restaurant: Ael-y-Bryn on
A496 ☎(01341) 247701

Benar Beach Camping and Touring Park, Talybont LL43 2AR ☎Dyffryn (01341) 247571 OS map
   124/574227 1m W of Dyffryn Ardudwy off A496 (Barmouth) at Llanddwywe, by beach Open Mar-
   Oct 230 pitches Level grass, sheltered 🔲⊛ satellite and TV hook up £4.00-£10.00

Dyffryn Seaside Estate, LL44 2HD ☎(01341) 247622 OS map 124/573232 1m W of Dyffryn
   Ardudwy via Station road, by beach Open Easter-Oct 548 pitches (248 static)
   🔲🔲🔲🔲🔲🔲🔲🔲 lic club, sauna, jacuzzi, bowling green, private beach £7.50

Islawrfford Farm, Tal-y-Bont LL43 2BQ ☎(01341) 247269 OS map 124/590212 ½m S of Dyffryn
   Ardudwy on right of A496 (Barmouth) Open Easter-Oct 241 pitches (216 static) Level grass
   🔲🔲🔲🔲🔲🔲🔲 (heated) 🔲🔲 £5.00-£15.00

Murmur-yr-Afon Touring Caravan Camping Park LL44 2BE ☎(01341) 247353 OS map
   124/588234 In Dyffryn Ardudwy near service station Open Mar-Oct 67 pitches Level grass and
   hard standings 🔲🔲🔲🔲⊛🔲🔲🔲🔲 £5.50-£9.25

Parc Isaf, Cors-y-Gedol Drive LL44 2RJ ☎(01341) 247447 OS map 124/595226 ½m S of Dyffryn
   Ardudwy off A496 (Barmouth) on right of Cors-y-Gedol road Open Easter-Oct 30 pitches 3½
   acres part level grass, sheltered 🔲🔲⊛🔲 farm produce £4.00-£8.00
See also Barmouth and Llanbedr

DYSERTH, Clwyd   **Map F3**
Pop 350 Restaurant: New Inn, Waterfall Rd ☎(01745) 570482

Longacres Caravan Park, Trelawnyd LL18 6BP ☎Dyserth (01745) 570531 OS map 116/098794 2½m E of Dyserth on right of A5151 (Holywell) at rear of petrol station Open Mar-Oct 12 pitches Level grass sheltered ⬛🚾⌀⊕ £5.00

Penisar Mynydd Caravan Site, Caerwys Road, Rhuallt LL17 0TY ☎(01745) 582227 OS map 116/094769 2m SE of Dyserth–signposted on A55 expressway (Conway-Chester) Open Apr-Oct, 30 pitches–no tents 2 acres grass and hard standing, sloping, sheltered 🗑🚾⌀⊕⌀⌣ £7.00-£9.25

FAIRBOURNE, Gwynedd   **Map D6**
Pop 250 EC Sat Little-known resort on S shore of Mawddach estuary facing Barmouth on N SEE beach, railway to Penrhyn Point (ferry to Barmouth) Restaurant: Springfield, Beach Road ☎(01341) 250378

Garthyfog Camp Site, Arthog LL39 1AX ☎Fairbourne (01341) 250338 OS map 124/638143 2m NE of Fairbourne on A493 (Dolgellau) Open all year 30 pitches Level/sloping grass and hard standings, sheltered 🖛 farm produce, walks £2.50-£5.00

Graig-wen Camping, Arthog LL39 1BQ ☎Fairbourne (01341) 250482/250900 OS map 124/656158 3m NE of Fairbourne on right of A493 (Dolgellau) Open Mar-Oct 210 pitches 42 acres partly level grass and hard standings ⌀⊕⌀🖛 B&B £4.00-£5.00

See also Barmouth

HARLECH, Gwynedd   **Map C5**
Pop 1,200. SEE castle, pottery 🅩 Gwyddfor House, High Street ☎Harlech (01766) 780658 Restaurant: Castle Cottage ☎(01766) 780479

Barcdy Touring Park, Talsarnau LL47 6YG *Quiet park near sea and mountains* ☎(01766) 770736 OS map 124/622371 4m NNE of Harlech on A496 (Maentwrog) Open Easter-Oct 80 pitches (30 static) Grass, part level, part sheltered ⬛🗑🚾⌀⊕⌀❀🖛 some provisions, freezer pack service £8.00-£10.00 (Mastercard/Visa)

Cae Cethin, Llanfair LL46 2SA ☎Harlech (01766) 780247 OS map 124/578287 1m S of Harlech off A496 (Barmouth) near slate caverns Open Easter-Nov 40 pitches 2½ acres terraced, grass and hard standing Farm produce £3.00-£4.00

Min-y-Don Ideal Caravan Park LL46 2UG ☎Harlech (01766) 780286 OS map 124/575317 ½m N of Harlech off A496 (Talsarnau) Open Easter-Sept 250 pitches ⌀❀🖛 £2.00-£3.00

Woodlands Caravan Park, LL46 2UE ☎Harlech (01766) 780419 OS map 124/582313 In Harlech, entrance adj castle car park–signposted Open Mar-Oct 37 pitches–no tents 4 acres level grass and hard standings, sheltered ⬛🗑🚾⌀⊕🏠 £5.00-£7.00

HAWARDEN, Clwyd   **Map G4**
Restaurant: Corkers Wine Bar 6m W at Mold ☎(01352) 59642

Greenacres Farm Park, Mancot, Deeside CH5 2AZ ☎Deeside (01244) 531147 OS map 117/318672 1m N of Hawarden off A550 (Queensferry) Open Easter-Sept, 45 pitches 3½ acres, level grass ⬛✖ (café), 🚾⊕⌀⌣♿ farm animals centre £13.00

HOLYHEAD, Anglesey, Gwynedd   **Map B3**
Pop 12,000. EC Tues, MD Fri, Sat Terminus of ferries from Ireland. Main town of Holy Island linked to Anglesey by causeway and bridge. SEE harbour, Holyhead mountains, South Stack Lighthouse 🅩 Marine Square, Salt Island Approach ☎Holyhead (01407) 762622 Restaurant: Beach 2m S at Trearddur Bay ☎(01407) 860332

Bagnol Caravan Park, Trearddur Bay LL65 2AZ ☎Trearddur Bay (01407) 860223 OS map 114/260780 3m S of Holyhead off B4545 (Four Mile Bridge) at Bagnol Open Mar-Oct, 200 pitches (150 static)–must book (caravans) 28 acres, level grass 🗑🚾⌀⊕⌀⊙🖂 beach access £12.00

Cliff Hotel Holiday Centre, Trearddur Bay LL65 2UR ☎Trearddur Bay (01407) 860634 OS map 114/260777 2m SE of Holyhead on B4545 (Trearddur Bay) Open Easter-Oct 15, 250 pitches (100 static) ⬛✖🅟🗑🚾⌀⊕ £4.00-£6.50

Gwynfair Caravan Site, Ravenspoint Road, Trearddur Bay LL65 7AX ☎Holyhead (01407) 860289 OS map 114/256777 1½m S of Holyhead off B4545 (Trearddur Bay) Open Mar-Oct 100 pitches 12 acres level grass ✖🗑🚾⌀⊕⌣🚽🖛 £4.00-£7.00

Valley of the Rocks Caravan and Camping Park, Porthdafarch Road, Trearddur Bay LL65 2LD ☎Holyhead (01407) 765787 OS map 114/236807 1½m S of Holyhead off B4545 (Trearddur Bay) Open Mar 14-Oct 25, 95 pitches Grass, level, sheltered ⬛🔌🗑⌀🖛 lic club £3.50-£7.50

For other sites near Holyhead see Rhosneigr and Valley

LLANBEDR, Gwynedd   **Map C6**
Pop 550. SEE Cwm Bychan lake and Roman steps, Shell Island, Harlech Castle 3m N Restaurant:
Plas Café 3m N at Harlech ☎ (01766) 780204

Hendy Touring Caravan Park, Hendy LL45 2LT ☎ (01341) 247263 OS map 124/587258 ½m S of
Llanbedr on left of A496 (Barmouth) Open May-Sept 20 pitches–no tents Level grass ▣◪⊕
£5.00

See also Dyffryn Ardudwy

LLANBEDROG, Gwynedd   **Map B5**
Pop 350 Village on E shore of Lleyn peninsula sheltered by promontory SEE views of St Tudwals
island Restaurant: Ship Inn, Pig St ☎ (01758) 740270

Bolmynydd Touring Camping Park, Refail LL53 7NP ☎ (01758) 740511 OS map 123/324313 1m
S of Llanbedrog off A499 (Abersoch) Open Easter-Sept 48 pitches 2 acres gently sloping grass,
sheltered ▤ (mobile) ▣◪◪⊕◪◪▣ £8.00-£9.00

Crugan Caravan Park, LL53 7NL ☎ (01758) 712045 OS map 123/335324 ½m N of Llanbedrog on
left of A499 (Pwllheli) Open Mar-Oct 120 pitches (100 static)–no tents or motor caravans ▣⊕◪◈
beach access £8.25-£10.50

Refail Touring Camping Park, Refail LL53 7NP ☎ (01758) 740511 OS map 123/327319 In
Llanbedrog near junct of A499 and B4413 (Aberdaron) Open Easter-Sept 33 pitches 3 acres
level/sloping grass, sheltered ▣◪◪⊕◪◪▣◪& shop calls £8.00-£9.00

LLANBEDRGOCH–see Benllech

LLANBERIS, Gwynedd   **Map C4**
Pop 3,500. SEE Snowdon (rack railway to summit), Dolbadarn Castle, lake Padarn, Bryn Bras
castle 3m NW ▨ Museum of the North ☎ (01286) 870765 Restaurant: Lake View Hotel at Tan-Y-
Pant ☎ (01286) 870422

Snowdon View Caravan-Camping Park, Brynrefail LL55 3PD ☎ Llanberis (01286) 870349 OS
map 114/562633 1m NW of Llanberis off A4086 (Caernarfon) on B4547 (Brynrefail) Open Mar-
Oct 436 pitches (174 static) ▤♀▣▱ (indoor heated) ⤸▣ £5.00-£8.00

LLANDRILLO, Clwyd   **Map F5**
Pop 350 Restaurant: Tyddyn Llan ☎ (01490) 440264

Hendwr Caravan Park LL21 0SN ☎ (01490) 440210 OS map 125/035386 1½m N of Llandrillo off
B4401 (Corwen) near river Dee–signposted Open Apr-Oct 150 pitches (80 static) 4 acres level
grass sheltered, some hard standings ▤▣◪◪⊕◪◪▣◪ farm produce £7.00-£8.00

LLANDUDNO, Gwynedd   **Map D3**
Pop 20,000. EC Wed SEE Rapallo House Museum, Haulfre Gardens, Happy Valley and Great
Ormes Head NW (by road or cabin lift) ▨ Chapel Street ☎ (01492) 876413 Restaurant: St Tudno,
North Par ☎ (01492) 574411

Penrhyn Hall Farm Caravan Park, Penrhyn Bay LL30 3EE ☎ Llandudno (01492) 549207 OS
map 116/820815 2m E of Llandudno off B5115 (Colwyn Bay) Open Mar-Nov 161 pitches (151
static) 7½ acres level/sloping grass and hard standings ▣◪◪⊕◪◪◪⤸ £11.30-£13.30

LLANDDULAS–see Colwyn Bay

LLANGEFNI, Anglesey, Gwynedd   **Map C3**
Restaurant: Anglesey Arms 7m SE at Menai Bridge ☎ (01248) 712305

Mornest Caravan Park, Pentre Berw, Gaerwen LL60 6HU ☎ Gaerwen (01248) 421725 OS map
114/475720 2m S of Llangefni on A5 (Menai Bridge-Holyhead) Open Mar 17-Oct 31 35 pitches
Level grass, sheltered ▤▣◪⊕◪▣▱ £6.00-£10.00

Trergof Caravan Park, Mona, Gwalchmai LL62 5EH ☎ Gwalchmai (01407) 720315 OS map
115/413744 2m SW of Llangefni off A5 (Menai Bridge-Holyhead) Open Mar-Oct, 48 pitches 7
acres, level grass, sheltered ▤▣◪⊕ £2.50-£5.00

LLANGOLLEN, Clwyd   **Map F5**
Pop 3,117. EC Thurs Small market town on S bank of river Dee best known as home of international
music festival SEE canal (by boat), Plas Newydd (home of `Ladies of Llangollen'), Dinas Bran
Castle, Vale of Llangollen, Int. Eisteddfod (Jul) ▨ Town Hall, Castle St ☎ (01978) 860828
Restaurant: Hand, Bridge St ☎ (01978) 860303

Ty Ucha Caravan Park, Maesmawr Road LL20 7PP ☎ Llangollen (01978) 860677 OS map
117/126/235425 1m E of Llangollen off A5 (Shrewsbury) Open Easter-Oct 40 pitches–no tents 4
acres level grass ▣◪⊕ £7.00

LLANRUG, Gwynedd   **Map C4**
Restaurant: Royal 3m W at Caernarfon ☎(01286) 673184

Brynteg Holiday Park LL55 4RF ☎(01286) 871374 OS map 115/544625 1m SE of Llanrug off
A4086 (Llanberis) near Bryn Bras Castle Open Mar-Nov, 455 pitches (286 static) 35 acres, part
sloping grass and hard standing 🛒❌🍴⚡🔌🚿🚰♿🅿🔥 (indoor heated) ⚡🛁🚻🏪♿ club,
fishing, boating £6.50-£13.00

Challoner Camping Caravan Park, Erw Hywel LL55 2AJ *Secluded park with views of Snowdon*
☎(01286) 672985 OS map 114/525635 ½m W of Llanrug on right of A4086 (Caernarfon) Open
Easter-Oct 35 pitches 2 acres level grass, sheltered 🛒🚿🔥♿🏪 £6.00

Plas Gwyn Caravan Park LL55 2AQ ☎(01286) 672619 OS map 115/525635 ½m W of Llanrug on
left of A4086 (Caernarfon) Open Mar-Oct, 60 pitches 3½ acres, grass, level and sloping,
sheltered 🛒⚡🔌🚿🔥♿🏪🚰 B and B £7.00-£10.00 (Mastercard/Visa)

Twll Clawdd Camping Caravan Park LL55 2AZ ☎(01286) 672838 OS map 115/530635 ½m W of
Llanrug on A4086 (Caernarfon-Llanberis) Open Mar-Oct, 40 pitches Level/sloping grass,
sheltered ⚡🔌🚿🔥♿ £7.00-£10.00

Tyn-y-Coed Farm LL55 2AQ ☎(01286) 673565 OS map 115/523630 ½m W of Llanrug on left of
A4086 (Caernarfon) Open Easter-Sept 80 pitches must book peak periods ⚡🔥🚰 £6.00-£8.00

LLANRWST, Gwynedd   **Map D4**
Pop 3,000. EC Thurs, MD Tues SEE parish church, Gwydir Park, Gwydir Castle, and gardens,
Bodnant gardens 6m N on A470 Restaurant: Meadowsweet ☎(01492) 642111

Bodnant Caravan Park, Nebo Road LL26 0SD ☎Llanrwst (01492) 640248 OS map 116/807608
½m S of Llanrwst on B5427 (Nebo) Open Mar-Oct 54 pitches Grass, level, part sheltered
🔥⚡🔌🚿🚰🚻🏪 (2) 📞 £8.00-£9.00

Glyn Farm Caravans, Trefriw LL27 0RZ ☎Llanrwst (01492) 640442 OS map 115781632 1½m
NNW of Llanrwst off B5106 (Conwy) Open Mar-Oct 28 pitches Level grass and hard standings,
sheltered ⚡🔥🚰 farm produce £6.50-£8.00

Maenan Abbey Caravan Park LL26 0VL ☎(01492) 640630 OS map 115/790658 3m N of
Llanrwst on A470 (Llandudno) Open Mar-Oct 105 pitches (72 static) 3 acres level grass sheltered
⚡🔥🔌🚿🚰 (£60) 🏪 £3.00-£6.00

Plas Meirion Caravan Park, Gower Road, Trefriw LL27 0RZ ☎Llanrwst (01492) 640247 OS map
115/783631 1½m NW of Llanrwst on B5106 (Conwy) Open Mar-Oct 31 pitches (26 static) 2
acres level grass, sheltered ⚡🔥🚿♻🏪 mountain bike hire £7.50-£11.00

LLANWNDA, Gwynedd   **Map C4**
SEE Caernarfon Bay W Restaurant: Stables ☎(01286) 830711

Tyn Rhos Farm LL54 5UH ☎Llanwnda (01286) 830362 OS map 115/455581 2m W of Llanwnda
off Saron-Llanfaglan road Open Mar-Oct, 20 pitches 2½ acres, level grass, sheltered ⚡🔥 farm
shop £6.00-£8.00

White Tower Caravan Park, Llandwrog LL54 5UH ☎Llanwnda (01286) 830649 OS map
115/458582 2m W of Llanwnda on Saron-Llandwrog road Open Mar-Oct, 106 pitches (54 static)
7 acres level grass and hard standings 🛒🍴⚡🔌🚿🔥♿🚰🛁🚻🏪🚰♿ fishing, lic club £5.00-
£10.50 (all cards)

LLANDWROG–see Llanwnda

LLIGWY BAY–see Moelfre

LLWYNGWRIL, Gwynedd   **Map C6**
Restaurant: Greenfield 4m S at Tywyn ☎(01654) 710354

Borthwen Farm LL37 2JT ☎(01341) 250322 OS map 124/588099 ½m W of Llwyngwril via level
crossing and road to station Open Mar-Oct 100 pitches (80 static) 8 acres level grass ⚡🔥
access to stony beach £4.00

**The distance and direction of a campsite is given from the centre of the key town under
which it appears, the place name in parentheses following the road number indicating which
route to take.**

MENAI BRIDGE, Anglesey, Gwynedd   Map C3
Pop 2,300. EC Wed, MD Mon Gateway to Anglesey, `The Mother of Wales', where Telford's 1000ft long suspension bridge crosses the Straits SEE Telford suspension bridge, St Tysilio church Restaurant: Liverpool Arms, St Georges Pier ☎(01248) 712453

Fron Caravan and Camping, Brynsiencyn LL61 6TX ☎(01248) 430310 OS map 114/472668 6m SW of Menai Bridge off A5 (Holyhead) on right of A4080 (Rhosneigr) Open Apr-Sept 79 pitches 5 acres level grass and hard standings, sheltered £9.00

Plas Coch Caravan Park, Llanedwen LL61 6EJ ☎(01248) 714346 OS map 114/512683 3m SW of Menai Bridge off A5 (Holyhead) on left of A4080 (Brynciencyn) Open Mar-Oct, 300 pitches (200 static) 200 acres, level grass, sheltered slipway £8.00

MOELFRE, Anglesey, Gwynedd   Map C3
Restaurant: Rhostrefor 3m S at Benllech ☎(01248) 852347

Capel Elen Caravan Park, Lligwy Beach LL70 9PQ ☎Moelfre (01248) 410670 OS map 114/484874 3m N of Moelfre off A5025 (Amlwch) at Brynrefail on Lligwy Beach road Open Mar-Oct, 75 pitches (45 static) 7 acres, gentle slope £6.50-£10.50

Melin Rhos Farm, Lligwy Bay, Dulas LL70 9HQ ☎(01248) 410213/410345 OS map 114/493864 ½m S of Moelfre off A5025 (Benllech) Open Easter-Oct 80 pitches 6 acres level grass and hard standings, sheltered £5.00-£8.00

Tyddyn Isaf Caravan Park, Lligwy Bay LL70 9PQ ☎Moelfre (01248) 410203 OS map 114/480849 ½m W of Moelfre off A5025 (Amlwch) Open Mar-Oct 80 pitches (50 static) Grass and hard standing, sheltered (£5/wk) lic club, private path to beach £6.00-£18.00

Tyn Rhos, Lligwy LL72 8NL ☎Moelfre (01248) 852417 OS map 114/509865 ¼m W of Moelfre on Lligwy road Open all year, 140 pitches (72 static) 16 acres, sloping £6.50-£10.00

MOLD, Clwyd   Map F4
Pop 8860 EC Thurs MD Wed, Sat Busy market town in Alyn valley SEE Theatr Clwyd, most advanced arts complex in Wales, parish church, Daniel Owen centre art gallery and museum Town Hall, East St ☎(01352) 759331 Restaurant: Bryn Awel, Denbigh Rd ☎(01352) 758622

Fron Farm, Hendre CH7 5QW ☎(01352) 741217 OS map 116/193678 4m NW of Mold on A541 (Denbigh) Open Apr-Oct 25 pitches Level/sloping grass, sheltered £7.00-£9.00

MORFA BYCHAN–see Porthmadog

NEFYN, Gwynedd   Map B5
Pop 1,150 SEE St Mary's church (now maritime museum) Restaurant: Caeau Capel near beach ☎(01758) 720240

Hirdre Fawr Farm, Edern LL53 8YY ☎(01758) 720278 OS map 123/249381 3m SW of Nefyn on right of B4417 (Tudweiliog) Open May-Oct 20 pitches 3 acres level grass, sheltered £5.00

Planning a tour in Europe?

Then choose one of the itineraries mapped and described in *Tour Europe* and have the homework done for you. Each chapter presents a complete holiday – a step by step account of how to enjoy touring for a fortnight through one of ten chosen regions in seven countries, each rewarding in itself, from the scenic splendour of the Austrian lake district adjoining Mozart's Salzburg to the wooded wonderland of the Ardennes/Eifel, from the castle-studded Loire valley to the sun-baked Italian Marches, and much more. Linking all the local information are touring directions and a sketch map, with each route forming a circuit so that it can be left and picked up again at any point.

Reserve your copy at a special pre-publication price by writing to Frederick Tingey (TE), Hillsboro, How Caple HR1 4TE.

NEWBOROUGH, Anglesey, Gwynedd   **Map C4**
SEE Newborough Warren, Llanddwyn island Restaurant: Bay 6m NW at Rhosneigr ℰ(01407) 810332

Awelfryn Caravan Park LL61 6SG ℰ(01248) 440230 OS map 114/425656 ¼m SW of Newborough off A4080 (Llanfairpwll) Open Easter-Sept 52 pitches 2 acres level grass ▣▨⊕ £6.00

PENMAENMAWR, Gwynedd   **Map D3**
Pop 4,050. EC Wed Restaurant: Castle, 5m E at Conwy ℰ(01492) 592324

Tyddyn Du Farm, Conwy Old Road LL34 6RE ℰ(01492) 622300 OS map 115/729770 1m E of Penmaenmawr off A55 (Conwy) near golf course Open Mar-Oct 100 pitches Level/sloping grass, hard standings, sheltered ▣▨⊕▨⊡ £8.00-£10.00 (most cards)

Woodlands Camping Park, Pendyffryn Hall LL34 6UF ℰ(01492) 623219 OS map 115/741776 1m NE of Penmaenmawr off A55 (Conwy) Open Mar-Oct–no adv booking 120 pitches–families and couples only Level grass and hard standings in woodland, sheltered ⵠↂ▣▣⊕▨⊡℗❀ lic club, woodland walks £8.00-£14.00

PENRHYNDEUDRAETH, Gwynedd   **Map D5**
Pop 1,820. EC Thurs SEE Portmeirion 2m S, nature reserve 2m NE, Ffestiniog railway Restaurant: Royal Sportsman 2m W at Porthmadog ℰ(01766) 512015

Blaencefn Caravan Park LL48 6NA ℰPenrhyndeudraeth (01766) 770889 OS map 124/620398 1m NE of Penrhyndeudraeth on left of A487 (Maentwrog) Open Easter-Oct 25 pitches 3 acres level grass *No showers* £3.00

Bwlchbryn Caravan Park LL48 6RY ℰ(01766) 771474 OS map 124/613395 ½m W of Penrhyndeudraeth off A487 (Porthmadog) Open Mar-Oct 49 pitches (42 static) ▣▨⊡ (8) £5.50

PENTRAETH–see Benllech

PONTRUG–see Caernarfon

PORTHMADOG, Gwynedd   **Map C5**
Pop 2,000. EC Wed, MD Fri Victorian town with extensive sandy beaches and safe port and harbour SEE Ffestiniog railway, Black Rock Sands, maritime museum ℹ High Street ℰPorthmadog (01766) 512981 Restaurant: Royal Sportsman, High St ℰ(01766) 512015

Black Rock Camping Site, Morfa Bychan LL49 9LD ℰPorthmadog (01766) 513919 OS map 124/531373 3m SW of Porthmadog at Black Rock Sands Open Mar-Oct 140 pitches Level grass ▣▣▨⊕▨⊕⤳ £10.00-£15.00

Cardigan View Park, Morfa Bychan LL49 9YA ℰPorthmadog (01766) 512032 OS map 124/542372 3m W of Porthmadog at Black Rock Sands Open Easter-Oct 224 pitches (192 static) Grass and hard standings, level ▣▨⊕▨ (indoor) ⊕⊡ £12.00

Garreg Goch Caravan Park, Morfa Bychan LL49 9YD ℰPorthmadog (01766) 512210 OS map 124/543372 2m SW of Porthmadog off Morfa Bychan road Open Mar-Oct 85 pitches (61 static) Level grass and hard standings ▤▣▨▨⊕▨⤳⊡⊡ £4.75-£7.85

Greenacres Holiday Park, Black Rock Sands, Morfa Bychan LL49 9YB ℰ(01766) 512781 OS map 124/546372 2m SW of Porthmadog on Morfa Bychan road Open Mar-Oct 947 pitches (870 static) Level grass and hard standings ▤ⵠ⤳ↂ▣▨⊕▨⊡⤳❀⊡ clubhouse, bowling £6.50-£11.75

Gwyndy Caravan Park, Black Rock Sands, Morfa Bychan LL49 9YB ℰPorthmadog (01766) 512047 OS map 124/543371 2m SW of Porthmadog off Black Rock Sands road at Morfa Bychan Open Mar 8-Nov 26 60 pitches (44 static) Level hard standing sheltered ▤▣▣▨▨⊕▨▣⊡⌂ super pitches £10.00-£13.50

Tyddyn-Adi Camping, Morfa Bychan LL49 9YW ℰ(01766) 512933 OS map 124/540377 3m SW of Porthmadog off road to Black Rock Sands via Morfa Bychan Open Mar-Oct 200 pitches 28 acres, level grass, sheltered ▤▣▣▨▨⊕⤳⊡ mini golf, games room £7.00-£9.50

Tyddyn Llwyn Caravan Camping Park, Black Rock Rd LL49 9UR ℰ(01766) 512205 OS map 124/561384 ½m SW of Porthmadog on right of Morfa Bychan road–signposted Open Mar-Oct 206 pitches (53 static) Level/sloping grass and hard standings ▤✕ⵠ▣▣▨▨⊕▨⤳⊡ games room £6.00-£9.00

Charges quoted are the minimum and maximum for two people with car and caravan or tent. They are given only as a guide and should be checked with the owner of any site at which you plan to stay.
Remember to ask whether hot water or use of the pool (if any) is extra and make sure that VAT is included.

Tan-y-Don Caravan Park

Victoria Road, Prestatyn   Tel (01745) 853749

West on A548 Rhyl road.

Open March-January. Level grass and hard standings.

£10-£12 per night for two (Mastercard/Visa/Switch)

PRESTATYN, Clwyd   **Map F3**
Pop 15,000. EC Thurs, MD Tues, Fri Popular resort with 3 beaches, once N terminus of Offa's Dyke
SEE Offa's Dyke Path ⓘ Scala Cinema, High St ✆(01745) 854365 Restaurant: Cross Foxes,
Meliden Rd ✆(01745) 854984

Nant Mill Farm LL19 9LY ✆Prestatyn (01745) 852360 OS map 116/074831 ½m E of Prestatyn on
A548 (Flint) Open Easter-Oct 150 pitches 5 acres level/sloping grass, sheltered
🛒▣▤⌀✲∅☻↲ £9.50-£11.50

Presthaven Sands Holiday Park, Shore Road, Gronant LL19 9TT ✆Prestatyn (01745) 856471 OS
map 116/095835 2m E of Prestatyn on A548 (Flint) Open Easter/May-Oct 1,200 pitches (1,100
static)–no tents 🛒✕⇿▣▤⌀✲▱ (out & indoor, heated) ↲▤⌂ hairdressing, sauna, solarium,
disco, amusements, lic and family clubs, entertainment £8.00-£12.00 (inc showers)

Talacre Beach Caravan Park, Talacre CH8 9RD ✆(01745) 852612/889616 OS map 116/182840
4m E of Prestatyn off A548 (Chester) Open Mar-Jan 620 pitches (600 static) Grass and hard
standing 🛒✕⇿▣▤⌀∅▱ (heated indoor) ↲⌂ lic club, barbecue, bowling green, tennis
£10.00-£20.00

Tan y Don Caravan Park, Victoria Road LL19 7UT ✆(01745) 853749/852563 OS map 116/055830
1m W of Prestatyn on A548 (Rhyl) Open Mar-Jan–must book peak periods 72 pitches (65 static)
Level grass and hard standings 🛒▣▤⌀✲∅↲▤✖▱ £10.00-£12.00 (Mastercard/Visa)

PWLLHELI, Gwynedd   **Map B5**
Pop 4,000. EC Thurs, MD Wed SEE Gimblet Rock ⓘ Y Maes ✆Pwllheli (01758) 613000
Restaurant: The Seahaven, West End Pier ✆(01758) 612572

Abererch Sands Holiday Centre, Abererch LL53 6PJ ✆Pwllheli (01758) 612327 OS map
123/403358 2m NE of Pwllheli off A497 (Criccieth) on Abererch Halt road Open Mar-Oct 155
pitches (85 static) Level grass 🛒▣▤⌀✲∅▱ (heated) ↲& £8.00-£11.00 (most cards)

Gimblet Rock Caravan Park, South Beach LL53 5AY ✆(01758) 712043 OS map 123/383346 ½m
S of Pwllheli on South Beach road Open Mar-Oct 140 pitches (115 static) 🛒♟▣✲∅✖▱⌂
£6.00-£8.25

Hendra Caravan Park, Efailnewydd LL53 8TN ✆Pwllheli (01758) 712793 OS map 123/350359
2½m W of Pwllheli off A497 (Nefyn) on B4415 (Aberdaron) Open Mar-Oct 150 pitches (120 static)
Hard standings ▣⌀▤ £9.00

See also Llanbedrog

RHOSNEIGR, Anglesey, Gwynedd   **Map B3**
Pop 1,560. EC Wed Restaurant: Minstrel Lodge, Station Rd ✆(01407) 810970

Bodfan Farm LL64 5XA ✆Rhosneigr (01407) 810563 OS map 114/342736 ½m N of Rhosneigr on
A4080 (Llanfaelog) near school Open Apr-Sept 60 pitches Level/sloping grass ▣⌀✲ freezer
pack service £5.00-£8.00

Plas Caravan Park, Llanfaelog LL63 5TU ✆Rhosneigr (01407) 810234 OS map 114/331738 1m
NE of Rhosneigr off A4080 near station Open Mar 15-Oct 31 72 pitches (55 static) 6 acres level
grass and hard standings ▣▤✲∅ £9.25-£12.75 (most cards)

Shoreside, Tyn Morfa Farm LL64 5QX ✆Rhosneigr (01407) 810279 OS map 114/324737 ½m NE
of Rhosneigr off A4080 (Llanfaelog) opp golf club Open Easter-Sept, 110 pitches 20 acres,
level/gentle slope ▤⌀✲↲▱⌂ pony trekking £8.00-£15.00 (inc hot water)

RHYL, Clwyd   **Map F3**
Pop 23,000. EC Thurs, MD Wed, Sat SEE Royal Floral Hall, Marine Lake Leisure Park, children's village ▯ Town Hall, Wellington Rd ☏Rhyl (01745) 355068 Restaurant: White Horse, Bedford St ☏(01745) 334927

Edwards Leisure Parks, Gaingc Rd, Towyn LL22 9HY ☏(01745) 342322 OS map 116/976797 2m SW of Rhyl on A547 (Abergele) Open Mar 21-Oct 21 432 pitches (400 static)–no tents, no adv booking 17 acres hard standings, level ▮⇴◙◘❀∅↩ £10.00 inc elect

Marine Holiday Park, Cefndy Road LL18 2HG ☏Rhyl (01745) 345194 OS map 116/003802 1m SW of Rhyl off A525 (Rhuddlan) near Marine Lake Open Apr-Oct, 491 pitches (466 static) ▮✗▯⇴◙∅∅▱ (indoor heated) ↩❀ (Jul-Aug) £5.70-£7.70

Sunnyvale Holiday Park (Camping Club), Foryd LL18 5AS ☏(01745) 339401 OS map 116/992807 1m W of Rhyl on right of A548 (Abergele) at rear of Ferry Hotel Open Apr 1-Sept 28, 120 pitches 5 acres, level grass ◙❀ £4.50-£5.30

See also Dyserth and Rhuddlan

RUABON, Clwyd   **Map G5**
Pop 2,500 SEE monuments in church, Wat's Dyke, Ruabon Mountain Restaurant: Wynnstay Arms ☏(01978) 822187

James Caravan Park LL14 6DW ☏(01978) 820148 OS map 117/302434 ½m S of Ruabon on A539 (Llangollen) near junct with A483 Open all year 40 pitches, some hard standings 8 acres, part level ◙∅❀⚃ £7.00-£8.00

RUTHIN, Clwyd   **Map F4**
Pop 4,330. EC Thurs, MD Tues, Thurs, Fri Historic town and one most picturesque in Wales on ridge above Vale of Clwyd SEE St Peter's church (panelled roof), castle (now hotel) ▯ Craft Centre, Park Rd ☏Ruthin (01824) 703992 Restaurant: Castle and Myddleton Arms, St Peter's Sq ☏(01824) 707215

Parc Farm Caravan Park, Llanarmon Yn lal CH7 4QW ☏(01824) 780666/780700 OS map 116/198556 6½m E of Ruthin off A494 (Mold) on B5430 (Wrecsam) Open Apt-Oct 220 pitches (200 static) Level/sloping grass, sheltered ▯◙◘∅❀∅▱◆ clubhouse £3.50-£14.00

Three Pigeons Inn, Craigfechan LL15 2EU ☏(01824) 703178 OS map 116/147545 3m SE of Ruthin off A494 (Mold) on B5429 (Craigfechan) Open Mar-Oct 14 pitches ✗▯❀∅❀ £4.00-£5.00

ST ASAPH, Clwyd   **Map F4**
Pop 3150 EC Thurs SEE Rhuddlan castle NW, Denbigh castle S Restaurant: Red Lion ☏(01745) 582716

Eryl Hall, Lower Denbigh Road LL17 0EW ☏St Asaph (01745) 582255 OS map 116/035729 1m S of St Asaph on right of B5381 Open Mar 21-Oct 7 301 pitches (240 static)–no tents Level grass and hard standings ▯◙◘∅❀∅❀↩❀ £9.50

TALYBONT–see Dyffryn Ardudwy

TOWYN–see Abergele and Rhyl

TREARDDUR BAY–see Holyhead

TREFRIW–see Llanrwst

Tour Regional France

224pp ISBN 1-870009-28-2 £7.50 post-free (in UK only)

Guided tours of 5-7 days duration through every region of France, with ample advice on what to see and do, route directions, maps, glossary and much more, such as what local specialities to look out for in shops and restaurants. The book is now in preparation and there will be a £2.00 reduction on the cover price for orders placed prior to publication.

Frederick Tingey, Mirador Books, Hillsboro, How Caple HR1 4TE.

TYWYN, Gwynedd   **Map C7**
Pop 2,800. EC Wed Seaside resort overlooking Cardigan Bay, with 6km of beach SEE church, railway museum, Tallylyn narrow gauge railway ⓘ High Street ☏ Tywyn (01654) 710070
Restaurant: Corbett Arms, Corbett Sq ☏ (01654) 710264

Pall Mall Farm LL36 9RU ☏ Tywyn (01654) 710384 OS map 135/595013 ½m NE of Tywyn on A493 (Dolgellau) Open Easter-Sept, 135 pitches Level grass ▣⌀ £3.50

Pant y Neuadd Caravan Park, Aberdovey Road LL36 9HW ☏ Tywyn (01654) 711393 OS map 124/597003 ½m SE of Tywyn on A493 (Aberdovey) Open Mar-Oct 99 pitches (67 static) Level grass, sheltered ▣▣⌀⊕⌀✓▭ £7.75-£9.75

Tynllwyn Caravan Camping Park, Bryncrug LL36 9RD ☏ Tywyn (01654) 710370 OS map 135/615023 2m N of Tywyn off A493 (Dolgellau) on B4405 (Abergynolwyn) via Bryncrug 7 acres, level grass Open Apr-Oct, 104 pitches (56 static) 7 acres, level grass ▤▣▣⌀⊕⌀✓▭ £4.00-£7.50

Waenfach Caravan Park, Llanegryn LL36 9SB ☏ Tywyn (01654) 710375 OS map 135/591050 3m N of Tywyn on A493 (Dolgellau) Open Apr-Oct, 60 pitches (40 static) Level/sloping grass, sheltered ▣▣⌀⊕⌀ £6.00

Woodlands Holiday Park, Bryncrug LL36 9UH ☏ Tywyn (01654) 710471 OS map 135/618035 4m NE of Tywyn off A493 (Dolgellau) on B4405 (Abergynolwyn) Open Apr-Oct–must book peak periods 142 pitches (122 static)–no tents Hard standings ▤✗♋▣▣⌀⊕⌀▭ (outdoor heated) ⊕✓▢▭ £6.00-£7.50

Ynysmaengwyn Park LL36 9RY ☏ Tywyn (01654) 710684 OS map 135/601021 1m NE of Tywyn on left of A493 (Dolgellau) in grounds of former manor house Open Apr-Oct, 195 pitches (115 static) 8 acres, mainly level grass ▤▣▣⌀⊕✓ fishing, adventure park £7.00-£12.00

VALLEY, Anglesey, Gwynedd   **Map B3**
Restaurant: Beach 4m W at Trearddur Bay ☏ (01407) 860332

Penrhyn Bay Touring Park, Llanfwrog LL65 4YG ☏ (01407) 730496 OS map 114/284847 5m N of Valley off A5025 (Amlwch) Open Easter-Oct 140 pitches (90 static) Grass, level, open ▤⋌▣▣⌀⌀▭ (indoor heated) ⊕✓▢▭ £4.00-£14.00

Pen-y-Bont Farm, Four Mile Bridge LL65 3EY ☏ Valley (01407) 740481 OS map 114/282787 1m SW of Valley on B4545 (Trearddur Bay) Open Whit-Oct 30 pitches 3½ acres level grass *No showers* £5.00-£6.00

Sandy Beach Touring Caravan Park, Llanfwrog LL65 4YH ☏ (01407) 730302 OS map 114/286848 4m N of Valley off A5025 (Amlwch) Open Mar-Oct 124 pitches (84 static) Level/sloping grass, sheltered ▤✗⌐▣▣⌀⊕⌀✓▢▭ £4.50-£8.50

Silver Bay Caravan Park, Pentre Gwyddel, Rhoscolyn LL65 2RZ ☏ Trearddur Bay (01407) 860374 OS map 114/287753 3m S of Valley off B4545 (Trearddur Bay) Open Easter-Jan–must book peak periods 176 pitches (160 static) Sloping grass, sheltered ▤▣⌀⌀✓✿▭ lic club, private beach £7.00-£10.00

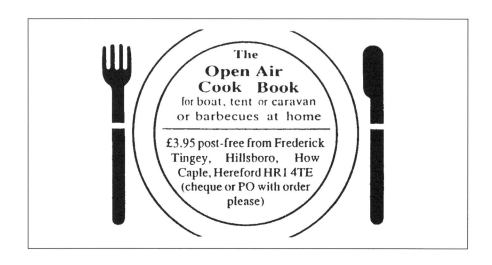

WAUNFAWR, Gwynedd   **Map C4**
Village 3m SE of Caernarfon Restaurant: Cwellyn Arms 4m SE on A4085 at Rhyd-Ddu ℰ(01286) 650537

Amos Jones Camping Site, Cynefin, Betws Garmon LL54 7YR ℰ(01286) 650537 OS map 115/545567 2m SE of Waunfawr on right of A4085 (Beddgelert) Open all year, 20 pitches Level grass, sheltered ✕♀🔥∅ fishing £5.00-£6.00

Bryn Gloch Caravan Camping Park, Betws Garmon LL54 7YY ℰ(01286) 650216 OS map 115/535575 1m SE of Waunfawr on right of A4085 (Beddgelert) Open all year, 180 pitches 12 acres level grass and hard standings, sheltered 🔥🏹🚽🔥∅⊕∅🔌➰🔥🏠♿🔥 fishing, mini-golf, mother and baby room £10.00 (most cards)

Tyn-yr-Onnen Farm LL55 4AX ℰWaunfawr (01286) 650281 OS map 115/535590 ½m W of Waunfawr centre on A4085–signposted Open Whitsun-Oct, 50 pitches 3½ acres grass, gentle slope, sheltered 🔥🚽🔥∅⊕∅⊕🔌➰🔥🏠 hill walks, fishing £6.00-£7.00

WRECSAM, (Wrexham) Clwyd   **Map G4/5**
Pop 41,570. EC Wed, MD Mon Most important industrial town in Wales on N bank of river Clywedog SEE St Giles church, Erddig mansion 1m S, Industiral Heritage Centre at Bersham 2m SW ℹLambpit St ℰWrexham (01978) 292015 Restaurant: Cross Lanes 3m SE on A525 ℰ(01978) 780555

Cae Adar Farm, Bwlchgwyn LL11 5UE ℰWrexham (01978) 757385 OS map 117/268529 4m NW of Wrecsam off A525 (Ruthin) Open May-Oct 12 pitches 2 acres, level grass, sheltered 🔥∅⊕ £6.00-£7.50

Plassey Touring Caravan and Leisure Park, Eyton LL13 0SP ℰ(01978) 780277 Fax (01978) 780019 OS map 117/351450 2m S of Wrecsam off A483 (Oswestry) on B5426 (Bangor-on-Dee)–signposted Open Mar-Nov 120 pitches Level grass and hard standing, sheltered 🔥✕♀⇆🏹🚽🔥∅⊕∅🔲 (heated indoor May-Sept) ⊕🔌➰🔥ℙ🔥 (1) ♿ 9 hole golf, pitch and putt, table tennis, badminton, sauna, craft workshops £12.00-£14.50 (inc elect) (Mastercard/Visa)

The Racecourse, Bangor on Dee LL13 0DA ℰ(01978) 781009 OS map 117/385448 4m SE of Wrecsam off A525 (Whitchurch) Open Mar 22-Nov 1 100 pitches 5 acres, level/sloping grass and hard standing, part sheltered 🚽🔥⊕∅♿ £4.30-£12.10 (Mastercard/Visa)

13 Central and South Wales

Covering two-thirds of the principality, Central and South Wales is made up of new counties with ancient regional names: Dyfed in the west, inland Powys in the east and Gwent and Glamorgan in the south.

Powys forms a long north–south rectangle along the border with England. The northern section is mainly a moorland plateau drained by the beautiful Lake Vyrnwy and trout-rich rivers flowing through deep valleys, the most attractive of which is the Dovey. The area is crossed in an east–west direction by only two roads but many routes for walkers. Central Powys is a district of hills and high moors dotted with isolated lime-washed farmhouses, cloaked on the east near New Radnor by a shady forest and occupied by four towns, none industrial: Presteigne, the once fashionable spas of Llandrindod and Builth Wells and Rhayader, gateway to the scenic Elan Valley and its series of reservoirs. Offa's Dyke Path passes near Knighton and Kington on a line which links the Severn and the Dee. In southern Powys is the wild Brecon Beacons National Park encircling the Black Mountains, with the Usk and its tributaries cutting through its wooded gorges. The south-eastern ramparts of Wales, the Black Mountains march east to the Wye, south to Crickhowell and northeast as far as Talgarth. Hay on Wye, half in England, is one gateway to the park, Abergavenny another.

Gwent, the former Monmouthshire, has an uninteresting coastline on the Severn Estuary, lofty hills mined for coal in the northwest and a pastoral landscape near the English border in the east—at its most inviting in the Wye Valley above Chepstow. A waymarked scenic drive through the Ebbw Forest starts at Cwmcarn near Newport.

Glamorgan is mountainous coalmining country in the north, pastoral and picturesque in the south. Popular seaside resorts like Porthcawl and Penarth alternate with industrial towns like Barry and Bridgend. West of Swansea is the wholly unspoiled Gower Peninsula ending in limestone cliffs.

Western Dyfed is noted for the sandy beaches of Cardigan, Aberporth and New Quay and the high cliffs between Aberystwyth and Aberaeron backed by bare moorland dotted with Iron Age hill forts, rough uplands and steepsided valleys. Local fishermen still use coracles of ancient design on the main waterway, the Teifi. A narrow-gauge railway operates between Aberystwyth and Devil's Bridge, a popular beauty spot.

The remote and thinly populated southwest corner of Wales has a romantic coastline of wild cliffs and windswept headlands, a mountainous north and a fertile and sunlit south. The Pembrokeshire Coast Path starts at St Dogmaels near Cardigan and follows the bay and inlets round to Amroth near Saundersfoot.

Campsites are well distributed along the south and west coasts, with the greatest concentrations around Saundersfoot, Laugharne, St David's and Pembroke in the south and Aberporth, Aberystwyth and Fishguard in the west. Inland campsites are most numerous around Narberth in the south, though there are two or more at each of the main centres in Powys. Coastal campsites are usually the best equipped.

ABERAERON, Dyfed   **Map D4**
Pop 1,445 EC Thurs Early 19c harbour town at mouth of river Aeron SEE Georgian houses and
harbour ◼The Quay ✆Aberaeron (01545) 570602 Restaurant: Feathers Royal ✆(01545) 570214

Aeron Coast Caravan Park, North Rd SA46 0JF ✆(01545) 570349 OS map 146/470634 In
  Aberaeron on A487 (Aberystwyth) Open Mar-Oct 200 pitches (150 static) Level grass
  🛒♿▣➓◪⊘➂⇲⊡♿ tennis £8.00-£11.00 (Switch)

Brynarion Caravan Park, Cross Inn SY23 5NA ✆(01974) 272231 OS map 146/540646 5m ENE
  of Aberaeron off A487 (Aberystwyth) on B4577 (Cross Inn) Open Mar-Oct 40 pitches (30 static)
  Grass, level, sheltered 🛒▣◪●⇲ £3.50-£4.50

Llanina Touring Park, Llanarth SA47 0NP ✆(01545) 580568 OS map 146/421574 4m SW of
  Aberaeron on A487 (Aberystwth-Cardigan) by Llanina garage Open Apr-Sept 45 pitches ➓◪➓
  £3.50-£4.50

Wide Horizons Caravan and Chalet Park SA46 0ET ✆(01545) 570043 OS map 135/440615 ¾m
  S of Aberaeron on right of A487 (Cardigan) by sea Open Apr-Oct 100 pitches (70 static) Grass
  and hard standings, sloping ➓▣◪●➓⊘➂⇲⊡⇲🏠 games room £6.50-£7.00

ABERCRAF–see Ystragynlais

ABERDARE, Mid Glam   **Map E6**
Restaurant: Glandover Arms, Gadlys Rd (B4275) ✆(01685) 872923

Dare Valley Country Park, Rhondda-Cynon-Taff CF44 7RG ✆(01685) 874672 OS map
  170/985026 ¼m SW of Aberdare off A4233 (Maerdy)–signposted Open Jan 2-Dec 23 35 pitches
  Level grass and hard standings ✖◪➓ serviced pitches £3.00-£7.50

ABERGAVENNY, Gwent   **Map G5**
Pop 12,000. EC Thurs, MD Tues, Fri SEE Castle Museum, St Mary's church, Sugar loaf mountain
4m NW, White Castle 5½m E via Llantilio Crosseny, Llanfihangel Court 5m N ◼Swan Meadow,
Cross St ✆Abergavenny (01873) 857588 Restaurant: Malthouse, Newmarket Close ✆(01873)
877842

Pyscodlyn Farm, Brecon Road NP7 7ER ✆Abergavenny (01873) 853271 OS map 161/266155
  2m W of Abergavenny on A40 (Crickhowell) Open Apr-Oct 60 pitches Grass, level, part sheltered
  ▣◪◪●⇲ £7.00-£8.00

The Offa's Tavern, Pandy NP7 8DL ✆(01873) 890254 OS map 161/332213 5½m N of
  Abergavenny on A465 (Hereford) Open all year 20 pitches Grass, part sheltered
  ✖➓◪◪➓⇲ dairy produce £9.00-£12.00

Wern-ddu Farm, Old Ross Rd NP7 8NG ✆(01873) 856223 OS map 161/322156 1½m NE of
  Abergavenny off A465 (Hereford) on right of B4521 (Skenfrith) Open Mar-Oct 20 pitches Level
  grass, sheltered ➓◪●◪➂ golf range and golf course £5.00 (Mastercard/Visa)

For other sites near Abergavenny see Crickhowell and Gilwern

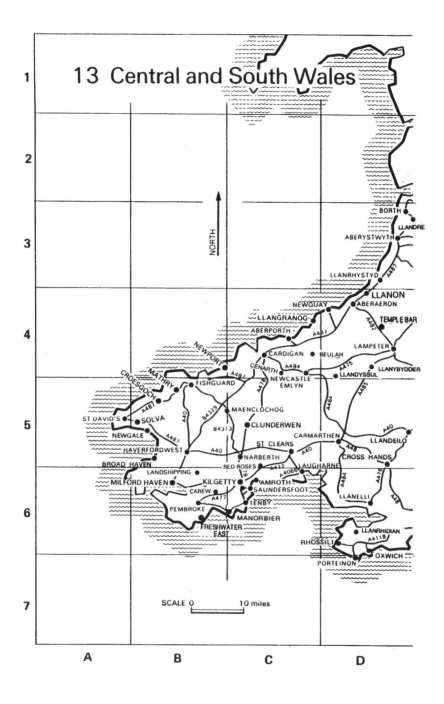

13 Central and South Wales

BORTH
LLANDRE
ABERYSTWYTH
LLANRHYSTYD
LLANON
NEWQUAY
ABERAERON
LLANGRANOG
TEMPLE BAR
ABERPORTH
LAMPETER
NEWPORT
CARDIGAN
BEULAH
CENARTH
LLANYBYDDER
CROESGOCH
MATHRY
FISHGUARD
NEWCASTLE EMLYN
LLANDYSSUL
MAENCLOCHOG
ST DAVID'S
SOLVA
CLUNDERWEN
NEWGALE
CARMARTHEN
LLANDEILO
HAVERFORDWEST
ST CLEARS
CROSS HANDS
NARBERTH
BROAD HAVEN
RED ROSES
LAUGHARNE
LANDSHIPPING
MILFORD HAVEN
KILGETTY
AMROTH
CAREW
SAUNDERSFOOT
LLANELLI
TENBY
PEMBROKE
MANORBIER
LLANRHIDIAN
FRESHWATER EAST
RHOSSILI
OXWICH
PORTEINON

SCALE 0   10 miles

NORTH

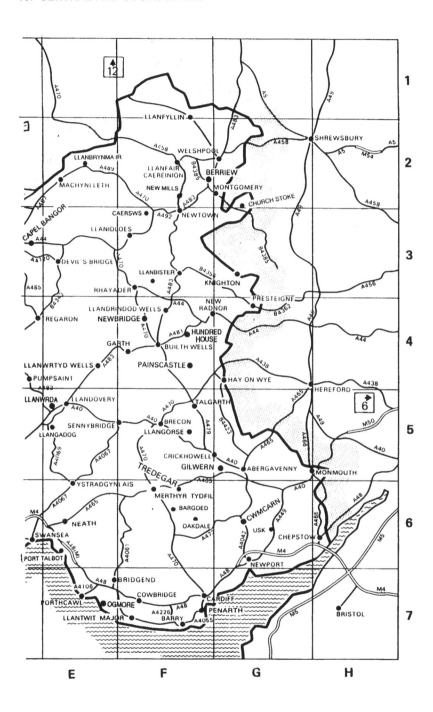

ABERPORTH, Dyfed   **Map C4**
Pop 800. EC Wed SEE natural harbour, Tresaith beach 2m E Restaurant: Morlan Hotel (01239) 810611

Brynawelon Touring Caravan Camping Park, Sarnau SA44 6RE (01239) 654584 OS map 145/322508 4m E of Aberporth off B4333 (Newcastle Emlyn) and A487 (Aberaeron) opposite Sarnau chapel Open Apr-Sept 30 pitches Grass, level, open   £7.50-£9.50

Caerfelin Caravan Park, SA43 2BY Aberporth (01239) 810540 OS map 145/257511 ¼m SW of Aberporth centre off B4333 (Cardigan) Open Mar-Oct 105 pitches (91 static) Grass, sheltered   £6.00-£10.50

Gwalia Falls Caravan Park, Tresaith SA43 2JL Aberporth (01239) 810361 OS map 145/272510 1m N of Aberporth off B4333 (Newcastle Emlyn) by sea Open Apr-Oct 58 pitches   £2.50-£3.00

Helyg Fach Farm SA43 2EB Aberporth (01239) 810317 OS map 145/269513 ½m E of Aberporth off B4333 (Newcastle Emlyn) Open Easter-Oct 290 pitches (200 static) 8 acres, level   lic clubs £3.50

Llety Caravan Park, Tresaith SA43 2ED (01239) 810354 OS map 145/273515 1m E of Aberporth in Tresaith near beach Open Mar-Oct 150 pitches 12 acres level/sloping grass   £7.00-£9.50

Manorafon Caravan Park, Penbryn, Sarnau SA44 6QH Aberporth (01239) 810564 Fax (01239) 810564 OS map 145/300520 2½m E of Aberporth off B4333 (Newcastle Emlyn) and A487 (Aberaeron) near Penbryn beach Open Easter-Oct 30 pitches Grass, part level, sheltered   £7.00-£10.00

Penrallt Hotel Caravan Park SA43 2BS Aberporth (01239) 810227 OS map 145/252504 1m SW of Aberporth on B4333 (Cardigan) Open Easter-Oct 100 pitches 10 acres, part level   (outdoor heated) nature trail £3.50-£5.00

Pilbach Caravan and Camping Park, Bettws Evan, Rhydlewis SA44 5RT (01239) 851434 OS map 145/308477 4m SE of Aberporth off B4333 (Newcastle Emlyn) Open Mar-Oct–must book peak periods 135 pitches (70 static) Grass and hard standings, part sloping, sheltered   bar snacks, clubhouse, games room £7.00-£10.00 (Mastercard/Visa)

Talywerydd Caravan Park, Penbryn, Sarnau SA44 6QY Aberporth (01239) 810322 OS map 145/298508 4m NE of Aberporth off A487 (Cardigan-Aberaeron) Open Feb-Oct, 40 pitches 4 acres, grass and hard standing, part sloping   (lic) 9 hole pitch and putt £7.00-£12.00 (Mastercard/Visa)

Treddafydd Farm, Sarnau SA44 6PZ (01239) 654551 OS map 145/305512 4½m NE of Aberporth off B4333/A487 (Aberaeron) and Penbryn beach road on left at Sarnau church Open Apr-Oct 40 pitches Grass, sloping, part sheltered   dry ice £6.00-£7.50

See also Llangranog

ABERYSTWYTH, Dyfed   **Map D3**
Pop 15,300. EC Wed, MD Mon Seaside resort, university town and admin centre for Cardigan Bay coast SEE Nat lib of Wales, Vale of Rheidol narrow gauge railway to Devil's Bridge Terrace Rd (01970) 612125 Restaurant: Castle, South Rd (01970) 612188

Aberystwyth Holiday Village, Penparcau Road SY23 1TH *Nearest site to town centre* Aberystwyth (01970) 624211 OS map 135/586810 ¼m S of Aberystwyth on A487 (Aberaeron) Open Mar-Oct–no adv booking 302 pitches (150 static) 30 acres level grass and hard standings, sheltered   (indoor) snack bar, lic club, fishing

Bryncarnedd Dairy Farm, SY23 3DG Aberystwyth (01970) 615271 OS map 135/603892 1m N of Aberystwyth on B4572 (Clarach Bay) Open all year 100 pitches Grass, level, part sheltered   dairy produce £5.50-£6.50

Glan-y-Mor Leisure Park, Clarach North Beach SY23 3DT Aberystwyth (01970) 828900 OS map 135/585841 2½m N of Aberystwyth off A487 (Machynlleth) Open Mar-Nov 235 pitches (160 static) 24 acres level grass   ten-pin bowling £7.50-£12.00 (Mastercard/Visa/Switch)

Midfield Caravan Park, Southgate SY23 4DX *Peaceful park with fine views of surrounding area* Aberystwyth (01970) 612542 OS map 135/596796 1½m ESE of Aberystwyth on A4120 (Devil's Bridge) Open Easter-Oct 132 pitches (57 static) Grass, part level, part sheltered   £4.80-£5.10

Morfa Bychan Holiday Park, Llanfarian SY23 4QQ Aberystwyth (01970) 617254 OS map 135/565771 4m S of Aberystwyth off A487 (Aberaeron) by beach Open Apr-Oct 264 pitches (214 static) Grass, sloping, open   (heated) club £6.00-£9.00

Ocean View Caravan Park, North Beach, Clarach Bay SY23 3DT *Small family-run site on land overlooking the sea* ☎Aberystwyth (01970) 828425 OS map 135/591842 2½m N of Aberystwyth off A487 (Machynlleth) on B4572 (Clarach) near beach Open Mar-Oct 74 pitches (24 static) Grass and hard standings, level 🔌⊕∅⊡🏠 £6.50-£9.50 (inc showers)

Rheidol Caravan Park, Felin Rhiw Arthen, Capel Bangor SY24 4EL ☎(01970) 880863 OS map 135/650802 4m E of Aberystwyth off A44 (Rhayader) at Capel Bangor near S bank of river Rheidol Open Mar-Oct 33 pitches Level/sloping grass and hard standings, sheltered 🔋⊕∅↵⊡ horse riding, narrow gauge railway £5.00

For other sites near Aberystwyth see Borth and Llandre

AMROTH, Dyfed   **Map C6**
Modest seaside resort fronted by sandy beaches Restaurant: Malin House 2m W at Saundersfoot ☎(01834) 812344

Meadow House Holiday Parc, SA67 8NS ☎(01834) 812438 OS map 158/150065 ¾m W of Amroth centre on Saundersfoot road Open Whitsun-Sept–no adv booking (families only, no motor cycles) 220 pitches (150 static) 🛒🔋∅⊕⊡ (indoor)⊛ (Jul-Aug) leisure centre £13.00-£16.00

Village Touring and Caravan Park, Summerhill SA67 8NS ☎(01834) 811051 OS map 158/155075 1m NW of Amroth centre at Summerhill Open Mar-Oct 42 pitches (22 static) Level/gently sloping grass 🔌⊕↵⊛ (Spring BH, Jul-Aug) ⊡ £5.00-£7.00

See also Kilgetty

ANGLE–see Pembroke

BARGOED, Mid Glam   **Map F6**
Restaurant: Tregenna 5m NW at Merthyr Tydfyl ☎(01685) 723627

Parc Cwm Darran, Cwm Llwydrew Farm, Deri CF8 9AB ☎Bargoed (01443) 875557 OS map 171/113037 3m NW of Bargoed off A469 (Rhymney) Open Mar-Oct, 30 pitches–booking advisable 3 acres part level, grass in country park with 3 lakes, waymarked walks. adventure playground, cycle track, BMX track and picnic sites 🔌∅♿ fishing £3.50-£7.00

BARRY, S Glam   **Map F7**
Pop 43,000. EC Wed Harbour town from which coal used to be exported, now lively resort and shopping centre SEE castle ruins, zoo, Porthkerry country park, Dyffryn House 🚩Barry Island (The Triangle, Paget Rd) ☎Barry (01446) 747171 Restaurant: Mount Sorrel, Porthkerry Rd ☎(01446) 740069

Fontygary Park, Rhoose CF6 9ZT ☎(01446) 710386 OS map 170/051660 5m W of Barry off B4265 (St Athan) Open Mar-Oct 484 pitches (430 static)–no tents Level grass and hard standings 🛒✗⨅↵🔋🔌∅⊕∅ ⊡ (heated) ⊛ tennis, fishing, fitness suite, games room £12.00-£20.00

Vale Touring Caravan Park, Port Road West CF62 3RT ☎Barry (01446) 719311 OS map 170/079679 1½m W of Barry on A4226 (Cardiff Airport) Open Apr-Dec 40 pitches, level grass 🔌∅⊕∅⊛↵ £7.50-£8.50

BERRIEW, Powys   **Map F2**
Restaurant: Royal Oak 5m NE at Welshpool ☎(01938) 572217

Maes yr Afon Caravan Park, Berriew SY21 8QB ☎Berriew (01686) 640587 OS map 136/161022 2m WNW of Berriew on B4390 (New Mills) near river Rhiw Open mid Mar-late Oct 96 pitches (76 static) Grass, level, sheltered 🔋🔌∅⊕∅⊛↵🔌 fishing £8.00 (inc showers)

KILGETTY near Saundersfoot

Stone Pitt Camping, Begelly

Small family-run park on A478 (Narberth-Tenby). Open March to January.

Telephone and Fax (01834) 811086

BORTH, Dyfed   **Map D3**
Holiday village on Cardigan coast ▨ High St ☏(01970) 871174 Restaurant: Friendship, High St
☏(01970) 871213

Cambrian Coast Caravan Park, Ynslas SY24 5JU *Seaside park with top-grade facilities* ☏(01970)
871233 OS map 135/620933 1m N of Borth on left of B4353 (Tre'r-ddol) near level crossing
Open Mar-Oct 175 pitches (125 static) 12 acres level grass ▤✗♀⊷♪▤▣◪◔∅⊡ (indoor)
◁▰▱& lic club, access to blue flag beach £7.00-£12.00 (Mastercard/Visa/Switch/Euro)

Glanlerry Camping and Caravan Park, SY24 5LU ☏Borth (01970) 871413 OS map 135/617886
½m SE of Borth on B4353 (Llandre) Open Apr-Oct 100 pitches Grass, level, sheltered
▣▰∅∅◁ £7.00-£8.50

Mill House Caravan Park, Dolybont, SY24 5LX ☏Borth (01970) 871481 OS map 135/623880 1m
SE of Borth off B4353 (Llandre) on Dol-y-Bont road Open Easter-Sept 40 pitches (15 static)
Grass, level, sheltered ▰∅◪▰ fishing £8.00-£9.00

Ty Craig Holiday Park, Llancynfelyn SY20 8PU ☏(01970) 832339 OS map 135/643922 4m NE of
Borth on B4353 (Machynlleth) Open Mar-Oct 75 pitches (30 static) Grass, level, part open
▤▣▰◪◔∅▱◩▱☎ £6.50-£7.50

Ty Mawr Caravan Camping Park, Ynyslas SY24 5LB *Quiet secluded park close to sea* ☏(01970)
871327 OS map 135/630927 3m NE of Borth on right of B4353 (Machynlleth) Open Easter-Sept
72 pitches (51 static) Level grass, sheltered ▣▰∅◪∅▰◩☎ £6.50-£12.00

BRECON, Powys   **Map F5**
Pop 7,000. EC Wed, MD Tues, Fri Cathedral town on ridge above confluence of 3 rivers and
popular touring centre for Brecon Beacons national park SEE Cathedral, castle ruins, county
museum, Welsh Borderers regimental museum (Zulu wars), whisky distillery ▨Cattle market car
park ☏Brecon (01874) 622485 Restaurant: Wellington, The Bulwark ☏(01874) 625225

Bishops Meadow Caravan Park, Hay Road LD3 9SW ☏Brecon (01874) 610000 Fax (01874)
614922 OS map 160/056300 1m NE of Brecon on B4602-A470 (Hay on Wye) adj motel Open
Apr-Oct 80 pitches Grass, level, sheltered ▤✗♀▣▰∅∅⊡◁& £6.00-£10.00 (Mastercard/
Visa)

Brynich Caravan Park, LD3 7SH *Family park in Brecon foothills* ☏Brecon (01874) 623325 OS
map 160/069278 1m E of Brecon on A470 (Builth Wells) near junction with A40 (Abergavenny)
Open Mar 28-Oct 28 130 pitches Grass and hard standings, level, open
▤♪▣▰◪∅◔◁▰& baby room £8.50-£10.00 (Mastercard/Visa/Delta)

Pencelli Castle Caravan Camping Park LD3 7LX *Immaculate site in Brecon Beacons* ☏(01874)
665451 OS map 161/095250 3m SE of Brecon off A40 (Abergavenny) on B4558 (Talybont)
Open all year 80 pitches 3 acres level grass and hard standings, sheltered ▣▰∅◪∅◁✿&
£9.00

Royal Oak Inn, Pencelli LD3 7LX ☏(01874) 86621 OS map 161/094250 3m SE of Brecon off A40
(Abergavenny) on B4558 (Talybont) Open all year, 30 pitches ¾ acre mainly level, hard standings
✗♀ fishing, boating, canoeing £6.00

See also Llangorse

BROAD HAVEN, Dyfed **Map B5**
Pop 600. EC Wed Restaurant: Druidstone ✆(01437) 781221

Broad Haven Caravan Park SA62 3JD ✆Broad Haven (01437) 781277 OS map 157/864141 ½m N of Broad Haven on B4341 (Haverfordwest)–approach from east Open Mar-Oct 210 pitches (175 static) Grass, level, sheltered ⛽🏊▦🚿◉∅◕⌄ £7.40-£9.00

Creampots Caravan and Camping Park SA62 3TU ✆Broad Haven (01437) 781776 OS map 157/882131 1½m E of Broad Haven off B4341 (Haverfordwest) at Broadway–2nd park 600 yds Open Apr-Oct 72 pitches Level grass, part sheltered ▦🚿∅◉◕⌄🚻🚮♿ £4.40-£8.40

Hasguard Cross Caravan Park, Hasguard Cross SA62 3SL ✆Broad Haven (01437) 781443 OS map 157/850107 2m S of Broad Haven on B4327 (Dale)–approach from east Open all year–must book 60 pitches (35 static) Grass, level, sheltered ✗🍽▦🚿∅◉∅🚻🚮 bar meals £6.50-£8.50 (1999)

Howelston Caravan Site, Little Haven SA62 3UU ✆(01437) 781253 OS map 157/850120 2m S of Broad Haven off Talbenny road–approach from south Open Apr-Sept 60 pitches (40 static) Grass, part sloping 🚿∅◉∅ freezer pack service £6.00-£8.00

Redlands Caravan Park, Little Haven SA62 3SJ ✆(01437) 781300 OS map 157/853109 2m S of Broad Haven on B4327 (Dale)–approach from east Open Apr-Sept–must book peak periods 63 pitches Grass and hard standings, level ▦🚿◉∅ £6.00-£8.50

South Cockett Touring Park, Broadway, Little Haven SA62 3TU ✆Broad Haven (01437) 781296 OS map 157/878134 2m E of Broad Haven off B4341 (Haverfordwest) at Broadway Open Easter-Oct 70 pitches 6 acres level grass, part sheltered ▦🚿∅◉∅🚻🚮☎ £5.65-£8.00

Steep hills between Little and Broad Haven make the route impassable for towed caravans

BRONLLYS–see Talgarth

BUILTH WELLS, Powys **Map F4**
Pop 1,500. EC Wed, MD Mon SEE Wyeside arts complex, Telford's iron bridge, riverside park, Wye Valley walk 🅸 Groe Car Park ✆Builth Wells (01982) 553307 Restaurant: Caer Beris Manor ½m W off A483 ✆(01982) 552601

Llewellyn Leisure Park, Cilmery LD2 3NU ✆Builth Wells (01982) 552838 OS map 147/010515 2m W of Builth Wells on A483 (Llandovery) adj inn Open all year 56 pitches Level/sloping grass and hard standing ⛽🚿∅◉⌄🚻 snooker, wet weather functions room, B&B £5.50-£7.50 (Mastercard/Visa)

Prince Llewellyn Inn, Cilmery LD2 3NU ✆Builth Wells (01982) 552694 OS map 147/002515 2m W of Builth Wells on A483 (Llanwrtyd Wells) Open all year 18 pitches ✗🍽🚮∅⌄ Fishing £3.00-£4.00

See also Hundred House

BURRY PORT–see Llanelli

CAPEL BANGOR–see Aberystwyth

CARDIFF, S Glam **Map F7**
Pop 281,300. EC Wed SEE national museum, Llandaff cathedral, St Fagan's castle (folk museum) 🅸 Bridge Street ✆(01222) 227281 Restaurant: Lincoln, Cathedral Rd ✆(01222) 395558

Pontcanna Caravan Park, Pontcanna Fields, Sophia Close, Llandaff CF1 9JL *Landscaped site near city centre* ✆(01222) 398362 OS map 171/171773 1m NW of Cardiff centre on right of A4119 (Llantrisant) near river Taff Open all year 43 pitches–no tents 2 acres level, hard standings ⛽▦🚿∅♿ £8.50

Vintage France

192pp ISBN 1-870009-04-5

Tours of the major vineyard areas make a celebratory start with Champagne in the north and end with Cognac and the Loire in the west. In between come Alsace, the Jura, Burgundy, Beaujolais, the Rhone Valley, Provence, Armagnac and the world-famous Bordelais around Bordeaux. Each vineyard area is described in terms of its history and landscape with individual wines related to the places where they are made and can be tasted. Most of these areas still provide quiet roads, fine scenery and local restaurant meals at local prices. **For details of publication and possible reductions on cover price write to Frederick Tingey at Hillsboro, How Caple HR1 4TE.**

CARDIGAN, Dyfed   Map C4
Pop 4,290. EC Wed, MD Mon, Sat SEE Mwnt viewpoint 6m N, castle and wildlife park at Cilgerran 4m SE ☑Theatr Mwldan, Bath House Rd ✆Cardigan (01239) 316230 Restaurant: Castle Kitchen 4m SE at Cilgerran ✆(01239) 615055

Blaenwaun Farm, Mwnt SA43 1QF ✆Cardigan (01239) 612165 OS map 145/204513 4m N of Cardigan off A487 (Aberaeron) at Penparc on Traeth-y-Mwnt road Open Easter-Sept, 80 pitches 10 acres, level/gentle slope 🏕🗑🚿🥘🚾 fishing £7.00-£8.00

Brongwyn Mawr Farm, Penparc SA43 1SA ✆(01239) 613644 OS map 145/209487 2½m NE of Cardigan off A487 (Aberystwyth) at Penparc on Ferwig/Mwnt road Open Mar-Oct, 20 pitches 2 acres, level grass, sheltered 🗑🚿⊕Ø🚾🛁🅿🔌🏠 £6.00-£9.50

Penralltllyn Farm, Cilgerran SA43 2PR ✆(01239) 682350 OS map 145/215413 4m SE of Cardigan off A484 (Newcastle Emlyn) at Llechryd on Boncath road Open Mar-Oct 20 pitches 1 acre, mainly level grass 🚿 £5.00-£6.50

CAREW, Dyfed   Map B6
Pop 400 SEE castle, high cross, tidal mill, museum, Cleddau valley Restaurant: Milton Manor 1m SW at Milton ✆(01646) 651398

Hazelbrook Caravan Park, Sageston Milton SA70 8SY ✆Carew (01646) 651351 OS map 158/058033 ½m E of Carew centre on right of B4318 (Tenby) via Sageston Open Mar 1-Jan 9, 120 pitches (50 static) 7½ acres level grass, hard standing 🏕⚡🗑🚿🥘⊕Ø🚾 £6.00-£10.50

Milton Bridge Caravan Park, Milton SA70 8PH ✆Carew (01646) 651204 OS map 157/040032 1m SW of Carew off A477 (Pembroke Dock) at Milton Brewery Inn Open Mar-Oct 38 pitches (23 static) 🏕🗑🚿🥘⊕Ø⊕🛁 £8.00-£12.00

CARMARTHEN, Dyfed   Map D5
Pop 12,470. EC Thurs, MD Mon, Tues, Wed, Fri, Sat SEE St Peter's church, county museum, Roman amphitheatre, Kidwelly castle 8m S ☑Lammas Street ✆Carmarthen (01267) 231557 Restaurant: Boars Head, Lammas St ✆(01267) 222789

Sunrise Bay Caravan Park, Llanstephan SA33 5LP ✆(01267) 241394 OS map 159/352106 9m SSW of Carmarthen off B4312 (Llanstephan) Open Apr-Oct 60 pitches (52 static) Hard standings, level grass, sheltered ✖🍴🔌🗑🚿🥘⊕Ø🚾 (heated) ⊕🔌🛁🏠♿ tennis, sailing, fishing £5.00-£15.00 (most cards)

CENARTH, Dyfed   Map C4
Pop 380 SEE falls, coracle fishing, museum, Teifi valley Restaurant: Three Horseshoes ✆(01239) 710119

Cenarth Falls Holiday Park SA38 9JS ✆(01239) 710345 OS map 145/265421 ¼m W of Cenarth on right of A484 (Cardigan) Open Mar-Oct 119 pitches (80 static)–booking advisable Grass and hard standings, sheltered 🏕✖🍴🗑🚿🥘⊕ØⓈ🔌🛁🚾♿ clubhouse, games room £8.00-£15.00 (Mastercard/Visa)

CHURCH STOKE, Powys   Map G2
Village at junction of A489 (Newton-Craven Arms) and A490 Restaurant: Dragon 3m NW at Montgomery ✆(01686) 668359

Bacheldre Watermill, SY15 6TE ✆Church Stoke (01588) 620489 OS map 137/243928 2m SW of Church Stoke on A489 at Bacheldre–signposted Open Mar-Oct 25 pitches 2 acres mainly level grass, sheltered, in grounds of working watermill 🏕🚿🥘⊕Ø🏠 flat rental £6.00

Daisy Bank Caravan Park, SY15 6EB ✆Church Stoke (01588) 620471 OS map 137/303929 2m SE of Church Stoke on A489 (Craven Arms) Open all year 40 pitches–adults only Level/sloping grass and hard standings, sheltered 🚿🥘⊕🔌🚿♿ serviced pitches, TV aerial hook-up, dog walk, putting green £10.00-£11.00 inc

Mellington Hall Caravan Park, SY15 6HX ✆Church Stoke (01588) 620456 OS map 137/259920 2m SW of Church Stoke off A489 (Newtown) and B4385 (Bishops Castle)–best approach Open Mar-Oct 180 pitches (136 static) Grass, level, sheltered 🏕✖🍴🔌🗑🚿🥘⊕Ø🛁🚿 £8.00-£9.00

The restaurants recommended in this guide are of three kinds – inns and pubs, restaurants proper and those forming part of hotels and motels. They all serve lunch and dinner – at a reasonable price – say under £10 a head. We shall be glad to have your comments on any you use this season and if you think they are not up to standard to have your suggestions for alternatives.

CLUNDERWEN, Dyfed   **Map C5**
Restaurant: Plas Hyfryd 3m S at Narberth ☏ (01384) 860653

Derwenlas Caravan Park, SA66 7SU ☏ Clunderwen (01437) 563504 OS map 158/122204 1m N
of Clunderwen on left of A478 (Cardigan) Open Mar-Oct 28 pitches Level grass, sheltered
🗑🚐🅿️⊕∅❸↲ £5.00-£6.00

Llandyssilio Caravan and Camping Site, Llandyssilio SA66 7TT ☏ (01437) 563408 OS map
158/128233 ½m N of Clunderwen on left of A478 (Cardigan) Open Mar-Oct 58 pitches Level
grass, sheltered 🗑🅿️🔌 (£20) 🔲 £9.00

CRICKHOWELL, Powys   **Map F5**
Pop 2,000. EC Wed, MD Thurs Country town in picturesque setting between Brecon Beacons and
Black Mountains SEE church, old bridge, castle ruins, Vale of Usk Restaurant: Bear, High St
☏ (01873) 810408

Bluebell Inn Caravan Park, Glangrwyne NP8 1EH ☏ Crickhowell (01873) 810247 OS map
161/240162 2m SE of Crickhowell on A40 (Abergavenny) at rear of inn Open Apr-Oct 10 pitches
Level grass *No showers* ✗🍴🅿️⊕∅ fishing £5.00 (Mastercard/Visa/Switch)

Cwmdu Camping and Caravan Site, Cwmdu NP8 1RU ☏ Bwlch (01874) 730441 OS map
161/176242 4m NW of Crickhowell on A479 (Talgarth) Open Mar-Oct 100 pitches Grass and
hard standings, sheltered 🔌➹🅿️🚐⊕∅🔌 £6.00-£8.00

Riverside Caravan Park, New Road NP8 1AY ☏ Crickhowell (01873) 810397 OS map 161/215186
¼m W of Crickhowell off A4077 (Gilwern) and A40 (Brecon) Open Mar-Oct 65 pitches (20
static)–no children under 18 yrs Hard standings and grass, level, sheltered 🚐🅿️⊕∅ £8.00-
£15.00

CROESGOCH, Dyfed   **Map B5**
Village short way inland of rocky Pembrokeshire coast SEE Baptist chapel, Porthgain harbour 2m
NW, Abereiddi Bay 2m W, Pembrokeshire coast path Restaurant: Old Cross 3m W at St David's
☏ (01437) 720387

Prendergast Caravan and Camping Park, Cartlett Lodge, Trefin SA62 5AL ☏ Croesgoch (01348)
831368 OS map 157/842324 2m NE of Croesgoch off A487 (Fishguard) in Trefin village Open
Apr-Sept 37 pitches Level/sloping grass, sheltered 🚐🅿️🔌🔲 £6.00-£8.00

Torbant Caravan Park SA62 5JN ☏ Croesgoch (01348) 831261 OS map 157/843308 1m NE of
Croesgoch on right of A487 (Fishguard) Open Easter-Oct 7–must book peak periods 131 pitches
(91 static) 🗑🚐🅿️∅🔲❸🔲🔌🏨 £3.50-£6.50

CROSS HANDS, Dyfed   **Map D5**
Restaurant: Cobblers, 3m NE at Llandybie ☏ (01269) 850540

Black Lion Caravan Camping Park, Black Lion Road, Gorlas SA14 6RU ☏ (01269) 845365
Fax (01269) 831882 OS map 159/575133 1m N of Cross Hands at Gorlas on Ammanford road,
near W terminus of M4 Open Apr-Oct 46 pitches 12 acres grass and hard standings
🍴🚐🅿️⊕↲🔌🔲 clubhouse £5.00-£10.00

Marlais Caravan Park, Carmel SA14 7UF ☏ (01269) 842093 OS map 159/585168 4m N of Cross
Hands on A476 (Llandeilo) Open Mar-Oct 60 pitches 🔌✗🍴🗑🚐🅿️⊕❸↲🔌🏨 fishing £4.50

CROSS INN (Dyfed)–see New Quay

CROSS INN (Powys)–see Llandovery

CWMCARN, Gwent   **Map G6**
SEE Cwmcarn Forest Drive, Caerleon Roman Fort 8m SE; Caerphilly Castle 10m SW Restaurant:
Michael's 3m S at Risca (01633) 614300

Cwmcarn Forest Drive Campsite, Nantcarn Road NP11 7FA ☏ Cross Keys (01495) 272001 OS
map 171/229937 1m E of Cwmcarn on forest drive Open all year, 40 pitches 3 acres, part
sloping, grass and hard standings 🗑🚐⊕∅ £5.00-£10.20 (Mastercard/Visa)

DEVIL'S BRIDGE, Dyfed   **Map E3**
SEE railway to Aberystwyth, nature trails Restaurant: Hafod Arms ☏ (01970) 890232

Erwbarfe Farm, SY23 3JR ☏ (01970) 890665 OS map 135/748784 1m N of Devil's Bridge on
A4120 (Ponterwyd) Open Mar-Oct 75 pitches (50 static) Grass, level, sheltered 🗑🚐∅❸🔌
(£40) 🔲 £5.00-£7.00 (all cards)

Woodlands Caravan Park SY23 3JW ☏ (01970) 890233 OS map 135/746773 ½m NE of Devil's
Bridge on A4120 (Ponterwyd) Open Mar-Oct 132 pitches (100 static) Grass and hard standings,
level, part sheltered 🔌✗🚐➹🗑🚐🅿️⊕∅↲🔌♿ fishing £7.00-£7.50 (2000)

DINGESTOW–see Monmouth

FISHGUARD, Dyfed   **Map B5**
Pop 4,980. EC Wed, MD Thurs SEE Strumble Head lighthouse and cliffs 4m N ⓩ Hamilton St
☎(01348) 873484 Restaurant: Cartref, High St ☎(01348) 872430

Fishguard Bay Caravan and Camping Park, Garn Gelli SA65 9ET ☎(01348) 811415 OS map
  157/991388 3m E of Fishguard off A487 (Cardigan) Open Mar 1-Jan 10 100 pitches (50 static)
  Grass, level, part sheltered 🐕🏹🔋💢⊕∅😊↩🏠🎱🎲 pool table, games room £8.00-£11.00
  (most cards)

Gwaun Vale Caravan Park, Llanychaer SA65 9TA ☎Fishguard (01348) 874698 OS map
  157/973357 1m SE of Fishguard on B4313 (Gwaun Vale) Open Mar-mid Jan, 30 pitches 3 acres,
  terraced, grass, hard standings 🐕🔋💢⊘⊕∅↩♿ £7.00-£8.00

Tregroes Touring Park, Manorowen SA65 9QF ☎Fishguard (01348) 872316 OS map 157/943361
  1m SW of Fishguard off A40 (Haverfordwest) on Manorowen road Open Easter-Oct 45 pitches
  💢⊘⊕↩ lic clubhouse £6.00-£7.00

FRESHWATER EAST, Dyfed   **Map B6**
Pop 420 SEE crescent beach, ruined Lamphey palace, Hodgeston church NE, Swanlake Bay E
Restaurant: Freshwater Inn ☎(01646) 672329

Upper Portclew Farm SA71 5LA ☎(01646) 672112 OS map 158/013988 ½m W of Freshwater
  East off B4584 (Lamphey) Open May 1-Sept 10, 40 pitches Level grass 🔋💢⊕ £7.00-£10.00

GARTH, Powys   **Map F4**
Pop 320. Restaurant: Neuadd Arms 4m SW at Llanwrtyd Wells ☎(01591) 610236

Irfon River Caravan Park, Upper Chapel Road LD4 4BH ☎(01591) 620310 OS map 147/959495
  ¼m SE of Garth on B4519 (Upper Chapel) by river Open Easter-Oct 75 pitches (45 static) Grass
  and hard standings, part level, part open 🔋💢⊘⊕∅🎲🏠 fly fishing £8.00-£9.00

Riverside Caravan Park, Llangammarch Wells LD4 4BY ☎(01591) 620629 OS map 147/935471
  2m SW of Garth off A483 (Llanwrtyd Wells) Open Easter-Oct 30 pitches Grass and hard
  standings, level, part open 🐕🔋💢⊘⊕↩🎲🏠 fishing £3.50

GILWERN, Gwent   **Map G5**
SEE Brecon and Abergavenny canal, Heads of Valleys road Restaurant: Somerset Arms 4m SE at
Abergavenny ☎(01873) 852158

Aberbaiden Caravan Camping Park, The Lodge NP7 0EF ☎Gilwern (01873) 830157 OS map
  161/259146 ½m E of Gilwern off A465 (Abergavenny) near junct with A4077 (Crickhowell) Open
  Apr-Oct, 60 pitches 6 acres, grass and hard standings, part sloping, sheltered ∅⊕↩ *No
  showers* £4.00

Clydach Gorge Touring Caravan and Camping Park, Station Road, Clydach NP7 0HD ☎(01633)
  838838 OS map 161/233137 1½m SW of Gilwern off A465 (Merthyr Tydfil) in Clydach Open Apr-
  Sept, 25 pitches 2 acres, level grass and hard standings 💢⊕ £3.00-£6.00

HAVERFORDWEST, Dyfed   **Map B5**
Pop 9,200. EC Thurs, MD Tues SEE Castle remains, county museum, St Mary's church (13c), priory
ruins ⓩ Old Bridge ☎(01437) 763110 Restaurant: Mariners, Mariners Sq ☎(01437) 713353

Pelcomb Cross Farm, Pelcomb Cross SA62 6AB ☎Camrose (01437) 710431 OS map
  157/919179 3m NW of Haverfordwest on right of A487 (St David's) near Pelcomb Cross Inn
  Open Mar-Dec 30 pitches 2 acres grass mainly level secluded ∅⊕↩ £6.00-£11.00

The Rising Sun Inn, Pelcomb Bridge, St David's Road SA62 6EA ☎Haverfordwest (01437)
  765171 OS map 158/933171 1½m NW of Haverfordwest on A487 (St David's) Open Mar-Oct 30
  pitches Grass, part level, part open 🍴🔋💢⊕∅🏠🏨 bar meals, B&B £6.00-£9.00

Scamford Caravan Park, Keeston SA62 6HN ☎Haverfordwest (01437) 710304 OS map
  158/912198 4m NW of Haverfordwest off A487 (St David's) Open Apr-Oct 30 pitches (25 static)
  Grass, level, open 🔋💢⊘⊕😊↩🏠 £5.50-£7.50

HAY ON WYE, Powys   **Map G4**

Pop 1,300. EC Tues, MD Mon, Thurs Historic border stronghold famous as the `town of books' SEE bookshops, river Wye, Hay Bluff (4m S), 2220 ft cliff in Black Mountains Restaurant: Lions Corner House, Lion St ☎(01497) 820175

Fforest Cwm Farm, Clyro HR3 5SG ☎ Hay on Wye (01497) 820649 OS map 161/201438 1½m NW of Hay on Wye off B4351 (Clyro) and Paincastle road Open Mar 15-Oct 20 pitches Grass, sloping, sheltered £2.00-£3.00

Harbour Farm, Newchurch HR5 3QW ☎(01544) 370248 OS map 148/188518 6m NNW of Hay on Wye off B4594 (Painscastle- Newchurch) on Glascwm road Open Easter-Oct 30 pitches (1) farm produce £2.00

Holly Bush Inn HR3 5PS ☎(01544) 370371 OS map 161/195404 2m SW of Hay on Wye on B4350 (Brecon) by river Open Apr 12-Oct 31, 22 pitches Grass, level, sheltered slipway, bar meals £7.00

Radnors End HR3 5RS ☎ Hay on Wye (01497) 820780 OS map 148/224431 ½m NW of Hay on Wye off B4351 (Clyro) by river Wye Open Mar-Oct 15 pitches—no trailer caravans 1 acre level grass, sheltered £6.00

HUNDRED HOUSE, Powys   **Map F4**

Pop 60 Restaurant: Hundred House Inn on A481 ☎(01982) 570231

Fforest Fields Camping Caravan Park LD1 5RT ☎(01982) 570220 OS map 148/114544 In Hundred House on A481 Open Easter-Oct 40 pitches (all with mains elect) 7 acres level grass £7.50

KILGETTY, Dyfed   **Map C6**

Pop 500 EC Wed MD Fri Inland village N of Saundersfoot SEE Carew Castle 6m SW ▧Kingsmoor Common ☎(01834) 813672 Restaurant: Kilgetty Arms ☎(01834) 813219

Croft Caravan Park, Reynalton SA68 0PE ☎(01834) 860315 OS map 158/090089 2m MW of Kilgetty off A477 (Pembroke) at Reynalton Open Easter-Nov 145 pitches (90 static) Grass, level, part open lic club £8.00-£12.00 (Mastercard/Visa)

Cross Park, Broadmoor SA68 0RS ☎(01834) 811244 OS map 158/098060 2m SW of Kilgetty at junction of A477 (Pembroke) and B4586 Open Apr-Oct 135 pitches (85 static) Sloping grass and hard standings, sheltered baths £6.00-£14.50

Heathfield Court Caravan Park, Pleasant Valley, Stepaside SA69 9BT ☎(01834) 812310 OS map 158/142074 1m E of Kilgetty on Stepaside road Open Mar-Oct 150 pitches Grass, level £5.00-£10.00

Little Kings Park, Longstone SA67 8PG ☎(01834) 831330 OS map 158/146092 2m NE of Kilgetty off A477 (St Clears) on Ludchurch road Open Easter-Sept—must book 75 pitches Grass and hard standing, level, sheltered (heated indoor) £7.00-£15.50

Masterland Farm Touring Caravan and Tent Park, Broadmoor SA68 0RH ☎(01834) 813298 OS map 158/123071 ½m W of Kilgetty on Pembroke road at Cross Inn Open Apr-Oct—must book peak periods 38 pitches Level grass and hard standings, sheltered refrigerators, baby room, games room £5.50-£13.00

Ryelands Caravan Park, Ryelands Lane SA68 0VY ☎(01834) 812369 OS map 158/125085 1m N of Kilgetty on right of Trewern road Open Easter-Oct 45 pitches 4 acres level/sloping grass sheltered £5.00-£9.00

Stone Pitt Camping, Begelly SA68 0XE ☎(01834) 811086 OS map 158/116077 1m NW of Kilgetty on left of A478 (Narberth-Tenby) Open Mar-Jan 30 pitches Level/sloping grass and hard standing, sheltered £6.00-£7.00

Windberry Top Farm, Begelly SA68 0XA ☎(01834) 812394 OS map 158/115089 1m NW of Kilgetty on A478 (Narberth) Open Whit-Sept 10 pitches £4.50

LAMPETER, Dyfed   **Map D4**

Pop 2,700. EC Wed, MD Alternate Tues SEE St David's college Restaurant: Black Lion Royal, High St ☎(01570) 422172

Moorlands Caravan Park, Llangybi SA48 8NN ☎(01570) 493543 OS map 146/598543 5m N of Lampeter off A485 (Tregaron) at Llangybi Open Apr-Oct 102 pitches (48 static) 4½ acres level grass and hard standings, sheltered lic club £6.00-£8.00

Red Lion Caravan Park, Pencarreg SA40 9QG ☎(01570) 480018 OS map 146/535451 3½m SW of Lampeter on A485 (Llanybydder) Open Mar-Oct 20 pitches Grass, part sloping, sheltered (2) £4.00 (inc showers)

LANDSHIPPING, Dyfed   Map B6
SEE river Cleddau Restaurant: Stanley Arms ☎(01834) 891227

New Park Caravan Site, SA67 8BG ☎Martletwy (01834) 891284 OS map 158/025112 1m E of
Landshipping on Templeton road Open Spring Holiday-Sept, 45 pitches Grass, part sloping, hard
standings ▨◪❂❂∅▣⬓ £5.50

Quay House, SA67 8BE ☎(01834) 651262 OS map 158/010110 ½m S of Landshipping centre on
Landshipping Quay road Open Easter-Sept 10 pitches 1½ acres mainly level grass £3.00

LAUGHARNE, Dyfed   Map C5
SEE grave and boathouse of Dylan Thomas, Pendine Sands 4m W Restaurant: Forge Motel 4m N
at St Clears ☎(01994) 230300

Ants Hill Caravan and Camping Park, SA33 4QN ☎Laugharne (01994) 427293 OS map
159/300119 ¼m N of Laugharne off A4066 (St Clears)–signposted Open Easter-Oct–must book
peak periods–120 pitches (60 static) Grass, level, part open ▤♀�−▨◪❂∅▣◩ (outdoor
heated) ❂⚐◪❉ (Jul-Aug) ⬓ first aid £6.00-£14.00

Broadway Caravan and Camping Site, SA33 4NU ☎Laugharne (01994) 427272 OS map
159/295103 ½m SW of Laugharne on A4066 (Pendine) Open Mar-Oct 36 pitches Grass, level,
sheltered ◪◍❂⬓ £5.00

LITTLE HAVEN–see Broad Haven

LLANARTH–see New Quay

LLANBISTER, Powys   Map F3
Restaurant: Park Motel 7m S at Cross Gates ☎(01597) 851201

Brynithon Caravan Site, Llandrindod Road LD1 6TR ☎(01597) 840231 OS map 136/103743 ½m
N of Llanbister on A483 (Newtown) Open Mar-Oct 25 pitches Hard standings, grass, level,
sheltered ◍❂◪⬓ rambling, fishing £4.00

LLANBRYNMAIR, Powys   Map E2
Restaurant: Wynnstay Arms on A470 ☎(01650) 521431

Cringoed Caravan Camping Park, SY19 7DR *Welcoming site in fine walking country* ☎(01650)
521237 OS map 135/886012 2m S of Llanbrynmair off B4518 (Llanidloes) Open Apr-Oct 70
pitches (20 static) 5 acres level grass and hard standings ▨◪◍❂∅◪⬓ £6.50

LLANDEUSANT–see Llandovery

LLANDOVERY, Dyfed   Map E5
Pop 2,100. EC Thurs, MD Fri SEE castle ruins, parish church, Usk reservoir 5m SE ▨Central Car
Park, Broad Street ☎Llandovery (01550) 720693 Restaurant: White Hart, Stone St ☎(01550)
720152

Black Mountain Caravan and Camping Park, Llandeusant SA19 9YG ☎(01550) 740621 OS map
160/772259 5m S of Llandovery via Myddfai–access by narrow mountain roads Open all year 60
pitches 5 acres level grass and hard standings ▤▨◪◍∅⚐⬓ £6.00-£7.00 (Mastercard/Visa)

Erwlon Caravan and Camping Park SA20 0RD ☎Llandovery (01550) 720332 OS map
146/779344 ½m E of Llandovery on A40 (Brecon) Open all year 40 pitches 8 acres level grass
and hard standings, sheltered ▨◪◍❂◪⚐□◪ (£1.50/wk) ⬓&⚒ pony trekking, fishing £6.00-
£7.50

Rhandirmwyn Park (Camping Club) SA20 0NT ☎(01550) 760257 OS map 146/779435 8m N of
Llandovery off A483 (Llanwrtyd Wells) on Rhandirmwyn road, by river Tywi Open Mar 20-Oct 30
90 pitches 11 acres, level grass, sheltered ▨◪◍❂◪❂& £11.80-£14.90 (Mastercard/Visa)

LLANDRE, Dyfed   Map D3
Restaurant: Felin Gyffin Watermill 1m S at Bow Street ☎(01970) 828852

Riverside Caravan Park SY24 5BY ☎(01970) 820070 OS map 135/631878 ¾m NNE of Llandre
on Glanfraid road Open Mar-Oct 100 pitches (76 static) Grass, level, sheltered–some hard
standings ▤▨◪◍❂∅⚐□◪⬓▣& fishing, dog walk £7.00-£8.50

FACTS CAN CHANGE

We do our best to check the accuracy of the entries in this guide but changes can and do
occur after publication. So if you plan to stay at a site some distance from home it makes
sense to ring the manager or owner before setting off.

LLANDRINDOD WELLS, Powys   Map E4
Pop 4,200. EC Wed, MD Fri SEE Spa, Castell Collen (Roman fort) 1m N, Elan Valley NW ℹ Old
Town Hall, Memorial Gdns ✆(01597) 822600 Restaurant: Bell Country Inn ½m W off A4081 at
Llanyre ✆(01597) 823959

Dalmore Caravan Park, Howey LD1 5RG ✆(01597) 822483 OS map 147/034582 2m S of
Llandrindod Wells off A483 (Builth Wells) Open Mar-Oct 41 pitches (21 static) 2 acres grass and
hard standings, part sheltered 🚐🚿⊙∅🏠🚾 £6.00-£8.50

Park Camping and Caravan Site, Cross Gates LD1 6RF ✆(01597) 851201 OS map 147/085650
3m NE of Llandrindod Wells off A483 (Welshpool) on A44 (Rhayader) by Park Motel Open Mar-
Oct 35 pitches Grass, level, sheltered 🚾✗🍴🔌🚐🚿⊙∅⊠🔧🚿🚮🏠 games room £6.00-
£6.75

See also Hundred House

LLANELLI, Dyfed   Map D6
Pop 45,000. EC Tues, MD Thurs, Sat Home of Welsh rugby, once prosperous harbour town SEE
Parc Howard museum (tinplate industry), Pembrey country park 7m W ℹ Public Library, Vaughan St
✆(01554) 772020 Restaurant: Diplomat 1m NE on A476 ✆(01554) 756156

Shoreline Leisure Home Park, Burry Port SA16 0HD ✆(01554) 832657 OS map 159/440005 4m
W of Llanelli off A484 (Carmarthen) at Burry Port near sea–signposted Open Mar-Nov–must book
250 pitches (210 static)–no tents Level grass and hard standing 🚾✗🍴🛢🚐🚿⊙∅⊠🔧🚿🚮🏠
£5.00-£8.00

See also Cross Hands

LLANFAIR CAEREINION, Powys   Map F2
Restaurant: Goat, High St (off A458) ✆(01938) 810428

Riverbend Caravan Park, Llangadfan SY21 0PP ✆(01938) 820356 OS map 125/013106 6½m W
of Llanfair Caereinion off A458 (Mallwyd) Open Apr-Sept 140 pitches (88 static) 7½ acres level
grass 🚐🚿⊙∅🔧🚮🚿 fishing, putting green £8.00 (1998)

LLANFYLLIN, Powys   Map F1
Pop 1,250 ℹ Council Offices, High St ✆(01691) 648868 Restaurant: Cain Valley, High St (A490)
✆(01691) 648366

Henstent Caravan Park, Llangynog SY10 0EP ✆(01691) 860479 OS map 125/060260 6½m NW
of Llanfyllin on B4391 (Llangynog) by River Tanat Open Mar-Oct 65 pitches (40 static) 4½ acres
gently sloping grass 🛢🚐🚿⊙∅🚿 fishing £6.00-£8.00

Vyrnwy Caravan Park, Llansantffraid SY22 6SY ✆(01691) 828217 OS map 126/218203 5m E of
Llanfyllin off A490 (Welshpool) and B4393 (Four Crosses) Open Apr-Oct 220 pitches (180 static)
Grass, level, part open 🚿⊙∅🚿 £10.00

LLANGADOG, Dyfed   Map E5
Pop 300 SEE Carn Goch Iron Age fort Restaurant: Cawdor Arms 6m SW at Llandeilo ✆(01558)
823500

Abermarlais Caravan Park, SA19 9NG ✆Llangadog (01550) 777868 OS map 146/160/695298
2m NW of Llangadog on left of A40/A482 (Llandovery) Open Feb-Nov 88 pitches Grass and hard
standings, sheltered 🚾🚐🚿⊙❸🔧🚿 (£10/mth) £7.50

Pont Aber Inn, Gwynfe SA19 9TA ✆(01550) 740202 OS map 160/238226 3m S of Llangadog on
left of A4069 (Brynamman) by river Open all year 30 pitches 1 acre mainly level grass, some
hard standings, sheltered 🚾✗🍴🚿⊙∅🔧🚿 fishing £6.00-£12.00

Pont Aber Inn

3m south of Llangadog on A4069 (Brynamman). Open
all year, 30 pitches on mainly level grass, sheltered.
Wide range of facilities including fishing.

Telephone 01550 740202

LLANGAMMARCH WELLS–see Garth

LLANGORSE, Powys   Map F5
Pop 400. SEE Lake Restaurant: Red Lion ☎(01874) 845238
Lakeside Caravan Camping Park, LD3 7TR ☎(01874) 658226 Fax (01874) 658430 OS map
    161/135275 ½m SW of Llangorse off Llanfihangel road near Llangorse Lake Open Apr-Oct 155
    pitches (82 static) Grass, level, sheltered ▯✕⚲▯▯▯▯▯▯▯▯▯▯▯ clubhouse, boat
    hire/launching, fishing, bike hire, pony trekking £7.00-£9.00 (Mastercard/Visa)
Llynfi Holiday Park LD3 7TR ☎(01874) 658283 OS map 161/125278 ½m NW of Llangorse off
    Llanfihangel road Open Apr-Oct 188 pitches (108 static) Level grass, sheltered
    ✕⚲▯▯▯▯▯▯▯ (heated) ⊕↩▯▯ lic club, slipway £7.00-£9.00
See also Brecon

LLANGRANOG, Dyfed   Map C4
Pop 150. EC Wed SEE cliffs, Ynys Lochtyn headland (NT) Restaurant: Y Gegin Fach ☎(01239)
654642
Arthen Caravan Park, Glyn Arthen SA44 6PP ☎Rhydlewis (01239) 851333 OS map 145/325485
    4½m S of Llangranog off B4334 (Rhydlewis) Open Mar-Oct 32 pitches 4 acres level grass,
    sheltered ▯▯▯▯▯↩▯▯ £5.50-£6.50
Greenfields Caravan and Camping Park, Plwmp SA44 6HF ☎Llangranog (01239) 654333 OS
    map 145/355523 3m SE of Llangranog on B4321 (Pentregat) at junction with A487 (Aberaeron-
    Cardigan) Open Mar-Jan 200 pitches (150 static) 33 acres level/gentle slope, grass, sheltered
    ▯⚲↩⚹▯▯▯▯▯▯▯↩▯▯▯▯▯▯▯ lic club, lake fishing, tennis, bowling green, golf
    £8.00-£12.00
Maes Glas Caravan Park, Penbryn SA44 6QE ☎(01239) 654268 OS map 145/302520 1m SW of
    Llangranog on coast above beach at Penbryn Open Mar-Oct 43 pitches Level grass, sheltered
    ▯↩▯▯▯▯↩▯ £7.50-£9.50
See also Aberporth

LLANGYNOG–see Llanfyllin

LLANIDLOES, Powys   Map F3
Pop 2,380. SEE market hall, museum, Llyn Clywedog lake ▯ Great Oak St ☎(01686) 412605
Restaurant: Red Lion, Great Oak St ☎(01686) 412270
Dol-Llys Farm SY18 6JA ☎Llanidloes (01686) 412694 OS map 136/962857 1m NE of Llanidloes
    off B4569 (Caersws) on Oakley Park road Open Easter-Oct 20 pitches Level grass ▯▯▯▯▯↩
    B&B, shooting, fishing £5.00-£6.00

LLANON, Dyfed   Map D4
Pop 350 SEE Llansantffraid village NW, Llanrhystyd church 2m N Restaurant: Bikerehyd Farm at
Pennant ☎(01974) 202365
Woodlands Caravan Park, SY23 5LX ☎Llanon (01974) 202342 OS map 135/511668 On W edge
    of Llanon Open Apr-Oct 100 pitches (60 static) Grass, level, sheltered–some hard standings
    ▯⚹▯▯▯▯▯▯ £8.50

LLANRHIDIAN, Gower, W Glam   Map D6
Restaurant: Welcome to Town (off B4295) ☎(01792) 390015
Llanrhidian Holiday Park, SA3 1EU ☎Swansea (01792) 391083 OS map 159/509933 1½m NE
    of Llanrhidian on B4295 (Crofty) Open Mar 1-Jan 10 390 pitches (240 static) Grass, level,
    sheltered ▯⚲↩▯▯▯▯▯▯▯↩▯▯▯ clubhouse £13.00-£22.50 (inc showers)

LLANRHYSTYD, Dyfed   Map D3
Restaurant: Black Lion 6m SW at Aberaeron ☎(01545) 570576
Morfa Farm Caravan-Camping Park SY23 5BU ☎(01974) 202253 OS map 135/524692 ½m S of
    Llanrhystyd off A487 (Aberaeron) Open Apr-Oct 170 pitches (150 static) level grass
    ▯▯▯▯▯▯↩▯ slipway, tennis, snooker £7.00-£9.00
Pengarreg Caravan Park, Pengarreg SY23 5DJ ☎(01974) 202247 OS map 135/533701 ½m SW
    of Llanrhystyd off A487 (Aberaeron) Open Apr-Oct–must book 150 pitches ▯▯ club fishing
    £4.00-£5.00
Penrhos Golf and Country Club, SY23 5AY ☎(01974) 202999 OS map 135/540698 ¼m E of
    Llanrhystd centre off A487 (Aberystwyth) Open Apr-Oct 150 pitches (135 static) ▯↩▯▯
    fishing, 18 hole golf course and leisure centre £12.00

LLANSANTFFRAID–see Llanfyllin

LLANTEG–see Red Roses

LLANTWIT MAJOR, S Glam   Map F7
Restaurant: West House, West St ☎(01446) 792406

Acorn Camping and Caravanning, Rosedew Farm CF61 1RB ☎(01446) 794024 Fax (01446)
794024 OS map 170/975675 ½m S of Llantwit Major off B4265 (Barry) Open Feb-Dec
105 pitches–bkg advisable Grass, level barbecue hire £6.50-£7.50

Llandow Touring Caravan Park, Llandow CF7 7PB ☎Llantwit Major (01446) 794527 and 792462
OS map 170/956713 2m N of Llantwit Major off B4270 (Cowbridge) Open Feb-Nov 100 pitches
5½ acres level grass and hard standing, sheltered £7.50-£9.00

LLANWRDA, Dyfed   Map E5
Pop 350 SEE Tywi and Dulais valleys, gold mines at Pumpsaint 6m NW Restaurant: Bridgend Inn
on A482 ☎(01558) 650249

Penlan Wen Caravan Park, Ciao SA19 8RR *Farm site near Pumpsaint gold mines* ☎(01558)
650667 OS map 146/705340 2m NW of Llanwrda on right of A482 (Lampeter) by river Cothy
Open Mar-Oct 20 pitches 3 acres grass ⊕ £2.00

LLANWRTYD WELLS, Powys   Map E4
SEE spa, Abernant lake ⓘThe Bookshop ☎Llanwrtyd Wells (01591) 610391 Restaurant: Neuadd
Arms ☎(01591) 610236

**Dol-y-coed Park LD5 4TH OS map 147/871470 ½m NW of Llanwrtyd Wells on Abergwesyn
road Open May-Sept**, 40 pitches–no adv booking 5 acres, level ✗ (snack), 🔲 fishing £4.00

LLANYBYDDER, Dyfed   Map D4
Restaurant: Cross Hands ☎(01570) 480224

Rhydcymerau Caravan Park, Rhydcymerau SA19 7PS ☎(01558) 685527 OS map 146/579389
5m SE of Llanybydder on B4337 (Llansawel) Open Apr-Oct 30 pitches Level grass, sheltered
lake fishing £3.50-£6.00

LONGSTONE–see Kilgetty

LUDCHURCH–see Narberth

LYDSTEP BEACH–see Manorbier

MACHYNLLETH, Powys   Map E2
Pop 1,900. EC Thurs, MD Wed Ancient town in lower Dyfi valley with spacious main street SEE
Owain Glyndwr Institute ⓘCanoflan Owain Glyndwr ☎Machynlleth (01654) 702401 Restaurant:
Skinners Arms, Main St (A487) ☎(01654) 702354

Dyffryn Dyfi Caravan Park, Brynmelyn, Llanwrin SY20 8QJ ☎(01650) 511252 OS map
124/808053 5m N of Machynlleth off A487 (Dolgellau) and B4404 (Cemmaes Road) Open Mar
27-Oct 31, 60 pitches 4 acres grass, level ⊘ 🔲 (£50) £5.00

MAENCHLOCHOG, Dyfed   Map C5
Remote village on S slopes of Preselly Hills, laced with rivers and footpaths. SEE Taf valley E
Restaurant: Wolfscastle 10m W at Wolf's Castle ☎(01437) 532225

Rosebush Caravan-Camping Park, Belle Vue House, Rosebush SA66 7QT ☎Maenchlochog
(01437) 532206 OS map 145/074293 1½m NW of Maenchlochog on B4313 (Fishguard) Open
Apr 1-Oct 14, 80 pitches (15 static) Grass and hard standing, level, sheltered ⊘ 🔲 £6.50-£7.50

Trefach Caravan Park, Mynachlog-ddu SA66 7RU ☎Hebron (01994) 419225 OS map 145/148290
4m NE of Maenchlochog off A478 (Cardigan-Tenby) near Glandy Cross Inn Open Easter-Oct 70
pitches (50 static) Grass, part sloping, sheltered (heated) lic
club, pony trekking £6.00-£10.00 (Visa)

CARAVAN STORAGE

Many sites in this guide offer caravan storage in winter but some will also store your caravan
in summer, which for those of us able to tour several times a year saves towing over long
distances. Sites most conveniently placed for this are those on or near popular routes to the
West Country and Scotland.

MANORBIER, Dyfed   Map C6
Pop 350. Village in centre of rugged headland built around ruins of impressive moated Norman Castle overlooking lovely bay, with a sandy beach on either hand. Other fine beaches are at nearby Lydstep and Jameston. SEE castle, church, King's Quoit burial chamber Restaurant: Castle Inn ☎ (01834) 871268

Buttyland Touring Caravan and Tent Park, SA70 7SN ☎ Manorbier (01834) 871278 OS map 158/068990 1m N of Manorbier centre on road to station Open Mar-Sept–booking advisable peak periods 50 pitches 10 acres level grass ⬛🛢🚿⊕⊘↩ £3.40-£6.00

Manorbier Bay Caravanserai, SA70 7SR ☎ Manorbier (01834) 871235 OS map 158/065989 1m N of Manorbier on A4139 (Tenby-Pembroke) Open Mar-Oct 84 pitches (65 static) Grass, level, open ⬛🛢⊘↩🚼 £8.81

Manorbier Country Park, Station Road, SA70 7SN ☎ Manorbier (01834) 871534 OS map 158/068993 1m N of Manorbier centre on road to station Open Apr-Oct 151 pitches (101 static) Hard standings and grass, level, sheltered ⬛🍴🍺🛢🚿⊕⊘🚻 (heated) ⊕↩🅿❀ (mid Jun-Aug) 🚼♿ tennis court, lic country club £10.00-£17.00 (Mastercard/Visa)

Park Farm Caravans SA70 7SU *Quiet site, own footpath to beach* ☎ (01834) 871273 OS map 158/063981 ½m NW of Manorbier off Pembroke road Open Easter-Oct 142 pitches (70 static) 25 acres level grass and hard standings, sheltered ⬛🛢🚿🛢⊕⊘ £3.50-£6.00

Tudor Glen Caravan Park, Jameston SA70 7SS ☎ Manorbier (01834) 871417 OS map 158/060990 1½m NW of Manorbier on A4139 (Tenby-Pembroke) Open Mar-Oct 56 pitches (20 static) Grass sloping, hard standings, sheltered ⬛🛢🚿🛢⊕⊘🚻 (outdoor) ⊕↩❀🚼 £5.50-£11.00

Whitewell Camping Park, Lydstep Beach SA70 7RY ☎ Manorbier (01834) 842200 OS map 158/095988 2m E of Manorbier on Tenby road at Whitewell near beach Open Apr-Sept 150 pitches (50 static) Level grass ⬛🍴🍺🛢⊘🚼

MATHRY, Dyfed   Map B5
SEE church with pre-Christian enclosure, Abercastle harbour and neolithic Carreg Samson capstone 2m NW Restaurant: Farmers Arms ☎ (01348) 831284 Nearest sites at Croesgoch 2m SW and Fishguard 4m NE

MERTHYR TYDFIL, Mid Glam   Map F6
Pop 42,000. EC Thurs, MD Tues, Sat SEE Cyfartha castle (museum) 🅸 Glebeland St ☎ (01685) 379884 Restaurant: Baverstock Hotel, Heads of Valley Rd ☎ (01685) 386221

Grawen Farm, Cwm Taff, Cefn Coed CF48 2HS ☎ Merthyr Tydfil (01685) 723740 OS map 160/016112 2m NW of Merthyr Tydfil on left of A470 (Brecon) Open Apr-Oct, 55 pitches 3½ acres level grass and hard standings, sheltered 🛢🚿🛢⊕↩🛢 forest walks, fishing, farm produce £7.00-£9.50

Rhydycar Sports and Leisure Centre, Rhydycar CF48 1UP ☎ Merthyr Tydfil (01685) 71491 OS map 160/050055 ½m S of Merthyr Tydfil off A470 (Brecon-Cardiff) Open May-Oct–no adv booking (max stay 3 nights) ✖🍺 bowls, squash, sauna Facilities available only at centre from 0730 to 2330–otherwise no charge

MILFORD HAVEN, Dyfed   Map B6
Pop 13,750 EC Thurs MD Fri Late 18c town above one of world's finest natural harbours thronged most days by supertankers delivering crude oil to nearby refineries SEE Dale and Marloes peninsulas SW guarding N side of harbour, with small villages and sandy beaches 🅸 Charles St ☎ (01646) 690866 Restaurant: Lord Nelson, Hamilton Terrace ☎ (01646) 695341

Sandy Haven Caravan Camping Park, Herbrandston SA73 2AL *Unspoilt site in beautiful location* ☎ (01646) 698844/694412/698083 OS map 157/856074 2½m W of Milford Haven by beach Open Easter-Sept 20 pitches Level/sloping grass, sheltered ⬛⊘⊕ boats accepted £8.00-£12.00

MILTON–see Carew

MITCHEL TROY–see Monmouth

CARAVAN STORAGE

Many sites in this guide offer caravan storage in winter but some will also store your caravan in summer, which for those of us able to tour several times a year saves towing over long distances. Sites most conveniently placed for this are those on or near popular routes to the West Country and Scotland.

MONMOUTH, Gwent   Map H5
Pop 7,350. EC Thurs, MD Mon, Sat Market town on English border with rich history and centre still retaining its medieval street plan SEE Monnow bridge (fortified gateway), museum with Nelson collection, Wye Valley, Skenfrith castle and church 6m NW ▮ Shire Hall, Agincourt Sq ☎ (01600) 713899 Restaurant: Punch House, Agincourt Sq ☎ (01600) 713855

Bridge Caravan and Camping Park, Dingestow NP25 4DY ☎ (01600) 740241 OS map 161/458103 4m SW of Monmouth off A40-A449 (Newport) on Dingestow road Open Easter-Oct 123 pitches Grass and hard standings, level, sheltered ▬ fishing £8.00-£10.00

Glen Trothy Caravan and Camping Park, Mitchel Troy NP25 4BD ☎ Monmouth (01600) 712295 OS map 162/495100 2m SW of Monmouth off new A40 (Raglan) and B4293 (Mitchel Troy) adj Glen Trothy hotel Open Mar-Oct—must book peak periods 140 pitches Grass, level, sheltered—some hard standings ▬ river fishing £7.00

Monnow Bridge Caravan Camping Park, Drybridge Street NP5 3AB ☎ Monmouth (01600) 714004 OS map 162/504124 ½m SW of Monmouth centre on right of B4233 (Abergavenny)– entrance at side of Three Horseshoes pub Open all year 33 pitches 1 acre level grass by river ▬ £5.00

MONTGOMERY, Powys   Map G2
Small Georgian town dominated by castle ruins. SEE castle, Montgomery canal, ruined Caersws fort 7m W, once hub of Roman road network in Wales Restaurant: Dragon ☎ (01686) 668359

Argae Hall Caravan Park, Garthmyl SY15 6RU ☎ (01686) 640216 OS map 136/194982 2m W of Montgomery off B4385 (Garthmyl) by river Severn Open all year 144 pitches (114 static)–no tents Grass, level, sheltered—some hard standings ▬ pub/club meals £10.00

Caerhowel Camping Caravan Park Caerhowel SY15 6HF ☎ Montgomery (01686) 668598 OS map 137/205981 2m NW of Montgomery off B4385 (Welshpool) on Forden road Open Easter-Oct, 24 pitches–no adv booking Level grass ▬ £5.00

See also Church Stoke

NARBERTH, Dyfed   Map C5
Pop 1,000. EC Wed SEE St Andrew's Castle 3m NW ▮ Town Hall ☎ (01834) 860061 Restaurant: Plas Hydryd, Moorfield Rd ☎ (01834) 860653

Allensbank Holiday Park, Providence Hill SA67 8RF ☎ Narbeth (01834) 860243 OS map 158/113134 1m S of Narberth off A478 (Tenby) Open Whitsun-Oct 15, 39 pitches (18 static) Grass, level ▬ games room £8.00-£14.00

Dingle Farm Caravan Park, Jesse Road SA67 7DP ☎ Narbeth (01834) 860482 OS map 158/113149 ½m N of Narberth centre on A478 (Cardigan) Open Easter-Sept 60 pitches (30 static) Grass, level, sheltered ▬ lic club £9.50-£11.00 inc elect and hot water

Noble Court Caravan Park, Redstone Road SA67 7ES ☎ Narbeth (01834) 861191 OS map 158/110155 ½m N of Narberth on B4313 (Fishguard) Open Mar-Nov 152 pitches (60 static) Grass and hard standings, level sheltered ▬ lic club, coarse fishing £9.00-£17.00 (Mastercard/Visa)

Redford Caravan Park, Princes Gate SA67 8TD ☎ Narbeth (01834) 860251 OS map 158/135132 2m SE of Narberth on B4314 (Princes Gate) Open Apr 19-Oct 15, 125 pitches (75 static) ▬ lic club, farm produce £7.00

Woodland Vale Caravan Park, Ludchurch SA67 8JE *Site with pitches attractively set between areas of water* ☎ (01834) 831319 OS map 158/140110 3½m SE of Narberth off A477 in Ludchurch Open Mar 1-Dec 1 110 pitches (80 static)–no tents Level grass, sheltered ▬ lic club, fishing £7.50-£12.00

Wood Office Caravan Park, Templeton SA67 8RR ☎ Narberth (01834) 860565 OS map 158/120128 2m SE of Narberth off A478 (Tenby) Open Mar-Oct 45 pitches Grass, level, open ▬ £6.00

For other sites near Narberth see Clunderwen and Kilgetty

FACTS CAN CHANGE

We do our best to check the accuracy of the entries in this guide but changes can and do occur after publication. So if you plan to stay at a site some distance from home it makes sense to ring the manager or owner before setting off.

NEATH, W Glam   Map E6
Pop 15,125. EC Thurs, MD Wed Restaurant: Castle Hotel, The Parade ☎(01639) 641119
Gelli Farm Caravan and Camping Park, Crynant SA10 8PP ☎Neath (01639) 750209 OS map
160/795066 6m N of Neath off A465 (Hirwaun) on Severn Sisters road beyond Crynant Open all
year 30 pitches ✗⊕ £2.50

NEWBRIDGE ON WYE, Powys   Map F4
SEE church, river Wye Restaurant: New Inn ☎(01597) 860211
Disserth Park, Howey LD1 6NL ☎(01597) 860277 OS map 147/035583 1½m E of Newbridge on
Wye off B4358 (Llandrindod Wells) near Disserth church Open Mar-Oct, 54 pitches (21 static)
Grass, level, sheltered ✗♀⊷◰🠶🠶⊘⊕⊘🠶 (£2/wk), 🠶 fishing £7.25-£8.50 (most cards)
Pont-ar-lthon Farm LD2 3SA ☎(01597) 860203 OS map 147/019572 1m S of Newbridge on Wye
on right of A470 (Builth Wells) immed after river bridge, by River Wye Open Mar-Oct, 44 pitches
4 acres, level grass 🠶 fishing £2.50-£3.50

NEWCASTLE EMLYN, Dyfed   Map C4
Pop 540. EC Wed, MD Fri SEE castle ruins, Teifi Falls, Cenarth Falls 2m W 🄸Market Hall
☎(01239) 711333 Restaurant: Emlyn Arms, Bridge St ☎(01239) 710317
Afon Teifi Caravan Camping Park, Pentre Cagal SA38 9HT *Well-run site in secluded valley*
☎Velindre (01559) 370532 OS map 145/338403 2m E of Newcastle Emlyn on A484
(Carmarthen) Open Apr-Oct 110 pitches Grass and hard standings, level 🠶🠶🠶⊘⊕⊘⊕🠶🠶⛾
£7.00-£8.00
Dolbryn Farm Campsite, Capel Iwan Road SA38 9LP ☎Newcastle Emlyn (01239) 710683 OS
map 145/296384 1¾m S of Newcastle Emlyn on Capel Iwan road Open Easter-Oct 40 pitches
Grass, part sloping, sheltered ♀🠶⊕⊕🠶⛾ £5.00
Moelfryn Caravan Camping Park, Pant-y-Bwlch SA38 9JG ☎Velindre (01559) 371231 OS map
145/321370 2½m S of Newcastle Emlyn off B4333 (Cynwyl Elfed) Open all year, 25 pitches 2
acres, level grass, part sheltered 🠶⊕🠶🠶 £4.50-£6.50
See also Cenarth

NEWGALE, Dyfed   Map B5
Restaurant: Cambrian Inn 3m NW at Solva ☎(01437) 721210
Brandy Brook Caravan and Camping Site, Roch SA62 5PT ☎Letterston (01348) 840272 OS
map 157/884239 3m NE of Newgale off A487 (Haverfordwest) via Roch Bridge Open Easter-Sept
95 pitches (36 static) 🠶⊕ £3.50-£9.00
Newgale Beach Holiday Park, SA62 6BD ☎(01437) 710675 and 710812 OS map 157/835212
1½m S of Newgale off A487 (Haverfordwest) on coast road adj beach Open Mar-Oct 90 pitches
(45 static) Grass, level, part sheltered 🠶✗⊷◰🠶🠶⊕⊘⊕🠶🠶 (£30) 🠶 surfing £7.00-£8.00
Park Hall Caravan Park, Maerdy Farm, Penycwm SA62 6LS ☎(01437) 721282 and 721606 OS
map 157/841244 2m N of Newgale off A487 (St David's) on 14 Signals Regiment road Open Mar-
Oct 120 pitches (60 static) Grass and hard standings, level, open 🠶🠶⊕🠶 (£50) fishing (5 acre
lake) £5.00-£7.00

NEW MILLS, Powys   Map F2
Restaurant: Bear 8m S at Newtown ☎(01686) 626964
Llwyn Celyn Caravan Park, Adfa SY16 3DG ☎(01938) 810720 OS map 136/055006 3m W of
New Mills off B4389 on road beyond Adfa Open Fri prior to Good Friday-Oct 71 pitches (55 static)
Grass, level, sheltered ⊷◰🠶🠶⊕⊘⊕🠶⛾ £7.50
Gwernydd Caravan Park, Gwernydd SY16 3NW ☎Tregynon (01686) 650236 OS map 136/087019
1m NW of New Mills off B4389 (Llanfair Caereinion) Open Mar-Oct 125 pitches (120 static) Grass
and hard standings, level, sheltered 🠶♀◰🠶🠶⊘🠶🠶🠶 £4.00-£6.00

Park Hall Caravan Park
Maerdy Farm, Penycwm SA62 6LS

2m north of Newgale off A487 St David's road

Open March–October   Grass and hard standings, level and open

Fishing in 5-acre lake   £6.50 for two

NEWPORT, Dyfed   **Map B4**
Pop 1,170 EC Wed SEE church, castle, hill fort, Pentre Ifan chambered tomb 2m SE Restaurant:
Llwyngwair Arms, East St ☎(01239) 820267

Llwyngwair Manor Holiday Park SA42 0LX ☎Newport (01239) 820498 OS map 145/072391 1m
    NE of Newport on A487 (Cardigan) Open Apr-Oct, 180 pitches (100 static) Level grass and hard
    standing, sheltered 🛎 (seasonal) ✗♀⊷🗐🐶🖉⊕∅⊑🐀⛊🚻 baths, lic hotel, fishing, tennis
    £6.00-£13.00 (Mastercard/Visa)

Morawelon, Parrog SA42 0RW ☎Newport (01239) 820565 OS map 145/050396 ½m NW of
    Newport at Parrog beach Open Easter-Oct, 85 pitches 6 acres, grass, level/gentle slope
    🛎✗⌇🗐🖉⊕∅ sailing, boat club, pony trekking £6.25-£8.95

NEWPORT, Gwent   **Map G6**
Pop 135,000. MD weekdays SEE St Woolos Cathedral, transporter bridge, Roman relics at
Caerleon 3m N 🅸Newport Museum, John Frost Square ☎Newport (01633) 842962 Restaurant:
Kings, High St ☎(01633) 842020

Tredegar House Country Park, Coedkernew NP1 9YW ☎Newport (01633) 815880 OS map
    171/285858 2m SW of Newport on A48 (Cardiff) at junction with A4072 (Bassaleg) near junction
    28 of M4–signposted Open Mar-Oct 50 pitches Grass and hard standings, sheltered
    ✗♀🗐⊕∅⊕🚽🚻 £5.00-£9.00 inc showers

NEW QUAY, Dyfed   **Map D4**
Small coastal town with history of smuggling on headland sheltering a sandy bay on either hand, with
cliffs on S providing a breeding ground for sea birds. The town is said to have been the model for
Dylan Thomas' *Under Milk Wood* 🅸Church St ☎(01545) 560865 Restaurant: Black Lion, Glanmor
Terr ☎(01545) 560209

Llwynon Farm, Cei Bach SA45 9SL ☎(01545) 580218 OS map 146/409596 2m E of New Quay
    off B4342 (Llanarth) Open Jul 16-Aug 13, 100 pitches Grass, sloping, part open ⊕⊑ £2.00

Pencnwc Holiday Park, Cross Inn SA44 6NL ☎New Quay (01545) 560479 OS map 145/383566
    2m S of New Quay on A486 (Synod Inn) Open Mar-Oct 225 pitches (175 static) Level grass and
    hard standings 🛎♀⊷🗐🐶🖉⊕∅⊑🚻 clubhouse, games room £8.00-£12.50

Wern Mill, Gilfachreda SA45 9SP ☎New Quay (01545) 580699 OS map 146/412588 2m SE of
    New Quay on B4342 (Llanarth) Open Easter-Oct 50 pitches Level grass, sheltered 🗐🖉⊕
    £4.00-£6.00

NEW RADNOR, Powys   **Map F4**
Pop 290. EC Wed Restaurant: Harp Inn 3m E at Old Radnor ☎(01544) 421655

Walton Court, Walton LD8 2PY ☎(01544) 350259 OS map148/255598 2½m ESE of New Radnor
    on A44 (Kington) Open all year 55 pitches Grass, level, sheltered 🛎🗐🐶🖉⊕🐀⊑ £4.00
See also Hundred House

NEWTOWN, Powys   **Map F2**
Pop 5,510. EC Thurs, MD Tues SEE Robert Owen and textile museums 🅸 Central Car Park
☎(01686) 625580 Restaurant: Bear, Broad St ☎(01686) 626964

Smithy Caravan Park, Abermule SY15 6ND ☎(01584) 711280 OS map 157/865033 9m N of
    Newtown on A483 (Welshpool) Open Mar-Nov 95 pitches (60 static) Level grass and hard
    standings, sheltered 🗐🐶🖉⊕∅🚽⊷🗆 fishing £5.50-£7.50

OAKDALE, Gwent   **Map F6**
Restaurant: Maes Manor 2m SW at Blackwood ☎(01495) 224551

Penyfan Caravan and Leisure Park, Manmoel Road NP2 0HY ☎Blackwood (01495) 226636 OS
    map 171/190011 1½m N of Oakdale off B4251 (Crumlin) on Manmoel road via Croespenmaen
    Open all year 75 pitches–booking advisable 4 acres grass and hard standing, level 🛎♀🗐🐶⊕🐀
    lic club, snacks £6.00

OXWICH, Gower, W Glam   **Map D6**
SEE nature reserve, Oxwich Burrows 1m E, Oxwich Point 1m SE Restaurant: Fairyhill 3m N at Reynoldston ✆(01792) 390139

Greenways Holiday Park SA3 1LY ✆Gower (01792) 390220 OS map 159/497860 ¼m S of Oxwich on Oxwich Green Open Apr-Oct 430 pitches (100 static) £10.00

Oxwich Camping Park SA3 1LS ✆Gower (01792) 390777 OS map 159/498865 ¼m SW of Oxwich in village Open Apr-Sept 180 pitches, no caravans Level/sloping grass and hard standings, sheltered (heated) club £10.00

See also Llanrhidian, Port Eynon and Rhossili

PAINSCASTLE, Powys   **Map F4**
SEE castle mound, village green, Llanbedr hill Restaurant: Harp 4m S at Glasbury ✆(01497) 847373

Rhosgoch Holiday Park, Rhosgoch LD2 3JB ✆Painscastle (01497) 851253 OS map 148/189467 2m NE of Painscastle on B4594 (Gladestry) Open Mar-Oct, 25 pitches–must book peak periods–no tents Grass, level, sheltered (£2/wk) (except small breeds), pony trekking, golf, tourist information £6.50

PANDY–see Abergavenny

PEMBROKE, Dyfed   **Map B6**
Pop 5,500. EC Wed SEE castle, Monkton Priory, Lamphey Palace ruins 2m SE ☒ The Commons Road Restaurant: Coach House, Main St (01646) 684602

Castle Farm Camping Site, Angle SA71 5AR ✆(01646) 641220 OS map 157/865033 9m W of Pembroke on B4320 (Angle) Open May-Oct 25 pitches Grass, part level, part open £3.00-£5.00

Windmill Hill Caravan Park, Windmill Hill Farm SA71 5BT ✆Pembroke (01646) 682392 OS map 158/979002 ½m S of Pembroke on B4319 (Bosherton) Open Mar-Oct 30 pitches 3 acres level grass milk £4.00-£9.00

For other sites near Pembroke see also Carew and Manorbier

PENARTH, S Glam   **Map F7**
Pop 22,500. EC Wed SEE Turner House art gallery, Penarth Head ☒ The Esplanade, Penarth Pier ✆(01222) 708849 Restaurant: Glendale, Plymouth Rd ✆(01222) 706701

Lavernock Point Holiday Estate, Fort Road CF6 2XQ ✆Penarth (01222) 707310 OS map 171/182682 2m S of Penarth off B4267 (Sully) on road to Lavernock Point Open Apr-Oct 200 pitches Level/sloping grass £5.00-£6.00

PORTEINON (PORT EYNON), Gower, W Glam   **Map D6**
Restaurant: Barrows 6m E at Mumbles ✆(01792) 361443

Bank Farm, Horton SA3 1LL ✆Gower (01792) 390228 OS map 159/472860 ¼m ENE of Porteinon at Horton Open Mar-Nov 230 pitches (100 static) £8.50-£16.50 (Mastercard/Visa)

Carreglwyd Camping, SA3 1NN ✆(01792) 390795 OS map 159/850466 On S edge of Porteinon off A4118 near beach Open Apr-Oct 280 pitches (80 static) Level/sloping grass, sheltered £7.00-£10.00

Gower Farm Museum and Caravan Park, Llandewi SA3 1AU ✆Gower (01792) 391195 OS map 159/462895 2m N of Porteinon off A4118 (South Gower) Open Apr-Oct 100 pitches 15 acres level/sloping grass £4.00-£5.50

Hillend Camping Park, Llangennith SA3 1JD ✆Llangennith (01792) 386204 OS map 159/418909 6½m NW of Porteinon on B4295 Open Apr-Oct 250 pitches–no touring caravans, no adv booking Grass level/sloping £7.00-£9.00

Newpark Holiday Park, SA3 1NP ✆Gower (01792) 390292 OS map 159/465858 ¼m S of Porteinon centre Open Easter-Oct 172 pitches Level grass and hard standings, sheltered £7.30-£9.50

Three Cliffs Bay Caravan and Camping Site, North Hills Farm, Penmaen SA3 2HB ✆Gower (01792) 371218 OS map 159/534886 5m E of Porteinon off A4118 (Swansea) Open Easter-Oct 95 pitches Grass, part sloping/level, sheltered £8.00-£10.00

PORTHCAWL, Mid Glam   **Map E7**
Pop 15,300, EC Wed Family resort once small fishing village, with sandy beaches and large amusement park SEE Porthcawl Point, St John's church at Newton 1m E, Merthyr Mawr Warren 2m E Old Police Station, John Street (01656) 786639/782211 Restaurant: Rose and Crown at Heol-Y-Capel (01656) 784850

Brodawel Camping Park, Moor Lane, Nottage CF36 3EJ (01656) 783231 OS map 170/816790 1m NW of Porthcawl off A4229 (Nottage) Open Apr-Oct 100 pitches Grass, level, part sheltered £7.00-£8.70

Happy Valley Caravan Park CF32 0NG (01656) 782144 OS map 170/852780 2m E of Porthcawl on A4106 (Bridgend) Open Apr-Sept 450 pitches (350 static) Grass and hard standings, sheltered lic club £7.00-£8.00 (Mastercard/Visa)

Kenfig Pool Caravan Park, Ton Kenfig CF30 9PT Porthcawl (01656) 740079 OS map 170/800814 3m NW of Porthcawl off B4283 (Port Talbot) Open Mar-Nov 78 pitches (75 static)–no tents 3½ acres sloping grass and hard standings £7.00-£10.00

PORT TALBOT, W Glam   **Map E6**
Pop 42,000 EC Wed MD Tues, Sat Restaurant: Aberavan Beach (01639) 884949

Afan Argoed Countryside Centre, Afan Forest Park, Cynonville SA13 3HG (01639) 850564 OS map 170/812952 6m NE of Port Talbot on A4107 (Cymmer)–latest time of arrival 1800 unless advance notice given Open Apr-Oct 10 pitches 1 acre grass and hard standing bike hire, fishing *No showers* £4.00 (Visa)

PRESTEIGNE, Powys   **Map G4**
Pop 1,330. EC Thurs Old Market Hall, Broad St (01544) 260193 Restaurant: Radnorshire Arms, High St (01544) 267406

Rockbridge Mobile Home and Holiday Park LD8 2NF (01547) 560300 OS map 137/295654 1m W of Presteigne on B4356 (Llangunllo) near river Open Easter-Sept 55 pitches (21 static) Grass, level, sheltered (25) £5.00-£10.00

PUMPSAINT, Dyfed   **Map E4**
Restaurant: Dowallcothi Arms (01558) 650547

Maesbach Caravan Park, Ffarmers Village SA19 8EX (01558) 650650 OS map 146/657451 2¾m N of Pumpsaint off A482 (Lampeter) Open Easter-Oct 35 pitches (9 static) Grass and hard standings, part level, part open £6.50-£8.00

RED ROSES, Dyfed   **Map C5**
Village at crossroads inland of Pendine Restaurant: Waungron Farm 4m N at Whitland (01994) 240682

Old Vicarage Caravan Park, SA34 0PG (01834) 831637 OS map 158/204117 In Red Roses at junct of A477 and B4314 Open Mar-Jan 40 pitches (24 static) Grass, level lic club, petrol £5.50-£12.00

Pantglas Farm, Tavernspite SA34 0NS (01834) 831618 OS map 158/175120 1½m NW of Red Roses off B4314 (Templeton) at Tavernspite Open Easter-Oct 75 pitches 7 acres level/gently sloping grass and hard standings, sheltered £6.50-£8.00

Rose Park Farm, Llanteg SA67 8QJ (01834) 831203 OS map 158/164098 2m SW of Red Roses on right of A477 (Pembroke) Open Whitsun-Oct 20 pitches–must book 3½ acres grass, part level, secluded £6.00-£8.00

South Caravan Holiday Park, Tavernspite SA34 0NL (01834) 831586/831451/831651 OS map 158/180127 2m NW of Red Roses on B4314-B4328 (Narberth) opp Alpha inn Open Mar-Oct 180 pitches (115 static) 10 acres level grass (indoor) bar meals £10.00-£14.00

RHAYADER, Powys   **Map F3**
Pop 1,180. EC Thurs, MD Wed SEE Elan Valley reservoirs SW Visitor Centre, North St Rhayader (01597) 810591 Restaurant: Elan Valley 2m SW on B4518 (01597) 810448

Gigrin Red Kite Caravan Site, South Street LD6 5BL Rhayader (01597) 810243 OS map 147/980678 ½m S of Rhayader off A470 (Builth Wells) Open all year exc Xmas/New Year 15 pitches 2 acres level grass sheltered indoor play area, fishing, nature trail, red kite centre £6.50-£8.00 inc elect

Wyeside Caravan Camping Park LD6 5LB (01597) 810183 OS map 147/968686 ¼m N of Rhayader on left of A470 (Llangurig) beside river Wye Open Feb-Nov 190 pitches pony trekking, fishing, bowls, putting, tennis £7.00-£8.00

RHOSSILLI, Gower, W Glam   **Map D6**
Pop 330. SEE Rhossili Bay ◪ Coastguard Cottages ☎ Gower (01792) 390707 Restaurant: Café Rendezvous ☎ (01792) 390645

Pitton Cross Caravan and Camping Park, SA3 1PH ☎ Gower (01792) 390593 Fax (01792) 391010 OS map 159/434878 1¼m E of Rhossilli on B4247 (Pilton Green) Open Apr-Oct 100 pitches 6 acres level grass and hard standings 🏪 🚻 ♨ ⊘ ⊕ ⊘ ⊙ ⤵ ⛟ ♿ £8.00-£11.25 (Mastercard/Visa)

RHYDLEWIS—see Beulah

ST CLEARS, Dyfed   **Map C5**
Pop 1,750. EC Wed, MD Tues SEE 12c church, Castle House Restaurant: Black Lion ☎ (01994) 230700

Afon Lodge Caravan Park, SA33 4LG ☎ St Clears (01994) 230647 OS map 158/274197 2m N of St Clears off Llanboidy road Open Mar-Dec 65 pitches (30 static) 5 acres part level grass and hard standings, woodland setting 🏪 ✗ 🍴 ⤴ 🚻 ♨ ⊘ ⊕ ⊘ ⤵ ⛟ ♿ ⛺ TV hook-up £5.00-£10.00

ST DAVID'S, Dyfed   **Map A5**
Pop 1,750. SEE cathedral, Bishop's Palace ruins Restaurant: Farmers Arms, Goat St ☎ (01437) 720328

Caerfai Bay Caravan and Tent Park SA62 6QT ☎ St David's (01437) 720274 OS map 157/760244 ½m S of St David's off road to Caerfai Bay adj coast path Open Easter-Oct 140 pitches (33 static) 10 acres level/sloping grass 🚻 ♨ ⊘ ⊕ ⊘ ⛺ beach £5.00-£11.00

Glan-y-Mor Tent Park, Caerfai Bay Road SA62 6QT ☎ St David's (01437) 721788 OS map 157/247756 ½m SE of St David's on Caerfai Bay road Open Apr-Sept 60 pitches–no trailer caravans ✗ 🍴 ♨ £7.00

Hendre Eynon Caravan Camping Park SA62 6DB ☎ St David's (01437) 720474 OS map 157/773280 2m NNE of St David's off B4583 (Whitesands) on Llanrian road Open Apr-Oct 85 pitches Grass level, part sheltered 🚻 ♨ ⊘ ⊕ ⊘ ⛟ farm produce, first aid £6.00-£10.00

Porthclais Farm, Porthclais Road SA62 6RR ☎ (01437) 721256 OS map 157/744243 1m SW of St David's off Porthclais road Open Mar-Oct 200 pitches 4 acres level grass ♨ farm produce £2.50

See also Croesgoch, Newgale and Solva

ST FLORENCE—see Carew

SAUNDERSFOOT, Dyfed   **Map C6**
Pop 2,500. EC Wed SEE harbour, Wiseman's Bridge 1m N, Monkstone Point 1m SE Restaurant: Old Chemist Inn, The Strand ☎ (01834) 813982

Heritage Court, Pleasant Valley, Stepaside SA67 8LN ☎ (01834) 812464/811063 1½m N of Saundersfoot off coast road via Wisemans Bridge Level grass, sheltered 🏪 ⤴ (to order) 🚻 ♨ ⊘ ⊕ ⊘ ⛺ (2) ⊕ ⛟ ⛺ clubhouse, games room, beach near £6.00-£12.00

Moreton Farm Leisure Park, Moreton SA69 9EA ☎ Saundersfoot (01834) 812016 OS map 158/118049 1½m W of Saundersfoot on A478 (Narberth-Tenby) opp chapel Open Mar 1-Nov 1 80 pitches (12 static) 12 acres level/sloping grass and hard standings, sheltered 🏪 🚻 ♨ ⊘ ⊕ ⊘ ⤵ ❀ 🏠 ♿ £5.00-£10.00

Trevayne Caravan and Camping Park, Monkstone Bay SA69 9DL ☎ Saundersfoot (01834) 813402 OS map 135/140030 2m S of Saundersfoot off B4316 (Tenby) on road to Monkstone Point Open Easter-Oct 200 pitches (80 static) Grass, part sloping ⛟ ⛺ farm produce, near beach £5.00-£12.00

See also Amroth and Kilgetty

SOLVA, Dyfed   **Map B5**
Restaurant: Harbour House ☎ (01437) 721267

Mount Farm, SA62 6XL ☎ (01437) 721301 OS map 157/828248 2m E of Solva on A487 (Haverfordwest) Open Apr-Oct 45 pitches Level grass, sheltered (20 static) 🏪 🚻 ♨ £6.00

Nine Wells Caravan Camping Park, Nine Wells SA62 6UH ☎ (01437) 721809 OS map 157/787248 ½m W of Solva on A487 (St David's) Open Easter-mid Oct 60 pitches Grass, level/sloping, part sheltered 🚻 ⊕ ⛟ £6.50-£8.00

STEPASIDE—see Kilgetty

SWANSEA, W Glam   **Map E6**
Pop 173,150. EC Thurs, MD Sat SEE museum, Clyne castle gardens, civic centre ⓘSingleton
Street ✆(01792) 468321 Restaurant: Annie's, St Helen's Rd ✆(01792) 655603

Blackhills Caravan and Camping Park, Fairwood Common SA2 7JN ✆Swansea (01792) 207065
OS map 159/581914 6m SW of Swansea off A4118 (Porteinon) Open Apr-Oct–must book peak
periods 300 pitches Grass and hard standings, level, sheltered ⌂🗗🖸🖉🖵🖳 £6.00-£10.00

Riverside Caravan Park, Ynysforgan Farm, Morriston SA6 6QL ✆Swansea (01792) 775587 OS
map 159/679991 3m N of Swansea on right of A4067 (Pontardawe) near junct 45 of M4, by river
Tawe Open all year, 120 pitches 7 acres, level grass and hard standings, sheltered
⌂🗗🖸🖉🖵🖳🖳🖳🖳🖳 jacuzzi, lic club, fishing £6.00-£14.00

TALGARTH, Powys   **Map F5**
Restaurant: Three Cocks 2m N at Three Cocks ✆(01497) 847215

Anchorage Caravan Park, Bronllys LD3 0LD ✆Talgarth (01874) 711246 OS map 161/142350 1m
NW of Talgarth off A479 (Bronllys) on A438 (Brecon) Open all year 193 pitches (77 static) Grass,
part sloping, sheltered, some hard standings ⌂🗗🖸🖉🖵🖳🖳🖳 Post office, baby bathroom,
hairdresser £8.00

Riverside International Caravan Camping Park, LD3 0HL ✆Talgarth (01874) 711320 OS map
161/148347 1m NW of Talgarth on A479 (Bronllys) Open Apr-Oct 84 pitches Grass and hard
standings, level, sheltered ✗♀🖳🖍🗗🖸🖉🖵🖳 (indoor) 🖳🖍🖵🖳🖳🖳🖳 lic snack bar,
fishing, sauna, jacuzzi, solarium, gym, putting green £7.50-£8.50

TAVERNSPITE–see Red Roses

TEMPLE BAR, Dyfed   **Map D4**
Pop 55 Restaurant: Vale of Aeron 1m NW on A482 at Ystrad Aeron ✆(01570) 470385

Hafod Brynog Caravan Park, Ystrad Aeron, Felinfach SA48 8AE ✆(01570) 470084 OS map
146/524565 1½m NW of Temple Bar on right of A482 (Aberaeron) Open Apr-Oct 42 pitches
Level/sloping grass and hard standings, sheltered 🖵🖉🖵🖳🖍 £6.00-£9.00

TENBY, Dyfed   **Map C6**
Pop 4,950. EC Wed SEE castle ruins, old town walls, Tudor Merchant's House, Caldy Island and monastery (men only) ▯ The Croft ☏ Tenby (01834) 842402 Restaurant: Coach and Horses, Upper Frog St ☏ (01834) 842704

Kiln Park Holiday Centre, Marsh Road, Kiln Park SA70 7RB ☏ Tenby (01834) 844121 OS map 158/126005 1m SW of Tenby on A4139 (Pembroke) Open Apr-Sept–must book (maximum stay 2 wks) 780 pitches (550 static) Level grass and hard standings ▮✕♀⌂⌐ 🗂❂∅⊗⊘▭⊕↵ (❀ Jun 21-Aug) ▱♿ lic club, petrol, amusements £9.00-£12.65

Lodge Farm, New Hedges SA70 8TN ☏ Tenby (01834) 842468 OS map 158/130029 1¾m N of Tenby on A478 (Narberth) Open Mar-Sept 105 pitches (40 static) Grass, level, open ♀🗂❂∅⊗⊕↵▱ games room £4.50-£14.00

Moysland Farm, Narberth Rd SA69 9DS ☏ (01834) 812455 OS map 158/127032 2m N of Tenby on A478 (Cardigan) near New Hedges roundabout Open Whitsun-Sept 14 pitches–must book 3 acres level grass, sheltered ❂❀ £6.00-£11.50

Rowston Holiday Park, New Hedges SA70 8TL ☏ Tenby (01834) 842178 OS map 158/132028 1½m N of Tenby off A478 (Narberth) Open Apr-Oct 240 pitches (130 static) Grass and hard standings, part sloping, part open ▮🗂❂∅⊗∅↵❀ (Jul-Aug) ▱ beach near £8.00-£14.00

Rumbleway Caravan and Tent Park, New Hedges SA70 8TR ☏ (01834) 845155 OS map 158/127028 1m N of Tenby off A478 (Cardigan)–signposted Open Apr-Oct 240 pitches (130 static) 25 acres level/sloping grass and hard standings, sheltered ▮♀⌐🗂❂∅⊗∅▭↵□▱❀▱♿ £8.00-£14.00

Well Park, New Hedges SA70 8TL ☏ Tenby (01834) 842179 OS map 158/129027 1½m N of Tenby on A478 (Narberth) Open Apr-Oct 150 pitches (42 static) Grass and hard standings, part level, part open ♀⌂🗂❂∅⊗⊘⊕↵□▱🏠 games room £6.00-£12.00

Windmills Camping Park, Brynhir Lane SA70 8TJ ☏ Tenby (01834) 842200 OS map 158/125020 ½m NW of Tenby on A478 (Begelly) Open Easter-Sept 65 pitches–booking advisable Grass, level ❂⊗∅

Wood Park Caravans, New Hedges SA70 8TL ☏ Tenby (01834) 843414 OS map 158/131130 1½m N of Tenby off A478 (New Hedges bypass) Open Easter-Sept–must book 150 pitches (90 static) Grass, level/sloping and hard standings, sheltered ♀🗂❂∅⊗↵ (❀ Jul-Aug) ▱ games room £5.00-£11.00

See also Carew and Manorbier

TREDEGAR, Gwent   **Map F6**
Pop 890 SEE memorial to Aneurin Bevan on A4047 1m NE, Sirhowy valley S, Bedwellte church 2m S ▯ Bryn Bach Country Park, Merthyr Rd ☏ (01495) 711816 Restaurant Tregenna 6m W at Merthyr Tydfil ☏ (01685) 723627

Parc Bryn Bach, Merthyr Road NP2 3AY ☏ Tredegar (01495) 711816 OS map 161/125102 1½m NW of Tredegar off A465 (Abergavenny-Merthyr Tydfil) Open Jan 2-Dec 24, 30 pitches Level grass and hard standing in 600 acre country park with water sports, hang gliding and fishing ✕🗂❂⊗∅↵♿ hostel £3.50-£6.00

TREGARON, Dyfed   **Map E4**
Pop 950 Remote hill town and popular trekking centre in Teifi valley ▯ The Square ☏ (01974) 298144 Restaurant: Talbot, The Square ☏ (01974) 298208

Hendrewen Caravan Park, Pencarw, Llangeitho SY25 6QU ☏ Tregaron (01974) 298410 OS map 146/642950 3m W of Tregaron off A485 (Lampeter) on B4342 (Llangeitho) Open Mar-Oct 40 pitches (35 static) 4½ acres grass level/gentle slope ▮✕♀❂∅ £3.50-£5.00-£6.50

TRESAITH–see Aberporth

USK, Gwent   **Map G6**
Pop 2,000 EC Wed SEE old inns, Usk Valley Restaurant: Three Salmons, Bridge Street ☏ (01291) 672133

Bridge Inn, Chainbridge NP5 1PP ☏ (01873) 880243 OS map 161/346054 3m N of Usk on B4598 (Abergavenny) by river Usk Open Mar-Oct 15 pitches 1½ acres mainly level grass ✕♀ fishing £3.00

The 180-mile long coast path is the highlight of the Pembrokeshire Coast National Park, giving views of wild rocks and sandy beaches, seal and bird colonies. *Pembrokeshire Coast National Park, County Offices, Haverfordwest SA61 1QZ – (01437) 710591.*

WELSHPOOL, Powys   **Map G2**
Pop 5,000. EC Thurs, MD Mon SEE Powis Castle, Powys Museum, old inns, narrow gauge railway
to Llanfair Caereinion 8m W ⛻Flash Leisure Centre ☏(01938) 552043 Restaurant: Royal Oak,
The Cross ☏(01938) 552217

Bank Farm Caravan Park, Middletown SY21 8EJ ☏(01938) 570526 OS map 126/294122 5½m E
   of Welshpool on A458 (Shrewsbury) Open Mar-Oct 56 pitches (34 static) Grass, part sloping, part
   sheltered ▣➋⌀⊛⌀➌⤻➊⊟⅃ first aid, trout fishing £6.50-£8.50

Severn Caravan Park, Kilkewydd Farm, Forden SY21 8RT ☏Forden (01938) 580238 OS map
   126/233025 3m S of Welshpool on A490 (Church Stoke) Open Apr-Oct 88 pitches (86 static)
   Grass and hardstanding level, sheltered ▣➋➌⤻➊ (£75) games room £4.00-£5.00

Valley View Caravan Park, Pentrebeirdd SY21 9DL ☏(01938) 500265 OS map 125/192142 5m
   NNW of Welshpool on A490 (Llanfyllin) Open Mar-Oct–no adv booking 100 pitches
   ▣⌀⌀⊛⌀⊟➌⤻⊡⌂⅃ £5.50-£6.00

YSTRADGYNLAIS, Powys   **Map E5**
Pop 8,400. EC Thurs, MD Fri SEE Craig-y-nos country park and Dan-yr-Ogof caves 6m NE
Restaurant: Copper Beech 2m NE at Abercraf (Heol Tawe off A4067) ☏(01639) 730269

Dan-yr-Ogof Caravan-Tenting Park, Abercraf SA9 1GT ☏Abercrave (01639) 730284/730693 OS
   map 160/840160 4m NE of Ystradgynlais on A4067 (Sennybridge) Open Easter-Oct–no adv
   booking 60 pitches Grass, sloping, sheltered ✗➋⌀ fishing, trekking, dry ski slope £8.00-£9.00

See listing under Carew

14 South Scotland

Just across the border with England, the two new counties of Borders on the east and Dumfries and Galloway on the west join up as South Scotland, a region in which few northbound travellers even stop, yet one with superb coastal scenery, a mild climate and uncrowded roads.

The Cheviots roll away to the west from Castle Bar, a popular gateway to the Borders. These and the heather-clad hills beyond provide extensive areas for gentle hill walking. On the east is a narrow and rugged coast inset with the fine sands of Coldingham Bay and the picturesque fishing ports of St Abbs and Eyemouth, famous for sea angling. In the centre of the country is Melrose, heart of Walter Scott country, for which Galashiels is a popular centre, Hawick, one of the largest Border textile towns and Jedburgh, with its museum housing the death mask of Mary Queen of Scots. Above the vast depression of the Devil's Beeftub near Moffat is the source of the Tweed, one of the most scenic of the country's many rivers and one of the most rewarding to fish. Further north it provides a beautiful setting for Peebles and nearby Niedpath Castle.

Dumfries and Galloway forming the western half of the region has a coastline that extends some 200 miles between the smithies of Gretna, where runaway couples used to get married, and Stranraer on the northwest. The lovely Solway coast in the south is indented with deep river estuaries at the head of which lie picturesque Newton Stewart, its houses lining both banks of the Cree, Dumfries with its memories of Bonnie Prince Charlie and the colourful market town of Kirkcudbright, dominated by the sixteenth-century MacLellan Castle.

North of Newton Stewart is the vast and hilly Glen Trool Forest Park centred on the 2764ft high Merrick Peak and mirrored in the tiny Loch Glen Trool. Criss-crossed by nature trails, the forest abounds in deer, red squirrel and less common species of birds, including the occasional golden eagle. An accessible yet rewarding vantage point is Robert the Bruce's victory stone.

To the southwest the sandy stretches of Wigtown and Luce Bay are a haven for sailing and sea angling and catches may sometimes even include a porbeagle shark. Whithorn, Sandhead and Portpatrick are good centres in this area, and the sub-tropical gardens at Logan are well worth visiting. Panoramic views follow one another on the cliff top run from Stranraer through Ballantrae to popular Girvan in the north. Inland, owing perhaps to the milder climate, towns and villages seem more cheerful and colourful than in other parts of Scotland.

Campsites are not too plentiful in the Borders and those that exist tend to be near the larger towns. In Dumfries and Galloway they are more plentiful on the coast but less frequent inland, especially in the west.

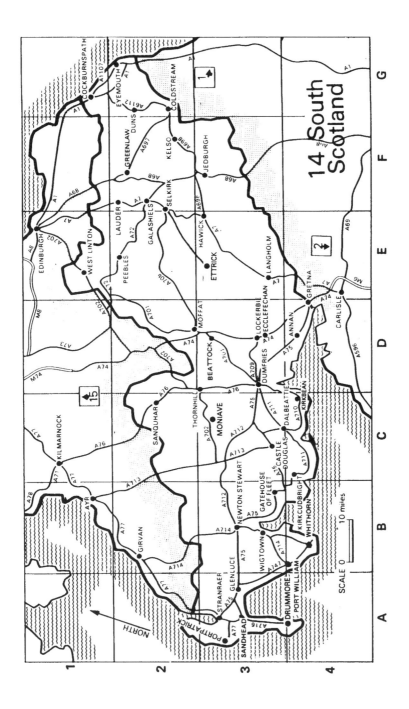

ANNAN, Dumfries & Galloway   **Map D4**
Pop 8,950. EC Wed, MD Fri, Sat SEE Moat House, old church Restaurant: Blue Bell Inn, High St
☎ (01461) 202385

Galabank Park, North Street DG12 6AQ *Well maintained site near centre* ☎ Annan (01556) 503806
OS map 85/194673 ½m N of Annan on B722 (Waterbeck) Open May-
Sept–no adv booking 30 pitches Grass, level, sheltered ▉❀ £6.25-£6.65

Queensberry Bay Caravan Park, Powfoot DG12 5PU ☎ (01461) 700205 OS map 85/138653
3½m W of Annan off B724 (Dumfries) on Powfoot road by Solway Firth Open Apr-Oct 172 pitches
(70 static) Hard standing and grass, level, open ▊⌇▉▉⌀❀⌀ fishing £8.00-£9.25

BEATTOCK, Dumfries & Galloway   **Map D3**
EC Wed Restaurant: Beattock House ☎ (01683) 300403

Beattock House Hotel Caravan Park, DG10 9QB *Pleasant wooded site in grounds of country
house adj main road* ☎ (01683) 300403 OS map 78/079027 ¼m N of Beattock centre near hotel
Open Apr-Oct 15 pitches Grass, some hard standings, level, sheltered ▉⌀⌇▉⌑ lic bar £5.50
(inc showers)

Craigielands Caravan Park DG10 9RB ☎ (01683) 300591 OS map 78/079019 ¼m S of Beattock
centre beyond railway bridge Open all year, 125 pitches (75 static) Level/sloping grass and hard
standings ✕⌇▉▉❀▉🏠 fishing, boating £6.00 (Mastercard/Visa/Delta)

BONCHESTER BRIDGE–see Hawick

CASTLE DOUGLAS, Dumfries & Galloway   **Map C3**
Pop 3,500. EC Thurs, MD Tues SEE ruined Threave Castle 1m W, Threave Estate gardens 1m SW,
Carlingwork Loch with bird sanctuary ℹ Markethill ☎ (01556) 502611 Restaurant: Douglas Arms,
King St ☎ (01556) 502231

Loch Ken Holiday Park, Parton DG7 3NE ☎ (01644) 470282 Fax (01644) 470297 OS map
84/685705 7m NW of Castle Douglas on A713 (Ayr) by Loch Ken Open Mar-Oct 85 pitches (35
static) Grass, part level, sheltered ▊⌇▉▉⌀❀⌀❀⌇▉⌑♿ fishing, canoe, dinghy and cycle
hire, windsurfing, sailing (launching facs) £7.00-£10.50

Lochside Park DG7 1EZ ☎ Castle Douglas (01556) 502949 OS map 84/765618 ½m S of Castle
Douglas off A75 (Gatehouse of Fleet) by Carlingwark Loch Open Easter-Oct–no adv booking 161
pitches Grass and hard standings, level ▉▉❀⌀⌇♿ boating, fishing, putting £7.95-£9.55

COCKBURNSPATH, Borders   **Map G1**
Restaurant: Harvesters 13m NW at East Linton ☎ (01620) 860395

Chesterfield Caravan Park, The Neuk TD13 5YH ☎ (01368) 830459 Fax (01368) 830394 OS map
67/770695 1m SW of Cockburnspath off A1 (Berwick) on Abbey St Bathans road Open Apr-Oct
75 pitches (40 static) Level grass ▉▉⌀❀⌀⌇▉⌑ £7.50-£10.00

Pease Bay Caravan Site, Pease Bay TD13 5YP ☎ (01368) 830206 OS map 67/794707 1½m SE
of Cockburnspath off A1 (Berwick on Tweed) Open Apr-Oct 321 pitches (307 static)–no tents
Level grass, sheltered, hard standings ▊✕⌇⌇▉▉⌀❀⌀❀⌇⌑ £9.00-£12.00

COLDINGHAM–see Eyemouth

CROCKETFORD–see Dumfries

DALBEATTIE, Dumfries & Galloway   **Map C3**
Pop 3,890. EC Thurs ⬛Town Hall ✆(01556) 610117 Restaurant: Douglas Arms 7m W at Castle Douglas ✆(01556) 502231

Barlochan Caravan Park, Palnackie DG7 1PF ✆(01556) 600256–bkgs (01557) 870267 OS map 84/819571 2½m S of Dalbeattie on A711 (Kirkcudbright) Open Apr-Oct 60 pitches (40 static) Level grass and hard standing, sheltered 🔣 fishing £7.50-£10.25

Beeswing Caravan Park, Drumjohn Moor, Kirkgunzeon DG2 8JL ✆(01387) 760242 OS map 84/885684 6m NE of Dalbeattie on A711 (Dumfries) Open Mar-Oct 60 pitches 🔣 donkey rides, fishing £4.90-£6.75

Castle Point Caravan Site, Rockcliffe DG5 4QL ✆(01556) 630248 OS map 84/855532 6m S of Dalbeattie off A710 (New Abbey) on Rockcliffe road, by sea Open Apr-Sept 37 pitches 3 acres, level grass 🔣 £8.50-£10.50

Islecroft Caravan Site, Mill Street DG6 4HE ✆Dalbeattie (01556) 610012 OS map 84/835614 ¼m E of Dalbeattie centre off A711 (Dumfries) by Colliston Park Open Easter-Sept 74 pitches–no adv booking Grass, level 🔣 £6.15-£7.30 (inc showers)

Kippford Holiday Park, Kippford DG5 4LF ✆(01556) 620636 Fax (01556) 620636 OS map 84/843564 3m S of Dalbeattie on A710 (Solway coast road) near junct with Kippford road Open Mar-Oct 184 pitches (108 static) Grass, part level, sheltered, some hard standings 🔣 pony trekking, fishing, sea trips, golf, cycle hire £7.00-£11.00

Mossband Caravan Park, Kirkgunzeon DG2 8JP *Small friendly park, family run* ✆(01387) 760208 OS map 84/872665 3½m NE of Dalbeattie on left of A711 (Dumfries) Open Mar-Oct 36 pitches Level grass and hard standings 🔣 tennis, pool room £4.50-£6.50

Sandyhills Bay Leisure Park, Sandyhills DG5 4PT ✆(01387) 780257 OS map 84/891549 6m SE of Dalbeattie on right of A710 (Dumfries) beyond golf course Open Apr-Oct 94 pitches (34 static) Level grass, sheltered 🔣 golf, beach £7.50-£10.95

DRUMMORE, Dumfries and Galloway   **Map A4**
Pop 390 EC Wed SEE church, ruined chapel, Mull of Galloway 2m S Restaurant: Queens, Mill St ✆(01776) 840300

Clashwannon Caravan Site DG9 9QE ✆(01776) 840632/840374 OS map 82/132374 ½m N of Drummore on A716 (Stranraer) Open Apr-Sept 20 pitches ½ acre level/sloping grass 🔣 £5.00

DUMFRIES, Dumfries & Galloway   **Map D3**
Pop 31,000. EC Thurs, MD Wed SEE Burns house and mausoleum, burgh museum, Globe Inn, Caerlaverock Castle and Wildfowl centre ⬛Whitesands ✆(01387) 853862 Restaurant: Jean Armour's Pantry, Robert Burns Centre, Mill Rd ✆(01387) 869079

Barnsoul Farm and Wildlife Area, Shawhead DG2 9SQ *One of Galloway's most scenic sites* ✆(01387) 730249 6m W of Dumfries off A75 (Castle Douglas) into Shawhead–signposted Open Apr-Oct 50 pitches (10 static) Level/sloping grass and hard standings, sheltered 🔣 campers' kitchen unit £6.00-£10.00

Courthill Caravan Park, Auldgirth DG2 0RR ✆(01387) 740336 OS map 78/926837 6m NW of Dumfries on A76 (Kilmarnock) Open all year–no adv booking 33 pitches Grass, level, open 🔣 £3.00-£5.00

Craigsview Caravan Site, 296 Annan Road DG1 3LN ✆Dumfries (01387) 753812 OS map 84/005762 1½m E of Dumfries on A780/A75 (Annan) 1½ acres, level Open Easter-Oct 20 pitches 🔣 £4.00

Galloway Arms, Crocketford DG2 8RA *Site with top facilities of adj hotel* ✆(01556) 690248 OS map 84/832729 9m W of Dumfries on A75 (Newton Stewart) in Crocketford adj hotel Open Apr-Oct 30 pitches Level grass, hard standings, sheltered 🔣 £6.00-£10.00

Mouswald Caravan Park, Mouswald DG1 4JS ✆(01387) 830226 OS map 84/060740 4½m ESE of Dumfries off A75 (Annan) Open Mar-Oct 50 pitches Grass, level, sheltered, hard standings 🔣 £7.50-£8.50

Newfield Caravan Park, Annan Road DG1 3SE ✆(01387) 740228 OS map 84/009759 2½m E of Dumfries on A75 (Annan) Open all year 40 pitches 2½ acres, level 🔣 dairy produce, fishing £3.75

Park of Brandedleys, Crocketford DG2 8RG ✆(01556) 690250 OS map 84/830725 9m W of Dumfries on A75 (Castle Douglas) Open all year 107 pitches (30 static) Grass, part level, hard standing, open 🔣 (35) 🔣 lic café, tennis, sauna £9.00-£15.00 (Mastercard/Visa/Switch)

Galloway Arms

Crocketford

West of Dumfries on A75 Newton Stewart road adjoining hotel.
Level grass and hard standings, sheltered.

Tel (01556) 690248

ECCLEFECHAN, Dumfries & Galloway   **Map D3**
Pop 800. EC Thurs SEE Carlyle's birthplace Restaurant: The Courtyard 3m SE at Eaglesfield
☎(01461) 500215

Cressfield Caravan Park DG11 3DR ☎and Fax Ecclefechan (01576) 300702 OS map 85/196744
¼m S of Ecclefechan centre on B7076 near junct 19 of A74(M)–signposted Open all year 115
pitches (48 static) Level grass, hard standing 🗗🗗🗗 dog exercise area, golf nets,
putting green, boules, giant chess and draughts, hotel adj £6.50-£8.50

Hoddom Castle Caravan Park, Hoddom Bridge DG11 1BE ☎(01576) 300251 OS map 85/155730
3m SW of Ecclefechan on right of B725 (Dalton) at Hoddom Bridge Open Apr-Oct 250 pitches
28 acres, part sloping, part hard standings, sheltered 🗗🗗🗗 golf,
fishing, tennis, nature trails, guided walks £5.50-£11.50 (Mastercard/Visa/Switch)

ETTRICK, Borders   **Map E2**
Restaurant: Etrrickshaws Lodge 10m NE at Ettrick Bridge ☎(01750) 52229

Angecroft Caravan Park, TD7 5HY ☎Ettrick Valley (01750) 62251 OS map 79/277135 ½m S of
Ettrick on B709 (Eskdalemuir) Open all year 49 pitches (41 static) Level grass and hard standing,
sheltered 🗗🗗🗗 £5.00-£10.00

Honey Cottage Caravan Park, Hope House TD7 5HU ☎Ettrick Valley (01750) 62246 OS map
76/295165 2m N of Ettrick on B709 (Selkirk) near junction with B711 (Hawick) Open all year 80
pitches (50 static) 7 acres, level grass, part open some hard standings
🗗🗗🗗 fishing, boating £6.50-£7.50

EYEMOUTH, Borders   **Map G2**
Pop 2,800. EC Wed SEE harbour, museum, memorial garden, Coldingham Priory 4m NW ℹ Auld
Kirk ☎Eyemouth (01890) 750678 Restaurant: Contented Sole at harbour ☎(01890) 750268

Coldingham Caravan Park, Coldingham TD14 5NT ☎(01890) 750316 OS map 67/896662 4m
NW of Eyemouth on A1107 (Cockburnspath) Open Mar-mid Nov, 180 pitches (150 static) hard
standings 🗗🗗🗗 £3.50

Eyemouth Holiday Park, Fort Road TD14 5ER ☎(01890) 751050 Fax (01890) 751462 OS map
67/941648 ½m N of Eyemouth on A1107 (Burnmouth) Open Mar-Nov 290 pitches (270 static)
Level grass and hard standings 🗗🗗🗗 children's room, barbecue
area, boat storage, private beach £10.00-£15.00 (Mastercard/Visa/Switch)

Highview Caravan Park, Coldingham TD14 5TX ☎(01890) 771221 OS map 67/843663 6m WNW
of Eyemouth on A1107 (Cockburnspath) Open Mar 31-Oct 31, 286 pitches (150 static) grass and
hard standing, level 🗗🗗🗗 chip shop £5.00-£7.00

Scoutscroft Caravan and Camping Park, Coldingham TD14 5NB ☎(018907) 71338 OS map
67/907662 2½m NW of Eyemouth off A1107 (Dunbar) on B6438 (Coldingham) Open Mar-Oct
160 pitches (100 static) Grass, level, sheltered 🗗🗗🗗 (50) 🗗🗗🗗 diving
centre £4.50-£14.00 (Mastercard/Visa)

GALASHIELS, Borders   **Map F2**
Pop 13,450. EC Wed SEE Mercat Cross, Old Gala House, Sir Walter Scott's home at Abbotsford 2m
SE, Melrose Abbey 4m E ℹ Bank Street ☎Galashiels (01896) 8255551 Restaurant: Abbotsford
Arms, Stirling St ☎(01896) 822517

Gibson Park, Melrose TD6 9RY ☎(01896) 822969 OS map 73/544341 4m SE of Galasheils on
right of A6091 (St Boswells) in Melrose Open all year 60 marked pitches 3 acres, level grass and
hard standings £12.30-£13.80 (Mastercard/Visa)

GATEHOUSE OF FLEET, Dumfries & Galloway　　　　　　　　　　**Map B3**
Pop 890. EC Thurs SEE ruined Cardoness castle, Anwoth churchyard ◪Car Park ☎(01557) 814212 Restaurant: Murray Arms ☎(01557) 814207

Anwoth Caravan Park, Garden Street DG7 2JU ☎(01557) 840333 OS map 83/595562 ¼m S of Gatehouse of Fleet off A75 (Newton Stewart) Open Apr-Sept 66 pitches Grass, level, sheltered (50) £4.00-£7.00

Auchenlarie Holiday Farm, DG7 2EX ☎(01557) 840251 OS map 83/536522 5m SW of Gatehouse of Fleet on A75 (Newton Stewart) Open Easter-Oct 447 pitches (160 static) 35 acres level grass part sheltered crazy golf £6.00-£7.00

Mossyard Caravan Site, Mossyard DG7 2ET ☎(01557) 840226 OS map 83/548519 4½m SW of Gatehouse of Fleet on A75 (Newton Stewart) Open Easter-Oct–must book peak periods 55 pitches 6½ acres, level/gentle slope private beach £6.00-£8.00

GLENLUCE, Dumfries & Galloway　　　　　　　　　　　　　　　**Map A3**
Restaurant: George 10m W at Stranraer ☎(01776) 872487

Cock Inn Caravan Park, Auchenmalg DG8 0JT ☎(01581) 500227 OS map 82/236518 5m SE of Glenluce on left of A747 (Port William) Open Mar-Oct–must book peak periods 120 pitches (70 static) Level/sloping grass and hard standings first aid, sauna £7.00-£11.00

Glenluce Caravan and Camping Park DG8 0QR ☎(01581) 300412 OS map 82/197574 ½m W of Glenluce centre off A75 (Stranraer) Open Mar-Oct–must book peak periods 45 pitches (27 static) Grass, level, sheltered, hard standings meals £6.70-£9.20

Whitecairn Farm Caravan Park DG8 0NZ ☎(01581) 300267 OS map 82/205598 1½m N of Glenluce on Penninghame Forest road Open Apr-Oct 50 pitches Grass, level, open (25) £7.50-£8.50

GREENLAW, Borders　　　　　　　　　　　　　　　　　　　　　**Map F2**
Pop 600. Restaurant: Purves Hall 4m SE on A697 ☎(01890) 840558

Greenlaw Caravan Park, Bank Street TD10 6XX ☎(01361) 810341 OS map 74/709461 ¼m N of Greenlaw on A6105 (Duns) by river Open Easter-Oct 115 pitches (90 static) 11 acres, level grass sep pitches, fishing £8.50-£11.50

GRETNA, Dumfries & Galloway　　　　　　　　　　　　　　　　**Map D4**
Pop 2,200. EC Wed SEE marriage smithy and museum at Gretna Green ◪ Old Headless Cross, Gretna Green ☎Gretna (01461) 337834 Restaurant: Gretna Chase 1m S on B721 ☎(01461) 337517

Braids Caravan Park, Annan Road CA6 5DQ ☎Gretna (01461) 337409 Fax (01461) 337409 OS map 85/318674 ¼m W of Gretna on B721 (Annan) Open all year–advisable book peak periods 86 pitches 5 acres level grass and hard standings, sheltered £6.00-£7.90

King Robert the Bruce's Cave Caravan-Camping Park, Kirkpatrick Fleming DG11 3AT ☎(01461) 800285 OS map 85/267703 3m NW of Gretna off A74 (Lockerbie) Open Apr-Oct 80 pitches Grass and hard standings, part sloping, sheltered (1) fishing £5.50

Old Toll Bar Caravan Park, Sark Bridge Rd DG16 5JD ☎Gretna (01461) 337439 OS map 85/327672 ¼m E of Gretna off A74 by river Sark Open Easter-Sept, 60 pitches (café) 5 acres level grass and hard standings, sheltered £5.00-£7.00 (Mastercard/Visa)

HAWICK, Borders　　　　　　　　　　　　　　　　　　　　　　**Map H3**
Pop 16,500. EC Tues SEE parish church, Goldielands Peel Tower, Wilton Lodge Park, museum ◪Common Haugh Car Park ☎Hawick (01450) 372547 Restaurant: Kirklands, West Stewart Pl ☎(01450) 372263

Bonchester Bridge Caravan Park, Bonchester Bridge TD8 9JN ☎(01450) 860676 OS map 80/586121 6m SE of Hawick on A6088 (Carter Bar) by Horse and Hounds Hotel Open Apr-Oct 20 pitches Hard standings and level grass, sheltered £5.00-£10.00

Riverside Caravan Park, Hornshole Bridge TD9 8SY ☎(01450) 373785 OS map 79/537169 2m NE of Hawick on left of A698 (Kelso) by river Teviot Open Mar-Oct 104 pitches (60 static) 8 acres hard standings and grass, level/gentle slope free fishing, campers lounge, games room £6.50-£7.50

JEDBURGH, Borders   **Map F3**
Pop 4,130. EC Thurs Border town set in beautiful landscape SEE abbey, Queen Mary's House, Jedburgh Castle (jail museum) ⓘ Murray's Green ☎ Jedburgh (01835) 863435 Restaurant: Fermiehurst Mill Lodge 3m S on A68 ☎ (01835) 863279

Eliot Park (Camping Club), Edinburgh Road TD8 6ED ☎ Jedburgh (01835) 863393 OS map 80/652210 ½m N of Jedburgh off A68 (Edinburgh) Open Apr 1-Sept 28, 45 pitches–adv booking min 3 nights 3 acres, level grass, sheltered � £8.00-£14.00

Jedwater Caravan Park, TD8 6PJ ☎ (01835) 840219 OS map 80/667160 3m S of Jedburgh on A68 (Carter Bar) Open Easter-Oct 135 pitches (60 static) Grass, level, open, hard standings ▣ (20) ▤ footballl pitch, giant trampolines £8.00-£10.00

Lilliardsedge Park, Ancrum TD8 6TZ ☎ (01835) 830271 OS map 74/620267 5m N of Jedburgh on A68 (St Boswells) Open Apr-Sept 140 pitches (90 static) ▣ bar meals, campers' kitchen, fishing £7.00-£7.50

KELSO, Borders   **Map F2**
Pop 5,210. EC Wed Attractive town on bend of river Tweed SEE abbey ruins, bridge, Floors Castle ⓘ Town House, The Square ☎ Kelso (01573) 223464 Restaurant: Cross Keys, The Square ☎ (01573) 223303

Kirkfield Caravan Park, Town Yetholm TD5 8RU ☎ (01573) 223346 OS map 74/821281 7m SE of Kelso off B6352 (Yetholm) Open Apr-Oct 31 pitches–no tents Level/sloping grass and hard standing, sheltered ▣ £8.50 inc elect

Springwood Caravan Park, Springwood Estate TD5 8LS ☎ Kelso (01573) 224596 OS map 74/720333 1m SW of Kelso on left of A699 (St Boswells) Open Easter-Oct 15 270 pitches (220 static) 30 acres level/sloping grass, sheltered ▣ (16 amp) ▣ £9.00-£11.00 (Mastercard/Visa)

KIPPFORD–see Dalbeattie

KIRKBEAN, Dumfries & Galloway   **Map C4**
Restaurant: Abbey Arms 5m N at New Abbey ☎ (01387) 880277

Lighthouse Leisure, Southerness DG2 8AZ ☎ (01387) 880277 OS map 84/550970 3m S of Kirkbean on A710 (Sandyhills) Open Mar-Oct 200 pitches (180 static) 8 acres level/sloping grass ▣ £6.50-£8.00 (Visa/Switch)

Southerness Holiday Village, DG2 8AZ ☎ (01387) 880256 OS map 84/976544 2m S of Kirkbean off A710 on road to Southerness Point Open Mar-Oct 600 pitches (400 static) Grass, level ▣ (heated) ▣ (25) ▤ lic club/bar, campers' kitchen private beach £7.00-£10.00

KIRKCUDBRIGHT, Dumfries & Galloway   **Map B4**
Pop 3,400. EC Thurs SEE Mercat Cross, museum, tolbooth, Broughton House, harbour ⓘ Harbour Square ☎ Kirkcudbright (01557) 330494 Restaurant: Selkirk Arms, High St ☎ (01557) 330402

Brighouse Bay Holiday Park, Borgue DG6 4TS ☎ (01557) 870267 OS map 83/626451 6m SW of Kirkcudbright off B727 (Borgue) on Brighouse Bay road Open all year 300 pitches (143 static) 24 acres, part sloping, part hard standings ▣ (indoor) ▣ (120) ▤ fishing, slipway, pony trekking, 18-hole golf par 72, jacuzzi, steam room, sunbed, quad bikes, 10-pin bowling £9.50-£12.75 (Mastercard/Visa/Delta)

Seaward Caravan Park, Dhoon Bay DG6 4TJ ☎ (01557) 331079 (bookings 01557 870267) OS map 83/664494 2½m SW of Kirkcudbright on right of B727 (Borgue) Open Mar-Oct 50 pitches (30 static) Some hard standings, level grass, sheltered ▣ (20) ▤ serviced pitches, mini golf, games room, 9 hole golf course, sea angling £8.25-£11.25

Silvercraigs Caravan-Camping Park, Silvercraigs Road DG6 4BT ☎ (01557) 330123 OS map 83/685510 ¼m S of Kirkcudbright off A711 (Dundrennan) Open Easter-Oct–no adv booking 50 pitches Grass, part sloping, open ▣ £7.95-£9.55

LANGHOLM, Dumfries and Galloway   **Map E3**
Pop 2500 EC Wed SEE remains of castle, Common Riding last Fri Jul, Gilnockie Tower 4m S ⓘ
High St ☎(01387) 380976 Restaurant: Eskdale, Market place ☎(01387) 380357
Whitshiels Caravan Park DG13 0HF ☎(01387) 380494 OS map 79/365854 ¼m N of Langholm
on left of A7 (Hawick) adj café Open all year 12 pitches ½ acre grass and hard standings,
sheltered ✕⚲🅿🍴⊕∅⌂ £4.00-£9.00

LAUDER, Borders   **Map F2**
Pop 810. EC Thurs SEE church, Thirlestane Castle (plasterwork ceilings). Border County Museum
Restaurant: Black Bull, Market Pl ☎(01578) 722208
Carfraemill Caravan Camping Park, Oxton TD2 6RD ☎(01578) 750215 OS map 73/508534 4m
NW of Lauder at junction of A68 (Edinburgh) and A697 adj hotel Open Easter-Oct 45 pitches
Level grass, sheltered 🅱🅿∅↩ £4.00-£6.50
Thirlestane Castle Caravan and Camping Park, TD2 6RU ☎Lauder (01578) 722254 OS map
74/538473 ¼m SE of Lauder off A697 (Coldstream) and A68 Open Easter-Oct 1, 60 pitches
Grass, part sloping, part open 🅱🅿⊕∅ £8.00

LOCHMABEN–see Lockerbie

LOCKERBIE, Dumfries & Galloway   **Map D3**
Pop 3,000. EC Tues, MD Tues, Thurs, Fri Pretty market town of red sandstone SEE lamb sales
market on Lamb Hill, Lochmaben Castle 3m W Restaurant: Blue Bell ☎(01576) 302309
Halleaths Caravan Park, Lochmaben DG11 1NA ☎Lochmaben (01387) 810630 OS map
78/098818 3m W of Lockerbie off A709 (Dumfries) Open Apr-Oct 70 pitches Grass, level,
sheltered ⚲🅱🅿🍴⊕∅↩🅿🅐 family facs £7.00-£10.50
Kirk Loch Brae Municipal Caravan Site, Kirk Loch Brae, Lochmaben DG12 6AQ ☎(01556)
503806 OS map 78/081826 4m W of Lockerbie on A709 (Dumfries) Open Apr-Oct 30 pitches–no
adv booking Grass and tarmac, level 🅱🅿⊕↩ golf, boating, fishing £6.45-£7.70

MELROSE–see Galashiels

MOFFAT, Dumfries & Galloway   **Map D2**
Pop 2,200. EC Wed SEE Macadam's grave, Devil's Beef Tub 5m N ⓘChurch Gate ☎(01683)
20620 Restaurant: Black Bull ☎(01683) 20206
Hammerlands Farm (Camping Club) DG10 9GL ☎Moffat (01683) 220436 OS map 78/085050
½m W of Moffat on right of A708 (Selkirk) Open Mar 23-Nov 2 180 pitches–adv booking min 2
nights Level grass, sheltered 🅱🅿🍴⊕∅↩🅐 £11.80-£14.90 (Mastercard/Visa)

MONIAVE, Dumfries and Galloway   **Map C3**
Pop 430 EC Thurs SEE fort, burial place of Annie Laurie Restaurant: Woodlea ☎(01848) 200209
Woodlea Hotel Caravan Park DG3 4EN ☎(01848) 200209 OS map 78/776895 1½m SW of
Moniave on A702 (New Galloway) in grounds of hotel Open Easter-Oct, 8 marked pitches 1 acre,
mainly sloping, hard standings ✕⚱⚲🅱🅿⊕∅⌂ (indoor) ↩🅿🅟 tennis, games room, croquet,
clay pigeon shooting, badminton, cycle hire, sauna, solarium £6.00-£12.00 (2000)
(Mastercard/Visa)

NEWTON STEWART, Dumfries & Galloway   Map B3
Pop 2,000. EC Wed, MD Thurs SEE church, museum, Galloway Forest Park ⓘDashwood Square
☎Newton Stewart (01671) 820431 Restaurant: Crown, Queen St ☎(01671) 820727

Caldons Campsite, Glentrool DG8 6AJ ☎Newton Stewart (01671) 820218 OS map 77/400790
13m N of Newton Stewart off A714 (Girvan) at Bargrennan via Glentrool (Forestry Commission)
Open Apr-Oct 160 pitches–no adv booking Grass, level, sheltered ▩▨▨▨▨▨▨▨ (20) ♿
£5.00-£5.50

Castle Cary Holiday Park, Creetown DG8 7DQ ☎(01671) 820264 Fax (01671) 820670 OS map
83/477576 7m S of Newton Stewart on left of A75 (Castle Douglas) Open all year 95 pitches–no
adv booking Grass and hard standing, level, sheltered ▩✗▨▨▨▨▨▨▨▨▨ (indoor and
outdoor, heated) ▨▨▨▨ (30) ▨♿ paddling pools, solarium, slipway, donkey park, nature
trails, games room, coarse fishing loch, crazy golf £8.45-£10.75

Creebridge Caravan Park, Minnigaff DG8 6AJ ☎Newton Stewart (01671) 402324/402432 OS map
83/415657 ¼m E of Newton Stewart off A75 (Gatehouse of Fleet) Open Mar-Oct 86 pitches (42
static) Grass and hard standing, sheltered ▩▨▨▨▨▨▨▨ £7.00-£8.00

Creetown Caravan Park, Creetown DG8 7HU ☎(01671) 82377 OS map 83/475585 6m SE of
Newton Stewart off A75 (Gatehouse of Fleet) Open Apr-Sept 66 pitches (50 static)
▨▨▨▨▨▨▨▨▨▨ £9.00-£10.75

Glentrool Holiday Park, Glentrool, Bargrennan DG8 6RN ☎Bargrennan (01671) 84280 OS map
76/77/353772 8m NW of Newton Stewart off A714 (Girvan) at Bargrennan on Glentrool road
Open Mar-Oct 60 pitches (24 static) Level grass and hard standings, sheltered ▩▨▨▨▨▨▨
games room, trout fishing, mountain bike hire £8.00-£9.00 (Mastercard/Visa/Amex)

Talnotry Campsite (Forest Enterprise) DG8 6AJ ☎Newton Stewart (01671) 402420 OS map
77/491715 6m NE of Newton Stewart on right of A712 (New Galloway) Open Apr-Sept, 60
pitches 15 acres, part sloping, hard standing and grass, sheltered ▨▨▨▨♿ fishing, forest trails
£7.00 (Mastercard/Visa)

Three Lochs Caravan Park, Balminnoch, Kirkcowan DG8 0EP ☎(01671) 830304 OS map
82/272654 9m W of Newton Stewart off A75 (Glenluce) Open Easter-1st Sat in Oct 145 pitches
(100 static) Level grass and hard standing ▩▨▨▨▨ (heated) ▨▨▨▨ children's playroom,
snooker, sailing, pitch and putt, fishing £9.00-£10.00

PEEBLES, Borders   Map E2
Pop 6,000. EC Wed, MD Fri SEE parish church, Neidpath Castle ⓘChambers Institute, High Street
☎Peebles (01721) 720138 Restaurant: Tontine, High St ☎(01721) 720892

Crossburn Caravan Park, Edinburgh Road EH45 8ED ☎Peebles (01721) 720501 OS map
73/250416 ½m N of Peebles on left of A703 (Edinburgh) Open Apr-Oct–must book 130 pitches
(80 static) Level grass and hard standing, sheltered ▩▨▨▨▨▨▨▨▨▨♿ barbecue,
fishing, mountain bike hire, putting green £9.00-£10.00 (Mastercard/Visa)

Rosetta Touring Caravan-Camping Park, Rosetta Road EH45 8PG ☎Peebles (01721) 720770
OS map 73/244414 ½m W of Peebles off A72 (Biggar) Open Apr-Oct 200 pitches (40 static)
Grass, level/sloping sheltered ▩▨▨▨▨▨▨▨▨▨▨ bowling green, putting green £4.00-
£10.50

Tweedside Caravan Site, Montgomery Street, Innerleithen EH44 6JS ☎Innerleithen (01896)
830260/830641 OS map 73/330564 6m SE of Peebles on A72 (Innerleithen) Open Apr-Oct–no
adv booking 80 pitches ▩▨ £4.00

PORTPATRICK, Dumfries and Galloway   Map A3
Pop 595 EC Thurs SEE Dunskey castle, parish church Restaurant: Harbour House ☎(01776)
810456

Castle Bay Caravan Park DG9 9AA ☎(01776) 810462 OS map 82/008536 ½m SE of Portpatrick
off A77 (Stranraer) Open Mar-Oct, 125 pitches (106 static) 22 acres, level grass and hard
standing, sheltered ▩▨▨▨▨▨▨▨▨▨▨ £7.00

Galloway Point Holiday Park, Portree Farm DG9 9AA ☎(01776) 810561 OS map 82/008538 ½m
SE of Portpatrick off A77 (Stranraer) Open Mar-Oct, 200 pitches (80 static) 16 acres, grass and
hard standings, part level, sheltered ✗▨▨▨▨▨▨▨▨▨▨▨ (£50) ▨ £8.00-£12.00

Sunnymeade Caravan Park DG9 8LN ☎(01776) 810293 OS map 82/005540 ½m SE of
Portpatrick off A77 (Stranraer) Open Easter-Oct 90 pitches (50 static) 8 acres, level/gentle slope,
grass and hard standings ▨▨▨▨▨▨ fishing £7.00-£9.00

PORT WILLIAM, Dumfries & Galloway   **Map B4**
Pop 520. EC Wed Restaurant: Monreith Arms, The Square ☎(01988) 700232

Knock School Caravan Park, Monreith DG8 8NJ ☎(01988) 700414/700409 OS map 83/368405
3m SE of Port William on A747 (Isle of Whithorn) near sea Open Easter-Sept–must book peak
periods 15 pitches Grass, part sloping, hard standing, sheltered ▨▨ golf, fishing £6.50

Monreith Sands Holiday Park, Monreith DG8 9LJ ☎(01988) 700218 OS map 82/365415 3m SE
of Port William on A747 (Isle of Whithorn) in village of Monreith Open Mar-Oct 60 pitches (45
static) Level grass, sheltered ▨⌀ near beach £6.00-£8.00

West Barr Farm Caravan Park, DG8 9QS ☎(01988) 700367 OS map 82/316462 2m NW of Port
William on A747 (Glenluce) Open Mar-Oct 30 pitches ▨▨⌀⊕ £8.00

SANDHEAD, Dumfries & Galloway   **Map A3**
Restaurant: North West Castle 8m N at Stranraer ☎(01776) 834413

Sandhead Caravan Park DG9 9JN ☎(01776) 830296 OS map 82/102508 ¼m NE of Sandhead
on right of A716 (Glenluce) Open Apr-Oct, 130 pitches (70 static) 10 acres, mainly level grass,
sheltered ▨▨⚲▨▨⌀⌀₺ by sea £8.00-£8.50

Sands of Luce Caravan Park, DG9 9JR ☎(01776) 830456 OS map 82/103510 1m N of
Sandhead on A716 (Stranraer) Open Apr-Oct 90 pitches (40 static) Grass, part level, part open
▨▨▨⌀⊕⌀♨☏ (25) ▯₺ games room, freezer pack service, private beach, boat launching
ramp £7.50-£9.50

SANQUHAR, Dumfries & Galloway   **Map C2**
Pop 2,070. EC Thurs SEE Tolbooth Museum, castle ruins, Riding of Marches Ceremony (Aug) ℹ
Tolbooth, High St ☎(01659) 550185 Restaurant: Nithsdale, High St ☎(01659) 550506

Castle View Caravan Park, Townfoot DG4 6AX ☎(01659) 50291 OS map 78/788094 1m S of
Sanquhar on A76 (Dumfries) Open Mar-Oct 30 pitches Grass, level, some hard standings
▨▨⌀ £8.00 (all cards)

SELKIRK, Borders   **Map F2**
Pop 6,000. EC Thurs SEE town hall, Flodden memorial, Bowhill House ℹHalliwell's House
☎Selkirk (01750) 20054 Restaurant: Cross Keys Inn, Market Place ☎(01750) 21283

Victoria Park, Buccleuch Road TD7 5DN ☎Selkirk (01750) 20897 OS map 73/465288 ¼m W of
Selkirk off A708 (Moffat) by Ettrick Water Open Apr-Oct 60 pitches Level grass and hard standing
▨▨⌀⊕⌀▯⊕♨ gym £6.00-£7.00

SOUTHERNESS–see Kirkbean

STRANRAER, Dumfries & Galloway   **Map A3**
Pop 10,000. EC Wed SEE Peel Tower, Lochinch, Kennedy Gardens 3m E, Logan Botanic Garden
10m S ℹPort Rodie Car Park ☎Stranraer (01776) 702595 Restaurant: George, George St
☎(01776) 702487

Aird Donald Caravan Park, London Road DG9 8RN ☎Stranraer (01776) 702025 OS map
82/074605 ¼m E of Stranraer off A75 (Newton Stewart) Open all year 100 pitches, grass and
hard standings ▨⚲▨▨⌀⊕⌀⊕♨ £7.00-£8.60

Cairnryan Caravan and Chalet Park, Cairnryan DG9 8QX ☎(01581) 200231 OS map 82/075674
5m N of Stranraer on A77 (Girvan) by Loch Ryan Open Apr-Oct–must book peak periods 110
pitches (83 static) Hard standings, level, sheltered ▨▨↦▨⌀▯⊕♨ (50) ▯ billiards £5.00-
£8.50

Drumlochart Caravan Park, Lochnaw DG9 0RN ☎(01776) 870232 OS map 82/998634 4½m NW
of Stranraer on B7043 (Lochnaw) Open Mar-Oct 120 pitches (90 static)–no tents 22 acres level
grass and hard standings, sheltered ▨▨▨⌀⊕⌀▯ (heated) ⊕♨▯🏠 lic club, pony trekking,
coarse fishing £8.50-£10.50

Ryan Bay Caravan Park, Cairnryan Road DG9 8QP ☎Stranraer (01776) 889458 OS map
82/084628 1½m NE of Stranraer on A77 (Girvan) by Loch Ryan Open Mar-Oct 200 pitches (170
static) Grass, level ▨▨⌀♨♨ (50) ▯ £5.00-£7.00

Wig Bay Holiday Park, Loch Ryan DG9 0PS ☎Kirkcolm (01776) 853233 OS map 82/034664 4¼
NNW of Stranraer on A718 (Kirkcolm) by Loch Ryan Open Mar-Oct 120 pitches (91 static) Level
grass and hard standings, sheltered ⚲▨▨⌀⊕⌀▯♨▯♨ dance hall £8.00-£10.00

Except where marked, all sites in this guide have flush lavatories and showers. Symbols for
these amenities have therefore been omitted from site entries.

STRANRAER

Wig Bay Holiday Park
Loch Ryan DG9 0PS

4m North of Stranraer on A718 (Kirkcolm)

Level pitches (grass and hard standing) near the sea
Open March to October

Tel (01776) 853233

THORNHILL, Dumfries & Galloway   **Map D3**
Pop 1,520. EC Thurs SEE 18c cross, Drumlanrig Castle Restaurant: George, Drumlanrig St
☎ (01848) 330326

Penpont Caravan Camping Park, Penpont DG3 4BH ☎ Thornhill (01848) 330470 OS map
78/850949 2m W of Thornhill on left of A702 (Moniaive) Open Apr-Oct 40 pitches (15 static)
Grass, level, open 🗑🅿🚿⊕∅🚮🏕 £6.50-£8.00

TOWN YETHOLM–see Kelso

WHITHORN, Dumfries & Galloway   **Map B4**
Pop 1,000. EC Wed SEE priory church, museum Restaurant: Steam Packet 3m SE at Isle of
Whithorn ☎ (01988) 500334

Burrowhead Holiday Village, Isle of Whithorn DG8 8JB ☎ (01988) 500252 OS map 83/450345
3m SE of Whithorn off A750 (Isle of Whithorn) on Burrowhead road Open Apr-Oct 300 pitches
(200 static) Grass and hard standings, part level, part open 🖩✗🍴⚲🗑🚿⊕∅🗄🚮⏛🏕🍺
(25) 🛏 (2) 📞 (10) tennis, football, mini golf, solarium, bubble spa, sauna £8.00-£11.00
(Mastercard/Visa)

Castlewigg Caravan Camping Park, DG8 8DP ☎ Whithorn (01988) 500616 Fax (01988) 500616
OS map 83/435450 2m N of Whithorn on A746 (Wigtown) Open Mar-Oct and winter w/ends 35
pitches Hard standing and grass, level, sheltered ✗🍴🗑🚿⊕∅🚮🏕 fishing £7.00-£8.00

15 Central Scotland

The regions of Tayside, Fife and Lothian on the east, Strathclyde on the west and Central in between join together as Central Scotland, a vast and geographically complex region.

Dominating the sunny southern shore of the Firth of Forth is the dramatically sited grey-stone city of Edinburgh, an eastern landmark in the busy industrial belt that stretches across Scotland to Glasgow and beyond. The main resort on the coast is Dunbar, backed by the Lammermuir Hills. The northern shore of the Forth estuary is more accessible, the fine sands running east from Aberdour all the way to St Andrews, with its golf courses and bottle dungeons. To the north is charming Loch Leven, a famous trout water ringed by the Lomond Hills.

In adjoining Tayside, the main resort on the coast north of the Tay estuary is Dundee, linked to the southern shore by two long bridges. Backing it and the more pleasant smaller resorts to the north is fertile farmland crossed by the Vale of Strathmore, with its views of the Grampian peaks. Pitlochry, north of Perth on the A9 to Inverness, is an enjoyable place to stay. In western Tayside are the Trossachs, a richly wooded gorge linking Lochs Achray and Katrine, with high mountains and forests on the north and rolling farmland on the south.

Central is Rob Roy country, in which the principal town is Stirling, dominated by its cliff-top castle above the Forth. And west of the densely populated industrial belt around Glasgow in mainland Strathclyde is the scenic holiday estuary of the Firth of Clyde. The best known resorts are Ayr, with miles of sands, Ardrossan, linked by ferry with the Isle of Arran, Dunoon, on the Cowal Peninsula, Gourock, from which there are cruises on the Firth, Largs, in a superb setting and with fine views of the islands, and Wemyss Bay, where ferries sail to Rothesay on the Isle of Bute.

North of Dumbarton, where the Clyde ceases to be industrial, is Loch Lomond, dotted with islands and with a length of twenty-four miles the largest stretch of inland water in Britain. Quiet places to stay around the loch are Aberfoyle, Ardgarten and Arrochar. North and west of the Firth of Clyde are the deep sea lochs, long peninsulas and romantic islands of westernmost Strathclyde, with their breathtaking scenery. In the upper half of the deeply indented coast is Oban, the hub of ferry services to the islands—Mull to the north, Jura and Islay to the west. The mainland capital is Inverary, and the head of Loch Fyne. West of the town is the Pass of Glencoe, scene of the infamous massacre in the seventeenth century, and to the south, on the tip of the peninsula, is Southend, ringed by prehistoric barrows and hill forts.

Campsites tend to be large and numerous on the east coast, small and infrequent on the west. Many of those within reach of the industrial belt or on popular through routes like the A9 tend to fill up early in season. Main concentrations are at the better-known places, like Stirling, Ayr, Pitlochry, Blairgowrie, Dunoon, Maybole and Oban. Many of the campsites on the west can only be reached by narrow single-track roads.

ABERFELDY, Tayside   **Map F2**
Pop 1,500. EC Wed Vacation resort beautifully set on river Tay between Pitlochry and Loch Tay
SEE Black Watch monument, Gen. Wade's Bridge (18c), Birks nature trail, Loch Tay 6m SW ⓘ The
Square ☎Aberfeldy (01887) 820276 Restaurant: Weem 1m NW at Weem ☎(01887) 820381

Aberfeldy Caravan Camping Park, Dunkeld Road PH15 2AF ☎Aberfeldy (01887) 820662 ¼m E
of Aberfeldy on A827 (Ballinluig) Open Apr-Oct 132 pitches (40 static) Grass, level
🗑️🍴⊕∅↵🍴& £7.00-£9.00 (Mastercard/Visa)

Glengoulandie Caravan and Deer Park, Foss PH16 5NL ☎(01887) 830261 OS map 51/768526
9m NW of Aberfeldy on B846 (Tummel Bridge) adjoining wildlife park Open Apr 1-Oct 10, 40
pitches (32 static)–no adv bkg Grass, level, open ⍾∅∅ £7.00-£8.00

ABERFOYLE, Central   **Map E3**
Village well placed for touring the Trossachs and Loch Lomond SEE Trossachs N, Queen Elizabeth
Forest Park (forest trails), Loch Katrine ⓘ Main St ☎(01877) 382352 Restaurant: Buchanan Arms
10m S at Drymen ☎(01360) 870588

Cobleland Caravan and Camp Site, Gartmore FK8 3RR ☎(01877) 382392 OS map 57/517972
2½m S of Aberfoyle off A81 (Glasgow) by river Forth Open Apr-Oct 140 pitches Grass, level,
sheltered ⍾🗑️🍴∅⊕∅↵& fishing £6.20

Trossachs Holiday Park FK8 3SA ☎(01877) 382614 3m S of Aberfoyle on left of A81 (Glasgow)
Open Apr-Oct, 99 pitches 40 acres, part sloping Grass and hard standing
⍾↗🗑️🍴∅⊕∅☻↵☐🍴🖵 mountain bike hire £8.00-£10.00

ABERLADY, East Lothian   **Map G4**
Pop 1200 SEE parish church, Mercat Cross, nature reserve Restaurant: Kilspindle House
☎(01875) 870682

Aberlady Caravan Park, Haddington Road EH32 08Z ☎(01875) 870666 OS map 66/476783 ½m
S of Aberlady on A6137 (Haddington) Open Mar-Oct 15 pitches Level grass and hard standings,
sheltered 🍴∅🍴🏠 £8.50

ABINGTON, Strathclyde   **Map F6**
Pop 200 EC Wed SEE Iron Age fort ⓘWelcome Break, A74 Northbound ☎(01864) 502436
Restaurant: Abington, Carlisle Rd ☎(01864) 502467

Crossburn Caravan Park, Douglas ML11 0QA ☎(01555) 851029 OS map 72/835305 10m NW of
Abington off M74 (Glasgow) on A70 (Douglas) Open all year 30 pitches 2 acres, terraced, hard
standings 🗑️∅⊕🍴 £6.00-£7.50

ALLOA, Central   **Map F4**
Pop 5,500 Restaurant: Royal 8m W at Bridge of Allan ☎(01786) 832284

Diverswell Farm, Fishcross FK10 3HL ☎Alloa (01259) 62802 OS map 58/892958 2m N of Alloa
off A908 (Tillicoultry) Open Apr-Oct 60 pitches 20 acres level hard standings 🗑️🍴∅⊕& £6.00-
£7.00

ANSTRUTHER, Fife   **Map H3**
Pop 3,260. EC Wed SEE Scottish Fisheries Museums, Chalmers House, Forth (by boat) ⓘScottish
Fisheries Museum, St Ayles ☎Anstruther (01333) 311073 Restaurant: Craw's Nest, Baukwell Rd
☎(01333) 310691

St Monans Caravan Park, The Common KY10 2DN ☎(01333) 730778 OS map 59/530018 2m
SW of Anstruther on A917 (Crail) Open Mar 21-Oct 31, 128 pitches (110 static) Grass, level,
sheltered 🗑️🍴⊕∅☻↵ £7.50-£9.00

ARBROATH, Tayside   **Map H2**
Pop 24,090. EC Wed SEE Vigeans museum, abbey church ruins, Signal Tower Museum ⓘMarket
Place ☎Arbroath (01241) 72609 Restaurant: Glencoe 8m SW at Carnoustie ☎(01241) 53273

Red Lion Caravan Park, Dundee Road DD11 2PT ☎Arbroath (01241) 72038 OS map 54/615393
1m S of Arbroath off A92 (Dundee) near West Links Open Mar-Oct 320 pitches (280 static) Level
grass ⍾✕🍴↵↗🗑️🍴∅⊕∅↵🖵& TV hook-ups £10.00 (all cards)

Seaton Estate Caravan Park, Seaton House DD11 5SE ☎(01241) 874762 OS map 54/660426
½m N of Arbroath off A92 (Aberdeen) Open Mar-Oct 150 pitches 60 acres level grass
⍾✕🍴🗑️🍴∅⊕↵☐ £11.00

**The distance and direction of a campsite is given from the centre of the key town under
which it appears, the place name in parentheses following the road number indicating which
route to take.**

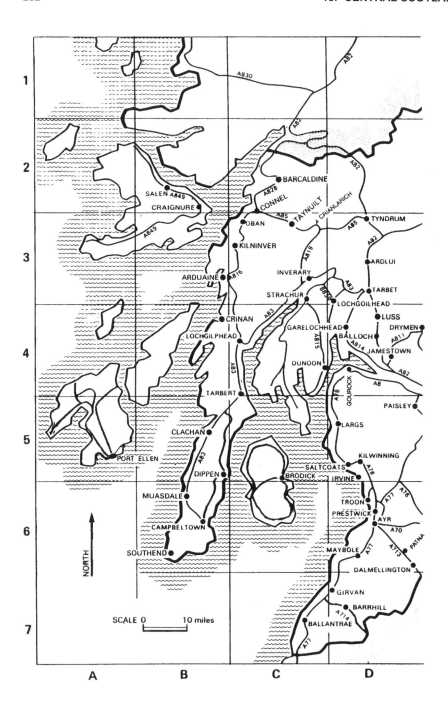

SCALE 0   10 miles

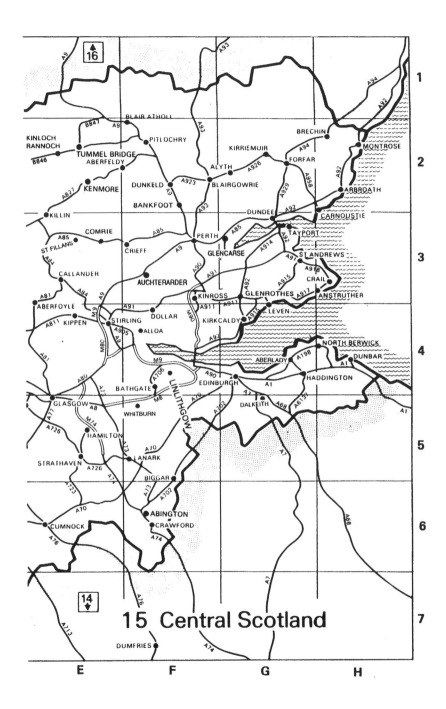

15 Central Scotland

ARDLUI, Strathclyde   Map D3
Pop 360. SEE Rob Roy's Cave, Pulpit Rock Restaurant: Ardlui ☎(01301) 704243
Ardlui Caravan Park, G83 7EB ☎(01301) 704243 OS map 56/315155 ¼m N of Ardlui on right of
   A82 (Fort William) on north shore of Loch Lomond Open Mar-Oct 96 pitches (84 static) Grass
   and hard standings, level ⬛✖♀⇆ ▯▤⌀⊕∅↲⬜▮⟐ boating (moorings), water skiing, fishing
   £10.00-£11.50

ARDUAINE, Strathclyde   Map B3
Restaurant: Culfail 5m NE at Kilmelford ☎(01852) 200274
Arduaine Caravan Camping Park PA34 4XQ ☎(01852) 200331 OS map 55/802102 ¼m S of
   Arduaine on right of A816 (Lochgilphead) near Arduaine Gardens Open Mar-Oct, 40 pitches
   Level/sloping grass and hard standings, sheltered ▮⊕ boating (jetty adj), fishing, moorings,
   dinghy launch £3.50-£13.50 inc showers

ARROCHAR–see Tarbet

AUCHINLECK–see Cumnock

AUCHTERARDER, Tayside   Map F3
Pop 360 Small town bypassed by A9 with main street almost 2m long SEE Heritage Centre,
Innerpeffray Library, founded 1691, 6m N ⓘ 90 High St ☎(01764) 663450 Restaurant: Coll Earn
House, High St ☎(01764) 663553
Auchterarder Caravan Park PH3 1ET *Friendly park at gateway to Highlands* ☎(01764) 663119
   OS map 58/964137 ½m NE of Auchterarder at junct of A824 (Aberuthven) and B8062 (Dunning)
   Open Jan-Dec 30 pitches 5 acres level grass and hard standings, sheltered ⬛▤▮⌀⊕∅⊛
   ▮⌂ private fishing, barbeques £8.00-£10.00

AYR, Strathclyde   Map D6
Pop 49,480. EC Wed, MD Mon, Tues Popular tourist and commercial centre on west coast with
many associations with Robert Burns, whose home town it was SEE Burns' cottage, Tam O'Shanter
inn museum, Auld Kirk, Auld Brig (bridge), Alloway church 3m S ⓘ 39 Sandgate ☎Ayr (01292)
284196 Restaurant: Balgarth 3m S at Alloway ☎(01292) 242441
Ayr Racecourse, Whitletts Road KA8 0JE OS map 70/352225 1m E of Ayr off A77 (Glasgow)
   Open Easter May 22-Sept 11–no adv booking 150 pitches Some hard standings ▯⊛ snacks
   £4.00-£5.00
Craigie Gardens (Caravan Club), Craigie Road KA8 0SS ☎Ayr (01292) 264909 OS map
   70/355214 ½m E of Ayr off A719 (Galston) Open Apr-Jan 90 pitches–no tents ▯▮⌀⊕&
   £9.00-£12.00 (Mastercard/Visa)
Crofthead Caravan Park, KA6 6EN ☎Ayr (01292) 263516 OS map 70/369205 2m E of Ayr off
   A70 (Holmston) Open Mar-Oct 156 pitches (60 static)–no adv booking Level/sloping grass and
   hard standings, sheltered ⬛⌁▯▮⌀⊕∅⊛↲⬜▮ £6.00-£6.50
Heads of Ayr Caravan Park, Danure Road KA7 4LD ☎Alloway (01292) 442269 OS map
   70/254158 5m SW of Ayr off A719 (Girvan) Open Apr-Sept 146 pitches (110 static) Grass, level,
   sheltered ⬛♀⇆▯▮⌀⊕∅↲▮ (20) ⊗⟐ meals, dancing £5.50-£7.00
Middlemuir Caravan Park, Tarbolton KA5 5NR ☎Tarbolton (01292) 541647 OS map 70/437257
   6m NE of Ayr off B743 (Mauchline) Open all year, 115 pitches (63 static) 19 acres, part sloping
   grass and hard standing, sheltered ▯▮⌀⊕∅⊛↲⬜▮⟐ £5.00-£9.00
Skeldon Caravan Park, Hollybush KA6 7EB ☎(01292) 560502 OS map 70/385145 6m S of Ayr
   off A713 (Dalmellington) on B7034 (Dalrymple) beside River Doon Open Apr-Sept 30 pitches
   Level grass and hard standings, sheltered ⬛▮⌀∅⊛↲▮⌂ fishing £7.50-£8.50
Sundrum Castle Holiday Park, Coylton KA6 6HX ☎Ayr (01292) 570057 OS map 70/404206 4m
   E of Ayr on A70 (Cumnock) near Coylton Open Mar-Nov 283 pitches (103 static) 11 acres, level
   grass and hard standings ⬛✖♀⇆⌁▯▮⌀⊕∅⬛ (indoor) ⊛↲⬜▯⊗⟐ lic club/bar,
   entertainment, cabaret suite, tennis, basket ball, putting green £7.00-£14.75

BALLANTRAE, Strathclyde   Map C7
Restaurant: Royal Hotel ☎(01465) 831555
Laggan House Leisure Park KA26 0LL ☎(01465) 831229 OS map 76/117835 3m SE of
   Ballantrae off A77 (Stranraer) on Heronsford road Open Mar-Oct 120 pitches (85 static) Level
   grass and hard standing, sheltered ♀▯▮⌀⊕∅⬛⊛↲⬜▮⟐⌂ solarium, sauna £5.00-
   £10.00

**Help us make CARAVAN AND CAMP IN BRITAIN better known to site operators – and thereby
more informative – by showing them your copy when booking in.**

BALLOCH, Strathclyde   **Map D4**
SEE Loch Lomond (boat trips), Cameron Estate gardens, wildlife park ⓘ Balloch Rd ✆(01389) 753533 Restaurant: Lomond Castle 2m N at Arden ✆(01389) 785681
Lomond Woods Holiday Park, Tullichewan, Balloch G83 8QP ✆(01389) 759475/755563 Fax (01389) 755000 OS map 56/382816 ½m E of Balloch centre at junction of A82 and A811 on S shore of Loch Lomond–signposted Open all year–booking advisable peak periods 200 pitches (40 static) Hard standings and grass, part sloping, sheltered ▣ (50) leisure suite with sauna, jacuzzi, sunbed, games room, table tennis, pool table, mountain bike hire £8.00-£12.00 (Mastercard/Visa/Switch)

BALMAHA–see Drymen

BARCALDINE, Strathclyde   **Map C2**
Restaurant: Rowan Tree 13m S at Oban ✆(01631) 562954
Barcaldine Garden Caravan Park PA37 1SG ✆(01631) 720348 OS map 49/950415 ¼m NE of Barcaldine off A828 (Fort William) Open all year, 75 marked pitches–adv booking min 3 nights Grass, level, sheltered–within 4 acre walled garden ▣ (£40) bar meals, boating, fishing £5.50-£7.00

BARRHILL, Strathclyde   **Map D7**
Restaurant: King's Arms 12m W at Girvan ✆(01465) 823322
Queensland Holiday Park, KA26 0PZ ✆(01465) 821364 OS map 76/216836 1m N of Barrhill on A714 (Girvan) Open Mar-Oct 49 pitches 8 acres grass and hard standings, level, sheltered ▣ £6.00-£8.00

BIGGAR, Strathclyde   **Map F5**
Pop 1,930. EC Wed, MD Sat SEE Boghall Castle ruins, 16c church, Gladstone Court Museum ⓘ High Street ✆Biggar (01899) 21066 Restaurant: Toftcombs ✆(01899) 20142
Biggar Park ML12 6JS ✆Biggar (01899) 20319 OS map 72/049380 ½m E of Biggar off A702 (West Linton) on B7016 (Broughton) Open Apr-Oct 60 pitches (40 static) Grass, level, open ▣ tennis, golf, boating £5.00

BLAIR ATHOLL, Tayside   **Map F2**
Pop 300. EC Thurs SEE Blair Castle, Garry Falls, Killiecrankie Pass Restaurant: Atholl Arms ✆(01796) 481205
Blair Castle Caravan Park PH18 5SR ✆(01796) 481263 OS map 43/872655 In Blair Atholl off A9 (Perth-Inverness) in Blair Castle grounds Open Easter-Oct–must book peak periods 283 pitches (112 static) Grass and hard standings, level, open ▣ pony trekking, fishing, serviced pitches £8.50-£10.50 (Mastercard/Visa)

BLAIRGOWRIE, Tayside   **Map F2**
Pop 5,760. EC Thurs SEE Ardblair Castle, Craighall Mansion, Fish Pass, Beech Hedge of Meikleour ⓘ Wellmeadow ✆Blairgowrie (01250) 872960 Restaurant: Angus, Wellmeadow ✆(01250) 872838
Ballintuim Hotel Caravan Park, Bridge of Cally PH10 7NH ✆Bridge of Cally (01250) 886276 OS map 53/103548 9m N of Blairgowrie centre off A93 (Braemar) on A924 (Pitlochry) in grounds of hotel Open all year, 90 pitches (60 static) Grass and hard standings, sloping ▣ salmon and trout fishing, pony trekking £6.00-£11.00 inc elect
Beech Hedge Caravan Park, Cargill PH2 6DU ✆Meikleour (01250) 883249 OS map 53/163373 5m S of Blairgowrie on A93 (Perth) Open Apr-Oct 20 pitches Grass and hard standing ▣ golf, fishing £5.00-£7.00
Blairgowrie Holiday Park, PH10 7AL ✆(01250) 876666 Fax (01250) 874535 OS map 53/181461 ½m N of Blairgowrie centre off A93 (Braemar) Open all year 180 pitches (135 static) Grass, level, hard standings, sheltered ▣ (30) putting green, bike hire £8.00-£10.50 (Mastercard/Visa/Switch)
Corriefodly Holiday Park, Bridge of Cally PH10 7JG ✆Bridge of Cally (01250) 886236 OS map 53/133514 6m N of Blairgowrie near junction of A924 (Pitlochry) and A93 (Braemar) Open all year exc Nov 100 pitches (50 static) Grass, sloping, hard standings, sheltered ▣ bar, games room, fishing £6.00-£10.50 (all cards)
Nether Craig Caravan Park, Alyth PH11 8HN ✆(01575) 560204 OS map 53/265527 6m E of Blairgowrie off A926 (Kirriemuir) on B954 (Bridge of Craigisla) Open Mar 15-Oct 31 40 pitches Level grass and hard standings, part sheltered ▣ £10.00-£12.00

BRECHIN, Tayside   **Map H2**
Pop 7,670. EC Wed SEE cathedral, Round Tower, Maison Dieu chapel ruins, Edzell castle 5m N ⓘ
St Ninian's Place ☏(01356) 623050 Restaurant: Balbirnie Mill, Montrose Rd ☏(01356) 624482

Glenesk Caravan Site, Glenesk by Edzell DD9 7YP ☏(01356) 647565 OS map 45/602717 7m N
of Brechin off A94 (Laurencekirk) and B966 (Fettercairn) beyond Edzell Open Apr-Oct 45 pitches
8 acres, level, sheltered Hard standings and grass 🛢🔌🖊⊕∅❸↙⊡🖫 £6.00-£9.00

East Mill Caravan Park, East Mill Road DD9 7AL ☏(01356) 628810 OS map 54/605594 ¼m SE
of Brechin off A933 (Arbroath) and A935 (Montrose) near Brechin bridge Open Apr-Sept 100
pitches (40 static) Level grass, sheltered 🎣✖🛢🔌🖊⊕ £4.50

BRODICK, Isle of Arran, Strathclyde   **Map C5**
Pop 810. EC Wed, MD Thurs ⓘThe Pier ☏(01770) 302140 Restaurant: Glencoy Farm ☏(01770)
302351

Middleton Camping Caravan Park, Lamlash KA27 8NN ☏(01770) 600251 OS map 69/025303
4m S of Brodick off A841 (Whiting Bay) Open Apr-Sept 72 pitches Grass and hard standings,
level, sheltered 🛢🔌🖊∅🖫 £7.00-£7.50

CALLANDER, Central   **Map E3**
Pop 1,760. EC Wed SEE Trossachs, Bracklin Falls, Loch Vennacher, Ben Ledi (2,875ft) ⓘVisitor
Centre, Ancaster Sq ☏Callander (01877) 330342 Restaurant: Myrtle Inn, Stirling Rd ☏(01877)
330919

Gart Caravan Park, Stirling Road FK17 8HW ☏Callander (01877) 330002 OS map 57/645070
½m SE of Callander on A84 (Doune) Open Apr 1-Oct 15, 200 pitches (70 static)–no tents Grass,
level, sheltered 🛢🔌🖊⊕∅↙♿ £12.00 (most cards)

Keltie Bridge Caravan Park, Cambusmore Estate FK17 8LQ ☏(01877) 330606 OS map
57/649069 1m SE of Callander on A84 (Doune) Open Apr-Oct 80 pitches (30 static) 12 acres
level grass 🛢🔌⊕∅♿ £7.50-£9.50

Mains Farm, Thornhill FK8 3QR ☏(01786) 850605 OS map 57/660000 6m S of Callander on
B822 (Kippen) Open all year 45 pitches 3½ acres grass and hard standings, gentle slope
🎣🛢🔌🖊⊕❸↙🖊🖫♿ £7.00

CAMPBELTOWN, Strathclyde   **Map B6**
Pop 5,500. EC Wed, MD Mon SEE Celtic cross, Davaar island, lighthouse ⓘ Mackinnon House,
The Pier ☏(01586) 552056 Restaurant: Ardshiel, Kilkerran Rd ☏(01586) 552133

East Trodigal Park (Camping Club), Machrihanish PA28 6PT ☏(01586) 810366 OS map
68/647208 5m W of Campbeltown on right of B843 (Machrihanish) Open Apr 1-Sept 28, 90
pitches–adv booking min 2 nights 10 acres, level grass and hard standings 🎣🍷🛢🔌🖊⊕ fishing,
games room £6.00-£9.00

Peninver Sands Caravan Park, Craigview, Peninver PA28 6QP ☏Campbeltown (01586) 552262
OS map 68/755245 4½m N of Campbeltown on B842 (Dippen) Open Apr-Oct–no adv booking
50 pitches (40 static) 3 acres level grass, sheltered 🛢🔌🖊⊕∅↙🖊🖫 £7.00

CARNOUSTIE, Tayside   **Map H2**
Pop 9,210. EC Tues SEE Buddon Ness, Waterwheel Mill ⓘThe Library, High St ☏Carnoustie
(01241) 52258 Restaurant: Glencoe, Links Par ☏(01241) 53273

Woodlands Caravan Park, Newton Road DD7 6HR ☏Carnoustie (01241) 854430 OS map
54/558350 ¼m N of Carnoustie centre off A92 (Dundee-Arbroath) Open Apr-Oct 120 pitches
Level grass, sheltered 🛢🔌🖊⊕∅↙♿ £4.00-£10.00

CARRADALE–see Dippen

CLACHAN, Strathclyde   **Map B5**
Restaurant: Old School (lunch only) 8m NE at Whitehouse ☏(01880) 740215

Kirkland Caravan Park PA29 6XL ☏(01880) 740200 OS map 62/767562 ¼m S of Clachan centre
on A83 (Campbeltown) Open Apr-Nov, 30 pitches (21 static) 3 acres, hard standings 🖊⊕🖊
fishing, pony rides, B&B £4.00

**Pitches must normally be vacated by 12 noon on the day of departure and at sites which do
not accept bookings arriving during the lunch hour usually gives the best chance of finding a
pitch.**

COMRIE, Tayside　　　　　　　　　　　　　　　　　　　　　　**Map E3**
Pop 1,400. EC Wed　SEE Museum of Scottish Tartans　Restaurant: Camus, Dundas St　☎(01764) 670917

Loch Earn Caravan Park, South Shore Road, St Fillans PH6 2NL　☎(01764) 685270　OS map 51/670235　5m W of Comrie off A85 (Lochearnhead)　Open Apr-mid Oct, 270 pitches (240 static)　Level grass, sheltered　🅿✕⬛⤾⤷🏕⬛⬛⊘⊕∅↩　£10.00 (Mastercard/Visa)

Riverside Caravan Park, Station Road, PH6 2EA　☎(01764) 670555 and 670207　OS map 52/58/780223　½m E of Comrie on A85 (Crieff)　Open Apr-Oct 155 pitches (125 static)　Grass, level and hard standing　⬛⬛⬛⊕∅↩⬛⬛　putting and bowling green　£11.50 (inc showers)

Twenty Shilling Wood Caravan Park PH6 2JY　☎Comrie (01764) 670411　OS map 52/762222　½m W of Comrie on A85 (Lochearnhead)　Open Easter-Oct, 90 pitches (35 static)–no tents (gates closed 2230-0800)　10 acres, hard standings, woodland　⬛⬛∅⊕∅⊕↩⬛　TV hookups　£8.00-£11.00 (Mastercard/Visa/Delta)

West Lodge, PH6 2LS　☎Comrie (01764) 670354　OS map 52/784225　1m E of Comrie on A85 (Crieff)　Open Apr-Oct, 60 pitches–booking advisable in season　3 acres level grass, sheltered　🅿⬛⬛⬛∅⊕∅⬛⬛　£8.00-£10.00

CONNEL, Strathclyde　　　　　　　　　　　　　　　　　　　　**Map C2**
Pop 250 EC Wed　SEE falls, bridge, Dunstaffnage Castle 3m SW, Ardchatten Priory 6m E　Restaurant: Falls of Lora　☎(01631) 710483

North Ledaig Caravan Site PA37 1RT　☎(01631) 710291　OS map 49/908369　1m N of Connel on left of A828 (Fort William)　Open Easter-Oct 260 pitches　Hard standings　🅿🏕⬛⬛⊕∅∅↩♿ baby room　£6.50-£12.50 (Delta/Switch)

CRAIGNURE, Isle of Mull, Strathclyde　　　　　　　　　**Map B2 Pop 50 EC Wed**
🅸 The Pierhead　☎(01680) 812377　Restaurant: Isle of Mull　☎(01680) 812351

Shieling Holidays PA65 6AY　☎(01680) 812496　OS map 49/724369　½m S of Craignure off A849 (Bunessan) by sea　Open Apr-Oct 42 pitches　Grass and hard standing, part level, sheltered　⬛⬛∅⊕∅⊕↩⬛⬛🏠　beach, boat hire　£10.00-£11.50 (Mastercard/Visa/Switch)

CRAIL, Fife　　　　　　　　　　　　　　　　　　　　　　　　**Map H3**
Pop 1,200. EC Wed　SEE Mercat cross, Balcombie castle ruins, Crail museum and heritage centre　🅸 Museum Marketgate　☎(01333) 450869　Restaurant: Croma, Nethergate St　☎(01333) 450239

Ashburn House, St Andrews Road KY10 3UL　☎Crail (01333) 450314　OS map 59/613080　¼m N of Crail centre on A917 (St Andrews) in grounds of country house　Open Mar-Oct 62 pitches (52 static)　3 acres level grass and hard standings, sheltered　⬛⬛∅⊕∅　serviced pitches　£8.50-£11.50

Sauchope Links Caravan Park KY10 3XJ　☎Crail (01333) 450460　OS map 59/626083　1m NE of Crail off Balcomie road　Open Mar-Oct, 150 pitches (100 static)　Level grass and hard standings　🅿⬛⬛⬛∅⊕∅⬛ (heated)⊕↩⬛　£12.20-£14.50 (2000) (Mastercard/Visa)

CRAWFORD, Strathclyde　　　　　　　　　　　　　　　　　**Map F6**
Pop 330 EC Wed　SEE castle, Roman forts and cairns　Restaurant: Crawford Arms　☎(01864) 502267

Crawford Caravan Camping Park, Murray Place, Carlisle Rd ML12 6TW　☎(01864) 502258　OS map 72/957204　In Crawford near junct 14 of M74　Open Apr-Oct 25 pitches　2 acres level grass and hard standings　🅿✕⬛⬛⊕↩　£5.00

CRIANLARICH, Central　　　　　　　　　　　　　　　　　　**Map D3**
Pop 600　Restaurant: Benmore Lodge　☎(01838) 300210

Glendochart Caravan Park, Glendochart FK20 8QT　☎(01567) 820637　OS map 51/479279　5m E of Crianlarich on right of A85 (Lochearnhead) past junct with A827 (Killin)　Open Mar-Oct 45 pitches　15 acres level grass and hard standings　✕⬛⬛∅⊕↩⬛　£6.50-£7.50

CRIEFF, Tayside　　　　　　　　　　　　　　　　　　　　　**Map F3**
Pop 5,100. EC Wed　SEE glass works, pottery, Drummond castle gardens 2m SW, Glenturret Distillery (tours)　🅸Town Hall, High St　☎Crieff (01764) 652578　Restaurant: George, King St　☎(01764) 652089

Braidhaugh Caravan Park, South Bridgend PH7 4HP　☎(01764) 652951　OS map 58/855210　¼m SW of Crieff off A82 (Dunblane)　Open Jan-Dec 36 pitches–no tents, must book peak periods　Hard standings, level　🅿✕⬛⬛⬛∅⊕⊕↩⬛⬛　£6.50-£8.00

Crieff Holiday Village, Turret Bank PH7 4JN　☎Crieff (01764) 653513　OS map 58/858226　½m W of Crieff off A85 (Comrie)　Open all year 106 pitches (40 static)　3 acres, terraced　Grass and hard standings, level, sheltered　🅿🏕⬛⬛⬛∅⊕∅⊕↩⬛⬛ (85) ⬛🏠　£7.00-£9.00 (Mastercard/Visa)

CRINAN, Strathclyde   Map B4
Pop 70 EC Sat SEE Donald Hill, Crinan canal Restaurant: Crinan Hotel ✆(01546) 870261

Leachive Caravan Park, Leachive Farm, Tayvallich PA31 8PL ✆(01546) 870206 OS map
  55/745875 7m S of Crinan on B8025 (Tayvallich) Open Apr-Sept, 52 pitches (37 static) 5 acres,
  level grass and hard standings, sheltered ▓✖♀↗❋❹⊕⚲ £6.00-£8.00

CULZEAN–see Maybole

CUMNOCK, Strathclyde   Map E6
Pop 9,610. EC Wed, MD Fri SEE Baird Institute, home of Keir Hardie ⓘ Glaisnock Street
✆Cumnock (01290) 420058 Restaurant: Royal, Glaishock St ✆(01290) 420822

Glenafton Park, Glenafton, New Cumnock KA18 4PR ✆(01290) 420405 OS map 71/617103 6m
  S of Cumnock off B741 (Dalmellington) Open all year 50 pitches (30 static)
  ▓✖♀↩↗❋❹⊕∅❸↩⌂☎ £5.00

DALKEITH, Lothian   Map G5
Pop 8,670. EC Tues MD Mon SEE St Nicholas church, King's Park, Dalkeith Palace, Newbattle
Abbey ⓘ The Library, White Hart St ✆(0131) 660 6818 Restaurant: Eskbank Motel, Dalhousie
Road ✆(0131) 663 3234

Fordel Camping Caravan Park, Lauder Road EH22 2PH ✆(0131) 663 3046/(0131) 660 3921 OS
  map 66/360668 1½m S of Dalkeith on left of A68 (Edinburgh-Newcastle) by Esso petrol station
  Open Mar-Sept, 45 pitches–no adv booking Grass and hard standing, sheltered
  ▓✖♀↩↗❋❹⊕∅❸↩☎ £7.50-£11.50 (Mastercard/Visa)

DIPPEN, Strathclyde   Map B5
Restaurant: Carradale 2m E at Carradale ✆(01583) 431223

Carradale Bay Caravan Park, Carradale PA28 6QG ✆(01583) 431665 OS map 68/805374 1m E
  of Dippen on B879 (Carradale) Open Apr-Oct, 60 pitches Grass on sand dunes, level, sheltered
  ❋❹⊕∅☎⌂↩ fishing (sea and river), canoeing £7.50-£12.80

Carradale Bay Caravan Park

On the east coast of Kintyre, a short drive from the busy port
of Campbeltown, with its Heritage Centre and whisky
distilleries (visits).

See listing under Dippen

DOLLAR, Central   Map F4
Pop 2,500. EC Thurs SEE Castle Campbell ruins Restaurant: Castle Campbell, Bridge St
✆(01259) 781519

Glendevon Caravan Park, Glendevon FK14 7JY ✆(01259) 781569 OS map 58/981052 6m NE of
  Dollar off A91 (Cupar) on A823 (Crieff) Open Apr-Oct 164 pitches (130 static) Level grass
  ▓✖♀❹↩ snack bar, disco dances, amusements, boating, fishing, shooting, quad bikes, gold
  panning, pony trekking (Jul-Aug) £5.00-£9.00 (Mastercard/Visa)

Riverside Caravan Park, FK14 7LX ✆Dollar (01259) 742896 OS map 58/926970 ½m S of Dollar
  on B913 by river Devon Open Apr-Sept 60 pitches (30 static) 7 acres level grass, sheltered
  ❋❹⊕❸ fishing £6.00-£9.00

DRYMEN, Central   Map D4
Pop 650. EC Wed SEE Loch Lomond, Potts of Gartness salmon leap ⓘ Library, The Square
✆(01360) 870751 Restaurant: Buchanan Arms ✆(01360) 870588

Cashel Caravan Camping Park, Balmaha G63 0AW ✆(01360) 870234 OS map 56/396939 7m
  NW of Drymen on Balmaha-Rowardennan road along E shore of Loch Lomond in Queen Elizabeth
  Forest Park Open Apr-Sept 200 pitches–adv booking min 7 nights Grass, part level, part open
  ▓❶❋❹⊕∅↩ fishing, boating £6.20

Millarochy Bay Park (Camping Club), Balmaha G63 0JQ ✆(01360) 870236 OS map 56/407927
  4m NW of Drymen on left of B837 (Rowardennan)–steep approach Open Mar 24-Nov 3 140
  pitches –adv booking min 3 nights 7 acres, level grass and hard standings, sheltered
  ▓❶❋❹⊕⚲ private beach, boating, fishing £9.20-£12.05

DUNBAR, Lothian Map H4
Pop 5,610. EC Wed Popular coast resort noted for its elegant main street (High St), with safe bathing from beaches of Bellhaven on W and White Sands on E. At Barns Ness, adj White Sands, are fossil-rich limestone cliffs. SEE castle ruins, parish church ■ Town House, High Street ☏ Dunbar (01368) 863353 Restaurant: Bayswell, Bayswell Park ☏ (01368) 862225

Barns Ness Park (Camping Club) EH42 1QP ☏ Dunbar (01368) 863536 OS map 67/720770 3m SE of Dunbar off A1085/A1 (Thornton Loch) on Barns Ness road Open Mar 20-Oct 30 80 pitches Level grass ▤∅⊕∅ £9.80-£12.40 (Mastercard/Visa)

Battleblent Hotel Caravan Park, West Barns EH42 1TS ☏ Dunbar (01368) 862234 OS map 67/660782 1m W of Dunbar on A1087 (West Barns) Open Apr-Oct, 10 marked pitches 1 acre level grass, sheltered ✗⚑▤∅□ £7.50-£9.50 (all cards)

Thurston Manor Holiday Park, Thurston, Innerwick EH42 1SA ☏ (01368) 840643 OS map 67/710730 2m SE of Dunbar off A1 (Berwick on Tweed) on Elmscleugh road Open Mar-Jan 500 pitches (400 static) Level grass and hard standing, sheltered ⚐✗⚑↵⚲▤⚑∅⊕∅◻↵□⚑& £8.00-£12.00 (Mastercard/Visa/Delta)

DUNDEE, Tayside Map G3
Pop 180,000. EC Wed, MD Tues SEE St Andrew's church, Camperdown park, cathedrals, Tay road bridge ■ City Square ☏ Dundee (01382) 527723 Restaurant: Invercastle, Perth Rd ☏ (01382) 569231

Inchmartine Caravan Park, Inchture PH14 9QQ ☏ Inchture (01828) 686251 OS map 59/265278 8m W of Dundee on A85 (Perth) Open Apr-Sept 45 pitches Grass, part open ⚑ £5.40-£6.50

Riverview Caravan Park, Monifieth DD5 4NN ☏ Monifieth (01382) 535471 OS map 54/501323 6m E of Dundee off A930 (Carnoustie) on Marine Drive by sea Open Apr-Oct 90 pitches Level grass and hard standing ▤⚑∅⊕∅⊕↵□& £10.00-£12.00 (most cards)

DUNKELD, Tayside Map F2
Pop 600. EC Thurs SEE cathedral, regimental museum, waterfalls ■ The Cross ☏ (01350) 727688 Restaurant: Atholl Arms, Bridge St ☏ (01350) 727219

Erigmore House Holiday Park, Birnam PH8 9XX ☏ Dunkeld (01350) 727236 OS map 53/038417 1m SE of Dunkeld off A9 (Perth) Open Mar-Nov 243 pitches (185 static)–no tents Grass, level, part open ⚐✗⚑↵⚲▤⚑∅⊕∅◻ (indoor heated) ↵□⚑ (25) Ⓟ□⚑ pony trekking, river swimming, fishing £11.00-£18.00 with all mains services

Inver Mill Farm Caravan Park, Inver Mill PH8 0JR ☏ (01350) 727217 OS map 52/015422 ½m W of Dunkeld on A822 (Inver)–signposted Open Apr-Oct–no adv booking 65 pitches Level grass ▤⚑∅⊕∅↵⚑& swimming, fishing, bike hire, tennis £8.00-£9.00

DUNOON, Strathclyde Map C4
Pop 8,750. EC Wed SEE Argyll national park, Kilman arboretum 6m N, Younger botanical gardens 7m NW, Cowal Highland gathering (Aug) ■ Alexandra Parade ☏ Dunoon (01369) 703785 Restaurant: Coylet Inn 5m N at Loch Eck ☏ (01369) 840322

Cot House, Kilmun PA23 8QS ☏ (01369) 840351 OS map 56/154831 3m N of Dunoon on A815 (Strachur) near junction with A880 Open Easter-Oct 40 pitches (20 static) 2½ acres level grass and hard standing ⚐✗⚑▤⚑∅⊕⚑ fishing, boating £4.00

Gairletter Caravan Park, Blairmore PA23 8TP ☏ (01369) 840208 OS map 56/195823 10m N of Dunoon on A880 (Ardentinny) on W shore of Loch Long Open Apr-Oct–must book peak periods 40 pitches Hard standings and grass, level ▤⚑∅⊕∅⊕↵⚑□& £6.50-£7.00

Glenfinart Park, Ardentinny PA23 8TS ☏ (01369) 810256 OS map 56/184884 13m NE of Dunoon off A885/A815 (Strachur) on A880 (Ardentinny) Open Apr-Oct 40 pitches Grass, level, sheltered ▤∅⊕⚑□ £4.00-£6.00

Invereck Countryside Holiday Park, Sandbank PA23 8QS ☏ (01369) 705544 OS map 56/148830 4½m N of Dunoon on left of A815 (Strachur) at head of Holy Loch Open Apr-Oct 30 pitches Grass and hard standing, level, sheltered ▤⚑∅⊕∅↵□⚑ (20) □⚑ fishing £6.00-£10.00

Stratheck Caravan Park, Inverchapel, Loch Eck PA23 8SG ☏ (01369) 840472 OS map 56/143865 7m NW of Dunoon on left of A815 (Strachur) by ferry Open Mar-Jan–must book peak periods 150 pitches (80 static) Hard standings and grass, level, sheltered ⚐⚑↵▤⚑∅⊕∅⊕↵□⚑□& fishing, country club, animal corner £5.50-£9.00

Some site operators make it a rule that cars must be left in a separate parking area away from caravans and tents, which can be inconvenient when shopping by car. But it does minimise traffic noise and the risk to children.

EDINBURGH, Lothian   **Map G4**
Pop 444,740. SEE castle, palace of Holyrood House, National Museum, Royal Scottish Museum, Royal Botanic garden, Tattoo (Aug-Sept) ⓘ Information Centre, Princes St ☎(0131) 557 1700 Restaurant: Alp Horn, Rose St ☎(0131) 225 4787

Drum Mohr Caravan Park, Levenhall, Musselburgh EH21 8JS ☎(0131) 665 6867 Fax (0131) 653 6859 OS map 66/371735 7m E of Edinburgh between B1361 (North Berwick) and B1348 (Prestonpans) Open Mar-Oct 120 pitches Grass, level, sheltered–some hard standings ⓛⓧⓞⓩⓔⓞⓞⓨⓓ £8.00-£10.00 (Mastercard/Visa)

Linwater Caravan Park, West Clifton, by East Calder EH53 0HT ☎(0131) 333 3326 Fax (0131) 449 3699 OS map 65/104696 7m W of Edinburgh off A8 (Newbridge) on B7030 (Linwater) Open Apr-Oct 60 pitches Level grass ⓞⓩⓔⓔⓞ sandpit, dog walk £8.00-£10.00 (Mastercard/Visa/Switch)

Mortonhall Caravan Park, Mortonhall Gate, Frogston Road East EH16 6TJ ☎(0131) 664 1533 OS map 66/262683 4m S of Edinburgh off city bypass at Lothianburn or Straiton junction–signposted Open Mar-Oct 250 pitches Grass and some hard standings, part sloping ⓛⓧⓩⓞⓩⓔⓞⓞⓨⓞⓓ serviced pitches £8.00-£11.00

Pentland Park Caravan Site, New Pentland, Loanhead EH20 9PA ☎(0131) 440 0697 OS map 66/264657 3m S of Edinburgh on right of A701 (Penicuik) Open Apr-Oct 242 pitches (180 static) ⓛⓞⓩⓔⓞⓔ £6.00

Seton Sands Holiday Centre, Longniddry EH32 0PL ☎Port Seton (01875) 811425 OS map 63/425758 10m E of Edinburgh off A1 (Dunbar) on B1348 (Port Seton) Open Mar 15-Oct 31, 720 pitches Level grass ⓛⓨⓤⓞⓩⓔ club room with entertainment, amusements £7.00-£8.00

Slatebarns Caravan Park, Slatebarns Farm, Roslin EH25 9PU ☎(0131) 440 2192 OS map 66/275635 6m S of Edinburgh off A701 (Peebles) in Roslin Open Easter-Oct 30 pitches–no tents Level grass and hard standing, sheltered ⓞⓩⓔⓞⓞⓓ £8.50-£11.00 inc elect

See also Aberlady and Dalkeith

FINTRY, Central   **Map E4**
Pop 150 Restaurant: Cross Keys 8m N at Kippen ☎(01786) 870293

Balgair Castle Caravan Park, Overglinns G63 0LP ☎(01360) 860283 Fax (01360) 860300 OS map 57/603886 1½m N of Fintry off Kippen road Open Mar-Oct 148 pitches (85 static) 38 acres level grass ⓛⓧⓨⓤⓧⓞⓩⓔⓞⓞⓨⓞⓔⓔ bar meals, pets corner, putting green, fishing £12.00-£14.95

FORFAR, Tayside   **Map G2**
Pop 12,740. EC Thurs SEE church, parks, castle and Angus Folk museum at Glamis 5m SW ⓘ The Library, West High St ☎(01307) 467876 Restaurant: Royal, Castle St ☎(01307) 462691

Lochside Caravan Park, Lochside DD8 1BT ☎Forfar (01307) 464201 OS map 54/450505 ½m NW of Forfar off A94 (Brechin) Open Apr-Oct 74 pitches Grass, level, open ⓞⓩⓔⓞⓨ leisure centre adjacent £6.30-£7.55

GARELOCHHEAD, Strathclyde   **Map D4**
Restaurant: Rosslea Hall 8m S at Helensburgh ☎(01436) 820684

Rosneath Castle Caravan Park, Rosneath G84 0QS ☎(01436) 831208 OS map 56/269821 7m S of Garelochhead off B833 (Kilreaggan) Open Apr-Oct 500 pitches (450 static) ⓛⓧ lic, ⓞⓞⓨ boating, sea angling £4.60

GIRVAN, Strathclyde   **Map D7**
Pop 7,690. EC Wed SEE Turnberry championship golf courses 5m N ⓘ Bridge Street ☎Girvan (01465) 894950 Restaurant: King's Arms, Dalrymple St ☎(01465) 893322

Benane Shore Holiday Park, Lendalfoot KA26 0JG ☎(01465) 891233 OS map 76/110884 8½m S of Girvan on A77 (Ayr-Stranraer) Open Mar-Oct 140 pitches (60 static) Level grass ⓛⓩⓔⓞⓔⓟⓔ private beach, boating £8.50-£10.00

Carleton Caravan Park, Carleton Lodge, Lendalfoot KA26 0JF ☎(01465) 891215 OS map 76/129901 7m S of Girvan off A77 (Stranraer) Open Mar-Oct–must book 60 pitches Grass, level, part open ⓔ (20) ⓔ (4) £5.00-£6.00

Jeancroft Holiday Park, Dipple KA26 9JW ☎Turnberry (01655) 31288 OS map 76/208043 3½m N of Girvan off A77 (Maybole) Open Mar-Oct 226 pitches (200 static) 11½ acres mainly level grass sheltered ⓛⓞⓩⓔⓨⓔⓔ £5.00

See also Barrhill

GLAMIS–see Kirriemuir

GLASGOW, Strathclyde **Map E5**
Pop 753,000. Largest city in Scotland made so partly by trade in tobacco and cloth in 18c and then by shipbuilding on the Clyde SEE cathedrals, Kelvingrove Park, Old Glasgow museum, Transport museum, botanic gardens, Kelvin Hall, 🛈 35-39 St Vincent Place ☎(0141) 204 4400 Restaurant: Babbity Bowster, Blackfriars St ☎(0141) 552 5055

Craigendmuir Park, Campsie View, Stepps F33 6AF ☎(0141) 779 2973 OS map 64/660697 3m NE of Glasgow off A80 (Stirling) at Stepps Open all year 40 pitches (24 static) Level grass and hard standing Tea room £7.50-£9.00 (Mastercard/Visa)

Strathclyde Country Park, 366 Hamilton Road, Motherwell ML1 3ED ☎Motherwell (01698) 266155 OS map 64/720584 10m SE of Glasgow near Junction 5 of M74 off A725 (Bellshill) Open Easter-Oct 15—max stay 14 nights 100 pitches 20 acres level grass and hard standing 🛉✖♀🗑🅱✪∅↩⚲🅀 sailing, boating, funfair, road train £3.70-£8.20 (2000)

GLENDARUEL—see Strachur

GLENCARSE, Tayside **Map G3**
Pop 50 EC Wed, Sat Restaurant: Newton House ☎(01738) 860250

St Madoes Caravan Park, Pitfour PH2 7LZ ☎(01738) 860244 OS map 58/203206 ½m E of Glencarse off B958 (Errol) in grounds of Pitfour Castle Open all year 20 pitches—no tents Hard standings 🗑🅱⦸🅱 £5.50-£6.50

GLENROTHES, Fife **Map G3**
Pop 36,200. EC Tues 🛈 Lion Square Kingdom Centre ☎(01592) 610784 Restaurant: Rescoble 3m W at Leslie ☎(01592) 742143

Balbirnie Park (Caravan Club), Markinch KY7 6NR ☎Glenrothes (01592) 759130 OS map 59/293018 2m E of Glenrothes off A911 (Leven) on Balbirnie Craft Centre road Open Apr-Sept, 90 pitches Grass, part hard standings 🗑🅱⦸✪∅ play frame, dog walk £6.20-£8.80

GOUROCK, Strathclyde **Map D4**
Pop 11,000 EC Wed Popular resort and centre for boat trips around coast and ferry port for Dunoon SEE coast on drive S to Ardrossan 🛈 Pierhead ☎(01475) 639467 Restaurant: Spinnaker, Albert Rd ☎(01475) 633107

Cloch Caravan Holiday Park, The Cloch PA19 1BA ☎(01475) 632675 OS map 63/204760 3m SW of Gourock on A770 coast road beyond ferry terminal opp lighthouse Open Apr-Nov 250 pitches (243 static)—no tents 18 acres hard standings and sloping gravel 🛉✖♀↩🗑🅱⦸∅↩🖭 games room £10.00-£12.00 (Mastercard/Visa)

HADDINGTON, Lothian **Map G4**
Pop 6,520. EC Thurs Restaurant: Bayswell 5m E at Dunbar ☎(01368) 862225

The Monks' Muir, EH41 3SB ☎(01620) 860340 Fax (01620) 861770 OS map 66/559760 3m E of Haddington on A1 (East Linton)—signposted Open all year 43 pitches Grass, part level, sheltered 🛉✖↩↗🗑🅱⦸✪∅↩🗖🅱🖭 barbecue area, golf package £11.40-£12.00 (Mastercard/Visa)

INVERARAY, Strathclyde **Map C3**
Pop 450. EC Wed SEE Castle, bell tower, Crarae gardens 9m SW 🛈☎ Front St (01499) 302063 Restaurant: Fernpoint near pier ☎(01499) 302170

Argyll Caravan Park PA32 8XT ☎Inveraray (01499) 302285 OS map 56/075054 2½m S of Inveraray on A83 (Campbeltown) Open Apr-Oct 300 pitches (200 static) Grass and hard standings, level, sheltered 🛉✖♀↩↗🗑🅱⦸∅🟢↩🅱🖭🛉 squash court, fishing £9.00-£11.00

IRVINE, Strathclyde **Map D5**
Pop 54,000. EC Wed Restaurant: Hospitality Inn 1m E on A71 ☎(01294) 874272

Cunningham Head Estate Camping Park, KA3 2PE ☎(01294) 850238 OS map 70/368416 3½m NE of Irvine on B769 (Stewarton) Open Apr-Sept—no adv booking 115 pitches (50 static) Grass, level, sheltered 🗑🅱⦸✪🟢↩🅱 (25) 🖭 £7.00-£9.00

KENMORE, Tayside **Map E2**
Pop 600 EC Wed Model village set round a green at E end of Loch Tay SEE church, 18c bridge, Loch Tay Restaurant: Kenmore, Village Sq ☎(01887) 830205

Kenmore Caravan and Camping Park, PH15 2HN ☎Kenmore (01887) 830226 OS map 51/52/774457 In Kenmore near bridge on right bank of river Tay Open Apr-Oct 180 pitches (90 static) Hard standings and grass, level, sheltered 🛉✖♀↗🗑🅱⦸✪∅🟢↩🗖🅱 (30) 🖭🛏🛉 par 70 golf course £10.00-£11.00 (Mastercard/Visa)

KILLIN, Central   **Map E2**
Pop 600 Community at head of Loch Tay, one of most beautiful in Scotland SEE Finlarig castle
ruins, healing stones in old mill, Dochart Falls, Loch Tay, MacNab clan chiefs burial ground, Ben
Lawers (3,984ft) ◨ Main Street ☏ (01567) 820254 Restaurant: Bridge of Lochay ☏ (01567) 820272

Cruachan Touring Park FK21 8TY ☏ Killin (01567) 820302 OS map 51/613358 3m NE of Killin on
A827 (Aberfeldy) Open Apr-Oct 80 pitches Grass and hard standing, part level, part open
🐾 ✗ ⟲ 🅱 🅿 ⊕ ∅ ☻ ↵ 🚏 🏠 fishing, forest walks £6.00-£7.00 (Mastercard/Visa)

Glen Dochart Caravan Park, Luib by Crianlarich FK20 8QT ☏ Killin (01567) 820637 OS map
51/477279 6m W of Killin on right of A85 (Crianlarich) Open Mar-Oct 90 pitches (30 static) Grass
and hard standings, level, part open 🐾 ⟋ 🅱 🅿 🅿 ⊕ ↵ 🖩 (20) 🚏 £4.50

High Creagan Caravan Park, FK21 8TX ☏ Killin (01567) 820449 OS map 58/594352 2½m E of
Killin on left of A827 (Aberfeldy) Open Apr-Oct 40 pitches Grass and hard standings, level,
sheltered 🐾 🅱 🅿 🅿 ⊕ ∅ 🚏 £7.00-£10.00

KILNINVER, Strathclyde   **Map C3**
Restaurant: Rowan Tree 9m N at Oban ☏ (01631) 562954

Glen Gallain Caravan Park PA34 4UU ☏ (01852) 316200 OS map 55/834195 2m S of Kilninver
off A816 (Loch- gilphead) at Scammadale signpost Open Apr-Oct, 65 pitches Grass and hard
standings, part sloping, part open 🐾 🅿 🅿 ⊕ ↵ £3.00-£6.00

KINLOCH RANNOCH, Tayside   **Map E2**
Pop 300. EC Wed Restaurant: Loch Rannoch ☏ (01882) 632201

Kilvrecht Caravan Camping Park (Forestry Commission), Lochend PH16 5QA ☏ (01882) 632335
OS map 42/617566 3m W of Kinloch Rannoch on Carrie road along S shore of Loch Rannoch
Open Apr-Oct–no adv booking 60 pitches Grass, level, sheltered ⊕ ☻ *No showers,* cold water
only, fishing boat hire £3.00-£5.00

KINROSS, Tayside   **Map F3**
Pop 4,500. EC Thurs SEE Loch Leven and Castle ◨ Kinross Service Area, M90 Junct 6 ☏ Kinross
(01577) 863680 Restaurant: Green ☏ (01577) 863467

Gairney Bridge Caravan Park, KY13 7JZ ☏ Kinross (01577) 862336 OS map 58/130985 3m S of
Kinross on B996 (Cowdenbeath) near Junct 5 of M90 Open Jun-Sept, 25 pitches Grass, level,
open 🐾 🅿 🅿 ⊕ £5.00-£7.50

Gallowhill Caravan Camping Park, Gallowhill Farm KY13 7RD ☏ (01577) 862364 OS map
58/106037 1m NW of Kinross off Dalqueich road Open Mar-Nov 50 pitches 5 acres level grass
and hard standings 🅱 🅿 🅿 ⊕ ↵ £8.50-£10.00

Turfhills Tourist Centre (Granada) KY13 7NQ ☏ Kinross (01577) 863123 OS map 58/106027 ½m
W of Kinross centre on A977 (Alloa) near Junction 6 of M90 Open all year 60 pitches–no adv
booking Hard standings 🐾 ✗ 🅱 🅿 ↵ £4.00

KINTYRE PENINSULA–see Campbeltown, Clachan, Dippen, Muasdale, Southend and Tarbert

KIRKCALDY, Fife   **Map G4**
Pop 49,820. EC Wed SEE Sailor's Walk, Ravenscraig Castle, Falkland Palace 10m NW ◨ Whytes
Causeway ☏ Kirkcaldy (01592) 267775 Restaurant: Parkway, Abbotshall Rd ☏ (01592) 262143

Dunnikier Caravan Park, Dunnikier Way KY1 3ND ☏ Kirkcaldy (01592) 267563 OS map
59/282940 1m N of Kirkcaldy off A910/B981 (Auchterderran) Open Mar-Jan 60 marked pitches
Level grass and hard standings 🐾 🅱 🅿 🅿 ⊕ ∅ 🍴 🅿 ⅙ £8.00-£10.00

Pettycur Bay Holiday Park, Kinghorn KY3 9YE ☏ (01592) 890321 and 890913 OS map
66/260864 3m SW of Kirkcaldy on A92 (Inverkeithing) Open Mar-Oct, 583 pitches (533 static)–no
adv booking Grass, level, sheltered–some hard standings 🐾 ✗ ￥ ⟲ 🅱 🅿 🅿 ∅ ☻ ↵ 🖵 🍴 (50) 🚏
£7.50-£10.50

Cause for Complaint

**If you have cause for complaint while staying on a site take the matter up with the manager or
owner. If you are still not satisfied set the facts down in writing and send photocopies to
anyone you think might be able to help, starting with the editor of this guide and the local
(licensing) authority for the area where the site is located.**

KILVRECHT CAMPING CARAVAN PARK

In unspoilt woodland setting 3m west of Kinloch Rannoch on south shore of Loch Rannoch

Tel (01882) 632335

Open April to October, level grass, sheltered

See listing under Kinloch Rannoch

KIRRIEMUIR, Tayside — Map G2
Pop 5,320 SEE JM Barrie's birthplace and Barrie Pavilion 🛈 High St ✆(01575) 574097
Restaurant: Royal 6m SE at Forfar ✆(01307) 462691

Drumshademuir Caravan Park, Glamis, Roundyhill by Forfar DD8 1QT ✆(01575) 573284 OS
map 54/382508 2m S of Kirriemuir on A928 (Dundee) Open all year 110 pitches (30 static) Hard
standings, grass, part sloping, sheltered 🏕✕🛇⤵🗎🔌🚿⊕∅🗐⊕↩🔥 (55) 🚐🏠♿ bar food,
putting £6.75-£9.75

The Glens Caravan and Camping Park, Memus by Forfar DD8 3TY ✆Foreside (01307) 860258
OS map 54/426591 4m NE of Kirriemuir off B955 (Dykehead) near Memus and Angus Glens
Open Apr-Oct 40 pitches 1½ acres, part sloping grass and hard standings
🏕🏹🗎🔌🚿⊕∅🔥🚐🏠 £8.00-£10.00

LANARK, Strathclyde — Map F5
Pop 9,770. EC Thurs SEE parish church, New Lanark, Craignethan castle ruins 4m NW
🛈Horsemarket, Ladycare Road ✆Lanark (01555) 661661 Restaurant: La Vigna (Italian), Wellgate
St ✆(01555) 664320

Newhouse Caravan Camping Park, Ravenstruther ML11 8NP ✆(01555) 870228 OS map
72/927457 3m NE of Lanark on left of A70 (Edinburgh) past junction with A743 adj golf course
Open Mar-Oct 45 pitches Grass and hard standings, level, sheltered 🏕🗎🔌🚿⊕∅🔥⊕↩🔥🚐♿
loch fishing £8.00-£10.00

LARGS, Strathclyde — Map D5
Pop 10,000. EC Wed SEE Skelmorlic Aisle 🛈Promenade ✆Largs (01475) 673765 Restaurant:
Glen Eldon, Barr Cres ✆(01475) 673381

Mains Caravan Camping Park, Skelmorlie PA17 5EU ✆(01475) 520794 OS map 63/200655 4m
N of Largs off A78 (Gourock) on Skelmorlie Castle road Open Mar-Oct 90 pitches (82 static)
Grass and hard standings, part level, part open 🔌🔥⊕∅↩🔥🚐🏠 £7.00-£12.00

LEVEN, Fife — Map G4
Pop 9,430. EC Thurs 🛈South Street ✆Leven (01333) 429464 Restaurant: Old Manor 2m E at
Lundin Links ✆(01333) 320368

Letham Feus Caravan Park, Letham Feus KY8 5NT ✆(01333) 351900 OS map 59/374049 3m N
of Leven on A916 (Cupar) Open Apr-Sept 151 pitches (125 static) Grass, sloping, sheltered
🏕🗎🔌🔥⊕∅⊕↩🔥 £9.00

Shell Bay Caravan Park, Elie KY9 1HB ✆(01333) 330283 OS map 59/465000 7m E of Leven off
A917 (Elie) on single track road near beach Open Mar-Oct 440 pitches (320 static) Grass, level
🏕✕🛇⤵🏹🗎🔌🔥⊕∅⊕↩ 🚐🚐 £8.50-£15.50 (Mastercard/Visa)

Woodland Gardens Caravan and Camping Park, Blindwell Road, Lundin Links KY8 5QG
✆(01333) 360319 OS map 59/418038 3m E of Leven off A915 (St Andrews) at eastern end of
Lundin Links Open Mar-Oct 25 pitches Grass, level, sheltered 🔌🔥⊕∅⊕↩🔥🚐🚐 £8.00-
£12.00

LINLITHGOW, W Lothian — Map F4
Pop 9,525 SEE site, Linlithgow Palace, old town, St Michael's church 🛈 Burgh Halls, The Cross
✆(01506) 844600 Restaurant Four Marys, High Street ✆(01506) 844535

Beecraigs Caravan Park, Beecraigs Country Park EH49 6PL *Modern site with serviced landscaped
bays* ✆(01506) 844516 Fax (01506) 846256 OS map 65/005746 2m S of Linlithgow off Bathgate
road–signposted Open all year 76 pitches Level grass and hard standings, sheltered
✕🗎🔌🔥⊕∅↩♿ country walks £9.00-£11.00

Loch House Caravan Camping Park, Loch House Farm EH49 7RG ✆Linlithgow (01506) 842144
OS map 65/993777 ½m N of Linlithgow on left of A706 (Bo'ness) beyond motorway bridge Open
all year 10 pitches Level/sloping grass 🗎🔌🔥⊕🔥 £3.50

BEECRAIGS

Linlithgow, west of Edinburgh

Modern site open all year with serviced landscaped bays in country park, within easy reach of the coast. Linlithgow palace is famous as the birthplace of Mary Queen of Scots.

LOCHGILPHEAD, Strathclyde   **Map C4**
Pop 1,900. EC Tues SEE church ◪Lochnell Street ☏Lochgilphead (01546) 602344 Restaurant: Stag, Argyll St ☏(01546) 602496
Lochgilphead Caravan Site, Bank Park PA31 8NX ☏Lochgilphead (01546) 602003 OS map 55/859881 ¼m S of Lochgilphead at junction of A83 (Ardrishaig) and A816 beside Loch Gilp Open Apr-Oct 70 pitches (30 static) Grass and hard standings, level, part open ⏚▣♨∅❂⤸❏♨ (30) ⌨ mountain bike hire £7.50 (Mastercard/Visa)

LOCH LOMOND–see Ardlui, Balloch, Drymen, Luss and Tarbet

LUSS, Strathclyde   **Map D4**
Pop 250 SEE Loch Lomond Restaurant: Lomond Castle 6m S at Arden ☏(01389) 850681
Inverbeg Holiday Park, G83 8PD ☏(01389) 850267 OS map 56/346982 4m NW of Luss on A82 (Crianlarich) by Loch Lomond Open Apr-Oct 180 pitches (100 static) Level grass and hard standings, sheltered ⏚➴▣♨∅❂❂⤸❏♨ £6.50-£9.00
Loch Lomond Park (Camping Club) G83 8NT *Site on banks of Loch Lomond* ☏(01436) 860658 OS map 56/360936 ½m N of Luss on A82 (Glasgow–Fort William) by Loch Lomond Open Mar 23-Nov 2, 90 pitches–tents only–adv booking min 2 nights 10 acres, level grass, sheltered ⏚∅❂❂ boat ramp, fishing £9.00-£10.00

MAIDENS–see Maybole

MAYBOLE, Strathclyde   **Map D6**
SEE Culzean Castle and country park 4m W Restaurant: Malin Court, 10m SW on A77 ☏(01655) 760457
Ardlochan House, Culzean KA19 8JZ ☏(01655) 760208 OS map 70/221090 6m W of Maybole off B7023-A719 (Turnberry) on Ardlochan road adj country park Open Easter-Oct 60 pitches (50 static) 4 acres level grass and hard standings ∅❂ £5.00
Culzean Bay Holiday Park, by Croy Shore KA19 8JS ☏(01292) 500444 OS map 76/248125 4m W of Maybole on B7023/A719 (Dunure) at Croy Shore Open Mar-Oct 130 pitches (100 static) Hard standings and grass, level, sheltered ⏚⤺▣♨∅❂⤸♨ (20) ⌨ games room £10.00
Glenside Farm, Culzean KA19 8JZ ☏(01655) 760020 OS map 70/246099 3m W of Maybole on left of A719 (Maidens) Open Apr-Oct 25 pitches 2 acres level grass and hard standings, sheltered ✕♨❂ £6.00-£7.00
Glenside Park (Camping Club), Culzean Castle KA19 8JX ☏(01655) 760627 OS map 70/247103 4m W of Maybole on right of B7023/A719 (Maidens) Level/sloping grass, sheltered ⏚▣♨∅❂⤸♿ £11.80-£14.90 (Mastercard/Visa)
Old Mill Caravan Site, Maidens KA19 8LA ☏(01655) 760254 OS map 76/223087 6m W of Maybole off A719 (Maidens) near beach Open Apr-Sept 26 pitches ✕▣♨∅🏠 £5.00-£6.00
Sandy Beach Caravan Park, Maidens KA26 9NS ☏(01655) 331456 OS map 76/2100083 6m SW of Maybole on A719 (Girvan) Open Apr-Oct 45 pitches (40 static) Grass, level ⏚▣♨∅❂♿ £9.00-£11.50

MEMUS–see Kirriemuir

MONTROSE, Tayside   **Map H2**
Pop 12,280. EC Wed SEE museum, Melville gardens ⓘ The Library, High Street ☎Montrose
(01674) 672000 Restaurant: Park, John St ☎(01674) 673415

East Bowstrips Caravan Park, St Cyrus DD10 0DE *Quiet coastal park with excellent facilities*
☎(01674) 850328 OS map 45/741653 6m N of Montrose on A92 (Stonehaven)–signposted
Open Apr-Oct 60 pitches 4 acres level grass and hard standings, part sheltered
🔣 £6.50-£8.00 (2000)

South Links Caravan Park, South Links DD10 8EJ ☎Montrose (01674) 672105 OS map
54/720575 ½m N of Montrose off A92 (Stonehaven) Open Apr-Oct 15 170 pitches
🔣 £6.50-£9.50 (2000)

MOTHERWELL–see Glasgow

MUASDALE, Strathclyde   **Map B6**
Restaurant: Putechan Lodge 4½m S on A83 at Bellochantuy ☎(01583) 421207

Muasdale Caravan Park PA29 6XO ☎(01583) 421207 OS map 62/683401 ¼m S of Muasdale off
A83 (Campbeltown) on seafront Open Apr-Sept, 30 pitches (10 static) Grass, part level, part
sheltered 🔣 ✕ (tea room) 🔣 £7.00

Point Sands Caravan Park, Tayinloan PA29 6XG ☎(01583) 441263 OS map 62/696485 4½m N
of Muasdale off A83 (Tarbert) Open Apr-Oct, 150 pitches (70 static) Level grass
🔣 (£50) 🔣 beach access £7.00-£10.50 (Visa)

NORTH BERWICK, Lothian   **Map H4**
Pop 5,220. EC Thurs SEE Tantallon Castle 3m E ⓘ 18 Quality Street ☎North Berwick (01620)
892197 Restaurant: Point Garry, West Bay Rd ☎(01620) 892380

Tantallon Caravan Park, Lime Grove EH39 5NJ ☎North Berwick (01620) 893348 OS map
67/566850 1m E of North Berwick on A198 (Dunbar) near golf course Open Mar-Oct 200 pitches
(60 static) 14 acres level grass 🔣 boating, fishing, golf, games room
£6.50-£10.00

OBAN, Strathclyde   **Map C3**
Pop 7,000. EC Thurs SEE cathedral, museum, Highland gathering (end Aug) ⓘ Boswell House,
Argyll Square ☎Oban (01631) 563122 Restaurant: Rowan Tree, George St ☎(01631) 562954

Ganavan Sands Caravan Park, Ganavan PA34 5TU ☎Oban (01631) 562179 OS map 49/862325
2m N of Oban on coast road to Ganavan, by sea Open Easter-Oct 80 pitches Grass and hard
standings, sheltered 🔣 £7.00-£11.00

Oban Caravan and Camping Park, Gallanach Road PA34 4QH ☎Oban (01631) 562425 OS map
49/831273 3m S of Oban on Gallanach road Open Apr-Oct 150 pitches–no adv booking Jul–Aug
Level grass and hard standing 🔣 £8.00-£9.00 (Mastercard/Visa)

Oban Divers' Caravan Park, Glenshellach Rd PA34 4QJ ☎Oban (01631) 562755 OS map
49/841277 1½m SW of Oban off coast road Open Mar 15-Oct 31, 45 pitches Grass and hard
standings, part sloping, sheltered 🔣 £8.00

PATNA, Strathclyde   **Map D6**
Pop 750 Restaurant: Balgarth 10m W at Ayr ☎(01292) 542441

Carskeoch Caravan Park KA6 7NR ☎Patna (01292) 531205 OS map 70/413079 ½m W of Patna
centre off Kirkmichael road Open Easter-Oct 150 pitches (90 static) 15 acres level grass and hard
standings 🔣 putting, fishing £5.00-£12.00

PERTH, Tayside   **Map F3**
Pop 40,090. EC Wed, MD Fri SEE St Ninian's Cathedral, Black Watch museum, leisure pool,
Greyfriars churchyard, Scone Palace 2m N ⓘ45 High St ☎Perth (01738) 638353 Restaurant:
Coach House, North Port ☎(01738) 627950

Cleeve Caravan Park, Glasgow Road PH2 0PH ☎Perth (01738) 639521 Fax (01738) 441690 OS
map 58/095227 1m W of Perth centre on A93 (Glasgow) Open Apr-Oct 100 pitches Sheltered,
level grass 🔣 £7.60-£9.00 (Mastercard/Visa/Switch)

Scone Racecourse, Scone PH2 6BE ☎Scone (01738) 635232 OS map 58/108274 2m N of Perth
off A93 (Braemar) at Old Scone Open Apr-mid Oct, 150 pitches–adv booking min 5 nights
🔣 fishing £7.00

**There's usually no objection to your walking onto a site to see if you might like it but always
ask permission first. Remember that the person in charge is responsible for safeguarding the
property of those staying there.**

PITLOCHRY, Tayside   **Map F2**
Pop 2,500. EC Thurs (winter) See Loch Faskally Dam (fish ladder and observation chamber),
Highland games (Sept), whisky distilleries, Blair castle and Blair Atholl 7m NW, Queen's View 6m
NW ⬛22 Atholl Road ☎Pitlochry (01796) 472215 Restaurant: Birchwood, East Moulin Rd
☎(01796) 472477

Faskally Home Farm PH16 5LA ☎Pitlochry (01796) 472007 OS map 43/922598 2m N of
   Pitlochry off A9 (Inverness) on B8019 (old A9) Open Mar 15-Oct 31, 315 pitches (80 static)
   Level/sloping grass, sheltered 🔂✖️⬛⬛⬛⬛ (indoor heated) ⤴ fishing £8.00-£9.90

Milton of Fonab Caravan Park PH16 5NA ☎Pitlochry (01796) 472882 OS map 52/944573 ½m S
   of Pitlochry off A9 (Perth) opp Bells distillery Open Apr 6-Oct, 150 pitches–families only, no motor
   cycles Level grass, sheltered 🔂⬛⬛⬛⬛⬛⬛⬛ free trout fishing, mountain bike hire £10.50

PITTENWEEM–see Anstruther

PRESTWICK, Strathclyde   **Map D6**
Pop 13,530. EC Wed SEE Cuthbert's church ⬛ Boydfield Gdns ☎Prestwick (01292) 79946
Restaurant: St Nicholas, Ayr Rd ☎(01292) 79568

Prestwick Holiday Park, KA9 1UH ☎Prestwick (01292) 479261 OS map 70/343278 1m N of
   Prestwick off A79 (Prestwick airport) on coast road–signposted Open Mar-Oct 186 pitches (155
   static) Grass, level 🔂⬛⬛⬛⬛⬛⬛⬛⬛ (35) ⬛ £10.00

ST ANDREWS, Fife   **Map G3**
Pop 13,490. EC Thurs SEE cathedral, chapter house and museum, botanic gardens, West Port,
Dutch village in Craigtown Park ⬛South Street ☎St Andrews (01334) 472021 Restaurant: Grange
Inn, Grange Rd ☎(01334) 472670

Cairns Mill Caravan Park, Largo Road KY16 8NN ☎St Andrews (01334) 473604 OS map
   59/498148 1m S of St Andrews on A915 (Largo) Open Apr-Oct 265 pitches (170 static) Grass
   and hard standings, level, open 🔂⬛⬛⬛⬛⬛⬛⬛⬛ (heated) ⬛⤴⬛⬛ (50) ⬛⬛ games room,
   coffee bar £8.50-£11.00 (Switch)

Clayton Caravan Park KY16 9YE ☎(01334) 870242 OS map 59/430183 5m W of St Andrews on
   A91 (Cupar) Open Apr-Oct 265 pitches (195 static) Level/sloping grass and hard standings,
   sheltered 🔂✖️⬛⬛⬛⬛⬛⬛⬛⤴⬛⬛⬛ £8.50-£9.00 (Mastercard/Visa)

Craigtoun Meadows Holiday Park, Mount Melville KY16 8PQ ☎St Andrews (01334) 475959 OS
   map 59/483153 1½m WSW of St Andrews off B939 (Pitscottie) on Craigtoun road Open Mar-Oct
   244 pitches (146 static) 🔂✖️⬛⬛⬛⬛⬛⬛ tennis, gymnasium, cycle hire £9.20-£10.25

Kinkell Braes Caravan Site KY16 8PX ☎St Andrews (01334) 474250 OS map 59/522157 1m SE
   of St Andrews on A918 (Crail) Open Mar 21-Oct 479 pitches (385 static) 30 acres level grass
   🔂✖️⬛⬛⬛⬛⬛⬛⬛⤴⬛⬛⬛⬛ café, games room £9.00-£15.00 (Mastercard/Visa/Switch/Delta)

ST CYRUS–see Montrose

ST FILLANS, Tayside   **Map E3**
Pop 250. EC Wed Sailing and mountaineering centre at E end of Loch Earn. SEE museum of
Scottish tartans (Easter-Sept) 5m E at Comrie Restaurant: Drummond Arms ☎(01764) 685212

Loch Earn Caravan Park, South Shore Road PH6 9NL ☎(01764) 685270 OS map 51/680238 1m
   W of St Fillans on South Lochearn road by private beach Open Apr-Oct 270 pitches 20 acres
   level grass, sheltered ⬛⬛⬛ £11.00 (Mastercard/Visa/Switch)

ST MADOES–see Glencarse

SCOTLANDWELL–see Glenrothes

SOUTHEND, Strathclyde   **Map B6**
Restaurant: Ardshiel 10m N at Campbeltown ☎(01586) 552133

Machribeg Caravan Site PA28 6RW ☎(01586) 830249 OS map 68/686085 ½m SW of Southend
   on road to Keil Point Open Easter-Sept, 140 pitches (60 static) 8 acres, grass, level, open
   ⬛⬛⬛⬛ boating, fishing, golf £5.00

CARAVAN STORAGE

Many sites in this guide offer caravan storage in winter but some will also store your caravan
in summer, which for those of us able to tour several times a year saves towing over long
distances. Sites most conveniently placed for this are those on or near popular routes to the
West Country and Scotland.

TAYNUILT

Crunachy Park, Bridge of Awe

by Loch Etive in scenic Argyll on A85 (Dalmally-Oban)
Owned and run by Angus Douglas

Open March to October

STIRLING, Central **Map E4**
Pop 26,770. EC Wed, MD Thurs SEE castle, Chapel Royal museum and art gallery, Darnley's house, Abbey Craig with Wallace monument 2m NE, Bannockburn memorial, Doune castle 6m NW ⚅ Dumbarton Road ☎ (01786) 475019 and Broad St ☎ (01786) 479901 Restaurant: Golden Lion, King St ☎ (01786) 475351

Auchenbowie Caravan Site Auchenbowie FK7 8HE ☎ (01324) 823999 OS map 57/795880 3m S of Stirling off A872 (Glasgow) south of Junction 9 of M80/M9 Open Apr-Oct–no adv booking 60 pitches Grass, part level, sheltered, some hard standings ⛟ (mobile) 🛒🚿⊗∅🔌☕🍴 (35) 🚉 £8.00-£9.00

Witches Craig Caravan-Camping Park, Blairlogie FK9 5PX ☎ Stirling (01786) 474947 OS map 57/822968 3m NE of Stirling on left of A91 (Dollar) Open Apr-Oct 60 pitches Grass and hard standings, level, sheltered 🛢🛒🚿⊗∅⊕☕🍴♿ £10.00-£14.00

STRACHUR, Strathclyde **Map C3**
Restaurant: Creggans Inn ☎ (01369) 820279

Glendaruel Caravan Park, Glendaruel PA22 3AB *Award-winning park in woodland garden* ☎ (01369) 820267 OS map 55/999868 10½m SW of Strachur on A886 (Colintraive) Open Apr-Oct 65 pitches (30 static) Grass and hard standings, level, sheltered–3 acres within 22 acre country park ⛟🚶🛢🛒🚿⊗∅⊕☕🍴🚉 cycle hire (adults only), fishing (salmon and sea trout), barbecue, under cover campers' kitchen £8.50-£10.50 (OAP discount) (Mastercard/Visa)

Strathlachlan Caravan Park, Strathlachlan PA27 8BU ☎ (01369) 860300 OS map 55/005955 6m S of Strachur off A886 (Tighnabruaich) on single track B8000 (Kilfinan) beside Loch Fyne Open Apr-Oct 104 pitches (96 static)–no tents Hard standings, level ⛟🛢🛒🚿∅🍴 (5) £4.50-£5.50

TARBERT, Strathclyde **Map C4**
Pop 220. EC Wed ⚅ Harbour St ☎ (01880) 820429 Restaurant: West Loch Hotel ☎ (01880) 840283

Point Sands Caravan Park, Tayinloan PA29 6XG *Quality site amid wonderful scenery* ☎ (01583) 441263 OS map 62/698484 8m S of Tarbert on A83 (Campbeltown) Open Apr-Nov 135 pitches (70 static) 15 acres level grass ⛟🛢🛒🚿⊗☕🍴🚉 £7.00-£12.00 (Mastercard/Visa)

Port Ban Park, Kilberry PA29 6YD ☎ (01880) 770224 Fax (01880) 770388 OS map 62/707655 15m W of Tarbert off A83 (Lochgilphead) on single track B8024 (Kilberry) Open Apr-Oct 92 pitches (62 static) Grass, part level, part sheltered ⛟✕🚐🛢🛒🚿⊗∅⊕🍴🚉 tennis, putting, boat hire, fishing £8.00-£9.00 (Mastercard/Visa)

See also Clachan

TARBET, Strathclyde **Map D3**
SEE Rest and Be Thankful Hill at Arrochar 2mW, Ben Arthur (2,891ft) NW ⚅ Main St ☎ (01301) 702260 Restaurant: Ardlui 8m N at Ardlui ☎ (01301) 704243

Ardgartan Campsite (Forestry Commission), Arrochar G83 7AL ☎ (01301) 702597 (season) 0131 314 6100 (out of season) OS map 56/275030 4m W of Tarbet on left of A83 (Inveraray) in Argyll Forest Park on west shore of Loch Long Open Apr-Oct 200 pitches Hard standings and grass, level, open ⛟🛢🛒∅⊗☕🍴 (50) ♿ pony trekking, rock climbing, boating, sea fishing £7.00-£9.00

Loch Lomond Holiday Park, Inveruglas G83 7DW ☎ (01301) 704224 OS map 56/320091 3m N of Tarbet on A82 (Fort William) beside Loch Lomond Open Mar-Oct and Dec-Jan 90 pitches (64 static) 1 acre level grass and hard standings ⛟🛢🛒🚿⊗∅⊕☕🍴🖵🚉🏪♿ all-weather pitches, fishing, beach, boating £6.50-£12.00

TAYINLOAN–see Tarbert

TAYNUILT, Strathclyde   Map C3
Pop 400 EC Wed SEE Nelson monument, Cruachan power station, old blast furnace, Loch Etive N,
Brander Pass E Restaurant: Brander Lodge ☎(01866) 822243

Crunachy Caravan Camping Park, Bridge of Awe PA35 1HT ☎(01866) 822612 OS map
50/032296 2m SE of Taynuilt on right of A85 (Dalmally-Oban) near Bridge of Awe Open Mar-Oct,
100 pitches 9 acres level grass and hard standings, sheltered ▨ ✗ (tea room) ⏁▨▨◪◉◪
◡▨▭& games room £9.50 (most cards)

TAYPORT, Fife   Map G3
Restaurant: Sandford Hill 6m W at Wormit ☎(01382) 541802

Tayport Links Caravan Park KY15 5RG ☎Tayport (01382) 552334 OS map 59/463285 ¼m E of
Tayport off B945 (Leuchars) on sea front Open Apr-Oct 100 pitches (70 static) Grass and hard
standings, level, sheltered ▨▨◪◉◪▭ (heated) ▭ £5.50-£12.00

TROON, Strathclyde   Map D6
Pop 14,250. EC Wed SEE Lady Isle bird sanctuary ▤Municipal Buildings, South Beach ☎Troon
(01292) 317696 Restaurant: Campbell's Kitchen, South Beach ☎(01292) 314421

St Meddans Caravan Site KA10 6NS ☎Troon (01292) 312957 OS map 70/332312 ¼m E of
Troon off A759 (Loans) Open Mar-Oct 26 pitches (18 static) Level grass sheltered ▨◪ £6.00

TUMMEL BRIDGE, Tayside   Map E2
Restaurant: Loch Rannoch 6m W at Kinloch Rannoch ☎(01882) 632201

Tummel Valley Holiday Park PH16 5SA ☎Tummel Bridge (01882) 634221 OS map 52/764592
¼m E of Tummel Bridge on left of B8019 (Pitlochry) Open Mar-Nov, 160 pitches (110 static) 50
acres, part sloping, part hard standings ▨✗▭⏁▨▨◪◉◪▭ (indoor) ▣▭▨ solarium,
entertainment (Jun-Aug), bike hire £5.90-£13.75

TYNDRUM, Central   Map D2
▤ Main St ☎(01838) 400246 Restaurant: Ardlui 13m S at Ardlui ☎(01301) 704243

Pine Trees Caravan Park FK20 8RY ☎(01838) 400243 OS map 50/327301 ¼m S of Tyndrum off
A82 (Tarbert) on road to lower station Open Jan-Oct 42 pitches Grass, level ▨◪◉▨ (50) ▭
£3.50-£4.00

WHITBURN, W Lothian   Map F5
Restaurant: Dreadnought 4m NE at Bathgate ☎(01506) 630791

Mosshall Farm Caravan Park, Blackburn EH47 7DB ☎(01501) 762318 OS map 65/975647 1m E
of Whitburn on A705 (East Calder) Open all year 25 pitches Level grass and hard standings,
sheltered ▨◉ £5.50-£6.00

16   North Scotland

North Scotland, made up of the new counties of Grampian on the east and Highland and the offshore islands on the west, contains what is probably the most beautiful scenery to be found anywhere in Britain.

The Highland coastline is most spectacular on the north and west, where giant arms of rock reach out towards the islands. Between them are deep lochs, linked from east to west by countless rivers and streams feeding innumerable lakes surrounded by wooded glens and majestic peaks. The most dominant inland feature in the country is the great rift which extends diagonally from Inverness to Fort William, in which the Caledonian Canal provides a continuous waterway from the North Sea to the Atlantic.

The best known centre in the south is Aviemore on the ski slopes of the Cairngorms. At nearby Kingussie is the Highland Wildlife Park where bison, beaver, lynx and even rarer osprey can be seen in a natural setting. Southwest lies Ben Nevis, at 4406ft Britain's highest mountain, and farther west still Loch Morar, our deepest lake.

Off the west coast is Skye, linked between Fort William and Mallaig by the famous Road to the Isles. Ferries to the island run from Glenelg and Kyle of Lochalsh as well as from Mallaig. Portree and Broadford are handy bases for exploring the island. From Uig, in northern Skye, boats leave for the Outer Hebrides. Facing Skye between the Kyle of Lochalsh and Ullapool is a wild and magnificently remote region of mountain peaks and forests, for which Applecross, Torridon, Gairloch and Kinlochewe are obvious centres. Further north is Lochinver, most famous of all the west coast fishing villages.

The northern coast has its own rugged grandeur and fine beaches at Balnakiel Bay, reached from Durness. Here too are the cliffs of Clo Mor, at 900ft Britain's highest, and the waterfall near Kylesku which plummets 660ft. The towns of Golspie, Dornoch, Helmsdale and Brora are each lively holiday centres with good beaches and facilities. Inland lie extensive nature reserves and national forest parks with awe-inspiring lochs and towering bens. Further south the Firths of Dornoch, Cromarty and Beauly flank not only high peaks but lush and fertile farmland and valleys brilliant with displays of wild flowers through the season.

The bold right angle of the Grampian coastline has many charming seaside villages and towns on its northern edge, while on the eastern edge after Peterhead fifteen miles of sands and dunes roll on towards the granite fishing port and resort of Aberdeen. West of Aberdeen is the pretty Dee Valley, with the royal hunting lodge of Balmoral and Braemar, home of the Highland Games. The Grampian is the main centre of whisky, too, and distilleries can be visited near Dufftown, Elgin and Keith.

Campsites on the west and north Highland are sparse. The eastern Highland is slightly better served, but the campsites all tend to be along the coast. The few inland often have primitive facilities and are very crowded in season. Sites in the Grampian are more regularly spaced, but are too few to cope with the high demand in season.

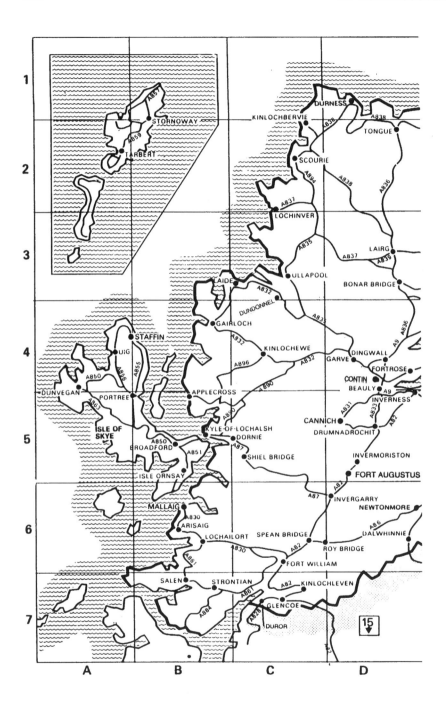

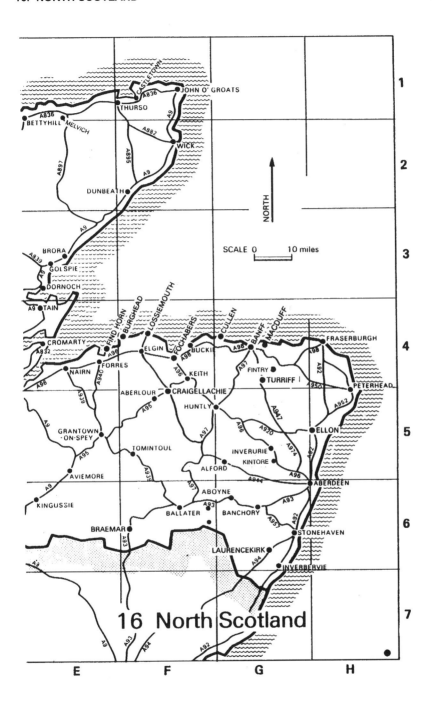

SCALE 0   10 miles

16 North Scotland

ABERDEEN, Grampian   **Map H6**
Pop 214,100. EC Wed, MD Fri SEE cathedral regional museum, fish market, Girdleness lighthouse
■ St Nicholas House, Broad Street ✆ Aberdeen (01224) 632727 Restaurant: Music Cellar, Union St
✆ (01224) 580092

Craighill Farm, Bridge of Dee AB1 5XJ ✆ Aberdeen (01224) 781973 OS map 38/923027 ¾m S of
Aberdeen on A90 (Stonehaven) Open Apr-Oct 20 pitches–no adv booking Grass, sloping, hard
standings, sheltered ▣∅⊛◗⊡ £5.00-£7.50

Hazelhead Caravan Park and Campsite, Groats Road AB1 8BL ✆ Aberdeen (01224) 321268 OS
map 38/894057 3½m W of Aberdeen off A944 (Alford) Open Apr-Sept 165 pitches Grass and
hard standings, level, sheltered ▤▣◗⊛∅↲ £8.55 (Mastercard/Visa)

Lower Deeside Caravan Park, Maryculter AB12 5FX ✆ Aberdeen (01224) 733860 OS map
38/860955 6m SW of Aberdeen off A93 (Banchory) adj hotel/restaurant Open all year 75 pitches
(45 static) Level grass and hard standings, sheltered ▤▣◗∅⊛∅↲⊡⊡☎ £8.50-£12.50
(most cards)

Skene Caravan Park, Mains of Keir AB32 6YA ✆ Aberdeen (01224) 743282 OS map 38/810082
7m W of Aberdeen off A944 (Alford) at Kirkton of Skene on B979 (Blackburn) Open Apr-Oct 10
pitches ▣◗⊛↲⊡ £8.00-£10.00

ABERLOUR, Grampian   **Map F5**
Pop 800. EC Wed SEE waterfalls on Aberlour Burn, Huntly Castle (heraldic carvings) 1m E,
Glenfiddich distillery 4m SE Restaurant: Dowans ✆ (01340) 871488

Aberlour Gardens Caravan Park AB38 9LD ✆ Aberlour (01340) 871586 OS map 28/282437 1m
N of Aberlour off A95 (Keith)–signposted on unclassed road–vehicles over 10ft 6in high use A941
(Dufftown) Open Mar-Oct 73 pitches (28 static) Grass, level, sheltered, some hard standings
▤⅄▣▣∅⊛∅◗↲◗⊡₫ milk, motorhome service point £6.50-£9.50

See also Craigellachie

ABOYNE, Grampian   **Map G6**
Pop 1,690. EC Thurs SEE winter sports centre, St Thomas's church, Aboyne games (Sept),
Glentaner deer forest, Craigievar Castle 7m NE ■ Ballater Road Car Park ✆ (01339) 886080
Restaurant: Birse Lodge, Charleston Rd ✆ (01339) 882243

Aboyne Loch Caravan Park, Aboyne AB34 5BR ✆ (01339) 886244 OS map 44/539995 ½m NE
of Aboyne on A93 (Aberdeen) near loch Open Apr-Oct–no adv booking 55 pitches (40 static) 8
acres, level, part hard standings ▤▣▣∅⊛∅◗↲⊡☎ fishing £8.50

Drummie Hill Caravan Park, Tarland AB34 4UP ✆ (01339) 881388 OS map 37/477044 5m NW of
Aboyne off B9094-A974 (Tarland) Open Apr-Oct 15, 98 pitches (67 static) Grass and some hard
standings, level, open ▤▣▣∅⊛∅◗₫ (40) ⊡ £8.00

ALFORD, Grampian   **Map G5**
SEE Haughton House 1m N ■ Railway Museum, Station Yard ✆ (01975) 562052 Restaurant:
Grant Arms 12m E at Monymusk ✆ (01467) 651226

Haughton House Country Park, AB33 8NA ✆ (01975) 562107 OS map 37/583168 1m N of Alford
on Montgarrie road Open Apr-Sept 175 pitches (40 static)–no adv booking Grass and hard
standings, level, sheltered ▤▣▣∅⊛∅◗↲⊡⊡ (2) putting green, guided walks, narrow gauge
railway £6.75

ALVES–see Burghead

APPLECROSS, Highland   **Map B5**
SEE Applecross forest Restaurant: Applecross Inn on A896 ✆ (01520) 744262

Applecross Campsite, Strathcarron IV54 8ND ✆ (01520) 744284 OS map 24/715446 ¼m E of
Applecross on Kishorn road–only poss approach for caravans from N via Kenmore Open Apr-Oct
60 pitches Level grass, sheltered ▤✗ (lic) ▣▣∅⊛⊡ wet weather area, tea room £8.00

ARISAIG, Highland   **Map B6**
SEE site, Sound of Arisaig, Silver Sands of Morar 6m N, islands (boat trips) Restaurant: Old Library Lodge ☎ (01687) 450651

Camusdarach Camping Site PH39 4NT ☎ and Fax (01687) 450221 OS map 40/663915 4m N of Arisaig on A830 (Mallaig) Open Mar 15-Oct 15–booking advisable Jul-Aug 42 pitches Grass, part level 🏠🚿🍴⊕∅🚻 adj sandy beach £7.00-£9.00 (inc showers)

Gorten Sands Caravan Site, Gorten Farm PH39 4NS ☎ (01687) 450283 OS map 40/640879 1m W of Arisaig off A830 (Mallaig) on Back of Keppoch road across cattle grid Open Apr-Oct 15, 45 pitches Grass and hard standings, level, part sheltered 🏠🚿🍴⊕∅🏪 adjacent to seashore £7.00-£9.50

Portnadoran Camping and Caravan Site, PH39 4NT ☎ (01687) 450267 OS map 40/652889 2m N of Arisaig off A830 (Mallaig) Open Apr-Oct 40 pitches Grass, level 🏠🚿⊕∅🧺🏪 adj sandy beach £6.00-£9.00

Skyeview Caravan Park PH38 4NJ ☎ (01687) 450209 OS map 40/654880 1m N of Arisaig off A830 (Mallaig) Open Apr-Oct, 20 pitches 2 acres, level/gentle slope, grass, sheltered 🚿🍴⊕ £5.00-£8.50 inc elect

AVIEMORE, Highland   **Map E5**
Pop 1,960. EC Wed Britain's premier skiing centre SEE Cairngorms centre, curling centre, reindeer herd, Ben Macdhui (4,296ft), Wildlife park, osprey sanctuary, Strathspey rlwy to Boat of Garten (5m), Craigellachic Rock (rallying point for the Clan Grant) 🚉 Grampian Road ☎ Aviemore (01479) 810363 Restaurant: Stakis Hotel ☎ (01479) 811013

Aviemore Mountain Resort Caravan Park, PH22 1PF ☎ Aviemore (01479) 810751 OS map 35/893122 ¼m S of Aviemore Centre off A9 (Kingussie) near tourist office Open Dec-Oct–must book peak periods 90 pitches Grass and hard standings level, part open 🚿 karting £6.00-£9.00 (Mastercard/Visa)

Campground of Scotland, Boat of Garten PH24 3BN ☎ (01479) 831652 OS map 36/939191 6m NE of Aviemore off A9 (Inverness) and A95 (Grantown on Spey) in Boat of Garten Open all year 97 pitches (60 static) Grass and hard standings, level, part open ⚡🏠🍴⊕∅🧺🏪 sep pitches £5.50-£11.50

Loch Garten Lodges and Caravan Park, Croft-na-Carn, Boat of Garten PH24 3BY *Site in picturesque setting overlooking Spey Valley and backed by Loch Garten nature reserve* ☎ (01479) 831769 OS map 36/965195 7½m N of Aviemore on B970 (Nethy Bridge) Open all year 30 pitches 3 acres level grass, sheltered ⚡🏠🚿🍴⊕🍺🏪 £7.00-£10.00

Dalraddy Caravan Park PH22 1QB ☎ Aviemore (01479) 810330 OS map 36/857083 3m S of Aviemore on right of B9152 (Kingussie) Open all year–must book 130 pitches (96 static) Level/sloping grass and hard standing, sheltered 🎣🏹🏠🚿🍴⊕∅🧺🍺🏪 fishing, clay-pigeon shooting, tennis £3.50-£6.50

Glenmore Forest Park Campsite PH22 1QU ☎ Cairngorm (01479) 861271 OS map 36/975097 7m E of Aviemore on B970 (Coylumbridge) by Loch Morlich Open all year–booking advisable 220 pitches Grass and hard standings, level, part open 🎣✕🏠🚿🍴⊕∅🧺🚪♿ forest trails £5.40-£6.60

High Range Touring Park, Grampian Road, PH22 1PT ☎ Aviemore (01479) 810636 OS map 35/36/894120 ½m S of Aviemore centre on B9152 (Kincraig) near junction with B970 Open Dec-Oct 60 pitches Hard standing and grass, level, sheltered ✕🍴⚡🏠🚿🍴⊕∅🍺🧺🏪♿🔔 £11.00 (Mastercard/Visa)

Rothiemurchus Camp and Caravan Park, Coylumbridge PH22 1QH ☎ Aviemore (01479) 812800 OS map 36/915106 1½m E of Aviemore off A951 in Coylumbridge Open all year 89 pitches (50 static) Level/sloping grass and hard standings, sheltered 🎣🏹🏠🚿🍴⊕∅🍺🍺🏪🔔 TV hook-up £7.00-£13.00 (Mastercard/Visa/Switch)

Speyside Caravan Park PH22 1PX ☎ Aviemore (01479) 810236 OS map 35/985115 ¼m S of Aviemore off B970 (Coylumbridge) beside River Spey Open all year 154 pitches (105 static) 10 acres, level grass and hard standings 🍴🏠🚿🍴🏪 (heated), serviced pitches, cycle hire, fishing £3.00-£7.50

BALLACHULISH–see Glencoe

BALLATER, Grampian   **Map F6**
Pop 1,180. EC Thurs SEE Falls of Muick, Loch Kinord 4m NE, Highland games (Aug) 🚉 Station Square ☎ Ballater (01339) 755306 Restaurant: Darroch Learg, Braemar Rd ☎ (01339) 755443

Ballater Caravan Site AB3 5QR ☎ (01339) 755727 OS map 37/370955 ¼m SW of Ballater off A93 (Braemar) near bridge over river Dee Open Easter-Oct–Jun-Aug maximum stay 14 nights 159 pitches (93 static) Grass and hard standing, level 🏠∅⊕∅🍺🧺🍺 £8.50-£9.50

BALMACARA–see Kyle of Lochalsh

BANCHORY, Grampian   **Map G6**
Pop 5,320. EC Thurs SEE Bridge of Feugh, Crathes castle 2m E, Deeside Heather Centre 7m E
🄸 Bellfield Car Park ☏ Banchory (01330) 822000 Restaurant: Burnett Arms, Main St ☏ (01330)
824944

Banchory Lodge Caravan Park, Dee Street, AB3 3HY ☏ (01330) 822246 OS map 38/698954 ¼m
SE of Banchory off A493 (Aberdeen) Open Apr-mid Oct–no adv booking Grass, level, sheltered
🖥 ⊕ ➋ (20) 🚮 £3.90-£4.65

Campfield Caravan Park, AB31 4DN ☏ (01339) 820250 OS map 38/652004 5m NW of Banchory
on A980 (Bridge of Alford) Open Apr-Sept 45 pitches (30 static) Grass, level, sheltered
🛒 🖥 ➋ ⌀ ➋ (30) 🚮 petrol £6.50-£7.50

Feughside Caravan Park, Strachan AB31 6NT ☏ Feughside (01330) 850669 OS map 38/643924
5m SW of Banchory off B976 (Aboyne) behind Feughside inn Open Apr-mid Oct 72 pitches (52
static) Grass, level, sheltered 🖥 ➋ ⌀ ⊕ ⌀ ⊕ ↩ ➋ (30) 🚮 ♿ £8.00-£8.50

Silver Ladies Caravan Park, Strachan AB31 3NL ☏ Banchory (01330) 822800 OS map 38/692936
1m S of Banchory on left of B974 (Strachan) Open Apr-Oct 105 pitches (88 static) 7 acres level
grass and hard standing 🛒 🖥 ➋ ⌀ ⊕ ⌀ ⊕ ↩ 🚮 £5.20-£7.10

BANFF, Grampian   **Map G4**
Pop 4,230. EC Wed SEE site, Mercat cross, museum, miniature railway from harbour, Duff House
1m S 🄸 Collie Lodge ☏ (01261) 812419 Restaurant: Banff Springs, Golden Knowes Rd ☏ (01261)
812881

Links Camping Park AB4 2JD ☏ (01261) 812228 OS map 29/675642 1m W of Banff off A98
(Portsoy) on B9139 (Whitehills) by sea Open Apr-Sept 145 pitches (85 static) Grass, level
🛒 ↩ 🖥 ➋ ⌀ ↩ 🚮 £5.00

BEAULY, Highland   **Map D4**
Pop 3,650. EC Thurs SEE Priory, Highland Craftpoint Restaurant: Priory, The Square ☏ (01463)
782309

Druimorrin Caravan Park, Orrin Bridge by Muir of Ord IV6 7UL ☏ (01997) 433252 OS map
26/506533 4½m NW of Beauly off A862/A832 (Contin) via Muir of Ord Open Easter-Sept 60
pitches Grass, level, part sheltered 🛒 🖥 ➋ ⌀ ⊕ ⌀ £6.00-£7.50

Lovat Bridge Caravan and Camping Park, IV4 7AY ☏ Beauly (01463) 782374 OS map 26/517450
1½m S of Beauly on A862 (Inverness) by River Beauly Open Apr-Oct 40 pitches 11½ acres, level
grass and hard standings ✕ ☕ ➋ ⌀ ⌀ ⊕ ↩ ⬚ ➋ bar meals, milk, fishing £8.00-£9.00

BETTYHILL, Highland   **Map E1**
🄸 Clachan ☏ (01641) 522342 (summer) Restaurant: Bettyhill ☏ (01641) 521352

Craigdhu Camping KW14 7SP ☏ (01641) 521273 OS map 10/709620 ½m E of Bettyhill centre on
A836 (Thurso) Open Easter-Oct, 90 pitches 5 acres, level/gentle slope, grass, sheltered ➋
£8.00-£10.00

BOAT OF GARTEN–see Aviemore

BRAEMAR, Grampian   **Map F6**
Pop 400 EC Thurs SEE castle, chairlift at Devil's Elbow, Linn of Dee, Malky Whisky Trail, Braemar
Gathering (1st Sat Sept), Balmoral Castle 8m E 🄸 The Mews, Mar Rd ☏ (01339) 741600
Restaurant: Invercauld Arms ☏ (01339) 741605

Invercauld Park (Caravan Club), Glenshee Road AB3 5QY ☏ (01339) 741373 OS map 43/153910
½m S of Braemar on right of A93 (Blairgowrie) Open mid-Apr-Sept, 75 pitches ➋ ⌀ ⌀ ↩ fishing
£8.00-£12.00

BRORA, Highland   **Map E3**
Pop 1,800. EC Wed SEE woollen mills Restaurant: Links ☏ (01408) 621225

Crakaig Caravan Park, Loth Beach KW8 6HP ☏ Brora (01408) 621260 OS map 17/960095 5m
NE of Brora off A9 (Helmsdale) at Crakaig near beach Open May-Sept 36 pitches 7 acres gentle
slope, sheltered £5.00

Riverside Croft Caravan Site, Stonehouse, Doll KW9 6NJ ☏ Brora (01408) 621819 OS map
17/885032 1½m SW of Brora off A9 (Golspie) at Doll Open May-Sept 18 pitches Grass, part
level, part sheltered 🖥 ⊕ ↩ 🚮 £3.50

Dogs are usually allowed but must be kept on a lead. Sometimes they have to be paid for.

BUCKIE, Grampian   **Map F4**
Pop 7,950. EC Wed SEE twin-towered church ◱Cluny Square ✆(01542) 834853 Restaurant:
Cluny, High St ✆(01542) 832922

Edindoune Municipal Site, Findochty AB4 1US ✆(01542) 835303 OS map 28/459679 3m NE of
   Buckie off A942 (Portnockie) near Findochty harbour Open May-Sept 22 pitches Grass, level,
   part open ▣ (35) ▨ £6.00

BURGHEAD, Grampian   **Map F4**
Pop 1,470 Fishing town on Burghead Bay SEE Burghead Well, Burghead Bulls (7-8c Pictish
stones) Restaurant: Torfness ✆(01343) 835663

Burghead Caravan Park, West Beach IV30 2UN ✆Burghead (01343) 835799 ¼m W of Burghead
   centre on west beach Open Apr-Sept 135 pitches (58 static) Grass, level, part open, hard
   standings ▣▣◒◈∅⌣▣▣▨ዼ adj sandy beach £4.00-£10.00

North Alves Caravan Park, Alves IV30 3XD ✆(01343) 850223 OS map 28/122623 3m S of
   Burghead on A96 (Elgin-Forres) Open Apr-Oct, 90 pitches (30 static) Level grass ▙▣▣◒◈▣
   £7.00-£10.00

Red Craig Hotel Caravan Camping Park IV30 2XX ✆Burghead (01343) 835663 OS map
   28/124689 ½m E of Burghead centre off B9012 (Hopeman) Open Apr-Oct, 38 pitches 4½ acres
   sloping/level grass ✗♀◒ጶ▣▣◒◈∅◐▣ weekend entertainment £9.00

Station Caravan Park, West Beach Road, Hopeman IV30 5RU ✆(01343) 830880 OS map
   28/145696 2m NE of Burghead off B9040 (Lossiemouth) Open Apr-Oct 85 marked pitches (50
   static) Level grass, sheltered ▣▣◒◈◐⌣▣▨ private beach £4.00-£10.00

CANNICH, Highland   **Map D5**
Pop 400 SEE Glen Cannich W, Glen Affric SW, Plodda Falls, Corrimony chambered cairn 3m E,
Loch Ness Monster exhibition 12m E at Drumnadrochit Restaurant: Glen Affric ✆(01456) 476214

Cannich Caravan Park IV4 7LN ✆(01456) 415364 OS map 26/341314 ¼m N of Cannich centre
   on A831 (Glassburn) Open Dec-Oct 100 pitches (15 static) Level grass and hard standings
   ▣▣◒◈◐⌣▣▣▨ዼ fishing, mountain bike hire £5.56-£9.56

CASTLETOWN, Highland   **Map F1**
Pop 2,850 Restaurant: Northern Sands 3m NE at Dunnet ✆(01847) 851270

Dunnet Bay Site (Caravan Club) KW14 8XD ✆(01847) 851319 OS map 12/219705 2m NE of
   Castletown on left of A836 (John O'Groats) adj sand dunes and beach Open mid-May-Sept 45
   pitches—peak booking essential 5 acres sand and level grass ∅ £7.00

CONTIN, Highland   **Map D4**
Pop 350 Village noted for its pleasant walks inc nearby Torrachilty forest trail SEE fish lift at
Torrachilty dam, spa of Strathpeffer 2m NE Restaurant: National Hotel 7m NE at Dingwall ✆(01349)
862166

Riverside Caravan Park, IV14 9ES ✆(01997) 421351 OS map 26/457559 In Contin on A835
   (Inverness-Ullapool) at junct with Strathpeffer road Open all year 30 pitches Grass, sloping
   ▙✗⌣▣▣◒◈∅▣ (£50/6mths) ▨▤ hot water, post office, fishing £6.00-£7.00

CRAIGELLACHIE, Grampian   **Map F5**
Restaurant: Aberlour 3m SW at Aberlour ✆(01340) 871287

Speyside Caravan Park (Camping Club), Elchies AB3 9SD ✆(01340) 810414 OS map
   28/257449 2½m NW of Craigellachie on left of B9102 (Archiestown) Open Jan 1-Oct 30
   75 pitches 3 acres, level, hard standings ▣∅◒∅ዼ £11.80-£14.90 (Mastercard/Visa)
See also Aberlour

CROMARTY, Highland   **Map E4**
SEE church, Hugh Miller's cottage Restaurant: Royal, Marine Terrace ✆(01381) 600217

Ferry Inn, Balblair IV7 8LG ✆(01381) 610250 OS map 21/703668 7m W of Cromarty on B9163
   (Conon Bridge) in Balblair Open Apr-Sept 7 pitches—booking advisable ♀ boating, fishing £4.50
Shore Mill IV11 8XU ✆(01381) 610216 OS map 21/750657 2½m SW of Cromarty on B9163
   (Conon Bridge) near beach Open Apr-Sept 15 pitches Grass, part level ▣ (20) ▨ £5.50

BURGHEAD – Station Caravan Park
West Beach, Hopeman

Family-run park near safe sandy beach with views of Moray Firth, haunt of dolphins.

Tel: 01343 830880   £4.40-£10.00 for two

CULLEN, Grampian   **Map G4**
Pop 1,400 EC Wed SEE Auld Kirk (carved panels) ⚊ Seafield St ☎(01542) 840757 Restaurant:
Seafield Arms, Seafield Street ☎(01542) 840791

Links Caravan Park, Portsoy AB4 2SS ☎Portsoy (01261) 842695 OS map 29/592662 5½m E of
   Cullen off A98 (Banff) Open Apr-Sept, 75 pitches 2½ acres, part level, grass 🖵🗑⊕∅↵🚐
   £7.10 inc elect

Cullen Bay Caravan Park AB5 2TZ ☎Cullen (01542) 840766 OS map 29/516676 ¼m W of
   Cullen off A98 (Fochabers) Open Easter-Sept 100 pitches (60 statics) 4½ acres, level, on clifftop 🖵🗑⊕∅🚐 £8.50

Sandend Caravan Camping Park, Portsoy AB45 2UD ☎Portsoy (01261) 842660 OS map
   29/555663 3m E of Cullen off A98 (Banff) adj sandy beach Open Apr-Oct, 72 marked pitches (25
   static) Level grass ⚟✕♀↵🖵🗑🗑⊕🖥 (£40) 🚐♿ £9.00-£9.75

CUMINESTOWN, Grampian   **Map G4**
Pop 560 Restaurant: Towie 4m SW on A947 at Auchterless ☎(01888) 511201

East Balthangie Farm AB53 5XY ☎(01888) 544261 OS map 29/841516 2m E of Cuminestown off
   B9027 (New Byth) Open Mar-Oct 13 pitches 7 acres level grass, sheltered 🖵🗑🗑⊕∅🖥🚐 dog
   walk £6.00-£8.50

DAVIOT–see Inverness

DINGWALL, Highland   **Map D4**
EC Thurs SEE museum, Highland games (Jul) Restaurant: Royal, High St ☎(01349) 862130

Black Rock Caravan Park, Evanton IV16 9UN ☎(01349) 830917 OS map 21/606665 5m NE of
   Dingwall off A9 (Tain) by River Glass Open Apr-Oct 107 pitches Level grass, sheltered
   🖵🗑🗑⊕∅🏵↵🖥🚐 tennis, fishing, forest walks £8.00-£12.00 (Mastercard/Visa/Delta/Eurocard)

DORNIE, Highland   **Map C5**
Pop 500. SEE Eilean Donan Castle Restaurant: Castle Inn ☎(01599) 555205

Ardelve Caravan Site, Dornie Bridge IV40 8DY ☎(01599) 555231 OS map 33/877268 ¼m W of
   Dornie on A87 (Kyle of Lochalsh) near Dornie Bridge by Loch Alsh Open May-Sept 33 pitches–no
   adv booking Level/sloping grass and hard standing, sheltered 🚐 £6.50

DORNOCH, Highland   **Map E3**
Pop 1,100. EC Thurs SEE cathedral, Skelbo Castle ruins, sandy beaches ⚊The Square
☎Dornoch (01862) 810400 Restaurant: Dornoch Castle, Castle St ☎(01862) 810216

Dornoch Links Caravan and Camping Site, The Links IV25 3LX ☎Dornoch (01862) 810423 OS
   map 21/800895 ¼m E of Dornoch centre, entrance via River Street Open Apr 1-Oct 28, 200
   pitches (80 static) Grass, level, pitches in bays on sand dunes ⚟🖵🗑🗑⊕∅↵🗆🚐♿ putting
   green, baby sitting £6.50-£7.50

Pitgrudy Farm, Poles Road IV25 3HY ☎Dornoch (01862) 810001 OS map 21/795911 1m N of
   Dornoch on B9168 (Golspie) Open May-Sept 40 pitches–no tents, no single sex groups, no motor
   cycles Grass, sloping, part sheltered 🖵🗑🗑⊕∅↵🖥 (no charge) 🚐 £5.00

Seaview Farm Caravan Park, Hilton IV25 3PW ☎Dornoch (01862) 810294 OS map 21/807916
   1½m NE of Dornoch on Embo road Open May-Sept–must book, 25 pitches Level grass,
   sheltered 🗑⊕ hot water–*No showers* £7.00

DRUMNADROCHIT, Highland   **Map D5**
Pop 360 EC Thurs SEE Urquhart Castle ruins, Corrimony Stone Circle, Cobb Memorial, Loch Ness,
Loch Ness Monster Exhibition Restaurant: Polmailly House (dinner only) 2m W on A831 ☎(01456)
450343

Highland Riding Centre, Borlum Farm IV3 6XN ☎Drumnadrochit (01456) 450220 OS map
   26/513293 1m S of Drumnadrochit off A82 (Fort William) Open May-Oct 25 pitches–no adv
   booking Grass sloping open, gravel level, sheltered 🖵🗑🗑⊕∅🖥 riding, fishing, boat trips on Loch
   Ness £7.80 (Mastercard/Visa)

DUNDONNELL, Highland   **Map C3**
Pop 100 Small resort at head of Little Loch Ryan Restaurant: Dundonnell ☎(01854) 633234

Badrallach Bothy and Campsite, Croft 9, Badrallach IV23 2QP ☎(01854) 633281 OS map
   19/065915 3m N of Dundonnell off A832 (Poolewe) by loch shore Open all year 15 pitches
   2½ acres level grass ∅🏠♿ games room, boat and bike hire £7.50

DUNVEGAN, Isle of Skye, Highland   **Map C4**
Restaurant: Harlosh 3m S on A863 ✆(01470) 521367

Dunvegan Caravan Park IV55 8WF ✆(01470) 521206 OS map 23/257477 ½m NE of Dunvegan on A850 (Portree) Open Apr-Sept 33 pitches–peak booking advisable 2 acres, level grass and hardstandings 🔲❸ £5.00-£7.00

DURNESS, Highland   **Map D1**
Pop 200 SEE Smoo Cave 1m E, Balnakeil Craft Village 1m W ℹ Sango ✆(01971) 511259
Restaurant: Kinlochbervie 20m SW at Kinlochbervie ✆(01971) 511275

Sango Sands Caravan Camping Park IV27 4PP ✆(01971) 511262 OS map 9/407677 ¼m S of Durness on A838 (Lairg) overlooking Sango Bay Open Easter-mid Oct–no adv booking 84 pitches Grass and hard standings, level, part sheltered 🔲✗♒◻🔲◔❸∅ campers' kitchen £7.50

DUROR, Highland   **Map C7**
SEE Loch Linnhe W Restaurant: Stewart ✆(01631) 740268

Achindarroch Farm PA38 4BS ✆(01631) 740277 OS map 49/992550 In village on A828 (Oban-Glencoe) Open Apr-Oct 25 pitches 3 acres level grass and hard standings 🔲◻🔲❸ £5.00-£6.00

ELGIN, Grampian   **Map F4**
Pop 19,240. EC Wed SEE site, cathedral (chapter house), museum, Braco's Banking House ℹ 17 High Street ✆(01343) 542666 Restaurant: Park House, South St ✆(01343) 547695

Riverside Caravan Park, West Road IV30 3UN ✆Elgin (01343) 542813 OS map 28/190625 ½m W of Elgin on A96 (Forres) by River Lossie Open Apr-Oct 82 pitches Grass, level, part open, some hard standings 🔲⚲◻🔲 (25) £8.00-£9.00

ELLON, Grampian   **Map H5**
Pop 6,600 EC Wed MD Mon Market town on river Ythan SEE castle ruins, old bridge, toll house, Haddon House 5m NW, Pitmeddan Gardens 4m SW ℹ Market Street car park ✆Ellon (01358) 720730 Restaurant: New Inn, Market St ✆(01358) 720425

Ythan Hotel, Newburgh AB41 6BE ✆(01358) 789257 OS map 38/988248 6m SE of Ellon off A975 (Foveran-Cruden Bay) Open Apr-Oct, 50 pitches (20 static)–no adv booking 3 acres, mainly level, hard standings ∅❸ £4.00-£6.00

EVANTON–see Dingwall

FINDHORN, Grampian   **Map E4**
Once a port, now a beach resort SEE Culbin Sands and Forest Restaurant: Crown and Anchor ✆(01309) 690243

Findhorn Bay Caravan Park IV36 0TY ✆Findhorn (01309) 690203 Fax (01309) 690203 OS map 27/048637/051635 1m S of Findhorn off B9011 (Forres) Open Apr-Oct, 150 pitches (50 static) 6 acres, level, grass and hard standings 🔲✗ (café) ⚲◻🔲◔❸∅ↄ🔲⊡ £4.00-£7.50

Findhorn Sands Caravan Park IV36 3YZ ✆(01309) 690324 Fax (01309) 690325 OS map 27/040645 ¼m N of Findhorn off B9011 Open Apr-Oct, 200 pitches (150 static)–no adv booking Level grass ◻🔲❸∅ £8.00-£9.00

FOCHABERS, Grampian   **Map F4**
Pop 1,400 EC Wed SEE parish church, Tugnet Ice House (fisheries museum), folk museum
Restaurant: Mill 4m NE on A98 at Tynet ✆(01542) 850233

Burnside Caravan Site IV32 7PF ✆(01343) 820511 and 820362 OS map 28/350580 ½m S of Fochabers on right of A96 (Aberdeen) Open Apr-Oct, 110 pitches (50 static) Grass, level, sheltered ◻🔲∅⊡ (heated) ❸ↄ⊡🔲 £7.50-£9.00

Spey Bay Caravan Park, Spey Bay IV32 7PJ ✆Fochabers (01343) 820424 OS map 28/356650 4m N of Fochabers on right of B9104 (Spey Bay) Open Apr-Sept, 35 pitches–no adv booking Level grass ✗♒◻🔲❸∅❸ↄ⊡🏠⛊ meals, golf, putting, driving range, tennis £4.25-£6.75

FORRES, Grampian   **Map E4**
Pop 7,440. EC Wed SEE Falconer museum, Witches' Stone, Sueno's Stone NE, Nelson Tower (view) ℹ Falconer Museum ✆(01309) 672938 Restaurant: Park, Victoria Rd ✆(01309) 672328

Riverview Leisure, Mundole Court IV36 0SZ ✆(01309) 673932 OS map 27/015600 1m W of Forres off A96 (Nairn) Open Apr-Nov 72 pitches (12 static) 50 acres level grass, sheltered 🔲✗♒◻🔲∅❸ↄ⊡ £8.00

FORT AUGUSTUS, Highland   Map D5
Pop 1,000 EC Wed See abbey, Gen Wade's road over Corrieyarrick Pass, Inchnacardoch Forest, Loch Ness, Caledonian Canal ■ Car Park ☎(01320) 366367 Restaurant: Inchnacardoch Lodge ☎(01320) 366258

Fort Augustus Camping, Market Hill PH32 4DH ☎ Fort Augustus (01320) 366360 OS map 34/373084 ½m S of Fort Augustus centre on right of A82 (Fort William) adj golf course Open Easter-Sept, 50 pitches 4 acres grass, part sheltered ▯🚐❄⊘⏚ㄥ £8.00

FORT WILLIAM, Highland   Map C6
Pop 4,270. EC Wed (winter) SEE Ben Nevis (4,418ft), West Highland Museum ■ Cameron Centre, Cameron Sq ☎(01397) 703781 Restaurant: Nevis Bank, Belford Rd ☎(01397) 705721

Glen Nevis Caravan and Camping Park, Glen Nevis PH33 6SX ☎ Fort William (01397) 702191 OS map 41/125723 2½m N of Fort William off A82 (Inverness) on right of Glen Nevis road Open Mar 31-Oct 31, 380 pitches Grass and hard standings, part level, part open 🛒✗🍴🍺 (season) 🏹▯🚐⊘❄⊘⏚ㄥ £7.40-£9.80

Linnhe Lochside Holidays, Corpach PH33 7NL ☎(01397) 772376 OS map 41/073771 5m NW of Fort William on left of A830 (Mallaig) Open Dec 17-Oct 31, 175 pitches (100 static) Hard standings, terraced 🛒🏹▯🚐⊘❄⊘❄⏚ 🍴🚻 slipway, sailing, free fishing, barbecue area, private beach, toddler's play room £8.50-£14.50 (all cards exc Amex)

Lochy Caravan Park, Camaghael PH33 7NF ☎ Fort William (01397) 703446 OS map 41/125764 2m N of Fort William off A830 (Mallaig) on Camaghael road Open all year–no adv booking 150 pitches 🛒✗▯🚐⊘ㄥ £6.00

FRASERBURGH, Grampian   Map H4
Pop 12,990. EC Wed SEE Wine Tower (16c), lighthouse ■ Saltoun Square ☎ Fraserburgh (01346) 518315 Restaurant: Alexander, High St ☎(01346) 328249

Esplanade Municipal Caravan Site, Harbour Road AB4 1US ☎ Fraserburgh (01346) 510041 OS map 30/001663 ¼m S of Fraserburgh off A92 (Aberdeen) adj beach Open Apr-Sept 50 pitches ▯🚐⊘❄⊘⏚ㄥ £5.50-£9.50

Kessock Road Camping AB4 4AE ☎ Fraserburgh (01346) 510042 OS map 30/999661 ¼m S of Fraserburgh off A92 (Aberdeen) Open Apr-Sept–120 pitches (50 static) ▯🚐⊘❄⊘⏚ £5.50-£9.50

Rosehearty Caravan Camping Park, Shore Street, Rosehearty AB4 4JQ ☎(01346) 861314 OS map 30/934676 5m W of Fraserburgh off A98 (Banff) on Rosehearty road Open Apr-Oct 40 pitches 1½ acres level on seafront ▯🚐⊘❄⊘❄⏚ £4.00-£8.75

GAIRLOCH, Highland   Map B4
Pop 1,000. EC Wed Fishing village, vacation resort and excellent touring centre for Wester Ross SEE Heritage museum, Loch Maree, Red Point (view), Victoria Falls, Inverewe gardens 5m NE ■ Achtercairn ☎ Gairloch (01445) 712130 Restaurant: The Old Inn, Flowerdale ☎(01445) 712006

Auchtercairn Farm Caravan Rest IV21 2BN ☎ Gairloch (01445) 712248 OS map 19/804770 ¼m N of Gairloch at junction of A832 (Poolewe) and B8021 (Melvaig) Open May-Sept 60 pitches 🛒✗ *No showers* £3.00

Gairloch Caravan Camping Park, Strath IV21 2BX ☎ Gairloch (01445) 712373 OS map 19/798774 ½m NW of Gairloch off B8021 (Melvaig) at rear of Millcroft Hotel Open Easter-Oct, 80 pitches 6 acres, level grass ▯🚐⊘❄⊘❄⏚🍴🚻 fishing and boating near £7.50-£9.00 (Mastercard/Visa)

Sands Holiday Centre IV21 2DL ☎ Gairloch (01445) 712152 OS map 19/760785 3m NW of Gairloch on left of B8021 (Melvaig) Open Apr-Sept 360 pitches 50 acres level/sloping grass 🛒🏹▯🚐⊘❄⊘⏚🚻 fishing, sandy beach adj £9.30 (Mastercard/Visa/Amex)

GLENCOE, Highland   Map C7
Pop 350. Scene of one of grimmest episodes in clan history when Campbells in league with
authorities massacred MacDonalds. The glen – traversed by A82 – is best approached from S to get
full impact of 3 Sisters peaks. SEE MacDonald memorial, Signal Rock Restaurant: Clachaig Inn
behind NT centre ☎(01855) 811252

Glencoe Camp Site (NT), Ballachulish PA49 4LA ☎Ballachulish (01855) 811397 OS map
   41/112576 1m E of Glencoe on left of A82 (Tyndrum) Open Apr-Oct 150 pitches Grass, part
   level, open ⬛🖫🅿🆕⊕⦸♿ fishing, forest trails £3.50-£9.00

Invercoe Caravan Park, PA49 4HP ☎Ballachulish (01855) 811210 OS map 41/099591 ½m N of
   Glencoe on B863 (Kinlochleven) near Glencoe crossroads by Loch Leven Open Easter-mid Oct
   60 pitches Grass, level, open ⬛🖫🅿🆕⊕⦸♿⤴🚎🚎♿ fishing £9.00-£11.00

Red Squirrel Camping Site PA39 4HX ☎(01855) 811256 OS map 41/120574 1½m SE of
   Glencoe off A82 (Glasgow) Open all year 200 pitches–no trailer caravans Grass and hard
   standings, level, part sheltered ⊕⦸🅿🏠 camp fires, swimming, fishing £8.00-£9.00

GRANTOWN ON SPEY, Highland   Map E5
Pop 1,400. EC Thurs Most elegant of Spey Valley resorts, founded 1776. Well placed for tours to E
coast as well as to the Great Glen and Inverness. The malt whisky trail passes near. ℹ54 High
Street ☎Grantown on Spey (01479) 872773 Restaurant: Rosehall, The Square ☎(01479) 872721

Grantown on Spey Caravan Park, Seafield Avenue PH26 3JQ ☎(01479) 872474 Fax (01479)
   873696 OS map 36/028283 ½m N of Grantown in Seafield Avenue Open Apr-Oct 154 pitches
   (50 static) Grass and hard standings, level/sloping, sheltered 🖫🅿🆕⊕⦸🅂⤴🐾 (15) 🚎 sep
   pitches £7.00-£10.50 (Mastercard/Visa)

HALLADALE–see Melvich

HOPEMAN–see Burghead

HUNTLY, Aberdeenshire   Map G5
Pop 4,500 Holiday resort and market town centred on two main streets and an attractive square. SEE
palatial castle ruins, museum, Leith Hall 8m S ℹ☎ (01466) 792255. Restaurant: Castle ☎(01466) 792696

Huntly Castle Caravan Park AB54 4UJ *Centrally located and well equipped park ideal for touring*
   castle and whisky trails ☎(01466) 794999 OS map 29/525405 ½m NW of Huntly near A96
   (Keith) Open Mar 23-Oct 28 126 pitches 15 acres level grass and hard standings
   🖫🅿🆕⊕⦸🅂♿ fully serviced pitches, indoor sports hall £8.50-£10.95 (Mastercard/Visa)

INVERBERVIE, Grampian   Map G6
Restaurant: St Leonards 10m NE at Stonehaven ☎(01569) 762044

Burgh Haugh Caravan Site DD10 0SP ☎(01561) 361182 OS map 45/830720 ½m S of
   Inverbervie off coast road Open Apr 5-Oct 31, 75 pitches Grass, level, sheltered 🖫🅿🆕⊕⦸🅂⤴
   putting green, tennis £6.00-£10.00

Lauriston Camping and Caravan Site, St Cyrus DD10 0DJ ☎(01674) 850316 OS map 45/736646
   7m SW of Inverbervie off A92 (Montrose) Open Apr-Sept 80 pitches (60 static) 7 acres level
   grass, sheltered ⬛➶🖫🅿🆕⊘⦸⤴🚎 £4.50-£6.00

Waird's Park, Johnshaven DD10 0HD ☎(01561) 362616/362280/362395 OS map 45/800672 5m
   SW of Inverbervie off A92 (Montrose) Level grass and
   hard standings ⬛🖫🅿🆕⊕⦸⤴🐾♿ first aid, putting, bowling, tennis £8.00-£9.50

INVERGARRY, Highland   Map D6
Pop 150. Village where Road to Isles begins and ends at Kyle of Lochalsh SEE Well of Seven
Heads monument, Loch Garry, Caledonian Canal Restaurant: Glengarry Castle ☎(01809) 501254

Faichem Park, Ardgarry Farm, Faichem PH35 4HG ☎(01809) 501226 Fax (01809) 501307 OS
   map 34/287015 1m W of Invergarry off A87 (Kyle of Lochalsh) on Faichem road Open Mar-Oct
   30 pitches Grass and hard standings, level and sloping, part open 🅂🆕⊕⦸🚎🏠 forest trails
   £7.00-£7.50

Faichemard Farm PH35 4HG ☎(01809) 501314 OS map 34/287018 2m W of Invergarry off A87
   (Kyle of Lochalsh) on Faichem road–signposted Open Apr-Oct 40 pitches 10 acres level grass
   and hard standings, sheltered 🖫🅂⊕⦸🏠 Sep pitches with picnic table, hill walking, fishing
   £6.00

INVERMORISTON, Highland   Map D5
Pop 400. EC Thurs SEE hydro-electric works, Glen Moriston, Loch Ness Restaurant: Glenmoriston
Arms ☎(01320) 351206

Loch Ness Caravan and Camping Park, Easter Port Clair IV3 6YE ☎(01320) 351207 OS map
   34/425151 1½m SSW of Invermoriston on A82 (Fort Augustus) beside Loch Ness Open Mar 15-
   Oct 15–adv booking min 3 nights 85 pitches 🖫🅂🆕⊕⦸⤴🔲 slipway, fishing £7.00-£9.50

INVERNESS, Highland   **Map D5**
Pop 41,000. EC Wed, MD Mon, Tues SEE cathedral, castle, museum, Northern Meeting Piping
Competition (Sept) Tonnahurich Cemetery (view), Culloden battlefield (visitor centre) 6m E, chapel
and regimental museum of Queen's Own Highlanders at Fort Grange 12m NE ▯ Castle Wynd
☎ (01463) 234353 Restaurant: Brookes, Castle St ☎ (01463) 225662

Auchnahillin Caravan Camping Park, Daviot East IV1 2XQ ☎ (01463) 772286 OS map
   27/740386 6m SE of Inverness off A9 (Aviemore) on B9154 (Moy) Open Mar-Oct 100 pitches
   Grass and hard standings, level ▯▯▯▯▯▯▯▯▯▯▯ (25) ▯ £5.70-£9.20

Balachladaich Farm, Dores IV1 2XP ☎ (01463) 751204 OS map 26/583329 9m SW of Inverness
   on B862 (Dores) at northern end of Loch Ness Open Apr-Oct 45 pitches *No showers,* boat hire,
   fishing £5.00

Bught Caravan Site, Bught IV3 5SR ☎ Inverness (01463) 236920 OS map 26/658438 1m SW of
   Inverness on A82 (Drumnadrochit) Open Easter-Sept 172 pitches Level grass sheltered
   ▯▯▯▯▯▯ £4.10-£10.80

Bunchrew Caravan Park IV3 6TD ☎ Inverness (01463) 237802 OS map 26/615600 3m W of
   Inverness on A862 (Beauly) Open Mar 15-Oct 15, 125 pitches Grass, level, sheltered
   ▯▯▯▯▯▯▯▯▯▯▯ £7.00-£7.50

Coulmore Bay Caravan Park, North Kessock IV1 1XB ☎ (01463) 731313 OS map 26/619482 3m
   N of Inverness off A9 (Cononbridge) by sea Open May-Sept 112 pitches ▯▯▯▯▯▯ boating,
   canoeing, sailing £4.50

Torvean Caravan Park, Glenurquhart Road IV3 6JL ☎ Inverness (01463) 220582/233051 OS map
   26/655483 1m SW of Inverness on A82 (Drumnadrochit) Open Apr-Oct 50 pitches–must book
   Jul-Aug–no tents, no single sex groups, no motorcycles 2 acres hard standings ▯▯▯▯▯▯
   £6.00

JOHN O'GROATS, Highland   **Map F1**
Pop 600 SEE Duncansby Head cliffs and lighthouse, Canishay church (tomb of Jan de Groot),
Orkneys (by day trip), Castle of Mey 6m W ▯ ☎ (01955) 611373 Restaurant: John O'Groats House
☎ (01955) 611203

John O'Groats Caravan Park, KW1 4YS ☎ (01955) 611329 OS map 12/382735 At northernmost
   point of A99 beside Last House in Scotland on seafront Open Apr-Oct 90 pitches Level grass and
   hard standings ▯▯▯▯▯▯▯▯ petrol, day trips to Orkney £7.50-£8.50

Stroma View, Huna KW1 4YL ☎ (01955) 611313 OS map 7/362731 2m W of John O'Groats on
   A836 (Thurso) Open Mar-Oct 30 pitches Grass and hard standings, level, sheltered
   ▯▯▯▯▯▯ farm produce £6.00 (inc showers)

JOHNSHAVEN–see Inverbervie

KEITH, Grampian   **Map F4**
Pop 4,460. EC Wed SEE Strathisla distillery, 17c bridge ▯ Church Road ☎ (01542) 882634
Restaurant: Royal, Church Rd ☎ (01542) 882528

Keith Caravan Site, Dunnyduff Road AB5 3JG ☎ (01542) 882078 OS map 28/434498 ¼m S of
   Keith on A96 (Huntly) Open Apr-Sept 50 pitches Grass, level, open ▯▯▯▯▯ fishing £4.50

KINGUSSIE, Highland   **Map E6**
Pop 1,300. EC Wed SEE Highland Folk Museum, china studios, Highland Wildlife Park 3m NE
▯ King Street ☎ (01540) 661297 Restaurant: Wood`n'Spoon, High St ☎ (01540) 661251

Kingussie Golf Club, Gynack Road PH21 1LR ☎ (01540) 661374 OS map 35/755015 ½m N of
   Kingussie centre off A9 (Aviemore) Open Apr-Sept 60 pitches–no tents Grass, level, open £4.00-
   £5.00

KINLOCHBERVIE, Highland   **Map C1**
Pop 420 Restaurant: Kinlochbervie ☎ (01971) 521281

Oldshoremore Caravan Site, Oldshoremore IV27 4RS OS map 9/211586 2m NW of Kinlochbervie
   on Oldshore road Open Apr-Sept 15 pitches–no adv bkg Part grass, part level, hard standings,
   sheltered ▯▯▯▯ £6.00-£7.50

**There's usually no objection to your walking onto a site to see if you might like it but always
ask permission first. Remember that the person in charge is responsible for safeguarding the
property of those staying there.**

KINLOCHLEVEN, Highland Map C7
Pop 1,620. EC Wed Restaurant: Tail Race ✆ (01855) 831777
Caolasnacon Farm PA40 4RS ✆ (01855) 831279 OS map 41/139607 3m SW of Kinlochleven on
B863 (Glencoe) Open Apr-Oct 70 pitches Grass, level 🔋🛒🅰️⊛∅⟳ (20) boat and fishing tackle
hire £4.75-£7.00

KINTORE, Grampian Map G5
Pop 2100 SEE Roman camp Restaurant: Kintore Arms, The Square (adj A96) ✆ (01467) 632216
Hillhead Caravan Park AB51 0YX ✆ (01467) 632809 OS map 38/777163 ½m SW of Kintore off
A96 (Aberdeen) and B994 (Kemnay) Open Apr-Oct 29 pitches 1½ acres level grass, sheltered
🔋✕🔋🛒🅰️⊛∅⊛⟳🔌⛺♿ fishing £7.50-£9.40 (Mastercard/Visa)

KYLE OF LOCHALSH, Highland Map B5
Pop 900. EC Thurs SEE harbour, Balmacara House 3m E, Eilean Donan Castle 9m E 🅸 Car Park
✆ (01599) 814276 Restaurant: Kyle, Main St ✆ (01599) 814204
Balmacara Woodland Campsite, Balmacara IV40 8DN ✆ (01599) 816321 OS map 33/803279 3m
E of Kyle of Lochalsh off A87 (Shiel Bridge) Open Easter-Sept, 55 pitches Level grass and hard
standing, sheltered 🛒⊛⊕ *No showers* £4.00-£5.00
Reraig Caravan Site, Balmacara IV40 8DH ✆ (01599) 566215 OS map 33/816272 3m E of Kyle of
Lochalsh on A87 (Dornie) at rear of Balmacara Hotel Open May-Sept 45 pitches–no adv booking
by phone–no awnings or large or trailer tents Grass, part level, part open, some hard standings
🛒⊛ £7.80 (Mastercard/Visa)

LAIDE, Highland Map C3
SEE Inverewe Gardens 8m S Restaurant: Aultbea 3m SW at Aultbea ✆ (01445) 731201
Gruinard Bay Caravan and Camping Park IV22 2ND ✆ (01445) 731225 OS map 19/903919 ¼m
E of Laide on A832 (Dingwall) Open Apr-Oct 55 pitches 3½ acres, level grass 🔋🔋🛒🅰️⊛⟳
£8.50 (Mastercard/Visa)

LAIRG, Highland Map D3
Pop 950. EC Wed SEE Falls of Shin, prehistoric hut circles 🅸✆ Lairg (01549) 402291 Restaurant:
Sutherland Arms, Main Rd ✆ (01549) 402291
Dunroamin Caravan Camping Park, Main Street IV27 4AR ✆ (01549) 402447 OS map 16/583066
At E edge of Lairg centre on A839 (Dornoch) at rear of Crofters Restaurant Open Apr-Oct 50
pitches Grass and hard standing, level, part sheltered ✕⟳🔋🅰️⊛∅⊛⟳🔌⛺ £5.50-£9.00
(Mastercard/Visa)
Woodend Caravan Site, Achnairn IV27 4DN ✆ Lairg (01549) 402248 OS map 16/558127 4m NW
of Lairg off A836 (Altnaharra) and A838 (Durness) Open Apr-Sept 55 pitches Grass, part sloping,
open 🔋🔋🛒🅰️⊛⟳⛺ (7), campers' kitchen £8.00

LAURENCEKIRK, Grampian Map G6
Restaurant: Thistle Inn at Auchenblae ✆ (01561) 320305
Brownmuir Caravan Park, Fordoun AB30 1SJ ✆ (01561) 320786 OS map 45/740772 5m NE of
Laurencekirk off A90 (Stonehaven) on Fordoun road Open Apr-Oct 60 pitches (45 static) Level
grass, sheltered 🔋🛒🅰️⊛∅⟳🔌♿ £6.00-£8.00
Dovecot Caravan Park, Northwaterbridge AB30 1QL ✆ (01674) 840630 OS map 45/646666 6m
SW of Laurencekirk off A90 (Forfar) on Edzell road Open Apr-Oct 75 pitches (45 static) Level
grass, sheltered 🔋🔋🛒🅰️⊛∅⊛⟳🔌⛺♿ £7.00-£8.00

LOSSIEMOUTH, Grampian Map F4
Pop 6,650 EC Thurs 🅸 Station Park ✆ (01343) 814804 Restaurant: Stotfield, Stotfield Road
✆ (01343) 812011
Silver Sands Leisure Park IV31 6SP ✆ Lossiemouth (01343) 813262 OS map 28/205712 2m W
of Lossiemouth on right of B9040 (Burghead) Open Easter-Oct, 350 pitches (200 static) Level
grass and hard standings 🔋🍴➘🔋🛒🅰️⊛∅⊛⟳🔌⛺ amusements, cycle hire £8.00-£12.00
(Mastercard/Visa)

**Some site operators make it a rule that cars must be left in a separate parking area away from
caravans and tents, which can be inconvenient when shopping by car. But it does minimise
traffic noise and the risk to children.**

LOTH–see Brora

MACDUFF, Grampian   **Map G4**
Pop 3,890 EC Wed SEE open air pool at Tarlair, Gardenstown harbour 5m E Restaurant: Fife
Arms, Shore Street ☎(01261) 832408

Myrus Caravan Park AB4 3QP ☎(01261) 812845 OS map 29/710633 1m SE of Macduff on A947
(Turriff) near junction with B9026 Open Apr-mid Oct, 60 pitches Level grass, sheltered ▮▯▯▯
cycle hire £6.50-£10.00

Wester Bonnyton Farm Camping and Caravan Park AB45 3EP ☎Macduff (01261) 832470 OS
map 29/740636 2m E of Macduff on right of B9031 (Fraserburgh) Open Easter-Oct, 30 pitches
Level/sloping grass ▮▯▯▯▯▯▯▯▯▯▯▯▯▯ £5.00-£7.00

MELVICH, Highland   **Map E1**
Resort noted for its views across Halladale estuary to Orkneys Restaurant: Melvich ☎(01641)
561032

Halladale Inn Caravan Park KW14 7YJ ☎(01641) 531282 OS map 10/391640 In Melvich near
Halladale estuary Open Apr-Oct 14 pitches Level grass and hard standings ▮✕▯▯▯▯▯▯▯
▯▯▯ £4.00-£10.00 (Mastercard/Visa/Delta)

MINTLAW–see Peterhead

NAIRN, Highland   **Map E4**
Pop 9,990. EC Wed SEE Cawdor Castle 5m SW, Fort George 10m W, Highland games (Aug)
▯King Street ☎Nairn (01667) 452753 Restaurant: Windsor, Albert St ☎(01667) 453108

Delnies Wood Camping Club, IV12 5NX ☎Nairn (01667) 455281 OS map 27/841555 3m W of
Nairn on A96 (Inverness) Open Easter-Oct 90 pitches Grass and hard core, level, sheltered
▮▯▯▯▯▯▯▯ £9.80-£12.40 (Mastercard/Visa)

Loch Loy Holiday Park, East Beach IV12 4PH ☎Nairn (01667) 453764 OS map 27/893572 ¼m
NE of Nairn on A96 (Forres) in Harbour Street near beach Open Mar-Nov 390 pitches (290 static)
Grass, level, open ▮✕▯▯▯▯▯▯▯▯▯▯▯▯▯▯ (25) ▯▯▯▯ £5.50-£15.00

Spindrift Caravan and Camping Park, Little Kildrummie IV12 5QU ☎Nairn (01667) 453992 OS
map 27/873537 2m SW of Nairn off B9090 (Cawdor) on Little Kildrummie road Open Apr-Oct 40
pitches 3 acres level/terraced grass ▯▯▯▯▯ fishing permits £6.50-£9.50

NEWTONMORE, Highland   **Map D6**
Pop 1,010 EC Wed ▯Newtonmore ☎(01540) 673274 Restaurant: Weigh Inn, Main Street
☎(01540) 673203

Invernahavon Holiday Park, Glentruim PH20 1BE ☎Newtonmore (01540) 673534 OS map
35/688950 3m S of Newtonmore off A9 (Perth) on Laggan road Open Easter-Oct 100 pitches
12½ acres level grass ▮▯▯▯▯▯▯▯▯▯▯ £8.00-£12.00

PETERHEAD, Grampian   **Map H5**
Pop 17,960. EC Wed SEE 12c church, museum, harbour, Ravenscraig Castle, Collieston visitor
centre (nature reserves) 10m SW ▯ Broad St ☎(01779) 471904 Restaurant: Waterside Inn 2m
NW on A952 ☎(01779) 471121

Aden Country Park, Aden Estate, Mintlaw AB42 5FQ ☎Mintlaw (01771) 623460/622857 OS map
30/985483 9m W of Peterhead on A950 (Banff) at Mintlaw station Open Apr-Oct 60 pitches
Grass, level, sheltered/woodland setting ▮▯▯▯▯▯▯▯▯▯ dog exercise area £6.00-£8.50

POOLEWE–see Gairloch

PORTREE, Isle of Skye, Highland   **Map C5**
Pop 1,800. EC Wed ▯Meall House ☎Portree (01478) 582137 Restaurant: King's Haven, Bosville
Terr ☎(01478) 582290

Loch Greshornish Caravan Camping Park, Arnisort by Edinbane IV51 9PS ☎(01478) 582230
OS map 23/349531 10m NW of Portree on right of A850 (Dunvegan) Open Apr-Oct 130 pitches
Grass and hard standings, part sloping, open ▮▯▯▯▯▯▯ £7.00 (2000)

Torvaig Caravan and Camping Site IV51 8BT ☎Portree (01478) 612209 OS map 23/481452 1m
N of Portree on A855 (Staffin) Open Apr-Oct 120 pitches Level/sloping grass and hard standings,
sheltered ▯▯▯▯ £7.00

ROSEHEARTY–see Fraserburgh

ROY BRIDGE, Highland   **Map D6**
Pop 200 SEE Glen Roy N, commando memorial 1m NW Restaurant: Spean Bridge 3m W at Spean Bridge ✆ (01397) 712250

Bunroy Caravan Park PH31 4AG ✆ (01397) 712332 OS map 34/274807 ¼m S of Roy Bridge off A86 (Newtonmore) beside River Spean Open Mar–Sept–no adv booking 30 pitches Grass, level, sheltered ▣▣▣▭ (1) 🏠 (8) swimming, fishing £4.50-£6.00

Glenspean Holiday Park PH31 4AW ✆ (01397) 712432 OS map 41/274807 In centre of village by Roy Bridge hotel Open all year 70 pitches 9½ acres part level, grass and hard standings ▣◢ £3.00-£4.00

Inverroy Camping Caravan Site PH31 4AQ ✆ (01397) 712275 OS map 34/257813 ½m W of Roy Bridge on A86 (Spean Bridge) Open all year 35 pitches Level grass and hard standing, sheltered ▣▣✿▭ £4.00-5.00

Kinchellie Croft Motel PH31 4AW ✆ (01397) 712265 OS map 34/290806 ¼m E of Roy Bridge on A86 (Aviemore) Open Apr-Sept 20 pitches–no advance booking £3.50-£4.50

SALEN, Highland   **Map B7**
Pop 100. EC Wed Restaurant: Kilcamb Lodge 4m E at Strontian ✆ (01967) 402257

Resipole Farm Campsite, Loch Sunart, Acharacle PH36 4HX ✆ (01967) 431235 OS map 40/723640 2m E of Salen on left of A861 (Ardgour) Open Apr-Sept 60 pitches Grass and hard standings, level, part open ✗♀▣◢✿∅▭🏠⚄ fishing, 9-hole golf, slipway £8.50-£10.00 (Mastercard/Visa/Switch)

SCOURIE, Highland   **Map C2**
Pop 280. SEE Handa Island bird sanctuary (boat trips) Restaurant: Anchorage ✆ (01971) 502060

Scourie Caravan and Camping Park, Harbour Road IV27 4TG ✆ Scourie (01971) 502060 OS map 9/155447 ½m S of Scourie at junction of A894 (Laxford Bridge) and Harbour Road Open Apr-Sept–no adv booking except by phone prior to arrival, 90 pitches Grass and hard standing, level, open ⚄ Meals £8.00

SHIEL BRIDGE, Highland   **Map C5**
Restaurant: Kintail Lodge ✆ (01599) 511275

Shiel Bridge Caravan Camping Park, Glenshiel IV40 8HW ✆ Glenshiel (01599) 511221 OS map 33/940185 ¼m S of Shiel Bridge on A87 (Invergarry) Open May-Sept 75 pitches Level grass and hard standings ⚓✗▣◢ £7.00-£8.00 (Mastercard/Visa)

Morvich Farm, Inverinate IV40 4HQ ✆ Glenshiel (01599) 511354 OS map 33/964210 3m N of Shiel Bridge off A87 (Kyle of Lochalsh) beside River Croe Open Apr 1-Oct 15, 75 pitches Fishing £6.60

ISLE OF SKYE–see Broadford, Dunvegan, Portree, Staffin and Uig

SPEAN BRIDGE, Highland   **Map C6**
Pop 130. EC Thurs ▣✆ (01397) 712576 Restaurant: Spean Bridge ✆ (01397) 712250

Gairlochy Holiday Park, PH34 4EQ ✆ (01397) 712711 Fax (01397) 712712 OS map 34/188835 1m NW of Spean Bridge off A82 (Inverness) on B8004 (Gairlochy) Open Apr-Oct 20 pitches Grass and hard standings, level, sheltered ▣✿∅⚲▭▣ (50) ▭ (6) 🏠 £7.50-£10.00

Stronaba Farm, Stronaba PH34 4DX ✆ (01397) 712259 OS map 34/208845 2½m N of Spean Bridge on A82 (Fort Augustus) Open Apr-Sept 25 pitches Grass, part sloping, sheltered, some hard standings ▣▣✿ £6.00-£7.00

STAFFIN, Isle of Skye, Highland   **Map A4**
Pop 200 Restaurant: King's Haven 17m S at Portree ✆ (01478) 612290

Staffin Caravan and Camping Park, Staffin IV51 9JX ✆ (01470) 562213 OS map 23/493672 1m S of Staffin on A855 (Portree) Open Apr-mid Oct 50 pitches Grass, level, sheltered, hard standings ▣◢✿∅▭🏠⚄ £8.00

STONEHAVEN, Grampian   **Map G6**
Pop 8,550. EC Wed SEE 16c tolbooth, old town, Muchalls castle 5m N, Dunnottar castle 1m S, Catterline fishing village 7m S ▣ Allardice Square ✆ (01569) 762806 Restaurant: St Leonards, Bath St ✆ (01569) 762044

Queen Elizabeth Caravan Park, Queen Elizabeth Park AB3 2GF ✆ Stonehaven (01569) 764041 OS map 45/875860 ¼m N of Stonehaven on A92 (Aberdeen) Open Apr-Oct 110 pitches (76 static) Hard standings, sheltered £6.50-£8.50

STORNOWAY, Isle of Lewis, Western Isles   **Map B2**
Pop 5,500. EC Wed ☒ South Beach Street ☏ Stornoway (01851) 703088 Restaurant: Royal,
Cromwell St ☏ (01851) 702109

Broad Bay Caravan Site, Coll Beach PA86 0HT ☏ Stornoway (01851) 702053 OS map 8/464385
5m N of Stornoway on B895 (North Tolsta) Open Apr-Oct 20 pitches Grass (sand dune area)
▤ ⊘ ▨ (30) ▭ beach £5.00

STRATHPEFFER–see Dingwall

STRONTIAN, Highland   **Map B7**
Pop 250. EC Wed Ferry to Fort William via Corran ▨ ☏ (01967) 402131 Restaurant: Kilcamb
Lodge ☏ (01967) 402257

Glenview Caravan Camping Park, PH36 4JD ☏ Strontian (01967) 402123 OS map 40/816613
¼m E of Strontian off A861 (Corran) Open Mar-Jan 41 pitches Grass and hard standings,
sheltered ▤ ⇢ ▨ ▨ ⊘ ⊕ ▭ pets corner £7.00-£9.00

TAIN, Highland   **Map E4**
Pop 2,200. EC Thurs SEE museum, distillery (Glen Morangie) Restaurant: Mansfield, Scotsburn Rd
☏ (01862) 892052

Meikle Ferry Caravan Park, Meikle Ferry IV19 1JX ☏ Tain (01862) 892292 OS map 21/762842
2m NW of Tain off A9 (Bonar Bridge) by new Dornoch Firth bridge Open all year 40 pitches
Grass, level, hard standings, part open ✖ ♀ ▨ ▨ ⊘ ⊕ ⊘ ⊕ ↵ ▨ ▭ £6.50-£10.00

TARBERT, Isle of Harris, Western Isles   **Map C1**
Pop 900. SEE quayside ▨ Pier Rd ☏ (01859) 502011 Restaurant: Harris ☏ (01859) 502154

Minch View Caravan Site, 10 Drinishadder HS3 3DX ☏ (01859) 511207 OS map 14/177940 4½m
SE of Tarbert off A859 (Leverburgh) Open all year 26 pitches Level grass and hard standing,
sheltered ▨ ▨ ⊕ ⊘ ▭ free fishing £5.00

THURSO, Highland   **Map F1**
Pop 8,000. EC Thurs SEE ruined bishops palace (13c), St Peter's church, botanic collection of
Robert Dick, Dunnet Bay and Dunnet Head 8m E ▨ Car Park, Riverside ☏ Thurso (01847) 892371
Restaurant: Pentland, Princes St ☏ (01847) 893202

Dunnet Bay Site (Caravan Club), Dunnet KW14 8XD ☏ (01847) 892319 OS map 12/219705 6m
E of Thurso on left of A836 (John O'Groats) adj sand dunes and beach Open May 15-Sept 30, 45
pitches 5 acres level grass ▨ ⊘ £7.00

Dunvegan Euro Camping and Caravan Site, Reay KW14 7RQ ☏ (01847) 811405 OS map
11/960647 11m W of Thurso on A836 (Tongue) Open Apr-Oct 15 pitches Grass, part level,
sheltered ▤ ↗ ▨ ⊘ ↵ £5.00-£6.00

Scrabster Road Caravan and Camping Site KW14 7JY ☏ Thurso (01847) 805503 OS map
11/12/112686 ¼m W of Thurso off A882 (Scrabster) Open May-Sept, 114 pitches Level/sloping
grass and hard standings Grass, level, open ✖ ⇢ ▨ ▨ ⊕ ⊘ ⊕ ↵ ▭ ▭ ৬ £7.80-£8.90

TONGUE, Highland   **Map D2**
Pop 150 SEE causeway across Kyle of Tongue (view), Ben Loyal (2,250ft), Loch Loyal 8m S
Restaurant: Tongue ☏ (01847) 611206

Bayview Caravan Site, 215 Talmine by Lairg IV27 4YS ☏ (01847) 601225 OS map 10/586627
4m N of Tongue off A838 (Durness) on Melness road Open Apr-Oct 15 pitches Hard standings,
sheltered £6.50-£7.50

Kincraig Caravan and Camp Park IV27 4XF ☏ (01847) 611218 OS map 10/593569 ¼m S of
Tongue centre off A836 (Lairg) Open Apr 1-Oct 8, 15 pitches–no adv bkg ▨ ⊕ £5.50-£6.50

TURRIFF, Grampian   **Map G4**
▨ High St ☏ (01888) 563001 Restaurant: Towie 5m S at Auchterless ☏ (01888) 511201

Turriff Caravan Park AB5 7ER ☏ Turriff (01888) 562205/562779 OS map 29/725494 ¼m S of of
Turriff on A947 (Aberdeen) Open May-Sept 45 pitches–must book Level grass, sheltered
▨ ▨ ⊕ ⊘ ↵ ▭ ▭ ৬ £6.50

On single track roads you need to drive further ahead than usual and pull into a passing
place whenever you see another vehicle coming, though many drivers will flash their
headlights to tell those towing caravans to come on. Keep an eye on your rear-view mirror
and if a queue of vehicles builds up behind you pull into a passing place to allow them to
overtake.

UIG, Isle of Skye, Highland   **Map A4**
Pop 200 SEE Skye Croft Museum, Hebrides (by organised boat trip). Restaurant: Uig ☎(01470) 542205

Uig Bay Camping IV51 9XU ☎Uig (01470) 542360 OS map 23/381637 ¼m W of Uig on A855 (Staffin) near ferry terminal Open Easter-Oct, 60 pitches 2½ acres, level, hard standings and grass 🐾 🗄 ♨ 🚿 ⊕ 🚐 boating, fishing, cycle hire £5.50-£8.50

ULLAPOOL, Highland   **Map C3**
Pop 1,000. EC Tues SEE waterfront, Summer Isles (boat-trips), Loch Broom, Corrieshalloch Gorge and Falls of Measach (12m S), Inverpolly nature reserve (info centre at Knockham) 10m N 🄸 West Shore St ☎Ullapool (01854) 612135 Restaurant: Ceilidh Place, West Argyle St ☎(01854) 612103

Ardmair Point Caravan Site IV26 2TN ☎Ullapool (01854) 612054 OS map 19/108984 3½m N of Ullapool off A835 (Elphin) Open Easter-Sept 45 pitches Grass, level, hard standings 🐾 ✕ ⚲ 🗄 ♨ 🚿 ⊕ Ø ↩ 🚐 🏪 ♿ boating by sea £8.00-£10.00 (Mastercard/Visa)

Broomfield Holiday Park, Shore St IV26 2SX ☎(01854) 612664 OS map 19/123939 In Ullapool near Ullapool Point Open Easter-Sept 140 pitches–no adv booking 11 acres level grass 🗄 🚿 ⊕ 🄶 ↩ £8.00-£11.00

WICK, Highland   **Map F2**
Pop 7,000. EC Wed, MD Thurs SEE rock scenery, Gala week (Jul), castle ruins, Sinclairs Bay, Caithness Glass works, Harrowhill 🄸Whitechapel Road off High Street ☎Wick (01955) 602596 Restaurant: Mercury, Riverside ☎(01955) 603344

Riverside Park (Caravan Club), Riverside Drive, Janetstown KW1 5SR ☎Wick (01955) 605420 OS map 12/361509 ½m NW of Wick off A882 (Thurso) Open Apr 25-Sept 90 pitches–peak booking advisable 6½ acres level grass and hard standing 🗄 🚿 ♨ ⊕ Ø £6.00-£10.00 (Mastercard/Visa/Switch)

Index